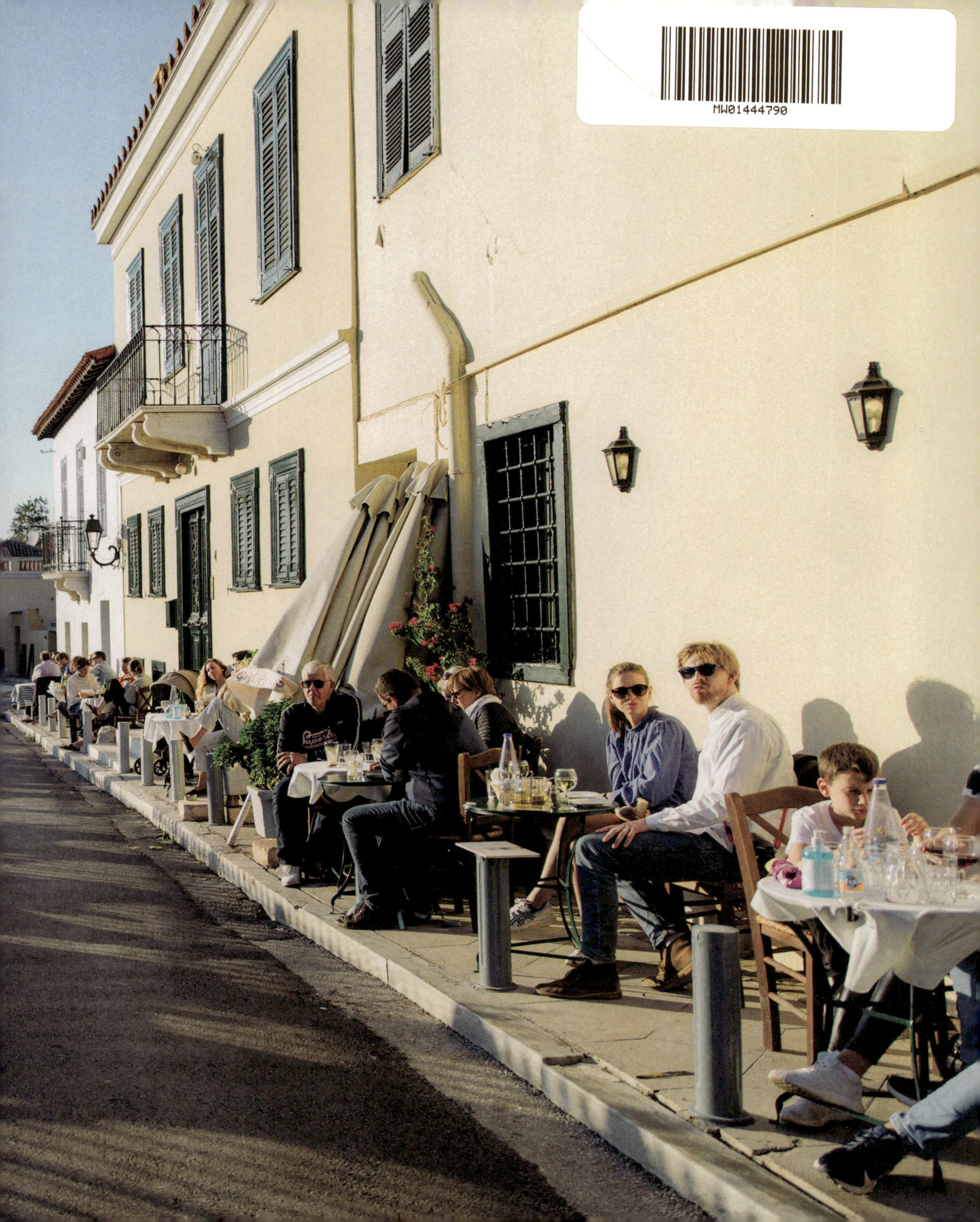

Athens

Also by Diane Kochilas

The Ikaria Way: 100 Delicious Plant-Based Recipes Inspired by My Homeland, the Greek Island of Longevity

My Greek Table: Authentic Flavors and Modern Home Cooking from My Kitchen to Yours

The Greek Vegetarian: More Than 100 Recipes Inspired by the Traditional Dishes and Flavors of Greece

The Food and Wine of Greece: More Than 300 Classic and Modern Dishes from the Mainland and Islands of Greece

Athens
Food, Stories, Love
A COOKBOOK

Diane Kochilas

ST. MARTIN'S GRIFFIN
NEW YORK

First published in the United States by St. Martin's Griffin, an imprint of St. Martin's Publishing Group

ATHENS. Copyright © 2025 by Diane Kochilas. All rights reserved. Printed in China. For information, address St. Martin's Publishing Group, 120 Broadway, New York, NY 10271.

www.stmartins.com

Design by Jan Derevjanik

Photography by Thomas Gravanis and Yiannis Sikianakis

Photo on p. 285: Copyright © 2023 AS Foodstudio/Shutterstock
Photo on p. 372 by Maria-Elpida Keridu

Food styling by Carolina Doriti

The Library of Congress Cataloging-in-Publication Data is available upon request.

ISBN 978-1-250-88002-4 (paper over board)

ISBN 978-1-250-88003-1 (ebook)

Our books may be purchased in bulk for promotional, educational, or business use. Please contact your local bookseller or the Macmillan Corporate and Premium Sales Department at 1-800-221-7945, extension 5442, or by email at MacmillanSpecialMarkets@macmillan.com.

First Edition: 2025

10 9 8 7 6 5 4 3 2 1

For my favorite Athenians, Kyveli and Yiorgo, with all the love in my heart.

*Maid of Athens, ere we part, give,
oh give me back my heart!*
—LORD BYRON

Contents

INTRODUCTION: ATHENS 1

Athens by Hand: Street Food Heaven 11

Good Morning, Athens: Breakfast 59

Dip into Athens 83

Sharing a Plate: Meze Heaven 101

Salad Days in Athens 143

Athens by the Spoon: Soups 169

The Taverna 193

The Great Bourgeois Dishes of Athens 211

A New Direction: Plant-Forward Athens 241

Carbs à la Athens 263

Athens & the Sea 289

Meat Me . . . in Athens 309

Desserts That Define Athens 333

Cheers to Athens: Drinks 367

ACKNOWLEDGMENTS 377
BIBLIOGRAPHY 379
INDEX 383

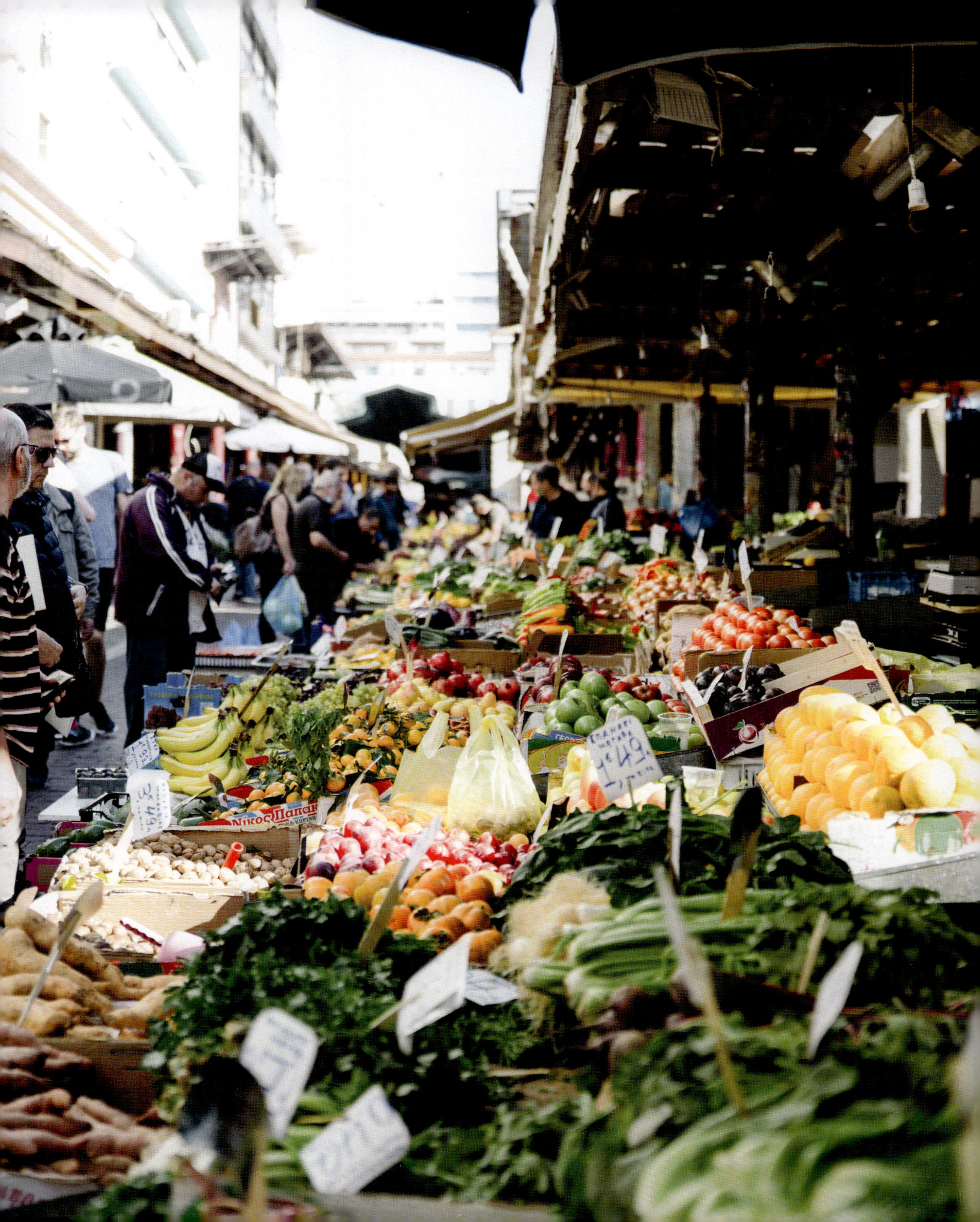

Introduction
Athens

Athens dances to its own vibe, and a fun, seductive, delicious vibe it is.

The Greek capital is one of the most vibrant cities in Europe, if not the world, with a food scene that is as multilayered and fascinating as its history, a city at once ancient and modern. It's also a city that takes some time to know, its charms not immediately apparent, especially if your visit is but a superficial one, a quick brush through the center, without time to explore. I hope, with this book, dedicated to my adopted city, that I can share a deep look inside its soul, documenting not only recipes and history, but my own experience of the city I've called home for a long time, the city that won my New York heart, drew me close, and seduced me enough to set down roots.

Athens Through (My) Youthful Eyes

I first came here as a young girl on the cusp of adolescence, in 1972, and returned almost every year thereafter, staying for a few days or a week or two, before boarding the hulking, greasy old ferries that took us to Ikaria, where my familial roots are. The city was exotic to my young eyes, and now, in retrospect, I see that I had yearned for Athens without really knowing it. A decade later, in 1982, after graduating from college and starting clumsily up the corporate ladder, I was looking for adventure, freedom, and something intangible—life's poetry, let's say—and I moved to Athens to find it.

And that I did, in a way. My only friend here was the boy who would become my husband and father of my children, and truth be told, I couldn't possibly have ever conceived of even writing this book if it weren't for Vasili, since so much of my experience of Athens is wedded to our life here together: My first long walks of discovery were together with him on sweet summer nights across the whole of Athens's terrain, from Kalithea, to the southwest of Syntagma Square, to Patissia, to the north, where we lived, sidewalks griddle-hot, laundry quivering in the breeze from the lines drawn across balcony railings above us, jasmine and honeysuckle mingling with the thick fumes of leaded gas. Even that seemed exotic, as did the spider's web of tram lines that are spun geometrically overhead, connecting the city's chaotic streets. They still form one of Athens's main means of mass transit.

To see Athens through loving, youthful eyes, regardless of one's age, is to find beauty in its chaos. I am forever the romantic.

The '80s

My early years as a young adult in Athens were delicious with endless nights in the tavernas around Exarcheia, the student, intellectual, and bohemian quarter back then, where cheap food and even cheaper rough wine fueled our youthful cure-the-world-of-its-ills cockiness. We took walks under the Acropolis on nights aglow with a full moon, unable to fathom, blinded as we were by youthful arrogance, the weight of the ancient on the explosive energy of the modern city. That contrast has haunted Greek writers and poets for centuries, and renews itself with every new historical upheaval.

We'd wind our way around Makriyianni and Koukaki, long before these most historic neighborhoods were pocked by Airbnbs, and dream of owning a neoclassical house on Tzami Karatasou Street, still one of my favorite streets in the city. Our walks under the Acropolis would take us up Dionysiou Areopagitou or Apostolou Pavlou and over to the stone church of Agios Dimitrios Loumbardiaris nearby, with the lovely café next to it, long gone, to sip a frothy frappe. Late on Sunday mornings, a jaunt to Dexameni, near Lycabettus Hill in Kolonaki, one of the city's favorite stomping grounds, was a must, if just to have a sip of ouzo and a small meze, before heading north for a family meal—that, too, an Athenian bourgeois, Greek, really, tradition.

The '80s were their own era here, one of optimism, growth, and wealth fed in large part by money from the European Union and the blustering bravado of the country's formidable PM, Andreas Papandreou. The city was also a hotbed of so much political activity. The Cold War raged its own proxy battle in Athens. I was a little tapped into this battle because I had networked among some of the international press in the city. Droves of middle-class and affluent Lebanese moved to Athens then, too, to escape the Lebanon War. (It's ironic that, as I write this book, droves of Israelis have bought a great deal of real estate in Athens, a safe haven for them, as it is both culturally and physically close.) And I landed my dream job, as an editorial assistant and sometime writer for *The Athenian*, a magazine published by Sloane and Drossoula Elliott and modeled after *The New Yorker*. As fate would have it, way back then I started writing about restaurants for the publication.

In that time in Athens, arm in arm with my beau, we'd spend fun nights at the city's open-air movie theaters, still one of the best things about this city, where you could and still can eat something simple and drink a beer or something harder, in rows of seats punctuated by folding metal tables on which to rest the likes of French fries and tyropites (cheese and phyllo pies), favorite movie snacks. The offerings have gotten a little more upscale all these years later. The seats, however, are still uncomfortable!

The '90s

I wax nostalgic about those few years in the early '80s, the ones that really forged my love of this city. We married in 1984 and left for my native New York, only to return full-time a decade later to a changed place, crackling with different energy and much vitality, a city once again in transition, shedding an older self for something more in tune with the times.

The 1990s in Athens were booming. By then, scars of the wars past and of the junta had finally begun to heal, softened with the balm of affluence, however ephemeral that eventually proved to be, and that affluence came part and parcel of the ever-growing ties to the EU, the cementing of which happened with the new millennium, when Greece became a full-fledged, if unready, member of the monetary union.

We moved back permanently in 1992, our first child was born in 1993, and I had another dream job, this one more serious and way more visible, as the food columnist and restaurant critic for the city's largest daily paper, *Ta Nea*, which I landed by chance. Over the twenty years I wrote my columns and documented Athens's food life for *Ta Nea*, I stood witness to immense social transformations. Vasili helped me a lot those first few years. My Greek was wanting at best, and Vasili's, being a native speaker, was rich with nuance and cultural references I could never hope to have as a transplant.

It was a fun time to be a food writer in Athens, with so many young Greeks, like ourselves, moving back from having studied abroad, and with them bringing the desire for new flavors and ethnic cuisines that had never before taken root in this, till then, provincial capital.

Athens had evolved. Tourism brought the enticements of affluence. A generation of Greeks returning to their homeland had become more sophisticated in their tastes. The once classless taverna, where rich and poor both enjoyed traditional food, was eclipsed by high-design restaurants where people could show off their ease with chopsticks and discuss whether a risotto was sufficiently al dente. By the mid-1990s, foreign cuisines were reaping the top prizes in nascent restaurant awards. Beyond the few lingering neighborhood tavernas, souvlaki joints, and tourist traps in the Plaka area, there were notably few Greek restaurants in the capital. In retrospect, the country was wholeheartedly forsaking its traditional cuisine and, by extension, its traditional values.

EU membership ushered in a torrent of new foods, many available for the first time on supermarket shelves. Restaurant menus from the 1990s read like a catalog of novel ingredients that were embraced more or less indiscriminately. In the early 1990s I reviewed dishes such as spinach-cheese pies in wonton wrappers, potato pancakes with smoked trout and heavy cream, and baked wheels of Camembert with berry sauce. There was smoked salmon or salmon roe on what seemed like every other plate of pasta, with the then-requisite vodka-cream sauce.

As the '90s progressed and the Athens stock market skyrocketed, restaurants reflected new wealth and unabashed hubris. Bouncers became fixtures at the doors, controlling who was allowed in. At one now-defunct restaurant, where my ancient Volkswagen Beetle was the only jalopy in a row of gleaming BMWs, the chef served forth a ridiculously pretentious fish fillet on a plate whose sole garnish was a large rock! Lavishly designed restaurants opened one after another. Mostly, the food was flashy with little substance, a metaphor for what was happening in the society. The stock market eventually crashed, and the well-guarded, oversized, and overdesigned eateries began to fizzle out. The bubble eventually popped.

The Olympics and a Greek Food Renaissance

Throughout this book, I mention the 2004 Olympics as a turning point, because they loomed fast and large on the collective conscience back then. With so much of the world's attention on Athens, chefs began to embrace their Greek roots with newfound pride. It was a hallelujah moment. Regional ingredients emerged from obscurity, and forgotten dishes were reworked to fit a modern nation brimming with excitement. Pride and provenance pervaded the restaurant scene almost to the point of excess, with menus reading like maps of the country's food products. Greek was *in*. The construction frenzy preceding the Olympics helped, too: Newer, better roads made it easier for regional delicacies to reach the city. It didn't take long for a whole crop of Greek gourmet shops to sprout.

I ran a magazine for the Hellenic Foreign Trade Board called *The Greek Gourmet Traveler*. We were a team of food and wine writers, chefs, pâtissiers, and food stylists who were on a mission to revamp our national cuisine, imbue it with a new identity, and share it with the world. We were also on a mission to bring it into the new century. Chefs found status as prized members of a newly desirable profession, and kitchens churned out plate after plate of creative, exciting Greek food. It was a thrilling, if sometimes excessive, time.

Hot Air

But the five years after the Olympics marked one of the most corrupt and decadent periods in modern Greek history. Scandal after government scandal soured headlines. Crooked officials cooked the books. The epitome of excess for me came at one of Athens's most fashionable restaurants, when I sampled, with (much justified) hesitation, a heaping mound of freeze-dried feta, numbingly cold, dry as sawdust, and about as flavorful. Like the tenuous foundations on which Greeks erected their glorious glitz, so did chefs serve food that was the culinary equivalent of a house of cards. They fashioned foams from the components of skordalia, the unapologetically garlicky classic dip. They fed us feta in myriad guises, including ice cream. And tumbled cubes of Greek salad–flavored gel and even sacrosanct moussaka in martini glasses.

To be fair, not all of it was bad, but most of it was intimidating, food that bullied even savvy diners into feeling that they had to like it in order to fit into some new socio-culinary order. The media, meanwhile, lavished praise on every spritz of foam. No one asked why so much of what had been a robust, earthy cuisine had been deconstructed into hot air, much like what was happening on a larger stage within the society.

The Crash

Then, suddenly, it all crashed. The crisis seared the pockets of ordinary Greeks and the Athens food scene retrenched. The bright side is that it was a time of much self-examination in a society not usually given to such ruminations. People had to figure out how to regain the dignity

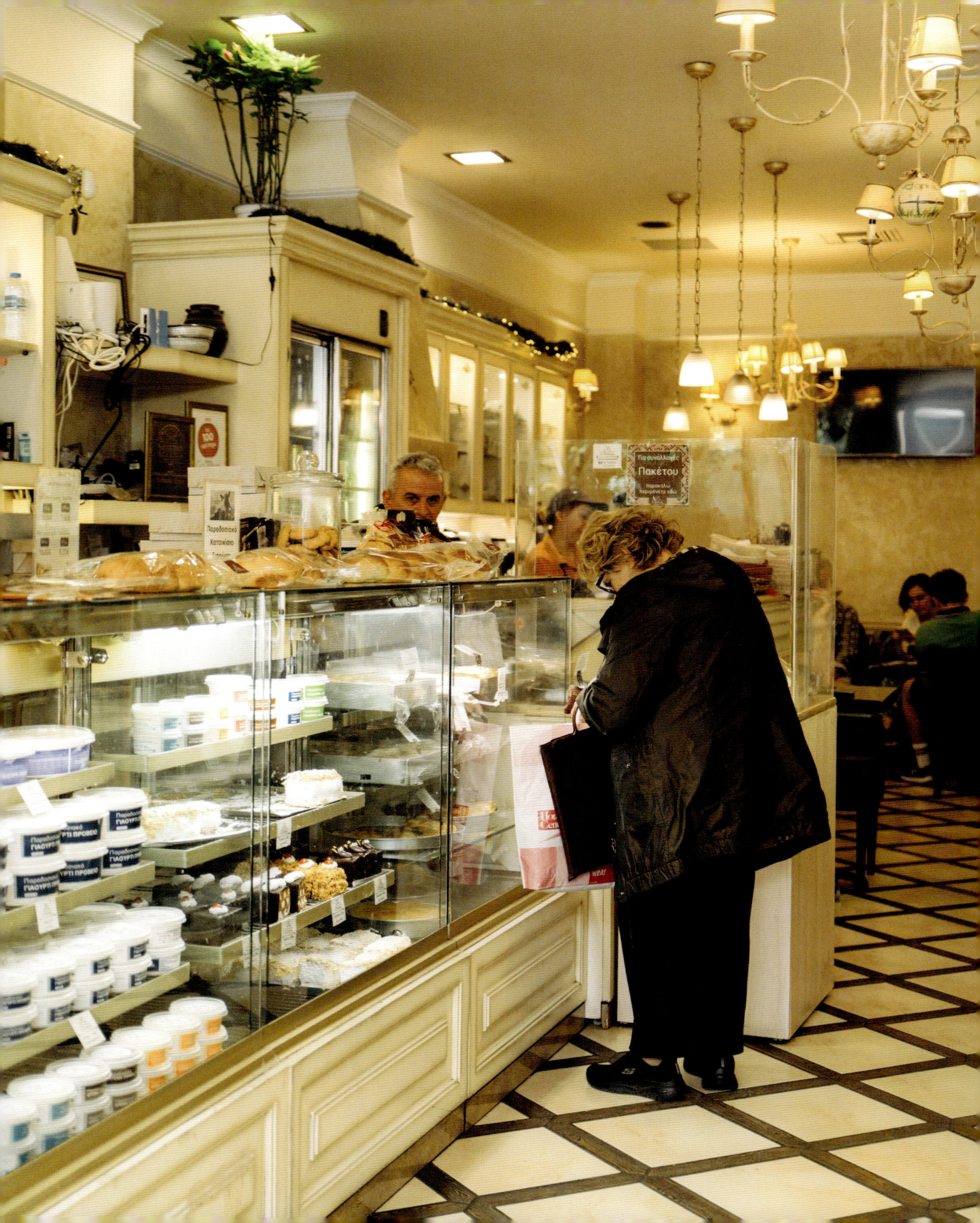
Για συναλλαγές
Πακέτου

and perseverance that have always fueled the Greek spirit.

What was happening in Greek society for the first decade of the twenty-first century was also happening in Greek kitchens: Chefs and home cooks alike were again embracing the understated splendor of their essential cuisine. The traditional fare is founded on real nutritional value and respect for the unadulterated flavors of seasonal ingredients. I saw it in a resurgence of casual tavernas with affordable prices and familiar, if more artful, foods, and in a food press that began catering to the needs of regular people who were looking for simple, healthy recipes to nourish them through hard times.

The Twenty-First Century: Globally Greek—Another Transformation

Things are different now. Athens has grown. Or, rather, it has grown up. For the first time in the three decades I've called this fascinating city home, I sense something in the air that's changed. Call it confidence. Call it a city finally comfortable in its own skin. A city finally at ease with what my youthful arrogance all those years ago, under the city's ancient temple, devoted to wisdom and aglow under the moon, couldn't put into words: Athens's most defining character trait is the natural, underlying, existential angst that has shaken its modern self, since its founding as the new Greek capital in 1830. Athens is a city that will always grapple with the towering reminder of its ancient glories, with every new generation forced to reckon with their contemporary city's imperfections, made more obvious by the daily grind and the constant, if romanticized, reminder of what most of us perceive as a perfect past.

In the last few years, I, too, am more comfortable in my Athenian skin. I am seeing the city for the first time, all over again. For most of my three decades here, I lived in a leafy suburb a few miles to the north. Then, in 2021, I moved downtown to the ancient heart of Athens. I walk everywhere, and that has enabled me to see Athens through fresh eyes, its startling contrasts revealed at every turn. I live where the ancient ceramicists once had their workshops, where Greece's first king, Otto of Bavaria, thought to fashion his palace in the middle of the nineteenth century (only to move uptown to where today's parliament sits) and where layer upon layer of architecture tells the story of this city. I can wolf down a gyro while resting on stumps of ancient marble in an empty lot across the way on Leonidou Street. I can surmise the optimism of a young nation each time I walk by the lumbering, if dilapidated, mansions of wealthy nineteenth-century merchants. I can imagine life in the silk factory, now the Municipal Gallery, every time I stroll down Marathonos Street, its colorful, humble, once-working-class houses now the abodes of hip and well-heeled visionaries who dared to move here before it was fashionable. I ruminate over the collage of city history in each weft and weave of its architectural tapestry, from exquisite neoclassical houses, to examples of lean modernist and Bauhaus buildings, to the brutalist 1960s and 1970s apartment houses and utilities buildings, all woven together in an urban jumble that's uniquely Athenian. The plateia (the Greek equivalent of the piazza) on which I live is a microcosm of both urban splendor and harsh urban reality, alive, on the one hand, with bars, cafés, restaurants, galleries, and theaters, and blighted on the other by the heroin addicts whose numbers speak to a problem of epidemic proportions. My neighborhood is an ethnic melting pot unlike most other neighborhoods in the city, and, despite its woes, it still has a spirit that every day renews my love affair with Athens and its formidable, awe-inspiring contrasts.

One needs time to understand Athens. For visitors, Athens once represented nothing more than a twenty-four-hour stopover en route to major tourist destinations like Santorini and Mykonos. But today the city is a great paradigm for good Mediterranean living and eating. In the last few years, it has become a hub for longer

Introduction: Athens 7

stays, with visitors increasingly interested in more than its famous antiquities. It's also become an amazing food city, an international food city, where Greek and global flavors mesh seamlessly, where the next generation of chefs, nurtured on the internet, have a much more fluid sense of Greekness when it comes to the food they're creating.

While the Parthenon crowns the city, visible from every direction, Athens's contemporary persona and less apparent charms are really what beguile. To navigate Athens is to discover a city obviously rich in history but also overflowing with new creative energy. Food, design, architecture, and nightlife all bubble with the creative juices pumping through the Greek capital.

Its neighborhoods are abuzz with young Greek and international artists, restaurants, bars, galleries, and more. Digital nomads are everywhere. Ever-social, Athens is home to some of the world's fifty top bars, named as such in major international publications. Drinks like the Aegean Negroni and Athens Spritz have become ubiquitous. Its markets reflect the ever-shifting demographics of this pulsating metropolis, so that even neighborhood farmers' markets carry international ingredients such as lemongrass, galangal, jicama, kale, ginger, and tamarind, to name a few. These were virtually unheard of in Athens just a few years ago, and they have been embraced by the Greek denizens of this city, too, whose life view skews toward the inclusive. My own daughter, nurtured on thirty years of traditional Greek cooking, thinks nothing of adding ginger or tamarind or curry or miso to a traditional Greek stew or trying a classic spanakorizo with quinoa or red rice that she picks up in bulk from her neighborhood open-air market. Her grandparents had never heard of, let alone imagined, such things.

Ancient traditions and global realities are everywhere in evidence. One can walk along the market area, down frenetic, crowded Athinas Street, which was imagined by nineteenth-century city planners as the connection between ancient Plaka at the foothill of the Acropolis and Omonoia Square, the very name of which means "unity" and was a beacon of the budding modern city, and find regional ingredients from all over Greece: fish varieties that were lauded by Aristophanes and savored in the Golden Era; honeys and teas and herbs and olives that have been part of the Greek culinary vernacular forever; beverages from Chios and Lesvos; olive oils from Sparta and Crete; cheeses much like the ones described in Homer. All of Greece culminates in the shops and eateries of Athens. One just needs to visit the Ancient Agora and National Archeological Museum to glimpse artifacts that evince how little has changed in the way of traditional cooking methods and ingredients from the time that philosophers roamed the city in wonder. Renowned American archeologist Dr. John Camp, who directed the Agora excavations for the American School of Classical Studies for fifty years, aptly said to me about the continuity of Greek cuisine, "Only the technology has changed," as he pulled ancient griddles and skewers from the catacombs of the Agora to show them to me. They looked remarkably modern.

But modern realities have shaped a modern city and its food, too. Three decades ago, the disintegration of the old Soviet bloc brought Poles, Bulgarians, Albanians, Georgians, and others to Athens in search of a better life, and more than a few have established restaurants, bakeries, and markets that contribute deliciously to the city's foodscape. That very same central market area is now home to Chinese, Sri Lankan, Pakistani, Arabic, and Egyptian food shops, restaurants, and bakeries. A golden visa program that brought throngs of Chinese, Israeli, Russian, and other foreign investors, and the refugee crisis that landed Iraqis, Afghans, Georgians, Syrians, Lebanese, Ethiopians, Senegalese, and others to a city still struggling to absorb them, have also helped shape Athenian food.

Side by side with tradition are all the new and exciting ingredients, flavors, and techniques being co-opted by both professional and home cooks in Athens. The local city press runs stories on the best Georgian flatbread makers and where to eat the best African, Asian, or Indian cuisine in the city, for example.

Athenian home cooks and chefs alike are managing an incredible balancing act, upholding and respecting their deeply rooted traditions, but also embracing the excitement of new ingredients and global trends. Some of the best Greek restaurant food in Athens is hyphenated, as in Greek-Japanese, one delicious example. Some of the most traditional dishes have been transformed to a more global Greek aesthetic. Classics like melitzanosalata, the roasted eggplant dip, for example, pop up all over the place, laced with new flavors such as miso and rice vinegar. These are but two of countless ways that the vibrancy of Athens, and its newly minted international face, is driving a delicious revolution in the kitchen.

Finding Balance

I hope in these pages that I, too, can deliver a complete portrait of the adopted city I have come to love and call home. Culled from my own experience as a transplanted Greek New Yorker expat in Athens these three past decades, this book, while focusing on recipes that represent both traditional Athenian dishes and contemporary Athenian flavors, is part memoir, part reporting, and part guide. There are more than a few iconic, historic dishes that represent long-standing Athenian classics or transformational milestones in the city's evolution from provincial backwater to robust Greek and, ultimately, European, capital.

My love of street food bubbles over into a serendipitous look at some of the best handheld treats the city has to offer, from handheld savory pies of every persuasion to koulouria, or simit rings, and roasted corn and chestnuts hawked from street carts, to the carnivorous pleasures in the souvlaki-gyro genre and, finally, to a look at the impressive array of literally wild street foods available for the picking: pink peppercorns that dangle from trees in many of the city's squares or the laurel, orange, olive, and fig trees that line Athenian streets. Urban foragers have much to find, too, wandering around any of the city's seven hills for wild herbs and greens, just about everything from stinging nettles and mallow to wild chicories and fennel.

Athens is also home to the majority of Greece's finest chefs, with twenty-seven Michelin stars to its name as of this writing. I've included recipes by a few of those chefs and others, whose contributions to Greek cooking have catapulted it to new levels. Among them: Lefteris Lazarou, the father of modern Greek cooking whose seaside restaurant Varoulko continues to seduce diners with delicate, artful, elegant seafood dishes and whose avuncular spirit captures part of the Greek soul. Nena Ismyrnoglou, one of the first women chefs in Athens, has been turning home cooking into an art form for the three decades I've known her. Christoforos Peskias was one of the first chefs to boldly embrace global ingredients and weave them seamlessly into Greek cooking. There are others, too, part of a newer, postcrisis generation, like Sotiris Kontizas, who is half Greek, half Japanese and who has created a genre all its own, in restaurants like Nolan, near Syntagma Square, and Proveleggios, in the trendy Kerameikos neighborhood.

The recipes in *Athens* are geared toward home cooks. While I've drawn inspiration from restaurant menus, my aim is always to provide recipes that can be cooked by just about anyone without too much difficulty. The dishes in this book represent a cross section from street foods you can create easily at home to vegan Greek fare, modern and traditional Greek, as well as hybrid Greek dishes. I couldn't leave out the classics that defined past generations of the Athenian table and are still beloved today, so many of those favorites are included in these pages, too.

Athens is my love song to this most fascinating city, presented plate by plate, and in words and pictures, too, for all to taste and enjoy!

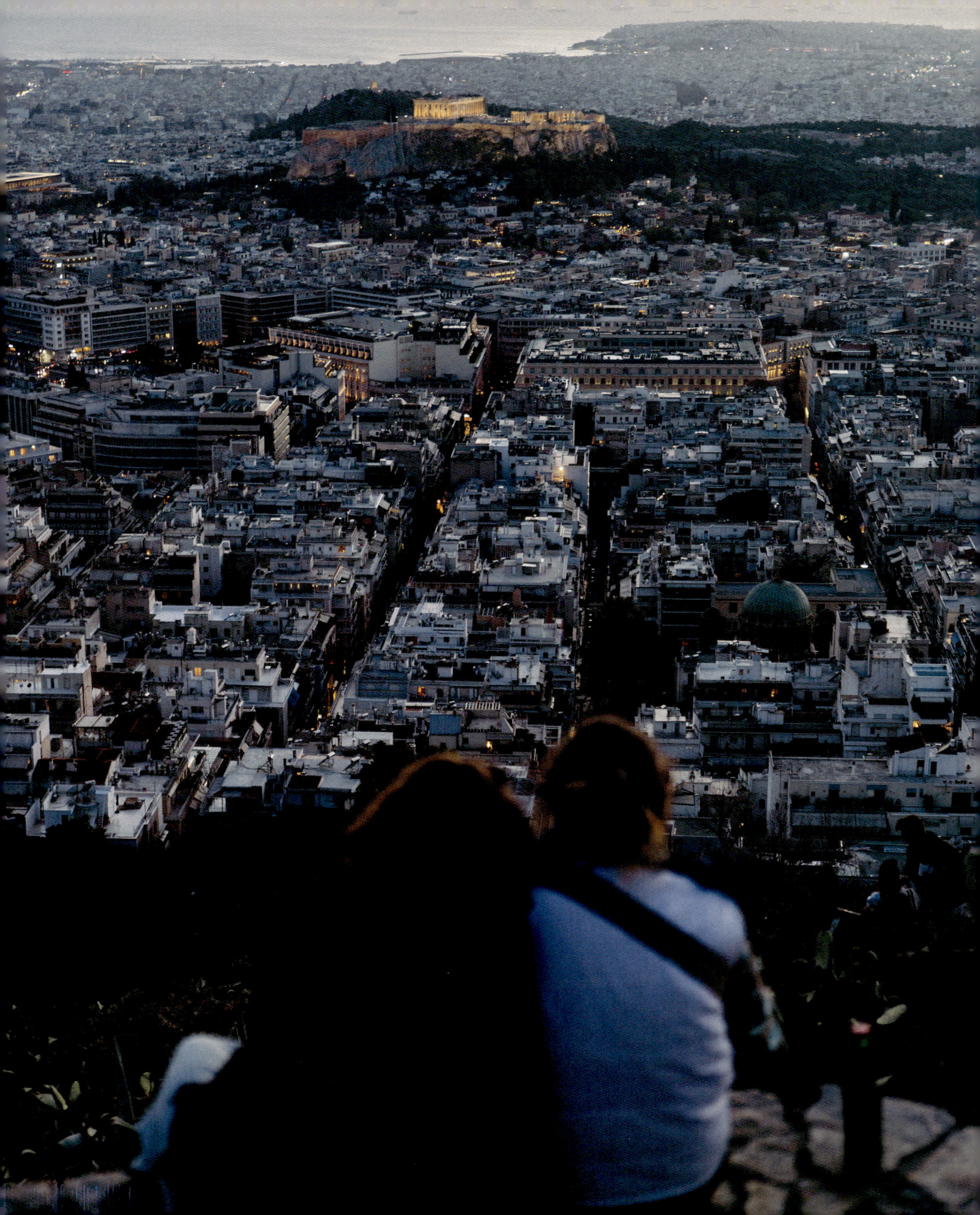

Athens by Hand

Street Food Heaven

Shopping bags in tow, stomach growling, I was on Karagiorgi Servias Street, which runs from Syntagma Square to Athinas Street in the heart of Athens, when I literally bumped into my friend Kyriako, a goldsmith whose workshop was a few feet away. It was lunchtime, the streets were packed, and he was rushing out for souvlaki. The best souvlaki, according to him, and so I followed. This was some twenty-five-plus years ago, the first time I found myself on the long line that was the telltale sign of this landmark souvlaki joint's popularity: Kostas on Pendelis Street, run by the grandson of the founder. His souvlaki stood out in the crowd as a paean to sublime simplicity (good, tender meat; plain, superthick yogurt; unapologetically sharp red onions; juicy tomatoes; and just the right amount of salt and oregano).

Athens was simpler then, the choices for handheld midday grub a toss-up between souvlaki and gyro, palm-sized savory pies differentiated by a few varying types of phyllo pastry, the filling, and the mastery of the makers, and, for those really in a hurry, a sesame bread ring or two called koulouria, which took but a few seconds to negotiate from any of the numerous carts stationed all day on busy street corners.

Fast-forward to the writing of this book. I made my way over to Pendelis Street a few weeks before finishing the manuscript, only to find that Kostas, historic Kostas, had moved, not squeezed out by rising rents, which is all too often the case, but spurred on by the owner's success to a bigger space nearby in a decidedly more touristy strip of the center. I used to love the old place, which was standing room only with a line that stretched twenty people long out the door for hours on end each day, its interior sparsely appointed with little decor beyond a few signs urging people to stay calm while they waited, old newspaper clippings, and some grainy black-and-white photos of Kostas's grandfather, who started with a souvlaki cart in 1948, then graduated to a shop on Adrianou in Plaka, before the current Kostas opened his hole in the wall in 2003. Evolution. Success. Bravo. And, yet, I was wistful and couldn't help but feel that yet another bit of old Athens was lost.

Younger generations than mine would probably beg to differ, at least if one is to judge by the youthful crowds and the palpable excitement in the air when strolling down historic Aiolou Street, which is to me the best place to grasp the breadth and spirit of the Athenian street food scene. Aiolou, named for the god of the wind, Aiolos, was the first street to be paved in the nineteenth century, when Athens had shaken off its Ottoman yoke and was emerging as the capital of the modern Greek state. It runs from the foothills of the Parthenon, at the Roman Agora, to Panepistimiou Avenue, and for most of the twentieth century it was home to the city's vibrant fabrics trade, reams of colorful cloth upright and flapping outside every small shop, as if waving to passersby to come in. We used to go to Aiolou when it was common to have one's clothing sewn by a seamstress, a custom that faded away in the 1980s.

Now, though, Aiolos's winds bring with them the seeds of change and every conceivable trend. Wafting on the breeze are the aromas of Athens's culinary evolution, from provincial capital to international hub, the fabric emporia mostly replaced by fast food and street food shops, cafés, and bars. In a way, this first paved street, so centrally located and with the symbolic Acropolis towering in the background at one end, also paved the way for Athens's new status as a food destination with global gustatory offerings. There are still a few stalwarts, and even another historic (it's a common name) Kostas souvlaki on Agia Eirini Square, which borders Aiolou and is one of the most picturesque plateias in the center, but mostly to stroll down the street of the winds is to see and be tempted by all the latest fads: Everything from reinvented souvlaki and gyros to really great Lebanese fare to the modern versions of Greek doughnuts—loukoumades—drizzled with a rainbow of syrup flavors. There's even bubble tea.

The evolution of street food was, of course, inevitable and mirrors the city's trajectory from a homogeneous society to a vibrant multiethnic European capital, where newly rooted immigrants do what many new arrivals do: scrape together some money and open a small food business.

The Athens street food scene began to mushroom in the early 1990s, with the first waves of immigrants from Eastern Europe. Polish pierogi, for example, called piroski in Greek, are sold in many a small storefront in downtown Athens. New immigrants from the Middle East have added delicious treats to the Athenian food scene, too, such as the tandoori flatbreads baked by recent arrivals from Georgia, who have settled in an area called Agios (Saint) Panteleimonas in lower Patissia, home to one of the largest Orthodox churches in the Balkans. Nowadays you can find pretty much everything from arepas to zongzi (sticky rice balls), the latter in my central Athens neighborhood of Metaxourgeio, which is also Chinatown.

In this chapter I focus on street food recipes that either have some Greek connection, such as pierogi filled with feta, or are the Greek favorites like phyllo pies and gyro-souvlaki wraps that continue to roll out to lines of adoring, hungry Athenians on the go. All the recipes are easy to reproduce in a home kitchen.

Peripatetic friends, should you wander the streets of Athens, you won't go hungry!

Athens by Hand: Street Food Heaven

Tyropitakia Kourou

A few places in Athens have long been known for their version of this unique cheese pie, kourou, among them Ariston on Voulis Street near Syntagma, and Dodoni. Kourou is a kind of tyropita (cheese pie) that is characterized by its short crust, as opposed to a cloak of phyllo pastry. The word comes from the Turkish kuru or kurig, which means "dry," and this pie is just that, but deliciously so: crumbly, buttery, and filled with tangy Greek feta.

MAKES 16 HAND PIES

For the pastry

4 to 5 cups all-purpose flour

½ teaspoon baking powder

½ teaspoon salt

Pinch sugar

¾ cup (6 ounces) cold unsalted butter, diced

¾ cup full-fat Greek yogurt

½ cup extra-virgin Greek olive oil

¼ cup canola oil

1 tablespoon grated kefalotyri or Parmigiano cheese

For the filling

½ pound Greek feta, crumbled

1 tablespoon Greek yogurt

1 tablespoon grated kefalotyri or Romano cheese

1 large egg, lightly beaten

2 tablespoons finely chopped fresh mint

Freshly ground black pepper to taste

For the glaze

1 large egg

1 teaspoon milk

½ to ¾ cup sesame seeds

1 teaspoons nigella seeds

In the bowl of a food processor outfitted with pastry blades, mix together 4 cups of the flour, the baking powder, salt, and sugar. Add the butter and pulse on and off until the mixture is mealy, 30 to 45 seconds. Alternatively, you can do this in a mixing bowl by hand, rubbing the flour mixture and butter together quickly with your fingertips.

In a medium bowl, whisk together the yogurt, olive oil, canola oil, and grated cheese. Add to the flour-butter mixture. If using a food processor, pulse it on and off until everything is combined, adding more flour 1 tablespoon at a time until the dough is dense and no longer sticky, being careful not to overwork. If it's by hand, mix in the liquid with a spoon until a soft, sticky dough forms and continue to knead it until a dough mass forms, adding more flour incrementally as needed, to form a dense, heavy dough that doesn't stick.

Shape the dough into a ball, cover with plastic wrap, and let it rest for at least 30 minutes in the refrigerator.

Make the filling: In a medium bowl, combine the feta, yogurt, grated cheese, egg, mint, and pepper, cover, and set aside until ready to use.

Preheat the oven to 375°F and line 2 rimmed baking sheets with parchment paper.

Remove the dough from the refrigerator and knead lightly on a floured work surface. Divide the dough into 16 equal pieces and shape each into a ball. Place in a floured bowl and cover with a kitchen towel.

Have a small bowl of cold water within reach. Take the first piece of dough, pat or flatten it into a circle with the palm of your hand, and roll it out to a circle 4½ to 5 inches in diameter. Place 2 teaspoons of the feta mixture in the center, dip your index finger in the water, and dampen around the inside rim. Fold the circle over to form a half moon. Press the pie closed using the tines of a fork or your fingers and place on a lined baking sheet. Repeat with the remaining dough and filling.

Make the glaze: Whisk together the egg and milk and brush the surface of the pies. Sprinkle with sesame and nigella seeds and bake for 15 to 20 minutes, or until deep golden. Remove, cool slightly, and serve.

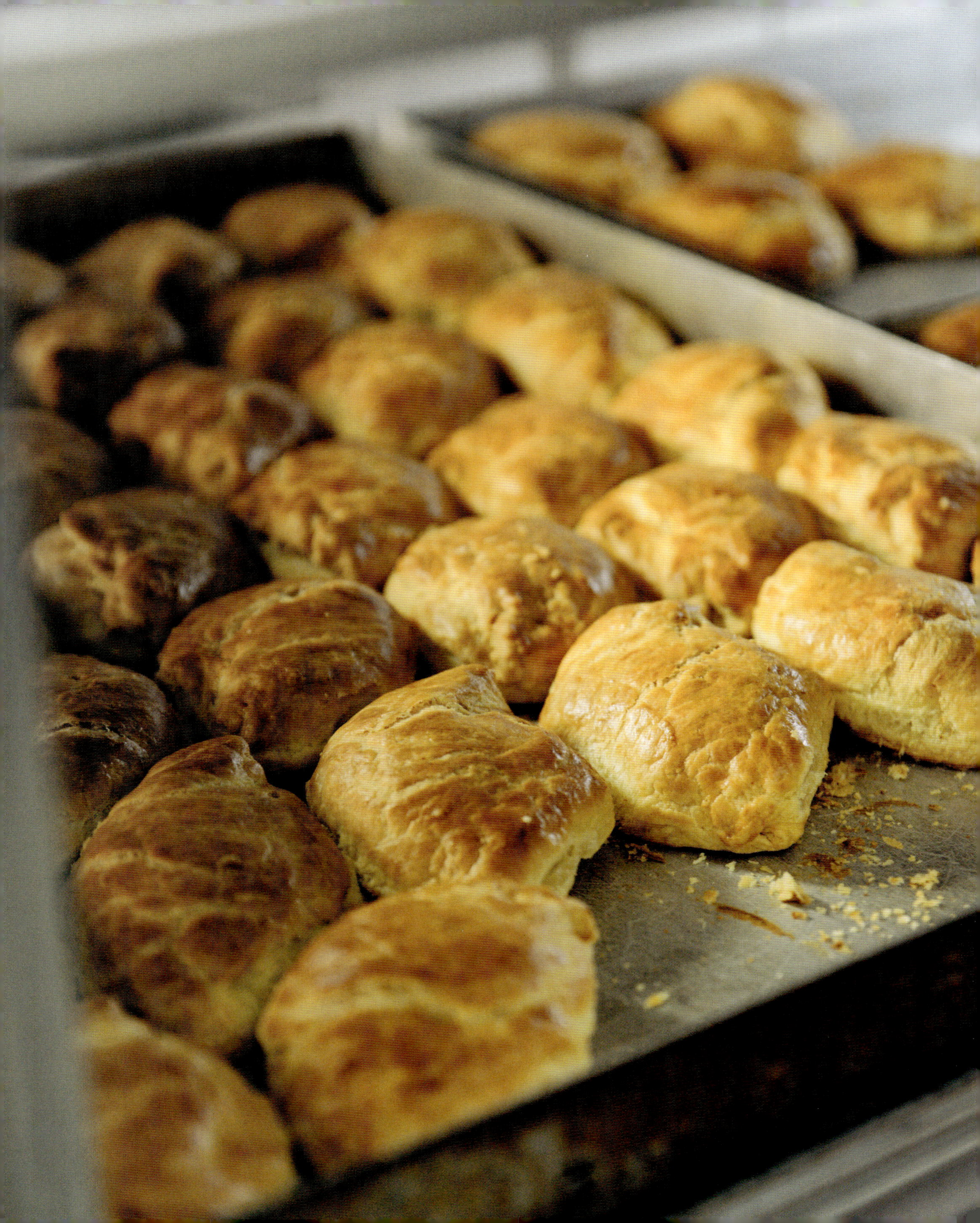

KOYPOY
CHEESE - PIE

Kasseropita Kourou

The most famous place in Athens for this insanely fattening but delicious cheese pie is a small shop called Dodoni, on Lykourgou Street, near Omonoia. The shop was opened in 1972 just across the street by four brothers who hailed from Arta, a coastal town in the southern part of Epirus, in northwestern Greece, where savory cheese pies are a long-standing tradition thanks to the history of shepherding and cheesemaking in the region. Now, a second generation of first cousins continues to run the operation, still making everything by hand. Their kourou is meltingly delicious, larger than most, shaped into a circle instead of a half moon, and filled with kasseri, a sweet and nutty yellow sheep's milk cheese that melts beautifully. They wouldn't, of course, part with the recipe that has kept two generations in business, so this is as close an approximation as possible!

MAKES 16 TO 20 SERVINGS

For the filling

1½ cups grated kasseri cheese

1½ cups crumbled graviera cheese

3 tablespoons heavy cream

2 large eggs, lightly beaten

Freshly ground black pepper to taste

For the pastry

1 recipe pastry for Tyropitakia Kourou (page 14)

For the glaze

1 large egg, lightly beaten

1 tablespoon milk

Make the filling: In a medium bowl, combine the kasseri, graviera, cream, eggs, and a little pepper.

Make the pastry: Remove the dough from the fridge and divide into 4 balls. Place in a floured bowl and cover with a kitchen towel.

Preheat the oven to 350°F and line 2 rimmed baking sheets with parchment paper.

Have a small bowl of cold water within reach. Take the first dough ball and roll it out on a floured surface to a circle about 14 inches in diameter. Using a 4-inch round cookie cutter, cut 8 to 10 circles out of the dough. Using your index finger, rub the perimeter of half of them with a little water. Place 2½ to 3 tablespoons of the cheese filling in the center of each. Fit the remaining circles over the filling, flush and even with the bottom circles, pressing to seal the rim. You can press around the rim decoratively with the tines of a fork or carefully roll up the perimeter to form a decorative rim about ⅛ inch wide. (It's easier to use the fork!) Place on a lined baking sheet and continue with the remaining dough balls and filling to make a total of 16 to 20 filled pies. If there is leftover pastry from cutting out the circles, put it all together and roll it out again to get a few more pieces out of the dough. Save a little filling for that, too.

Make the glaze: Whisk together the egg and milk and brush the surface of the pies. Bake for about 20 minutes, until golden and crispy. Remove, cool slightly, and serve.

Cheese Pies of Athens

They're called tyropites in Greek, literally translated as cheese pies, and their existence stretches way back in time. Ancient literature is peppered with mention of cheese pastries, sweet and savory. To this day, all over Greece, there are dozens of different regional variations.

But in Athens, the story of these handheld, filling treats oozing with feta, kasseri, and a few other Greek cheeses, which are sold by the piece as a snack or quick meal and meant to be eaten on the go, goes back to about the turn of the nineteenth century, when the Greek capital was young and people from the countryside and many parts of the diaspora still under Turkish rule flocked to it.

One such émigré happened to be an enterprising baker named Anastasios Lombotesis, who imported a recipe for what would become his signature pie, copied by many over the years: tyropita kourou, made with a buttery short pastry that's crumbly and bready at the same time. The year was 1910, and the shop, Ariston (which means "perfect"), has been in business ever since, now run by the husband of Lombotesis's granddaughter. It's an Athenian landmark on Voulis Street, up the road from the original Parliament in the heart of the commercial district of the city.

Decades would go by, though, before the cheese pie as a classic Athenian street food with many variations would take root in every corner of the city. That began to happen in the postwar years, with the arrival of a second wave of Greeks from Asia Minor who settled in a neighborhood called Nea Ionia, a few kilometers north of the center. To this day, there are still some great handmade tyropites to be found there.

The cheese pie elicits a lot of passion among local foodies. Which shop makes the best, and which is preferable—kourou, classic crispy layers of phyllo, or country-style dough that is breadier and more rustic? Which place has the creamiest filling? Feta or kasseri?

Thinking about tyropita places in Athens is a little like trying to find the best pizza in New York City. There are a handful of great places and a lot of mediocre ones.

ΖΑΧΑΡΟΠΛΑΣΤΕΙΟΝ
ΑΡΙΣΤΟΝ
ΔΙΟΝ. ΛΟΜΠΟΤΕΣΗΣ
Απο το 1910 Βουλης 10
ΤΥΡΟΠΗΤΕΣ
ΣΠΕΣΙΑΛ
ΤΥΡΟΠΗΤΕΣ
ΣΠΕΣΙΑΛ

Mouzilo's Fabulous Tyropita

I went on a reconnaissance mission to Glyfada, a suburb about 7 miles south of Athens, in an area newly minted as the Athenian Riviera, to seek out Mouzilo, a tiny shop that sells what I can honestly say are the best homemade pies I have ever tasted in the greater Athens area! Stefanos Vasilopoulos, who opened the shop a few years ago, named it for his remote mountain village in Karpenisi, an isolated pocket of northwestern Greece. Like much of that part of Greece, his hometown is renowned for its savory pies. His handmade phyllo is spectacular, crispy, not too thin, not too thick, crinkled, and rich with the flavor of very good olive oil. In his cheese pie, besides feta, he uses a few cheeses that are specialties of his village, namely tsalafouti, a soft, tangy sheep's milk cheese a little bit like a cross between cream cheese, and quark, and a soft goat's milk cheese. They're both impossible to find in the United States, so I have reworked the recipe to approximate the flavor.

MAKES 6 TO 8 SERVINGS

For the phyllo pastry

2 cups fine semolina

1 cup all-purpose flour, or more as needed

½ teaspoon salt

¾ cup water, or more as needed

½ cup extra-virgin Greek olive oil, plus more for brushing

2 teaspoons red wine vinegar

For the filling

2 cups crumbled Greek feta

⅔ cup northern Greek tsalafouti cheese, quark, or whipped cream cheese

⅓ cup soft chèvre

½ cup nigella seeds

Make the pastry: In the bowl of a stand mixer outfitted with a dough hook, combine the semolina, flour, and salt. Add the water, olive oil, and vinegar and mix at low speed to combine. Increase the speed to medium and knead until a smooth, pliant dough forms, about 8 minutes in total. Add a little more water or flour if needed to reach the consistency of a malleable dough. You'll know it's ready when the sides of the bowl are clean. Transfer the dough to a lightly floured surface, knead by hand for about a minute, then divide into 5 equal balls.

Oil the mixer bowl and place the dough balls inside. Cover with plastic wrap and let the dough stand for at least 30 minutes before using.

In the meantime, make the filling: Combine all the cheeses in a medium bowl and mix thoroughly.

Fill a shallow baking pan filled halfway with water, place it on the bottom of the oven, and preheat the oven to 375°F. Oil a 13- to 15-inch round pan. (In Greece, we use round pans about 1½ inches deep to make most savory pies; the closest approximation for an American cook would be a deep-dish pizza pan. A classic 14-inch one will do. A stainless steel paella pan will also work.)

Flatten one dough ball with the palm of your hand on a lightly floured work surface. Flour your rolling pin and roll out the disk to an ⅛-inch-thick circle about 2 inches larger than the circumference of the pan. Place it inside the pan, letting it overhang around the perimeter. Brush it generously with olive oil all over. Repeat with a second dough ball and place it over the first sheet, leaving some overhang, and brush that generously with olive oil, too.

Spoon about half of the cheese filling over the surface of the crinkled phyllo. Roll out another ball, again to a circle slightly larger than the circumference, place it in the pan, and, using your fingertips, crinkle it a little, so that the surface is wavy. Oil it generously and dot with the remaining cheese mixture.

One at a time, roll out 2 more balls the same way, slightly larger than the circumference, then crinkle them a little when you place them inside the pan and brush them generously with olive oil. Take the top and bottom dough overhang and press it inside the circumference of the pan, pinching it as you go along the inside perimeter, to form a nice rim.

Sprinkle the nigella seeds over the top. Score the pie into 6 or 8 wedges (like a pizza). Bake until the phyllo is set and the top is golden and even a little charred. Remove, cool slightly, and serve.

HARRY'S KITCHEN
HOMEMADE PIES

HARRY'S KITCHEN
HOMEMADE PIES

Harry's Strapatsada Boureki

Harry and his wife, Iouli, run a hole in the wall on Lekka Street in Central Athens, a small, winding pedestrian path that leads to Ermou, the city's main shopping street. There is a line out the door here pretty much all day, and with good reason. Harry hails from Poli (Constantinople, or present-day Istanbul), which holds a special (delicious) place in Greek culinary lore. He is usually in the tiny kitchen in back, visible from the street, hand-rolling pastry for his homespun pies. The fillings are unique, with the likes of mushrooms, spicy cheese, classic spinach, and chicken, but so is their pastry—the secret, according to Harry, being the addition of milk. My favorite is the strapatsada, basically tomato scrambled eggs, the perfect Mediterranean diet breakfast on the go.

MAKES 10 HAND PIES

For the pastry

3 to 4 cups all-purpose flour

½ teaspoon salt

½ cup whole milk

¼ cup extra-virgin Greek olive oil, plus more for brushing

¾ cup water

For the filling

3 tablespoons extra-virgin Greek olive oil

2 large, ripe tomatoes, diced (with juices) or grated

4 large eggs

1 scant teaspoon dried Greek oregano

Salt and freshly ground black pepper to taste

For the glaze

1 large egg, lightly beaten

1 tablespoon milk

3 tablespoons melted ghee or clarified butter

Make the pastry: In the bowl of a stand mixer outfitted with a dough hook, combine 3 cups of the flour and the salt. In a small bowl, whisk together the milk, olive oil, and water and add that to the flour. Knead at low speed at first to combine, and once a sticky dough mass forms, increase the speed to medium. If the dough is very sticky, add more flour 2 tablespoons at a time until a smooth dough forms that doesn't stick to the sides of the bowl. Remove the dough and divide it into 10 balls. Oil the mixer bowl, put the dough balls in the bowl, cover with plastic wrap, and leave to rest for at least 30 minutes.

While the dough is resting, make the strapatsada filling: In a nonstick skillet, warm the olive oil over medium heat. Add the tomatoes and cook until their juice cooks off and they're thick and jammy.

In a small bowl, whisk the eggs and pour them into the tomato mixture, pushing them around in the mixture with a wooden spatula to scramble them. They should be juicy but not runny. Season with the oregano, salt, and pepper and remove from the heat. Let the mixture cool.

Preheat the oven to 350°F. Line a baking sheet with parchment paper.

On a lightly floured surface, roll out the first dough ball to a circle about 5 inches in diameter. Brush the surface with a little olive oil and place a heaping tablespoon of the filling in the center. Fold in half to form a half moon and press or roll the edges together to seal the pastry. Place on the lined baking sheet and continue with remaining dough and filling.

Make the glaze: Whisk together the egg and milk. Brush the surface of each piece with a little melted ghee and the egg wash. Bake for about 20 minutes, until golden. Remove and serve, or wrap tightly and store for a day or two at room temperature.

You can make these ahead and freeze them, then bake directly from the freezer in a preheated 350°F oven for 20 to 25 minutes.

Edible Athens, Literally

For about a decade, when our daughter was a child, we lived in the suburb of Holargos, in a rented 1950s maisonette replete with the most beautiful jade-green mosaic floors and a balcony perched high over the street, from which I could sit to nurse and then, later, play with her, unnoticed, while watching the neighbors go about their day. The lady across the street hung her carpets off the balcony railing for a few days every October and May, readying them to be either rolled out or rolled up and stored for the summer, noisily, rhythmically beating the dust out of them with a long wicker carpet thingamajig, the kind with a paddle at one end shaped like the stencil of a rosette. I had never seen anything like that in the wall-to-wall carpeted world of my New York upbringing, so I thought it must be uniquely Greek.

Up the street from her was "Mama," the only name I knew of this bent-over yet spry grandma, because her fifty-something son would shout for her every afternoon to come home from her almost daily foraging expeditions among the olive, fig, mulberry, and bitter orange trees that lined our block and offered their bounty to those industrious enough to pluck their fruits gratis. Mostly, the fruits fell to the ground and blackened underfoot, at least the figs and olives did, speckling the sidewalk like a Jackson Pollock painting.

Mama was the first encounter I had had as an Athenian neophyte with a whole world previously unknown to me: street food in the literal sense. Edible Athens is a city not only of great restaurants and sidewalk treats, it's a city where wild greens grow in abandoned lots, and people like Mama go picking them—in season, of course. It's a city where in even the most urban, downtown, centrally located streets and squares, there's food to be had if you're willing to go for it. As a young reporter I once plucked bay leaves off a tree-line canopy of them in the cement jungle of Patissia, with the late, great Greek painter of gorgeous culinary still lifes, Panayiotis Testis, whose studio was nearby. I also once almost got arrested, or at least noticed, by the bull-chested guards outside the New Democracy Party's headquarters on Rigilis Street, because someone mentioned the pink peppercorn trees that grow there, and I went to look and pluck. That was years ago, and I had all but forgotten them until I discovered, luckily, that they also grow in my own edgy downtown neighborhood, right there in Plateia Avdi; once in a while, if I run out and it's the right season, oblivious to the packed bars and cafés bordering the plateia, I go get some from the source. It's very cool!

In that same square sit a few grassy, gated areas full of herb bushes, a cook's unintentional garden, but I steer clear of them for fear of seeming odd. But I have picked mustard greens, nettles, mallow, and many different wild chicories from nearby lots and up a ways around the less congested areas on the edge of the city.

I relay all this here because edible Athens is so much more than we are used to considering, a cornucopia not only of great, say, souvlaki and gyro cones and so much other delectable street food, but of real street food, Nature in the unlikeliest of places, and all the things a typical Mediterranean landscape has to offer. Mama had the right idea!

Crispy Fried Feta Triangles from Nea Ionia

These crispy fried cheese triangles with their crunchy, toothsome pastry are inspired by a destination cheese pie shop in Nea Ionia, a working-class suburb north of the city settled by Greek refugees from Asia Minor in the 1920s. The Gounarides family, originally from Asia Minor, have been rolling out their own crispy, bubbly phyllo pastry since 1945, and their fried, triangular pies draw fans from all over the city. I used to live nearby and would frequently stop off to pick up these way-too-tempting treats.

MAKES 20 TRIANGLES

For the pastry

3 to 4 cups all-purpose flour

1 scant teaspoon salt

1 egg, lightly beaten

1 cup water

2 tablespoons ouzo, grappa, strained fresh lemon juice, or red wine vinegar

¼ cup extra-virgin Greek olive oil

For the filling

1½ cups crumbled Greek feta

½ cup fresh Greek myzithra, anthotyro, or whole-milk ricotta cheese, drained

Freshly ground black pepper to taste

Pinch dried Greek mint, or to taste

Corn or sunflower oil, for frying

Make the pastry: Place 3 cups of the flour and the salt in the bowl of a stand mixer outfitted with a dough hook. Give the mixture a swirl to combine. Add the egg, water, ouzo, and olive oil and mix at low speed to combine. Increase the speed to medium and mix until a smooth but slightly sticky and relatively firm dough forms. Add more flour a tablespoon or two at a time, if needed, to reach the desired consistency. Shape the dough into a ball, oil the mixer bowl, and let the dough rest in the bowl for at least 30 minutes and up to 2 hours, covered with a kitchen towel or plastic wrap.

Make the filling: In a small bowl, combine all the ingredients for the filling, cover, and refrigerate until ready to use.

Have a small bowl of cold water within reach. Divide the dough into 2 balls and flatten each into a disk. Roll out the first piece on a lightly floured surface in as close to a rectangle shape as possible, about 15 by 8 inches. Cut the rectangle in half lengthwise. Cut each strip into pieces about 3 inches long. Place a heaping tablespoon of the cheese filling in the middle of each piece. Using your index finger, rub the perimeter of the dough with a little water, then fold the dough over to form a rectangle. Press the pie closed using the tines of a fork or your fingers and place on a lined baking sheet. Repeat with the remaining dough and filling.

Heat 1 to 1½ inches corn oil in a large, heavy skillet over medium-high heat and fry a few triangles at a time, turning with kitchen tongs to brown lightly on both sides, about 2 minutes per side. Remove and drain on paper towels. Repeat with the remaining triangles, replenishing the oil if necessary. Serve hot or warm.

Greco-Russian Piroski Stuffed
with Feta Mashed Potatoes

One of the most fascinating parts of Athens to explore is the area of Agios (Saint) Panteleimonas, named for the huge church, one of the largest in the Balkans, that anchors it. The neighborhood is in the northwestern part of the city center, about a 20-minute walk from Omonoia, between Victoria Square and Attiki Square. It's one of the most multiethnic parts of the city, home to Afghan, Syrian, Egyptian, Georgian, Polish, Nigerian, Senegalese, and Ethiopian immigrants, among others, and the aromas of all this global cooking emanates from bakeries, kebab and shawarma shops, falafel joints, and more. I tasted one of the best gyros I'd ever had in the city here, at a place called Al Zaim, run by Syrians, who stack their chicken pieces on a huge standup rotisserie and wrap the shavings in flatbread together with strips of pickled cucumber, yogurt, tomatoes, fries, lettuce, and pomegranate molasses.

Acharnon and Aristotelous, two of the main streets that run north-south in the neighborhood, are also home to exotic (for Athens) produce markets, where gourds, chiles, unfamiliar root vegetables, and other foreign fare are the stuff of daily meals. It's here, too, where some of the best piroski and Georgian flatbreads are found, in a few shops that draw a crowd all hours of the day. My favorite piroski fit my goal perfectly: a cross-cultural concoction that is a classic piroski pastry packed with comforting feta mashed potatoes.

MAKES 20 PIROSKI

For the pastry

1½ cups whole milk or water, warmed

1 tablespoon active dry yeast

1 teaspoon sugar

1 teaspoon salt

1 large egg

2 tablespoons extra-virgin Greek olive oil

3½ to 4 cups all-purpose flour

For the filling

2 large Yukon Gold potatoes

2 teaspoons salt, plus more to taste

¼ cup extra-virgin Greek olive oil or melted unsalted butter

1½ cups crumbled Greek feta

Freshly ground black pepper to taste

Sunflower oil, for frying

Make the pastry: In a large bowl, combine the warm milk, yeast, and sugar. Cover and let the mixture proof for about 5 minutes, or until it starts to bubble a little. Whisk in the salt, egg, and olive oil. Add the flour in 1-cup increments, stirring after each addition, until a soft, somewhat sticky dough forms. You will use at least 3½ cups of flour in the total mixture. Turn the dough out onto a floured surface and knead it a little more, sprinkling and working a little of the remaining flour into the dough, which should be soft and a little sticky. Oil the bowl, put the dough in it, cover with a kitchen towel, and let it rest and rise for 45 to 60 minutes.

In the meantime, make the filling: Peel and quarter the potatoes and place them in a pot with enough water to cover by 1 inch. Bring to a boil and add the salt. Boil until the potatoes are soft enough to pierce easily with a fork, 15 to 20 minutes. Drain the potatoes and place in a medium bowl. Add the olive oil and crumbled feta. Mash with a fork or potato masher until the mixture is smooth. Season to taste with salt and pepper. Set aside to cool.

Remove the piroski dough from the bowl and shape into a loaf about 30 inches long. Cut through the loaf at 1½-inch intervals to get 20 even-sized pieces. Keep them covered with a kitchen towel while you work.

On a lightly floured surface, roll out 1 piece of dough to a circle about 5 inches in diameter. Fill the center with about 1½ tablespoons of the filling. Bring the dough together from 2 sides of the circle and pinch to seal. Turn the sealed piroski over so the seam side is on the bottom and roll it out a little to shape into a flattish oval about 1 inch thick. Cover with a kitchen towel and repeat with the remaining dough and filling.

When they're all assembled, pour about 3 inches sunflower oil into a large, wide pot or deep skillet and heat to about 375°F. Using a slotted spoon, carefully slip a few piroski, seam side down, into the oil and cook, turning once, until golden brown, about 4 minutes. Have a double layer of paper towels spread out onto a platter or tray and drain the piroski. Continue frying and draining, replenishing the oil and using more paper towels as needed. Serve hot.

Graviera Cheese and Ham Pie

Ham and cheese fillings for phyllo pies make for one of the most popular street foods. Getting the creaminess just right is the secret, and the best ones are usually a combination of a quick béchamel sauce with a variety of cheeses and bits of ham mixed in.

MAKES 12 SERVINGS

For the filling

2 tablespoons unsalted butter

2 tablespoons all-purpose flour

2 cups whole milk, warmed

½ cup heavy cream

½ teaspoon freshly grated nutmeg, or more to taste

Salt and ground white pepper to taste

2 large eggs

1½ cups crumbled Greek feta

1½ cups diced or coarsely grated kasseri, graviera, or other mild, semi-soft sheep's milk cheese

1 cup diced good-quality ham

For the pastry

1 pound frozen phyllo, thawed and at room temperature

Extra-virgin Greek olive oil or melted clarified butter, for brushing

Make the filling: In a deep skillet or small, wide pot, warm the butter over medium heat until it melts and bubbles. Add the flour and whisk for 3 to 5 minutes, until the flour is cooked but before it starts to brown. Add the warm milk in a slow, steady stream, whisking until it starts to thicken, 6 to 8 minutes. Whisk in the cream and continue whisking until the mixture is luscious and thick, almost the consistency of pancake batter. Season with the nutmeg, salt, and white pepper.

In a medium bowl, whisk the eggs until frothy, then vigorously whisk in about ¼ cup of the béchamel, in 1-tablespoon increments, to temper the eggs (keep them from curdling). Then, slip the beaten, tempered eggs into the béchamel, whisking vigorously so they don't cook. Stir in the cheeses and ham and adjust the seasoning with more nutmeg, salt, and white pepper, as desired.

Preheat the oven to 375°F. Lightly oil a 9 x 13-inch baking pan.

Place 6 sheets of phyllo on the bottom of the pan, brushing each with olive oil. Spread the filling evenly over the last sheet and top with another 4 or 5 sheets, brushing each with olive oil, too. Roll the edges in to form a decorative rim. Score the pie into 12 pieces and bake for about 50 minutes, or until golden and crisp. Serve warm for the cheeses to ooze out pleasantly and the filling to retain its creaminess.

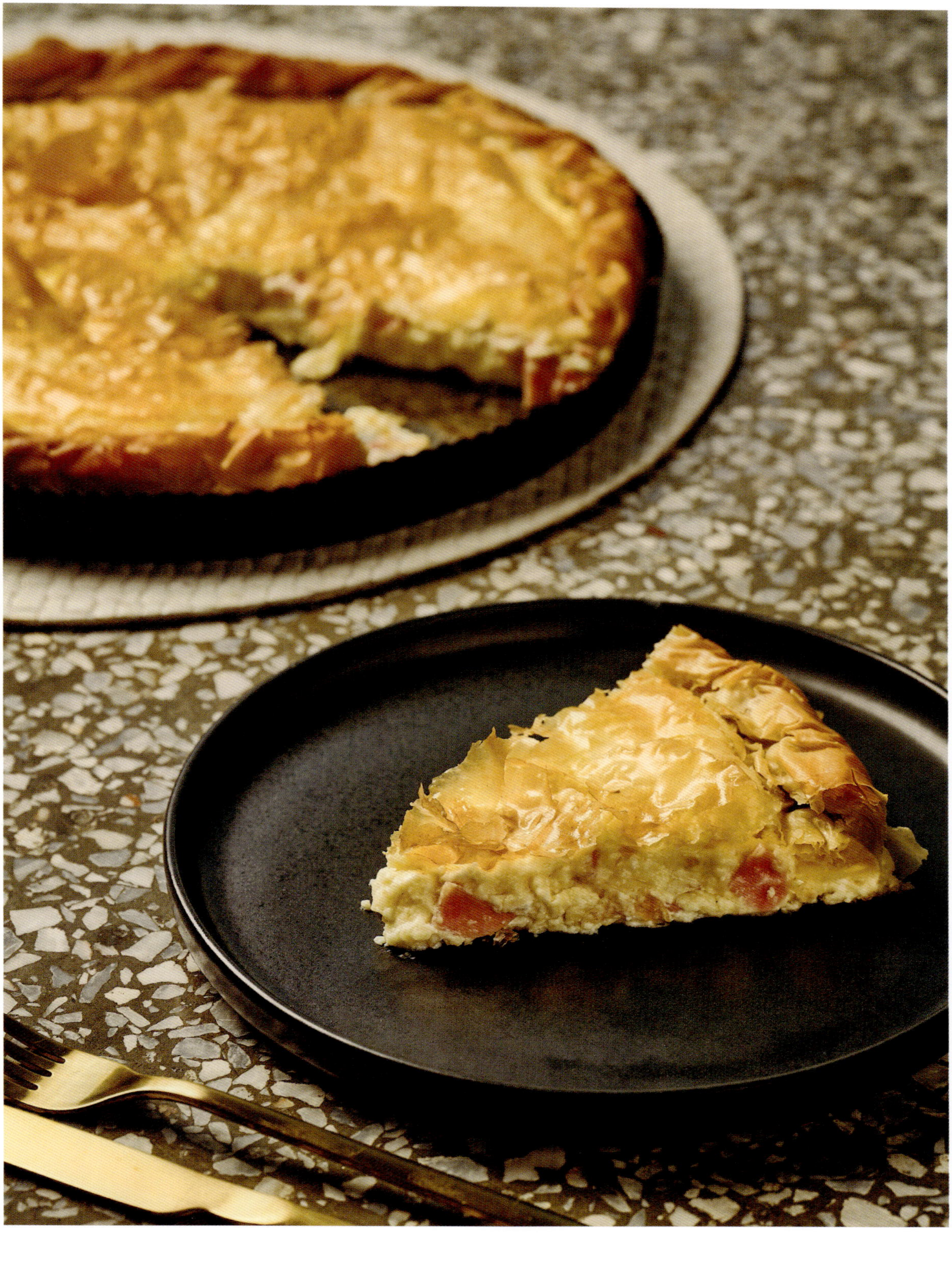

The Sandwich, Athens Style

Sandwiches are a huge topic. I still recall so fondly my very first years visiting Athens, as a girl, and discovering the tost places. These were small storefronts with an open display of ingredients, everything from lettuce and tomatoes to olives, bacon, meatballs, boiled eggs, fried peppers and eggplants, and a variety of yogurt-, mayonnaise-, or cheese-based spreads. You could pick and choose and the guy behind the counter would slap it all together on an oval white bun and grill it in what was essentially a panini maker. This was Athens when it was a simpler city, with limited street food options that made tost seem exciting, especially to a young palate like mine.

Tost, in its simplest form, is still one of the most popular after-school snacks or quick meals, and most moms are happy to offer their kids a "tostaki," referring to what is basically a grilled cheese sandwich that sometimes also contains sliced ham or turkey and tomatoes. Panini makers are a common kitchen appliance in Athens.

But at the commercial level, there's been a sandwich revolution in the city, and it's in evidence on many downtown streets. Everything Italian is looked upon with reverence, so many sandwich stops have a gourmet selection of Italian charcuterie, cheeses, and condiments, and many still offer up a kind of make-your-own combo sandwich, grilled or not.

There are a few destination sandwich shops around town where the offerings are Greek, international, and creative. I've culled from many of them when thinking about the sandwiches that define the unique Athenian interpretation of that universally loved hand-held food.

Kimadopita

GROUND BEEF AND VEGETABLE PIE

Savory pies can be filled with almost anything, but ground meat pies are especially esteemed because they can easily double as a substantial meal. Most recipes originate in either Epirus, the mountainous region in northwestern Greece, or among the Greeks of the Black Sea, known as Pontos. In recent years, a few pie shops around Athens have rebirthed the idea of a meat pie to include fillings like beef bourguignon! I bow to a more classic rendition here, a sort of amalgam of the various meat pies I've known and loved on the streets of Athens.

MAKES 8 TO 10 SERVINGS

For the filling

3 tablespoons extra-virgin Greek olive oil

3 large onions, very finely chopped

1 large carrot, peeled and minced

1 celery stalk, trimmed and minced

Salt and freshly ground black pepper to taste

½ teaspoon ground allspice

½ teaspoon freshly grated nutmeg

½ teaspoon ground cinnamon

½ teaspoon sweet paprika

½ teaspoon smoked paprika or cayenne

2 pounds ground beef

1 bay leaf

1 tablespoon tomato paste

1½ cups grated kasseri cheese

1 large egg, lightly beaten

1 cup chopped fresh flat-leaf parsley

For the pastry

1 pound frozen phyllo, thawed and at room temperature

Extra-virgin Greek olive oil, for brushing

To make the filling, heat the olive oil in a large, wide pot or deep skillet over medium heat. Add the onions, carrot, and celery, salt very lightly, and cook, stirring occasionally, for about 10 minutes, until soft and glistening. Add the spices and stir them around for a few seconds. Add the ground beef, breaking it up in the pan with a wooden spoon. Add the bay leaf. Stir in the tomato paste and cook, stirring, until the meat is browned and the pan juices have been absorbed, 12 to 15 minutes.

Remove the pan from the heat and let the mixture cool. Remove the bay leaf, add the grated cheese, and adjust the seasoning with salt and pepper. Add the lightly beaten egg and parsley and mix well.

Preheat the oven to 375°F. Oil a 9 x 13-inch baking pan.

Place 8 sheets of phyllo on the bottom of the pan, leaving the phyllo overhanging around the rim of the pan and brushing each sheet with olive oil as you go. Spread the meat filling evenly over the top and pat down with a spatula.

Place another 6 sheets of phyllo over the top, brushing each with olive oil. Taking the phyllo that hangs over the edge of the pan from both the bottom and top layers, roll them together and turn them into the pan as you go, along all four edges, to form a decorative rim. Score the pie into serving pieces and bake for about 50 minutes, or until golden and crisp. Remove, cool completely, and serve.

Spinach Pie Meets Croissant

Not too far from my home in downtown Athens is Praxitelous Street, named after the legendary marble sculptor of the ancient world and home for most of its modern life to small shops that sell all kinds of paper and lighting fixtures. There are some exquisite buildings and stoas—the Greek equivalent of porticos, or long, covered walkways on the ground level of many old buildings—along this street, and the tradesmen's spaces that once occupied them have morphed into bars, cafés, restaurants, and, of course, temporary rentals for hip tourists. Most of the lighting shops have gone dark. That said, there's a youthful spark to this old Athenian street, and you can see it in the morning in the line spilling outside Overoll, a croissant shop, and at night at the Clumsies, which is consistently voted one of the best bars in the world. Overoll is where Greek savory pies meet French puff pastry. Their hand-held spinach-feta croissant has taken the city by storm, and the recipe below is my homage to this Greco-French borderless treat.

MAKES 10 PIECES

For the filling

1 (10-ounce) package frozen chopped spinach, thawed

2 tablespoons extra-virgin Greek olive oil

1 tablespoon unsalted butter

1 leek, trimmed and very finely chopped

1 garlic clove, minced

1¼ cups crumbled Greek feta, plus more for serving

3 tablespoons chopped fresh dill, plus more for serving

½ teaspoon freshly grated nutmeg

Salt and freshly ground black pepper to taste

For the pastry

1 large egg, lightly beaten

1 tablespoon water

All-purpose flour, for dusting

½ (17.3-ounce) package puff pastry (1 sheet), thawed

2 tablespoons sesame seeds

Make the filling: Place the spinach in a fine-mesh sieve or colander and squeeze out as much of the liquid as possible. Alternatively, you can do this in a thin cotton kitchen towel. It's important for the spinach to be dry.

Heat the olive oil and butter in a medium skillet over medium heat. Add the leek and sauté until soft, about 7 minutes. Stir in the garlic. Transfer to a medium bowl and add the well-drained spinach, 1 cup of the crumbled feta, the dill, nutmeg, salt, and pepper. Mix well.

Preheat the oven to 400°F.

For the pastry, whisk the egg and water in a small bowl. Sprinkle a work surface with flour. Unfold the pastry sheet on the work surface. Brush the pastry sheet with a little of the egg mixture. Top with the spanakopita mixture, leaving about ½ inch of pastry along the edges. Starting at a short side, roll up like a jelly roll. Cut into about 10 (1-inch) slices. Place the slices, cut side down, onto 2 rimmed baking sheets. Brush the slices with the egg mixture and sprinkle with the sesame seeds. Bake for 15 minutes, or until the pastries are golden brown. Remove the pastries from the baking sheets and let cool on wire racks for 10 minutes. Garnish with additional crumbled feta and chopped dill and serve.

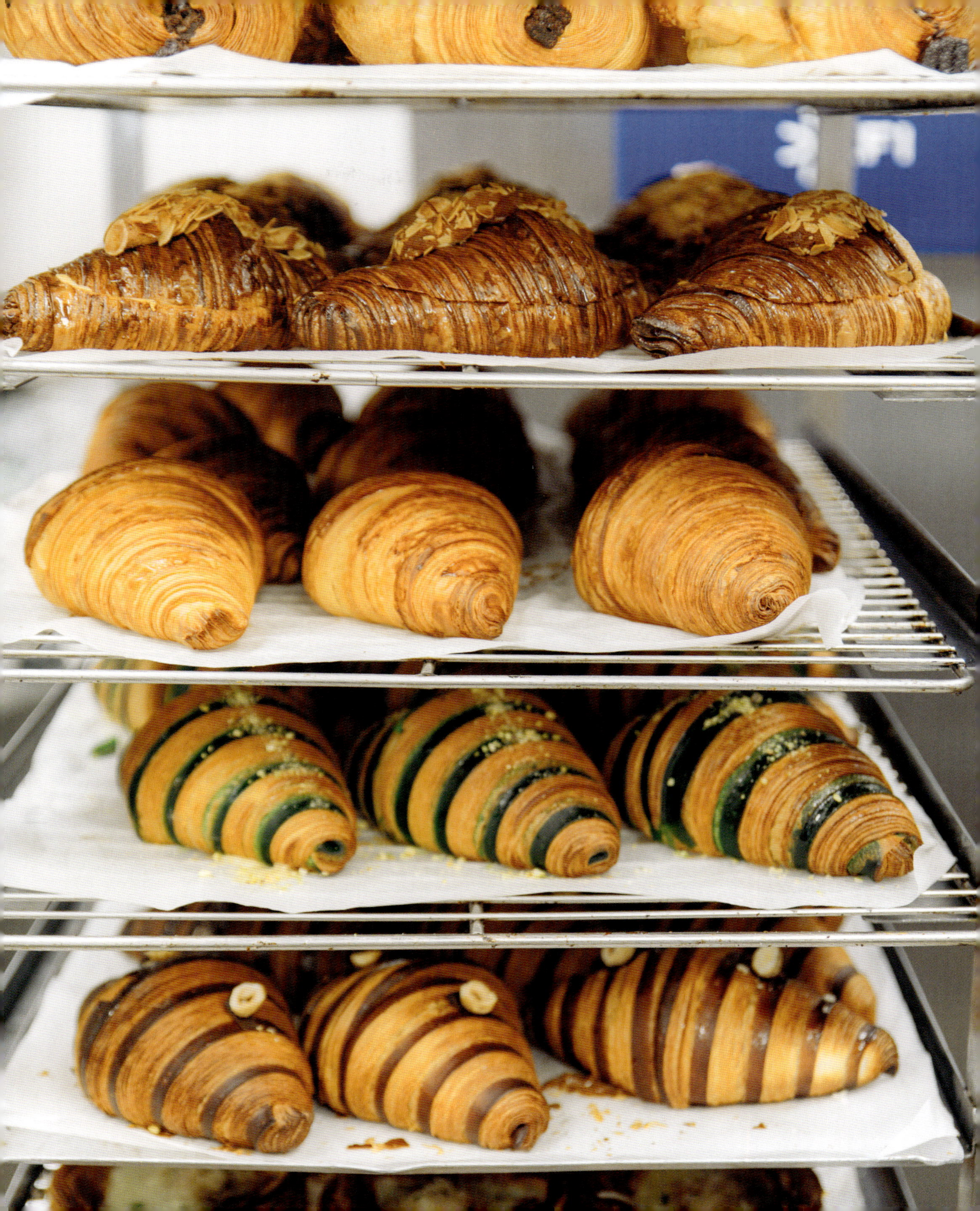

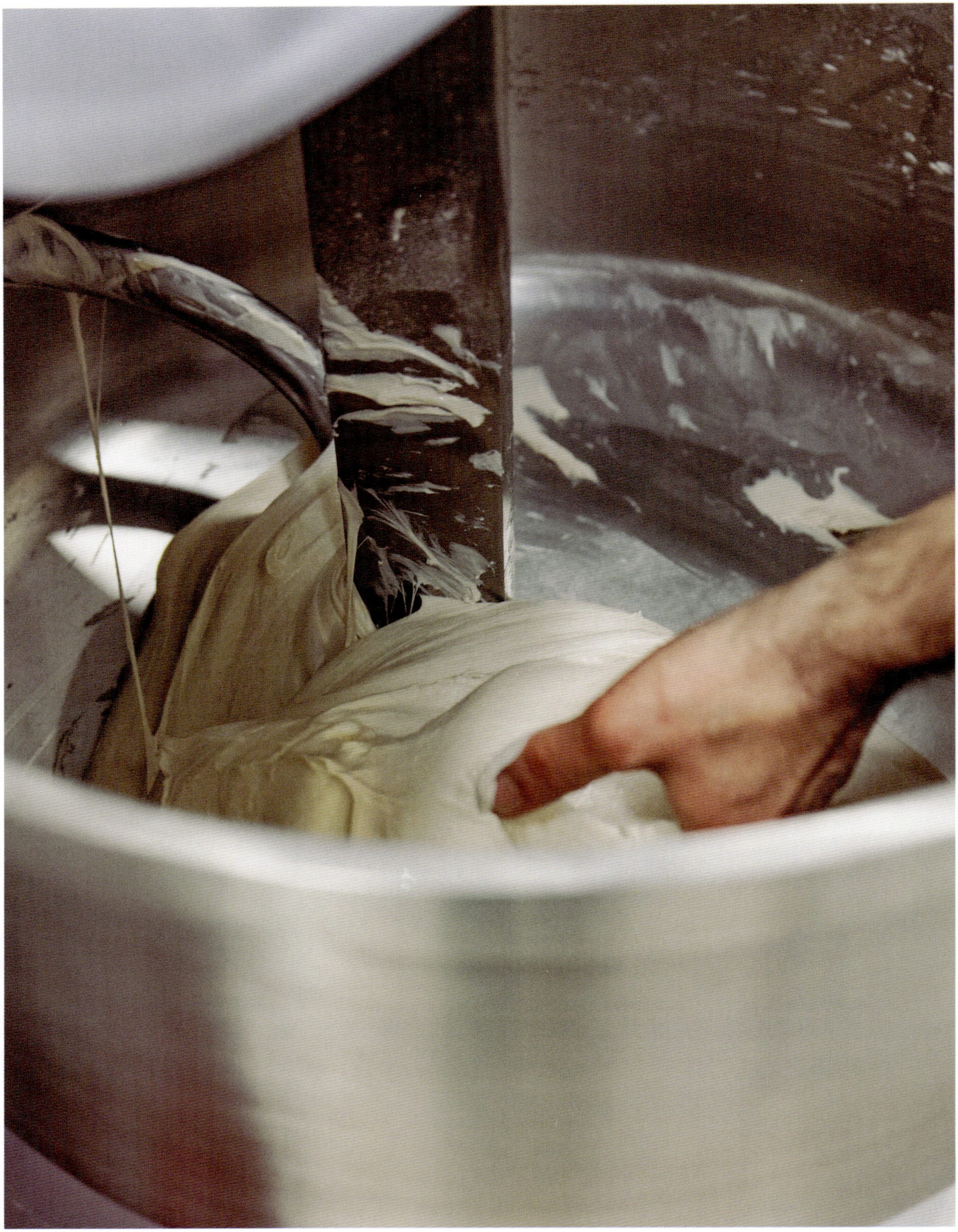

FOCACCIA SANDWICHES

As I researched the street foods of Athens, I began to notice some trends that hadn't been part of the city's food tapestry even just a short time ago. In Athens's newfound life as a multicultural city, many delicious hybrids have been born there. Indeed, my goal when looking at the international face of Athens wasn't to record the recipes for classic fare from other places, such as Russian piroski or Italian focaccia, that are available all over the city. Instead I sought out the overlaps where Greek and international meet, hence the following handful of fun sandwiches that call for focaccia but are filled with Greek ingredients. Many have been inspired by a place called Black Salami that has been all the rage since it opened a few years ago in the downtown neighborhood of Exarcheia, itself one of the greatest points of cultural change and transformation the city has ever seen. I've tweaked the following few sandwiches to make them easier to prepare in a home kitchen anywhere.

Grilled Spanakopita Focaccia

Spanakopita has inspired many iterations beyond the classic Greek phyllo pie. The spinach-leek-onion-feta-dill filling is so universally liked and such a timeless classic that it's found its way into everything from crepes (page 72) to salads (page 143) to this Gallic-Grecque creation that draws a crowd all day long at the sandwich shop Black Salami.

MAKES 2 SANDWICHES

Filling for Spinach Pie Meets Croissant (page 32)

½ cup well-drained Greek anthotyro or ricotta cheese

3 tablespoons grated pecorino, Parmigiano, or Greek kefalograviera cheese

2 (4-inch) focaccia squares, halved horizontally

2 tablespoons extra-virgin Greek olive oil, plus more for frying (if not using a panini maker)

In a medium bowl, combine the spanakopita filling with the additional cheeses.

Brush the inside of each of the 4 focaccia pieces with olive oil (save a little for the top, too). Spread the spanakopita filling evenly between the 2 bottom halves. Cover with the top 2 halves and press down. Brush the tops with the remaining olive oil.

Grill in a hot oiled skillet or in a panini maker until the outside is lightly browned, maybe a little charred in a few places, and crispy. Serve hot.

Grilled Focaccia Sandwich
with Greek Olives, Manouri Cheese, Tomato Vinaigrette, and Fresh Basil

This oversized sandwich is the perfect example of a Graeco-Roman marriage made in food heaven! Manouri is a mild, buttery whey cheese very similar to ricotta salata, which would be an easy replacement. The tomato vinaigrette with Greek honey is yet another example, however simple, of some of the new combinations of traditional ingredients that define Athens today.

MAKES 2 SANDWICHES

¼ cup extra-virgin Greek olive oil, plus more for frying (if not using a panini maker)

1 heaping tablespoon tomato paste

2 teaspoons balsamic vinegar

1 teaspoon honey (ideally Greek pine honey), or more to taste

Salt and freshly ground black pepper to taste

1 tablespoon toasted pine nuts or coarsely chopped toasted hazelnuts

3 tablespoons chopped pitted kalamata, Greek Halkidiki, or other green olives, 10–12 in all

2 (4-inch) focaccia squares, halved horizontally

4 slices manouri or ricotta salata cheese, about ½ inch thick and 2½ inches in diameter

4 to 6 (¼-inch-thick) tomato slices

6 to 8 fresh basil leaves

In a small bowl, whisk together the olive oil, tomato paste, balsamic vinegar, and honey until smooth. Season lightly with salt and pepper.

Pulse the nuts and olives together in the bowl of a small food mill or processor for a few seconds, until mealy and well combined.

To assemble the sandwiches, spread the tomato paste vinaigrette on the inside of each of the 4 focaccia pieces. Place the manouri and tomato slices on the 2 bottom halves, then divide the olive-nut mixture evenly over them. Place the basil leaves on top and cover the sandwich with the 2 top halves of the focaccia. Grill in a hot skillet lubricated with a teaspoon or two of olive oil or in a panini maker until the focaccia is crispy and lightly browned. Serve.

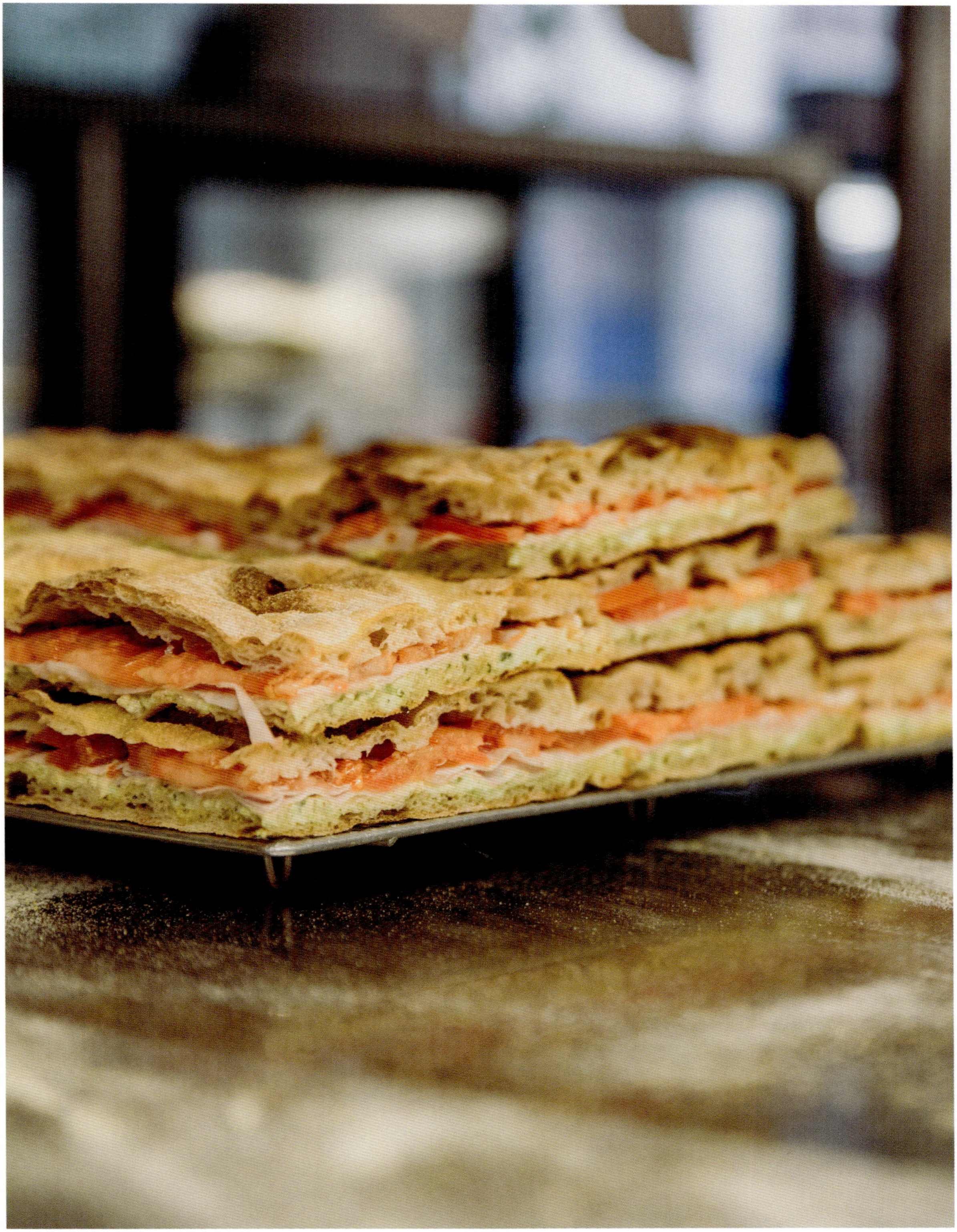

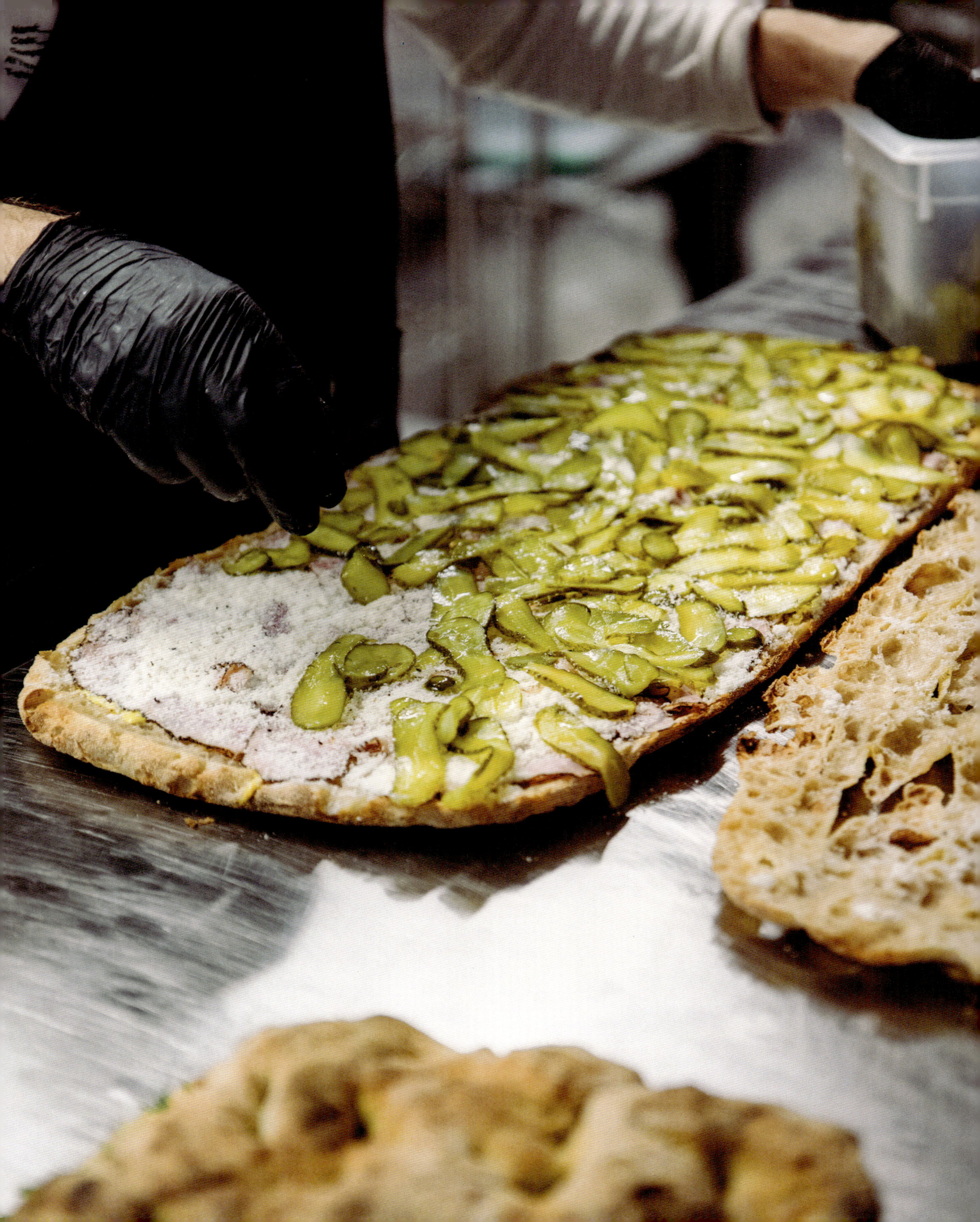

Focaccia Sandwich
with Fava, Arugula, and Grilled Eggplants

Fava is a very common Greek bean spread, akin to hummus but made from yellow split peas and not chickpeas. I used it as a sandwich spread in many recipes because it adds substance and is creamy, almost like mayo, but denser and much more nutritious. I was glad to see the use of fava as a sandwich spread take root in a very trendy shop in Exarcheia and love the idea of this vegan sandwich composed of real food and nothing fabricated in a lab. You can substitute hummus, homemade or ready-made from the grocery store, if you don't feel like making the fava or can't find it already made in a specialty Greek food shop.

MAKES 2 SANDWICHES

½ bunch arugula, trimmed

8 tablespoons extra-virgin Greek olive oil, plus more as needed

Sea salt to taste

2 tablespoons balsamic vinegar

1 teaspoon grape or pomegranate molasses

1 small red onion, coarsely chopped

1 small eggplant, trimmed and cut lengthwise into ½-inch slices

½ teaspoon minced garlic

¼ cup Yellow Split Pea Fava (page 97) or hummus

2 (4-inch) focaccia squares, halved horizontally

Coarsely chop the arugula and toss in a medium bowl with 2 tablespoons of the olive oil, a pinch of salt, 1 teaspoon of the balsamic vinegar, and the grape molasses. Set aside to marinate until you're ready to use it in the sandwich.

Heat 2 tablespoons olive oil in a medium nonstick or cast-iron skillet over low heat. Add the onion, sprinkle with a little salt, and cook for about 20 minutes, until golden.

In the meantime, heat a ridged grill pan over medium heat. In a large bowl, whisk together 2 tablespoons olive oil, the remaining 1 tablespoon balsamic vinegar, and the garlic. Brush the eggplant slices with the remaining 2 tablespoons olive oil. Place in the grill pan in a single layer, in batches if necessary, and grill, turning once, to brown lightly, soften, and acquire lines on both sides, 4 to 5 minutes. Remove and transfer to the bowl with the oil, vinegar, and garlic. Turn the slices gently in the marinade and let them stand for about 10 minutes.

To assemble the sandwiches, spread the fava on the inside of each of the 4 focaccia pieces. Divide the eggplant slices evenly between the 2 bottom halves of the focaccia, then top with an equal portion of caramelized onions and marinated arugula. Place the 2 top halves of the focaccia over the arugula, pressing down a little. You can serve this as is or toast it in a panini maker, fresh arugula and all. Either way, it's a great tostaki.

Bean Soup Sandwich

Athens has seen a huge explosion in street food concepts these past few years. Many are skewer-centric, such as souvlaki and gyro every which way, but there are now countless offerings both Greek and international. One of the more creative stops is a place I stumbled upon in the northern suburb of Agia Paraskevi, called Oursa, the Greek word for "bear." A bear is the defining animal of northern Greece whence chef-owner Dimitris Stratis hails. This little place is basically a glorified shack or canteen, where he combines comfort with convenience by serving up traditional Greek recipes like oregano chicken, pork and celery, and even the classic Greek bean soup between the bread. He has a penchant for pickled veggies and hot peppers, so tradition is spiced up at Oursa. This recipe is inspired by one of his delicious offerings. Beans on toast, move over!

MAKES 2 TO 4 SANDWICHES

½ cup extra-virgin Greek olive oil

1 large red onion, peeled and finely chopped (about 1 cup)

1 large carrot, chopped

1 celery stalk, chopped

2 garlic cloves, finely chopped

1 (15-ounce) can good-quality, low-sodium cannellini beans, drained

1½ cups canned diced tomatoes

2 bay leaves

1 to 2 cups water

2 long dried chiles

Salt and freshly ground black pepper to taste

1 tablespoon balsamic vinegar

¼ cup chopped fresh flat-leaf parsley

¼ cup chopped fresh oregano

1 cup sliced cooked pork or beef sausage (optional)

½ cup crumbled Greek feta (optional)

2 to 4 sourdough buns or rolls

Heat ¼ cup of the olive oil in a large pot over low heat. Add the onion, carrot, and celery and cook until softened, about 10 minutes. Stir in the garlic. Add the beans and toss to coat in the oil. Pour in the tomatoes with their juices, bay leaves, and 1 cup of the water. Add the chile peppers. Raise the heat and bring to a boil. Reduce the heat to low and let the beans simmer for about 30 minutes, or until the mixture is thick and creamy and the beans and vegetables are very soft. Add more water as needed, checking the liquid content on the beans as they simmer.

About 10 minutes before removing from the heat, season with salt and pepper to taste. Add the balsamic and stir in the parsley and oregano. Add the sausages and/or feta (if using).

Heat a nonstick or cast-iron skillet over high heat. Open the buns without separating the bottoms and tops completely. Brush the inside surfaces with some or all of the remaining olive oil and sear, cut side down, in the hot skillet. Place the buns on plates and spoon the bean filling inside. Serve.

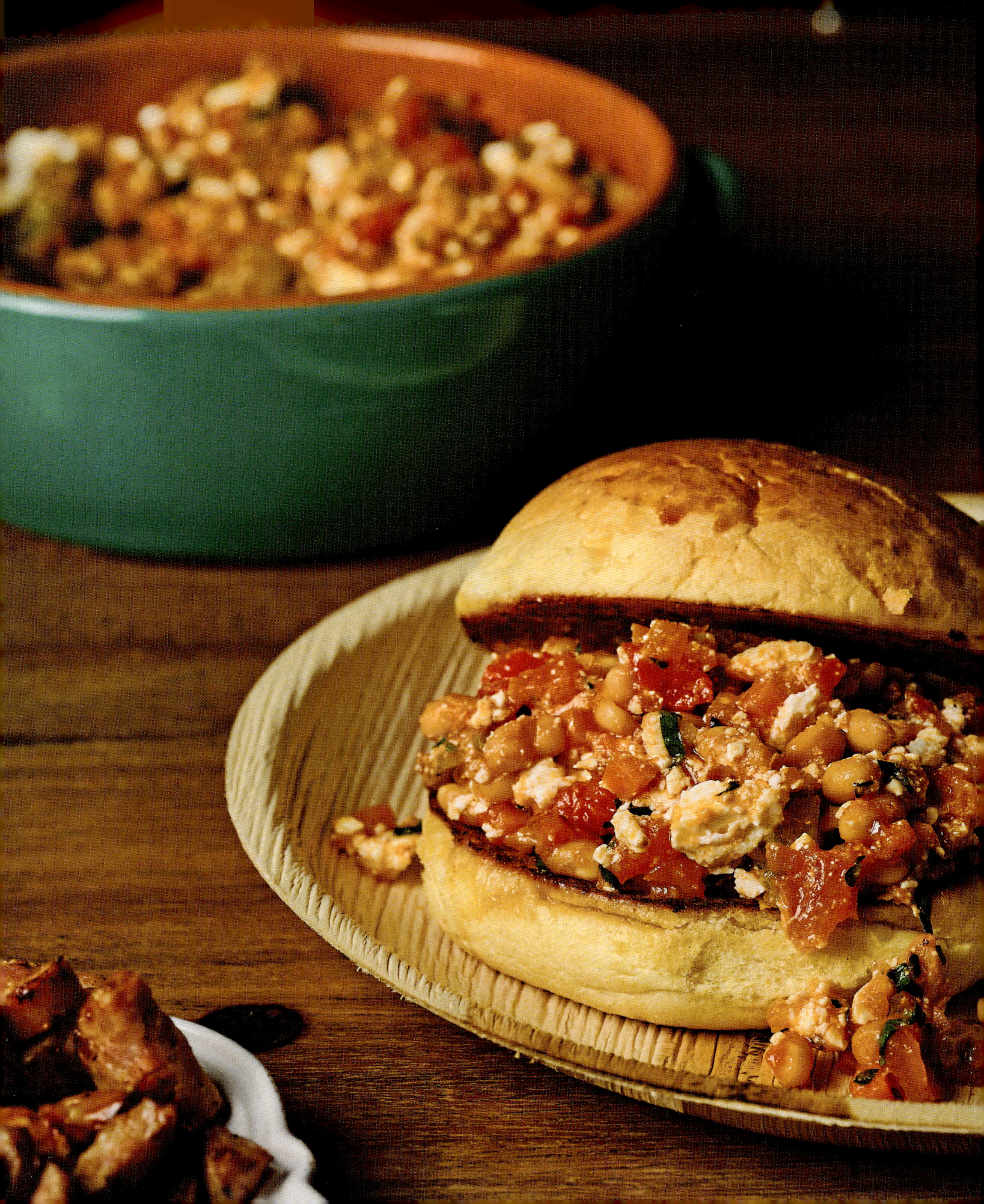

Coca-Cola
ORCHIS MASCULA
סחלב חם
וטרי
ברוכים הבאים!
WILD
ROOT
ΣΑΛΕΠ

Greek Simit-Koulouria

The koulouri, or sesame bread ring, is one of the most enduring symbols of Greek urban food life. In Greek we call them *koulouria Thessalonikis*, in reference to Greece's second largest city, where the koulouri is something of an urban legend, either having arrived there with the legions of Asia Minor immigrants a hundred years ago or going back much further, to the days of Byzantine Empire, where it was called *kollikion*, a word sometimes said to be the root of the present Greek word *koulouri*. They're also a popular morning snack in Turkey, where they're called *simit*.

Some people refer to the koulouri as the Greek bagel, mostly because of the ring shape, but they couldn't be more different in flavor, texture, and preparation. Koulouria are firmer and thinner than bagels, and slightly sweet.

They are sold on downtown Athenian street corners from carts often worked by older men; in my day as a journalist at one of the city's largest papers, they were delivered every morning and set on the desks of everyone in the newsroom; schoolkids a generation ago would grab one on their way to school, gobbling it down with a soft, glossy wedge of La Vache Qui Rit cheese, the "traditional" accompaniment.

Now, they've become the stuff of food chains and have morphed into a sandwich bread, despite the thinness of the rings, which leaves little room for filling. They're covered with more than sesame seeds these days, too—one finds koulouria blanketed with sunflower seeds, filled with tahini, made from whole wheat flour, and more. But on any morning in the Psyrri neighborhood of downtown Athens you can still smell and see the fresh koulouria coming out of the oven and being loaded up on street carts to be sold in the traditional way, as a snack on every other corner.

As for their place in the sandwich lore of Athens, a few years ago industrious bakers began to see them as something that could be filled, thus broadening their appeal. There are even a few chains now that specialize in koulouri sandwiches. Typical fillings are cream cheese, turkey or ham, lettuce, and tomatoes; or sliced yellow cheeses and turkey or ham. You'll also find the koulouri equivalent of a bagel with lox, as smoked salmon is popular in Athens, too.

Koulouria

Make these at home and use your imagination when it comes to the seed toppings. Koulouria, or bread rings, always have a subtle underlying sweetness and can be halved and spread with something soft like cream cheese or hummus. They make a great snack and are fun to prepare.

MAKES 12 RINGS

For the dough
1 (0.25-ounce) envelope active dry yeast (2¼ teaspoons)
1½ cups warm water
½ teaspoon sugar
1 teaspoon salt
4 to 4½ cups all-purpose flour

For the sesame seed coating
5 tablespoons sugar
1½ cups warm water
2 cups sesame seeds

To make the dough, in a large bowl, dissolve the yeast in the warm water and stir in the sugar. Cover and let the yeast proof and bubble for about 10 minutes. Add the salt and 4 cups of the flour, stirring, then kneading, until a firm but pliant dough takes shape, 8 to 10 minutes total kneading time. Add a little more flour if necessary. (Alternatively, you can do this in the bowl of a stand mixer outfitted with a dough hook.) Cover the dough with a kitchen towel and let it rest and rise for about 1 hour.

Preheat the oven to 375°F. Line 2 rimmed baking sheets with parchment paper.

To make the sesame seed coating, in a wide bowl, whisk the sugar and warm water together until the sugar dissolves. Place the sesame seeds in a shallow baking pan lined with parchment paper.

Remove the dough and punch down on a lightly floured surface, then divide into 4 equal balls. Roll out each ball into a rope about 24 inches long and cut at 8-inch intervals. Shape each piece into a ring and pinch together at both ends to secure closed. Quickly dip the rings into the sugar water, then press them lightly into the sesame seeds, turning so that both sides are covered with sesame seeds. Place on the lined baking sheets. Continue until all the rings are formed and covered in sesame. Bake for about 15 minutes, or until golden and firm. Remove, cool, and store in an airtight container. The koulouria will last for a few days.

Variations

You can replace the flour with whole wheat, or a combination of whole wheat and all-purpose.

Experiment with seed toppings. Many koulouria sold in Athens nowadays have coverings of sunflower or pumpkin seeds, which you can either keep whole or crush a little in a mortar with a pestle.

Try twisting the dough rope as you form the ring, to give the koulouri attractive folds, then proceed to dip and cover it in sesame seeds. You can even make thinner ropes, braiding two into one koulouri.

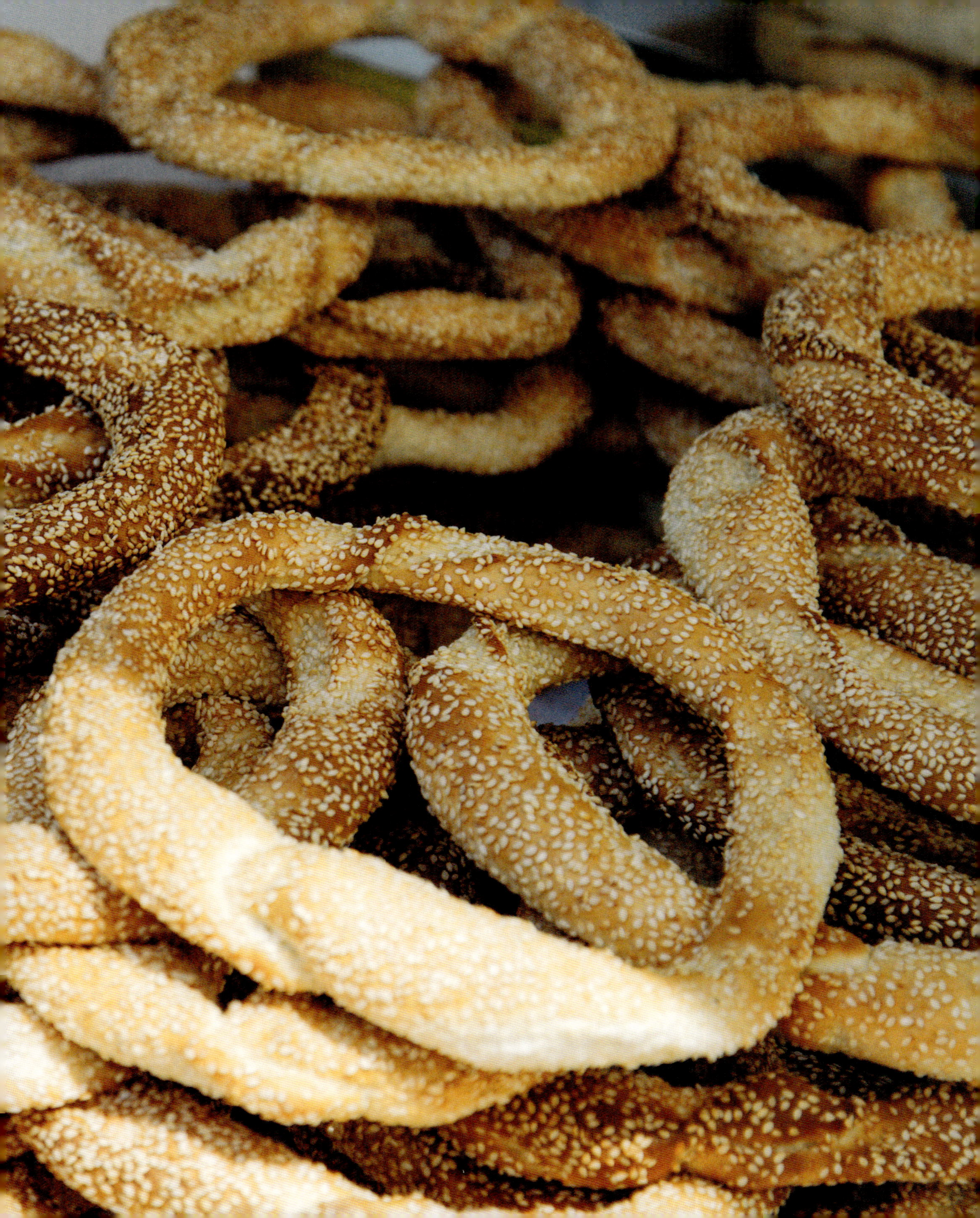

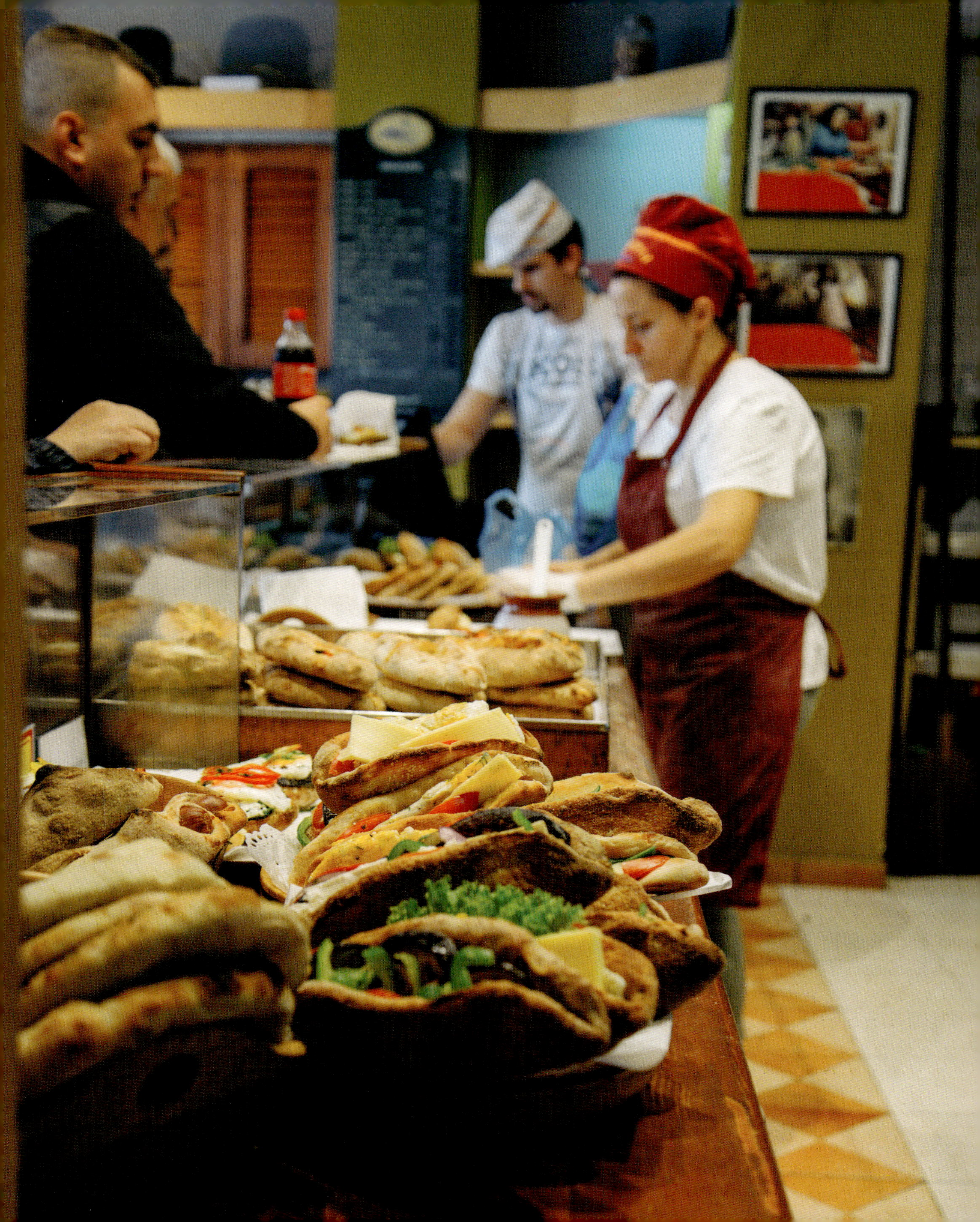

Peinirli

My memories of peinirli—doughy, smoky, cheesy comfort food that belongs to the annals of Anatolian specialties brought to Greece by refugees from Asia Minor in the 1920s—overlap like the folds in pastry with memories of youthful love and the carefree approach of a skinny twenty-something eating very fattening food.

Peinirli is a boat-shaped pizza-like concoction, the name of which derives from the word for cheese in Turkish, *penir*. It is traditionally filled with kasseri and butter in its most basic iteration, or with spicy soutzouk sausage or pasturma and a sunny-side up egg in its more robust traditional form.

In the late 1970s and early '80s I'd walk with the big V, as I liked to call my husband, to Fokionos Negri, a once-grand pedestrian street in Kypseli, now seeing a revival, that was home to a couple of great peinirli restaurants, or we'd drive our sputtering old VW Fox up to Drossia, a suburb some 20 kilometers north of Athens, where many refugees from Asia Minor had settled and, as a result, the most renowned peinirli places were located. Many are still there.

We were young, with little money, and peinirli made for an affordable outing. And a delicious one. And the experience of breaking apart the chewy bread and laughing while separating the stubborn, elastic strands of melting cheese, was one of many first experiences of a shared, if often, tense life that followed. Fokionos Negri took a plunge for the worst as the Kypseli neighborhood changed in the late 1980s, the old peinirli places closed up, and Drossia lost its luster as we gravitated toward the culinary renaissance of the 1990s in Athens. The oversized, overstuffed comfort food of our younger days morphed, too, into a more self-conscious iteration, smaller and filled with highfalutin tidbits like quail eggs, caviar, and prosciutto, where once regular old hen's eggs, robust pasturma, and kasseri reigned supreme. The original kimadopita (ground meat pie, page 31) was most likely originally a dough boat of peinirli oozing with lightly spiced ground meat sauce.

For a time in the early 2000s, the peinirli was downsized to a four-bite dough boat filled with fanciful cheffy things, and as of this writing it's seeing a resurgence, larger and both traditional and "creative." One place in downtown Athens makes a tasty version with béchamel, mushrooms, and a dash of truffle oil, and others with mozzarella or vegan cheese, prosciutto, pesto, and other non-Greek ingredients. You can experiment with fillings, too, once you make and shape the dough. Found on the peinirli trail around greater Athens are fillings such as hummus or Greek fava; pesto; any good melting cheese or vegan cheese, if that's your thing; and fresh toppings like basil leaves, baby spinach, or watercress, to name a few.

If you do visit the city and want to taste what is considered by many to be the best peinirli in town, head to a place called Peinirli Ionias on Panormou Street. You will be smitten, for sure!

Traditional Peinirli

If you like making bread and pizza, you'll love making peinirli. Use these dough boats as a vessel for your own imagination, filling them in as fanciful or simple way as you like.

MAKES 6 PEINIRLI

For the dough

1 teaspoon active dry yeast

1¼ cups warm water

1 scant teaspoon salt

4 to 5 cups all-purpose flour

For the filling

1 pound kasseri cheese, or ½ pound each mozzarella and provolone, coarsely grated

½ cup water

6 teaspoons unsalted butter, preferably sheep's milk

Optional additions

Greek or Armenian soutzouk (aged, spicy sausage), cut into thin rounds

Pastourma—about 1 slice, chopped, per peinirli (Pastourma, a spiced, cured beef, is usually covered with a sticky spice rub. Remove this, if desired, before chopping the meat.)

Large eggs—1 per peinirli

To make the dough, combine the yeast and the warm water in a large bowl, stir it gently, and let it proof for 10 minutes. Mix in the salt. Add 4 cups of the flour, mix together, and start kneading, adding a little more flour in increments of ¼ cup, until a soft, somewhat sticky dough takes shape, 8 to 10 minutes total kneading time. Cover the bowl and let the dough rest for 20 minutes.

Preheat the oven to 400°F. Line a rimmed baking sheet with parchment paper. Place a shallow pan of water on the bottom of the oven to create steam, which will help create a crunchy finish on the dough as it bakes.

Mix together the kasseri and water.

Divide the dough into 6 equal balls. On a lightly floured surface, using either your palms and fingertips or a rolling pin, open or roll out each ball one at a time to an oval about 10 inches long. Place each piece on the lined baking sheet.

Divide the kasseri mixture into 6 equal portions and spread onto the center of the dough ovals, spreading it evenly in the center with the back of a spoon or spatula and leaving a border of dough about 1½ inches wide all around. If you are adding sausage or pastourma, add it now. Fold the two long sides of the oval over the edges of the filling, allowing most of the filling to remain uncovered, and pinch together the tips of the oval to form a boat.

Bake for 8 to 10 minutes, or until puffed, browned, and ready. If you want to add eggs to the peinirli, pull them out of the oven after 4 minutes and carefully break 1 egg into the center of each, then return them to the oven for the full baking time. No matter which variation you choose, add a dab of butter to each piece as soon as it comes out of the oven, and serve hot.

Vegan Peinirli
with Hummus

This classic Anatolian snack and street food is finding its way back to center stage if the few new shops specializing in it that have opened in Athens as of this writing are any indication. One in my downtown neighborhood created a vegan variation, which I have adapted here.

MAKES 6 PEINIRLI

For the filling

6 tablespoons extra-virgin Greek olive oil

2 medium red onions, coarsely chopped

Salt and freshly ground black pepper to taste

1½ cups halved teardrop tomatoes

3 cups good-quality store-bought hummus

6 tablespoons chopped pitted kalamata olives

2 cups baby arugula, trimmed

For the dough

1 recipe dough for Traditional Peinirli (page 48)

To make the filling, in a nonstick or cast-iron skillet, warm 2 tablespoons of the olive oil over medium-low heat. Add the onions and a pinch of salt and cook slowly for about 20 minutes, until the onions are caramelized. Remove and cool slightly.

Meanwhile, in a separate skillet, heat 1 tablespoon olive oil over medium-high heat. Add the tomatoes and cook until they burst and start to blister a little, and their juices start to evaporate, 10 to 12 minutes. Set aside.

Preheat the oven to 400°F. Line a rimmed baking sheet with parchment paper. Place a shallow pan of water on the bottom of the oven to create steam, which will help create a crunchy finish on the dough as it bakes.

Divide the dough into 6 equal balls. On a lightly floured surface, using either your palms and fingertips or a rolling pin, open or roll out each ball one at a time to an oval about 10 inches long. Place each piece on the lined baking sheet.

Spread ½ cup hummus over each oval, spreading it with the back of a spoon or a spatula and leaving 1 inch of dough around the entire rim. Spoon the caramelized onions, blistered tomatoes, and chopped olives on top. Season lightly with salt and pepper, as desired. Fold the two long sides of the oval over the edges of the filling, allowing most of the filling to remain uncovered, and pinch together the tips of the oval to form a boat shape.

Bake for 8 to 10 minutes, until the dough is puffed, browned, and crisp. Remove, drizzle the remaining olive oil over each piece, and top with a small bunch of arugula. Serve immediately.

The Ultimate Street Food: Souvlaki

This is the story of how Greece's most iconic street food, the one dish recognizably Greek all over the world, came to be in Athens. A few years ago, while I was filming an episode of *My Greek Table* called "Ancient Foods for Modern Cooks," I had the good fortune to visit with Dr. John Camp, who at the time had been the director of the excavations at the ancient Agora in the center of Athens. We were in the storerooms when he pulled a few rough metal skewers out of a box. They were about 14 inches long and dated to 450 BC. "Nothing's new except the technology," he said. Skewered meat, called *oveliskos* or *ovelia* in antiquity, was as beloved then as it is now.

Indeed, the history of skewered, fire-roasted meats is a long and glorious one in Greece, but it's modern souvlaki and its close cousins, gyro and kebab, the ultimate street foods, that captured and enraptured me as I dug deeper into their roots. One has to know a little of the history of the city in the early part of the twentieth century, when the Balkans were in turmoil, borders were still fluid, and the upheavals of the Asia Minor Catastrophe in 1922 saw more than a million mostly Greek refugees expelled from the shores of Turkey, bringing a tragic, bloody, and abrupt close to three thousand years of Greek life there. And one has to know a little of the country's more recent history, because the story of souvlaki and gyro in their present forms is unexpectedly entwined with the Greek military dictatorship more than half a century ago. In a moment of ethnic cleansing of the edible kind, the colonels simply outlawed ground lamb gyro and kebab, deeming these two delicious and popular street foods too Eastern, and in their place forced pork onto the plate, hence its prevalence as the meat of "classic" Greek souvlaki. To this day, it's almost impossible to find ground lamb even in butcher shops in Athens and greater Greece.

In their wonderful book *Souvlaki*, Athenian journalists Tasos Brekoulakis and Marina Petridou trace the origins of modern souvlaki to 1924, when an Armenian refugee named Misak Aniskipian, originally from the town of Adana, Turkey, who had fled Asia Minor before 1922 and settled briefly in Egypt, makes his way to Greece and opens the country's very first souvlaki joint, in Nikaia, near Piraeus, where many refugees had settled. He called it Aigyptiakon (the Egyptian), perhaps nostalgic for the few years he had spent in then cosmopolitan Egypt. (The early 1920s also saw the exodus of hundreds of thousands of Armenians from Turkey, many of whom settled in Greece, too.) Aniskipian, a shrewd businessman, changed his name to a more Greek sounding Isaac Meraklidis, *meraklis* being the word for a person especially skilled in a particular craft, and his grilled lamb kebab served with tomato and pita bread became famous all over the neighborhood.

It wasn't long before he opened a second place in the heart of old Athens, right on Monastiraki Square, leaving his teenage son to run the original shop. Anyone who has ever visited the Greek capital will likely have noticed this restaurant. It's called Bairaktaris today, after the young man who came to work for Meraklidis in the 1950s and eventually bought him out. He was catapulted to instant renown when Greece's first post-junta prime minister, Konstantinos Karamanlis, famously ate there with a gaggle of his ministers. Just a peek inside Bairaktaris will give you a sense of how popular the place has been over its decades in business.

Indeed, to this day, that corner of Monastiraki Square and Mitropoleos Street, which leads into it, are still home to the three most renowned souvlaki-gyro-kebab places in Athens: Bairaktaris, of course, but also Thanasis and Savvas, the family founders of which who also got their start and honed their knowledge of the trade while working as young men for Meraklidis. There was a time just a few decades ago, before tourism suffocated the square, when the Monastiraki was where the best traditional music in Athens could be heard, and in their heyday these shops served souvlaki to the stars of Greek rebetika music and their acolytes.

In many ways, even at this writing, the point of reference for Athenian souvlaki is still the Monastiraki. Besides lower Mitropoleos Street and Monastiraki Square, there is Kostas on Plateia Agias Eirinis, famed for his spicy sauce, but whose family also influenced the history of souvlaki in the Greek capital. Kostas's father is said to have been one of the original street vendors of kalamakia, small chunks of meat threaded on wooden skewers and grilled over hot coals, a trend that was brought to Athens in the 1950s after some enterprising entrepreneur borrowed the idea from vendors who did a bristling business at the Rio-Antirio boat crossing, across the Corinth Canal from the Peloponnese into mainland Greece. In Athens, the first brick-and-mortar kalamaki place still stands and is still popular: Leivadia, on Plateia Klathmonos, a little ways from Omonoia.

In my time here over three decades of chronicling Greek food, souvlaki and its close relative, gyro—cones of stacked meat grilled on an upright rotisserie—have also been tweaked and rethought, spun and chopped, and turned into a plethora of modern choices. Chicken is as popular as pork, but now there's vegan souvlaki, pulled pork souvlaki, fish gyro, mushroom gyro, vegetable souvlaki, and countless other renditions seasoned with the sprinklings of the global palette, everything from soy sauce to ginger to star anise.

Athens by Hand: Street Food Heaven 51

My tastes still run to the traditional, and there really is nothing quite as delicious and satisfying as a great souvlaki or gyro, dripping garlicky yogurt sauce, unapologetically stacked with raw onions, made more refreshing with tomatoes, and stuffed (not to my liking) with French fries, a trend that took root in poorer days when it was easier for many people to fill their bellies with an overloaded potato-stuffed wrap than to order, say, two, without the spuds.

What Makes Great Souvlaki and Gyro?

It's the meat, of course! But it's other things, too, such as the marinade, extra sauces, and garnishes.

The most popular souvlaki meat in Greece is pork, with chicken probably second in line. Beef and lamb are relatively rare, at least among the more casual street food vendors of the genre. Regardless of the meat of choice, it should be a tender cut and then should be well marinated to make it as juicy and succulent as possible.

Tzatziki (Greek yogurt–cucumber–garlic sauce), plain yogurt, and something simply called "sauce"—usually a combination of mayo and ketchup, often with a little cayenne or other spice thrown in—are the most popular ways to dress up a souvlaki or gyro wrap. The wrap is also filled with a choice of sliced or diced tomatoes, raw red onions, and fried potatoes, which adds heft but to my mind detracts from the purity of the wrap!

As far as gyro goes, that's a somewhat more contentious subject because the differences between the commercially prepared meat cones and the ones made by hand are huge. Almost all gyro now found on the streets of Athens is of the former variety, produced in large scale by combining ground meat (usually pork, but also chicken, and, at least in Greece, less often lamb and beef) with seasonings, and some kind of binder in the starch family, and building this mixture around an upright spit that fits into the rotisserie. It's easier for restaurants to work with this, for sure. As the meat cooks, it self-bastes in its own fat, which drips down, and the result is a good down-and-dirty gyro, with the shavings characterized by somewhat grainy texture.

But the handmade stuff is a work of art when done well. In my experiences in Athens, this has all but disappeared but is starting to resurface in some of the gyro places opened up in recent years by immigrants from Syria and elsewhere. Thin slices of seasoned meat are stacked on the upright spit, and the cone of meat turns and cooks slowly. There is less uniformity than one finds with the commercially made cones, but there is more skill needed as one has more control over the seasonings and the grilling.

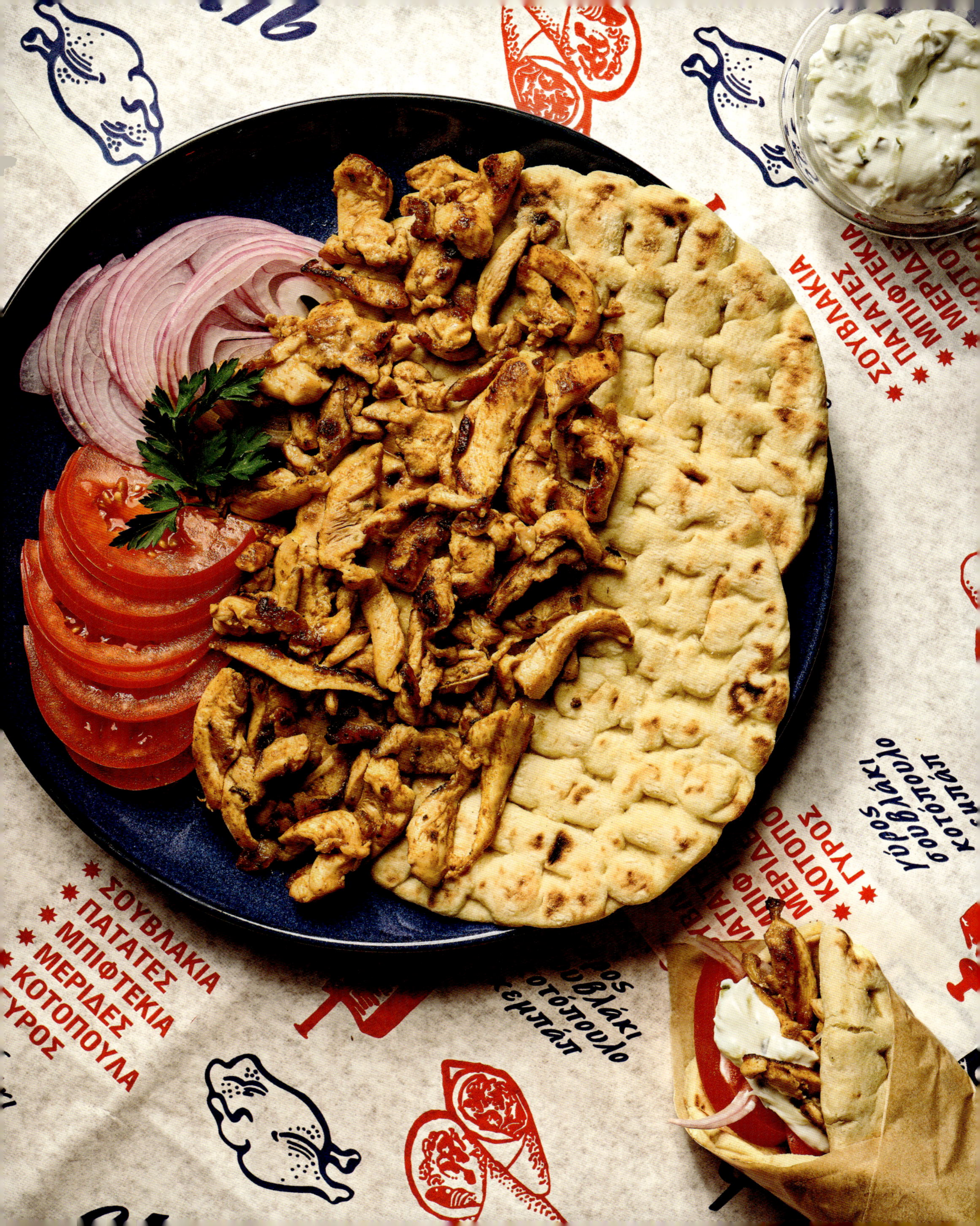
ΣΟΥΒΛΑΚΙΑ
ΠΑΤΑΤΕΣ
ΜΠΙΦΤΕΚΙΑ
ΜΕΡΙΔΕΣ
ΚΟΤΟΠΟΥΛΑ
ΓΥΡΟΣ

Homemade Chicken Gyro

Gyro saw its moment in the light of gourmet interpreters a few years ago, when the likes of fish gyro and a few other physics-defying affectations emerged from the kitchens of Athens's more creative chefs. Gyro is a cone of stacked protein, most often pork or chicken. There are still a handful of places that season and stack their own meat, but by and large this once masterful art has been supplanted by commercially produced cones, ready to click into place on the upright grill. To make this at home the traditional way is all but impossible, but to get the shavings off a few tasty skewers is totally doable.

MAKES 6 SERVINGS

For the chicken

2½ pounds boneless, skinless chicken breasts, pounded to thin them out a little

½ cup extra-virgin Greek olive oil

½ cup dry white wine

1 tablespoon Dijon mustard

1 tablespoon minced garlic

Grated zest of 1 lemon, preferably organic

1 tablespoon smoked paprika

1 tablespoon dried Greek oregano

1 tablespoon dried thyme

Salt and freshly ground black pepper to taste

6 to 8 (12-inch) metal skewers

For the garlic sauce

1½ cups Greek yogurt

2 teaspoons of minced garlic

2 tablespoons extra-virgin Greek olive oil

Cut the chicken breasts into quarters. Rinse and pat dry.

In a large bowl, whisk together the olive oil, wine, mustard, garlic, lemon zest, paprika, oregano, thyme, and pepper. Place the chicken breasts in the marinade and turn to coat. Cover the bowl and place in the refrigerator to marinate for at least 1 hour and up to 3.

Preheat the oven to 400°F.

Season the chicken in the marinade with salt and turn well. Remove the chicken from the marinade and roll up each piece like a jelly roll, then thread each roll onto the skewers. You'll probably get around 4 rolled-up fillets per skewer. Season with additional salt and pepper, if desired.

Place the skewers over a metal or ovenproof glass or ceramic baking dish so that the chicken isn't touching the bottom of the pan but rather is set over it, with the skewers' ends on either side of the pan. If your skewers are 12 inches long, a shallow 8-inch square pan is perfect for this. Bake, basting the skewers a few times with the pan juices and turning them at least once to brown evenly, until cooked through, about 30 minutes.

In the meantime, make the yogurt-garlic sauce (if not using tzatziki): Mix together the yogurt, garlic, olive oil, salt, and pepper.

Remove the chicken from the oven. Lower the oven temperature to 200°F and place the pita rounds on the oven rack to warm them up. Place the skewers on a cutting board. Using a sharp knife, "shave" the rolled-up chicken from each end so that the pieces that fall off look very much like the shavings of gyro, or thin ribbons of meat. When you get near the skewer, push the remaining pieces off with the knife.

For serving

2 cups Classic Tavernisio Tzatziki (page 98) or the garlic sauce

6 (8-inch) pita rounds

1 to 2 red onions, halved and thinly sliced

3 firm, ripe tomatoes, cored, halved, and thinly sliced

Optional finishing ingredients

Cayenne pepper

Grilled green chiles

Chopped fresh flat-leaf parsley

French fries

Dried Greek oregano

Remove the pita from the oven. To serve, spread a little of the tzatziki or yogurt-garlic mixture on each of the warm pita rounds. Place about ⅔ cup meat over the tzatziki or yogurt, then the onion and tomato slices. Add any of the optional finishing extras you'd like now: Toss in some cayenne or a grilled chile if you like heat. Add a sprinkling of parsley for something fresh. If you want a heartier gyro, add a fistful of fried potatoes. As always, a little more dried oregano is a nice last touch, if you want an extra flavor boost. Roll up the wrap and serve.

Calamari Souvlaki

Hoocut, an upscale souvlaki place on Agia Eirini Square, took the city by storm when it opened a few years ago, the brainchild of the successful restaurant team that opened a place called Cookoovaya ("owl," as in the symbol of the city) near the old Athens Hilton. In addition to a long list of inventive, if classic, souvlaki, they also wrapped a grilled squid skewer that is absolutely delicious, so much so, in fact, that it inspired this recipe! As for the name of this innovative souvlaki joint, it recalls the owl, too, by making a play on words with the sound of its calling, "hoo," or as in Who Cut!

MAKES 2 TO 4 SERVINGS

4 (12-inch) skewers

For the yogurt sauce

6 tablespoons Greek yogurt

1 teaspoon minced garlic

2 tablespoons chopped fresh mint

½ teaspoon finely grated lemon zest

Dash hot sauce

Salt and freshly ground black pepper to taste

For the calamari

2 tablespoons balsamic vinegar

⅓ cup extra-virgin Greek olive oil

2 large garlic cloves, minced

1½ teaspoons dried Greek oregano

Salt and freshly ground black pepper to taste

4 (6- to 8-inch-long) whole fresh squid, viscera removed

For serving

1 medium red onion, halved and cut into 1½-inch squares

2 red bell peppers, seeded and cut into 1½-inch squares

6 (8-inch) pita bread rounds

Dash hot sauce

If using wooden skewers, place them in a small pan with water and leave them to soak until you're ready to grill.

In a small bowl, combine the yogurt, garlic, mint, lemon zest, hot sauce, salt, and pepper. Cover and refrigerate until ready to use.

In a medium bowl, whisk together the balsamic vinegar, olive oil, garlic, oregano, and salt and pepper to taste and set aside until ready to use.

Rinse the cleaned squid under cold running water and pat dry. Cut the squid body into 1½-inch rings. Cut the tentacles in half. Place the squid pieces in a large bowl and toss with half of the marinade. Cover and refrigerate for 30 minutes.

At the same time, place the onion and pepper pieces in the bowl with the remaining marinade and toss. Cover and refrigerate for 30 minutes.

Preheat the grill or broiler to medium and remove the skewers from the water. Oil the grill rack if necessary. Remove the yogurt mixture from the fridge.

Thread alternating pieces of the marinated squid and onion and pepper onto the skewers. Try to save the tentacles for last on each skewer. Place on the grill or, if using the broiler, on a pan large enough for the skewers to rest on the rim without touching the bottom. Brush with any remaining marinade left in the bowls. Grill or broil for 5 to 8 minutes, until the squid and vegetables are charred and cooked.

About 3 minutes before removing the skewers, place the pita rounds on the grill or on the second rack under the squid if using the broiler, just to warm them through.

Spoon a little of the yogurt mixture onto each warm pita round and pull the squid and vegetables off the skewers onto the pita. Spoon a little more of the yogurt on top if desired and sprinkle with a few drops of hot sauce. Roll up the pita, wrap the bottom with parchment and aluminum foil, and serve.

Moussaka Pita Wrap

This reinvention of moussaka as a wrap pops up in various street food joints around Athens, and it is something between a wrap and a sloppy Joe, a deconstructed moussaka that morphs into street food.

MAKES 4 SERVINGS

- 8 tablespoons extra-virgin Greek olive oil, divided
- 1 small red onion, chopped
- 2 garlic cloves, minced
- ½ pound ground beef or a combination of ground beef and pork
- 1 tablespoon tomato paste
- ⅔ cup dry white wine, divided
- Salt and freshly ground black pepper to taste
- 1 cinnamon stick
- ½ teaspoon ground allspice
- 1 bay leaf
- 2 Yukon Gold potatoes, peeled and cut into ½-inch cubes
- 1 small to medium eggplant, trimmed and cut into ½-inch cubes
- 1 large zucchini, trimmed and cut into ½-inch cubes
- 1 teaspoon dried Greek oregano
- ½ to 1 cup Greek yogurt
- 4 (8-inch) pocketless pita wraps

Heat 2 tablespoons of the olive oil in a large skillet over medium heat. Add the onion and cook, stirring, until wilted and glistening, about 7 minutes. Stir in the garlic, then add the ground meat, and cook, breaking up the meat until it turns brown. Add the tomato paste and ⅓ cup of the white wine, season lightly with salt and pepper, and add the cinnamon stick, allspice, and bay leaf. Cover and simmer for about 30 minutes, until the mixture is thick and jammy.

In the meantime, prepare the vegetables: In a separate skillet or wok, heat 3 tablespoons olive oil over medium-high heat. Add the potato cubes and cook until lightly browned and about halfway done, 10 to 12 minutes. Add the eggplant cubes and stir until they begin to soften. Add the zucchini. Pour in the remaining ⅓ cup wine, season lightly with salt and pepper, and cook until the vegetables are tender, about 15 minutes total. Season with the oregano and set aside.

While the vegetables and meat are cooking, whisk the yogurt with the remaining 2 tablespoons of olive oil to loosen it, then season it lightly with salt.

Either preheat the oven to 325°F or heat a nonstick skillet over low heat. Drizzle the pita rounds with the remaining 1 tablespoon olive oil and brush it over one side of each. Place in the skillet or bake on a parchment-lined rimmed baking sheet for a few minutes, flipping once, until warmed through.

To assemble the wraps, divide the vegetables evenly among the wraps and spoon them over the oiled side of the wrap. Divide the meat mixture and do the same. Drizzle the yogurt over the top and fold the bread into a wrap. Serve hot.

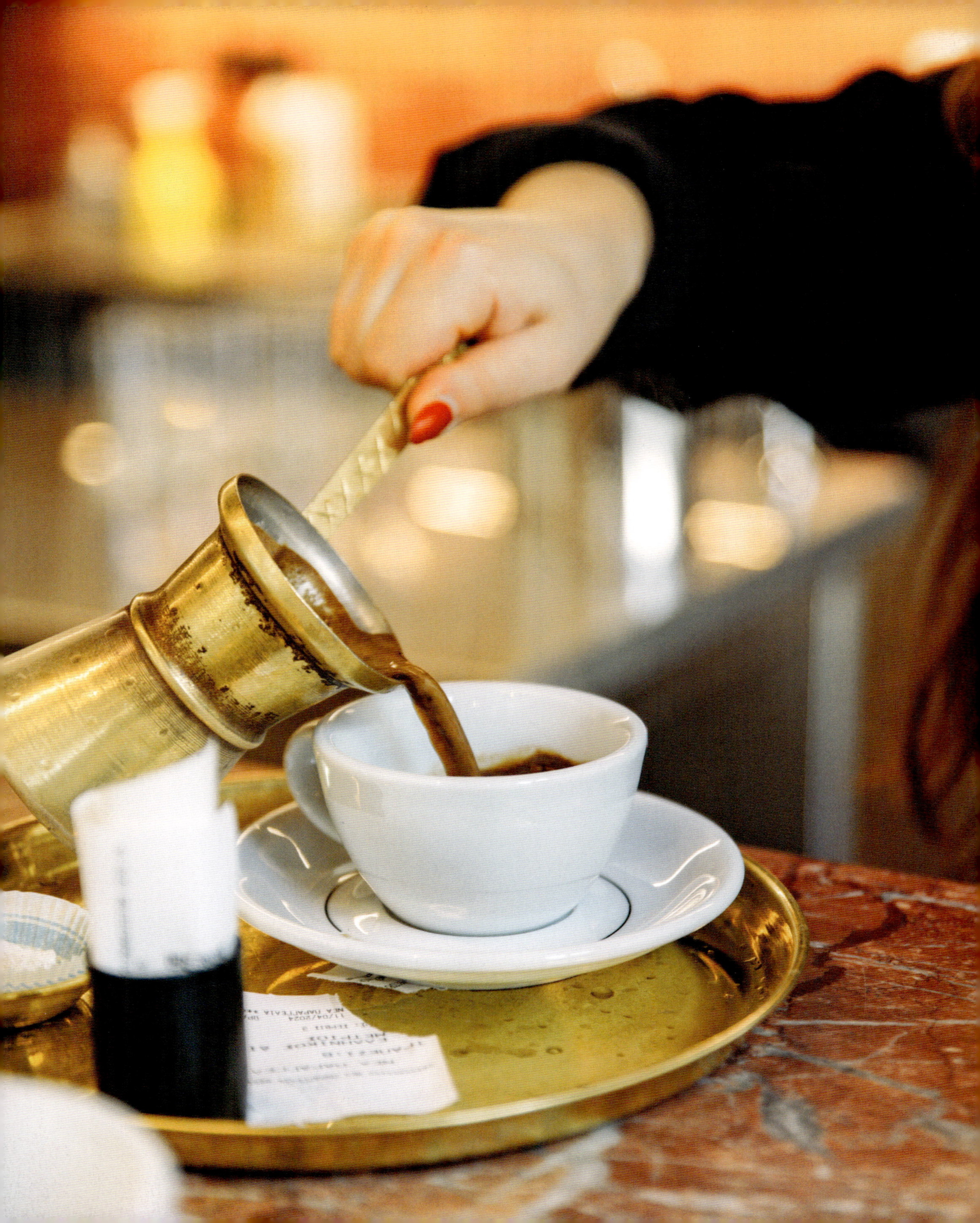

Good Morning, Athens

Breakfast

"Coffee and a cigarette" was my usual, sarcastic answer when non-Greek colleagues would ask me over the years what a traditional Greek breakfast is in the birthplace of the Mediterranean diet. Thankfully, that was only half a joke (Greeks are still, unfortunately, big smokers), because over the past decade or so there's been a concerted, official effort to codify and brand Greek breakfast, mostly aimed at encouraging hotels to broaden the range of great Greek breakfast options, beyond yogurt and honey, to sweet and savory pastries, regional egg dishes, cheeses, charcuterie, and more. The effort has worked, as many hotels now offer a much richer and more varied breakfast than was ever imagined even a decade ago. Museum cafés have caught on, too, and one of the best places in the city to have breakfast is the Acropolis Museum Café.

Brunch has gotten big in Athens, too, especially on the weekends, and the last few years have seen a proliferation of eateries that focus on morning menus, which have gotten more creative, with chefs culling from both global and Greek regional traditions. Pancakes with a Greek twist (or traditional Greek pancakes, called *tiganites*), avocado toast, homemade granola, and a whole world of egg dishes are among the many ways in which breakfast items have evolved, folding trends and Greek traditions together. Ancient foods like trahana, a dairy-based grain product that was often the breakfast porridge of Greek farmers, have found new life in breakfast bowls, garnished with fruits, nuts, honey, grape molasses, or cheese and charcuterie. In neighborhoods like Kypseli, about a mile from the center, where a younger and often international demographic has taken root in the last few years, transforming what looked for years like permanent urban decay into hipster attractiveness, brunch and cool coffee places are all the rage.

Athens has always had a vibrant café society, too, and on any given morning it's fairly obvious that stopping—and sitting—for a sip is part of the city's urban culture. Kolonaki Square, in one of the most affluent parts of downtown Athens, with long-standing places like Da Capo, is where you might see clusters of the city's political and media elite chattering, plotting their day, and sipping an espresso or two.

I love to head out in the morning and order a coffee at one of my favorite plateias, be it at Agias Eirinis, one of the most beautiful city circles, or on Plateia Avdi, a large square abutting the Athens Municipal Gallery and a stone's throw from my apartment. Like every meal of the day, just sipping a coffee becomes a social affair, greeting people you know, chatting with the waitperson, watching the cats, dogs, and birds frolic.

My favorite breakfast continues to be one that needs neither an introduction nor a real recipe: great Greek yogurt with some seasonal fruit and a teaspoon of dark Greek pine honey. But my morning jaunts around town have revealed a much richer breakfast-scape than that simple, beloved combo. The recipes that follow include lots of bready things, especially pancakes and creative crepes, as well as a few of my favorite egg dishes, homemade granola (trending at this writing), and a country porridge that's found new life in hipster Athens.

The breadth of a Greek breakfast as expressed in hotel menus would include much more, embracing phyllo pies both sweet and savory, olives, Greek cheeses and cured meats, a host of jams, and lots of different toppings for classic Greek yogurt, including a bevy of fruit preserves called spoon sweets.

Coffee is de rigueur, too, and the quaff of choice has shifted decidedly away from the once ubiquitous frappe (shaken, iced instant coffee) to espresso and cappuccino, hot or freddo, cold brew—a newcomer to the Athens coffee club—and Elliniko, or Greek coffee, made with finely ground lightly roasted coffee in a briki, a tapered pot with a long handle.

Kalimera to all!

Homemade Granola
with Greek Flavors

Granola has captured the imagination of countless Greek chefs and shop owners and it stands to reason, since it's the perfect pairing for a cup of real Greek yogurt. While this medley of oats, dried fruits, and nuts hardly existed even a few short years ago in Athens, now it's everywhere, from the international breakfast menus of downtown hotels to small neighborhood cafés. Many small food shops also sell Greek versions of granola, which tend to be excellent, mostly because of the superior quality of nuts and dried fruits in Greece.

MAKES 3 CUPS

4 cups rolled oats

1 cup coarsely chopped unsalted raw almonds

1 cup coarsely chopped walnuts

1 cup coarsely chopped Greek pistachios

1 cup chopped dried Greek figs

½ cup dark seedless raisins

½ cup chopped dried apricots

½ cup sesame seeds

1 teaspoon salt

2 teaspoons ground cinnamon

½ teaspoon ground cloves

4 tablespoons extra-virgin Greek olive oil

6 tablespoons Greek pine honey

3 tablespoons apricot or orange marmalade

3 tablespoons tahini

Preheat the oven to 350°F. Line 2 rimmed baking sheets with parchment paper.

In a large bowl, combine the oats, nuts, dried fruits, sesame seeds, salt, and spices.

In a medium saucepan, combine the olive oil, honey, marmalade, and tahini and cook over medium-low heat, whisking to combine. Drizzle this mixture into the dry ingredients and stir to combine. Spread the mixture evenly over the lined baking sheets and bake for 30 to 40 minutes, stirring every 10 minutes or so, until the granola is crunchy but not too dark. Remove, cool slightly, and break apart any clumps that are too big. Cool completely and store the granola in well-sealed jars at room temperature. It will keep for up to 1 month.

Trahana Breakfast Bowl

Trahana, easily found online (in my e-shop and elsewhere) as well as in Greek and Middle Eastern food shops, is one of the oldest foods in the eastern Mediterranean. Essentially a way to preserve milk in the centuries before refrigeration, trahana, in its most common iteration (there are many versions), is made by cooking flour, cracked wheat, or bulgur with milk to get a thick, almost solid porridge, which is then broken into clumps, dried in the sun, and passed through a fine-mesh sieve to a pebbly consistency. It's the original farmer's breakfast, a hearty porridge meant to keep one sated for hours of calorie-burning chores; it's also captured the imagination of Athenian chefs for decades now, and is reappearing on menus across the city as of this writing in a kind of modern swing back to its breakfast roots. This recipe is inspired by the trahana bowl at a small, trendy place called Santo Belto in the ultra-trendy Kypseli neighborhood. They serve a sweetened version of trahana, which I have adapted here.

MAKES 2 SERVINGS

1 cup sweet or sour trahana

2 cup almond, coconut, or cow's milk

1 cup water, or more as needed

8 dried apricots, finely chopped

6 dried Greek figs, thinly sliced or chopped

2 tablespoons raw almonds, coarsely chopped

Greek pine honey to taste

Pinch dried mint (optional)

In a medium saucepan, combine the trahana, milk, and water and simmer over medium heat for about 12 minutes, adding more liquid as needed to reach a thick porridge-like consistency.

Remove from the heat and divide into serving bowls. Garnish with the dried fruits and almonds, drizzle with honey to taste, season with a pinch of mint (if using), and serve.

Stani and Greek Yogurt in Athens

When I moved downtown, south of Omonoia Square, in 2021, fresh from the leafy northern suburbs of Athens, I found myself navigating the backstreets of my new, if edgy, neighborhood a few times a week in order to procure one of this city's greatest treasures: real Greek yogurt from a century-old establishment called Stani, which means "the pen," as in the place where sheep are held.

This fabulous galaktokomeio, or dairy emporium, with its old-world charm, sits in one of the seediest parts of the center, but despite that, it draws crowds of locals and an ever-growing parade of foodies on walking tours, all ready to enjoy some of the best yogurt in Greece, replete with a thin, papery skin on top that is pure heaven to eat, as well as a handful of other renowned specialties: delicately tart cultured sheep's milk butter served up as a generous slab on a plate and drenched in a thick, golden bath of Greek honey; anthogalo, or cow's milk cream, served with honey and walnuts in a parfait glass, and a dense, dreamy rice pudding, all creamy with cinnamon umami.

Mostly, though, this stalwart is known for its history and is one of the few food businesses to have survived and flourished for so long in ever-changing Athens. Athens, like all of urban Greece, was once dotted with galaktokomeia in every neighborhood, places that sold milk and other daily necessities and that flourished from the 1950s to the 1980s. They were often named EBGA, an acronym for the Greek Milk Industry co-op, but there were others, too, not part of the chain.

Stani was one. The original shop first opened its doors in Piraeus in 1931, then moved to the present location in 1949, after the original location was bombed during World War II. The original owner's grandson, Thanasis Karagiorgos, presides over the current location on Marika Kotopouli Street, named after a famous turn-of-the-century stage actress. (The National Theater of Greece is a short walk from here.) The same family of dairy farmers from a mountain village in Corinth who supplied his grandfather continue to supply Stani's milk today. They make the yogurt and other dairy delights in the basement.

While Athenians sip their freddos and wax poetic about "WA-fless" (waffles pronounced in Greek!), I happily meander the grimy back streets of Omonoia for a glorious taste of the past. Luckily, you don't have to stay in situ to enjoy Stani's delights. They pack to go as well.

Pancakes, Athens Style

Greeks call pancakes tiganites, *from the word for frying pan,* tigani. *They've taken up a newfound place of importance as brunch becomes more and more popular in Athens. As for toppings, you find just about everything from Greek honey and yogurt to Merenda and Nutella to savory sauces like béchamel and cheese toppings speckled with ham.*

MAKES ABOUT 12 (4-INCH) PANCAKES

1½ cups all-purpose flour

2 teaspoons baking powder

½ teaspoon sugar

½ teaspoon salt

1¼ cups milk

3 tablespoons melted unsalted butter or extra-virgin Greek olive oil, plus 1 teaspoon oil for the pan

1 large egg

Optional toppings

Tahini whisked with honey

Tahini whisked with grape molasses (petimezi)

Honey, sesame seeds, and ground cinnamon

Merenda or Nutella

Greek feta melted with a little heavy cream and butter

Béchamel

Greek yogurt with fruit

Sift together the flour, baking powder, sugar, and salt in a large bowl and make a well in the center. Add the milk, melted butter, and egg and whisk to form a thick, smooth batter.

Brush a nonstick or cast-iron skillet with 1 teaspoon oil and heat over medium-high heat. Using a ¼-cup measure or small ladle, pour the batter into the frying pan. You should be able to fit at least 2 and probably 3 for each batch. Cook for 2 to 3 minutes on the first side, then use a spatula to flip over. Cook on the other side until golden brown. Remove and set aside, covered, to keep warm. Serve with your desired toppings.

Café Society

Starbucks, Greek chains like Mikél, and delivery guys who'll bring a single cup of coffee on a motorbike to your front door—environmental concerns be damned—have taken the place of the grand old cafeneia and cafeterias in Athens, but coffee culture and café society are still alive and thriving. Indeed, coffee is woven deep into the social fabric of this city.

Every neighborhood plateia has at least one, but usually multiple, cafés, and these are gathering places for every facet of society. On any given morning, you can stroll through Kolonaki Square in the city's poshest neighborhood and spot politicians sipping their morning brew before heading off to run (or ruin, depending on one's point of view!) the country.

Coffee has been at the center of Athens's cultural, intellectual, and social life since at least the late nineteenth century. Many coffee emporia began as kafekopteia, or coffee grinding and roasting shops, and a few still exist. Some, like the gorgeous old Neon at Omonoia Square, with its toweringly high painted ceiling (now a bakery chain), Zaharatos near the Palace and Parliament at Syntagma, and Zonar's on Panepistimiou (renovated in 2016) opened as grand cafés in the European tradition more than a century ago and stood witness to Greek history. Café Neon was immortalized by the Greek painter Yannis Tsarouchis, and frequented by some of the city's most famed men of letters, such as the poet Yannis Ritsos. A small place on Voukourestiou Street, Brazil, was still famous as recently as the start of the twenty-first century. Indeed, when I first moved to Greece in the 1980s as a young journalist, I used to spot the Nobel laureate poet Odysseas Elytis in his characteristic black fisherman's cap sipping his morning coffee there.

Other, simpler shops occupied, and still do, a decidedly masculine place in neighborhoods, basic storefronts where men could escape the perceived banalities of life at home and gather with their buddies to shoot the breeze and maybe play some poker.

Now, the vast majority of the grand old places have faded into extinction, replaced by bustling, noisy chains and "all-day cafes" with thudding music and elaborate espresso machines.

Coffee preferences, along with the establishments that serve it, have similarly evolved dramatically over the years. Until the 1960s, most people drank tourkiko, or Turkish coffee, which morphed into Elliniko (Greek) after the Turkish invasion of Cyprus in 1974.

The Frappe Cult

Then, in 1957, thanks to a serendipitous stroke of genius by one Dimitris Vakondios, an employee of the Nestlé company, purveyors of Nescafé instant coffee, a whole new phase in Greek coffee history was born: the frappe. Vakondios was working for the company at the annual Thessaloniki International Fair and couldn't find hot water to make a cup of instant coffee, so he shook some together with a little cold water and, voilà, the foamy frappe was born. It became a Greek cultural icon, one that was perfected in Athens a few years later, thanks to the late, great Christos Lentzos, whose legendary pastry shop—Lentzos—on Eftichidou Street in Pangrati, served up a frappe with cult status from 1964, when it first opened, to 2013, when he finally shuttered the place. Songs have been written about Lentzos's frappe! What made it special was its creamy texture, sweetness, and strength. The typical recipe calls for 1 teaspoon instant Nescafé, 1 teaspoon sugar (for medium), and 1 cup water. Lentzos's is said to have contained ¼ cup coffee, 1 cup sugar, and 1½ cups water, all mixed in the glass container of a blender, to make four coffees. While other cafeterias followed the standard recipe, getting about a thousand frappes out of a 5-pound bag of coffee, Lentzos is said to have gotten about three hundred, so the coffee was strong and sweet, and it kept people coming back for more.

The love affair with the frappe lasted until globalization brought an outpouring of cappuccino, espresso, freddo, and, sadly, Starbucks (in 2002, just before the Athens Olympics) with it.

Still, meeting up for coffee is a big pastime in Athens, both for a morning jolt of caffeine or just socially in the middle of the day. Walking the city and stopping at one of its many plateias is a great way to see Greek urban life in action and to understand that even now, as Athens becomes more and more international, coffee time still seems to be a universal hour.

Good Morning, Athens: Breakfast 67

Pancakes
with Baklava-Flavored Greek Yogurt

The warm-spice flavors of baklava and the crunch of nuts combine perfectly with the tart, satisfying taste and texture of Greek yogurt. This topping is a favorite.

MAKES ABOUT 12 PANCAKES

4 to 6 tablespoons coarsely ground walnuts

1 teaspoon ground cinnamon

Pinch salt

1 recipe Pancakes (page 65)

1½ cups Greek yogurt

4 to 6 tablespoons Greek pine honey

Combine the walnuts, cinnamon, and salt in a bowl.

Stack 3 pancakes per serving on a plate and dollop a tablespoon of Greek yogurt, the nut mixture, and a drizzling of honey over each as you stack them. Serve.

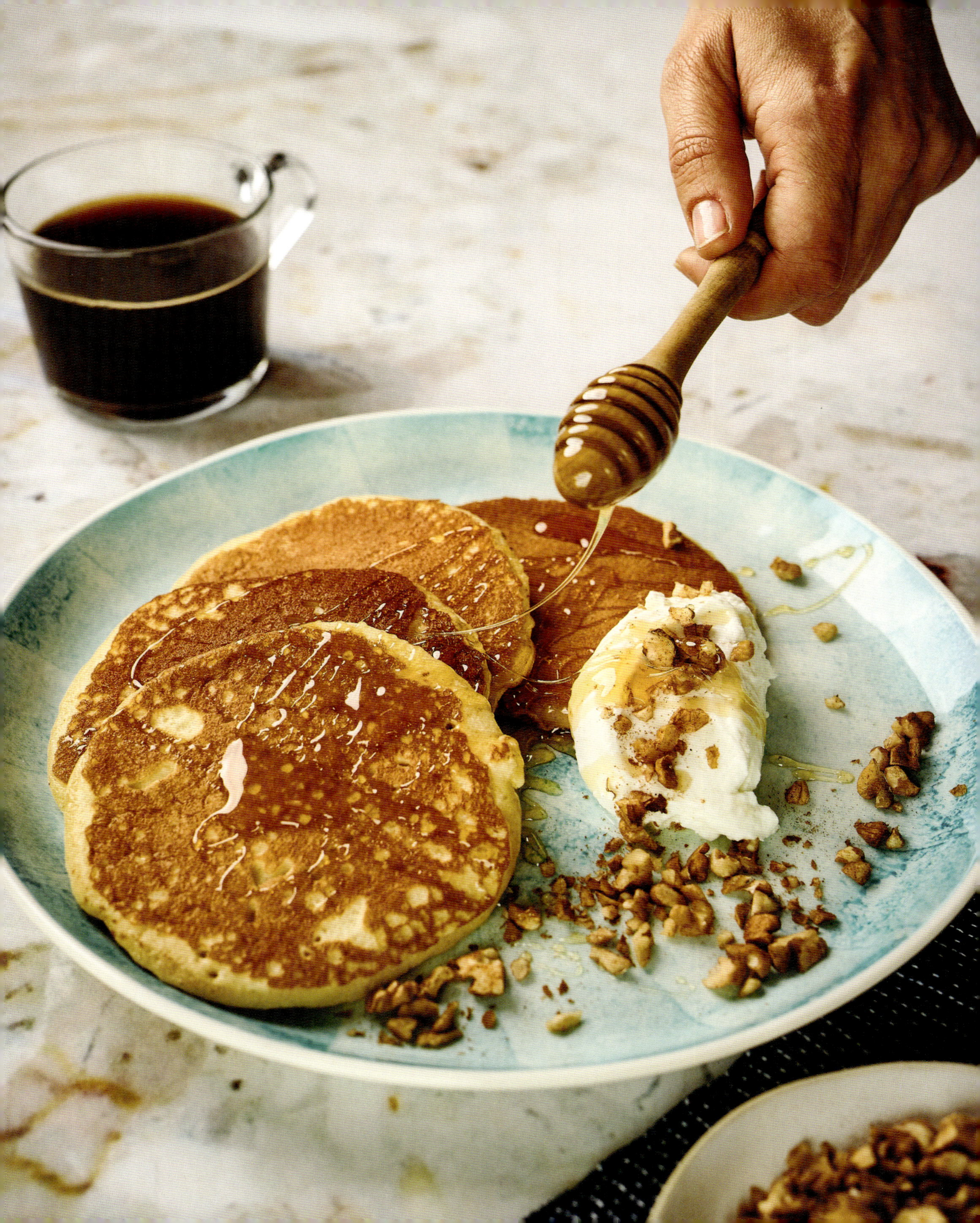

Pancakes Stacked
with Ham and Feta Cream

I like to meet up with friends for late breakfast or brunch on Sunday mornings, especially when the weather is sunny and Athens is all ripe for a walk. One of my favorite areas to walk to is called Plateia Proskopon, or Boy Scout Square, in Pangrati, a particular pocket of the city that's about a half-hour jaunt on foot from Syntagma. There are many small restaurants and cafés and the vibe is relaxed and hip. One time we couldn't get into the hottest ticket, which would have been the restaurant Akra, without a reservation, even for brunch, so we ended up in a bright, pleasant café around the corner, and ordered a stack of these totally over-the-top pancakes to share.

MAKES ABOUT 12 PANCAKES

1 tablespoon unsalted butter or extra-virgin Greek olive oil

1 scant tablespoon all-purpose flour

1½ cups whole milk, warmed

½ cup light or heavy cream

1 cup crumbled Greek feta

Salt and freshly ground black pepper to taste

Pinch grated nutmeg

1 recipe Pancakes (page 65)

1½ cups diced smoked ham

¼ cup finely chopped fresh flat-leaf parsley

Heat the butter or olive oil in a deep skillet, add the flour, and whisk for about 3 minutes, until the flour begins to turn light golden. Add the milk, cream, and feta, whisking until smooth and creamy. Season to taste with salt, pepper, and nutmeg.

To serve, stack the pancakes, add a spoonful of the feta cream to the center of each as you stack them, and sprinkle some of the chopped ham over it. Drizzle a bit more of the cream over the last pancake in the stack so that it cascades down dramatically. Sprinkle with chopped parsley and serve.

Cornmeal Pancakes
with Grape Molasses

Cornmeal pancakes are not a new thing—in fact, they're culled from one of the most traditional regional Greek recipes, called tsaletia, *a specialty of Corfu. I love these pancakes because they're the perfect blend of Greek tradition and modern Athenian sensibilities.*

MAKES 4 SERVINGS

1½ cups fine cornmeal

½ cup whole wheat flour

2 teaspoons baking powder

1 teaspoon salt

1 cup milk

⅓ cup water

¼ cup extra-virgin Greek olive oil, plus 2 to 3 tablespoons for frying

1 tablespoon grape molasses (petimezi) or Greek pine honey

¼ teaspoon vanilla extract

2 large eggs

½ cup Greek currants or seedless dark raisins

For the topping

⅔ cup grape molasses (petimezi)

1½ tablespoons tahini

Mix together the cornmeal, flour, baking powder, and salt in a large bowl.

In a separate bowl, whisk together the milk, water, ¼ cup of the olive oil, grape molasses, and vanilla. Whisk in the eggs.

Add the flour mixture to the liquid, whisking all the while, to form a thick batter. Add a little more flour, cornmeal, milk, or water as needed to reach the consistency of a typical pancake batter. Stir in the raisins.

To make the topping, whisk together the grape molasses and tahini and set aside.

In a nonstick skillet, warm 2 more tablespoons of olive oil over medium heat. Pour in a ladleful of the batter, about ½ cup. Cook until set and lightly browned on one side, then flip with a spatula to cook on the other side. Remove and set aside, covered, to keep warm. Continue until the batter is all used up, replenishing the pan with a little extra olive oil as needed. Serve the pancakes hot, drizzled with a little of the petimezi-tahini mixture.

Crepes, Exciting Generations

My friend Melina Milionis, pastry chef extraordinaire and Greek American lover of Athens, reminded me of crepes in a conversation right about the time I was finishing up this book. "Athens is heavy on the crepe scene," which surprised me since creperies were no longer the kind of eatery I'm naturally drawn to.

Her newer perspective sent me back decades, though, and I recalled so many fond memories of my time in this city way back in the early 1980s, when the first creperies began to open, usually in quaint old neoclassical houses that were just starting to be transformed into eating establishments. They were all the rage and were inexpensive enough to attract streams of young twenty-somethings, among them, myself, my soon-to-be-husband, and our friends. Crepes made for an exotic night out, when we'd head to the old quarters of Exarcheia and sit for hours in cozy venues outfitted with crocheted curtains, lumbering old dining hutches, and antique wall lamps that invariably cast a warm, golden hue on the space.

The city was more innocent then, just a decade or so past the end of the junta, and we were coming of age, some of us having already studied, others about to. Creperies tempered our youthful wanderlust vicariously. Ironically, they still capture the imaginations of yet more waves of young people, something I saw in my own kids; the very first recipe they ever learned to make on their own was for crepes, almost always filled with globs of chocolate-hazelnut cream.

Creperies are still around, but they're tempered, too, into yet another mirror of Greekness mixed with the global palate, so that now one finds crepes filled not so much with French cheeses as with feta, and more than a few other local ingredients.

Spanakopita Crepes

Is this the ultimate Franco-Grecque collaboration? The classic Greek filling and the classic French crepe are a match made in heaven.

MAKES ABOUT 8 CREPES

For the spanakopita filling

3 tablespoons extra-virgin Greek olive oil

1 leek, trimmed and chopped

2 scallions, trimmed and chopped

1½ pounds baby spinach

1 cup snipped fresh dill

⅓ cup chopped fresh mint

1½ cups crumbled Greek feta

Freshly grated nutmeg, to taste

Salt and freshly ground black pepper to taste

For the crepes

1 cup all-purpose flour

2 large eggs

Pinch salt

½ cup milk

½ cup cold water

1 tablespoon extra-virgin Greek olive oil

Prepare the filling: Heat the olive oil in a large, deep skillet or wide pot over medium heat. Add the leek and scallions and sauté until wilted, about 7 minutes. Add the spinach, raise the heat a little, and cook, stirring, until wilted, reduced considerably in volume, and relatively dry. We want to cook off the water that the spinach will exude. Stir in the dill and mint 1 minute before removing from the heat. Let cool for 10 minutes, or cool completely, cover, and refrigerate for up to a full day ahead of time. If necessary, drain the mixture in a colander. When it cools down, add the feta and season with nutmeg, salt, and pepper.

Make the crepes: In a large bowl, whisk together the flour, eggs, and a pinch of salt. Add the milk and cold water, 1 tablespoon at a time, and mix until the batter is smooth and pourable.

Heat a nonstick skillet over medium heat and brush it with olive oil. Pour about ¼ cup batter into the skillet for each crepe. Cook until the crepes are golden brown and crispy around the edges, 2 to 3 minutes per side.

Place the cooked crepes on a serving platter and spoon equal amounts of the spinach-feta mixture evenly on half of each crepe. Fold the crepes in half and serve immediately.

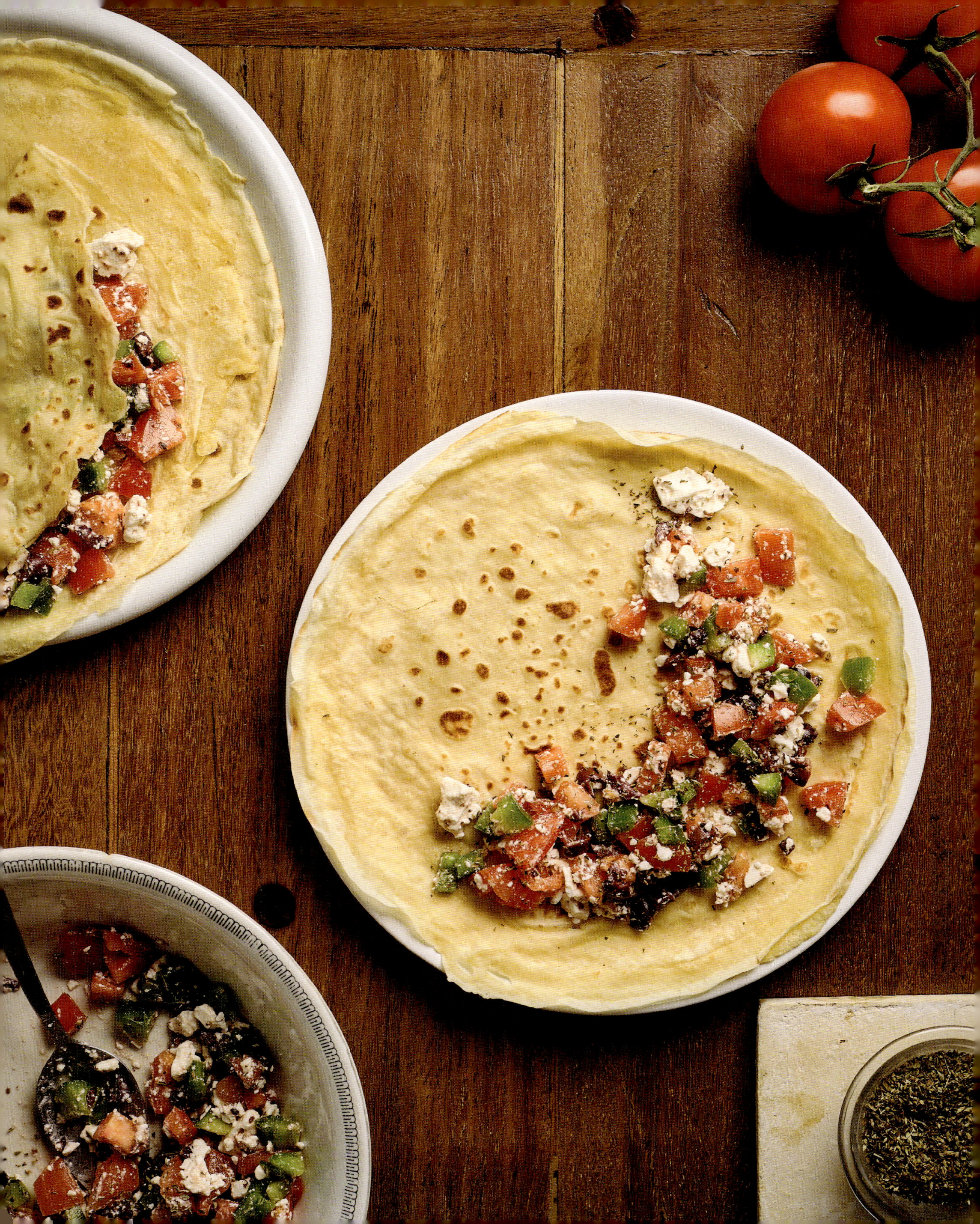

Greek Salad Crepes

It doesn't take a huge leap of faith to marry the basic ingredients of a robust Greek salad with a delicate crepe. This easy recipe might just become your new favorite quick breakfast.

MAKES ABOUT 8 CREPES

For the crepes
1 cup all-purpose flour
2 large eggs
Pinch salt
½ cup milk
½ cup cold water
1 tablespoon olive oil

For the filling
⅔ cup crumbled Greek feta
½ cup chopped pitted kalamata olives
1 large, firm ripe tomato, diced
1 green bell pepper, seeded and diced
1 tablespoon fresh, chopped oregano or 2 scant teaspoons dried Greek oregano
Salt and freshly ground black pepper to taste

Make the crepes: In a large bowl, whisk together the flour, eggs, and salt. Add the milk and cold water, 1 tablespoon at a time, and mix until the batter is smooth and pourable.

Heat a nonstick skillet over medium heat and brush it with olive oil. Pour about ¼ cup batter into the skillet for each crepe. Cook until the crepes are golden brown and crispy around the edges, 2 to 3 minutes per side.

Make the filling: In a small bowl, mix the feta, olives, tomato, green pepper, oregano, salt, and pepper.

Place the cooked crepes on a serving platter and spoon equal amounts of the feta mixture evenly on half of each crepe. Fold the crepes in half and serve immediately.

Athens-Style Avocado Toast
with Mashed Feta, Tomatoes, and Jammy Eggs

Avocado toast took Athens by storm a few years ago, with an immediate Greek spin, most commonly the addition of feta. It has countless variations around the Greek capital, with sunny-side up eggs, poached or soft-boiled eggs, scrambled eggs with and without tomato, but also with additions like spinach or arugula, tomatoes, olives, and, of course, dried Greek herbs.

MAKES 2 SERVINGS

- 2 large eggs
- 2 to 4 slices good whole-grain or multigrain bread
- 1 ripe avocado, peeled, pitted, and halved
- ½ cup crumbled Greek feta
- ½ teaspoon dried Greek oregano
- Smoked sea salt to taste
- 6 teardrop tomatoes, sliced or quartered lengthwise
- 1 teaspoon extra-virgin Greek olive oil

Bring a small pot of water to a gentle simmer and submerge the eggs in the pot with a slotted spoon, carefully, so they don't crack. Cook for exactly 7 minutes for a softly set yolk or 8 minutes for a jammy yolk. Remove and cool slightly before cracking open.

While the eggs are cooking, toast the bread. Mash together the avocado pulp, feta, oregano, and smoked salt. Spread this mixture evenly over the toasted bread slices. Garnish with the tomato slices and top each piece with half an egg. Drizzle with a little olive oil and serve.

Kayianas on Toast 2 Ways

Kayianas is a simple, traditional scrambled egg and tomato recipe from the Peloponnese that is synonymous with easy, everyday seasonal cooking but that has also captured chefs' attention in restaurants all over the city. It means "omelet," from the Persia kaygana, *and is similar to another scrambled egg dish called stapatsada (from the Italian* strapazzare*). In summer, it's invariably made with fresh tomatoes, while in winter, good-quality canned tomatoes are more popular. There are a few variations on the traditional versions, with additions like feta cheese or sfela, a hard brine cheese from the Peloponnese, and sometimes with a little pasto, or cured pork, another specialty of the region.*

But it's really what chefs have been doing to kayianas that has shaped this simple dish into something menu-worthy. Additions like an onion-thyme duet, or a savory sausage-studded panna cotta that melts into the scrambled eggs, or chicken, and even a couple of egg-white versions are some of the options I have encountered in Athenian restaurant outings. I offer up two simple versions below, dressed up with a little feta, or with arugula and cured pork, and served on toast.

MAKES 4 SERVINGS

2 tablespoons extra-virgin Greek olive oil, plus more for drizzling

3 large, ripe tomatoes, seeded and finely chopped, or 2 cups canned diced tomatoes, drained

Salt and freshly ground black pepper to taste

8 large eggs, lightly beaten

1 cup crumbled Greek feta

Dried Greek oregano or thyme to taste

4 slices sourdough bread, about 1 inch thick, toasted or grilled

Heat the olive oil in a 10-inch skillet over medium heat. Add the tomatoes, season with salt and pepper, and cook for about 10 minutes, or until they're no longer runny. Pour in the eggs and push around with a wooden spoon or spatula to make a loose scramble. Add the feta and oregano. Cook to the desired firmness, 7 to 8 minutes. Drizzle a little olive oil over the toasted bread and spoon equal amounts of the kayianas over each slice. Serve.

Variation

Omit the feta, if desired. Have a bunch of trimmed baby arugula washed, spun dry, and set aside, and 4 to 8 thin slices of Greek pasto (cured pork) or pancetta. Serve over the toasted bread. Place a slice or two of the pasto or pancetta over the eggs and a little arugula on top. Drizzle some olive oil over the arugula, season lightly with salt and pepper, and serve.

Cycladic Eggs on Toast

One of my favorite breakfast spots in Athens is the café inside the atrium of the Cycladic Museum in Kolonaki. It's a secret little oasis with natural light pouring in and an air of civility and peace that pervades the space. In keeping with the theme of the museum, some of the café's offerings are infused with ingredients that are native to the Cyclades Islands, such as capers and great goat's milk and cow's milk cheeses. The purely regional cheeses of the Cyclades are still practically impossible to find in the United States, so I've re-created a favorite breakfast using ingredients that are available.

MAKES 2 SERVINGS

3 heaping tablespoons katiki cheese or soft chèvre, or a combination of 2 tablespoons crumbled Greek feta and 1 tablespoon well-drained ricotta or fresh Greek anthotyro

1 teaspoon capers, preferably Santorini, drained and coarsely chopped

3 tablespoons extra-virgin Greek olive oil, divided

2 large eggs

2 slices whole-grain sourdough bread, toasted or grilled

1 medium, firm ripe tomato, cored and cut into 6 rounds

Salt and freshly ground black pepper to taste

A few pieces of pickled sea fennel (aka rock samphire or kritamo), if available

Mash the cheese(s), capers, and 1 tablespoon of the olive oil together until creamy and thick.

Heat the remaining 2 tablespoons olive oil in a small nonstick skillet over medium heat. Break the eggs carefully into the pan and cook until the whites are set and the yolks are cooked to desired consistency.

Spread the cheese mixture evenly over each piece of toasted bread. Place 3 tomato slices over the cheese and then carefully add a sunny-side up egg over the tomatoes. Season with a little salt and pepper and, if desired, garnish with a few sprigs of pickled sea fennel.

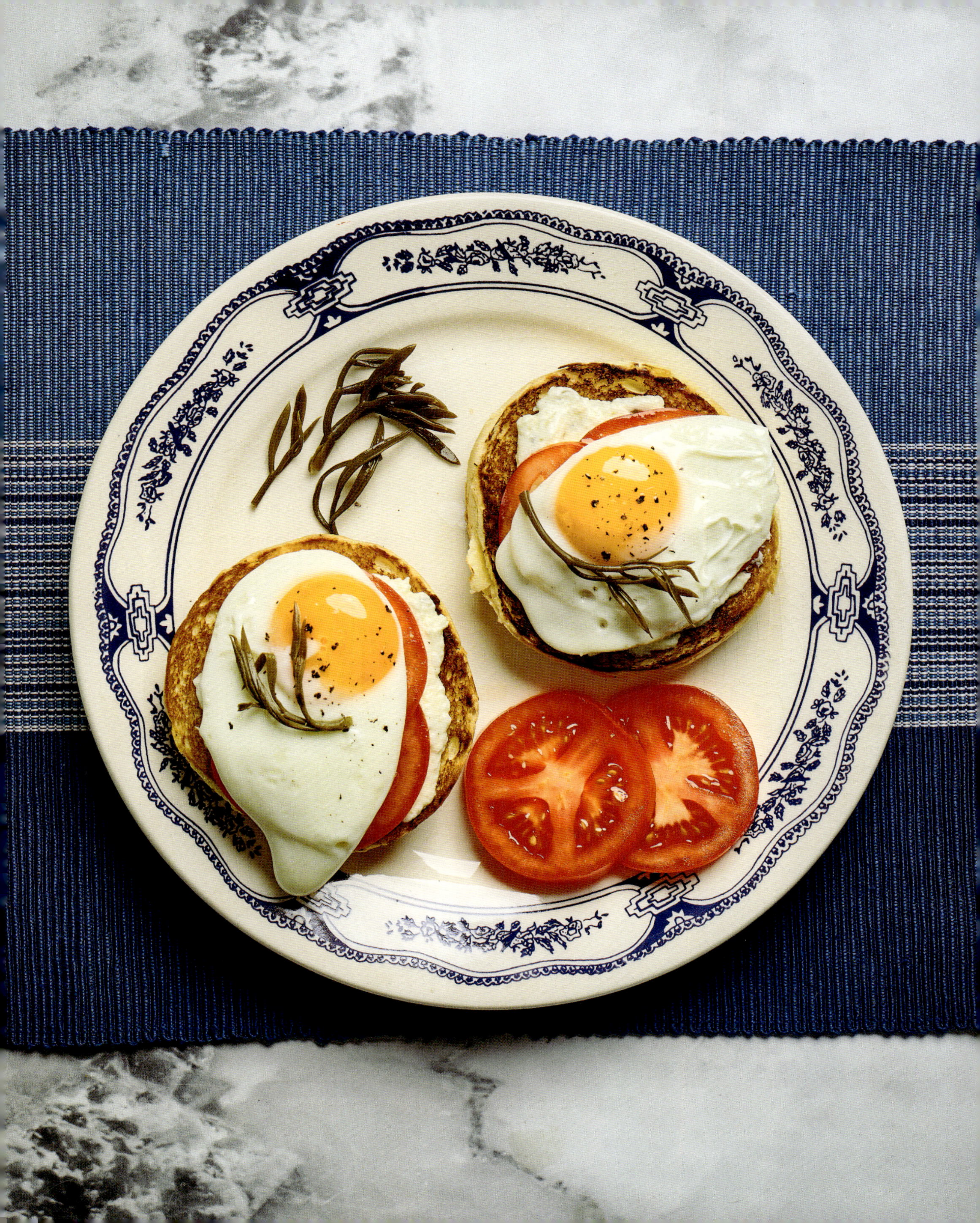

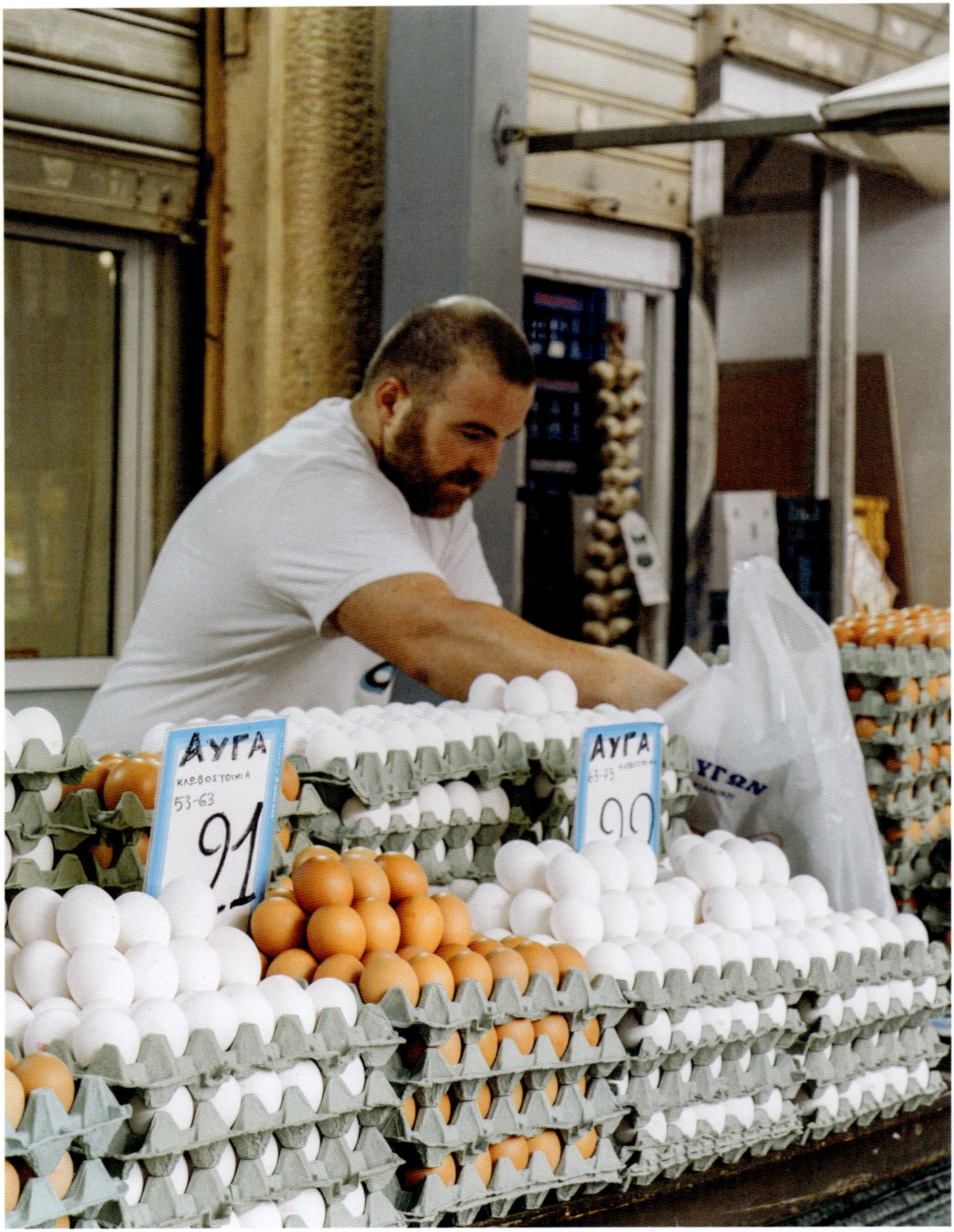
ΑΥΓΑ
53-63
91
ΑΥΓΑ
63-73

Hangover Eggs

This fun breakfast and brunch recipe was born in my daughter's Athenian kitchen, and as she says, it's her absolutely favorite way to cook eggs. You'll need plenty of olive oil, which you spoon over the whites as they cook in the frying pan. As for the name, I guess it's something she has come to see as her personal cure for a wine-induced headache from the night before.

MAKES 1 SERVING

⅓ cup extra-virgin Greek olive oil

2 large eggs

Salt and freshly ground black pepper to taste

½ cup coarsely crumbled or sliced Greek feta

1 or 2 slices whole-grain bread

Heat the olive oil in a nonstick skillet over medium-low heat. Carefully break the eggs into the pan, so as not to break the yolks. Cook, spooning the oil over the whites as you go. Once the whites start to congeal but are still fairly loose, season lightly with salt and pepper. Spoon some more of the olive oil in the pan over the whites, then add the feta, spooning it over the whites and trying to contain it so it doesn't spill off and burn or melt in the frying pan.

Cover and cook for about 45 seconds, until the feta melts but before the yolks solidify too much. Carefully transfer to a serving plate, raise the heat a little, and fry the bread in the remaining olive oil, flipping once, to brown on both sides. Serve hot!

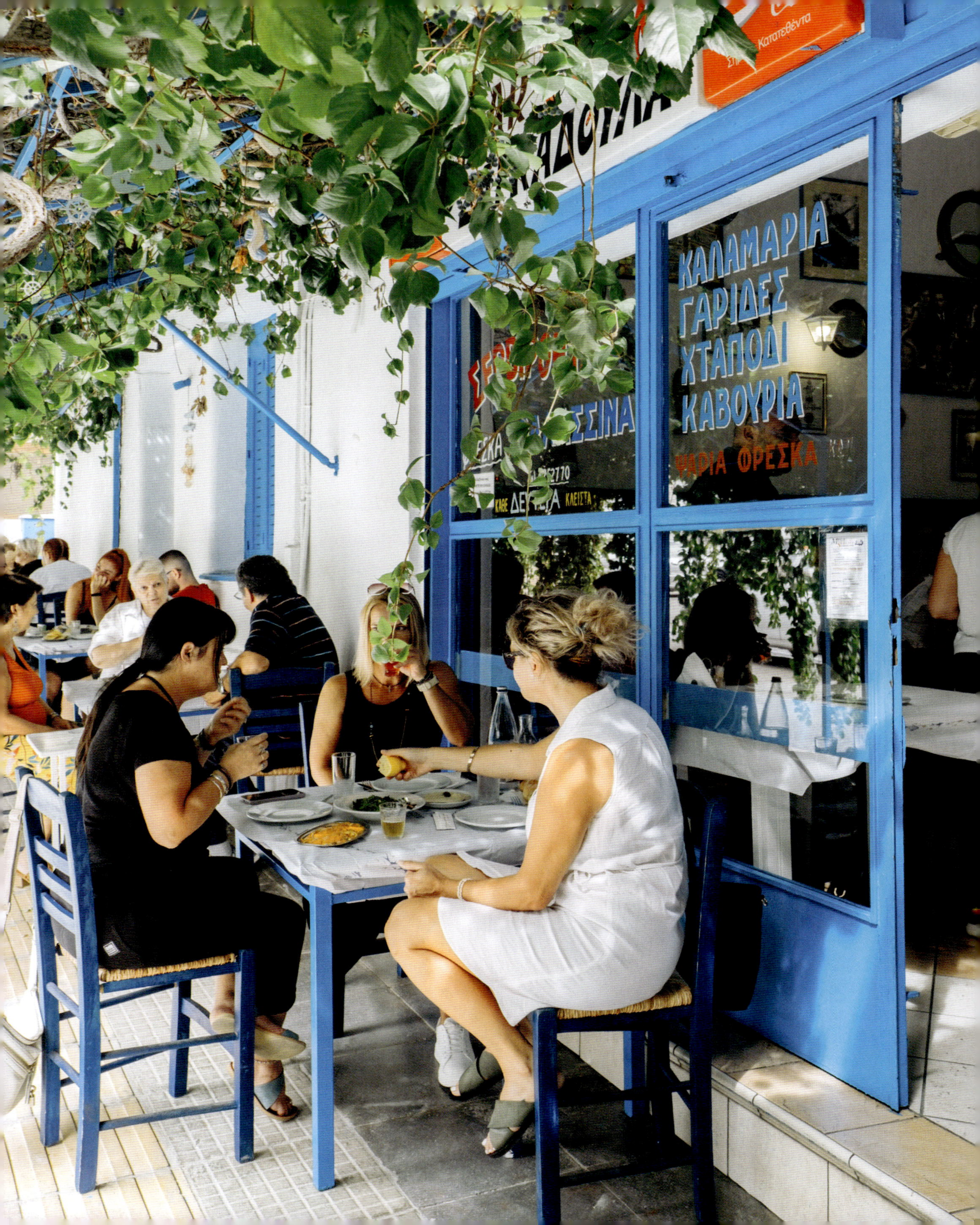

Dip into Athens

Greece, a country of bread lovers even in these gluten-bashing times, boasts the perfect way to enjoy one of the world's most ancient and revered foods: a whole array of dips, traditional and contemporary, spread far and wide in the Greek and Athenian kitchens. The story of dips is inherently linked to the story of bread, for it was the opson—bread and condiment course—of ancient Athenian symposia that first brought together bread and something savory with which to serve it, a nosh considered the epitome of civilized culture, and that is a notion that stands tall even today.

Dips fall into a few basic categories beyond traditional and contemporary: There are those that are dairy based (think Greek yogurt and whipped soft cheeses); bean based, such as fava; and vegetable based, with eggplant, roasted peppers, and, these days, avocado leading the way. Inspirations from the sea, especially taramosalata (fish roe dip), abound, too. Nuts frequently play a role, if not as a base then as an addition that lends texture or acts as a binder.

Athenian restaurant outings provide the best way to plunge into the dipping bowls, so to speak, and understand how classics like taramosalata or tzatziki (the yogurt-cucumber-garlic trio) have evolved. And evolved they have, sometimes unrecognizably so. Ingredients that were long held to be sacrosanct in their use, with the exception of regional, traditional iterations—say, a taramosalata with almonds (northern Greece) or a roasted eggplant spread with capers and tomatoes (Cyclades)—are now fodder for the creative food mill, as a new generation of chefs, unfettered from tradition, sees them in a totally new light. Hence, I've dipped into the likes of taramosalata whipped with avocado or tomato paste or even with sweet potato, and melitzanosalata (roasted eggplant) mixed with miso. As the palette of ingredients grows more global, so does the palate. Maybe because dips are easy, getting creative with them is easy, too.

In the offerings that follow, you'll find both traditional taverna stalwarts and vibrant new interpretations of the classics, most of them culled from restaurant outings these past few years.

TARAMOSALATA REVOLUTION

Taramosalata is the emulsified mixture of fish roe, fat (olive oil or another, less-expensive and more neutrally flavored oil), acid (usually lemon juice), and typically—but not always—some sort of base, such as bread, potatoes, or almonds. In my travels around Athens these last few years I've noticed an undeniable trend: Tarama (cod or carp roe) is now the stuff of experimentation, and chefs are mixing it with just about everything from tapenade to tomato paste to sweet potatoes. It's fun to see all the ways tarama, a most traditional ingredient, can be transformed, a whole rainbow of fish roe dips that take their cue from a classic and run with it.

Note that most Greeks, whether home cooks or professional chefs, prefer the undyed version of tarama, not pink but a creamy ecru color. Pink tarama is mostly what is available stateside, and the two are interchangeable.

A Fish Taverna's Taramosalata

There used to be a time, decades ago, when Pezoulas was arguably the most famous fish taverna in Athens. When it opened in 1951, there was still a racetrack nearby. It began as an ultrasimple eatery first opened by the grandparents of the current owners, who turned the ground level of their home into an oinomageirion. There aren't many oinomageiria left, the name of which translates simply as a place for wine and cooked food. Pezoulas underwent a facelift a few years ago, losing much of its old-world charm, and in an attempt to stay relevant they now serve all the fashionable raw fish options that Athenians have come to embrace. But I like to come here for the traditional fare, among which is a classic taramosalata made, from what I can tell, without a base of bread or potato, and for their kakavia, or traditional fish soup. More on that in the soup chapter, though!

MAKES ABOUT 3 CUPS

5 ounces tarama, preferably white

2 tablespoons finely chopped red onion

½ cup strained fresh lemon juice

2 to 2½ cups sunflower or canola oil

In the bowl of a food processor, pulverize the tarama, minced onion, and lemon juice until it becomes a paste.

With the motor running on high, slowly add as much of the oil as possible through the feed hole so that the tarama completely absorbs it and the resulting texture is a smooth and silky paste. Remove and serve.

Sweet Potato Taramosalata
with Bottarga

The combination of sweet potato and salty fish roe yields a surprisingly harmonious result, especially at the hands of agile and able chefs like Nikos Mihail of Argoura, a favorite fish place in the Kallithea neighborhood of Athens. Seltzer adds springiness, and bottarga, an ancient delicacy in Greece, brings an element of sophistication to one of the most recognizable Greek dips.

MAKES ABOUT 2 CUPS

- 1 medium sweet potato, scrubbed
- ½ cup finely chopped fennel bulb
- 1 small red onion, finely chopped
- 1½ tablespoon tarama (preferably white), or more if desired
- ½ cup extra-virgin Greek olive oil
- ½ to 1 cup canola or sunflower oil, as needed
- Strained juice of ½ lemon, or more as desired
- Seltzer or carbonated water, as needed
- Pita chips or bread, for serving
- 4 to 6 razor-thin slices Greek avgotaraho (bottarga) (optional)

Put the sweet potato in a small pot of cold water and bring to a boil. Cook until the flesh is soft and creamy and the skin bursting. Remove and cool slightly.

Peel the warm sweet potato, break it up or cut it into pieces, and place in the bowl of a food processor. Add the fennel and onion. Process for a few seconds on high speed until smooth.

Add the tarama and pulse to combine. With the processor motor running, add the olive oil and about half of the lemon juice, alternating between each, then continue to add canola oil and lemon juice, processing all the while, until the taramosalata is creamy and smooth. Loosen it, if desired, with a little seltzer, pulsing on and off to combine.

Serve the taramosalata with pita chips or bread, garnished, if desired, with a few slices of bottarga.

Taramosalata
with Tomato Paste

One of my favorite neighborhoods in Athens, despite the fact that it can get rather touristy, is Koukaki, around the Acropolis Museum and stretching down toward Syngrou Avenue, which unites the southern suburbs with the center of the city. There are lots of interesting wine bars and restaurants that run the gastronomic gamut from traditional to modern Greek places as well as ones that feature the cuisines of many nations. At one modern Greek seafood place I had visited with a colleague, my eye was instantly drawn to a taramosalata whisked with tomato paste. The density and sweetness of the tomato paste was a pleasant counter to the salty, robust flavor of the roe. It looks interesting, too!

MAKES ABOUT 2 CUPS

2 medium potatoes (about ½ pound total), peeled and cubed

2 heaping tablespoons tarama (preferably white)

Strained juice of 2 lemons

1½ tablespoons good-quality tomato paste

¾ to 1½ cups extra-virgin Greek olive oil

Put the potatoes in a small pot of cold water and bring to a boil. Turn the heat down and simmer until cooked, 20 to 25 minutes.

Remove the potatoes from the water with a slotted spoon and transfer to the bowl of a food processor. Reserve the hot liquid.

Add the tarama and lemon juice to the food processor and pulse on and off continuously until the mixture is pureed. Add the tomato paste and ½ cup of the hot liquid and pulse a few more times. Pulsing all the while, add the olive oil, slowly drizzling it into the mixture, for about 4 minutes total. The amount of olive oil will vary depending on the starchiness and variety of the potatoes. The mixture should be very creamy and fluffy, and that texture is achieved by adding ample oil. If the mixture is dense, add a few more drops of the hot liquid and pulse on and off again.

Taste, and if the taramosalata is too sour because of the lemon juice, add more olive oil. Serve.

Nena Ismyrnoglou's Beet Taramosalata
with Lime and Mint

Nena and I have been friends since I first moved to Greece in the 1990s, and she was chef-partner in Kallisti, one of the first gourmet Greek restaurants to open in Atismyrhens. She has since gone on to cook in many other places, and Kallisti is now just a fond memory. She also is one of the major contributors to Gastronomos, *the Greek food magazine. This dish is inspired by one of her published recipes in the magazine.*

MAKES ABOUT 2 CUPS

10 ounces country-style sourdough bread, crusts removed

5 ounces tarama

1 small cooked beet, chopped*

1 small red onion, chopped

1 cup extra-virgin Greek olive oil

5 to 8 tablespoons strained fresh lime juice

1 teaspoon balsamic vinegar

1 or 2 radishes, cut into paper-thin slices and crisped in ice water

4 or 5 small fresh mint leaves

1 teaspoon salmon roe

* If your market doesn't carry vacuum-packed cooked beets, you can cook the beet yourself: Trim the root and stem ends and scrub well. Place the beet in a small pot with enough water to cover by 2 inches. Add 1 tablespoon red wine vinegar, which helps preserve the beet's color, and bring to a simmer. Cook until tender but al dente, about 25 minutes. Remove, drain, and cool. Put on gloves and peel the beet, then chop.

Dampen the bread under the tap or in a bowl of cold water and squeeze out the excess moisture very well.

Place the tarama and beet in the bowl of a food processor and process until well combined. Add the onion and continue to process to combine well. Crumble the dampened bread and add it to the food processor, pulsing on and off to combine. Add the olive oil, 5 tablespoons of lime juice, and the balsamic vinegar, pulsing on and off until the mixture is smooth and creamy. Taste and adjust the acidity as desired with a little more lime juice. Loosen the mixture if necessary with a little water.

Serve in a bowl garnished with the radish slices, fresh mint, and the teaspoon of salmon roe sprinkled over the surface.

Katsogiannis's Grilled Eggplant Dip
with Roasted Red Peppers

The historic old tavernas of Athens are disappearing with alarming speed as the city changes rapidly, becoming ever more international with each passing day. But some places, at least as of this writing, are still happily going strong a few generations since their founding. One such place is Katsogiannis Taverna in Drapetsona, a working-class and once-industrial area on the fringes of the Port of Piraeus, which was settled by Greek islanders and then, in 1922, by the thousands of Greek refugees who poured into Athens as the result of the Asia Minor Catastrophe. This throwback to another era started off as a milk and dairy shop in 1930 and then morphed into a taverna a few years later. What I love most about it, besides its newfound status as a cultural landmark (because it has remained unchanged for almost a century), is the mix of clientele, everyone from guards at the nearby Averoff Prison to artists, lawyers, and intellectuals. The menu is a simple one of classic taverna fare and simple seafood.

MAKES ABOUT 4 CUPS

4 medium eggplants

2 red bell or Florina peppers

1 garlic clove, minced

4 to 6 tablespoons extra-virgin Greek olive oil

½ cup finely chopped fresh flat-leaf parsley

Salt and freshly ground black pepper to taste

Preheat the grill or broiler to high. If using the broiler, line a rimmed baking sheet with aluminum foil. Using a fork, puncture the eggplants in a few different places all around.

Grill or broil the eggplants and whole peppers until charred and soft, 25 to 35 minutes for the eggplants and about 20 minutes for the peppers. You'll need to turn them as they cook to make sure that they char evenly all over. Remove them with kitchen tongs, immediately place in a bowl, and cover so that they steam a little, enabling you to peel the peppers and loosen the skin around the eggplant pulp more easily.

Split the eggplants down the middle lengthwise, score the flesh, and scoop it out with a spoon, transferring it to a colander set over a bowl. Let the eggplant pulp drain for about 1 hour. Peel, seed, and finely chop the peppers.

Place the drained eggplant pulp on a cutting board and finely chop it. Transfer it to a medium bowl, add the chopped peppers and their juices, and mix well. Stir in 4 tablespoons of the olive oil, the garlic, and the parsley and season to taste with salt and pepper. Add the remaining olive oil if desired to make the consistency a little more velvety. Serve.

Melitzanosalata
with Miso, Tahini, and Petimezi

To the best of my knowledge, the first chef in Athens to mix Japanese miso paste into a traditional Greek melitzanosalata (roasted eggplant salad) was Christoforos Peskias. As of this writing, he heads the kitchen at one of the city's most beautiful restaurants, Balthazar, as well as at a meze place in central Athens called Dopio. The fermented, umami flavor of miso adds an incredible depth to the smoky, satisfying flavor of grilled eggplant.

MAKES ABOUT 3 CUPS

- 3 large eggplants
- ½ cup tahini, preferably from unhulled sesame seeds
- 1 tablespoon white or red miso paste
- 2 to 8 tablespoons extra-virgin Greek olive oil
- 2 tablespoons strained fresh lemon juice
- 1 tablespoon balsamic vinegar
- 1 tablespoon grape molasses (petimezi), or more, as desired
- Salt to taste

Preheat the broiler to high. Line a rimmed baking sheet with aluminum foil.

Pierce the eggplants all over with a fork, place on the lined baking sheet in the middle or lower third of the oven, and broil on high for 35 to 45 minutes, turning several times with kitchen tongs, to roast and blister all over. The eggplants should be very soft. Remove and let cool for 10 minutes.

Cut the eggplants in half lengthwise. Scoop out the flesh of each eggplant and transfer to the bowl of a food processor. Add the tahini and miso and pulse on and off to combine. Add 2 tablespoons of the olive oil, the lemon juice, balsamic vinegar, and petimezi and pulse on and off until very smooth and creamy. Adjust the texture with additional olive oil and the seasoning with a little salt.

Transfer to a bowl, cover, and refrigerate for at least 30 minutes before serving.

Sweet Potato Skordalia

Sweet potatoes, low on the glycemic index, are high on the minds of so many Athenian chefs, who have been using them in place of conventional potatoes as part of a trend I've been witnessing for years now, to make tradition more compatible with contemporary health and diet perspectives. The result is a subtler and lighter skordalia, the pungency of the garlic offset by the subtlety of the sweet potatoes.

MAKES ABOUT 2 CUPS

2 large sweet potatoes, peeled and cut into large chunks

Sea salt to taste

3 to 5 garlic cloves, roughly chopped

½ to ¾ cup extra-virgin Greek olive oil

2 tablespoons white wine vinegar or cider vinegar

Put the sweet potatoes in a pot with enough cold water to cover them by about 1 inch and bring to a boil. Season generously with salt. Reduce the heat to a simmer, cover, and cook the sweet potatoes until fork-tender.

Transfer the sweet potatoes to the bowl of a food processor, add the garlic, and process to puree, adding the olive oil and vinegar as you go. If the puree can absorb a little more olive oil, drizzle some in and continue processing. Season to taste with salt and serve.

To Kafeneion's Delicious Eggplant Dip
with Olives and Honey

On an unusually warm Sunday in January, I met up with a friend who was passing through Athens en route to Tel Aviv, and we had lunch at a quaint retro spot in the Plaka called To Kafeneion. It's not unusual to sit in a four-hundred-year-old building in the Plaka, at the foothills of the Parthenon, but what is, admittedly, unusual is to have a really good meal! This is the most touristy part of the city and all too often restaurant food is not the best. We ordered a few mezedes, and this delicious, slightly sweet eggplant dip was one of them.

MAKES 3 CUPS

3 medium eggplants

½ to ⅔ cup extra-virgin Greek olive oil

2 tablespoons golden raisins or 4 large Greek dried figs, soaked in water to soften

5 sun-dried tomatoes, soaked in warm water for 20 minutes

⅓ cup extra-virgin Greek olive oil

⅔ cup sliced pitted kalamata olives

1 tablespoon Greek pine honey, or more to taste

Salt to taste

Preheat the grill or broiler to medium-high.

Using a fork, puncture the eggplants all around. Place on the grill rack or on a rack over a pan about 8 inches from the broiler and grill or broil, turning on occasion, until charred all over, 25 to 35 minutes. Remove and transfer to a bowl, cover, and let them cool and steam so the skins peel off easily.

In the meantime, drain the raisins or figs and the sun-dried tomatoes. If you're using figs, trim off the stems and chop the figs. Chop the sun-dried tomatoes.

Pour the olive oil into a large bowl.

Place the eggplants on a cutting board and split lengthwise down the middle with a knife. Score the flesh. If the seed beds are very dense, remove them (I usually don't bother). Scoop out the eggplant pulp with a spoon, careful not to get charred bits of skin, and drop it into the bowl with the olive oil.

Add the figs, sun-dried tomatoes, olives, and honey, mixing to combine well. Season to taste with salt and serve.

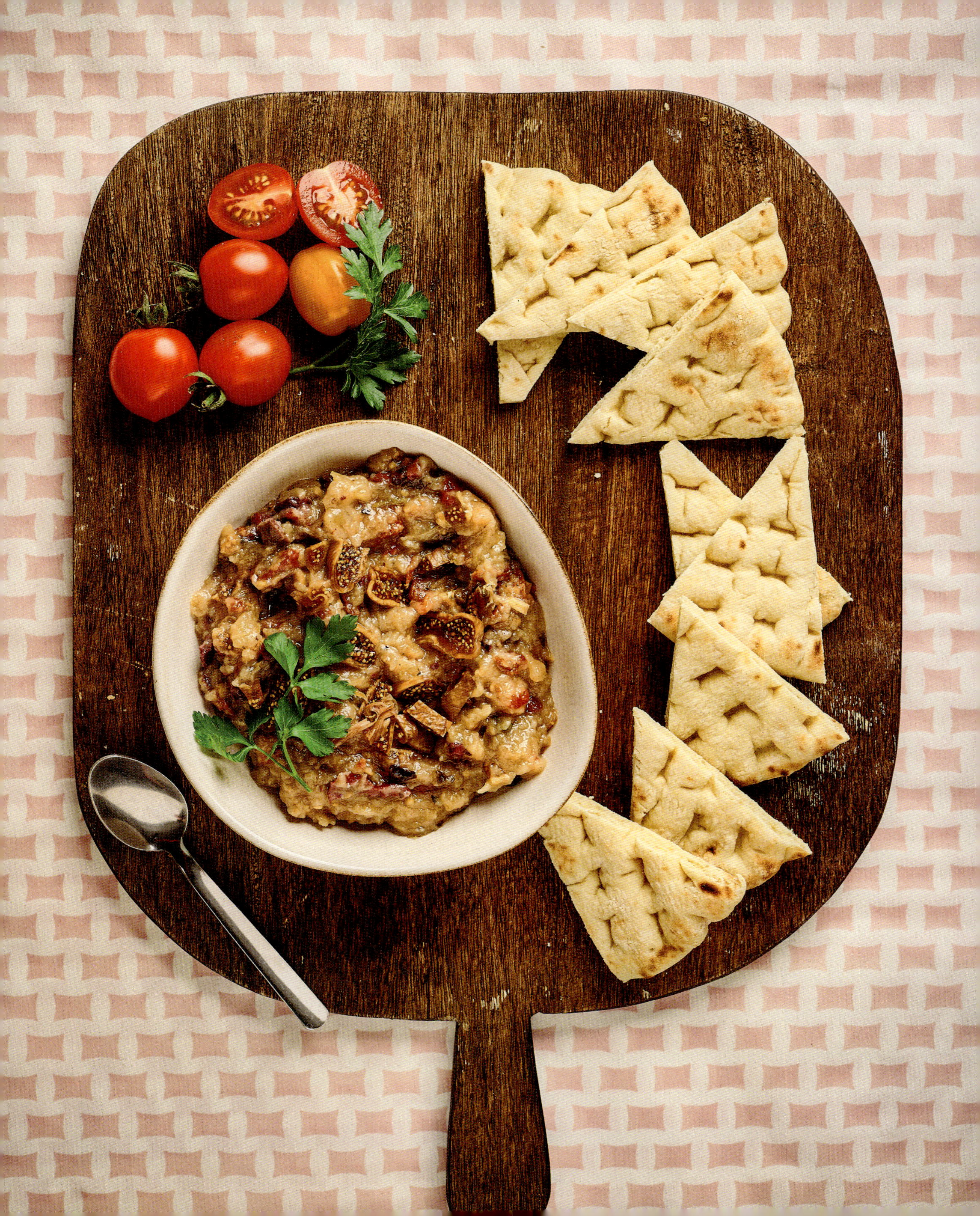

Mung Bean Fava with Tahini and Za'atar

Mung beans are not native to Greece, and only in the past decade or so have they become somewhat popular, thanks to the thriving community of Southeast Asians who have become part of the tapestry of multiethnic Athens. The first Indian and Pakistani restaurants started to open in the 1990s on the rundown streets around the Central Market. I loved wandering those streets back then and still do, but things have changed dramatically along those once rundown streets. The market area bustles day and night and there are many well-established Southeast Asian businesses now, a supermarket stocked with Egyptian products, and a whole world of Chinese shops and merchants who sell everything from tofu to sandals up and down streets like Evripidou and Sophocleous (named for two of the most important tragedians in ancient Greece). Greek shops that sell some of the best cheeses and charcuterie in town, a renowned honey shop, spice emporiums, and more crowd these side streets. A few sell nothing but dried goods like beans and rice, and it is there, as well as in the shops selling Southeast Asian ingredients, that mung beans first made their appearance. This recipe is a rendition of Greek fava, a split pea puree, with clearly Anatolian flavors, in a nod to the multiethnic side of Athens.

MAKES 6 SERVINGS

3 tablespoons plus ½ cup extra-virgin Greek olive oil, or more as needed

1 red onion, coarsely chopped

1 cup chopped fennel bulb

1 carrot, peeled and chopped

½ pound mung beans

2 garlic cloves, chopped

2 tablespoons tahini

3 to 5 tablespoons strained fresh lemon juice, to taste

1 teaspoon ground cumin

Salt and freshly ground black pepper to taste

2 teaspoons za'atar

1 or 2 scallions, trimmed and very thinly sliced

Pinch cayenne

Heat 3 tablespoons of the olive oil in a wide pot over medium heat. Add the onion, fennel, and carrot and cook until glistening and softened, 10 to 12 minutes. Add the mung beans and give them a turn in the oil to coat. Stir in the garlic and swish around for about 45 seconds.

Heat water in a kettle or pot to boiling, and add enough of it to the mung beans to cover by about an inch. Bring to a boil over high heat, reduce the heat to medium, and skim the foam off the top. Lower the heat to a slow simmer and cook the mung beans until very soft, about 30 minutes. Replenish the mixture with more hot water if needed.

Drain the mung beans and vegetables, reserving the liquid. Transfer the mung bean–vegetable mixture to the bowl of a food processor and pulse on and off to make a chunky paste.

Add the tahini and 2 tablespoons of the lemon juice and pulse on and off until a thick, smooth paste forms. Add ½ cup olive oil, 1 tablespoon at a time, pulsing after each addition, as much as you need for the mixture to be very velvety and smooth. Season with the cumin and salt and pepper, pulsing on and off to combine well, and adjust the seasoning with additional lemon juice as needed; if the mixture is still dense, you can loosen it with a bit of the mung bean cooking liquid.

To serve, spread the mung bean fava onto a platter, swirling it with the back of a spoon. Garnish with the za'atar, finely sliced scallion, and a sprinkling of cayenne.

Garlicky Fava
with Red Wine and Herbs

There are so many variations on the fava theme trending in Athens as of this writing that it's hard to keep up. Chefs are taking the basic recipe for this traditional puree of yellow split peas, one of the most ancient foods in Greece, to new places by adding fermented black garlic, squid ink, soy sauce, and tomato paste, among other ingredients. They're also experimenting with different beans and legumes in the place of yellow split peas, such as red lentils, a relative newcomer that arrived in Athens with the wave of Southeast Asian immigrants a few years ago. I've seen fava made with black giant beans or whisked with roasted red peppers. The combinations are endless, and so are the toppings, from Thai-spiced carrots to tomato salsa, to the usual array of grilled seafood, especially squid and octopus. The recipe below is a trendy one, too, combining two classic Greek dips into one. I guess it was only a matter of time before that happened!

MAKES 6 SERVINGS

⅓ cup extra-virgin Greek olive oil, plus ½ to ⅔ cup, or even a bit more for pureeing

1 large red onion, finely chopped

2 cups yellow split peas

1 cup dry red wine

Hot water or vegetable stock as needed

1 bay leaf

3 or 4 fresh oregano sprigs

4 to 7 garlic cloves, minced

1 to 4 tablespoons red wine vinegar

Sea salt to taste

1 teaspoon dried Greek oregano (optional)

Heat ⅓ cup of the olive oil in a wide pot over medium heat. Add the onion and cook, stirring, until soft and translucent, about 8 minutes. Add the yellow split peas and toss to coat in the oil. Add the red wine. Stir until the wine is absorbed and the alcohol has cooked off, about 5 minutes. Add enough hot water to cover the yellow split peas by 1 inch. Add the bay leaf and oregano sprigs. Simmer until the water is absorbed, then add another increment of water, again covering the split peas by about 1 inch. Keep adding water incrementally as the fava absorbs it, until the split peas are tender enough to mash against the side of the pot with a spatula or wooden spoon and the liquid is totally absorbed. The split peas should be the texture of chunky mashed potatoes.

Remove the bay leaf and oregano sprigs from the pot. Add the garlic and a tablespoon or two of the hot fava mixture to the bowl of a food processor and puree at high speed to get a very smooth paste. Transfer the remaining hot fava to the food processor bowl and puree, drizzling in the remaining olive oil and a tablespoon or two of vinegar, alternating between each, to reach a consistency that is silky and smooth. Season to taste with salt and test for balance, adding more vinegar if the mixture needs a little more acidity. It will absorb a lot of olive oil as you puree it, upwards of nearly a cup. Transfer the fava to a serving bowl, cool slightly, and serve, sprinkled with a little dried oregano, if desired.

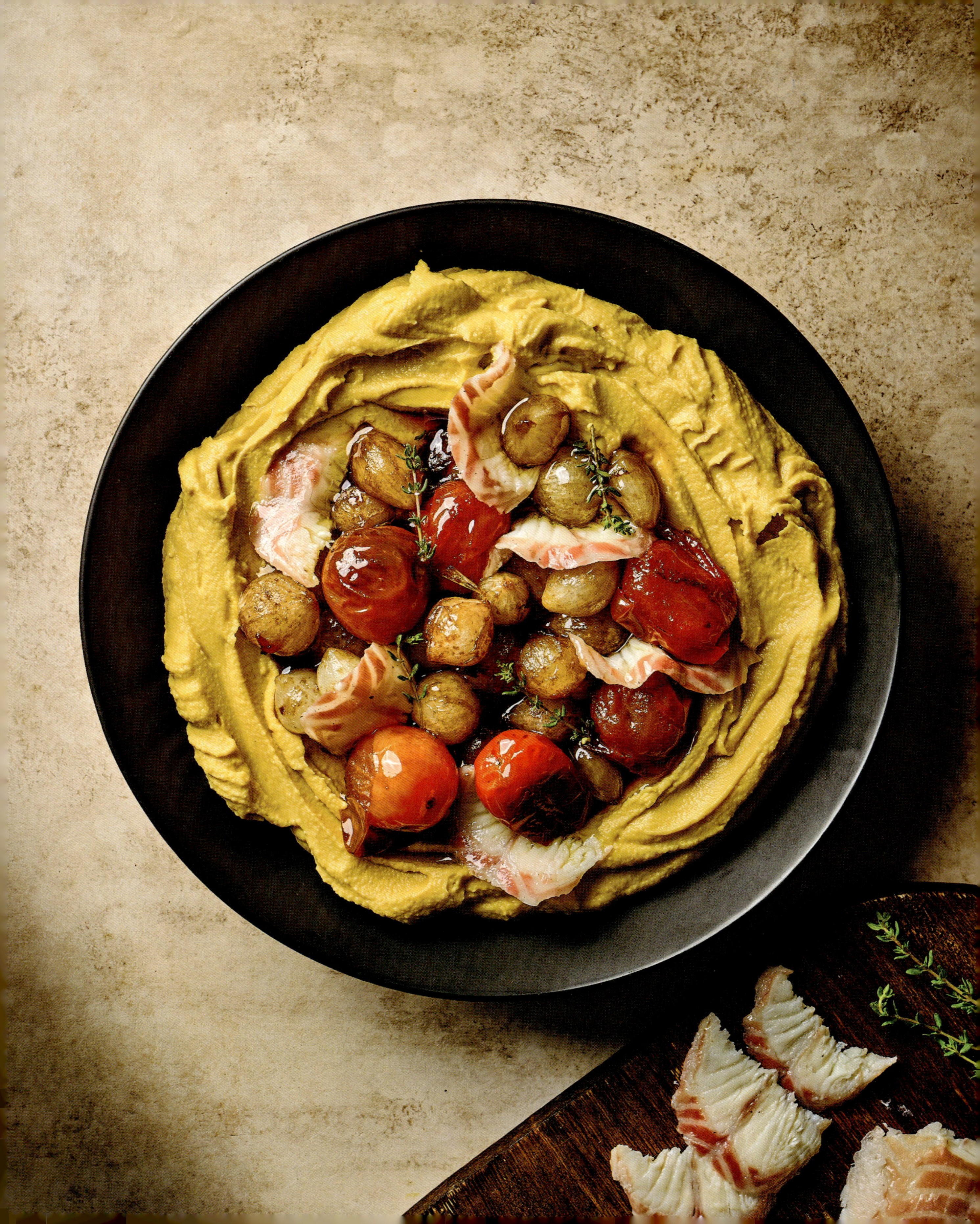

Yellow Split-Pea Fava
with Smoked Eel, Caramelized Tomatoes, and Onions

Most Americans know smoked eel only if they've encountered it as unagi in a Japanese restaurant. Much of what is available in the US is farmed in Maine. In Greece, eels flourish in many parts of the country, and one of the most beloved ways to enjoy them is smoked as a garnish for salads and purees such as fava. This recipe is inspired by a dish at one of Athens's most renowned seafood tavernas, Pezoulas, in Kallithea. If you're using canned smoked eel for this, save a little of the olive oil from the can to drizzle into or over the fava for extra flavor.

MAKES 6 SERVINGS

For the fava

3 tablespoons extra-virgin Greek olive oil, plus ½ to ⅔ cup for whipping into the fava and drizzling as garnish

1 small red onion, coarsely chopped

2 cups yellow split peas, preferably Greek from Santorini or Feneos

1 bay leaf

4 fresh thyme sprigs

Hot water as needed

Salt to taste

Strained juice of ½ to 1 lemon, to taste

4 ounces butterflied or canned smoked eel, thinly sliced

For the onion-tomato topping

2 tablespoons extra-virgin Greek olive oil

2 cups pearl onions

Pinch salt

1 cup teardrop or cherry tomatoes (any color or mixture of colors)

2 teaspoons balsamic vinegar

2 teaspoons grape molasses (petimezi)

Make the fava: Heat 3 tablespoons of the olive oil in a wide pot over medium heat. Add the onion and cook, stirring, until soft and translucent, about 8 minutes. Add the split peas and give them a swirl to coat in the oil. Add the bay leaf and thyme sprigs and enough hot water to come up about 1 inch over the fava. Bring to a boil, then reduce to a simmer and cook for about 40 minutes, replenishing with a little more hot water several times during cooking to keep the fava from scorching. Toward the end, the fava will be soft enough to mash against the side of the pot with a spoon, most of the water will have been absorbed, and the bubbles on the surface will be large. Remove the pot from the heat and cover for a few minutes with a kitchen towel.

While the fava is cooking, prepare the onion-tomato topping. Heat the olive oil in a heavy, preferably cast-iron, skillet over medium heat. Add the pearl onions and salt and cook, shaking the pan back and forth on occasion, until they start to caramelize, 15 to 20 minutes. Add the tomatoes and raise the heat a little. Shaking the pan back and forth, cook the tomatoes and onions until the tomatoes start to blister but still retain their shape, another 7 to 10 minutes. Add the balsamic vinegar and petimezi, shake the pan back and forth to distribute evenly, and remove from the heat.

Remove the bay leaf and thyme sprigs from the fava and transfer the fava and vegetables to the bowl of a food processor. Season lightly with salt. Puree, drizzling in some of the remaining olive oil and the lemon juice in alternating increments, until the fava is very velvety. If you're using canned smoked eel, you can drizzle in a little of the olive oil it is preserved in, which is very flavorful and intense. Use it judiciously.

Cut the smoked eel into thin slices. Spread the fava onto a platter or plate and top with the tomato-onion mixture. Tuck the smoked eel pieces between the tomatoes and onions and drizzle a little olive oil (and a little of the can juices, too, if using) over the top. Serve.

Classic Tavernisio Tzatziki

A great tzatziki has a few basic rules: Start with excellent, full-fat Greek yogurt, don't skimp on the garlic, and make sure to add both acid and fat. Athenian tavernas usually present tzatziki that's unapologetically garlicky, as is the one below! It's served as a dip with bread, or as an accompaniment to fried vegetables such as zucchini and eggplant, or with vegetable fritters. Tzatziki also finds its way into gyros and souvlaki, a pungent, creamy buffer between the smoky meats and the pillowy pita wrap.

MAKES ABOUT 2 CUPS

1 large cucumber, peeled and seeded

2 to 4 garlic cloves, minced

1½ cups full-fat Greek yogurt

3 tablespoons extra-virgin Greek olive oil

2 tablespoons red wine vinegar

2 heaping tablespoons fresh chopped mint or dill

Salt to taste

Grate the cucumber on the coarse side of a hand grater. Place the grated pulp in a colander and let it drain for 30 minutes. Transfer it to a cheesecloth and wring it dry again and again until you've squeezed out all the liquid.

Mix the cucumber, garlic, yogurt, olive oil, vinegar, mint or dill, and salt in a bowl. Serve, or cover and refrigerate to serve chilled.

Fiery Feta Cream

Tyrokafteri is one of the classics in Greek tavernas, a spicy combo of feta and various kinds of hot peppers, hot pepper flakes, or hot sauces, sometimes loosened or made creamy with the addition of Greek yogurt. It's a dip but it also serves as a filling for everything from roasted peppers to burgers. There are a few ancient tavernas in Athens renowned for one specialty or another; this version of tyrokafteri is inspired by an old taverna in Pangrati (home to many old tavernas) called To Koutouki tou Marathonitis.

MAKES ABOUT 4 CUPS

1 red bell pepper

3½ cups crumbled Greek feta

1 cup Greek yogurt

5 to 6 tablespoons extra-virgin Greek olive oil

1 tablespoon finely chopped fresh green or red chile

2 turns freshly ground black pepper

Roast the bell pepper under the broiler or on the grill, turning until it is soft and blistered all over. Transfer to a small bowl with a plate or lid on top. Let the pepper cool, then peel, seed and chop it, reserving its juices.

In the bowl of a food processor, place the feta and yogurt. Pulse to combine. Add the roasted red pepper and its juices, olive oil, chile, and pepper and pulse on and off until the mixture is creamy and smooth. Transfer to a bowl and serve.

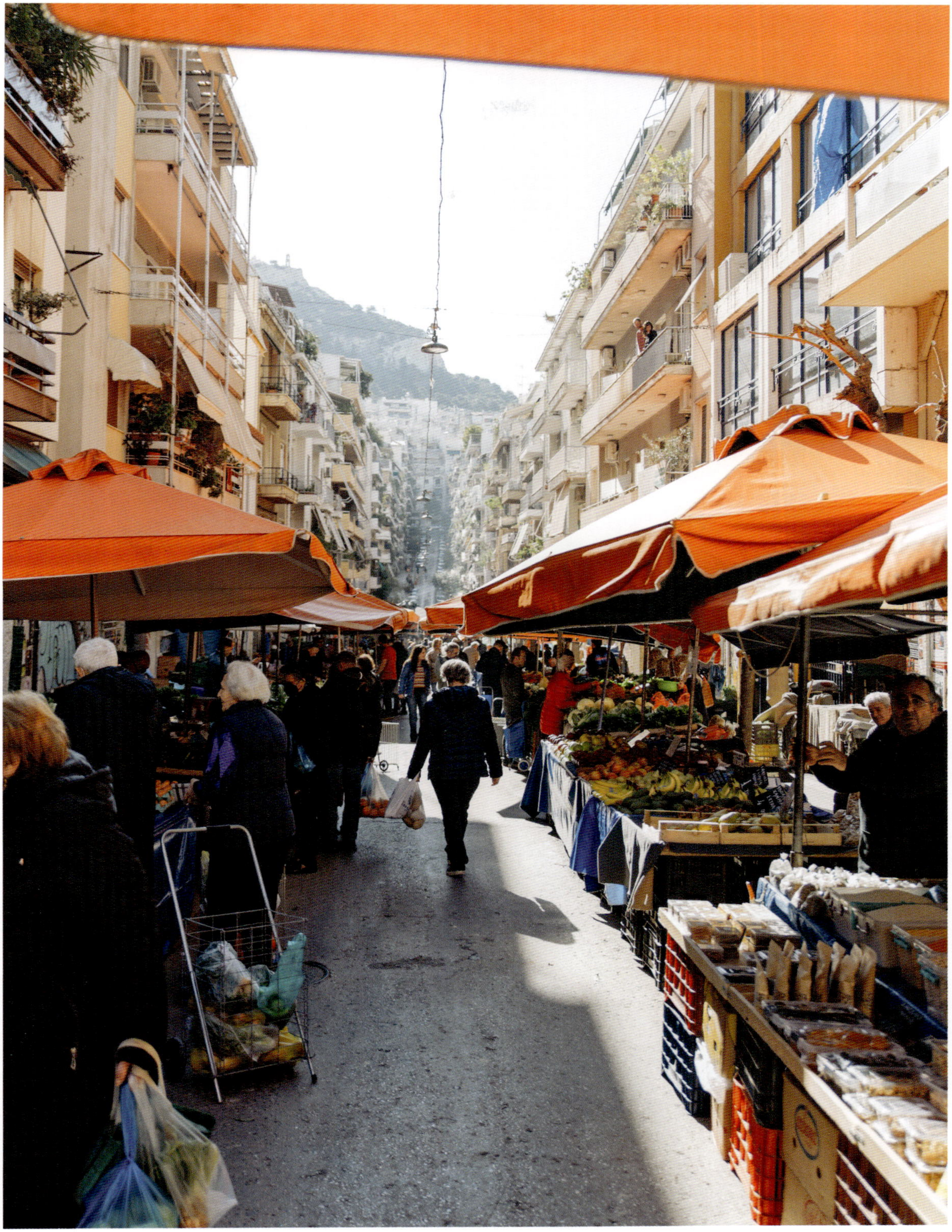

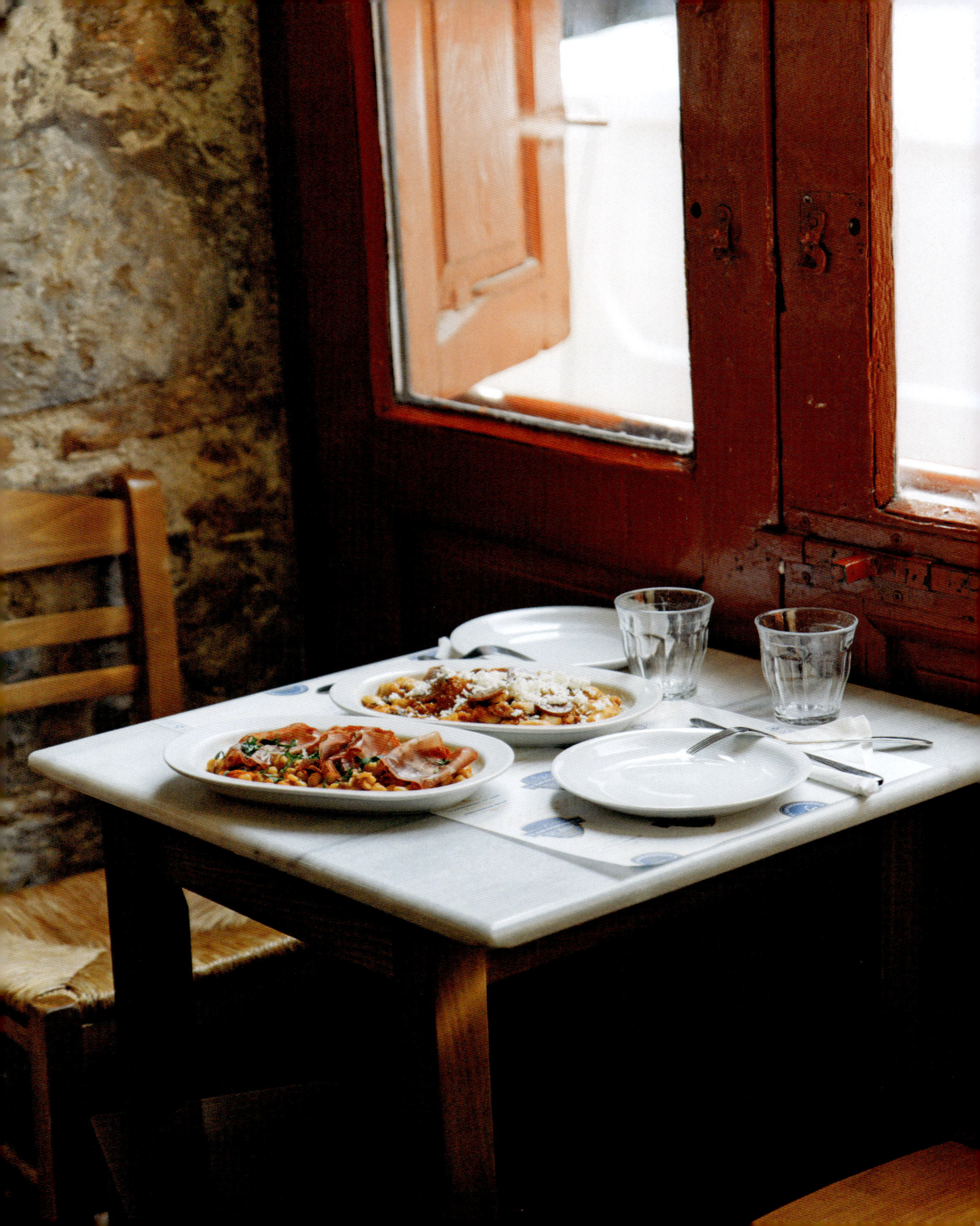

Sharing a Plate

Meze Heaven

One of my favorite things to do in Athens is to head to the Varvakeios fish market, both to shop and to nosh. If there's a friend in tow, all the better. I squeeze into the bustling, narrow corridor just across from the Korakis fish stall on the east side of the market, near the main entrance, in hopes of finding an empty stool or two at the sliver of a high-top, essentially an extension of the sill outside the window pass of this tiny place's even tinier kitchen. But I am happy to stand, too. From that hot box of a space, with speed, flair, and flavor, emerge some of the best mezedes in the city: Dolmades, saganaki, fried shrimp, langoustines, keftedes awash in tomato sauce, and simple plates of olives and feta are among their offerings I love.

There are a few other spots I gravitate to as well to share a plate and a sip with a friend or two, among them Avli, a once-hidden, now all-too-often tourist-trodden inner courtyard in Psyrri; To Ouzerie tou Laki off Victoria Square; and Athinaikon, Kapetan Mihalis, and Lesvos, all in Exarcheia.

The meze tradition of enjoying small plates of savory food, accompanied by wine, ouzo, raki, or tsipourio, permeates the cultures all around the eastern Mediterranean. At first glance, this most convivial food tradition has Anatolian roots; the word itself derives from the Persian, *maza*, which means "taste."

But the truth is that the concept of sharing small plates of savory delights while imbibing in the company of friends was actually born in the Athens of classical antiquity, specifically at the symposia. The word *symposium* means "to drink together." It was considered barbaric—and still is—to descend into drunkenness; what were essentially drinking parties, in which male Athenian citizens partook in wine, philosophical discussions, music, song, and sex (both hetero, with courtesans, and homoerotic), were always accompanied by food, typically served on small plates at the beginning of the evening, before anything else began. Over time, as the ancient world frayed and Greece segued into Hellenistic, Roman, and Ottoman eras, the symposia evolved, too. Cafeneia and tavernas eventually became the venues for drinking (mostly all-male events until pretty recently), socializing, and discussing the issues of the day, and shared plates of small, savory treats continued to be a part of that experience. When Greece was under Ottoman rule, raki, ouzo, and tsipouro were the allowed quaffs, as wine is prohibited in Islam.

Fast-forward to modern Athens, a city of small plates served forth both at home and in countless hospitality settings, from the central market and old neighborhood cafeneia like the ones mentioned above, a few of which have morphed into modern legends, to designated meze and ouzo restaurants (mezedopoleia and ouzeries, respectively). Most full-service restaurant meals start with a choice of shared plates, too, as the custom is so deeply entrenched in Greek food traditions.

Mezedopoleia, ouzeries, and tsipouradika (places specializing in tsipouro—Greek grappa) started to take their current form in the 1960s. Sharing a glass of humble ouzaki (a little ouzo) was and still is an act of friendship, and the simplest things, like a salted cucumber or a few olives, are always served as an accompaniment. Going for a meze was something mostly men did after work and before arriving home, where a meal awaited them. By the 1980s, the simple offerings turned into a sprawl, and it's not uncommon for mezedopoleia to have forty or fifty items at a time on their menus. Now, the older custom of having a very small nosh over something alcoholic, to stave off inebriation, has mushroomed into a full meal. One goes out in Athens these days specifically for a meze experience, ordering everything from dips to fried foods to meats and seafood, retaining the convivial essence of the experience with company and conversation. Dialectics and dinner are truly in the Greek DNA.

The recipes in this chapter are a mix of things, some traditional, some twists on tradition, and some thoroughly modern affectations, such as the new world of raw seafood treats that Athenians have embraced with alacrity this past decade or so. There's much here, I promise, that you'll want to share!

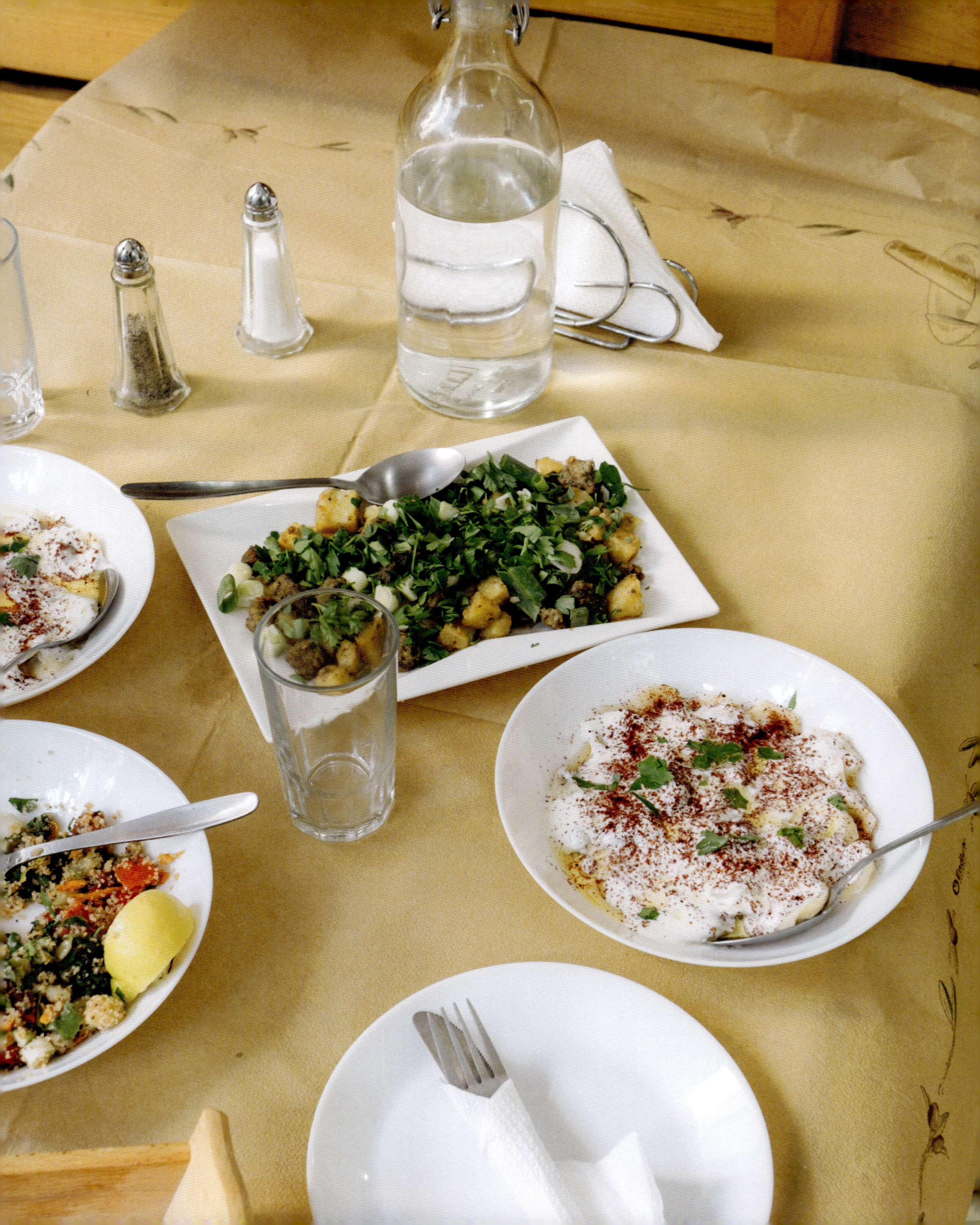

THE SAGANAKI CHRONICLES

Saganaki most commonly refers to a wedge of floured and fried cheese, which, in its most flamboyant iteration, is flambéed by pouring ouzo or brandy over it and bringing it to the table with flaming drama. That version, popularized in Greek restaurants all over America, was invented in Chicago at the Parthenon restaurant, but the true story of saganaki is much older and more complex.

The word comes from the Turkish sahan, a two-handled round-edged shallow frying pan. Technically, anything prepared in it is called saganaki. Cheese, traditionally hard Greek cheeses like kefalotyri and kefalograviera, are the most popular and widespread versions of saganaki, but the genre is a flexible one.

Chewy cheeses like halloumi and Mastelo, a regional cheese from the island of Chios, are probably just as popular now as the traditional hard cheeses mentioned above. Mastiha liqueur has become a popular finish, whether set alight or not. Saganaki can also be decidedly Anatolian, with ingredients like eggs and pasturma, so long as they're cooked in the right pan. Chefs are getting creative with the saganaki pan, by warming to newcomers like sweet potatoes and sausages.

Finally, seafood is a favorite, with dishes like Shrimp Mikrolimano (page 122), aka shrimp saganaki. Mussels, octopus, and other sea creatures are popular, too.

Saganaki with Pasturma and Eggs

This simple combination of the spicy cured beef pasturma and eggs is a testament to both the timeless appeal of Anatolian flavors among contemporary Greek cooks and the range of saganaki recipes, defined by the two-handled, round-rimmed shallow pan the word refers to and to anything cooked in it. Thinks scrambled eggs with bacon here, but replaced with pasturma, and think of bread to dip into those soft yolks. You might be wondering why this sunny-side up egg concoction isn't in the breakfast chapter—it's the pasturma, way too spicy and pungent, at least for this palate, as a breakfast food. You can substitute pastrami for pasturma, but there is nothing that will taste exactly like it.

MAKES 1 TO 2 SERVINGS

2 tablespoons unsalted butter

4 slices pasturma, trimmed of the spice rub and coarsely chopped

2 large eggs

Salt, freshly ground black pepper, and sweet or hot paprika, to taste

Melt the butter in a small saganaki pan or skillet over medium heat and add the pasturma. Carefully break the eggs into the pan, season lightly with salt, and spoon some of the melted butter over them. Cook until the whites are set and the yolks soft. Season with pepper and paprika and serve.

Sharing a Plate: Meze Heaven

Panko-Crusted Saganaki

Oats. Seeds. Phyllo. Flour. These have all been used in twenty-first-century Athens to coat a wedge of cheese, typically feta or one of Greece's firm yellow cheeses, before pan-frying and serving, most often with a side of something sweet, like marmalade, honey, or preserves. Panko is a newer addition to the crust, and it's been popping up as a coating for all sorts of Greek and Cypriot cheeses. It's especially good as a coating for haloumi, and haloumi sticks have become a popular meze. Regardless of the cheese of choice, a crust of panko imparts crunchiness without stodginess.

MAKES 4 SERVINGS

½ pound firm Greek feta, well drained, or hard yellow cheese such as kefalotyri, kefalograviera, or halloumi

1 large egg

½ cup panko bread crumbs

3 tablespoons extra-virgin Greek olive oil

Optional toppings or accompaniments

Tomato jam or chutney

Fig jam or preserves

Olive jam

Quince jam

Cut the cheese into rectangles about 1½ inches wide, ½ inch thick, and 2 to 3 inches long. Lightly beat the egg in a wide, shallow bowl. Spread out the panko on a large, flat plate.

Heat the olive oil in a nonstick skillet over medium-high heat.

While the oil is warming, dip the cheese pieces into the egg on both sides, then into the panko, pressing gently so that the bread crumbs stick. Carefully place them in the pan, working in batches as necessary, and cook on one side until golden and crisp, about 2 minutes. Using a spatula or kitchen tongs, carefully turn over to cook and brown on the other side. Remove and serve immediately, with any of the suggested accompaniments.

Sweet Potato Saganaki

As of this writing, there is a trend afoot regarding vegetable-based saganaki, which are essentially quick stir-fries made not in a wok but in the two-handled saganaki pan. Sweet potato and pumpkin have captured the imagination of chefs across Athens. These new interpretations are a bit too virtuous for my saganaki taste, unless you add a little down-and-dirty sausage!

MAKES 4 SERVINGS

6 ounces chilled fresh pork or beef sausage, cut into ½-inch rounds

2 tablespoons extra-virgin Greek olive oil

1 leek, trimmed and thinly sliced

2 medium sweet potatoes, peeled and cut into ¾-inch cubes

2 garlic cloves, minced

⅓ cup dry white wine

Sea salt to taste

½ teaspoon finely grated lemon zest

1 small, whole red chile

1 teaspoon dried Greek oregano

Heat a 12-inch saganaki, paella pan, or skillet over medium heat and add the sausage. Cook, stirring, until browned lightly, then transfer to a plate. Keep the sausage fat in the pan. Add the olive oil and raise the heat to medium-high. Add the leek and sweet potatoes and cook, stirring, until softened and lightly browned, 7 to 8 minutes. Add the garlic. Return the sausage to the pan, mix it gently, and pour in the wine. Season with the salt and add the lemon zest and chile, cover partially, and cook until the sweet potato is tender, about 7 more minutes. Sprinkle in the oregano and serve.

Octopus Saganaki

All of Greece is in this octopus saganaki: the sea, the iconic cephalopod that so defines Greek meze dishes, fresh vegetables, feta cheese, ouzo, and, of course, EVOO. I recommend the small musky octopus, Eledona moschata, far less intelligent than its larger cousin, the common octopus, and requiring much less time to cook. There are many variations on the seafood saganaki theme, the most famous of which call for mussels or shrimp.

MAKES 6 SERVINGS

3 small musky octopuses

5 tablespoons extra-virgin Greek olive oil

1 red bell pepper, seeded and cut into ¼-inch strips

1 green bell pepper, seeded and cut into ¼-inch strips

2 garlic cloves

3 firm, ripe tomatoes, diced

1 teaspoon sweet paprika

½ teaspoon red pepper flakes

3 tablespoons ouzo

½ pound Greek feta, cubed

Salt and freshly ground black pepper to taste

Trim the hoods and viscera from the octopuses and cut each in half. Place in a large saganaki or 12-inch round-edged frying pan and drizzle in 2 tablespoons of the olive oil. Cover and cook over medium heat for about 45 minutes, or until the octopuses are deep pink and tender but still a little al dente.

Push the octopuses to one side of the pan and carefully pour or ladle off the pan juices, transferring them to a bowl and setting the bowl aside. Add another tablespoon or two of olive oil to the pan. Add the pepper strips and cook for 7 to 8 minutes, stirring, to soften. Stir in the garlic and then the tomatoes.

Raise the heat a little and bring to a quick simmer. Add the paprika, red pepper flakes, and ouzo. Cook, stirring a little, for 5 minutes for the alcohol to cook off. Add 3 tablespoons of the pan juices and discard the rest. Add the feta cubes to the pan, shake back and forth, and cook for a few minutes, until the feta starts to melt. Season with salt and pepper and serve immediately.

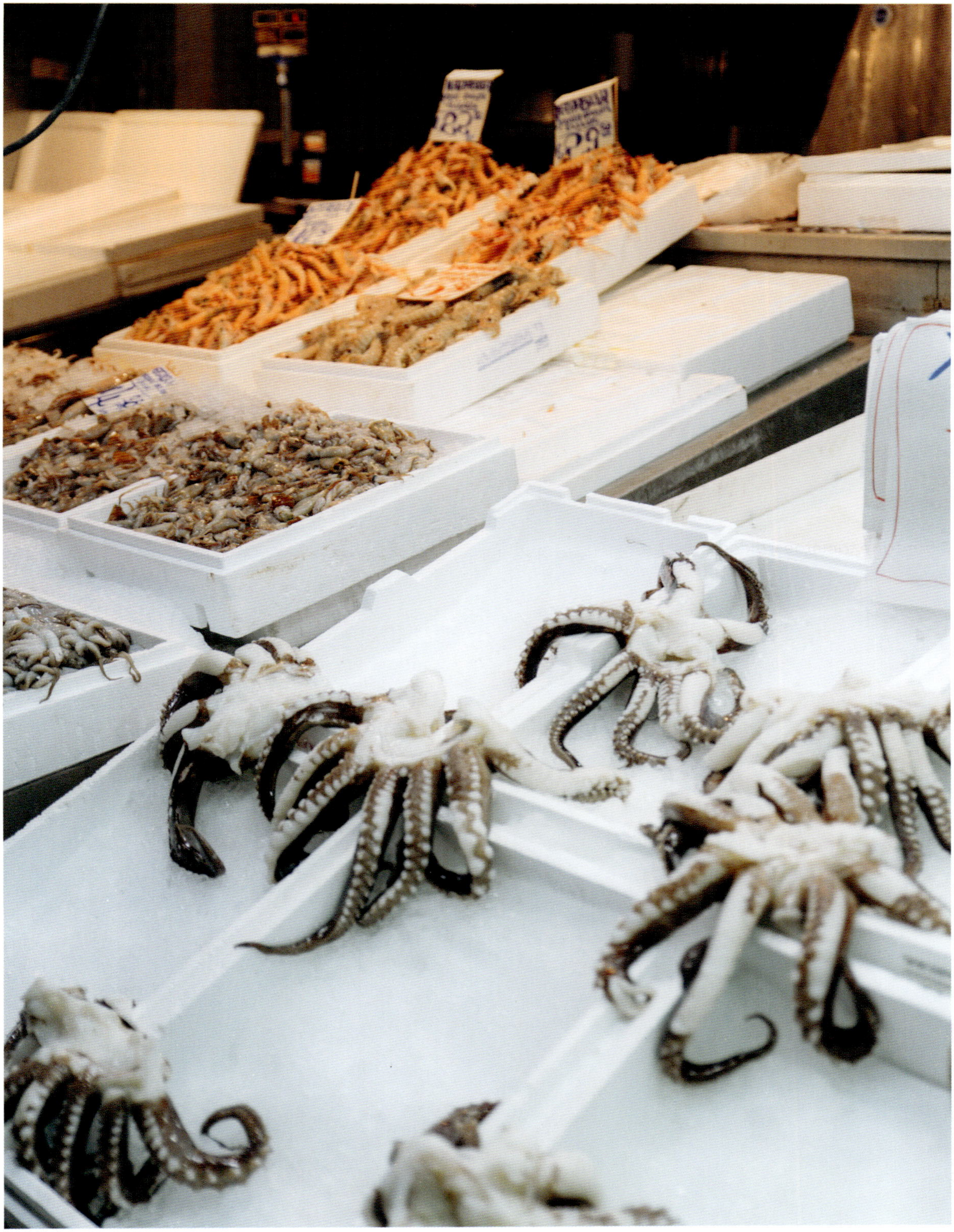

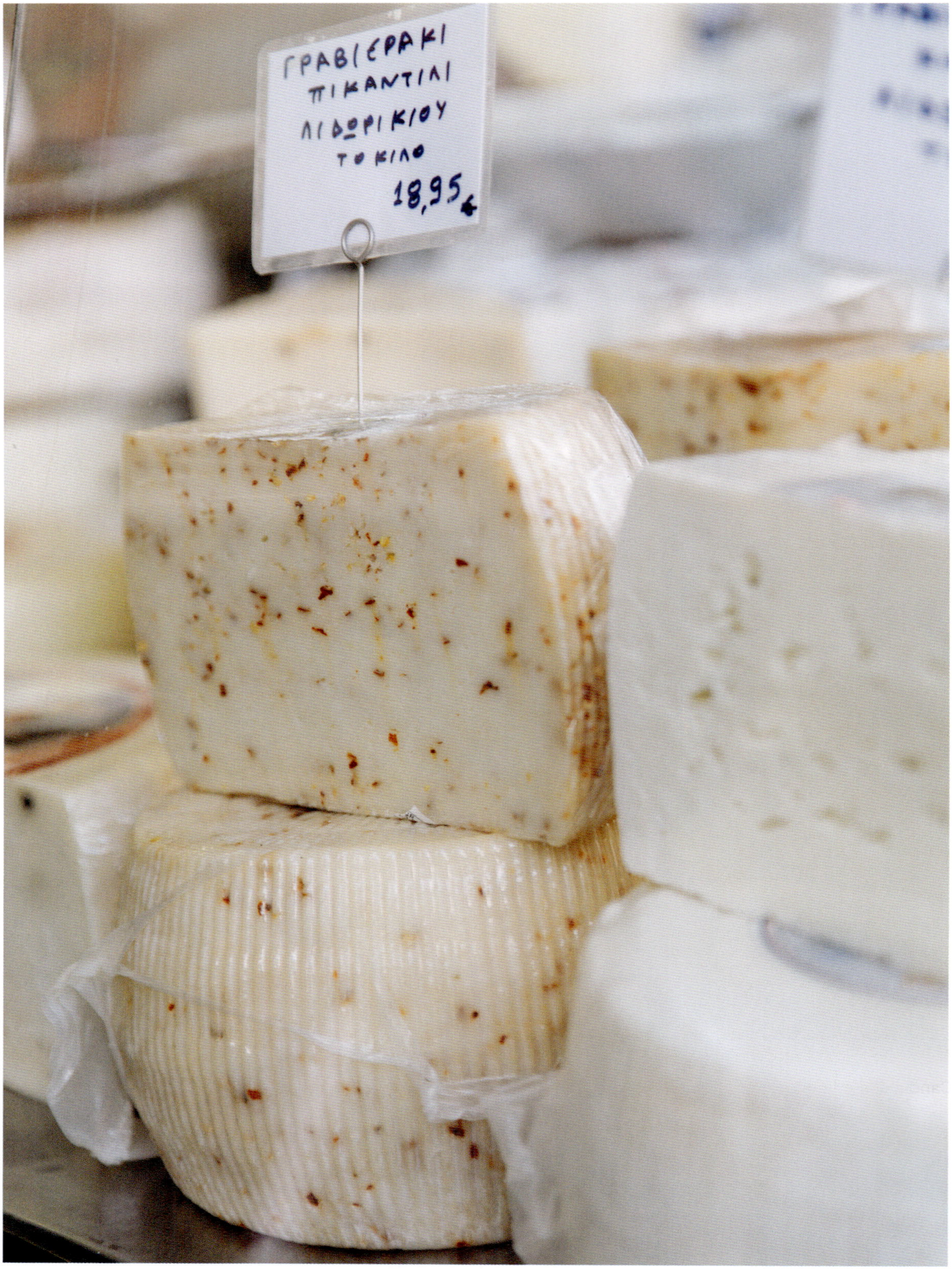
ΓΡΑΒΙΕΡΑΚΙ
ΠΙΚΑΝΤΙΛΙ
ΛΙΔΟΡΙΚΙΟΥ
ΤΟ ΚΙΛΟ
18,95 €

Crunchy Feta in Phyllo
with Tahini and Berry Sauce

Feta phyllo packets have spread like wildfire across Athenian (and other Greek) restaurant menus, mostly served with a generous drizzling of honey. As of this writing, that combo is looking exhausted, and chefs are seeking out new ways to dress a most beloved modern meze. Enter tahini, itself seeing a renewed purpose in the kitchen beyond its role as a fat reserved for the strictest fasting days, and some imports like blueberries, not native to Greece but grown now in its northern climes. The variations on this theme are endless!

MAKES 4 SERVINGS

For the tahini sauce

⅓ cup tahini

2 to 4 tablespoons warm water

2 tablespoons lemon juice

1 tablespoon extra-virgin Greek olive oil

Pinch of salt

For the blueberry sauce

½ teaspoon cornstarch

2 tablespoons water

½ cup fresh blueberries

2 tablespoons Greek honey

½ teaspoon grated lemon zest

For the feta

4 frozen phyllo sheets, thawed and at room temperature

4 rectangular slices Greek feta, about ¼ inch thick

2 tablespoons melted butter or extra-virgin Greek olive oil

Canola or sunflower oil, for frying

Make the tahini sauce: In the bowl of a small food processor, pulse together the tahini, 2 tablespoons of the water, the lemon juice, olive oil, and salt. Add a little more water if necessary to make the sauce pourable. Set aside.

Make the blueberry sauce: Mix the cornstarch into the water in a small saucepan and add the blueberries, honey, and lemon zest. Cook, stirring, over medium-low heat until the blueberries start to burst apart and the liquid thickens, 5 to 6 minutes. Set aside.

Make the feta packets: Stack the phyllo sheets and cut down the middle into two strips. Brush one strip lightly with melted butter, then place a second strip on top. Keep the remaining phyllo covered with a kitchen towel while assembling the packets. Place one feta rectangle on the bottom, leaving an inch border from the bottom and sides. Fold the bottom and sides over the phyllo to cover the edges, then fold up to form a packet. Set aside and repeat with the remaining phyllo, melted butter, and feta.

Heat about 1 inch of canola oil in a large, heavy skillet and place one phyllo packet gently in the pan. Fry it on one side over medium-high heat until golden, about 4 minutes, then, using kitchen tongs and/or a spatula, gently flip it to brown on the other side. Remove and drain on paper towels. Repeat with the remaining packets, replenishing the oil as needed.

Serve the packets individually or on a platter, drizzled with the tahini sauce and blueberries.

Pan-Fried Cheese
with Mastiha and Lemon

Mastiha, a resin and natural gum produced solely in twenty-one villages on the south side of the island of Chios, is held in high esteem among cooks and chefs. It started to become part of the modern Athenian and greater Greek kitchens as the 2004 Athens Olympics loomed. The two or so years leading up to the Olympics saw a radical transformation in the food scene, and the games sparked a frenzy not only of Greek pride but of the reinvention and repurposing of traditional ingredients. Mastiha became trendy, and it still is.

It's no wonder why. Its piney flavor is surprisingly compatible with a whole range of foods, from citrus to tomatoes to chocolate to cheese. The liqueur, called for below, is one of the best Greek digestifs and the quaff of choice after countless meals, both at home and at all levels of dining.

MAKES 2 TO 4 SERVINGS

2 tablespoons extra-virgin Greek olive oil

2 (½-pound) rounds Mastelo or halloumi cheese or 2 wedges Indian paneer or any other mild, squeaky cheese, about ½ inch thick

Finely grated zest and strained juice of 1 lemon

¼ cup mastiha liqueur

2 tablespoons finely chopped fresh mint

Freshly ground black pepper to taste

Lemon wedges, for serving

Lemon marmalade, for serving (optional)

2 teaspoons Greek pine honey, for serving (optional)

Heat the olive oil in a medium nonstick skillet over high heat. Add the first round of cheese and sear it until browned and crusty on one side, about 2 minutes. Using a spatula, flip it over to brown and form a crust on the other side. Transfer the cheese to a plate or small serving platter. Quickly fry the next piece in the same way and transfer that, too, to the plate.

Reduce the heat to low and carefully add the lemon zest and juice and the mastiha liqueur to the skillet. Cook until the alcohol evaporates, about 2 minutes, stirring a little to scrape up any pieces of cheese that might be stuck to the pan. Stir in the mint and add a turn or two of black pepper. Remove the pan from the heat. Pour the mastiha-lemon sauce over the cheese and serve, with a wedge or two of lemon and an optional spoonful of lemon marmalade and drizzling of honey.

Nena's Grilled Squid
with Smoked Eggplant Salad

Nena Ismyrnoglou, the chef who created this recipe, is one of the most important female chefs working in Athens. I've known her and loved her food since she first opened Kallisti, a groundbreaking restaurant and one of the early pioneers of modern Greek cooking. That original restaurant is now long closed, but Nena has gone on to leave her mark on numerous Athenian eateries, most recent of which is Elia, in the heart of Syntagma.

The marriage of roasted eggplant salad, melitzanosalata, and seafood has been a long-standing trend in Athens, reinterpreted by every chef who, like myself, loves this combination. This simple, elegant recipe is one of my friend Nena's classics.

MAKES 4 SERVINGS

For the eggplant salad

2 medium eggplants

¼ cup extra-virgin Greek olive oil

1 tablespoon strained fresh lemon juice

½ teaspoon brown sugar or 1 teaspoon grape molasses (petimezi)

1 drop mastic oil, 2 tablespoons mastic water, or ½ teaspoon ground mastic

Salt and freshly ground black pepper

For the squid

¾ pound fresh or thawed frozen squid, viscera removed and discarded

¼ cup extra-virgin Greek olive oil

½ teaspoon grated lemon zest

3 tablespoons strained fresh lemon juice

¼ cup finely chopped fresh herbs of choice, such as basil, flat-leaf parsley, cilantro, oregano, and/or thyme

Salt and freshly ground black pepper to taste

Prepare the eggplant salad: Prick the eggplants, with a knife in 2 or 3 places. Roast them one by one over a low flame on a gas stove or under the broiler in the oven until they soften and their skin is charred, 20 to 25 minutes.

Lay the eggplants on a cutting board, cut them in half, and use a spoon to remove the pulp. Place the pulp in a fine-mesh sieve and let it drain. Be careful not to include the charred skin.

Transfer the eggplant flesh to a blender, add the olive oil, lemon juice, brown sugar, mastic oil, salt, and pepper and pulse on and off for a minute or two to blend. Taste and adjust the seasoning.

Prepare the squid: Preheat the broiler to high.

Oil the squid and place on a nonstick broiler-safe pan, such as cast-iron. Broil for 3 minutes on each side, cooking the tentacles a bit longer. Cut the squid body into thin rings or strips depending on the size of the squid and place in a bowl, along with the tentacles. Toss with the olive oil, lemon zest and juice, herbs, salt, and pepper and mix well.

Spread the eggplant salad on 4 plates, divide the squid in equal portions over the eggplant, and serve.

Gilt-Head Bream in Citrus Juice
with Tomato, Olives, and Red Onion

Heady, robust ingredients like red onions and Greek olives spike up this otherwise delicate fish.

MAKES 4 SERVINGS

Strained juice of ½ lemon

Strained juice of ½ lime

6 tablespoons extra-virgin Greek olive oil, divided

Coarse sea salt

2 gilt-head bream, sea bass, fluke, or striped bass fillets

1 medium ripe tomato, peeled, seeded, and cut into ½-inch dice

6 kalamata olives, pitted and quartered

1 small red onion, halved and thinly sliced

2 turns freshly ground black pepper

Whisk together the citrus juices, 4 tablespoons of the olive oil, and a pinch of sea salt in a wide, shallow bowl. Using a sharp, clean knife, cut the fillets against the grain into ¼-inch slices and place in the bowl. Marinate the fish pieces in the citrus mixture for 5 minutes in the fridge.

Arrange the fish slices in two rows or two concentric circles on a rectangular or round plate, respectively. Drizzle over any remaining marinade.

Spoon the tomato pieces and olives over and around the fish. Place the onions in a pile in the center of the plate. Drizzle over the remaining 2 tablespoons olive oil and turn the peppermill twice over the platter. Serve immediately.

Crudo, Athenian Style

A generation ago, it would have been impossible to imagine Athenians, or any other Greeks for that matter, embracing a plate of raw fish, no matter how artfully presented. Sure, there have been a few regional delicacies that are almost raw, specifically the sardines of Kalloni in Lesvos, put up in salt for a few hours before being savored, or the well-known meze called gavros marinatos, fresh anchovies marinated in salt and vinegar.

Until the post-junta and baby-boomer generations of Greeks returned from abroad, where they had gone either in self-imposed exile or to study, the notion of eating almost anything raw was downright anathema. But Greeks who had lived in other parts of the world, mostly in cosmopolitan metropolises like London, Paris, and New York, encountered the global cuisines that had long taken root in those cities. When they started to filter back to their homeland, they created a demand for new kinds of restaurants.

The first Japanese restaurant to open in Athens was Kyoto, in 1977. By 1992, when I moved to Greece from New York, the first casual sushi bars started to open—indeed, the very first place was simply called Sushi Bar. It took a few years before Greek chefs started to experiment with raw fish, and one of them, Costas Tsingas, who had owned an epic New York Greek restaurant called Agrotikon, was among the first. His spanakorizo sushi became an Athenian legend and took several forms: as classic sushi, with raw fish over a mound of spanakorizo; as dolmades, using sheets of nori; and as grape-leaf dolmades, with a filling of tuna and sushi rice, minus the spinach. All were delicious novelties.

With Greece's seafood traditions and excellent-quality fresh fish, the idea of crudo—raw fish and seafood—was a natural evolution. Brilliant chefs like Varoulko's Lefteris Lazarou was among the first to create thin, pristine, almost surgical fillets of local fish and to marinate them with a budding new world of accessible regional ingredients, from citrus fruits to mastiha. Another master of the craft is Nikos Mihail of Argoura, an exquisite, casual seafood restaurant in the working-class neighborhood of Kallithea. He's a burly guy with a delicate touch, and his raw creations are truly inspired. There are others, of course, too many to list here, and even a sushi restaurant with a decidedly Greek identity, called Sushi Mou (My Sushi), where Greek and Japanese traditions make for a beautiful marriage of East and West, perhaps the true evolution of that first inspired spanakorizo sushi from way back when.

Greek Sushi Dolmades

Argoura, where this recipe is from, is one of my favorite places in Athens to eat seafood. Chef-owner Nikos Mihail is a big teddy bear of a man, and his appreciation of obscure ingredients from far afield in Greece, but also from around the globe, make every meal there a delicious surprise, especially for regulars like me. His combinations are equally surprising, as in these sushi dolmades, which are elegant, simple, and a great new take on such an iconic Greek dish.

MAKES 48 PIECES

24 grape leaves

½ cup sushi rice or Greek Carolina rice, cooked according to package directions

2 tablespoons ouzo

2 tablespoons rice vinegar

4 ounces raw sashimi-grade tuna

4 scallions, trimmed and chopped

¼ cup finely chopped fresh dill

¼ cup extra-virgin Greek olive oil

Sea salt and freshly ground black pepper to taste

1 cup Greek yogurt, or more to taste

Bring a medium pot of water to a rolling boil and blanch the grape leaves for 1 minute to soften. Remove with a slotted spoon and transfer immediately to a bowl of ice water. Remove and pat dry with paper towels. Set aside until ready to use.

Transfer the cooked rice to a bowl. Mix the ouzo and vinegar into the rice.

Dice the tuna and add to the rice, together with the scallions, dill, and olive oil. Mix together well but gently. Season to taste with salt and pepper.

Place the grape leaves vein side up in rows on a clean work surface. Take 2 teaspoons of the tuna mixture at a time (or more, if it fits) and place in the center of each leaf. Fold in the sides and roll up into a tight cylinder. When all the rolls are completed, take a sharp chef's knife and slice through the middle of each dolma, on the bias, to get two cylinders with a slanted, angled opening. Serve two per portion, one overlapping the other if desired, with a little Greek yogurt on the side.

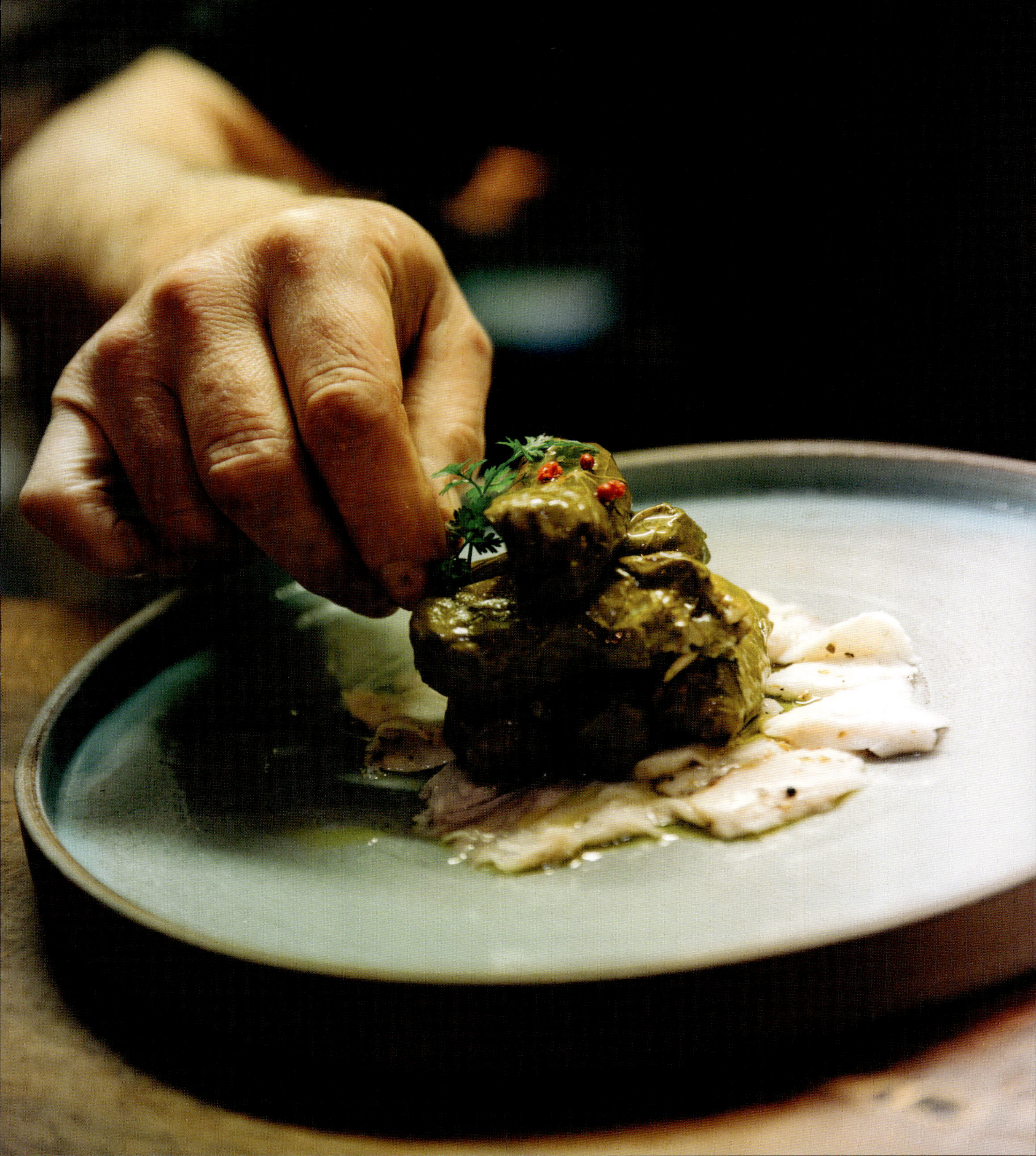

Sea Bass Carpaccio over Grape Leaves

I frequent Argoura, mostly with a friend of mine, Ilias, who is also a chef. This well-respected fish taverna in the neighborhood of Kalithea draws a crowd from all over Athens because chef-owner Nikos Mihail creates some of the most creative seafood fare in the city. He's a big man with big appetites, but his food is delicate and refined, and his penchant for experimentation and for sourcing obscure ingredients seems to know no bounds. On a jaunt there one weeknight, he brought out a row of light and delicious stuffed grape leaves punctuated with pieces of uber-fresh sea bass carpaccio. This is his recipe.

MAKES 12 MEZE SERVINGS OR 6 MAIN COURSE SERVINGS

For the rice filling

¼ cup extra-virgin Greek olive oil

6 onions, finely chopped

1 fennel bulb, finely chopped

1½ cups Carolina rice or other long-grain white rice

3 cups seafood stock or water

2 star anise (optional)

Salt and freshly ground black pepper to taste

1 (16-ounce) jar grape leaves (70 to 80 leaves), drained

1 bunch fresh wild fennel fronds, finely chopped (optional)

1 bunch fresh dill, finely chopped

1 bunch fresh mint, finely chopped

Strained juice of 1 large lemon, plus 1 lemon, sliced into thin rounds

Make the rice filling: Heat the olive oil in a large, deep skillet or wide pot over medium heat. Add the onions and fennel and sauté until translucent and softened, about 8 minutes. Add the rice and toss to coat in the oil. Add the seafood stock and star anise (if using) and bring to a simmer. Season with salt and pepper, reduce the heat to low, cover, and simmer until the rice is al dente, about 15 minutes.

While the rice is simmering, bring a large pot of water to a rolling boil and fill a large bowl or basin with ice water. Add batches of grape leaves at a time to the boiling water and blanch for 1 minute to soften. Remove with a slotted spoon and submerge immediately in the ice bath.

When the rice is done, remove the star anise (if used). Stir the wild fennel (if using), dill, and mint into the rice. Let the mixture cool slightly.

Separate out any grape leaves that might be torn or too small to roll. Lightly oil a clean, wide pot. Place the irregular grape leaves on the bottom.

Line as many of the usable grape leaves as will fit on a clean work surface, vein side up. Snip any stems that might be too long. To the bottom, wider part of each grape leaf, add 1 scant tablespoon of the rice filling. Use your judgment because not all the leaves will necessarily be the same size, so some will take a bit more filling, others a bit less. To roll them, fold in the sides, then fold the bottom over the sides and roll up like a cylinder, using your index and middle finger to fold in and taper the upper, narrower part of each leaf. The idea is to not have errant snippets of the leaves sticking out from the final rolled cylinder.

For the carpaccio

1 very fresh (2½-pound) whole Mediterranean sea bass, scaled, gutted, thoroughly boned, and filleted, or about 1 pound sea bass fillets

Salt and freshly ground black pepper to taste

Strained juice of 2 lemons

⅓ cup extra-virgin Greek olive oil

To finish

3 scallions, finely chopped

Extra-virgin Greek olive oil, for drizzling

Lemon slices or wedges, for serving

Place the stuffed leaves seam side down in the prepared pot, placing them very snugly next to each other in a concentric circle starting from the perimeter. You can make layers if they don't all fit in a single layer inside the pot. Continue until the leaves and rice filling are used up.

Pour in the lemon juice and place the lemon rings decoratively over the top. Pour in enough water to come about two-thirds up the height of the stuffed leaves. Place an inverted plate over the stuffed leaves to hold them in place and cover the pot. Bring to a simmer over medium heat, then reduce the heat to low and gently simmer for 35 to 40 minutes, until the liquid has been absorbed and the leaves and rice are tender. Let the stuffed leaves cool down as desired inside the pot. You can serve them warm, at room temperature, or chilled.

About 20 minutes before serving, prepare the carpaccio. Cut each fillet into about 36 pieces, each about 1 inch square. They won't be perfectly even, so don't worry. Place in a shallow dish, in layers, season each layer with salt and pepper, and add the lemon juice and olive oil, gently tossing to combine. Marinate for 15 minutes.

To serve, place 6 or 12 dolmades on a plate, then place 3 or 6 slices of the carpaccio, one after every other rolled grape leaf respectively, between them. Sprinkle some of the chopped scallions on top and garnish with a drizzling of olive oil and a couple of raw lemon slices or wedges.

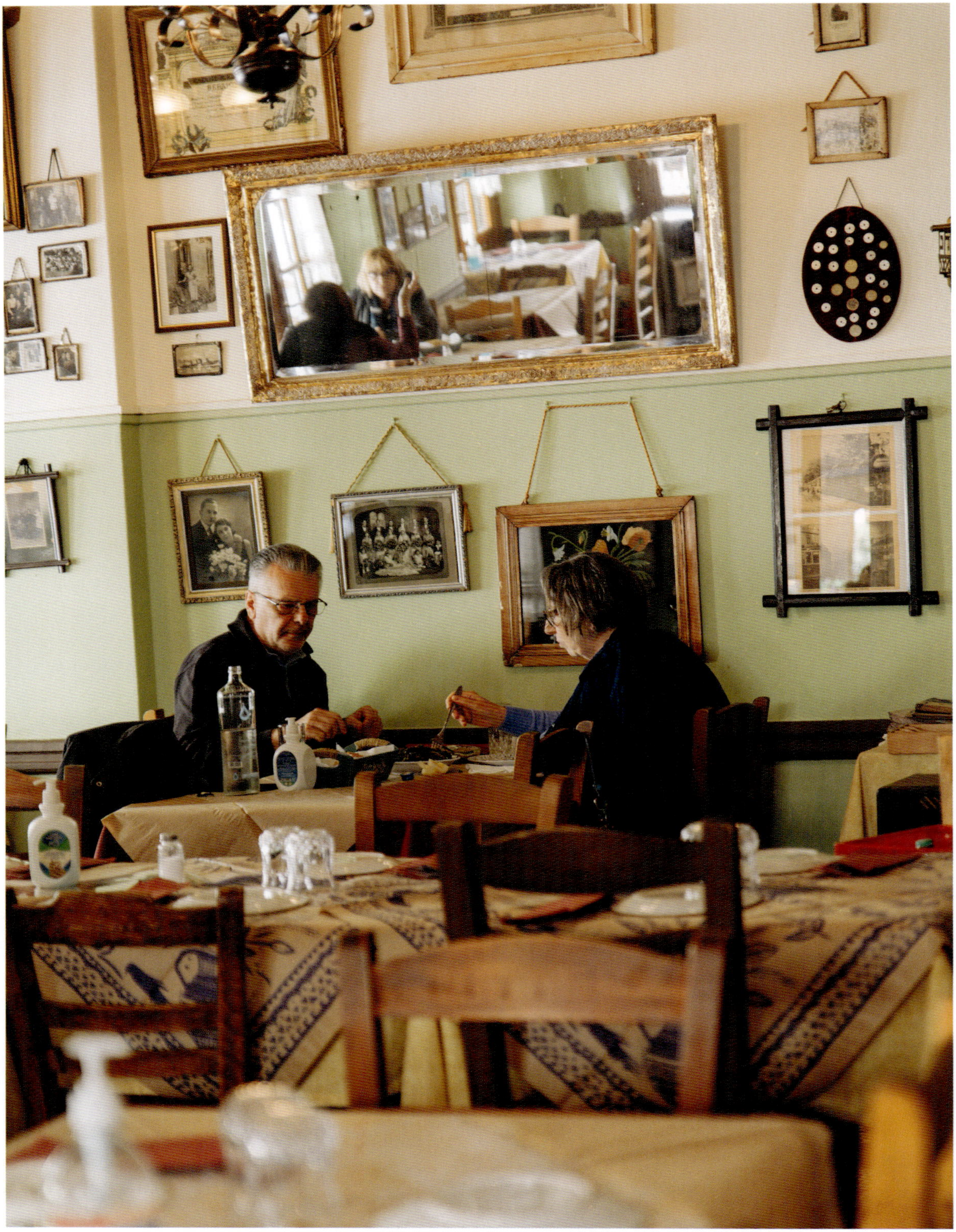

The Lightest Shrimp Meze
with Capers, Ouzo, and Orange

A recipe I ran across in Gastronomos, *a popular Greek food magazine, by my friend, Nena Ismyrnoglou, one of Athens's pioneering women chefs, inspired this dish. Nena uses tangerines in many of her recipes, spearheading a trend to explore citrus beyond the ubiquitous lemon in so much Greek cooking.*

MAKES 4 TO 6 SERVINGS

5 tablespoons extra-virgin Greek olive oil, divided

1 pound medium shrimp, heads and tails on, peeled and deveined

3 scallions, trimmed and chopped

3 garlic cloves, cut into slivers

1 fresh chile, seeded and cut into thin rings (optional)

2 tablespoons capers, preferably Santorini, rinsed and drained

½ cup ouzo

Grated zest of 1 orange

Strained juice of 2 oranges

1 tablespoon strained fresh lemon juice

Salt and freshly ground black pepper to taste

1 small fennel bulb, trimmed and cut into thin slices

2 tangerines, peeled and sectioned

2 tablespoons snipped fresh dill

Pinch cayenne

Heat 2 tablespoons of the olive oil in a large skillet over medium-high heat. Add the shrimp and sauté until bright pink, about 3 minutes. Using a slotted spoon, transfer the shrimp to a bowl.

Turn the heat down to medium and replenish the oil with 1 more tablespoon. Add the scallions, garlic, chile (if using), and capers, and sauté for 3 to 4 minutes, until bright and translucent. Carefully add the ouzo, orange zest, and orange and lemon juices. Cook for 1 minute or 2, until the alcohol in the ouzo cooks off. Return the shrimp to the pan and heat through. Season to taste with salt and pepper.

Toss the shaved fennel, tangerine slices, and dill together with the remaining 2 tablespoons olive oil, cayenne, and sea salt to taste. Mound evenly on 4 plates or on a platter and place the seared ouzo shrimp on top. Serve.

Shrimp Mikrolimano

Imagine postwar Greece, a decade and more having passed since its bloody civil war, too, and a new fervor to rebuild the country and enjoy life permeating just about everything. Greece of the early 1960s was an optimistic tiger economy and a time of rapid transformation and development. Athens and its environs were being reimagined and remade, and the city's population grew by about 700,000 people during the 1960s, from about 1.8 million in 1961 to about 2.6 million in 1971.

It was right about then that Mikrolimano, the small, historic port on the Saronic Gulf of Piraeus, began to perk up, too, having been settled by Greek refugees from Asia Minor who could boast the richest culinary traditions of any other Greek community in the diaspora.

*Mikrolimano—Little Harbor—has always been a port. In antiquity it was a naval and commercial port called Mounihas; by the Byzantine era it had been rechristened Lanterna or Fanari, which is the word for "lighthouse," and then, for several hundred years as Greece was under Ottoman rule, it became known as Tourkolimano—the Turkish port—or Pasalimani, the Pasha's Port. After Greek independence, it was named Akti Koumoundourou, after Alexandros Koumoundouros, an early Greek prime minister whose seaside mansion is now the home of the Yacht Club of Greece. And, finally, in the 1960s, this picturesque little harbor morphed once again and acquired its current name. Mikrolimano was a small fishing port, and wherever a fresh catch comes in, fish tavernas soon follow. It became famous for its shrimp dishes—as big as lobsters—so much so that the strip is still referred to as Ta Garidadika (*garida *being the Greek word for "shrimp"). The most historic taverna here was Botsaris, named for Markos Botsaris, a Greek revolutionary during the Greek War of Independence. It opened in 1960 and closed five decades later, but its most famous dish, Shrimp Mikrolimano, copied by all the seafood tavernas up and down the coast, lives on and is one of the greater Athens region's most iconic recipes and one of the great ouzo mezedes of Greece.*

MAKES 4 TO 8 SERVINGS

- ½ cup extra-virgin Greek olive oil, divided
- 1 large red onion, finely chopped
- 3 garlic cloves, minced
- 5 firm, ripe tomatoes, grated on the coarse side of a stand grater
- ½ teaspoon sugar
- 2 pounds large shrimp, peeled and deveined, heads and tails left on
- ½ cup ouzo
- Sea salt and freshly ground black pepper to taste
- ½ pound Greek feta, cut into ½-inch cubes

Heat ¼ cup of the olive oil in a large skillet over medium heat. Add the onion and cook, stirring, for about 12 minutes, until soft and lightly golden and translucent. Stir in the garlic. Add the grated tomatoes and simmer for 10 to 15 minutes to thicken up the sauce a little. Stir in the sugar.

About 5 minutes before the sauce is ready, heat the remaining ¼ cup olive oil in another large skillet over medium-high heat. Add the shrimp and sauté for about 2 minutes, turning once, until they start to color on both sides. Carefully and slowly pour the ouzo into the frying pan and deglaze the shrimp, cooking until the alcohol in the ouzo burns off.

Pour the thickened tomato sauce into the pan with the shrimp. Season with salt and pepper to taste. Add the feta and cook for 3 to 5 minutes, until the shrimp are completely cooked and the feta is melting but not liquid. Remove and serve immediately.

Shrimp Croquettes
with "Sos Pikant"

This recipe doesn't sound Greek at all, but it's a classic on the menu of one of the oldest meze restaurants in Athens, Athinaikon, which traces its history way back to 1932, when three Greek chefs from Smyrna (present-day Ismir), a city renowned for its food culture, first opened up near the old courthouse on Santarosa Street in the heart of the city. Much has changed in nearly a century, including the ownership, and now Athinaikon, with two locations, one in Exarcheia and one near Syntagma on Mitropoleos, is still a great place to sample a wide array of meze plates in the city. What I love most about this dish is its unapologetically retro sauce, a mix of mayonnaise and ketchup, which for a time in the '80s was all the rage.

MAKES 6 SERVINGS

For the sauce

⅔ cup mayonnaise

½ cup ketchup

2 tablespoons whisky

1 tablespoon brandy

2 teaspoons strained fresh lemon juice

For the croquettes

1 cup all-purpose flour

Salt and freshly ground black pepper to taste

½ pound shrimp (any size), peeled, deveined, and coarsely chopped

½ pound fresh crabmeat, coarsely chopped

Corn or sunflower oil, for frying

Whisk together all the ingredients for the sauce, cover, and refrigerate until ready to use.

Place the flour in a wide, shallow bowl and season with salt and pepper. Place the shrimp and crabmeat on a paper towel–lined plate with a couple of paper towels on top to absorb as much dampness as possible. Let the seafood sit for about 10 minutes between the paper towels.

Heat 3 inches of corn oil in a large, heavy pot over medium-high heat.

Mix the seafood together in a bowl and take a heaping tablespoon at a time of the mixture in the palm of your hand, shaping it into a clumpy, amorphous ball about the size of a golf ball. Roll in the flour and shake off the excess through your fingers. Carefully slide the seafood ball into the hot oil. Repeat with remaining mixture, frying in batches of three or four at a time, until golden and crisp, 3 to 5 minutes. Drain on paper towels and serve immediately with the "sos pikant."

ΟΥΖΟΜΕΖΕΔΟΠΩΛΕΙΟΝ
Το ΑΘΗΝΑΪΚΟΝ
Το ΟΥΖΕΡΙ της οδου Σανταροζα
απο το 1932
ARGOS SECURITY

Ο ΤΑΧΥΔΡΟΜΟΣ
ΕΙΚΟΝΕΣ
ΕΙΚΟΝΕΣ
Η ΓΥΝΑΙΚΑ

ΕΝΑ - ΨΑΡΙΑ
No 54
ΚΑΣΙΔΟΚΩΣΤΑ
ΦΡΕΣΚΑ ΨΑΡΙΑ
MOWI
psaria.g
freska

Mussels with Turmeric

Theatrou Street on the other side of the Central Market isn't the place one would expect to find surprisingly great, if simple, fare. But a few places in this rather rundown part of the market area offer up some delicious food. One such place is Diporto, the oldest taverna in Athens, and the other is To Steki tou Theatrou, roughly translated as the Hangout on Theater Street. It was here, at lunch one day with my friend Yiani, that I tasted a steaming bowl of turmeric mussels.

MAKES 4 SERVINGS

¼ cup extra-virgin Greek olive oil

1 teaspoon minced garlic

2 pounds fresh mussels, cleaned

1 cup dry white wine

½ cup ouzo

2 teaspoons ground turmeric

Pinch sea salt

Pinch grated nutmeg

⅔ cup chopped fresh flat-leaf parsley

Crusty sourdough bread, for serving

In a Dutch oven or large pot with a tight-fitting lid, heat the olive oil over medium-high heat and swirl in the garlic. Add the mussels, cover the pot for 30 seconds, then add the wine, ouzo, turmeric, salt, and nutmeg. Cover again, shake the contents of the pan back and forth over the heat, and cook for 4 to 5 minutes, or until the mussels have opened. Discard any that have not. Transfer to a large bowl with all the pan juices, sprinkle with the parsley, and serve with good bread.

Anchovies Sofrito from Laki's Ouzerie

Anyone who lives in Athens usually has their favorite spots, and they're typically places that are "secret" as much as that is possible these days. One of mine is To Ouzerie tou Laki (Laki's Ouzo Restaurant) just off Victoria Square, where one can find some of the best and most creative seafood mezedes in the city.

My daughter introduced me to this little place, astonished that it had been around for "so long." It turns out her idea of "so long" is 1984, when Lakis first opened, and the truth is that back then this neighborhood was truly edgy, and Laki was, indeed, a pioneer, not only because he opened in an unlikely cul-de-sac but because his cooking was way ahead of its time. Ouzo restaurants are by default meze places, and almost equally by default seafood places, because that's what goes best with Greece's milky, anise-flavored national quaff. His menu is filled with unusual offerings, and this recipe is inspired by one of them, and a personal favorite. Sofrito is a traditional dish from Corfu made with veal and characterized by a garlicky, tangy, vinegar-laced sauce. I loved the idea of using fresh anchovies instead, as Laki does on his menu, and so I re-create it below.

MAKES 4 SERVINGS

1 cup all-purpose flour

Salt and freshly ground black pepper to taste

1½ cups extra-virgin Greek olive oil (or a combination of olive and canola oils), plus more as needed

1 pound fresh anchovies (15 to 20), gutted, heads on, and rinsed well in a colander

6 garlic cloves, minced

½ cup dry white wine

1 cup water or vegetable stock

3 tablespoons white wine vinegar, or more, to taste

1½ cups chopped fresh flat-leaf parsley

Season the flour with salt and pepper in a large, wide, shallow bowl, so you can toss the anchovies in it without the flour spilling out.

Heat the olive oil in a large skillet over medium-high heat. Toss a handful at a time of the anchovies in the seasoned flour and fry in batches in the hot oil, until golden, turning on both sides to brown and crisp evenly, 7 to 8 minutes. Remove the fish with a slotted spoon and drain on paper towels. Continue with the remaining fish and replenish the oil if needed.

Remove the pan from the heat and drain off all but about 3 tablespoons oil. Warm the pan over medium-low heat and add the garlic, stirring it to keep it from burning. Carefully pour in the wine and deglaze the pan, scraping the flour and any fishy bits that are stuck to the bottom. Add the water and 3 tablespoons of vinegar and cook until about half of the liquid has evaporated and the sauce is thickened, 5 to 7 minutes. Season with salt and pepper to taste. Adjust seasoning with a little more vinegar if desired. Stir in the parsley and continue cooking for another 5 minutes.

Return the anchovies to the pan and shake back and forth so they're evenly distributed among the sauce. Transfer to a platter, spooning any sauce left in the pan over them.

Potatoes Yiahni
with Smoked Herring

I just love this recipe. It's so rustic and elegant at the same time, made with simple, everyday ingredients, with a nod to one of the Greek kitchen's most beloved imports, smoked herring, which has been part of the Greek larder for decades. It typically is turned into a meze on its own, its oily skin burnt off over a live flame on the stovetop and its flesh pulled apart into thin strips before being softened in olive oil. Here, the potatoes help counter the strength and saltiness of the fish.

MAKES 4 SERVINGS

½ cup extra-virgin Greek olive oil, divided

1 large red onion, halved and thinly sliced

3 garlic cloves

1 pound Yukon Gold potatoes, peeled and quartered

Salt and freshly ground black pepper to taste

½ cup dry white wine

½ cup tomato puree

2 teaspoons red wine vinegar

1 teaspoon dried Greek oregano

½ teaspoon smoked paprika, or more to taste

Pinch cayenne (optional)

1 (3- to 4-ounce) smoked herring fillet, broken apart into small pieces

2 tablespoons chopped fresh flat-leaf parsley

In a wide pot, heat ¼ cup of the olive oil. Add half of the onion and all of the garlic and cook until soft and translucent, about 8 minutes. Add the potatoes and turn to coat in the oil. Season to taste with a little salt. Add the wine and bring to a simmer. Add the tomato puree and enough water to bring the liquid to about halfway up the depth of the potatoes. Cover and cook until the potatoes are fork-tender but not mushy, 20 to 25 minutes. Taste and adjust the seasoning with salt and pepper. About 5 minutes before removing from the heat, gently stir in the vinegar and oregano.

Let the potatoes cool to warm, then transfer to a serving plate. Dust with the paprika and cayenne (if using), add the herring bits, remaining raw onion slices, and parsley on top. Drizzle with the remaining ¼ cup olive oil and serve.

Mushroom Chickpea Tigania
with Soy Sauce and Honey

Tigania, from tigani, the word for "frying pan," usually refers to a dish of quickly seared small pork cubes finished with wine that is one of Greece's favorite carnivorous mezedes. But vegetarians and vegans are having their day in Athens, too, and despite the incredible wealth of traditional plant-based dishes that are part of Greek cuisine, there's also a move toward redesigning the classics to appeal to a growing audience of vegetarians. This dish in so many ways represents the new Athens: Greek but international, too, culled from tradition but changed, a mix of well-known Greek ingredients like honey, with newcomers like soy sauce, which would have been an unthinkable, even unknowable, addition a generation ago.

MAKES 6 TO 8 MEZE SERVINGS

1 pound button mushrooms or a mix of portobellos, oyster mushrooms, shiitakes, cepes, and porcini

3 tablespoons extra-virgin Greek olive oil

1 large red onion, finely chopped

3 garlic cloves, minced

Salt to taste

1 (15-ounce) can good-quality, low-sodium chickpeas, rinsed and drained

⅓ cup dry white wine

2 tablespoons soy sauce

2 teaspoons Greek honey

3 tablespoons chopped fresh thyme

Pinch cayenne

Trim and wipe the mushrooms clean. Cut them into halves, thick slices, chunks, and/or strips, depending on the variety (they should all be about the same size; if using morels, keep whole).

Heat the olive oil in a large skillet over medium heat. Add the onion and sauté, stirring, until soft, 8 to 10 minutes. Stir in the garlic. Add the mushrooms, in batches if necessary, season with a little salt, then cover and cook until they lose about half their volume.

Add the chickpeas and wine and cook until the alcohol in the wine evaporates, then add the soy sauce, honey, thyme, salt, and cayenne. Cook for a few more minutes, stirring gently, then transfer to a bowl or plate and serve.

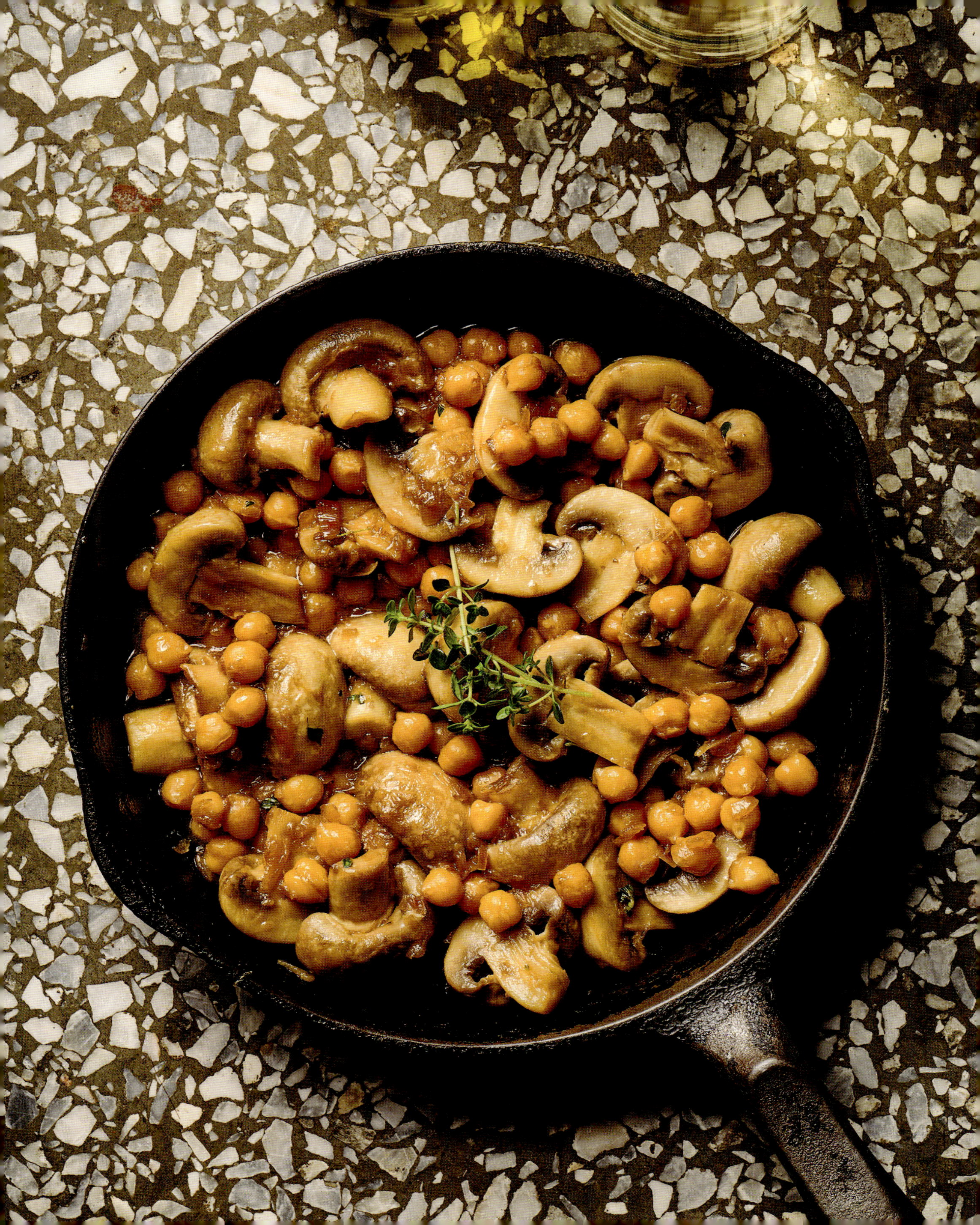

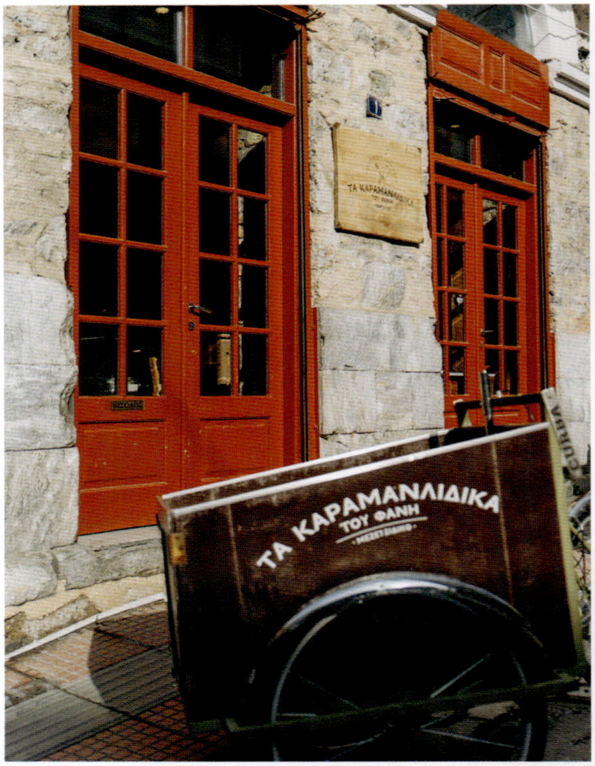
ΤΑ ΚΑΡΑΜΑΝΛΙΔΙΚΑ
ΤΟΥ ΦΑΝΗ

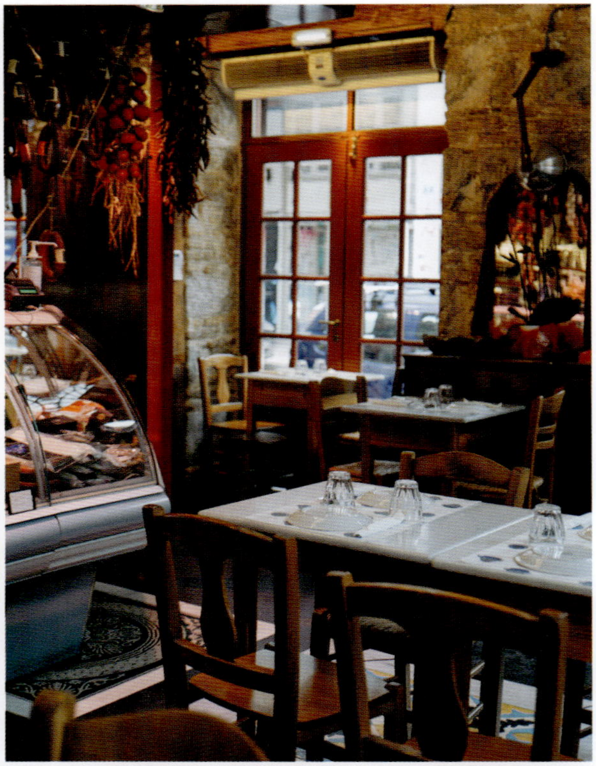

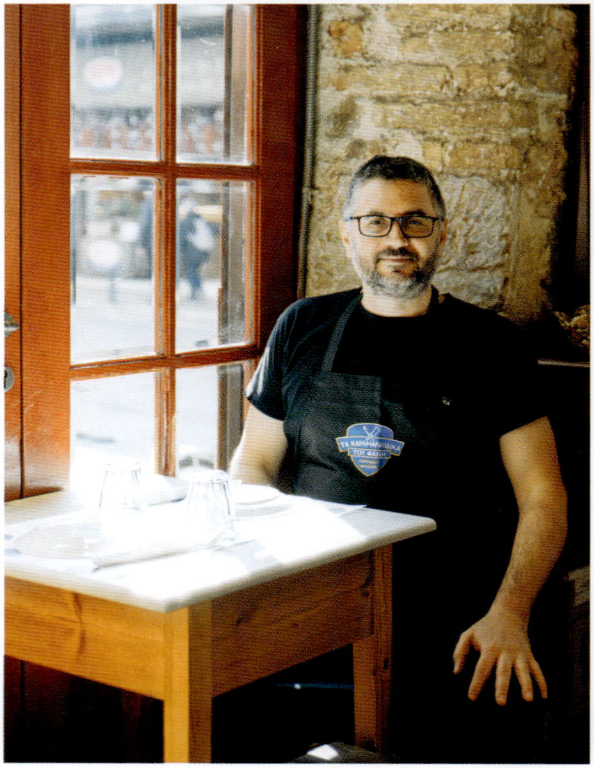
ΤΑ ΚΑΡΑΜΑΝΛΙΔΙΚΑ
ΤΟΥ ΦΑΝΗ

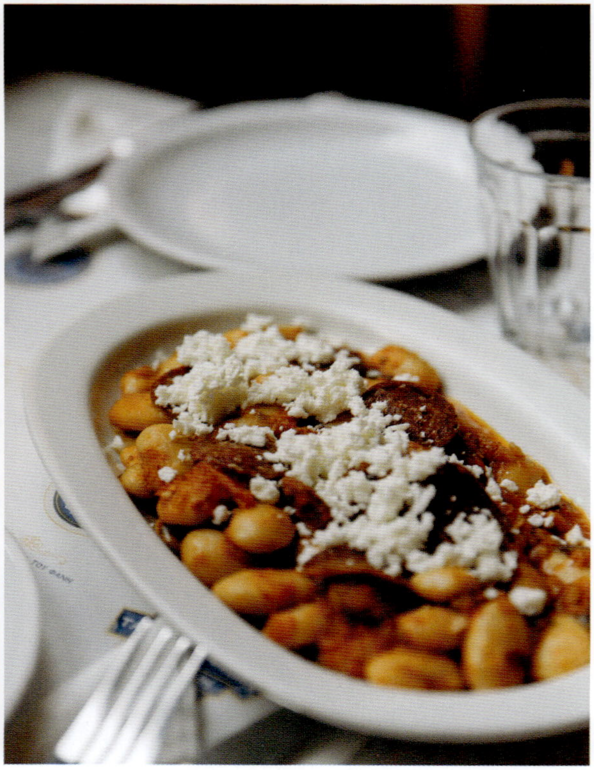

Karamanlidika's Giant Beans Bouryioundi
with Feta and Spicy Sausage

Fani, the ever-smiling, food-loving owner of Ta Karamanlidika, which is luckily located about a seven-minute walk from my apartment, has one of the great palates of Athens. His original tiny shop, across the street from the restaurant that bears his name, is the place to go for the finest artisanal cheeses, charcuterie, and other delicacies sourced from all over Greece. Athenian gourmands line up here daily for their pasturma fix, or to pick up a few hundred grams of smoked feta or tart, creamy anevato cheese, among the many offerings in this food lover's heaven.

So successful has this tiny delicatessen been that Fani was able to open his dream restaurant across the street (as well as another one on Ermou Street, also in Central Athens). His dream restaurant has a menu redolent of the flavors of the East that he loves so much, flavors and ingredients that wove their way into Greek kitchens from the spice markets and perfumed pots of the Greeks of Asia Minor. This recipe (pictured on the opposite page, bottom right) is one such example, bouryioundi being the original baked feta, long before such things went viral on the internet.

MAKES 6 SERVINGS

1 pound Greek giant beans, soaked overnight in ample water and drained

¾ cup extra-virgin Greek olive oil

1 large red or yellow onion, finely chopped

10 cups finely chopped tomatoes

2 teaspoons salt

1 teaspoon freshly ground black pepper

½ teaspoon red pepper flakes

1 to 2 teaspoons sugar (optional)

6 slices very spicy Adana sujuk, spicy beef chorizo, andouille sausage, or spicy Italian sausage per serving

¾ cup finely chopped fresh flat-leaf parsley

¾ cup crumbled or coarsely grated Greek feta, preferably barrel-aged

Put the giant beans in a large pot and pour in enough water to cover by 3 inches. Bring to a simmer over medium heat and cook, skimming the foam off the surface, for about 1½ hours, until tender but al dente. Drain.

While the beans are cooking, heat the oil in a large pot over medium heat. Add the onion and sauté until lightly browned, 15 to 20 minutes. Add the tomatoes and season the mixture with the salt, black pepper, and red pepper flakes. Add a bit of sugar if the tomatoes are too acidic and need to be balanced with some sweetness. Simmer for at least 1 hour, or as needed for the sauce to thicken and reduce by about a third. Season the beans with salt to taste 15 minutes before removing from the heat.

Preheat the oven to 375°F.

Add the giant beans to the tomato mixture and transfer to a casserole or baking dish. Gently stir in the sausage pieces. Bake for 15 minutes for the flavors to meld. Stir in the parsley and half of the feta. Remove and serve in individual plates, sprinkled with about a tablespoon more of grated or crumbled feta per portion.

Pasturmadopita from Karamanlidika

These crisp, pungent pastry cigars are a logical specialty of Fanis's restaurant, Ta Karamanlidika, because he sources and sells the absolute best pasturma in Athens. This is the spiced, cured beef redolent of fenugreek and other Anatolian spices. These pastries are a classic meze. As for the yufka, it's a Turkish pastry like phyllo but thicker and sturdier, which you can find online or in Turkish food shops. It comes in a variety of shapes, one of which is as ready-cut triangles.

MAKES 10 PIECES

5 ounces pasturma, finely chopped

5 ounces Turkish soutzouk, finely chopped

5 ounces kasseri cheese, grated or finely chopped

2 large, firm ripe tomatoes, diced

1 large bell pepper, seeded and diced

10 triangular sheets yufka pastry

Corn or sunflower oil, for frying

⅔ cup Greek yogurt

Mix the pasturma, soutzouk, and kasseri cheese in a bowl until well combined. Divide into 10 equal portions. Halve the diced tomatoes, then divide one of the halves into 10 equal portions. Divide the diced pepper into 10 equal portions as well. Set aside the remaining diced tomatoes for serving.

Place one yufka sheet on a clean surface. Place one portion of the filling mixture in the center. Top the filling with a portion of the tomato and a portion of the pepper. Carefully roll up the yufka, starting from the wide end, folding in the sides as you go to create a cigar-like shape. Repeat with the remaining yufka sheet and fillings.

Heat about an inch of oil in a large, deep skillet over medium-high heat. Working in batches, fry the rolled pastries until golden brown on one side, turn with kitchen tongs to fry on the other side, about 3 minutes. Replenish the oil as needed, straining out any burnt bits of pastry with a slotted spoon. Drain on paper towels. Serve hot with the remaining diced tomatoes and a dollop of yogurt.

Warm Giant Beans
with Smoked Mackerel and Red Onions

GHEE-ghan-dez is how we pronounce the big white Greek giant bean that is a bestseller on Greek restaurant menus the world over. Its most popular iteration is baked in a casserole with vegetables and tomato sauce, but there are plenty of other wonderful recipes for this hearty bean, too. The combination of beans and fish or seafood appears in many forms throughout the Greek kitchen, and the recipe below, which combines earthy giant beans with unctuous, smoky mackerel makes not only a great meze but a meal, too. You could easily swap out the giant beans for navy beans, black-eyed peas, or chickpeas.

MAKES 4 TO 6 SERVINGS

2 cups Greek giant beans, soaked overnight in ample water and drained

1 bay leaf

Salt and freshly ground black pepper to taste

⅔ cup extra-virgin Greek olive oil, divided

1 large red onion, minced

5 garlic cloves, minced

1½ cups tomato puree

1 fresh rosemary sprig

1 scant teaspoon za'atar

1 tablespoon balsamic vinegar or pomegranate molasses, or more to taste

½ cup snipped fresh dill

For serving

1 (4- to 6-ounce) smoked mackerel fillet

1 medium red onion, halved and thinly sliced

1 lime, halved

Put the giant beans in a medium pot and pour in ample fresh water to cover by 2 inches. Bring to a simmer, add the bay leaf, and cook for about 1½ hours, or until tender but al dente. Season to taste with salt about 30 minutes before removing from the heat.

In a large, wide skillet, heat ⅓ cup of the olive oil over medium heat. Add the onion and cook, stirring, until soft and translucent, about 7 minutes. Stir in the garlic, tomato puree, rosemary sprig, za'atar, and salt and pepper to taste. Bring to a simmer and cook for about 15 minutes, until thickened. Stir in the balsamic vinegar and dill.

Drain the giant beans and reserve 1 cup of their cooking liquid. Add the giant beans to the skillet with the tomato mixture and heat through, adding a little of their cooking liquid if needed to keep the beans moist but not soupy. Stir in half of the remaining olive oil.

Serve the giant beans on a platter and place the mackerel fillet over it. Top with the raw onion, remaining olive oil, and a squeeze of fresh lime and serve.

Leloudas's Poor Man's Plate of Greek Fries
with Ground Meat Sauce and Grated Myzithra

The first time I ever visited Leloudas Taverna in the neighborhood of Botanikos, I was with my neighbor Konstantinos and we walked from Kerameikos, our neighborhood in downtown Athens, past industrial zones and urban no-man's-lands to arrive at what looked at first sight like a truck stop. Leloudas. This little place has warmed with the patina of age and has been attracting nearby factory workers, truckers, and neighborhood folks since Dimitris Leloudas first opened it in 1928. A few recipes, including the one below, were the brainchild of the current chef's grandmother, a Greek refugee from Asia Minor.

Today, Leloudas's grandson Dimitris runs the place, and the crowds includes all of the above plus its share of the curious and the hipsters in search of lost, old Athens. Places like these seem to be disappearing with alacrity as the city experiences a profound transformation, and Botanikos, too, is slated for gentrification, as the home to a new soccer stadium. The area takes its name from the Athens Botanical Garden nearby.

As for this dish of spiced ground meat served over fries and topped with grated hard myzithra cheese, it's a classic here, created almost a century ago.

MAKES 4 TO 6 SERVINGS

4 tablespoons extra-virgin Greek olive oil, divided, plus more for frying

3 large onions, finely chopped

1 large garlic clove, minced

1½ pounds ground beef

3 cups canned diced tomatoes

1 cup dry white wine

1 cinnamon stick

6 allspice berries

1 scant teaspoon ground nutmeg

10 to 15 black peppercorns, crushed

Salt to taste

6 large Yukon Gold potatoes

⅔ cup grated dried Greek myzithra or pecorino cheese

In a large skillet, heat 2 tablespoons of the olive oil over medium heat. Add the onions and sauté until translucent, 5 to 7 minutes. Stir in the garlic. Add the ground beef and cook, stirring until the meat begins to brown, 10 to 15 minutes. Add the tomatoes, wine, cinnamon, allspice, nutmeg, peppercorns, and salt. Lower the heat, cover, and simmer for 35 to 40 minutes, until the liquid has been absorbed and the meat is cooked. Remove the pan from the heat and let meat cool slightly. Remove the cinnamon and allspice.

Meanwhile, prepare the potatoes: You can peel them or leave them unpeeled, especially if they're organic. Cut the potatoes in half lengthwise, then into ½-inch slices. Stack the pieces and cut into ½-inch sticks. Place in a bowl of ice water.

About 20 minutes before taking the meat off the stove, start preparing the fries. Heat about 2 inches of oil in a large skillet. Take about two handfuls of potatoes from the ice bath and blot them dry on a kitchen towel. Add the potatoes to the hot oil and fry until golden, turning once with a slotted spoon, 7 to 8 minutes. Using a slotted spoon, transfer them to a plate lined with paper towels to drain. Season while hot with a little salt. Repeat with the remaining potatoes, replenishing the oil if necessary.

Serve the potatoes on individual plates or on a platter and spoon the ground meat sauce on top. Grate some traditional aged Greek myzithra on top and serve.

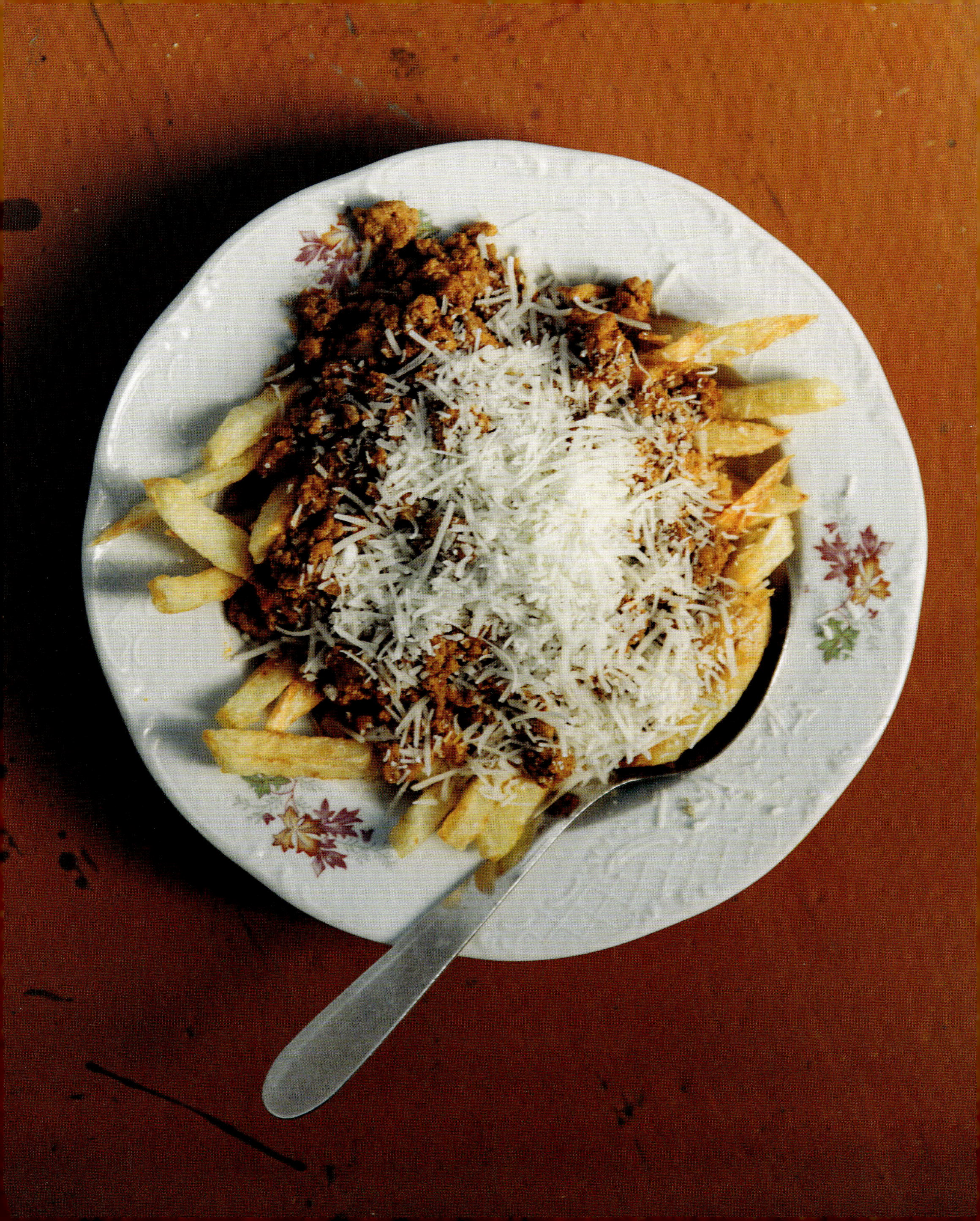

Grilled Sausage "Plaki"

Ntylan, yes, named after Bob but spelled phonetically in Greek, had recently opened as I was researching and writing this book. It's a tiny place on a pedestrian path in Kypseli, a historic neighborhood about a mile from the center of Athens, whose main drag, Fokionos Negri, was once the city's equivalent of Park Avenue before people started to move north to the suburbs. It has been one of the most densely populated parts of Athens since the apartment-house building boom of the mid-1960s to early 1980s, but as its affluent denizens moved out, Kypseli declined and became ever more populous. It is one of the most multiethnic neighborhoods in the city, and in the last few years, as Athens reclaimed its pre-crisis glory, Kypseli has seen a change of fate, too. It's now home to a burgeoning thirty-something population, a lot of foreign and Greek artists, and some great galleries and hip restaurants.

Ntylan, a small gem of a place on Agias Zonis Street, is among them, opened by the former chef at Vangelis Beis and his partner Virginia Christoforidi, who runs the front of the house. The menu is small and it changes often, and when I dine there I usually end up ordering just about everything. Ntylan is the paradigm of new Athens cooking, unfettered by traditions but undeniably Greek. The chef cross-references Greek cooking in his dishes, taking, in just one example, the tomato sauce for a fish dish called plaki, *for example, and marrying it with sausage.*

I don't know if creative freedom, perfunctory nods to traditional dishes, and the tenets of Greek cooking are all mutually compatible. The litmus test is always taste, and at Ntylan, with a free-wheeling spirit in every plate, the food definitely tastes good.

MAKES 4 SERVINGS

⅓ cup extra-virgin Greek olive oil

2 medium onions chopped

3 garlic cloves, chopped

1 (15-ounce) can diced tomatoes

2 tablespoons tomato paste

1 cinnamon stick

6 whole cloves

5 allspice berries

Salt and freshly ground black pepper to taste

2 large Yukon Gold potatoes, scrubbed

1 pound pork or beef sausages

For the roasted red pepper cream

2 good-quality roasted red peppers in brine, rinsed, drained, and chopped

3 garlic cloves, lightly smashed

3 tablespoons extra-virgin Greek olive oil, or more as needed

In a large skillet, heat the oil over medium heat. Add the onions and sauté, stirring constantly, until wilted, about 10 minutes, then add the garlic and stir for a few seconds. Add the tomatoes with their juices and bring to a boil, then reduce the heat to a simmer and add the tomato paste, cinnamon, cloves, allspice, salt, and pepper. Cover and simmer for 15 to 20 minutes, or until the onions are very soft. Remove the cinnamon stick, allspice berries, and cloves.

While the sauce is simmering, put the potatoes in a pot and pour in enough water to cover by 2 inches. Bring to a boil, add a heaping teaspoon of salt, and simmer the potatoes over medium heat until fork-tender, 20 to 25 minutes.

Place the sausages in a ridged grill pan and cook over medium heat, turning every so often, until seared and browned on all sides and thoroughly cooked through, about 20 minutes.

While everything is simmering, put the roasted red peppers, garlic, and olive oil in the bowl of a food processor and puree at high speed until creamy. Add a little more olive oil and/or a few drops of water if needed to achieve the desired consistency.

Drain the potatoes, peel if desired, and mash with a little salt and olive oil in a bowl, using a fork. They should be chunky. Cut the sausages on the bias into 1½-inch pieces.

To serve, spread the chunky potatoes on a platter or individual serving plates, top with the tomato sauce and grilled sausage pieces, and spoon or pipe the roasted red pepper cream on top.

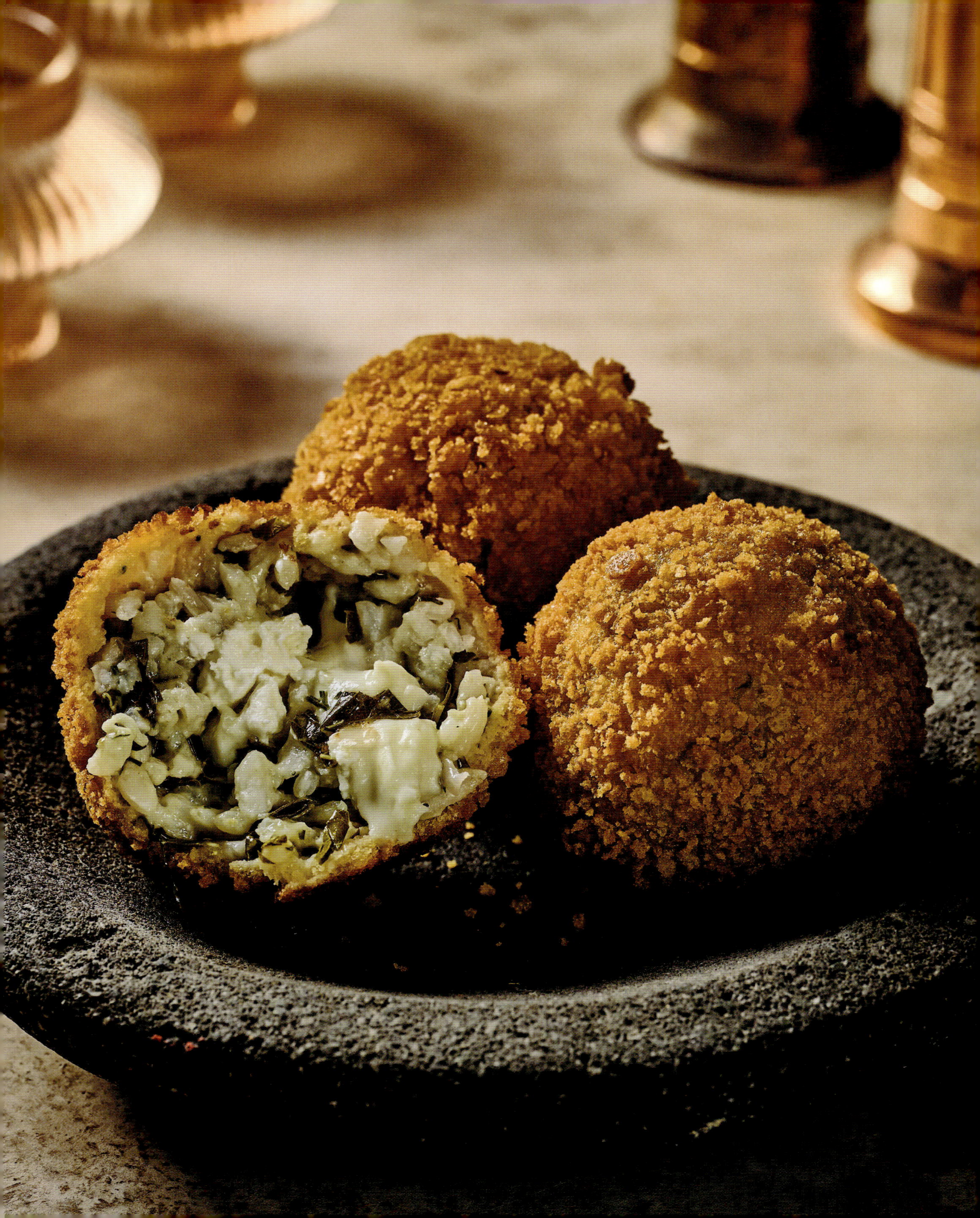

Grape Leaf Arancini

My Athens neighborhood, Metaxourgeio, south of Omonoia, is in the midst of dramatic transformation, from a once working-class hub to hipster heaven, filled with bars, restaurants, cafés, and theaters. There is one place I like to frequent for a quiet glass of wine and a few small plates called Karla, and on one outing with a friend we were pleasantly surprised to find this most grecophied version of arancini on the menu.

MAKES 6 SERVINGS

For the risotto

6 grape leaves, either fresh or brined

3 tablespoons extra-virgin Greek olive oil

1 medium red onion, finely chopped

2 garlic cloves, minced

1½ cups Arborio or Greek Carolina rice

Salt and freshly ground black pepper to taste

3 cups vegetable stock or water

2 tablespoons unsalted butter

½ cup grated kefalograviera or parmesan cheese

For the arancini

½ cup all-purpose flour

1 teaspoon fine salt

⅛ teaspoon freshly ground black pepper

2 large eggs

2 cups panko bread crumbs

2 ounces mozzarella cheese, cut into ½-inch cubes and chilled

2 ounces Greek feta, cut into ½-inch cubes and chilled

2 cups extra-virgin Greek olive oil or vegetable oil, for frying

Prepare the risotto: Bring a small pot of water to a rolling boil and have a separate bowl with ice water nearby. Blanch the grape leaves for 1 minute to soften, then submerge immediately in the ice bath. Remove, pat dry, and chop. Set aside.

Heat the olive oil in a large, wide skillet over medium heat. Add the onion and sauté until translucent, 7 to 8 minutes. Stir in the garlic. Add the rice and stir it to coat in the oil for about a minute. Add the salt and pepper, stock, and butter, reduce the heat to low, cover, and cook for 20 to 25 minutes, or until the liquid is absorbed and the rice tender but al dente and the liquid is fully absorbed. About halfway through simmering the rice, stir in the chopped grape leaves.

Prepare the arancini: Set up three medium bowls: the first with the flour seasoned with the salt and pepper, the second with the eggs, whisked, and the third for the bread crumbs. Line 2 rimmed baking sheets with parchment paper.

When the rice is done, turn off the heat and stir in the kefalograviera. Carefully spread the rice onto one of the prepared baking sheets and let it cool for 10 minutes.

When the rice is cool enough to handle, wet the palms of your hands to keep the rice from sticking to them, and form into twelve 1½-inch balls. Insert a cube of each cheese, side by side, into the center and press the rice around it so the cheese is completely enclosed.

Carefully dredge each ball in the seasoned flour, then in the eggs, then in the bread crumbs. Place on the other lined baking sheet.

Pour the olive oil into an 8-inch saucepan (it should be about ½ inch deep) and heat to 350°F. Be careful not to overheat the oil to the smoking point. Fry 4 to 6 balls at a time, turning gently, until golden brown, 3 to 4 minutes, then transfer to a paper towel–lined plate.

Let the arancini cool for about 5 minutes before serving.

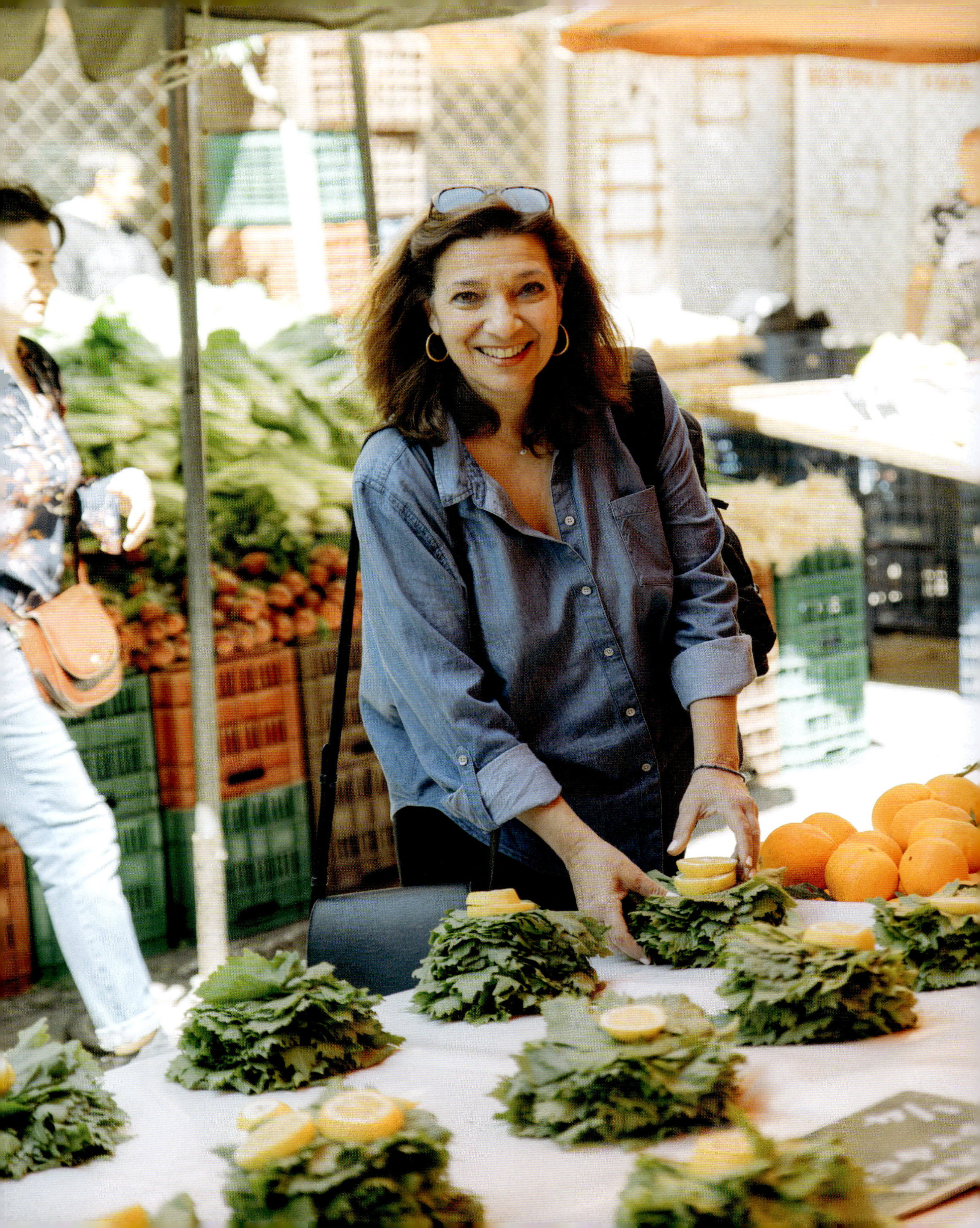

Salad Days in Athens

It used to be that the salad offerings on Greek tables, whether at home or in tavernas, were defined by the specific offerings of each season, with protagonists being the classics: tomato-cucumber or Greek salad in summer; cabbage-carrot slaw in winter; lettuce-dill-tender green onions in spring.

There were a few all-weather salad specialties that spoke to the entertainment needs of Athenian (and Greek) families, especially as far back as my memory serves me, in the 1970s and '80s. These were the likes of rossiki salata, a potato salad studded with capers, pickled cornichons, boiled carrots, and hard-boiled eggs, dressed in mayonnaise, homemade in the best circumstances to show off the skill of the cook. Tuna salad with a thick coating of mayo and/or mixed with rice (page 163) and vegetables is another retro salad that people made at home for holiday or company buffets. And the most famous of all Athenian "salads" is aptly named Athinaiki Salata (page 162), a dish that requires poaching a whole grouper with potatoes, carrots, and celery, meticulously removing and deboning it, and then reconstructing its flesh into a fish-shaped presentation with capers, cornichons, and carrots—the stuff of eyes, mouth, and scales. A homemade mayonnaise was de rigueur if one wanted to enjoy the oohs and aahs of family and friends.

But the salad bowl is arguably the first place that traditions got tossed and a global palette of ingredients added to the mix. Now, salads are an anything-goes expression of everything, every whimsy, every reinvention of the classics, every influence under the sun.

There is still a seasonal bent in evidence, because of the sheer quality of produce in Athenian and Greek markets and the fact that things are, well, cheaper in season. But there's also a world of "new" produce grown in Greece, from kale to red lettuces to goji berries and a free-spirited use of traditional ingredients like tahini (in dressings) and fresh and dried fruits tossed with greens and veggies. The mixing and matching of a broader spectrum of ethnic traditions, such as a "Greek" salad dripping with plush burrata cheese, is also among the newfound ways salads are tossed across the Athenian (and Greek) table.

Salad has been liberated and anything goes, so enjoy!

The Not-So-Classic Greek Horiatiki Salata

Horiatiki salata, aka the Greek salad, is on almost every menu in Athens in one form or another. Greeks know to stay shy of it before tomato season, disparaging the bland flavor and mealy pulp of winter greenhouse tomatoes, but there are plenty of versions that call for more intensely flavored small tomatoes, such as teardrops and cherry tomatoes. The salad below calls for a quintet of different tomato varieties, in an effort to distinguish it among a crowded field.

MAKES 6 SERVINGS

1 cup cherry tomatoes, halved

1 cup red teardrop tomatoes, halved

1 cup yellow teardrop tomatoes, halved

2 perfect juicy large summer tomatoes, such as Jersey Beefsteaks, cut into wedges

2 black tomatoes, cut into wedges

1 red onion halved and cut into ⅛-inch slices

1 green bell pepper, seeded and cut into rings

1 large seedless cucumber, peeled, halved lengthwise, and sliced ⅛-inch-thick

4 to 6 pepperoncini

Coarse salt or sea salt

12 kalamata olives in brine, rinsed and drained

2 teaspoons Greek or other small capers, rinsed and drained

⅓ cup extra-virgin Greek olive oil

5 ounces Greek feta, cubed

2 teaspoons fresh oregano or ½ teaspoon dried Greek oregano

Place the tomatoes, onion, green pepper, cucumber, and pepperoncini in a large bowl. Season with salt. Add the olives and capers. Toss gently with half of the olive oil. Top with the feta and sprinkle the oregano over the feta. Drizzle the remaining olive oil over the feta and into the salad. Serve.

The Birth of Greece's Flagship "Village" Salad: Horiatiki

There's everything practical and nothing romantic about the origins of Greece's most iconic salad!

According to the late Greek food historian Alexandros Yiotis, the Greek salad was born in the 1960s in the Plaka, the old historic area under the Acropolis, by wily taverna owners. The up-to-then classic summer salad was a medley of tomatoes, cucumbers, onions, and peppers, sans feta, but it was subject to price regulation and thus restaurant operators couldn't charge "free market" prices for it. Growing tourism and regulated prices were not a happy couple. Someone came up with the idea of adding a slab of feta, which essentially changed the definition of the salad and rendered it unaffected by any price limitations. Taverna could now charge what they wanted for it. Thus the horiatiki, or village salad (*horio* means "village" in Greek), was never associated with any village, but it caught on quickly. Nowadays, the horiatiki is embedded in the lingo of practically every Greek in the world and probably on every Greek restaurant menu, too. This salad should be served in the summer, when tomatoes are at their peak.

And, speaking of tomatoes... It wasn't but two hundred years ago that the star of Greece's iconic salad appeared for the very first time—that, too, in the Plaka area, but within the walls of a Capuchin monastery on Tripodon Street, one of the oldest streets in the world. One Father Frangisko had brought tomato seeds with him from abroad in 1818 and planted them as a decorative fruit. It took a few years for the tomato to make it from decorative to edible, but by the early twentieth century it had been embraced and started to appear in countless Greek dishes.

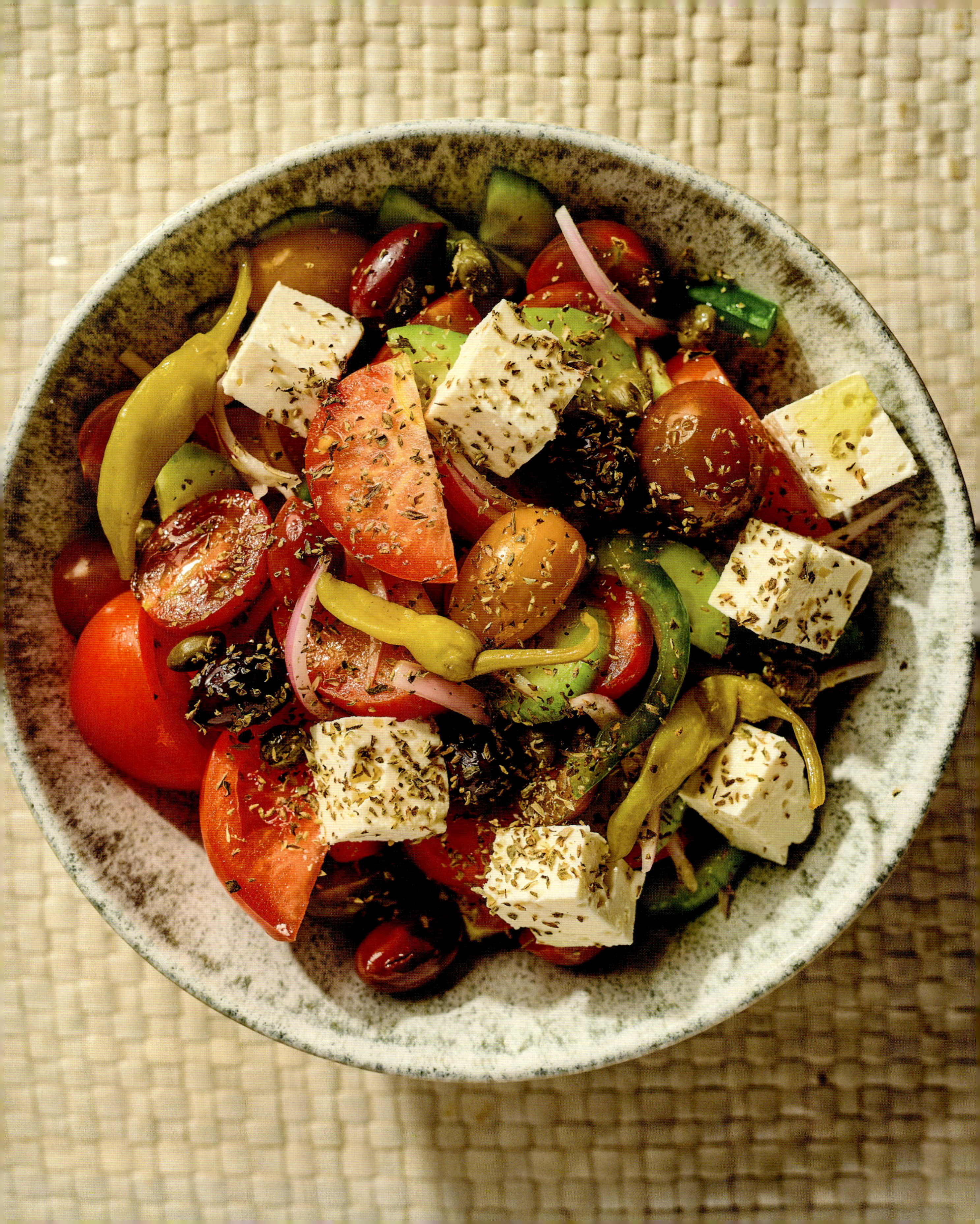

VARIATIONS ON THE GREEK SALAD

It is only natural that on the ever-evolving Greek table, Athenian chefs would start to look at a classic Greek salad with an eye to adding their own interpretations to the bowl.

Hence the likes of Greek salad granita, the brainchild in various iterations by a handful of cutting-edge Greek chefs, among them Georgianna Hiliadaki, Christoforos Peskias, and Sotiris Kontizas. I first tasted a rendition of this back in the early 2000s, as Athens geared up for the Olympics. Then, while filming season 2 of My Greek Table, *I visited the now-defunct Funky Gourmet in the Metaxourgeio neighborhood of Athens, where chef-owner Hiliadaki pureed then strained all the fixings of a Greek salad and spun it to granita in a state-of-the-art ice cream maker, shockingly tossing all the solids in the rubbish bin! At Nolan, near Syntagma, Kontizas serves up a fruity Greek salad with cherries, tomatoes, and cucumber granita, the plating of which is a work of art. The list goes on, but the concept of turning the salad into ice is a popular one, at least as of this writing. At the other end of the spectrum are drinkable Greek salads, as a light consommé and as gazpacho.*

Olive dust, ground koulouria (see page 44) powder, and creamed feta are a few other new ingredients that have helped reshape the horiatiki salata as it appears on Athenian menus. So have additions like strawberries and basil.

I don't know where I stand on any of this—a rose-by-any-other-name kind of question. What I do know is that one of life's greatest pleasures is to dip into an original Greek salad, fully in season, and with a piece of good bread to soak up all the juices that lie in wait at the bottom. We call this action papara, which also happens to be the word for nonsense, as in trying to recast a classic that doesn't need fixing—just fixings, and good, seasonal ones at that! That said, all the creativity around Athenian Greek salads is fun, and so I present a few new classics here.

Greek Salad
with Cucumber Granita

Here's a new Greek salad bowl inspired by one of the signature dishes at Nolan, a popular restaurant serving up Greco-Japanese cuisine in the heart of the city. The original, with blanched, peeled, then dehydrated tomatoes that are later slowly cooked in olive oil until they become confit, is hard to replicate at home. I've re-created a version below that calls for a spicy cucumber granita with marinated tomatoes and a few other gems of Greek summer, in a bowl.

MAKES 4 SERVINGS

For the cucumber granita

4 large cucumbers

1 tablespoon strained fresh lime juice

1 tablespoon rice vinegar

½ teaspoon matcha green tea powder

½ teaspoon chili powder or freshly ground black pepper to taste

¼ teaspoon sea salt

For the salad

3 cups teardrop tomatoes, halved lengthwise

1 cup fresh firm cherries, pitted and halved

1½ cups purslane

5 tablespoons extra-virgin Greek olive oil, divided

Sea salt to taste

¾ cup crumbled Greek feta

¼ cup full-fat Greek yogurt

½ teaspoon finely grated lemon zest

2 tablespoons fresh mint chiffonade

Start several hours ahead or the day before, and make the granita: Take a vegetable parer and peel the cucumbers in alternating strips, leaving some of the green skin intact. Halve the cucumbers lengthwise, remove the seeds, and cut into 1-inch chunks.

In a blender or food processor, puree the cucumbers to a fine pulp. Add the lime juice, rice vinegar, green tea powder, chili powder, and salt. Season with more salt and lime juice, if desired. Transfer to a large metal baking pan and freeze until solid.

Place the tomatoes, cherries, purslane, 3 tablespoons of the olive oil, and a little sea salt in a large bowl and marinate for a few minutes while you prepare the feta mixture.

Place the feta, yogurt, remaining 2 tablespoons olive oil, and lemon zest in the bowl of a food processor or powerful blender and puree to a smooth cream.

Scrape out a mound of the cucumber granita into each of 4 serving bowls. Toss the mint into the tomato-cherry mixture just before serving. Spoon the mixture next to the granita in each bowl and, using either a teaspoon or a pastry bag, dot the salad with some of the feta cream. Serve.

Greek Gelatin Salad

I am not quite sure if this actually fits into a chapter on Greek salad except that it's one of the more creative renditions of a Greek icon that I've come across in my perusings through restaurant menus and Greek food magazines. It's actually quite elegant, if aspic is your thing!

MAKES 6 SERVINGS

3 pounds (about 12) firm, ripe tomatoes

2 scant teaspoons powdered gelatin, divided

½ cup chopped pitted kalamata olives

1 teaspoon dried Greek oregano

Salt and freshly ground black pepper to taste

Pinch sugar (optional)

1½ cups crumbled Greek feta

1 cup Greek anthotyro or ricotta cheese, drained

½ cup cream cheese

½ cup milk

For the salad

1 green bell pepper

1 medium seedless cucumber

¼ cup extra-virgin Greek olive oil

1 teaspoon capers, rinsed, drained, and chopped

1 teaspoon finely chopped fresh oregano

Salt (optional)

4 kalamata olives, pitted

Hold a tomato at the stem end and grate it from its base on the coarse side of a box grater. Do this by hand—you'll end up with a fresh tomato concasse and a butterflied tomato skin, which you can discard. Repeat with all the tomatoes.

Place the tomato pulp in a fine-mesh sieve set over a bowl to strain out the excess liquid for about 20 minutes. Set the pulp aside and gently warm the liquid in a small saucepan. Don't boil it, just warm it, then stir in half of the gelatin, whisking until it is dissolved.

In a medium bowl, combine the tomato juice and gelatin, tomato pulp, chopped olives, oregano, salt, and pepper. Taste the mixture. If it is too acidic, add a pinch of sugar.

Line an 8 x 3-inch rectangular terrine with plastic wrap, leaving 3 to 4 inches of wrap hanging over the edge. Spread the tomato mixture on the bottom of the terrine and freeze for 20 minutes.

In the meantime, make the feta cream. Place the feta, anthotyro, and cream cheese in the bowl of a food processor and pulse on and off to combine.

Warm the milk and dissolve the remaining gelatin in it, whisking until smooth. Add the milk and gelatin to the cheeses, pulsing to combine well. Spread the feta mixture over the chilled tomato base inside the terrine. Cover with the plastic wrap overhang and refrigerate for 6 hours or overnight until set.

Just before ready to serve, seed the bell pepper and dice it. Take a vegetable parer and shave the cucumber into thin strips. Roll these up into curls.

Whisk together the olive oil, capers, and oregano. Season if desired with a pinch of salt.

Unwrap the top of the terrine and place a platter over the top. Invert it carefully, remove the mold, and carefully pull away the plastic wrap. Garnish with the cucumber rolls, olives, and diced pepper. Drizzle the dressing over the top. Slice and serve.

Fresh Tomato-Onion Salad
with an Extra Grated, Juicy Tomato

I ventured to this famous old place in a famously working-class neighborhood of Athens called Moschato with my dining buddy, Ilias. The taverna is immaculate and very simple, with a few photos here and there on the wall and a few shellacked fish carapaces for color and gloss nailed to the columns. Mother and son run this old taverna, which has been serving forth simple, fresh seafood in the form of a very limited menu since the 1950s. What I love about this place is that it embodies the very same philosophy that luxurious restaurants like New York's Milos have built an empire on—simplicity and ultrafresh ingredients at, of course, a literal fraction of the cost. The tomato salad that follows, coupled with a plate of olives, a slab of feta, and a minced cabbage slaw are the only starters. The rest is about the fish and seafood—select offerings there, too, with an eye to consummate freshness and simplicity of preparation.

You need really ripe, firm tomatoes for this.

MAKES 2 TO 4 SERVINGS

4 large tomatoes in season, very ripe and sweet, but firm

Sea salt to taste

1 red onion, halved and thinly sliced

1 large pinch Greek dried oregano

4 to 6 tablespoons extra-virgin Greek olive oil, or as desired

Hold one tomato at the stem end, grate it from its base on the coarse side of a box grater. Discard the skin.

Core the remaining tomatoes and cut them into 1½-inch chunks. They won't be completely even or all the same size. It doesn't matter. Season the tomato pieces lightly with a pinch of sea salt. Spoon the grated tomato over the tomato chunks, season lightly with salt, and top with the onion slices and oregano. Drizzle on as much olive oil as you want. Serve.

ΚΡΙΘΙΝΗ	ΚΡΙΘΑΡΟΚΟΥΛΟΥΡΑ	ΚΑΛΑΜΠΟΚ
ΚΡΗΤΗΣ	ΑΦΡΑΤΗ	
2,50 /τμχ	7,90/kg	7,90/kg

ΠΑΞΙΜΑΔΙΑ	ΠΑΞΙΜΑΔΙΑ
ΝΤΑΚΟΣ	ΝΤΑΚΟΣ
ΚΡΙΘΙΝΟΣ	ΚΡΙΘΙΝΟΣ
7,90/kg	7,90/kg

ΚΡΗΤΙΚΗ ΜΠΟΥΚΙΑ

ΒΡΩΜΗΣ

8,90 €/kg

Carob Rusk Tomato Salad
with Burrata, Olive Oil, and Herbs

Rusks, or paximadia, *as they are called in Greek, are an ancient way to preserve bread by baking it twice so that it's dehydrated and rock hard. It was one of the most rustic and agrarian foods of sustenance in Greece, with every region boasting its own variety or variations, some with barley, others with wheat or chickpea flour, some seasoned with spices and aromatic seeds. Then, sometime in the 1990s, there was, well, a rusk explosion, and the first place it hit was the Greek capital. As chefs began to look inwards to their own traditions, the interest in this delicious hardtack, for that is what it is, grew. By the next decade, every supermarket had a wall-length selection of regional rusks and chefs were putting them on the menu with abandon, as the base of salads akin to panzanella and as the base for countless other toppings, too. Carob flour, once the stuff of the wartime Greek diet and an absolute survival food, saw a rebirth. Carob rusks caught on. Today they're immensely popular thanks to a texture that is softer than those made with barley and wheat, and to their inviting chocolate color and subtly sweet taste.*

MAKES 4 TO 6 SERVINGS

6 to 8 small carob rusks

2 large, ripe summer tomatoes, cored and cut into chunks

2 tablespoons fresh basil chiffonade

1 tablespoon chopped fresh oregano

Sea salt to taste

6 tablespoons extra-virgin Greek olive oil, divided

1 (½-pound) chunk burrata cheese, drained

Place the carob rusks in a serving bowl. In a separate bowl, toss the tomatoes, basil, oregano, sea salt, and 4 tablespoons of the olive oil together and let the mixture stand at room temperature for 10 to 15 minutes. Spoon it over the rusks, making sure to use all the juices, too. Let the rusks soften under the tomatoes for 5 minutes.

Top with the burrata, season with a little additional sea salt, and drizzle the remaining 2 tablespoons olive oil over the cheese and salad. Serve.

Watermelon Salad
with Jalapeños, Avocado, and Feta

I love this salad. Watermelon and feta have enjoyed a decades-old love affair, but the addition of avocados, jalapeños, and cilantro to this dish speaks to the way flavors and ingredients from other cultures, in this case Mexico, have seeped into the vernacular.

MAKES 2 TO 4 SERVINGS

4 cups ripe, firm sweet watermelon cubes, seeds removed or seedless

1 large or 2 small ripe avocados

1 tablespoon chopped fresh cilantro or mint

Fleur de sel to taste

1 red onion, halved and thinly sliced

1 jalapeño, seeded and sliced into thin rings

⅔ cup crumbled Greek feta

¼ cup extra-virgin Greek olive oil

1 tablespoon sherry vinegar

Place the watermelon cubes in a large shallow bowl. Halve the avocado(s) lengthwise, remove the pit(s), and score the flesh into ½-inch squares. Using a teaspoon, scrape the avocado cubes directly into the bowl with the watermelon. Sprinkle the cilantro and a pinch of flaky salt on top. Add the onion and jalapeño. Spoon the crumbled feta on top.

Whisk together the olive oil, vinegar, and a pinch more salt. Pour over the salad, toss gently, and serve.

Bibb Lettuce Salad
with Winter Fruit and Walnuts

When I make this salad, it's usually after a walk through my neighborhood farmers' market, grabbing a few tender heads of Bibb lettuce, seasonal crisp apples and pears, and all the other harbingers of cool weather on display. It's easy and filling. If your market carries vacuum-packed precooked beets, simply rinse the beet under cool water and then dice.

MAKES 4 TO 6 SERVINGS

1 large Bibb lettuce

1 Golden Delicious apple, cored and cut into ½-inch cubes

1 large, firm ripe pear, cored and cut into ½-inch cubes

2 celery stalks, trimmed and chopped

1 cooked beet, cut into ½-inch dice*

6 tablespoons extra-virgin Greek olive oil

1 tablespoon red wine vinegar

1 tablespoon strained fresh lemon juice

1 garlic clove, minced

Salt to taste

½ cup walnuts, very coarsely chopped

---

*If your market doesn't carry vacuum-packed cooked beets, you can cook the beet yourself: Trim the root and stem ends and scrub well. Place the beet in a small pot with enough water to cover by 2 inches. Add 1 tablespoon red wine vinegar, which helps preserve the beet's color, and bring to a simmer. Cook until tender but al dente, about 25 minutes. Remove, drain, and cool. Put on gloves and peel the beet, then dice.

Tear apart the lettuce leaves, wash and spin dry, and tear into large, amorphous pieces in a serving bowl. Add the apple, pear, celery, and beet.

Whisk together the olive oil, vinegar, lemon juice, and garlic. Season to taste with salt.

Pour the dressing over the salad, sprinkle the coarsely chopped walnuts on top, and serve.

Greek Taverna Cabbage-Carrot Salad
with a Tomato Rose

This retro taverna salad was all the rage when Athens was still very much a homogeneous city. The tomato rose, a testament to TLC taverna style, crowned many a simple cabbage salad! It's important to use a very well-sharpened knife when making the rose.

MAKES 4 TO 6 SERVINGS

1 firm, ripe tomato

2 cups coarsely shredded red cabbage

2 cups coarsely shredded green cabbage

2 carrots, peeled and coarsely grated

2 teaspoons capers, rinsed and drained

6 tablespoons extra-virgin Greek olive oil

2 tablespoons strained fresh lemon juice

Sea salt to taste

With the tomato in one hand and holding the circular base in place, use a sharp paring knife to start to peel around the tomato without severing the continuum of the peel. It's similar to peeling an apple in one concentric spiral. You want to end up with a single strip of tomato peel that's about ½ inch thick. Cut all around the tomato, trying to keep the peel at the same thickness as you go. As you get toward the stem, use the upper part of the paring knife to try to make the strip a little narrower. Coil the strip over the wide circular part, which is the original base cut to shape the rose. Set it aside. This is easier than it sounds!

In a large, shallow salad bowl, place the shredded red cabbage, shredded green cabbage, and carrots in separate mounds. Strew the capers on top. Place the tomato rose in the center.

Whisk together the olive oil, lemon juice, and salt. Pour the dressing over the salad and serve.

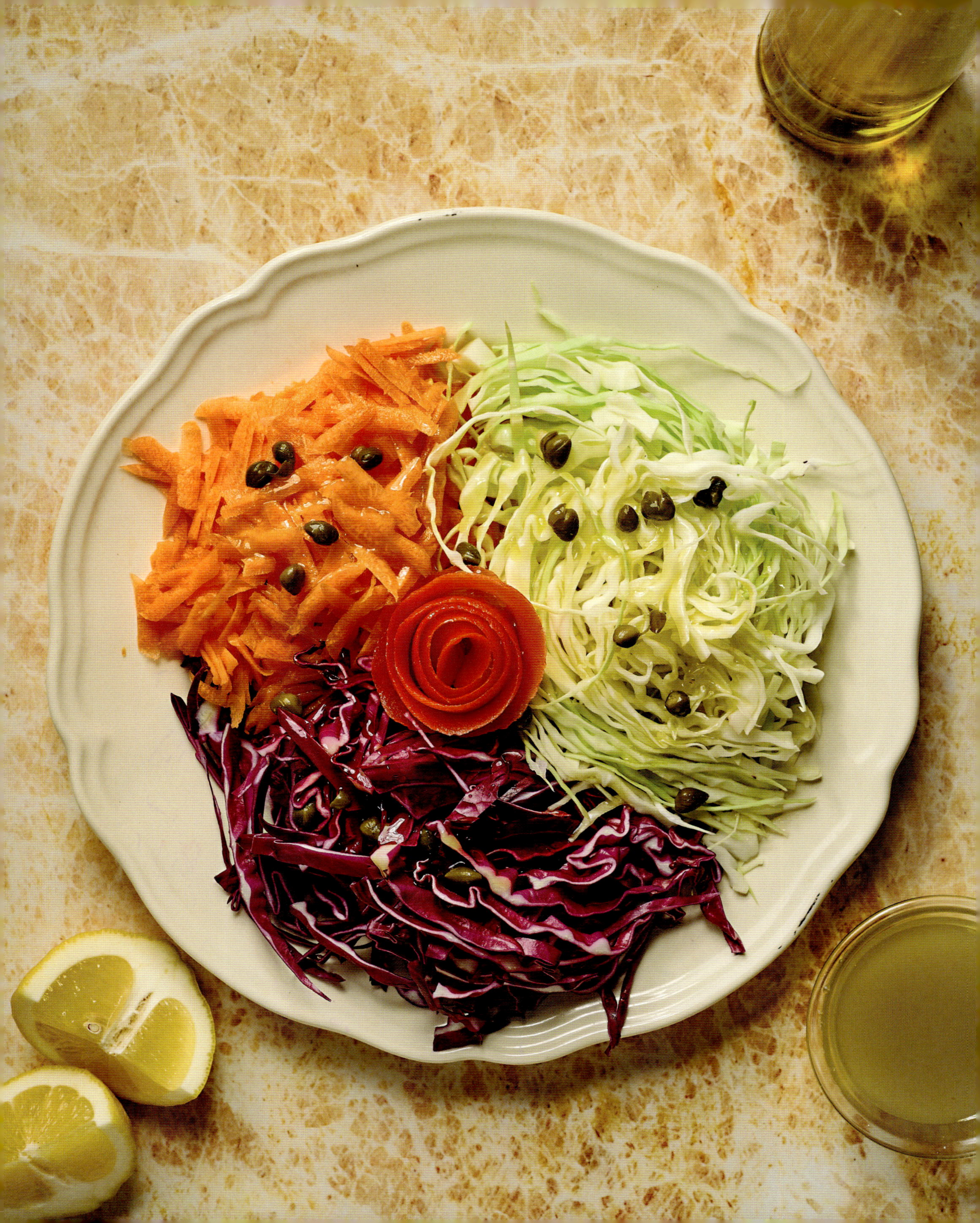

Beet and Arugula Salad
with Sultanas and Chèvre

Something that exists as pretty standard fare on Athenian menus these days, which was almost unheard of, or at the very least, exotic, when I arrived in the city more than thirty years ago, is the sweetening up of salads with additions like dried or fresh fruits, honey, and petimezi. At markets here, besides the year-round availability of fresh beets, a beloved root vegetable, there are always vacuum-packed cooked fresh beets in the produce section, one of many Mediterranean-diet convenience products that helps everyday cooks make eating healthier easy!

MAKES 2 TO 4 SERVINGS

Strained juice of ½ lemon

½ medium celery root

2 small bunches arugula, trimmed and torn

2 cooked beets, cut into ½-inch dice

2 to 3 tablespoons sultanas (golden raisins)

3 tablespoons toasted walnuts, hazelnuts, or pine nuts*

4 ounces soft chèvre or mashed Greek feta

For the dressing

¼ cup extra-virgin Greek olive oil

2 tablespoons fresh orange juice

1 tablespoon sherry vinegar

1 teaspoon Greek pine honey

1 teaspoon Dijon mustard

Salt to taste

*The best pine nuts in terms of flavor and texture are either Italian, Greek, or American. They're expensive, but well worth it because they're sweet and intensely flavored, as opposed to the most commonly found Chinese pine nuts, which sometimes have a metallic taste.

Fill a bowl with ice water and add the lemon juice. Peel the celery root and cut into matchsticks. Place in the bowl of lemon ice water.

Cut off and discard the stems from the arugula. Tear the arugula into pieces and place in a serving bowl. Drain the celery root and pat dry. Add the celery root, beets, raisins, and nuts to the salad. Use a teaspoon and break apart the chèvre into small dabs. Add these to the salad.

Whisk together all the ingredients for the dressing and pour over the salad just before serving. Toss and serve.

Baby Arugula and Chickpea Salad
with Raw Red Onion, Hard-Boiled Eggs, and Tahini Ladolemono

Here's a great example of the kind of salad that has cropped up in Athens of late: wholesome, hearty, main-course material with ingredients like tahini that speak of tradition put to new uses.

MAKES 4 SERVINGS

8 cups baby arugula

1 (15-ounce) can good-quality, low-sodium chickpeas, rinsed and drained

1 red onion, halved and thinly sliced

8 to 10 wrinkled black Moroccan olives or Greek throumbes olives

3 hard-boiled eggs, peeled and halved

1 tablespoon toasted sesame seeds

For the dressing

6 tablespoons extra-virgin Greek olive oil

2 to 4 tablespoons water

2 tablespoons strained fresh lemon juice, or more to taste

2 teaspoons tahini

½ teaspoon Greek pine honey

Pinch ground cumin

Pinch paprika

Salt to taste

Place the arugula, chickpeas, and onion in a serving bowl. Toss gently. Place the olives and hard-boiled eggs on top.

In the bowl of a small food processor, combine the olive oil, 2 tablespoons of the water, the lemon juice, tahini, honey, cumin, paprika, and salt. Pulse until smooth and creamy, adding a little more water if necessary to reach the desired consistency.

Pour the dressing over the salad, sprinkle with sesame seeds, and serve.

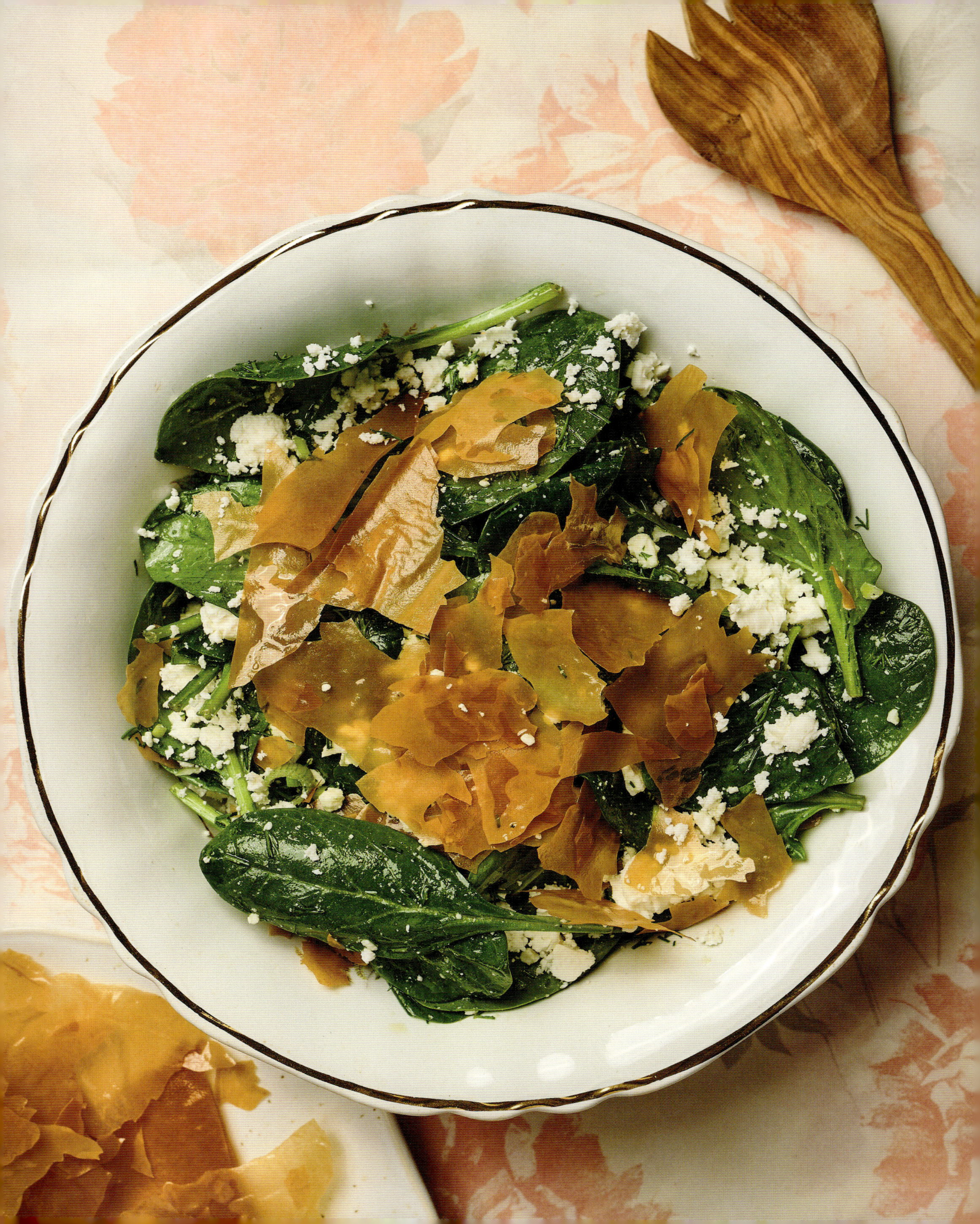

Spanakopita Salad

There's a spanakopita-everything trend running through Greek kitchens, and so the ingredients in this Greek classic are reimagined as croissants (page 32), focaccia sandwiches (page 35), and more, like this fun salad that calls for breaking up the crunchy baked phyllo as garnish over a bowl of spinach and feta. Enjoy!

MAKES 4 SERVINGS

2 #7 frozen phyllo sheets, thawed and at room temperature

5 tablespoons extra-virgin Greek olive oil

4 cups baby spinach

3 scallions, trimmed and chopped

½ cup snipped fresh dill

⅔ cup crumbled Greek feta

Sea salt and freshly ground black pepper to taste

Preheat the oven to 375°F. Line a rimmed baking sheet with parchment paper.

Place one sheet of phyllo over the parchment, brush with olive oil, and place the other sheet on top. Brush that one with a little olive oil, too. Place a second baking sheet over the phyllo and bake for 15 to 20 minutes, or until golden and crisp. Remove the top sheet and let the phyllo cool.

Mix the spinach, scallions, dill, and feta together in a serving bowl. Toss with the remaining olive oil, salt, and pepper.

Break apart the phyllo into amorphous pieces and sprinkle over the salad. Serve.

Athinaiki Salata Reimagined

The name of this dish, which translates as "Athenian salad," is sometimes also called "Athenian mayonnaise." It is one of the classics of "bourgeois" Greek cooking, and something Athenian ladies of a certain generation made for company and special occasions, showing off their skills in the kitchen. See the classic rendition on page 217. The version below is an amalgam of reimagined versions I've seen here and there over the last few years in Athens. The additions of shrimp, saffron, and a ring mold are not part of the original.

MAKES 6 TO 8 SERVINGS

1 (2-pound) whole red snapper, grouper, haddock, or monkfish, cleaned

4 Yukon Gold potatoes, peeled and quartered

2 celery stalks, trimmed

2 carrots, peeled

1 small celery root, peeled, halved, and cubed

Salt and freshly ground black pepper to taste

½ cup extra-virgin Greek olive oil

1 pound small shrimp, peeled and deveined

For the saffron mayonnaise

2 large egg yolks, at room temperature

1 tablespoon white wine vinegar

1 teaspoon Dijon mustard

Large pinch Greek saffron (krokos Kozanis)

Salt and freshly ground black pepper to taste

1 cup extra-virgin Greek olive oil

1 teaspoon strained fresh lemon juice

For garnish

1 tablespoon snipped fresh dill or chopped chives

Pink peppercorns

Wrap the whole fish in cheesecloth and tie it closed.

Layer the potatoes, celery, carrots, and celery root in a pot large enough to hold the fish without bending or breaking it. Lightly salt the vegetables as you layer them in the pan. Drizzle in the olive oil.

Place the wrapped fish over the vegetables and pour in enough water to cover by 2 inches. Cover and bring to a simmer. Cook for 14 minutes from the minute the water starts to boil. Skim the foam off the surface of the liquid if necessary, then add the shrimp and continue simmering for another 4 minutes or so, until the shrimp are cooked through and bright pink.

Carefully remove the fish and transfer it to a platter to cool until you can handle it. Strain the soup into a bowl, reserving the solids and liquid separately. Transfer the solids to another bowl.

Carefully debone the fish and shred it as you go. Transfer the shredded fish to the bowl with the vegetables and shrimp.

Make the mayonnaise: Add the egg yolks to the bowl of a food processor and process for 20 seconds. Add the vinegar, mustard, saffron, and salt to taste and process for another 20 seconds. Add the oil, very slowly, drop by drop, processing all the while, until it is completely absorbed. Add the lemon juice and adjust the seasoning with salt and pepper.

Stir the mayonnaise and chopped chives or dill into the fish, shrimp, and vegetable mixture and gently spoon into a ring mold. Cover and refrigerate for 1 hour before serving.

Reheat the fish broth and adjust the seasoning with additional salt and pepper. Serve hot with the fish salad as an accompaniment. Sprinkle the fish salad with the pink peppercorns just before serving.

Retro Rice and Tuna Salad

I love this salad! I can almost see it in one of those newspaper inserts from the 1960s, replete with the ink drawing of a slim, happy homemaker holding it up next to the printed recipe. This belongs to the genre of "modern" Greek cooking of that decade as well as the 1970s, when the country was opening up and inching toward a more contemporary version of itself. The idea of rice in a salad was a leap of faith away from, say, a pilaf, something new to bring to the family table.

MAKES 4 TO 6 SERVINGS

1½ cups long-grain white rice

1 cup frozen corn kernels

1 (5- or 6-ounce) can tuna in water, drained

10 teardrop tomatoes, halved lengthwise

2 scallions, trimmed and chopped

2 tablespoons capers, rinsed and drained, or 1 medium dill pickle, trimmed and diced

½ cup chopped fresh flat-leaf parsley

5 tablespoons extra-virgin Greek olive oil

2 tablespoons strained fresh lemon juice

Salt and freshly ground black pepper to taste

Cook the rice according to the package directions. About 5 minutes before removing the rice from the heat, gently stir in the corn kernels.

Transfer the rice and corn to a serving bowl. Break up the tuna and add it to the rice. Add the tomatoes, scallions, capers, and parsley.

Whisk together the olive oil, lemon juice, and salt and pepper to taste and pour over the salad. Toss gently and serve.

Bulgur Salad
with Fresh Fruit and Figs

This unusual fruit salad could easily belong in the breakfast chapter, as I ran across it at an Athenian café where overnight oatmeal and homemade granola kept it company in a glass display of healthy morning options. But I also like to enjoy this as a salad course in its own right.

MAKES 4 SERVINGS

1 cup coarse bulgur

1 cup of water

1 Fuji or McIntosh apple, cored and cut into ½-inch cubes

1 large pear, such as Anjou, Bartlett, or Comice, cored and cut into ½-inch cubes

6 dried Greek figs, either Kymi or kalamata, trimmed and chopped

1 scallion, trimmed and finely chopped

⅔ cup shelled salted pistachios, preferably Greek from Aegina, coarsely chopped

½ cup chopped fresh mint

½ cup extra-virgin Greek olive oil, or more as needed

2 tablespoons aged balsamic or Greek raisin vinegar

1 to 2 tablespoons grape molasses (petimezi)

Pinch salt

Pinch ground cinnamon

Place the bulgur in a bowl and pour in the water. Cover with a kitchen towel and let the bulgur soak until the water is completely absorbed, about 1 hour.

Add the apple, pear, figs, scallion, pistachios, and mint to the bulgur.

Whisk together the olive oil, balsamic vinegar, petimezi, and salt. Mix into the bulgur, add the cinnamon, and toss to combine. Serve immediately.

ΜΠΑΡΜΠΟΥΝΙΑ
ΦΑΣΟΛΙΑ
ΕΙΣΑΓΩΓΗΣ
€: 3,50 Kg
ΓΙΓΑΝΤΕΣ
ΚΑΣΤΟΡΙΑΣ
€: 7,80 Kg

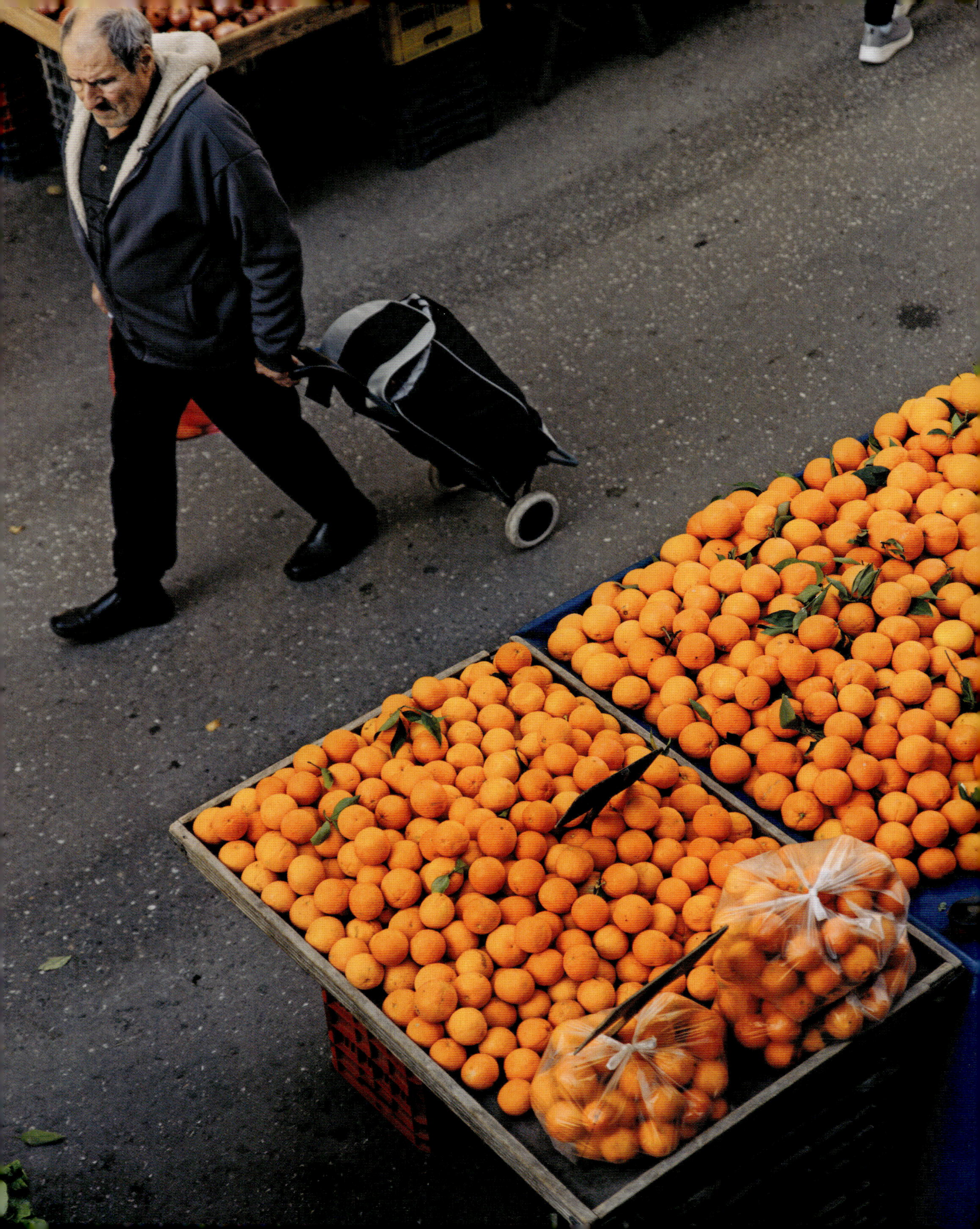

Mixed Greens Salad
with Tangerine–Olive Oil Dressing

Rifts on the traditional ladolemono, the lemon–olive oil dressing that is the most classic of all Greek dressings, started to make a show in Athenian restaurants when I was still writing about food in the 2000s for Ta Nea *newspaper. It was a great time to be a food writer in Greece because with the 2004 Olympics looming large, Greek traditions suddenly emerged as inspiration for a new generation of chefs eager to modernize the cuisine. Even something as simple as this dressing got a face lift with the advent of tangerine juice in lieu of most of the more acidic lemon juice. It's yummy!*

MAKES 6 SERVINGS

For the salad

1 small head radicchio, trimmed, halved, and cut into thin ribbons

2 endives, trimmed and cut crosswise into ¼-inch strips

2 cups shredded red cabbage

2 cups shredded white cabbage

1 fennel bulb, trimmed, halved, and cut crosswise into ¼-inch strips

3 tablespoons chopped fresh marjoram or oregano

3 tablespoons fresh mint chiffonade

3 tangerines, peeled and separated into sections or cut into rounds

¼ cup salted pistachios, preferably Greek from Aegina

For the dressing

½ cup strained fresh tangerine juice

2 tablespoons strained fresh lemon juice

2 teaspoons finely grated tangerine zest

½ cup plus 2 tablespoons extra-virgin Greek olive oil, or more as desired

1 scant teaspoon Greek pine honey

½ teaspoon Dijon mustard

Sea salt to taste

Place the radicchio, endive, cabbages, and fennel in a serving bowl. Mix in the marjoram and mint. Scatter the tangerine pieces and pistachios on top.

Whisk together all of the ingredients for the dressing until emulsified. Pour the dressing over the salad just before serving. Toss and serve.

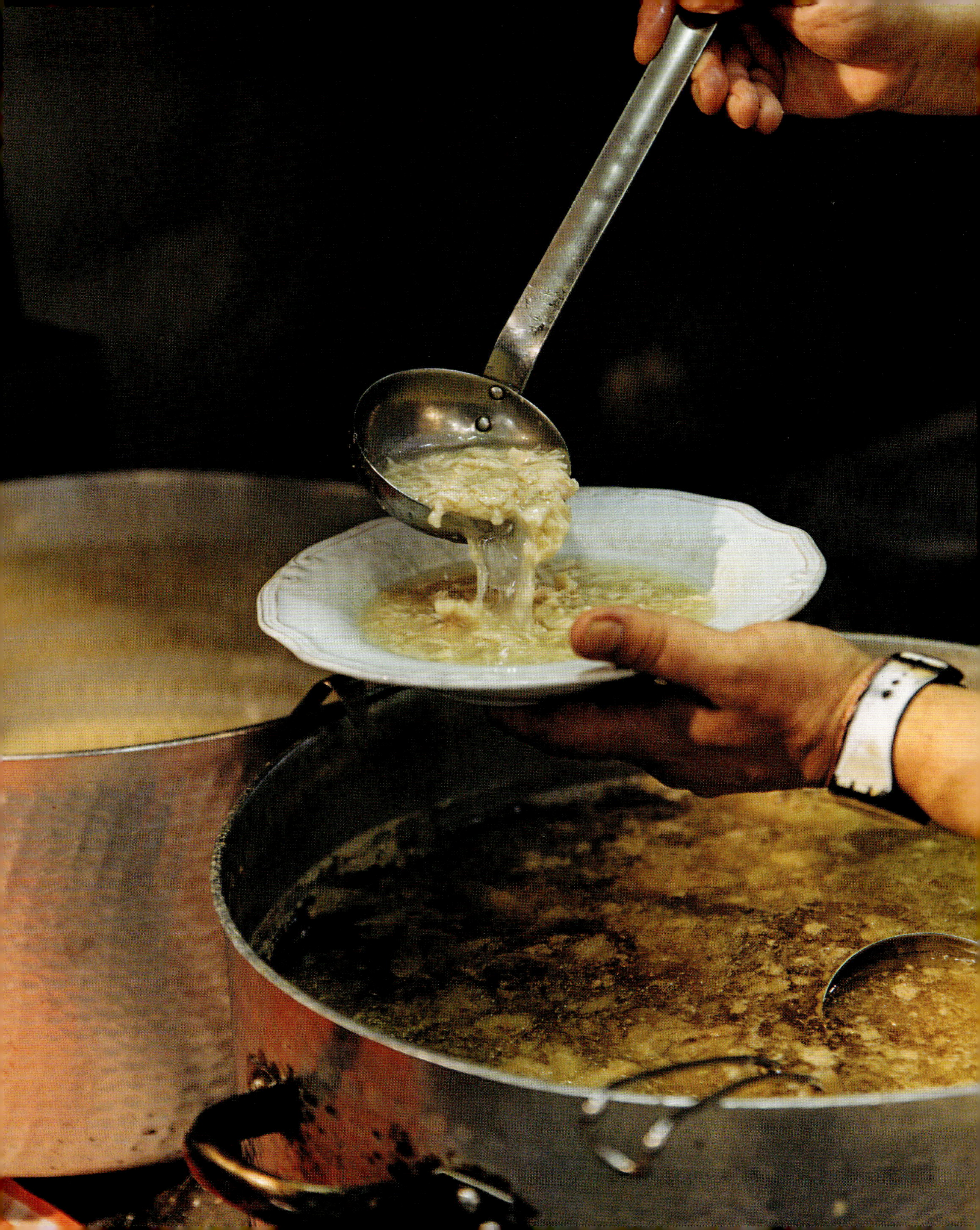

Athens by the Spoon

Soups

Something's astir in the world of Athenian soups, and has been for a long while now. When I think of soup in Athens, I travel back a little ways, to the image of tall, old hammered tin pots gurgling on the stained and well-worn stovetops of the mageiria or soupadika, the places with open kitchens, dishes of the day still in their pots and pans in steam-table displays, and cooks who seemed to have a cigarette permanently dangling from the upper corner of their lips, ladling out bowls of nourishment to the likes of cabbies and workers of every ilk and repute. The soups were standard fare: patsas (tripe soup), a beef or chicken soup or two, maybe a bean soup, maybe yiouvarlakia, a lemony meatball-and-rice dish that's somewhere between a soup and a stew. Fish soups could also occasionally be counted among the regular fare. It was all traditional and mostly pretty rustic.

But the Athens soup scene is very different now. The city's soup pot is a true melting pot. Greece has a temperate clime, and soups as a general rule have never been a huge part of the country's cuisine. Sure, there are many traditional soups, but their place on the table was mostly seasonal, with the exception of fish soup and patsas, the former a year-round delight and the latter a salve for the working classes and the hung over. Then, chefs, ever on the lookout for new frontiers, began to embrace soups and get creative with them, so much so that nowadays the très American or European likes of silky carrot, pumpkin, and cauliflower veloutés are commonplace on menus across the city, partly thanks to the love affair many chefs now have with a cutting-edge tool called the Thermomix, which heats and purees simultaneously (among other things), creating creamy textural elixirs, often without the typical addition of butter and cream, a feat unachievable with ordinary blenders.

Then, of course, there is the whole globalization of the soup pot, as of everything, really, thanks to the internet and social media, but also to realities on the ground, so to speak. Athens, a fairly homogeneous city when I first arrived here to settle in 1992, is now an international capital. I live, for example, in an ancient part of town, its unofficial Chinatown, and I can walk up the street to buy tofu in various forms, rice noodles, fish sauce, vegetables whose names and identity are a mystery to me, and other foods once unimaginable in the Greek capital.

This confluence of traditional and international flavors has created a delicious new chapter in the Athenian soup story. Magazine articles sing the praises of the best pho in the city, and in the next issue write of where to slurp the best taverna fish soups or heady, soothing patsas. There's a little crossover between Greek and global flavors, too, and that, at least in my experience eating out, is mostly in the veloutés, where ingredients once exotic, like curry and coconut milk, are easy to incorporate. At least one chef, Sotiris Kontizas, known for his Greco-Asian cooking, has blurred the boundaries with recipes like his pho avgolemono, a brilliant blending of two completely different traditions.

In the pages that follow, the choice of soups ladled out is a mix of old and new, with plenty of pots dedicated to the timeless classics and their particularly Athenian stories.

Beef Cheek and Mushroom Soup

Beef cheeks make me smile. Cheeks were a cut that went directly from the butcher block to the rubbish bin until the Greek financial crisis spurred chefs to look for cheaper raw ingredients to keep costs down and customers coming. Beef cheek stifado cropped up then, and so did a few soups, like this sating brew of vegetables, mushrooms, and beef cheeks that is perfect for a winter day.

MAKES 6 SERVINGS

½ cup extra-virgin Greek olive oil

3 large onions, coarsely chopped

3 celery stalks, coarsely chopped

2 tablespoons tomato paste

3½ pounds beef cheeks, trimmed and halved

1 large carrot, peeled and whole

10 fresh thyme sprigs

2 bay leaves

10 black peppercorns

2 allspice berries

⅔ cup dry red wine

2½ quarts water

3 large potatoes, peeled and cut into 1-inch cubes

Salt and freshly ground black pepper to taste

1 pound button mushrooms, trimmed and halved

Strained juice of ½ lemon (optional)

In a large, heavy pot, heat the olive oil over low heat. Add the onions and cook until deep golden and tender, about 1 half hour, stirring occasionally.

Stir in the celery and cook for 10 minutes to soften. Stir in the tomato paste, swirling it to spread evenly throughout the onions and celery. Add the beef cheeks, carrot, thyme, bay leaf, peppercorns, and allspice to the pot. Pour in the wine, raise the heat to medium-high, and bring to a boil. Add the water, then reduce heat to low. Simmer the soup for about 3½ hours, or until the beef cheeks are tender.

Remove the beef cheeks from the pot. Cut or break apart the beef cheeks into chunks and return them to the pot, together with the potatoes. Season to taste with salt and pepper and cook for 15 minutes, until the potatoes are tender but still a little al dente. Add the mushrooms and continue simmering the soup for another 15 to 20 minutes. Adjust the seasoning with salt, pepper, and the lemon juice (if desired), and serve.

Athens Central Market Beef Soup

I head to Epirus in the Central Market for this. It's so characteristically Athens, timeless Athens, unsexy Athens, real Athens. Epirus sits on a corner of the market, within breathing distance of the meat hawkers shouting for your attention while hacking away on bloodied butcher blocks, no frills and no decorum in sight. The market is not for the faint of heart, that's for sure, but to walk through it is to step back a few decades, when Athens was still a provincial city. Restaurants like Epirus abounded. It is what Greeks call a mageirio, from the verb "to cook," mageirevo, *and refers to a specific type of traditional eating establishment with an open kitchen where a dozen or so different Greek classics sit in steam-table basins for diners to see and choose from. The beef soup is soul-warming and hearty, made even more so by the use of beef shoulder, which contains a good amount of collagen and connective tissue that breaks down with long, slow cooking to create a flavorful broth.*

MAKES 6 SERVINGS

1¾ pounds bone-in beef shoulder

½ pound beef bones, if available

2 carrots, peeled and cut into ½-inch rounds

2 celery stalks, trimmed and chopped

2 large red onions, coarsely chopped

2 garlic cloves, minced

3 medium potatoes, peeled and cut into chunks

3 firm, ripe tomatoes, peeled and cubed

3 Chinese celery stalks with leaves, chopped

1 scant teaspoon black peppercorns

5 fresh thyme sprigs

2 bay leaves

5 allspice berries

Salt and freshly ground black pepper to taste

1 large zucchini, trimmed and cut into 1-inch cubes

½ cup extra-virgin Greek olive oil

Place the beef and bones (if using) in a large soup pot and cover with cold water by 3 inches. Bring to a simmer over medium heat and cook for about 1 hour, or until the meat is halfway cooked.

Add the carrots, celery, onions, garlic, potatoes, tomatoes, Chinese celery, peppercorns, thyme, bay leaves, and allspice to the pot. Season to taste with salt and pepper. Continue simmering at least another hour, or until the meat falls off the bone. Remove the meat and bones and transfer to a plate or bowl to cool slightly. Shred the meat and return it the soup. Stir in the zucchini cubes and cook for another 15 to 20 minutes, until the zucchini is tender. As soon as you turn off the heat, stir in the olive oil. Serve.

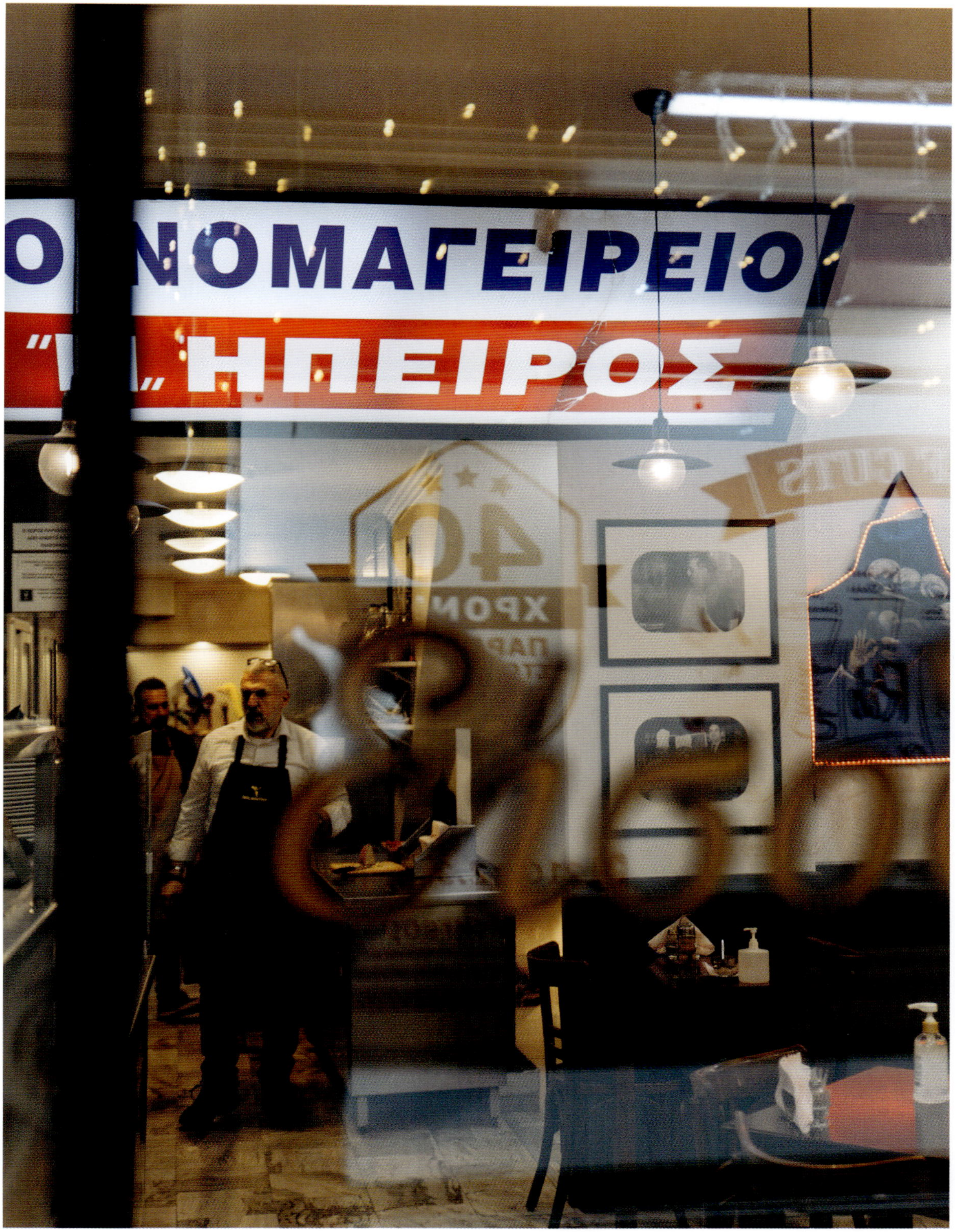
ΝΟΜΑΓΕΙΡΕΙΟ
ΗΠΕΙΡΟΣ

Roasted Butternut Squash Soup
with Greek Figs

Winter squash soups, though not a Greek tradition, are now a common offering both at home and in restaurants. Perhaps the advent of so many Greek Americans or Greeks who spent time in the US and celebrate Thanksgiving abroad helped give rise to such a wholehearted embrace of winter squash soups, but there's usually some kind of Greek twist, whether it's the addition of local honey, grape molasses, feta cheese, or, in this case, Greek figs.

MAKES 4 TO 6 SERVINGS

- 1 (3-pound) butternut squash
- 6 tablespoons extra-virgin Greek olive oil, divided, plus more for drizzling
- Salt and freshly ground black pepper to taste
- 4 fresh thyme sprigs
- 1 large onion, finely chopped
- 1 leek, trimmed and chopped
- 2 garlic cloves, minced
- 1 large Yukon Gold potato, peeled and cubed
- 1 teaspoon ground cumin
- Grating of fresh nutmeg, to taste
- 1½ to 2 quarts vegetable stock
- ½ cup light cream
- ½ cup Greek yogurt
- 4 dried Greek figs, finely chopped
- 2 tablespoons pumpkin seeds, lightly toasted

Preheat the oven to 400°F. Line a rimmed baking sheet with parchment paper.

Trim the stem and base off the butternut squash, cut it in half lengthwise, and remove the seeds and fibrous part of the cavity.

Place the squash halves cut side up on the baking sheet. Brush the flesh with 3 tablespoons of the olive oil and season lightly with salt. Place 2 of the thyme sprigs inside or on top of the flesh. Roast until soft, about 35 minutes. Remove and cool.

Heat the remaining 3 tablespoons olive oil in a large pot over medium heat. Add the onion, leek, and garlic and cook until soft and glistening, about 7 minutes. Stir in the potato cubes, cumin, and nutmeg. Add the stock and bring to a simmer.

Scoop out the flesh from the roasted butternut squash and transfer it to the simmering soup. Season to taste with salt and pepper and cook for about 20 minutes, for the flavors to all meld.

Puree the soup using an immersion blender or by transferring it to the bowl of a food processor or blender and processing until smooth. Transfer, if necessary, back to the pot and heat gently, whisking in the cream and yogurt.

In a small, dry skillet, toast the chopped figs and pumpkin seeds over low heat until the seeds are lightly toasted, 3 to 5 minutes, stirring.

Ladle the soup into bowls, garnish with the fig–pumpkin seed mixture, and drizzle a little olive oil over each serving.

To Oinomageireio Epirus

Rania gives me a hug whenever I stop in on her famous Athenian landmark, which is oftentimes with a few American guests in tow, and then points to the wall of fame, packed with celebrity photos and a framed yellowed old newspaper article from three decades past, the one I wrote of this place when I was a young reporter for *Ta Nea*.

To Oinomageireio Epirus sits at the back corner of the Varvakeios Agora, aka Athens Central Market, near the meat stalls, and is one of the oldest continuously operating restaurants in the city. It was born in 1898 and christened back then To Monastiri (the Monastery), opening in the newly minted market, which had been established just a little over a decade earlier, in the heart of the young Greek capital. Rania is the daughter of famed, late Athenian restaurant operator Tzimis, who bought the place in the 1980s and renamed it To Oinomageireio Epirus, after the beloved part of northwestern Greece where he was from. To this day, through times of feast and famine, Epirus has remained a steadfast beacon of traditional Greek cooking, treasured, among other things, for its soups. It is still the heart and pulse of Athens, attracting everyone from its longtime customers to ladies who lunch to the Birkenstock-clad young, and, of course, most famously of all, to the night owls who crave salvation through a few sips of soup, namely patsas, the traditional Greek hair-of-the-dog. Indeed, everyone who comes here is looking for a taste of something real and Greek, and its wall of fame shows Andrew Zimmern, Anthony Bourdain, and Jamie Oliver among those who've been customers over the years.

Tzimis passed away in the 1990s, and Rania decided to take up the reins, doing so with laudable devotion to the traditions that have always made this corner of the market a popular spot. It's almost a museum piece now, one of the last such places left, and lucky for its location, location, location, since the Varvakeios continues to be the traditional culinary heart of the city, where rich and poor shop for the freshest meats and fish, but is also now a destination where tourists flock, in guided groups or as sole adventurers, on that ephemeral search for the authentic.

Epirus is still an anchor of certainty in the hustle and bustle of the market. Its beige-tiled floors are calming; its characteristic red, white, and blue sign shines bright; and its open kitchen speaks to a lost era when such restaurants were a part of every neighborhood. It's one of the few places in Athens still open twenty-four hours a day, and to visit at all hours is to see the lifecycle of the city itself.

On Easter Saturday, one of the great food traditions of Athens plays out here, with people queuing up from the morning, their fingers curled around the handles of the pots they've brought from home, as they wait in line for mageiritsa, Greek Easter soup, one of the things for which this simple restaurant is known. They take it home to warm up after the midnight church service. The restaurant serves it after church in situ, too, and fills up with Athenians of every socioeconomic background, who spill in with their lighted candles waiting to be served a plate of this filling, lemony, herbaceous rice and offal soup. Rania and her staff start making it weeks before, hand-chopping something like half a ton of lamb's viscera to meet the demand.

Mageiritsa and its cousin, patsas, tripe soup, are the two most famous soups made here. Indeed, on every table, day and night, is a small bowl of boukovo, Greek red pepper flakes, and a cruet of skordostoumbi, garlic cloves steeped in red wine vinegar, the condiment most often drizzled into patsas.

But this humble old place mostly serves forth a daily repertoire of Greek classics, simply plated, in an unpretentious atmosphere, for everyone to enjoy.

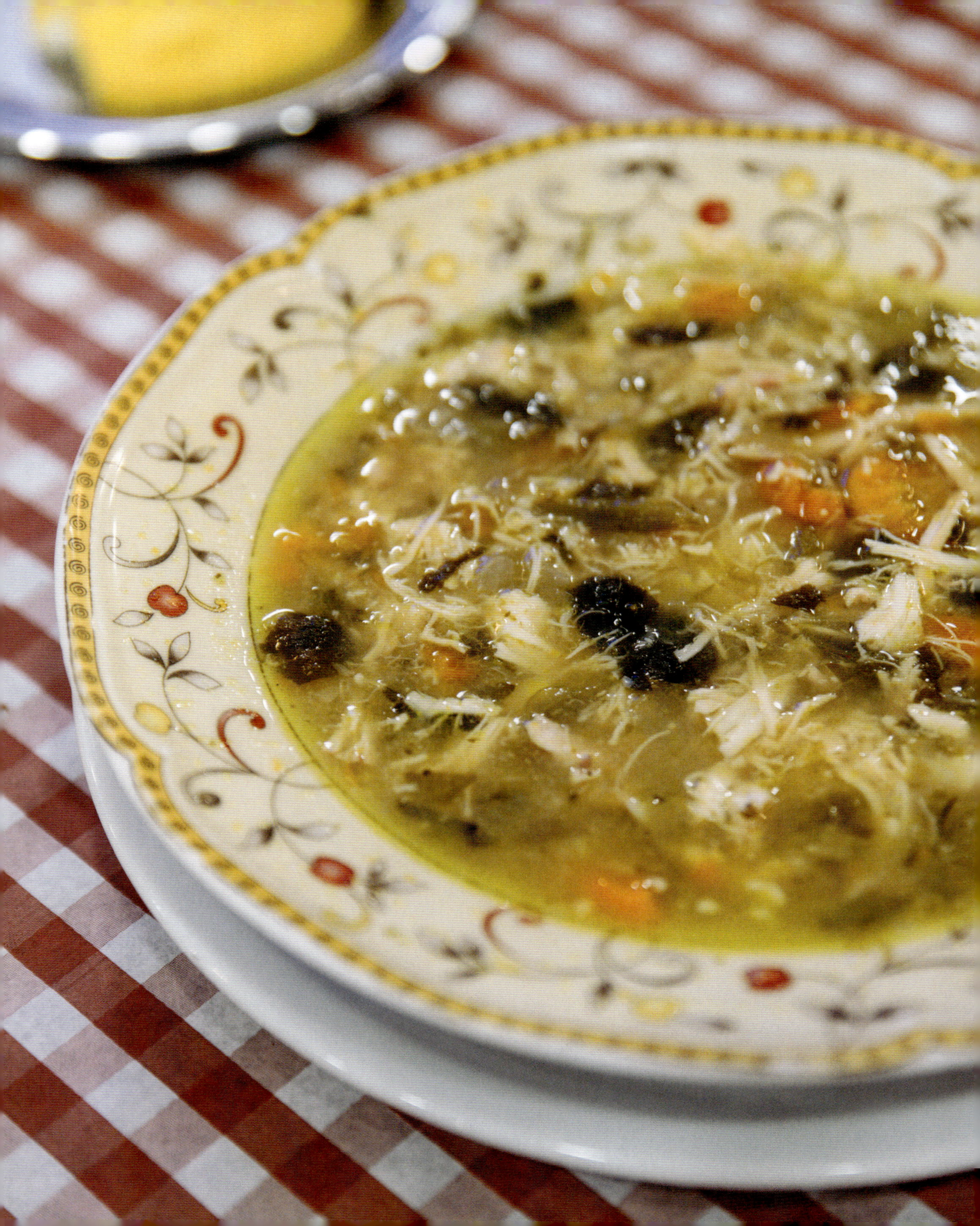

Epirus's Lemony Pulled Chicken Soup

If you're like me, you have a natural affinity for food markets, especially when you travel. As I said, the Athens Central Market has changed dramatically over the years from rough-and-tumble to tame and somewhat gentrified (sushi bars and fresh pasta restaurants line one part of it), but there's still enough grit and old-city charm to draw an adventurous eater to places like Epirus, one of the few working-class restaurants left in the capital. It's here that you'll see the steam-table displays of everything the cooks made on a given day, among their frequent offerings this tangy chicken soup, slurped with comforting pleasure by a motley mix of everyone from fresh-faced college students on a study-abroad program to market scamps who crawl out from the woodwork to grab a bite at Epirus.

MAKES 6 TO 8 SERVINGS

1 (5-pound) chicken, cut into large pieces, skin removed if desired

3 carrots, 1 left whole and 2 peeled and chopped

2 onions, 1 left whole and 1 minced

1 garlic clove, peeled

2 bay leaves

Salt and freshly ground black pepper to taste

6 tablespoons extra-virgin Greek olive oil, divided

1 large potato, peeled and diced

1 celery stalk, trimmed and finely chopped

Strained juice of 1 lemon

1 cup chopped fresh flat-leaf parsley

Place the chicken, whole carrot, whole onion, garlic clove, and bay leaf in a large pot. Pour in enough water to cover by 3 inches and bring to a boil over medium-high heat. Season lightly with salt and pepper. Turn the heat down to a gentle simmer, cover partially, and cook for about 1½ hours, or until the chicken is falling off the bones.

Remove the chicken pieces and vegetables with a slotted spoon and discard the vegetables and bay leaves. Let the chicken cool until you can handle it, then shred or pull the meat into thin threads; discard the skin and bones. Strain the broth through a fine-mesh sieve or cheesecloth-lined colander into a bowl.

Wipe the pot dry, but don't wash it. Add 2 tablespoons of the olive oil and heat over medium heat. Add the chopped carrots, minced onion, potato, and celery, cover, and cook, stirring on occasion, until softened and translucent, about 8 minutes. Return the shredded chicken to the pot and pour the broth back in. Simmer for 45 minutes, or until the vegetables are very soft.

Whisk together the remaining 4 tablespoons olive oil and the lemon juice and stir that into the soup. Season to taste with additional salt and pepper, stir in the parsley, and serve.

All-Nighter's Patsas (Tripe Soup) Inspired by Epirus Restaurant

"Look at this city," my friend Peter Poulos said to me many years ago, while we were stuck in Athens traffic on a Tuesday night, at around 3 a.m. "It's life-affirming, that people are out in the middle of the week, and we're honking to move!" It's a comment that has stayed with me all these years, because if Athens is anything, it's a late-night city. And in a late-night city, night owl revelers often need to fill their bellies with something soothing, coating, and nutritious. That something is patsas, the tripe and/or trotter soup that divides the world into very black and white love-it or hate-it categories. Whatever one's feelings about this ancient elixir, said to be the descendent of the black broth (melanos zomos) of Spartan warriors, it's a traditional late-night hair-of-the-dog kind of thing that's given a flavor boost with skourdostoumbi, a sort of homemade garlicky condiment. The places that serve it are usually open 24–7, catering to taxi drivers, working folk, and those late-night partyers who hope to allay a looming hangover.

MAKES 8 TO 12 SERVINGS

For the skordostoumbi

8 garlic cloves, peeled

1 tablespoon coarse sea salt

2 cups red or white wine vinegar

For the patsas

3 pounds beef trotters, well rinsed

½ cup extra-virgin Greek olive oil

3 large red onions, chopped

4 garlic cloves, minced

2 pounds beef tripe, well rinsed and cut into small squares

2 bay leaves

6 whole cloves

Sea salt and freshly ground black pepper to taste

1 to 4 tablespoons paprika

½ cup red pepper flakes

Make the skordostoumbi: Using a mortar and pestle, gently smash the garlic cloves, salt, and a few tablespoons of the vinegar together to make a paste. You can do this in a small food processor, too. Transfer it to a glass jar or cruet and add the remaining vinegar. Let it rest overnight.

Make the patsas: Place the trotters in a large pot, cover with ample cold water, and bring to a boil. Drain and rinse.

Wipe the pot dry, add the olive oil, and heat over medium heat. Add the onions and cook until wilted, 8 to 10 minutes, then stir in the garlic. Return the trotters to the pot, add the tripe, and sauté a little. Add enough water to cover the ingredients by 2 inches. Add the bay leaves, cloves, and pepper to taste.

Turn the heat down to low, cover partially, and simmer for 3 to 3½ hours, adding boiling water as needed to keep the mixture liquid. Skim the fat off the surface of the soup over the course of cooking it. The soup is done when the meat pulls off the bones easily. About 15 to 20 minutes before removing the pot from the heat, season to taste with salt. Redden the soup to your liking with as much or as little paprika as you like, stirring it in just before serving. Serve with the red pepper flakes and the skordostoumbi.

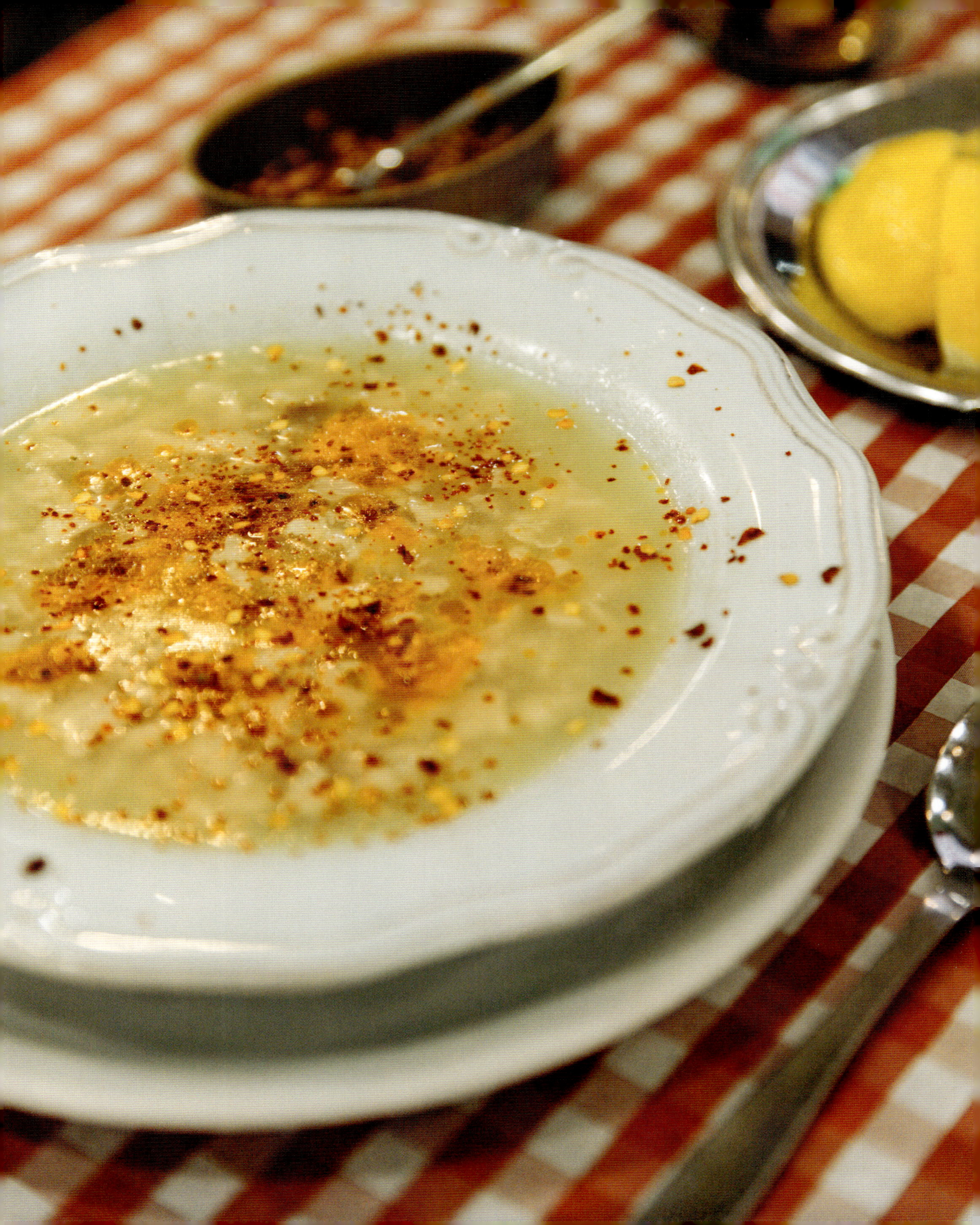

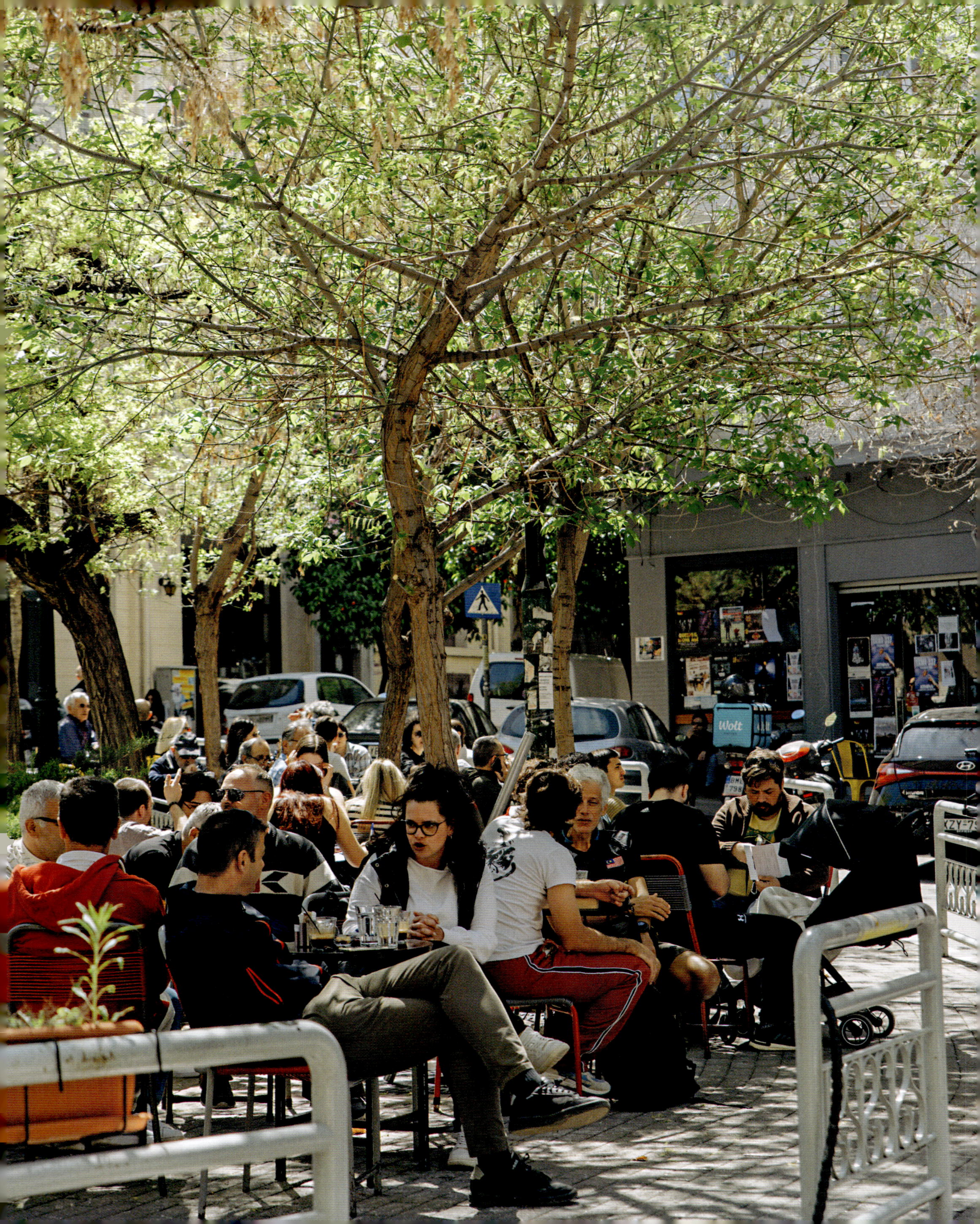
Wolt

Diporto and Barba Mitsos

Enter. Order. Eat. Leave. That's the gruff but endearing way of things at Diporto ("Two Doors"), an Athenian cult taverna, at once excitingly shabby and delicious and, as of this writing, teetering on extinction, to the uproar of a city that is selling its old soul and replacing its hidden charms with bland boutique hotels for more and more tourists to fill. News accounts of its closing, one more victim of gentrification, spread like fire through the city. The phenomenon is a facet of the Athenian zeitgeist, circa 2024, and this beloved basement taverna, on the corner of Socratous and Theatrou streets in the heart of the Central Market area, is yet another victim.

Like a Caravaggio painting, light spills into subterranean Diporto, creating drama and contrast. Barba Mitsos, the eighty-something-year-old owner, wrapped in his characteristic knee-length white chef's coat, is aglow in its dusty rays as he moves from table to table, slapping down plates of his time-tested simple Greek recipes to a crowd that has morphed over the years from market scamps, newspaper reporters, and lawyers to a more incongruous mix of locals, hipsters, and tourists, all hungry for a glimpse of the past. Giant wine barrels filled with the retsina Mitso makes himself at the end of every summer in nearby Mesogeia line the darkened walls and an ancient marble counter on one end of the space shimmers silvery like a full moon on a clear night.

Diporto first opened its doors in 1911 and has been in the same family ever since. Mitsos, aka Dimitris Koliolios, is the adopted son of the original owner, and he's been the taciturn, shuffling presider of things in this renowned eatery since 1957. In the last decade or so, his nephew has worked side by side with him. I've been coming here since I was a young newspaper reporter, too, introduced to the place by the old-timers at *Ta Nea*, in the 1990s. Back then, there were a handful of places like Diporto around the market area, but they've all since shut their doors.

The menu here is gloriously simple and consistently delectable, square one of Athenian gastronomy: legendary soups of chickpeas, beans, or beef; potatoes yiahni, a casserole that makes a main course of the world's most popular tuber; grilled anchovies or sardines; fava (puree of yellow split pea); a perfect horiatiki salata; horta (boiled greens); and, to finish, a slab of homemade semolina halva.

Rumors come and go. The building, erected in 1880, may have been bought by a fund and is soon slated for either demolition or a major facelift. Or maybe it wasn't. Diporto will be part of a new boutique hotel. Or maybe not. Barba Mitso is retiring and his nephew will continue the legacy. Perhaps. Time will tell what the fate of these two doors will be, but one thing is for sure: Old Athens is fading, and with it morsels of its history are, too.

Chickpea Soup That Emulates Diporto's Legendary Revithada

In case Diporto does not survive gentrification, here is my version of Barba Mitso's recipe for the absolute best chickpea soup in Athens. It's epic.

MAKES 6 TO 8 SERVINGS

⅔ cup extra-virgin Greek olive oil, divided

1 large onion, minced

2 garlic cloves, minced

1 pound dried chickpeas, soaked overnight and drained

Salt to taste

2 teaspoons dried Greek oregano

Strained juice of 1 large lemon

In a large pot, heat ⅓ cup of the olive oil over medium heat. Add the onion and garlic and cook until wilted, 7 to 8 minutes. Add the chickpeas and enough water to cover by about 2 inches. Bring to a simmer, partially cover the pot, and cook for 2½ to 3 hours, until the chickpeas are very tender.

Using an immersion blender and a good eye, puree about 1 cup of the mixture inside the pot. Alternatively, transfer 1 cup of the chickpeas to the bowl of a food processor and puree, then return the pureed chickpeas to the pot.

Season to taste with salt, bring back to a simmer, and stir in the oregano, lemon juice, and remaining ⅓ cup olive oil. Serve.

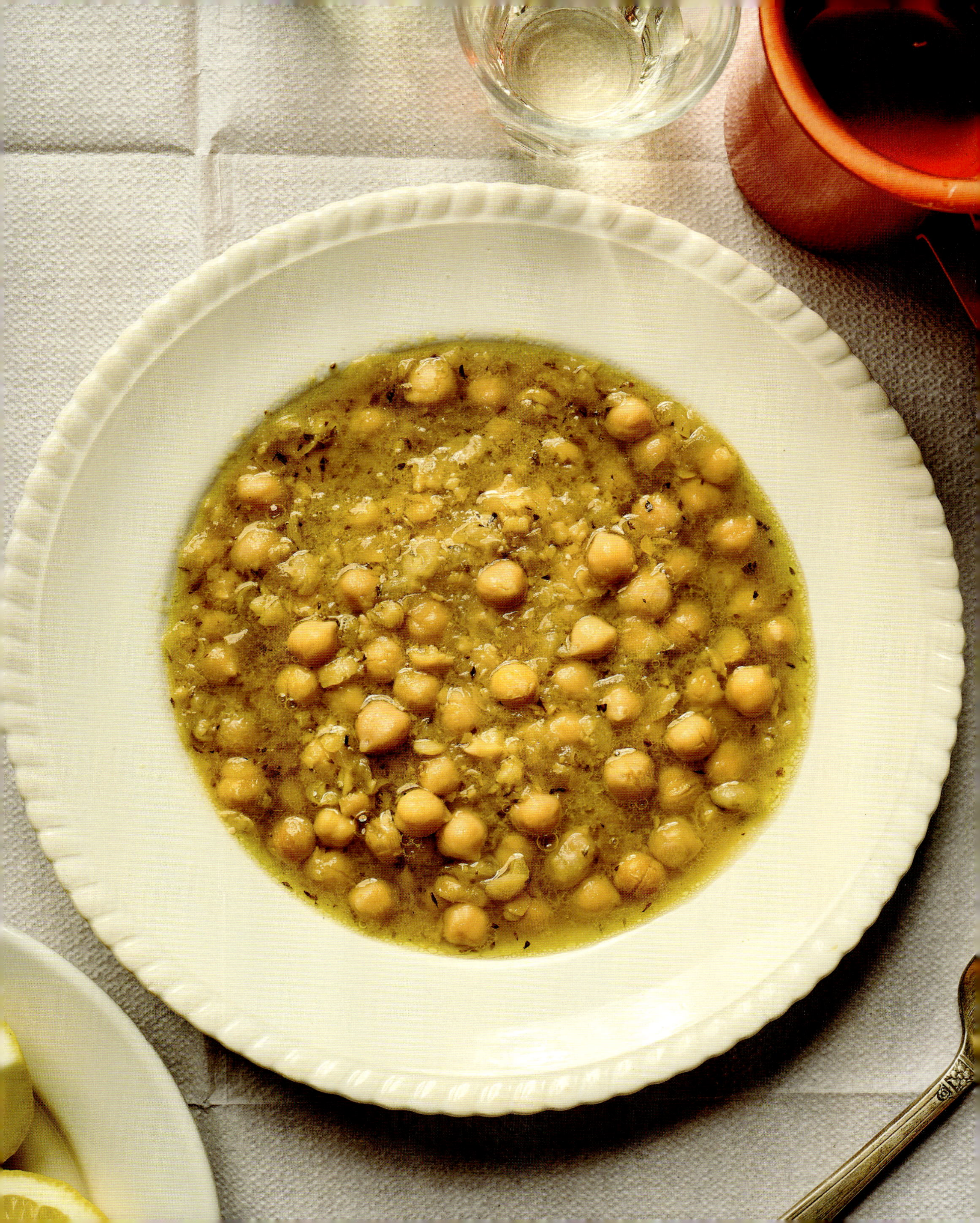

Chickpea Soup
with Pasturma from Fani's Ta Karamanlidika

This hearty winter soup, created in the meat-heavy kitchen of Fani's Ta Karamanlidika on Evripidou Street in central Athens, combines the best of intentions into something delicious, traditional, and modern all at once: thick chickpea soup, a Greek classic, speckled with bits of the best pasturma in Athens, found at Fani's charcuterie counter.

MAKES 4 TO 6 SERVINGS

1 pound dried chickpeas or 4 (15-ounce) cans good-quality, low-sodium chickpeas

Salt and freshly ground black pepper to taste

½ cup extra-virgin Greek olive oil, divided

2 red onions, finely chopped

1 cup canned diced tomatoes

Pinch sugar

5 slices pasturma, trimmed and finely chopped

1 teaspoon ground sumac

⅔ cup chopped fresh flat-leaf parsley

If you're using dried chickpeas, leave them to soak overnight in ample water, then drain the following day. Put them in a large pot, cover with fresh water, and simmer for 1½ to 2 hours, until they're very tender but still retain their shape. Season with salt and pepper about 15 minutes before removing from the heat. Drain and set aside. If using canned chickpeas, rinse and drain them in a colander under running water and set aside.

Heat ¼ cup of the olive oil in a wide pot over medium heat. Add the onions and cook until translucent and soft, about 10 minutes. Add the tomatoes and sugar, turn the heat down to medium-low, and cook, stirring, for 8 minutes. Add half the pasturma and the chickpeas, turn the heat back up to medium, and bring to a simmer. Add the sumac and pepper. Season to taste with a little salt, if necessary. Stir in the remaining ¼ cup olive oil and the chopped parsley and serve, garnished with the remaining pasturma.

Creamed Trahana
with Dried Figs and Bottarga

In the years leading up to the 2004 Athens Olympics, chefs seemed to be in their own Olympian race to explore traditional, often peasant ingredients and reinvent them for a modern age. It was an incredibly exciting time to be a food writer in Greece. I recall vividly the first time I tasted a recipe similar to this, for a kind of velouté soup made with trahana, one of the most ancient foods in the Eastern Mediterranean, a granular, cooked, wheat-and-dairy-based delight originally "invented" as a way to preserve milk. It was at the nimble hands of Christoforos Peskias, a star chef in Athens for almost three decades now. I just recall that first spoonful of velvety, satisfying tanginess for an ingredient that until then had been relegated to farmers' breakfast porridge and grandmothers force-feeding reluctant kids, for whom trahana is often a much-derided yuk food. I was transported by the sheer simplicity of the chef's idea, to just puree the thing to a texture that catapulted it to gourmetdom and to pair it with bottarga and figs, the kinds of sumptuous treats worthy of an ancient Greek banquet.

MAKES 6 SERVINGS

¼ cup extra-virgin Greek olive oil, plus more for drizzling

1 red onion, finely chopped

1 fennel bulb, trimmed and finely chopped

2 large garlic cloves, minced

1 large carrot, left whole

2 cups sour trahana

8 to 12 cups chicken stock, as needed

Sea salt and freshly ground black pepper to taste

6 fresh thyme sprigs

4 fresh oregano sprigs

1 cup Greek yogurt

Strained juice of ½ to 1 lemon

12 thin slices Greek avgotaraho (bottarga)

6 dried kalamata figs, stemmed and thinly sliced

In a large, wide pot, heat the olive oil over medium heat. Add the onion, fennel, garlic, and carrot and cook until soft and translucent, about 8 minutes. Stir on occasion to keep from burning.

Add the trahana and stir to coat in the oil. Add 8 cups of the stock and season with salt and pepper. Tie together the thyme and oregano sprigs and add them to the soup. Bring to a simmer, then reduce the heat to low, and simmer until the trahana granules have disintegrated completely into a thick porridge, 25 to 30 minutes. Because trahana absorbs up to six times its volume in liquid, and every brand is a little different, keep an eye on the soup and add more stock as needed.

Remove the pot from the heat. Remove and discard the herb sprigs and carrot. Transfer the soup, in batches as necessary, to the bowl of a food processor or powerful blender and puree the soup at the highest speed until it is really creamy, adjusting the viscosity judiciously by adding more stock as you go. Pulse a few tablespoons of the Greek yogurt into each batch. When done, pour the soup back into the pot and stir in the lemon juice to taste and, if desired, a little more olive oil. Adjust the seasoning with salt and pepper.

Serve the soup garnished with the bottarga and dried figs, a divine combination when eaten all together. Drizzle with more olive oil, turn the pepper mill once or twice over each bowl, and enjoy.

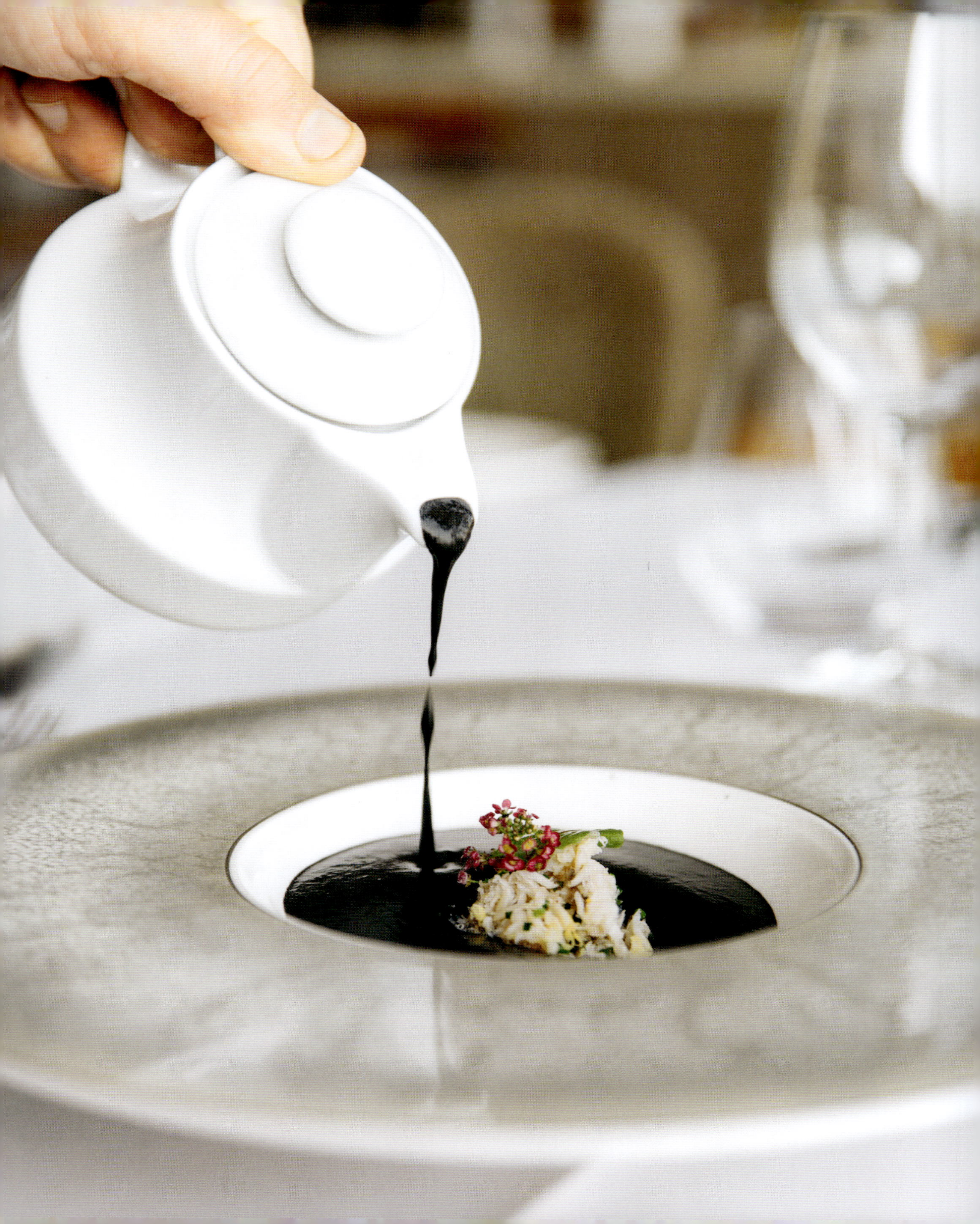

Lefteris Lazarou's Cuttlefish Ink and Crab Soup

The very first time I sipped a spoonful of this signature Lazarou soup it was like taking a swim in the dark—mysterious, a little adventurous, and absolutely delightful. The bowl was filled with an elixir the color of obsidian, a liquid perfectly creamy and rich to its depths with the flavor of the sea. It was a revelation. Lazarou has created many renditions of this soup over the years, and I am not quite sure where the following recipe, with crab and asparagus, falls in the lineup, but in any form, his cuttlefish ink and seafood soups are an Athenian legend.

MAKES 4 SERVINGS

7 tablespoons extra-virgin Greek olive oil

1⅓ cups thinly sliced leeks

2 cups minced onions

1 small bunch asparagus, trimmed and halved crosswise

4 cups heavy cream

4 cups fish stock

½ cup cuttlefish ink

1 teaspoon strained fresh lemon juice

1 teaspoon salt

1 scant teaspoon cornstarch, diluted in ¼ cup water

8 teaspoons canned lump crabmeat

In a large pot, heat the olive oil over medium heat. Add the leeks and onions and sauté until they are soft, 8 to 10 minutes. Add the asparagus and continue to sauté for a few more minutes. Pour in the heavy cream and fish stock bring the mixture to a boil.

Transfer the soup, in batches as necessary, to a blender and blend until completely smooth. Return the pureed soup to the pot. Stir in the cuttlefish ink to give the soup its characteristic black color. Adjust the flavor with the lemon juice and salt.

Gradually add the cornstarch mixture, stirring all the while, to thicken the soup to the desired consistency.

Ladle into 4 bowls, top each serving with a portion of crabmeat, and serve.

Taverna Fish Soup

I've slurped many a fish soup around this city in the thirty-plus years I've called Athens home. Some are consommé-like, clear and light, with bits of white-fleshed fish and vegetables suspended in broth. Others are made hearty with rice or trahana, and thickened with avgolemono. Some are pureed to creamy comfort. This one, a kind of amalgam of my fish soup memories, culled from many taverna meals, is a combination of all of the above.

MAKES 6 TO 8 SERVINGS

½ cup extra-virgin Greek olive oil

2 carrots, peeled and cut into thin rounds

2 leeks, trimmed and chopped

2 celery stalks, trimmed and chopped

2 Yukon Gold potatoes, peeled and cubed

1 strip lemon zest

10 fresh flat-leaf parsley sprigs

3 fresh thyme sprigs

Salt and freshly ground black pepper to taste

2 pounds mixed whole fresh fish, such as gurnard, snapper, scorpionfish, monkfish, haddock, cod, mullet, mahi-mahi, and/or grouper, gutted and scaled

¼ cup strained fresh lemon juice

In a large, deep pot, heat ¼ cup of the olive oil over medium-low heat. Add the carrots, leeks, celery, potatoes, lemon zest, parsley, and thyme. Season with a little salt, cover, and sweat the vegetables until they're translucent and softened, about 8 minutes. Check on them occasionally and stir them up a bit. Season lightly with salt and pepper.

Place the fish in a cheesecloth, salting them lightly and layering them so that the largest fish are on the bottom and the smaller ones on top. Tie the cheesecloth loosely to make a wide bundle and place it gently over the vegetables.

Pour in enough water to cover the contents of the pot by 2 inches. Cover the pot and simmer until the fish are tender, 12 to 15 minutes. Carefully remove the cheesecloth bundle and transfer it to a platter. Continue simmering the stock until the vegetables are tender, about 20 more minutes. Remove and discard the lemon zest and herb sprigs.

When the fish is cool enough to handle, debone each one and shred the flesh. Make sure there are no bones in the cleaned and shredded fish. Add the shredded flesh to the pot and simmer for 5 minutes.

Using an immersion blender or food processor, puree the soup until it is thick and creamy. Add boiling water if needed to thin the soup a little. Mix in the lemon juice and remaining ¼ cup olive oil and pulse to combine. Adjust the seasoning with salt and pepper and serve.

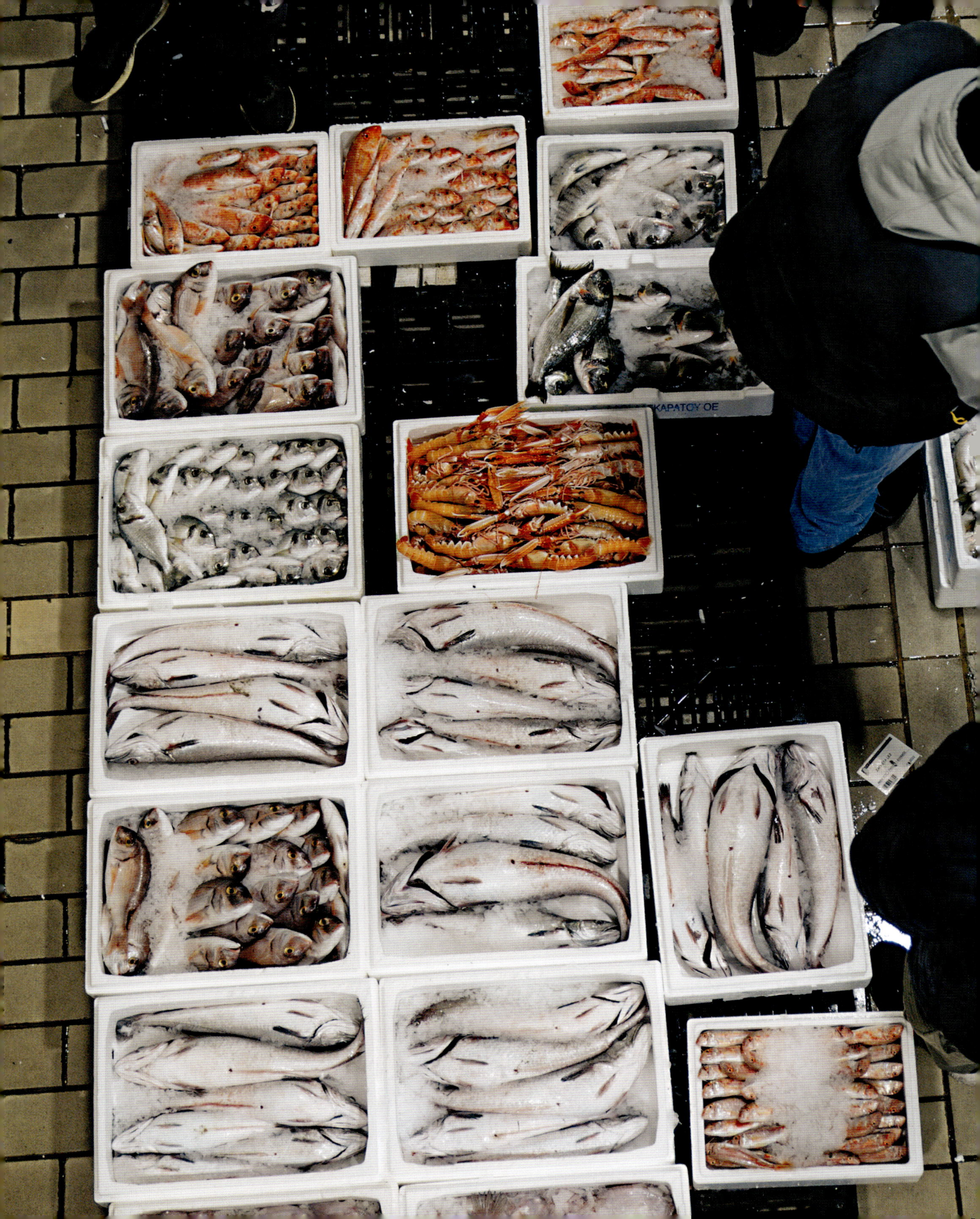

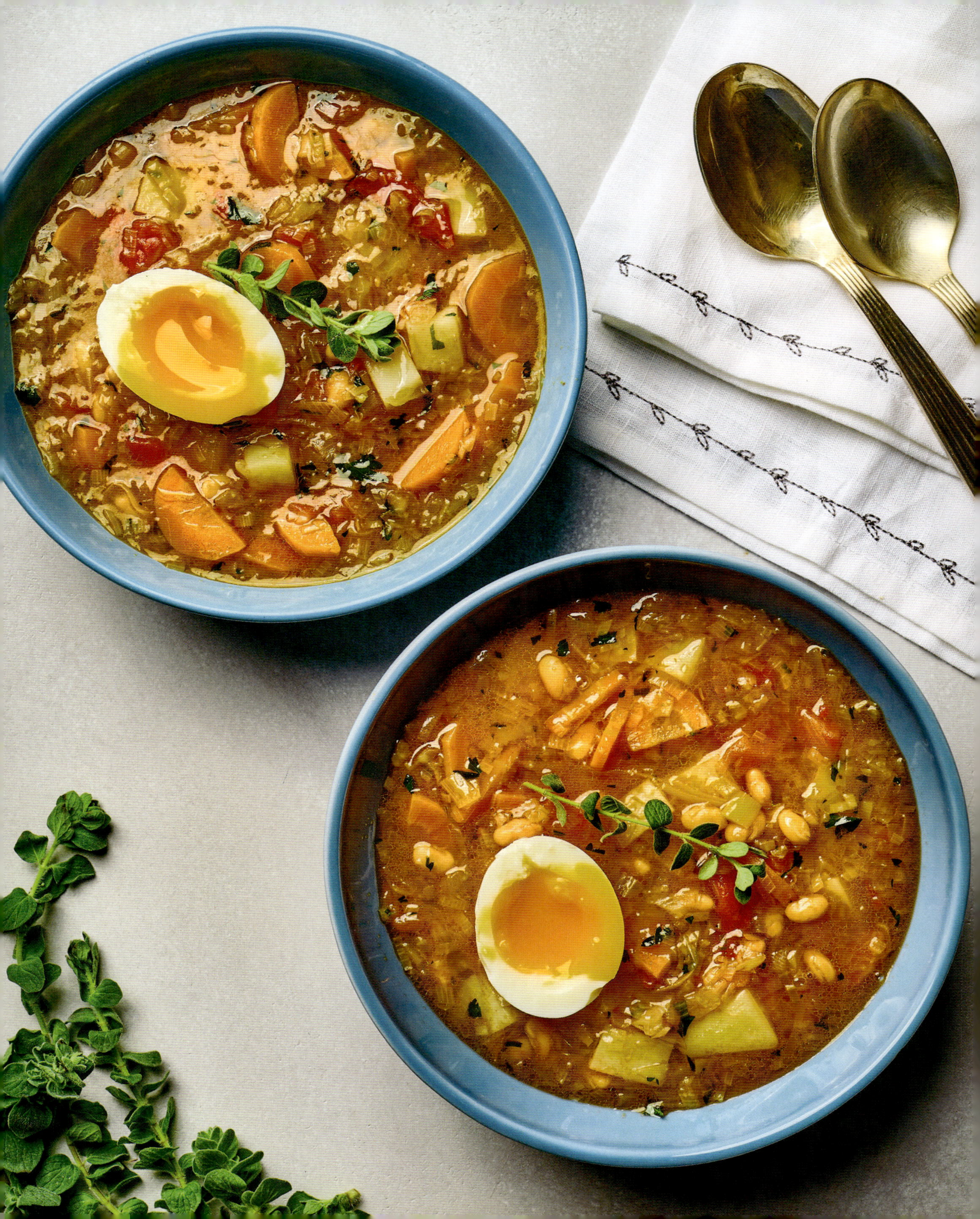

Greek Vegetable Soup
with Jammy Eggs

Soft-boiled and/or jammy eggs made their appearance on Greek menus sometime in the 1990s, when it was all the rage to dress up dishes with an oozing soft egg, which added drama and trendiness to many a dish, transforming something as pedestrian as, say, a vegetable soup into something fashionable and fun.

MAKES 4 TO 8 SERVINGS

½ cup extra-virgin Greek olive oil, plus more for drizzling

3 celery stalks, trimmed and chopped

2 large onions, chopped

1 leek, trimmed and chopped

3 large carrots, halved lengthwise and sliced crosswise ¼-inch thick

3 garlic cloves, finely minced

2 large potatoes, peeled and cubed

Sea salt and freshly ground black pepper to taste

1 (15-ounce) can diced tomatoes

1½ quarts vegetable stock or water

1 (15-ounce) can cannellini beans. drained and rinsed

1 large bunch Swiss chard, trimmed and cut into thick ribbons

1 cup fresh flat-leaf parsley, finely chopped

3 tablespoons finely chopped fresh oregano

4 large eggs, at room temperature

In a large soup pot, heat ¼ cup of the olive oil over medium heat. Add the celery, onions, leek, and carrots, lower the heat to medium-low, and cover the pot. Sweat the vegetables for 6 to 7 minutes, until softened. Stir in the garlic. Add the potatoes and turn to coat in the olive oil. Season with salt and pepper.

Add the canned tomatoes with their juices and stir to combine with the vegetables. Pour in the vegetable stock. Raise the heat to medium-high, add the beans, and bring to a simmer. Reduce the heat to medium and simmer the soup for about 30 minutes. Add the Swiss chard and continue cooking for another 15 to 20 minutes, or until the soup is thick and rich and all the ingredients have melded. Stir the parsley and oregano, adjust the seasoning with additional salt and pepper, and stir in the remaining ¼ cup olive oil.

About 10 minutes before serving the soup, place the eggs in a medium pot with enough cold water to cover by 1 inch. Bring to a gentle simmer and cook the eggs to soft, about 4 minutes. Remove and rinse under cold water. Peel the eggs and cut them in half lengthwise, being careful not to spill the yolk, which should still be almost liquid. You have to time this so that you can serve the eggs when the soup is also ready to be served.

To serve, ladle the hot soup into individual bowls and garnish with 1 or 2 soft-boiled egg halves in each.

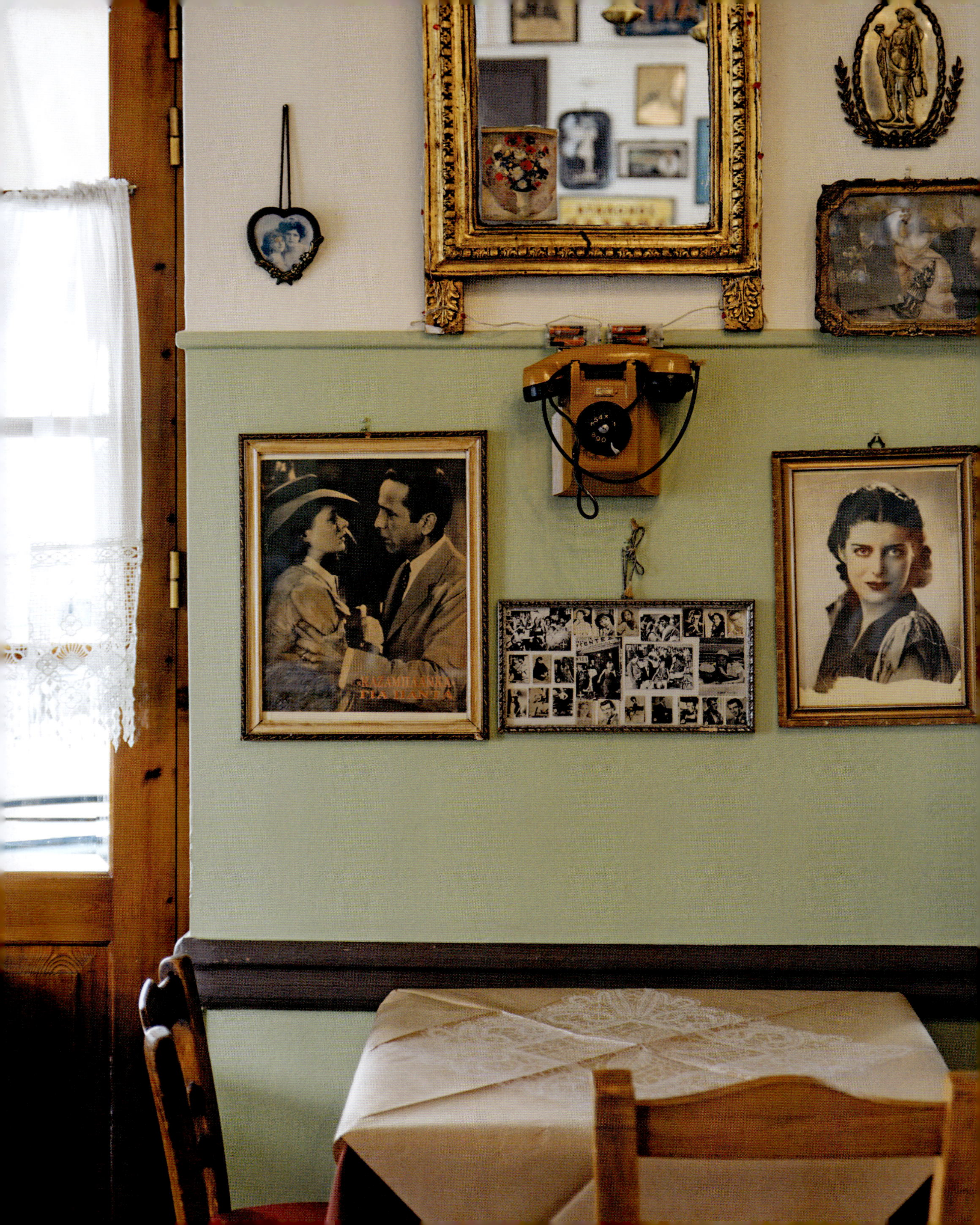
ΓΙΑ ΠΑΝΤΑ

The Taverna

No book about Athens could possibly omit the taverna and the role this simple, working-class eating establishment has played in the life and evolution of the city. When I moved here in my early twenties, full of excitement and very much in love, Vasili and I would head to the local tavernas of Exarcheia with his gaggle of friends, mostly young artists who were studying in the ateliers of one or another of the professors at the nearby School of Fine Arts. It was a great life for a twenty-something-year-old, cheap and lively, our endless conversations sharpened by glass after glass of acrid retsina and fueled by plates of traditional Greek food like snails, keftedes, and fried anchovies. There was always music, either blaring from loudspeakers or live. It was easy to be a bohemian in 1980s Athens.

Yet, the taverna is ancient in all but name, its path threading back to the bustling lanes of the ancient Agora, circa 2000 BC. Imagine a boisterous market packed with hawkers of every kind, from sandal makers to oil merchants, under the shadow of the Parthenon, abutting present-day Adrianou Street just between the Monastiraki and Plaka. The daily needs for a thirst-quenching quaff and a nibble were met with the emergence of the kapileio, ancestor to today's taverna, essentially makeshift thatch-roofed stalls set up by farmers who sold their wine and products—a place to stop, in other words, to drink a glass and satisfy an ancient midday hunger with a bite of cheese or perhaps some olives. Simple stuff. The kapileio morphed into the taverna, so named after the Latin *taberna*, for "hut" or "stall," which continued to flourish into the Byzantine era, during which time its offerings grew to include slightly more embellished menus. But wine was always central to the taverna experience, and it still is.

The taverna as we know it today, a simple neighborhood place, typically lined with retsina barrels and serving up traditional Greek food, is tied to the birth of the modern Greek state and the emergence of the working class. Its present form started to take shape in the middle of the nineteenth century, with the exodus of thousands of people from the Greek hinterlands who spilled into Athens, the country's newly minted capital. Whole neighborhoods with people from specific regions of Greece started to take shape, like the Maniatika in Piraeus (people from the Mani); Anafiotika in the Plaka (from Anafi island), and so on, and in each neighborhood tavernas sprang up, morphing into hangouts for working-class men, who could stop in for a glass of wine and a small bite after work, to shoot the breeze and talk of the news of the day. The first tavernas were in those working-class neighborhoods, specifically Metaxourgeio (where the silk factory was located), Gazohori (near the old gas works), Anafiotika, and Psyrri (which housed small shops of metal and leather workers, among other things). In Exarcheia, where the School of Fine Arts and Greek National Technical University were established in 1837 and where the magnificent National Archeological Museum is located, tavernas catered to students and intellectuals, and I was happily among them in my twenties, side by side with my artist husband and his artist friends.

The anchor in each and every taverna, dating to its earliest manifestations, wasn't the food as much as it was the wine—specifically, in modern times, the retsina swimming in all those thick wine barrels lining the walls. Eating out, a middle-class construct, was not a thing, so to speak, in nineteenth- and early twentieth-century Athens; going to a taverna was more about the social gathering, mostly of men, and centered around wine drinking. Not much different, in other words, from the ancient kapileio. And, importantly, the taverna evolved as a kind of hoi polloi counterweight to the life of the aristocratic, educated upper classes, who swarmed around the court of the newly imposed Greek king Otto of Bavaria, frequenting the young city's grand hotels, dining on rich European foods and downing Bavarian brews. Instead of béchamel and beer, poorer Athenians chomped on small fry and chicken gizzards. They sipped retsina, made anew each September with grapes collected and vinified from nearby Mesogeia, Attica's sprawling vineyard since the days of those makeshift wine stalls, where the Savatiano grape still blankets the land. Savatiano is the predominant grape varietal in retsina production, and the resin needed to give this unique Greek wine is culled from the sap of Aleppo pine, which once covered the area, too.

Enter 1922 and the Asia Minor Catastrophe, when approximately 1.2 million Greek refugees thronged the country, forced out of the homes they knew for millennia. By the end of the war, by some accounts, the Mikrasiates accounted for about 50 percent of the Athenian population. And they changed the face of the table and the life of the city with their delicious Anatolian foods and music. The refugees settled by default in tiny houses and apartments provided by the Greek state, so small that congregating indoors was almost impossible, and so they breathed new life into the story of the taverna, where they'd meet, not only to sip and eat, but to sing and listen to the rebetika music of the homeland they left behind. More often than their conservative Greek peasant counterparts from the hinterlands, these new arrivals had their women in tow. The taverna started to morph from a men's-only club to a more inclusive version of itself, still anchored by wine, still working class, but with fuller and fuller menus and a touch of feminine mystique. By the early twentieth century every working-class neighborhood in Athens had its tavernas, and to this day the best ones are still located in what was until just a few years ago the city's working-class hubs, like Petralona, Votanikos, Pangrati, Metaxourgeio, and Patissia.

There is also a whole category of fish tavernas, mostly located on stretches of the Attica coast or in neighborhoods near the sea. They're called psarotavernes (*psari* is the singular form of the word for "fish"), and their offerings are as simple as those that specialize in meat and other Greek traditional foods.

The taverna was, in a way, what the lunch counter and original diners were to urban American neighborhoods: places where locals could go for some respite and decent food, where the owner knew everyone by name and face and acted as confidant and counselor. Those aspects have been diluted in global Athens, but we still love our tavernas, even though nowadays there are fewer and fewer of the very old, traditional places left. But a number of century-old establishments do still exist, rediscovered with every new generation and written about in the press.

This chapter is but a partial paean to the taverna and its delicious fare, with a few twists and some modern takes, as this ancient eating concept reinvents itself to stay relevant with the times. It is by no means a complete account of every popular dish on offer, so forgive the omissions of dishes you might have wanted to find. Take note, too, that there are more than a few designated "taverna" recipes tucked into other chapters, such as the Taverna Fish Soup (page 188) and Leloudas's Poor Man's Plate (page 136).

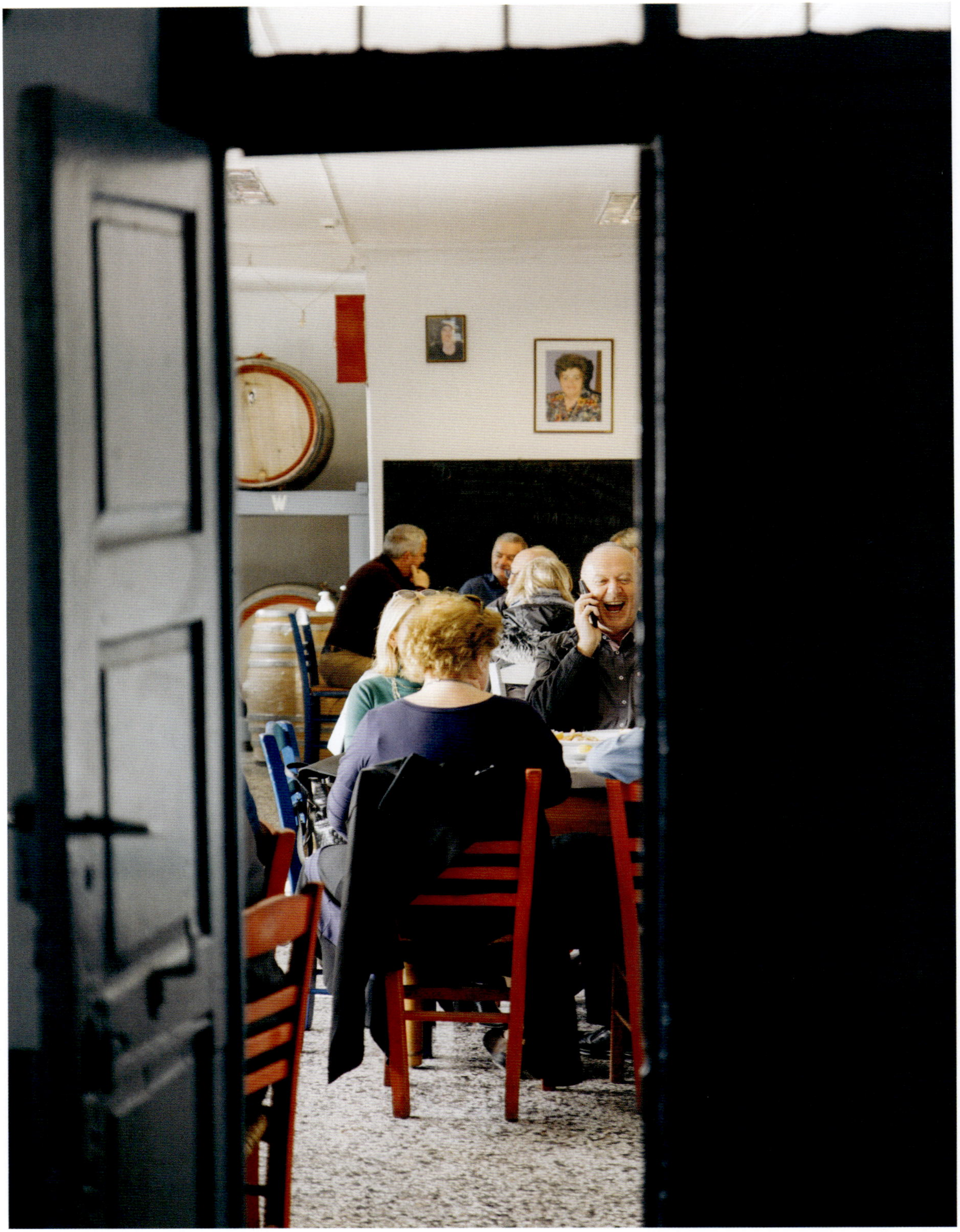

Clay-Baked Whole Eggplants
with Feta and Tomatoes

This classic eggplant dish, oozing with feta and other melted cheeses, is a bestseller on countless taverna menus. It's a universally loved recipe, and the skill of the cook who makes it is finding the right balance between the eggplants, tomatoes, and cheese(s), so that the latter doesn't completely overpower everything else. Sometimes the dish is a layered affair and sometimes, as below, the eggplants are split and stuffed whole with this comforting mixture.

MAKES 6 TO 8 SERVINGS

4 medium eggplants

⅓ cup extra-virgin Greek olive oil, plus more for the baking dish

1 large red onion, finely chopped

3 garlic cloves, minced

3 medium, firm ripe tomatoes, diced

1 scant teaspoon dried Greek oregano

Pinch sugar

Salt and freshly ground black pepper to taste

1½ cups crumbled Greek feta

Heaping ¼ cup coarsely grated graviera or other mild, nutty yellow sheep's milk cheese, or Gruyère

4 teaspoons chopped fresh flat-leaf parsley

Preheat the oven to 400°F.

Using a sharp knife, slit the eggplants lengthwise down the middle, keeping the stem intact. You don't want to halve the eggplants, just to open them so that you can fill them whole once they're soft enough.

Oil a clay or ovenproof ceramic baking dish large enough to hold the eggplants in one layer. Place in the hot oven and bake until their flesh is soft and the skin slightly charred, about 20 minutes.

While the eggplants are baking, heat the olive oil in a large, deep skillet or wide, shallow pot over medium heat. Add the onion and sauté until translucent, 8 to 10 minutes. Stir in the garlic and diced tomatoes and season with the oregano, sugar, salt, and pepper. Cook for about 10 minutes, until the mixture is thick without the tomatoes losing their shape too much. Remove from the heat.

Remove the eggplants from the oven and gently pry open each one, being careful not to tear the bottom. Think of them as eggplant boats with the stem intact. Gently mash the flesh inside the eggplant skins a little, using a fork. Spoon the tomato-onion mixture into each eggplant, not worrying if it spills over. Spoon the feta over the tomato-onion-eggplant pulp inside the "boat," and sprinkle with the graviera. Return the baking dish to the oven and bake for another 12 to 15 minutes, until the cheeses melt. Remove, sprinkle with the parsley, and serve.

The Simplest Fried Whole Shrimp

Head to the garidadika—shrimp houses—that line the Piraiki Coast along the Saronic Gulf and you'll find this dish in various renditions on every menu. To make this as close as possible to its truest iteration, it's definitely best to use fresh and not frozen shrimp.

MAKES 4 SERVINGS

Extra-virgin Greek olive oil or vegetable oil, for frying

¾ cup all-purpose flour

2 tablespoons plain fine bread crumbs

Salt and freshly ground black pepper to taste

1 pound shrimp, peeled and deveined, heads and tails left on

Lemon wedges, for serving

Heat a large, heavy nonstick skillet over high heat and pour in about ⅛ inch olive oil.

Combine the flour, bread crumbs, salt, and pepper in a shallow bowl. Toss a small handful of the shrimp in the flour and bread crumb mixture. Shake out the excess flour on the shrimp either by bouncing a few at a time in your hands or inside a fine-mesh colander over a plate, so as not to make a mess. Add the lightly dusted shrimp to the hot oil in a single layer and fry until bright pink, turning once. They need only 2 to 3 minutes in total. Transfer to a plate lined with paper towels and continue until all the shrimp are dusted and fried.

Serve with lemon wedges.

Fried Mussels

Mussels are farmed mostly in the Thermaiko Gulf in northern Greece, outside Katerini and Thessaloniki. They make their way to Athenian tavernas and are loved either steamed with ouzo and lemon, or fried. You might find these crunchy mollusks spilling out of a paper cone or in a basket at casual seafood places around town, usually with a ramekin of some heady dip. I like these with Mung Bean Fava (page 94) or Sweet Potato Skordalia (page 91).

MAKES 4 TO 6 SERVINGS

4 cups all-purpose flour

4 cups rice flour or cornstarch

1½ tablespoons baking powder

1 scant teaspoon salt

1½ cups seltzer water

1 (12-ounce) can beer

¼ cup ouzo

¼ cup extra-virgin Greek olive oil

1 teaspoon paprika

½ to 1 teaspoon cayenne (optional)

1½ pounds shelled fresh or thawed frozen mussels

Vegetable oil, for frying

Combine the flour, cornstarch, baking powder, and salt in a large bowl. Slowly mix in the seltzer, beer, ouzo, and olive oil. Taste and season with additional salt if necessary. Stir in the paprika and cayenne (if using). The batter should be roughly the consistency of a thick pancake batter. Cover and refrigerate for 1 hour or up to 3.

Rinse the mussels under cold water in a colander and pat dry.

Heat about 3 inches vegetable oil in a large, deep skillet. Using a slotted spoon, dip a few mussels into the batter and remove, sliding them immediately into the hot oil. Fry the mussels for 2 to 3 minutes, turning to crisp and brown on all sides. They should be crunchy and golden. Transfer with a clean slotted spoon to a platter lined with paper towels. Repeat until all the mussels are battered and fried. Serve immediately.

Cheese-Stuffed Taverna Burgers

Sunday lunch is still family time for many Greeks, and that usually means either a long lunch at the parents' or in-laws' or a meal out with the kids in tow at a local taverna, the kind that often abuts a playground so everyone is happy. Biftekia, Greek burgers, are a classic, and shaping them so that there's a little surprise melting out of the middle is a sign of love, especially when cubes of ripe tomatoes spill over the top and there's warm grilled bread nearby.

MAKES 4 TO 6 SERVINGS

1 pound ground beef

½ pound ground pork

1 large egg, slightly beaten

2 scant teaspoons Dijon mustard

½ to ⅔ cup coarse plain bread crumbs

4 large garlic cloves, minced

3 tablespoons dried mint

2 tablespoons dried Greek oregano

Salt and freshly ground black pepper to taste

4 to 6 tablespoons extra-virgin Greek olive oil

1 cup crumbled Greek feta crumbled

½ cup coarsely grated graviera or other mild, nutty yellow sheep's milk cheese, or Gruyère

1 tablespoon strained fresh lemon juice

2 large, firm ripe tomatoes, diced

Combine the ground meats, egg, mustard, ½ cup of the bread crumbs, garlic, mint, oregano, salt, and pepper in a large bowl and knead well. Add 2 tablespoons of the olive oil to the mixture while kneading to create a soft, succulent mass. The mixture should be dense but slightly unctuous; add more bread crumbs or olive oil as needed to achieve that. Cover and refrigerate for at least 30 minutes or up to 2 hours.

Preheat the oven to 350°F. Oil a large baking pan.

Mash the feta, graviera, and lemon juice together in a bowl using a fork, or pulse on and off in a food processor, to form a thick paste. Divide the mixture into 8 equal portions, about 2 tablespoons each, and squeeze together to compress and shape into small balls.

Divide the ground meat mixture into 8 equal parts. Rub the palms of your hands with a little olive oil and shape each portion into a burger. Using your thumb, make an indentation in each burger and fill with a cheese ball. Pinch together the meat to seal the indentation so that the cheese is not exposed.

Place the burgers in the oiled pan. Cover with parchment paper and then aluminum foil and bake for 35 to 40 minutes, until well done. Remove the parchment and foil about 10 minutes before removing from the oven so the burgers get some color.

While the burgers are baking, season the tomatoes with a little salt and pepper and a tablespoon or two of olive oil. Serve the burgers with the diced tomatoes spooned on top.

Keftedes of Athens

Keftedes are Greek meatballs, and in Athens they're something of a cult food, sought out in tavernas far and wide across the city, each vying for a place on the list of "best" keftedes in town.

One of the most famous places is the century-old Karavitis taverna in Pangrati, which attracts a loyal clientele for all its meaty offerings but especially for its keftedes, which are perfectly fried and crunchy but also juicy. A little farther north there's the eighty-year-old Kitsoulas taverna in Halandri, the place to go for some of the best traditional Greek food in the city, especially for lunch.

Every taverna renowned for its meatballs also, of course, has its own particular recipe. For some, that's the addition of ouzo to the meat mixture; for others, it's the meat itself: lamb, beef, pork, or some combination thereof? The most traditional keftedes recipes call for mint, but nowadays one is just as likely to find keftedes seasoned with parsley, oregano, and so much more, especially as younger chefs experiment with this Greek classic, adding spices their grandmothers would never have imagined. There's also a trend afoot to dress up the meatballs with sauce, and everything from cheese to creamy turmeric to ouzo-infused tomato sauces is finding a place over this ultimate comfort food.

What makes a great kefte? You need a mixture of meat that contains some fat so that the meatball is juicy. Fresh herbs and some dried bread crumb or bread help the meatballs retain moisture and a light, fluffy texture. They can be baked or fried; the latter is tastier, of course, and the oil should be hot enough to cook the meatballs to a crusty, lightly charred exterior without burning but also not so hot that the outside cooks before the inside has a chance to.

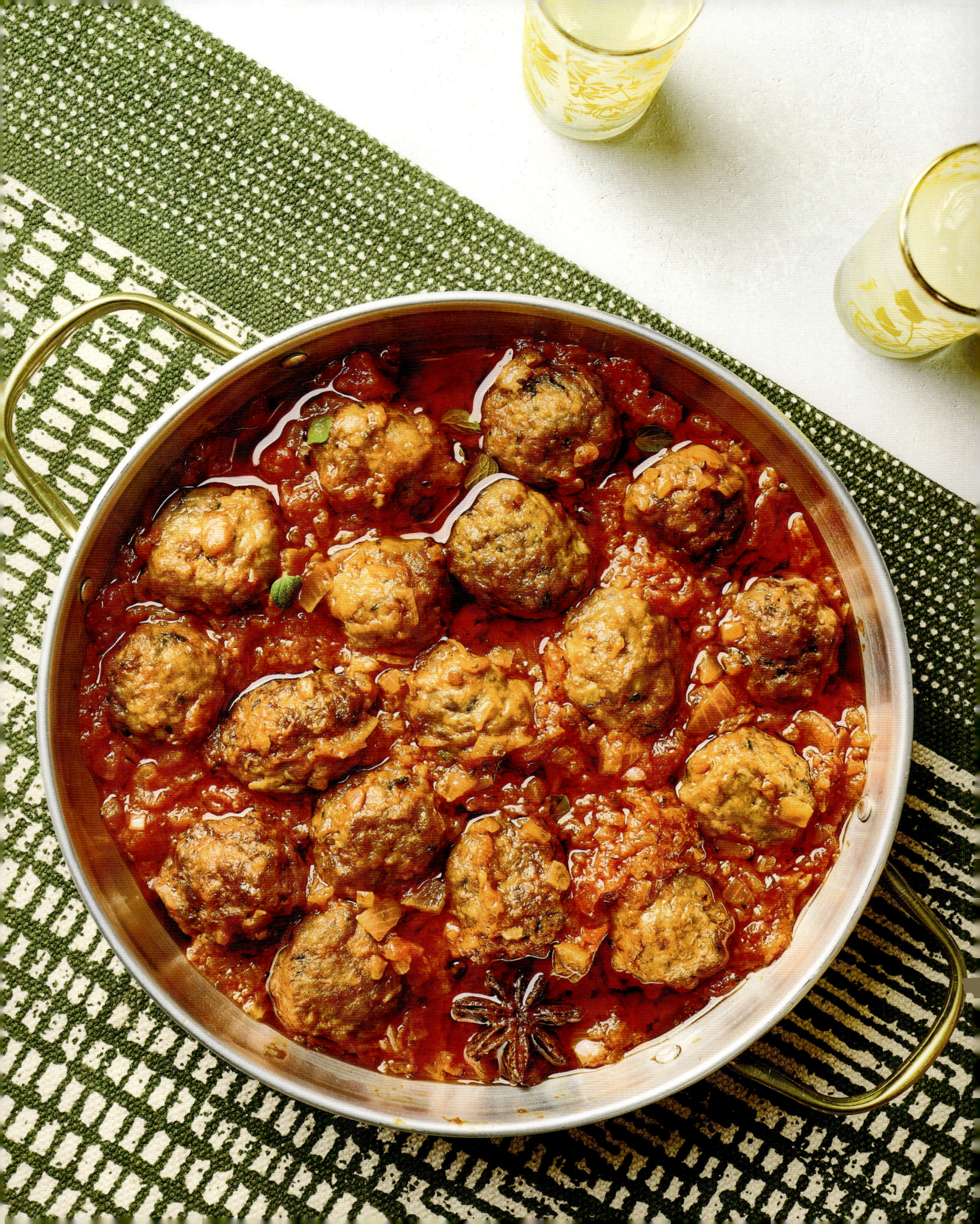

Keftedes
with Ouzo and Diced Tomatoes

I love to read about the evolution of family food businesses, and one of the most telling is that of the Katsogiannos family taverna in Drapetsona, a working-class neighborhood in southwestern Piraeus. Drapetsona means "the place of refuge for runaway slaves"— fitting to a degree, as this area was transformed by the establishment of a huge fertilizer factory in the early twentieth century and then by the arrival of the Greek refugees from Asia Minor in 1922. The taverna traces its roots to a decade later when its founder, Grigoris Katsogiannos first opened a little shop selling milk, butter, other dairy products, and a unique pudding made with grape must called moustalevria. *The little shop slowly began to sell more and more prepared foods until it became a full-fledged taverna by 1939. The family ran it for decades and eventually sold it to a passionate cook named Dora Stavridou, who kept the name and the old-world atmosphere intact. The food is still excellent, and these lovable Greek meatballs in an ouzo-infused tomato sauce are an especially delicious specialty!*

MAKES ABOUT 36 KEFTEDES

For the meatballs

3 to 4 slices stale white bread, crusts removed

1 cup milk

1½ pounds ground beef

½ pound ground pork

1 large onion, minced or grated

⅓ cup ouzo

½ cup chopped fresh mint

2 teaspoons dried Greek oregano

2 tablespoons extra-virgin Greek olive oil

2 large eggs, lightly beaten

Salt and freshly ground black pepper to taste

Vegetable oil, for frying

Flour, for dusting

For the sauce

¼ cup extra-virgin Greek olive oil

1 large onion, diced

1 carrot, finely diced

3 garlic cloves, finely chopped

2 cups canned diced tomatoes

½ cup ouzo

1 star anise

1 cup water

Salt and freshly ground black pepper to taste

2 strips orange zest

2 teaspoons dried Greek oregano

-recipe continues-

Make the meatballs: Line a rimmed baking sheet with parchment paper. Tear the bread into pieces and dampen it in a bowl with the milk, then squeeze the pieces to get as much moisture as possible out of them.

Place the ground meats, squeezed bread, onion, ouzo, mint, and oregano in a bowl and knead lightly to combine. Add the eggs and season with salt and pepper. Knead lightly. Take about 1 tablespoon at a time of the mixture and shape into balls the size of golf balls. Place the keftedes on the lined baking sheet, and when you're done with shaping the entire mixture, place the sheet in the fridge for 30 minutes so that the meatballs firm up a bit.

Meanwhile, make the sauce: Heat the olive oil in a large, wide pot over medium heat. Add the onion and sauté until soft and translucent, about 8 minutes. Stir in the diced carrot and cook for 2 minutes, then stir in the garlic. Add the tomatoes and bring to a boil. Add the ouzo and star anise and simmer for 5 minutes for the alcohol to cook off. Add the water and season to taste with salt and pepper. Add the orange zest and oregano and simmer for 15 to 20 minutes, until it starts to thicken.

While the sauce is simmering, fry the meatballs. Heat about 1 inch vegetable oil in a wide, deep skillet over medium heat. While the oil is heating, spread some flour on a large plate, season lightly with salt and pepper, and lightly dredge the first few keftedes, shaking off the flour by bouncing the keftedes one at a time in the palm of your hand. Using a spatula or kitchen tongs, carefully place 5 or 6 keftedes in the pan, being careful not to crowd them. Fry until browned on one side, then turn with the tongs to fry on the other side. Remove with a slotted spoon and drain on paper towels. Repeat with the remaining keftedes.

Carefully slide the keftedes into the sauce and continue cooking the sauce for about 25 more minutes, until thick and the meatballs are cooked through. Serve.

Tigania

PORK AND LEEKS WITH RED PEPPER FLAKES AND HERBS

There are still a few cafeneia left in Athenian neighborhoods that serve more than coffee or beer. Indeed, some of the best, if simplest, food can be found in these places, which are inexpensive neighborhood hangouts that usually attract a loyal and consistent clientele. You'll find things like black-eyed pea salad and fava on the menu, and simple meat dishes like tigania, bits of pork or sometimes chicken cooked up in a frying pan (tigani is the word for "frying pan," hence the name of this dish). Leeks and spices like red pepper flakes and even curry nowadays are typical additions to the meat.

MAKES 6 SERVINGS

1 cup water

3 leeks, whites only, halved lengthwise and cut crosswise ⅛ inch thick

½ cup extra-virgin Greek olive oil

1½ pounds boneless pork shoulder or leg, cut into 1-inch cubes

Salt and freshly ground black pepper to taste

½ to 1 teaspoon red pepper flakes

1 cup dry red wine

2 teaspoons Dijon mustard

1 teaspoon dried Greek oregano

Bring the water to a simmer in a large skillet over medium heat. Add the leeks and cook until the water evaporates, about 5 minutes.

Add the olive oil and heat over medium-high heat. Add the cubes of pork and cook, stirring, until the pork starts to brown. Season with salt and pepper. Sprinkle in the pepper flakes and add the red wine and mustard. Continue cooking until the pork is tender, about 20 minutes, and stir in the oregano about 5 minutes before removing from the heat. Serve.

The Last Resin Tappers of Attica

Necessity is the mother of invention. So it goes with what is arguably Greece's most famous and one of its most misunderstood wines: retsina, a white or rosé wine flavored with pine resin. Athenian tavernas would not exist without it, and Attica would not be known as a major wine-producing region if it weren't for this oft-maligned Greek wine.

Retsina is one of two officially designated traditional wines in Greece. It was born in ancient Greece when the most common way to store anything, from olive oil to wheat to wine, was in large clay amphora, or jugs. It didn't take long to discover that wine shipped or stored in these earthenware containers went bad quickly, because clay is porous and the wine oxidized.

The thick resin from the plentiful Aleppo pine trees was discovered to be a perfect sealant. But by the third century AD, the Romans had invented the wooden barrel, which even today stores wine best, and which the Greeks adopted, too. But they had grown fond of the piney resin in their wine, so they began adding it, not to prevent oxidation, but as an aroma. And so it is that the tradition invented thousands of years ago is still alive today.

Retsina, once maligned for its overtly rustic flavor, sometimes compared to turpentine, is now enjoying a renaissance. Because of its robust flavor, it is still considered by many to be the best wine to pair with a varied array of mezedes that are such a big part of the Greek table.

Just south of Athens lies the Kouvaras pine forest, where the Aleppo pine trees carpet the hilly landscape. It is here, a few years ago, that I met Ioannis and his son Harilaos, among the last resin tappers of Attica. In his mid-eighties, Ioannis has been tapping trees and collecting resin for sixty years. When we met, he was one of a small group of traditional vintners who still tap the local pine.

A tin is installed just below the cut to catch the slowly flowing resin. After a week, the resin is collected. The resin from the tins is transferred to a box. Any that has hardened is scraped out. A single tree can produce around 15 pounds of resin in a single year. They reserve some of the resin for their own retsina production, but most is sold to commercial wineries in the area. Classic retsina is made just like any white wine: from pressing to fermentation in steel tanks. The only difference is that a small amount of pine resin specifically from the Aleppo pine is added at the start of fermentation.

Retsina is produced in Attica, Viotia, and Evia, mainly from the regions' local Savatiano and Rhoditis grape varieties. There is also a rosé retsina called Kokkineli made with either the Rhoditis grape or more recently with Xinomavro or Assyrtiko.

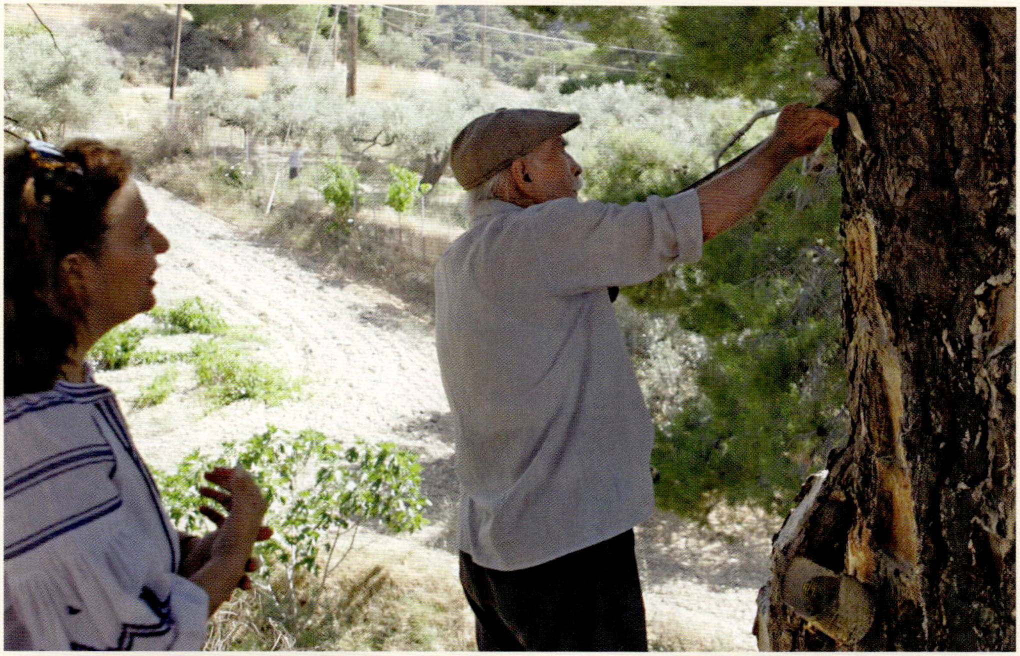

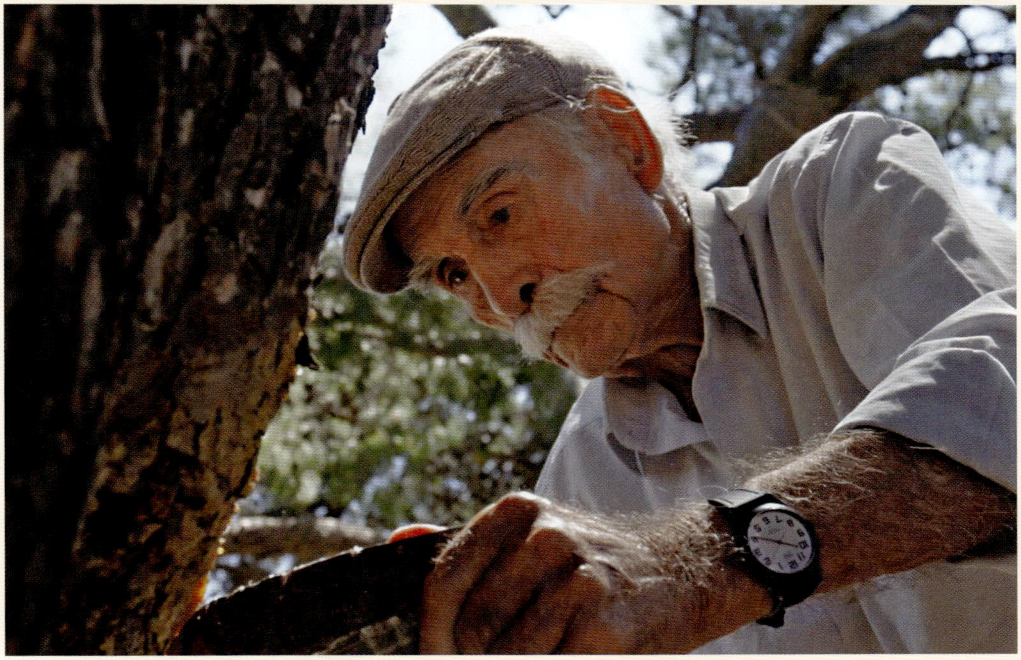

The Simplest Pan-Seared Lamb Chops

Chops, aka paidakia (pa-ee-DA-kia) are sometimes the stuff of near religious devotion for Athenians. Indeed, grilling is not something people typically do at home. Instead, they head to grill houses, called psistaries. *Some of the best are concentrated on the outskirts of the city, in places like Vari, along the Athenian Riviera, or Kalyvia, inland from the coast in Mesogeia. The city itself has its fair share of these smoky havens, too, some of them around for decades. The offerings are many, but chops are always top of the list, and they are most commonly cut from lamb or mutton.*

When I first moved to Greece, I always used to chuckle at another common menu item, chicken chops or ribs. Obviously, these don't really exist on the anatomy of a chicken, but in Greek tavernas they're strips of chicken usually cut from the thigh, then marinated and grilled.

Below, bowing to the unlikelihood of finding lamb or any other chops for that matter, on a balcony barbecue in Athens, the recommended cooking method is in a stovetop ridged grill pan, with a little olive oil and all the classic fixings.

MAKES 4 TO 6 SERVINGS

Extra-virgin Greek olive oil, as needed

2 pounds single-rib lamb chops

Salt and freshly ground black pepper to taste

1 to 2 tablespoons dried Greek oregano

3 lemons, cut into wedges, to serve

Drizzle enough olive oil to barely cover the surface of a 12- to 15-inch heavy, ridged grill pan and heat over high heat.

Place as many lamb chops as will fit in one layer in the pan, being careful not to crowd them, and sear on one side for 2 to 3 minutes. Season generously with salt and pepper. Using tongs, turn over to the other side. Sear for another minute or two, season the other side with salt and pepper, too, and transfer to a platter. Sprinkle with oregano, then tent with aluminum foil. Repeat with the remaining lamb chops, replenishing the oil as needed. Serve hot, with lemon wedges.

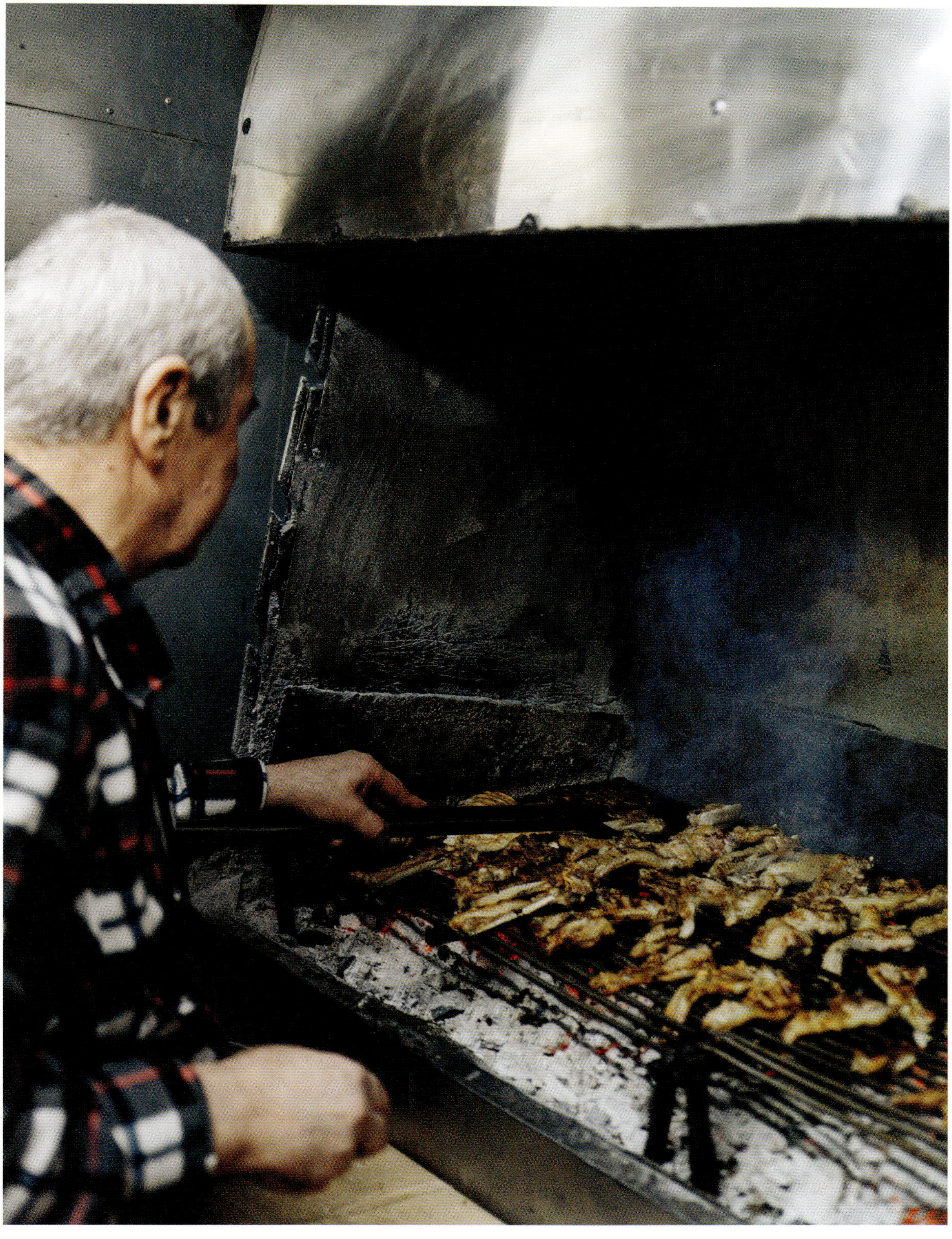

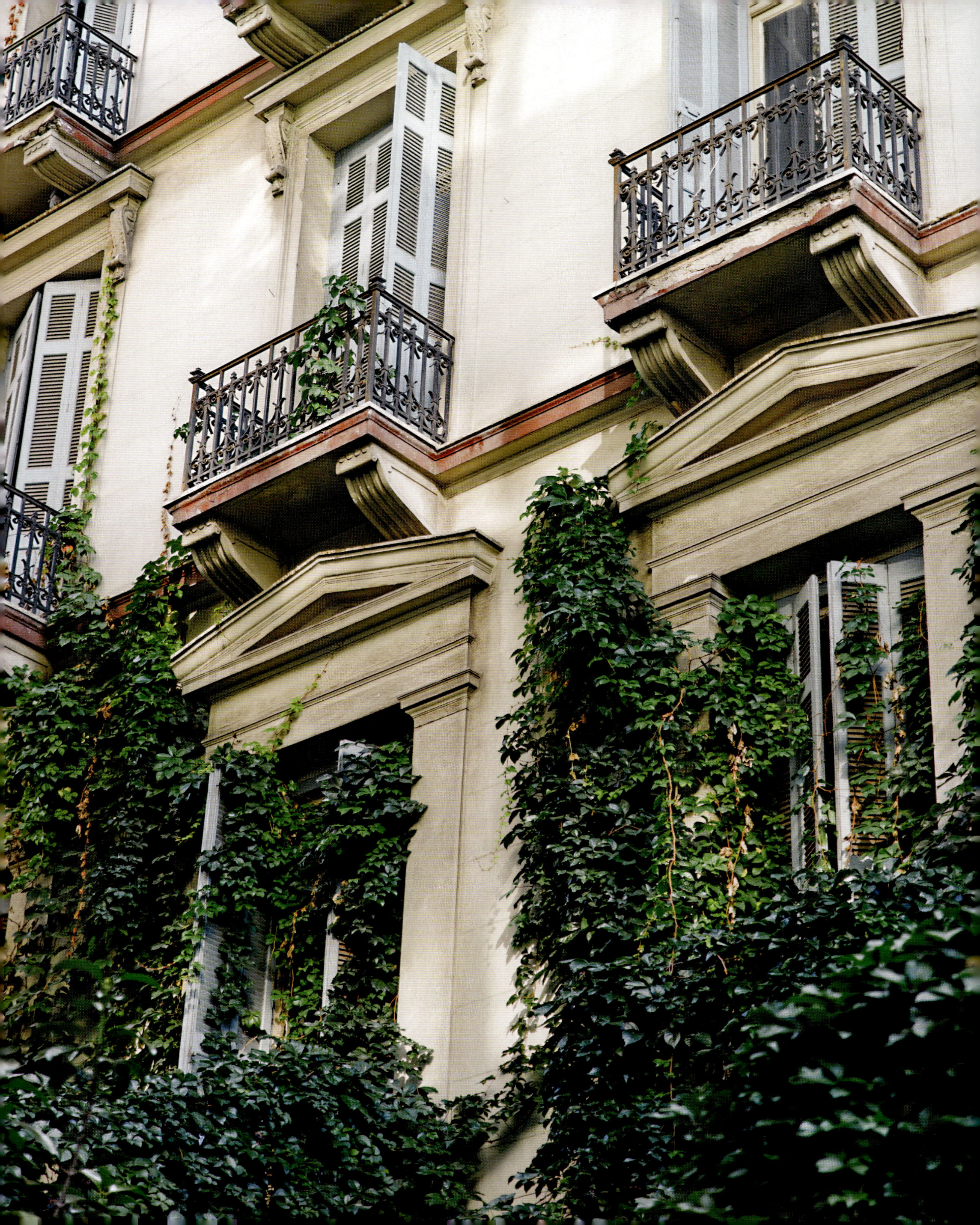

The Great Bourgeois Dishes of Athens

Athenians speak fondly of their urban, or "bourgeois," cuisine with dishes that call to mind Sunday meals, family values, and solid social mores, but also something less tangible: optimism and security. The great bourgeois dishes of Athens and Greece were born of hope, and a look to the future; but they were also born of a desire to shed parts of a collective past that were extraordinarily painful, impoverished, rural, and, finally, rife with war and hunger.

The bourgeois cuisine of Athens and other urban centers in Greece is, by most accounts, the cuisine that evolved on the heels of World War II and the Greek Civil War, and coincided both with the mass migration of Greeks from the countryside to Athens, as they searched for a better, more affluent, and modern life and with the segue from an agrarian to a more industrialized society. But the story is deeper than that and starts with the founding of the Greek state in 1830. To think about the bourgeois, or urban, cuisine of Athens is to think about the story of Greek food from its ancient roots to its rural depths and, finally, to its transformation, replete with European aesthetics and a little French flair, in the first part of the twentieth century, then again after the two world wars, and, finally, today in our anything-goes barrier-free e-world. Inherent in those trajectories are complexities that go way beyond the dinner plate, straight to the heart of Greek national identity as it is expressed through food.

The First Flavors of the West

The Greek Revolution, which began in 1821, led to Greece's emancipation from four hundred years of Ottoman rule. When the Greek state was founded in 1830, the European powers that supported the Greek cause installed a Bavarian prince, Otto, then only seventeen, as king. The year was 1832. His reign lasted thirty years, and the palace was what is now the Greek parliament building at Syntagma Square. The establishment of his rule brought with it a new focus, toward the West, and around his court a whole new social class, mostly of wealthy diaspora Greeks, swarmed. They embraced European mannerisms and foods, and by doing so planted the seeds of what I like to describe as delicious culinary conflict, between Greece's rural—peasant—traditions and the newfound flavors of the West. That pull between tradition and modernity, East and West, old and new has provided the fodder for a tasty tug-of-war playing out in the Greek kitchen ever since, in various transformations and waves.

Syntagma Square in the nineteenth century was a place of energetic construction, from the center of a nascent dusty small town to the heart of the European capital it finally is today. The courtly swarms made for good business, and by the 1840s, cafés, restaurants, and pastry shops filled the streets around the palace. Some were famous for more than a century. The most iconic paean to the look-West embrace of the Greek upper classes still stands: Athens's most opulent hotel to this day is the 150-year-old Grande Bretagne, one of the finest neoclassical buildings in the city, situated directly across the square from present-day Parliament. A few cafés, in particular Anatoli ("Dawn," open from 1845 to 1969) and Zaharatos (1888 to 1963), became *the* places for powerbrokers of the era, the latter so much so that it was dubbed a second, more democratic parliament. For nineteenth- and early twentieth-century chefs and pâtissiers, to cook in the palace kitchens or hone one's skills at Cecil, the most famous patisserie of the day, was among the highest honors and a fast lane to success.

But for ordinary people, the diet was still agrarian and simple, with hints of ancient foods that had survived, flourished, and nourished Greeks through the ages. Beans and legumes, greens, trahana, olives, seasonal vegetables, sheep and goat's milk cheeses, and lamb, goat, or rooster (with homemade noodles—still a popular comfort food today) were the telltale ingredients of Greek cooking, which was derived from the land and from the country's rural heritage. These age-old staples were disparaged as barnyard backwardness by courtly, snobbish Athenians of the time, whose tastes ran to all things European, from French, Dutch, and other Western European charcuterie and cheeses to imported Bordeaux and Burgundy wines.

In food, this story of forfeiting rural Greekness for some notion of Europeanness was to repeat itself a few more times, catapulted by historical upheavals like the Asia Minor Catastrophe in 1922, two world wars and the Greek Civil War, migrations en mass, entrance into the EU, and the pervasive influence nowadays of the internet. But what Greeks refer to so fondly as their urban or bourgeois cuisine is the food seasoned with western brushstrokes that evolved with postwar reconstruction in the 1950s and '60s.

Some History

The aftermath of World War I and the Asia Minor Catastrophe saw more than a million Greek refugees, many from thriving urban centers like Smyrna and Constantinople, pour into Greece from present-day Turkey, bringing with them a culinary sophistication and cosmopolitan aesthetic that was perfumed with all the spices of Anatolia. Around that time, Nikos Tselementes published his first cookbook, single-handedly shifting the direction of traditional Greek cooking into something hybrid and Eurocentric, all in the name of modernity. His legacy is controversial, but his recipes are still a big part of our culinary vernacular. The Greek table was suddenly laden with a heady mix of rural traditional foods, Anatolian exoticism, and béchamel sauce, all melding together but also competing to be the definitive lexicon of a national culinary identity.

Starvation changed things. Many Greeks in their sixties, myself included, joke lovingly about our parents and grandparents, who were obsessed with feeding us, and our visions of them chasing us and our children around the house or playground with a spoon, lest we feel the slightest pang of hunger, seem funny now. But overnourishing was a sign of love, spawned by the palpable fear of hunger. More Greeks died of starvation during World War II than of wartime injuries; Athens was hit particularly hard, with more than forty thousand people starving to death during the German occupation between 1941 and 1944.

Those memories, seared forever into the consciousness of the war generation, ironically helped usher in the era of *astiki kouzina*—the rich, more European (read that as French) urban or bourgeois cuisine that so many in my generation associate with family meals and emotional as well as physical security. For our parents and grandparents, *astiki kouzina* was their nod to and embrace of everything that was modern in their heyday, everything that would help them turn the page from a war-torn or backward rural past toward a new future, filled with optimism and hope.

The postwar years marked the second time in recent history when Greeks turned their backs on rurality in favor of some notion of European-seasoned modernity. My in-laws, for example, who were teenagers during the occupation and lucky enough to survive, couldn't bring themselves ever again to eat the likes of cornmeal (bobota), black-eyed peas, or carob because these were virtually the only foods they had for the three long years between 1941 and '44. Cooking them in a postwar kitchen just brought back the harrowing memories they had set their minds and psyches on forgetting. In yet another twist of irony, the last two decades have seen a resurgence of these traditional foods, absent from the collective psyche of younger Greeks with no such wrenching memories, and resuscitated as neotraditional foods. Ancient, agrarian foods and recipes have gotten a facelift in today's Athenian kitchens, appearing in newfangled ways that our ancestors couldn't possibly have imagined. But that's a story for another time.

During the years of postwar reconstruction, in the 1950s and '60s, hundreds of thousands of Greeks from the countryside emigrated to Athens, looking for economic opportunity and a better way of life. Within a decade a solid middle class had been established. In the 1950s, too, Athens saw the arrival of another wave of urbane Greeks, this time not from Asia Minor but from Egypt, when President Abdel Nasser expelled all foreigners in 1956. The migrations from rural areas to cities, the influx of Egyptian Greeks, and the earlier arrival of Asia Minor Greeks, coupled with a newfound spirit of hope as Greeks rebuilt the country, all had a profound effect on cuisine. Lifestyles and eating habits changed, but so did kitchen equipment. Modernity entered the kitchen in the guise of convenience: Blenders, mixers, electric ovens, and pressure cookers were the newfound accoutrements of a postwar, contemporary Greek home.

New ingredients heralded in an era of modern convenience, too, among them flavor cubes for making broth, frozen phyllo pastry, and a hideous concoction called Morfat, an alabaster-white, paste-like, sweet pastry "cream" made of skim milk and vegetable fat that was spread onto celebratory tortes with abandon. Meat consumption increased exponentially; rice, once an expensive import, was now grown on Greek soil thanks to agronomists from the Marshall Plan who taught Greek farmers how to cultivate it; new herbs and spices and a wider range of produce were all becoming more readily available. Urbanization also brought the supermarket to Athens (and all of Greece), which had forever been characterized by the neighborhood shops of countless independent small merchants.

These next pages are devoted to the bourgeois, Western-facing foods of optimism and to a nostalgia for the values that came with cooking, serving, and enjoying them. The recipes speak to the comingling of familiar Greek ingredients with new ones and with new techniques, and to the desire to shed some of the relics of an agrarian past and forge ahead with a modern mindset and menu.

Whether that was or is truly possible among a people for whom the past is so palpably visible is another question. Are moussaka and pastitsio, comforting affectations, slathered in a French cream sauce, really Greek? Are honey, olives, oil, and a whole host of other foods that trace back to antiquity the real—and only—stuff of true Greek cooking? Should the Greco-bourgeois likes of beloved dishes such as Kotopoulo (Chicken) Milanese, a famed "Greek" dish of the 1960s and '70s (page 237); Noua, aka noix, or pot roast (page 224); and a uniquely Hellenic interpretation (some might say slaughter) of the classic French soufflé (page 227) that would have Carême turning in his grave, even be included into the national cuisine we call Greek? In my humble opinion, honed from a spirit of expansiveness, the answer is a resounding *yes*, so long as the most basic question of all is also answered in the positive: "Does it taste good?" *Yes!*

Fish à La Spetsiota

Fish à la Spetsiota, or "in the manner of Spetses," an island in the Saronic Gulf, not too far from Athens, is one of the most beloved traditional ways to prepare fish, especially in the summer, when tomatoes are ripe. This dish is often made with fish like red pandora, similar to snapper, or gilthead bream, both common in the waters around Spetses. It was popularized by the great early-twentieth-century Greek chef Nikos Tselementes, who was the first to add bread crumbs to the recipe, the better for making it a little heartier, giving it some texture, and soaking up any excess liquid from the tomatoes, which, when picked ripe from a Greek summer crop, are quite juicy.

MAKES 4 TO 6 SERVINGS

6 ripe tomatoes, peeled, cored, and coarsely chopped

3 garlic cloves, chopped

⅓ cup chopped fresh flat-leaf parsley

½ cup dry white wine

Salt and freshly ground black pepper to taste

2 pounds fish fillets, preferably from red snapper, bream, porgies, cod, or halibut

½ cup plain bread crumbs

½ cup extra-virgin Greek olive oil, plus more for the pan

Drain the tomatoes in a colander for 15 minutes. Transfer to a medium bowl, add the garlic, parsley, and wine, and let stand for 30 minutes.

Meanwhile, lightly salt the fish and let it stand, refrigerated, for 30 minutes.

Preheat the oven to 350°F.

Season the fish with a little additional salt and pepper. Place in a lightly oiled baking dish. Spoon the tomato mixture over the fish and top with the bread crumbs. Drizzle with the olive oil. Bake for 20 to 25 minutes, until the fish is fork-tender, the tomato topping dense and juicy, and the bread crumbs golden. Serve.

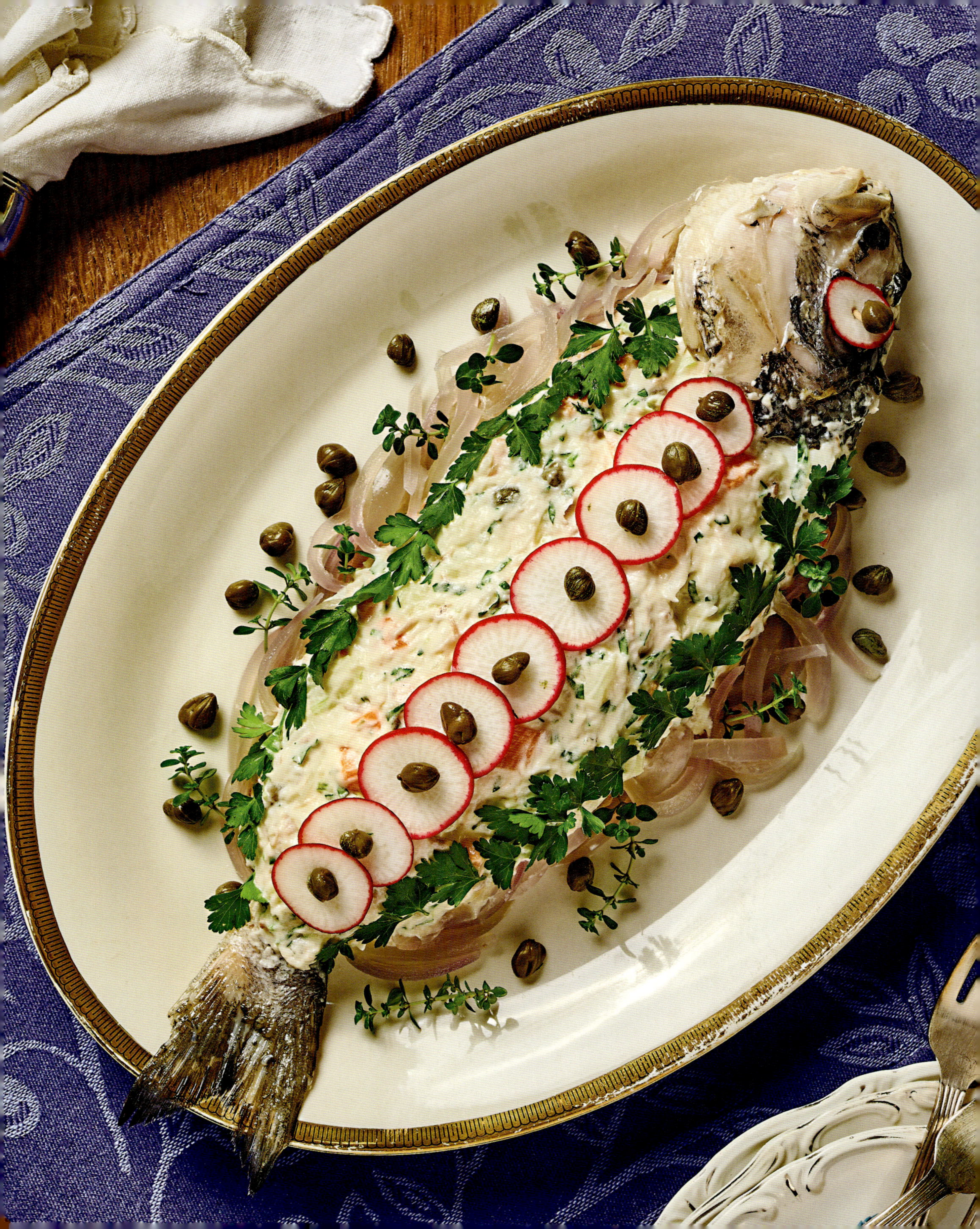

Athinaiki Mayioneza
ATHENIAN MAYONNAISE

It's hard to pinpoint when, exactly, this classic dish, one of the few, if only, recipes to be identified as Athenian, first made its appearance in the local kitchens of Athenian homemakers. It was very popular in the 1970s and was the star of special-occasion buffets. I vividly recall my mother-in-law making it for holiday and Sunday tables, bringing it to the table all sculpted in the shape of a fish and set on a platter, with capers, cornichons, and carrots to look like eyes, mouth, and scales. It might seem ironic that the name of the dish mentions the mayonnaise but not the fish, and that's because to make mayonnaise at home was considered difficult, and so the dish was a test of sorts by which the skill of a home cook was gauged.

By some accounts, Athenian mayonnaise was a way to make good use of leftover fish, by dressing it up the next day and transforming it into something special and visually appealing. It wasn't necessary to use expensive fish for that. Bakaliaros (cod) was common, although if it was part of a truly special occasion, a more expensive catch, such as grouper, was preferred.

The recipe is, by many accounts, a combination of the innate sense of economy of traditional Greek home cooks and the fusion of a beloved salad called Rossiki ("Russian"), a potato salad studded with carrots, capers, and cornichons and dressed, of course, in the very best renditions with homemade mayo.

One thing is for certain: Athinaiki mayoneza is the one of the handful of bourgeois recipes that defined a generation, creating food memories strong enough to keep the dish alive today, sometimes transformed into twenty-first-century renditions. The following version honors the classic!

MAKES 4 TO 6 SERVINGS

1 onion, cut in half

8 to 10 medium celery stalks

2 carrots

½ bunch fresh flat-leaf parsley

2 potatoes, cut in half

Sea salt and freshly ground black pepper to taste

2 pounds fresh whole grouper, sea bream, or cod, gutted and cleaned

Capers and cornichons, for garnish

For the Greek mayonnaise

1 large egg yolk

2 teaspoons strained fresh lemon juice

1 teaspoon mustard powder or Dijon mustard

1 cup extra-virgin Greek olive oil

Sea salt and freshly ground black pepper to taste

-recipe continues-

Add the onion, celery, carrots, parsley, and potatoes to a pot, cover with water to by 2 inches, and bring to a boil. Season to taste with salt and pepper and reduce to a simmer. Cook the vegetables for about 30 minutes, or until everything is tender but still a little al dente.

Meanwhile, prepare the mayonnaise: In a bowl, whisk together the egg yolk, lemon juice, and mustard until smooth. Very slowly, a few drops at a time, whisk in about ¼ cup of the olive oil, allowing time for it to emulsify after each addition. Going slowly is very important, lest the mayonnaise break up. Once about ¼ cup oil has been worked in and emulsified, add the remaining ¾ cup oil in a slow, steady stream, whisking all the while. At the end, when it all comes together, season with salt and pepper. Cover and refrigerate until ready to use.

Wrap and tie the fish in cheesecloth to keep it from falling apart while poaching. Carefully place the whole fish in the pot with the vegetables and simmer it gently to poach for 15 to 20 minutes, depending on the size of the fish. A general rule of thumb is about 10 minutes per pound.

As soon as it's ready, using two large slotted spoons, transfer the fish very carefully to a cutting board. Let it cool a little, remove the cheesecloth, and clean the fish thoroughly, removing the central bone and other, smaller bones, but keeping the head and tail intact. As you clean and shred the flesh, try to keep the fish flesh in largish chunks.

Place the fish in a mixing bowl and add the capers and 2 tablespoons of the mayonnaise, or more as needed to make a moist mixture that holds together.

Reconstruct the fish on a platter, placing the head and tail at either end, and use the boiled vegetables as a garnish around the fish. Top the fish with the rest of the mayonnaise and create eyes, a mouth, and, if desired, scales using capers, cornichons, and thinly sliced boiled carrots from the stock. Serve.

ΛΑΥΡΑΚΙΑ
ΚΕΦΑΛΟΝΙΑΣ
6 98
ΛΑΥΡΑΚΙΑ
ΚΕΦΑΛΟΝΙΑΣ
4.98
ΤΣΙΠΟΥΡΑ
ΚΕΦΑΛΟΝΙΑΣ
5 98

Lahanodolmades Avgolemono
CABBAGE ROLLS WITH EGG-LEMON SAUCE

This dish, variations of which are popular all over the Balkans and into Eastern Europe, is considered one of the great dishes of Greek bourgeois cooking. Perhaps because it requires skill, time, and dexterity at every level is it considered so special. The cook has to know the right kind of whole cabbage head to buy, and how to prepare and break apart the leaves to roll them properly, trimming around the thick vein. Then there is the egg-lemon sauce, and how to best temper it in order to achieve the desired result: emulsified creamy perfection. Stuffed cabbage is a winter dish in Greece, and as the fall progresses into cooler and cooler weather, cabbages appear at the neighborhood markets with more and more frequency, piled up like cannonballs on table after table at neighborhood produce markets. Accommodating (and shrewd) merchants will cut a couple down the middle to show their hearts: the tight-leaved ones are best for salad, while those whose inner leaves are loose and airy are best suited for lahanodolmades because it's easier to break them apart.

MAKES 6 TO 8 SERVINGS

For the cabbage rolls

Salt and freshly ground black pepper to taste

1 large or 2 medium whole cabbage heads (about 5 pounds total)

2 tablespoons extra-virgin Greek olive oil, plus more as needed

1 tablespoon unsalted butter

2 large onions, finely chopped

1 pound ground beef

½ pound ground pork

½ cup short-grain white rice

½ cup chopped fresh flat-leaf parsley

½ cup chopped fresh dill

1 large egg, lightly beaten

1 cup sauerkraut, drained (optional)

For the avgolemono

3 large eggs yolks

Strained juice of 2 lemons

Bring a large pot of water to a rolling boil and season with salt. Cut into the cabbage at its base to remove the stem. Gently plunge the cabbage head into the water and simmer it for 8 to 10 minutes, until the leaves are softened and translucent. Remove with a slotted spoon and set aside to cool.

While the cabbage is simmering, prepare the filling. Heat the oil and butter in a large skillet over medium heat until the butter melts. Add the onions and cook until translucent and soft, about 8 minutes. Add the ground meats and sauté, turning, until browned, 12 to 15 minutes. Season with salt and pepper. Remove from the heat and let cool slightly. Add the rice, parsley, dill, and egg. Knead to combine and set aside.

By now the cabbage should be cool enough to handle. If not using sauerkraut, remove the small, unusable cabbage leaves from the boiled head and shred. Oil the bottom of a large, wide pot and strew the sauerkraut or shredded small cabbage leaves on the bottom.

Gently pull apart the remaining leaves from the cabbage head. Halve the largest leaves if desired. Place 2 to 3 teaspoons of the meat filling inside each cabbage leaf, depending on its size. Roll up the leaves to make cylinders, folding in the edges to keep the filling from spilling out. Place seam side down in the pot. Continue to form the rolls, placing them snuggly next to each other. If there are more rolls than fit in one layer, start a second layer.

Add enough water to cover the rolls by 1 inch and cover with an inverted plate. Bring to a simmer over medium heat, then reduce and simmer gently for about 1½ hours, or until the cabbage is very tender and the rice is cooked. There should be 1½ to 2 cups of liquid total left in the pot, which you'll need to make the avgolemono.

In a medium bowl, whisk the egg yolks until very frothy, then slowly whisk in the lemon juice. Take a ladleful of the hot pot juices and drop by drop add them to the egg-lemon mixture, whisking vigorously all the while, until you've incorporated the full ladle. Repeat with a second ladleful. Pour the avgolemono into the pot, tilt it back and forth to distribute it evenly, and serve hot.

Moscharaki Lemonato

LEMONY BRAISED BEEF

Meat stews and roasts, especially veal or beef, were almost always reserved for a Sunday or holiday meal, and there are many variations on the stew theme, from lemony to tomato-based. This comforting dish is grandma food at its finest.

MAKES 6 TO 8 SERVINGS

½ cup extra-virgin Greek olive oil

2½ pounds boneless beef shoulder or neck, cut into 2-inch cubes and patted dry with paper towels

Salt and freshly ground black pepper to taste

2 large yellow onions, finely chopped

4 garlic cloves, minced

½ cup dry white wine

1½ cups beef or chicken stock

3 bay leaves

4 to 6 fresh thyme sprigs

Grated zest and strained juice of 1 large lemon

Heat the oil in a large, wide pot over medium-high heat. Using kitchen tongs and working in batches as necessary, add the beef pieces in a single layer. Sear on one side for about 7 minutes, then turn carefully to brown on the other side and all around. Season with salt and pepper, then transfer the beef with a slotted spoon to a bowl or plate. Add the onions to the pot, reduce the heat to medium, and cook until wilted and translucent, 7 to 8 minutes. Stir in the garlic. Deglaze by carefully and slowly pouring in the white wine and scraping the bottom with a wooden spoon or spatula to get all the tasty bits.

Return the beef and any accumulated juices to the pan and add the stock, bay leaves, thyme sprigs, and a little more salt and pepper. Bring to a simmer. Skim the foam off the surface of the liquid as the beef simmers for the first 10 minutes or so. Cover the pan and simmer the beef for 2 to 2½ hours, or until it's meltingly tender and left with very little juice in the pan, which should be thick, almost gelatinous, by the end of the cooking.

Remove the bay leaves and thyme sprigs and add the lemon zest and juice. Simmer for 5 more minutes. Remove from the heat and serve.

Moscharaki Kokinisto

BEEF STEW

Melting. Syrupy. Lush. These might be some words, roughly translated from the Greek, to describe this most beloved of meat stews on the Sunday table.

MAKES 6 TO 8 SERVINGS

⅓ cup extra-virgin Greek olive oil

2 to 2½ pounds beef chuck, cut into 1½- to 2-inch cubes and patted dry with paper towels

Sea salt to taste

2 large red onions, finely chopped

3 garlic cloves, finely chopped

1 carrot, left whole

2 celery stalks, coarsely chopped

3 cups canned diced tomatoes

½ cup dry white wine

2 cups chicken, beef, or vegetable stock

2 bay leaves

4 fresh oregano sprigs

3 allspice berries

1 small cinnamon stick

Heat the olive oil in a large, wide pot over high heat. Using kitchen tongs and working in batches as necessary, add the beef pieces in a single layer. Sear until one side is browned, for about 7 minutes, then turn carefully to brown on the other side and all around. Season with salt, then transfer the meat with a slotted spoon to a bowl or plate.

Add the onions to the pot, turn the heat down to medium, and cook, stirring, until translucent, about 8 minutes. Stir in the garlic. Return the meat and any accumulated juices to the pot. Add the whole carrot and celery stalks and nestle them between the pieces of meat. Pour in the canned tomatoes, wine, and enough stock to come about three-quarters of the way up the meat. Add the bay leaves, oregano, allspice berries, and cinnamon stick. Season with salt and pepper. Turn the heat down to low, cover, and simmer for about 2 hours, or until the meat practically melts on the fork when pierced. Serve.

Noua

ATHENIAN POT ROAST

If there is one retro meat dish that epitomizes the optimistic tables of the 1960s and '70s in Athens (and Greece), it's noua, or pot roast, sometimes made with a lemony sauce, but most often made with a tomato-based sauce and the occasional addition of mushrooms, if one happened to be a tad more adventurous. They were usually canned!

Noua was one of the recipes that spoke of growing affluence in an ever-more-urbanized city, and it denoted having "arrived" economically. The fact that it was always referred to by its French name (from noix, *which literally means "walnut," but also refers to the round or eye round of beef) also spoke to this dish's clear place among the bourgeois class; I still have clear memories of Greek ladies with their gray-blue coiffed hair and their de rigueur pearls and pumps, sipping coffee and speaking French together at the cafés in the well-heeled northern suburb where we raised our family. French was the language of the upper classes who prepared their noua for Sunday lunch, knowing just how to cook this lean, boneless cut (typically eye of round, chuck, or rump roast) so that it was succulent but well done, which is how Greeks prefer their meats, and how to slice it thin enough to be elegant but not so much so as to crumble, and in such a way that every piece had a generous but judicious spoonful of pan juices and a large side of buttery Bundt-pan molded pilaf to go with it. I sometimes like to serve it with simple roasted or mashed potatoes.*

MAKES 6 TO 8 SERVINGS

½ cup extra-virgin Greek olive oil

1 (2½-pound) beef eye round, rump, or chuck round, at room temperature

2 yellow onions, chopped

2 medium carrots, peeled and cut into ½-inch rounds

2 celery stalks, chopped

2 canned whole plum tomatoes

Salt and freshly ground black pepper to taste

2 bay leaves

¾ cup dry white wine

4 cups low-sodium chicken stock or bone broth, heated

Heat the olive oil in a large Dutch oven over medium-high heat. Add the meat and cook, turning it as it browns until all sides are nicely seared. Carefully remove it with kitchen tongs or a slotted spoon and transfer to a plate. Tent it with aluminum foil to keep it warm.

Reduce the heat to medium and add the onions, carrots, and celery. Cook, stirring, for 8 to 10 minutes, until translucent and softened. Squeeze the tomatoes over the other vegetables. Return the meat to the pot along with any accumulated juices, season it generously with salt and pepper, and add the bay leaves and wine. When the wine cooks off, add enough stock to come about halfway up the meat. Cover, turn the heat down to low, and simmer for 1½ to 2 hours, or until the meat is very tender.

Transfer the meat to a platter and tent again with aluminum foil. Remove the bay leaves. Puree the pot juices with an immersion blender or transfer to the bowl of a food processor and puree until very smooth, then return to the pot. Reduce over medium heat and simmer until thick, about 5 minutes.

To serve, cut the beef into thin slices and spoon the pot juices on top.

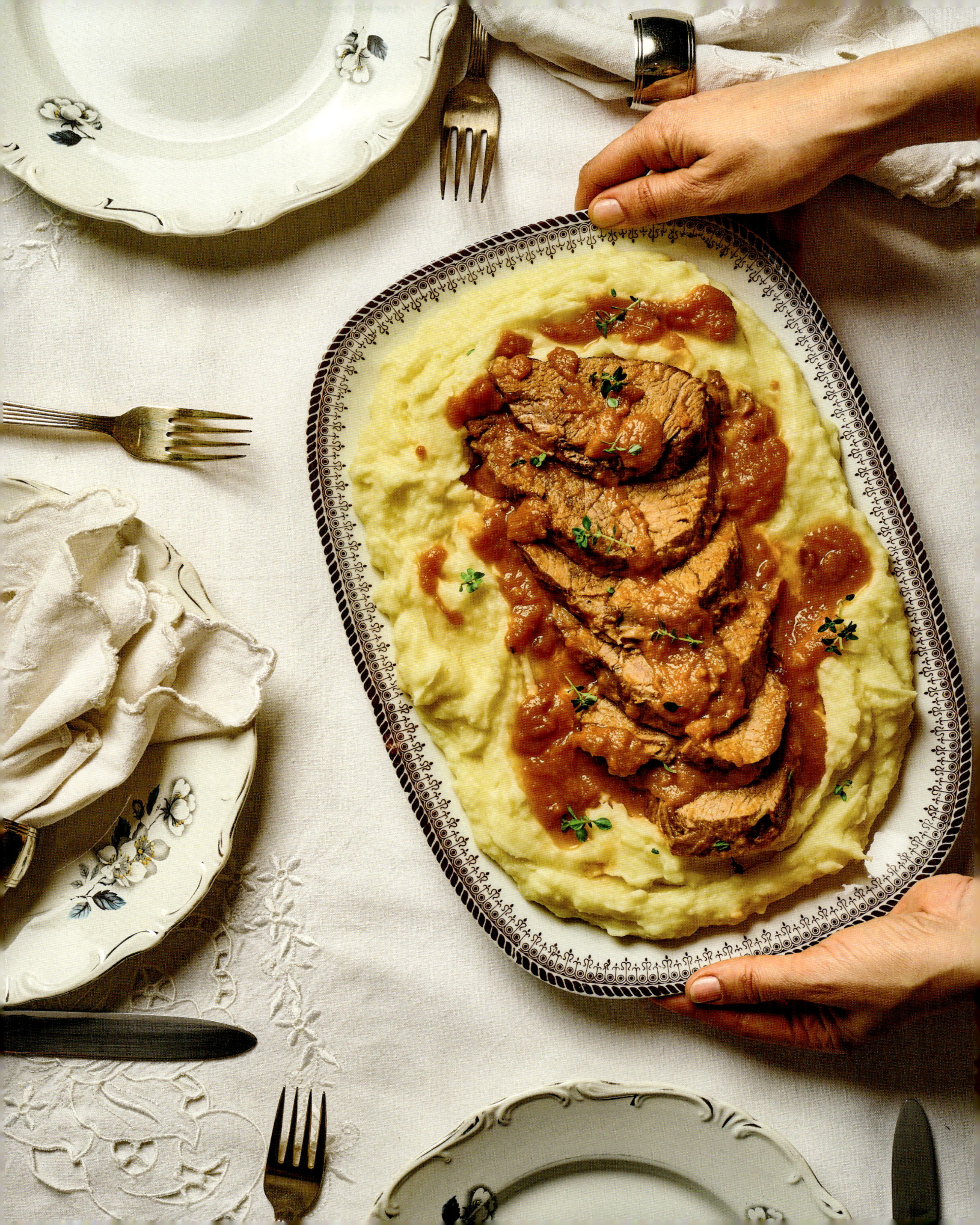

Yiouvetsi

HOMEY, COMFORTING BEEF BAKED WITH ORZO

Although the word yiouvetsi *comes from the Turkish* guvec, *which means "clay pot," referring to the vessel in which it is traditionally prepared, yiouvetsi (beef, chicken, or lamb baked with orzo and an aromatic tomato sauce) is the summation of all that is comforting in the Greek kitchen. It still is often the stuff of a Sunday meal, the kind that housewives prepared at home but men carried to the local bread baker on Sunday morning to cook, because it was the wife's "day off." Indeed, the custom of carrying a tray of Sunday lunch to be baked at the local fourno faded as recently as the late 1980s.*

Yiouvetsi quickly segued from the annals of Ottoman cooking and into the Greek vernacular, becoming a classic Greek dish distinguished by the addition of orzo, so much so that it was immortalized as early as 1903 in a famous short story by the Greek novelist Alexandros Papadiamantis, who describes the protagonist in "O Kakomis" ("The Porter") heading to the baker every day at noon, when yiouvetsi came out of the oven, and enjoying it cross-legged on a small table in the shop before taking his afternoon siesta.

These days, yiouvetsi is up for grabs at the hands of contemporary chefs and food writers who make it in countless new ways, with mushrooms or squid in place of meat, or with sausages or wild boar. The clay-pot reference has succumbed to obscurity; now yiouvetsi pretty much means almost anything baked with orzo. The following recipe, though, pays homage to the classic, so if you've got a clay pot, dust it off.

MAKES 6 TO 8 SERVINGS

½ cup extra-virgin Greek olive oil

1 large onion, finely chopped

2½ pounds boneless beef chuck, cut into 2-inch cubes

½ cup dry red wine

Salt and freshly ground black pepper to taste

1½ cups canned diced tomatoes

2 tablespoons tomato paste diluted in ½ cup water

2 bay leaves

1 cinnamon stick

4 allspice berries

2 to 5 cups vegetable stock, bone broth, or water

1 pound orzo

Boiling water, as needed

Heat the olive oil in a large, wide, flameproof clay pot or ovenproof pot, such as cast iron or enamel, over medium-high heat. Add the onion and sauté until translucent and softened, about 8 minutes. Add the meat and let it brown on all sides, turning the pieces with tongs. Deglaze with the red wine, pouring it into the pan and letting the alcohol cook off, 3 to 5 minutes, stirring with a wooden spoon. Season with salt and pepper, then stir in the tomatoes and diluted tomato paste. Add the bay leaves, cinnamon stick, and allspice berries.

Add enough stock to come about two-thirds of the way up the pot. Bring to a fast simmer, then reduce the heat to low, cover, and simmer slowly for about 1 hour 15 minutes, until the meat is tender.

Preheat the oven to 375°F.

Add the orzo to the pot, spreading it evenly around the morsels of meat, then add enough boiling water to cover by 2 inches. Season the pasta with salt and pepper. Cover and place in the hot oven. Bake for 45 minutes or so, until the pasta is tender and the meat meltingly so. Remove the bay leaves and serve.

Athenian Housewife's False Soufflé

Sunday meals with the family were once long and lingering affairs. The tradition is still alive, if a little more anemic, as people are busier and the family structure isn't as ironclad as it once was. But when I was a young bride and then a young mother, it went without saying that we'd go to my in-laws' for Sunday lunch. The array of recipes in this chapter were the kinds of dishes my mother-in-law would prepare, always with a keen, if hopelessly indiscreet eye to making her one and only son happy! Soufflé was among them, a source of pride, even if it wasn't exactly what Antonin Carême would have envisioned. A Greek soufflé, straight out of the magazine pages of the time, was about excess and not technique, a superfluous overflowing concoction of cheeses and ham and béchamel baked in a relatively shallow pan between layers of white bread! But it was great in its own way, too.

MAKES 4 TO 6 SERVINGS

1 cup (2 sticks) unsalted butter, softened

1 (1-pound) loaf white bread, sliced

¾ pound coarsely grated kasseri cheese

¾ pound coarsely grated graviera or other mild, nutty yellow sheep's milk cheese, or Gruyère

½ pound coarsely grated Greek kefalotyri or other hard, yellow grating cheese

1 cup grated Parmigiano

½ pound sliced deli ham, diced

4 large eggs, slightly beaten

6 cups whole milk

Salt and freshly ground black pepper to taste

Grated nutmeg to taste

Preheat the oven to 350°F. Lightly butter a 9 x 13-inch glass or ceramic baking dish.

Place enough bread slices in one layer, trimming them if necessary, on the bottom of the baking dish. Generously butter the surface of the bread.

Combine the cheeses and ham, tossing to mix well, and sprinkle half the mixture over the bread. Cover the surface with another layer of bread, trimming as needed. Butter the surface of the second layer of bread and sprinkle the remaining cheese-and-ham mixture on top.

In a medium bowl, whisk together the eggs, milk, salt, pepper, and nutmeg and pour the mixture over the surface of the pan, tilting so that it is evenly distributed. Bake for about 30 minutes, or until golden and bubbling. Serve hot.

The Legacy of Nikos Tselementes and the Reinvention of Greek Cuisine

In a chapter on the bourgeois cuisine of Greece—indeed, in any discussion of Greek food over the last century and some—it would be an oversight to omit mention of Nikos Tselementes, the country's first celebrity chef and someone who single-handedly reshaped Greek cuisine, edging it westward, away from its peasant roots and Ottoman influences by imbuing it with French sauces and techniques that forever changed the table. His influence was so great and lasted so long that his surname became synonymous with cookbooks, whether or not he was the author.

Tselementes was born in 1878 in the village of Exambela on the Cycladic island of Sifnos, the son of a chef, but he grew up in Athens, where he finished high school. His first taste of the cooking life came from his experience working in his father's and uncle's restaurant in Faliro, along the coast just outside the center of the Greek capital. He then went on to study cooking in Vienna, returned, and cooked for various embassies. In 1910, he started publishing a cooking magazine called *Odigos Mageirikis* (*Cooking Guide*), which was a combination of recipes, nutritional information, and tips, all aimed at the literate, therefore upper-crust, Greek homemaker who was finding her way in an evolving new nation eager to embrace a new identity more closely associated with the West.

Almost a decade later he managed the Hotel Hermes in the center of the city, then left in 1920 for the United States, where he cooked in some of the finest restaurants of the era before returning to Greece permanently in 1932. He set up a cooking and pastry school in Athens and published a cookbook that showcased both savory and sweet recipes, but in its pages, replete with explicit drawings and photos, he instilled French techniques, recipes, and sauces, such as the now-ubiquitous béchamel, into traditional Greek cooking, forever changing it. He encouraged the use of butter over olive oil and is credited with inventing pastitsio and moussaka as we know them today, layers of pasta or eggplant-zucchini-potato covered in a spiced ground meat sauce and topped with a thick layer of béchamel. Imagine Greek restaurant menus without that?

His contributions to the evolution of Greek cuisine are undeniable, but his Francophile refiguring of what had always been an agrarian-based cuisine sowed the seeds of controversy that would sprout decades later. For much of the twentieth century, Greeks looked to and embraced all things foreign, unsure of their own place on the world stage, looking to "improve" their identity with seemingly modern affectations brought in from abroad. Cuisine and cultural identity are intrinsically intertwined in every culture.

While Tselementes's book went on to dozens of reprints over the years, was literally synonymous with the word *cookbook*, and became the cooking bible of almost every homemaker in Greece from the 1920s when it was first published until at least the 1970s, it started to lose luster as Greeks became more comfortable in their own proverbial skins. It took time—decades—for that to happen, and for the country and its national identity to heal and evolve, after World War II, the Civil War, the junta, and the entry into the EU.

Today, the culinary landscape is shaped by an openness and an anything-goes mindset, but the look to our roots, relatively newfound, is a deep one, and starting from around the late 1990s, as the Athens Olympics approached, all things regional, agrarian, and Greek suddenly came into focus. Cuisine evolves.

Pastitsio

Pastitsio shed its traditional pastry crust and donned a coat of béchamel instead under the guidance and reinvention of Nikos Tselementes, who also reworked the classic French sauce to include cheese. In its best-known iteration with that creamy béchamel sauce, it's a great dish, satisfying and sophisticated but also extraordinarily comforting. It's no accident that it has come to become one of the defining dishes of Greek cuisine.

MAKES 8 TO 10 SERVINGS

4 tablespoons extra-virgin Greek olive oil, divided

3 large onions, finely chopped

1 large garlic clove, minced

1½ pounds ground beef

3 cups canned diced tomatoes

1 cup dry white wine

1 cinnamon stick

6 whole allspice berries

1 scant teaspoon ground nutmeg

10 to 15 black peppercorns crushed

Salt to taste

1 pound thick tube spaghetti, such as bucatini

4 ounces kefalotyri cheese, grated

For the Greek béchamel

8 tablespoons (1 stick) unsalted butter

Scant ½ cup all-purpose flour

7 cups whole milk, heated

1 cup heavy cream

Salt and ground white pepper to taste

Grated fresh nutmeg to taste

2 large whole eggs plus 2 large egg yolks, lightly beaten

⅔ cup fresh Greek anthotyro, ricotta, or fresh myzithra, drained

⅔ cup crumbled Greek feta

½ cup grated kasseri cheese

In a large skillet, heat 2 tablespoons of the olive oil over medium heat. Add the onions and sauté until translucent, 7 to 10 minutes. Stir in the garlic. Add the meat and cook, stirring, until the meat begins to brown, 10 to 15 minutes. Add the tomatoes, white wine, cinnamon, allspice, nutmeg, peppercorns, and salt. Lower the heat, cover, and simmer for 35 to 40 minutes, until the liquid has been absorbed and the meat is cooked. Remove the pan from the heat and let meat cool slightly. Remove the whole spices.

While the meat is simmering, bring a large pot of water to a boil and cook the pasta according to the package directions until al dente. Drain the pasta and shock in cold water, then drain again. Toss the pasta in a large bowl with the remaining 2 tablespoons olive oil and half of the grated kefalotyri cheese.

Preheat the oven to 350°F. Lightly oil a 9 x 13-inch baking pan.

Make the béchamel: In a large saucepan, melt the butter over medium heat until it starts to bubble but before it browns. Add the flour and whisk vigorously for a few minutes, until the flour turns a pale golden color. Slowly add the hot milk, whisking all the while. Add the cream. Season with salt, white pepper, and nutmeg. Whisk continuously until thick, 10 to 15 minutes, being careful not to scorch the bottom of the pot. Vigorously whisk in the lightly beaten eggs and yolks. Stir in the anthotyro, feta, and half of the grated kasseri cheese.

Toss the pasta with a little of the béchamel. Spread half of it on the bottom of the prepared baking pan. Pour in the meat sauce, spreading evenly over pasta. Sprinkle with 1 to 2 tablespoons of the remaining grated kasseri cheese. Make a second layer of the pasta. Pour the béchamel over the pasta, making sure it's evenly spread over the top. Sprinkle with the remaining grated kasseri cheese. Bake for 45 to 60 minutes, until the béchamel thickens and swells and a golden-brown crust forms on top. Remove from the oven, let it cool slightly, then cut into squares and serve.

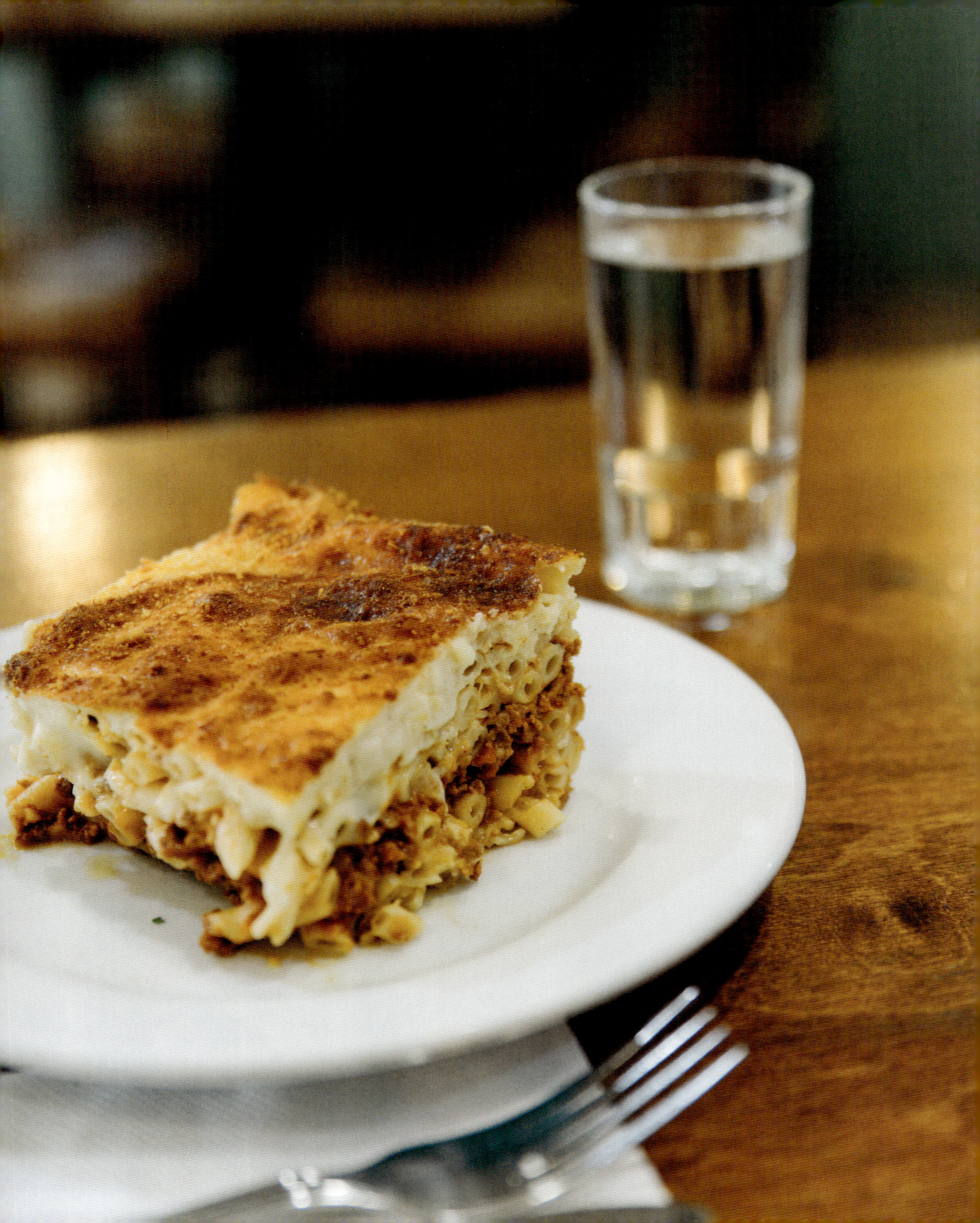

Pastitsio Past and Present

Pastitsio, the most celebrated Greek pasta dish, is literally a mess. That's what the root of its name, from the Italian *pasticcio*, actually means. Anyone who's ever been to a Greek restaurant or eaten in a Greek home has probably come across this famous baked pasta dish, one of the most iconic of all Greek recipes.

Its roots go back to sixteenth-century Italy and the Renaissance, where this mess was a delicious concoction of pasta and various meats, wrapped in a slightly sweet pastry. It was a celebratory dish, as the sugar used to sweeten its pastry cloak was imported and dear. The most revered pasticcio of the era was the pasticcio di maccheroni or pasticcio alla ferrarese, from Ferrara, a town between Venice and Bologna, where it became popular among Italian nobles. It's still made there.

It traveled from the environs of Venice to the Venetian outposts of the Ionian, namely Corfu and later Kythera, where it changed slightly, mirroring whatever was available on each of these islands. In Corfu it was called pasticcio tsi nonas (grandmother's pasticcio) and sometimes venetetsianiko pastitsio, which is the name it is known by in Kythera. Both versions emulate the original, with bits of meat and cheese, usually the week's scraps from the tables and estates of the aristocratic class, tossed between pasta and cloaked in a sweetened short crust. Sometimes it was made in grander style, with game, boiled eggs, meatballs, and more. It has survived the centuries and on Kythera is the traditional dish on the Sunday before Lent starts.

Pastitsio made its way through the Venetian strongholds of Greece, landing a place in the first cookbook, published in Syros in 1828. In that recipe, pasta is tossed with a heady beef ragù dotted with prunes and richly spiced.

Then, almost forty years later, a Greek chef in Constantinople named Nikos Sarantis published the pastitsio recipe that broke with the traditions to date, and suggested fish or game as the protein(s) of choice.

But it wasn't until at least another four decades later that pastitsio took on its current form, the one we know in Greek restaurants the world over, and for that we have, as I've already written, Greece's first celebrity chef and her most influential culinarian ever to thank: Nikos Tselementes. Taking features of pastitsios past, he created a spiced ground meat sauce, tossed it with the pasta, nixed the pastry cloak, and poured a very français béchamel on top. And, voilà, a legend was born.

Pork Fricasse with Celery and Leeks

Fricasse, a combination of protein, greens and/or vegetables, and egg-lemon (avgolemono) sauce, is a dish with many variations all around Greece. In Athenian eateries one finds it mostly in old mageiria (traditional, usually working-class restaurants with open kitchens and a steam-table counter for all to see the offerings of the day) or in classic tavernas like Oikonomou in Petralona, Filipou in Kolonaki, and Vlassis around the Hilton area, almost the last of the Mohicans, so to speak, as far as eateries with classic Greek fare go. The most common iteration of fricasse is with pork, but one also finds it made with chicken and fish. Emulating a taverna trick, this recipe calls for stabilizing the avgolemono with cornstarch.

MAKES 6 TO 8 SERVINGS

Sea salt and freshly ground black pepper to taste

1½ pounds celery, with leaves, trimmed and chopped

2 bunches Chinese celery, trimmed and chopped

1 (3-pound) bone-in pork shoulder, cut into stewing-size pieces

½ cup extra-virgin Greek olive oil

1 tablespoon unsalted butter

2 bunches scallions, trimmed and chopped

2 large red onions, finely chopped

3 leeks, trimmed and chopped

2 to 3 cups hot water or chicken or vegetable stock

3 large eggs, separated

Strained juice of 3 lemons

1 teaspoon cornstarch

Bring a medium pot of water to a rolling boil and salt generously. Add the chopped celery and Chinese celery and blanch for about a minute to soften. Drain and set aside.

Wipe the pot dry. Pat the pork pieces dry with a paper towel.

Heat the olive oil and butter together over medium heat in the pot until the butter starts to bubble. Using kitchen tongs and working in batches so as not to crowd the pan, add the pork pieces and sear, turning with the tongs, until browned on all sides, 8 to 10 minutes. Season the meat with salt and pepper and transfer to a bowl or plate.

Add the scallions, onions, and leeks to the pot and cook over medium heat, stirring, until softened and translucent. Add a pinch of salt to help the mixture cook more quickly.

Return the celery, Chinese celery, and meat, along with any accumulated juices, to the pot. Taste and season with salt and pepper. Stir so that the meat is more or less enveloped by the vegetables, the better to absorb all their delicious flavors.

Add enough hot water to barely cover the contents of the pot. Cover, turn the heat down to low, and simmer for about 1½ hours, or until the pork is very tender and falling off the bone.

To make the avgolemono, in a medium metal bowl, whisk together the egg whites until you get a firm meringue. Add the yolks, one by one, until they're thoroughly blended into the meringue. Very slowly, drop by drop, whisk in the lemon juice and then the cornstarch. Take a ladleful of the pot juices and very slowly add them to the avgolemono mixture, whisking all the while. Repeat with a second ladleful. Pour this mixture into the pot, swirl it all around, and serve immediately. Do not cover the pot—you'll end up with an omelet!

Moussaka with Metsovone Béchamel

There's another Greek dish famous the world over: moussaka. Here, I present to you a moussaka recipe I recall from my days as a young journalist. It is from a famous bar called 17, after the original address on Voukourestiou Street it called home from 1957 until 1990, before reopening as a bar-restaurant a few meters away on Lycabettus Street in Kolonaki. In its heyday, Bar 17 was deep Athens, the hangout for everyone who was anyone in the city, and for anyone who was visiting, including the likes of Frank Sinatra and other Hollywood stars. It was where the boss, a big someone, would go every day for lunch and a few dry martinis, so famous that even The New York Times *wrote about them a few decades back. The owner, Fotis Krikzonis, arrived in postwar Athens as a thirteen-year-old boy from the remote mountainous area of Agrafa in northwestern Greece, did just about everything from shining shoes to shoveling coal before he started waiting tables, and, finally, opened his own place, which quickly morphed into the stuff of urban legends. He passed away two decades ago, but his sons still run the place most days.*

MAKES 6 TO 8 SERVINGS

For the béchamel

6 tablespoons unsalted butter

6 tablespoons all-purpose flour

6 cups milk, warmed slightly

⅔ cup heavy cream

½ teaspoon freshly grated nutmeg

Salt and freshly ground black pepper to taste

2 large eggs

1 cup grated metsovone or smoked provolone

½ cup ricotta or Greek anthotyro

½ cup grated kefalotyri, kefalograviera, Romano, or Parmigiano

Make the béchamel: In a large saucepan, heat the butter over medium heat until melted and bubbling; be careful not to let it brown. Add the flour and whisk together for about 5 minutes, being careful not to brown the roux (butter-flour mixture). The aim here is to cook the flour so that the sauce doesn't end up with a pasty taste. Add the warm milk, whisking all the while.

Add the cream, nutmeg, salt, and pepper. Whisk the béchamel for 8 to 15 minutes, until it has the consistency of a medium-thick pancake batter. Remove from the heat and slide in the eggs, working fast and whisking to combine them without curdling them. Whisk in the cheeses. Cover and set aside until ready to use.

For the meat sauce

Extra-virgin Greek olive oil, as needed

4 medium to large onions, chopped

2 pounds lean ground beef

3 garlic cloves, finely chopped

2 whole cloves

1 cinnamon stick or ½ teaspoon ground

2 bay leaves

Pinch allspice

Salt and freshly ground black pepper to taste

½ cup dry red wine

3 cups canned diced tomatoes

3 tablespoons tomato paste

6 large eggplants, trimmed and sliced lengthwise into large ovals about ¼ inch thick

⅔ cup plain bread crumbs, or 2 large potatoes, peeled and sliced into ⅛-inch rounds

1 cup grated kefalotyri, kefalograviera, or Romano cheese

Prepare the meat sauce: In a large, heavy skillet, heat 2 tablespoons olive oil over medium heat. Add the onions and sauté until translucent, 7 to 10 minutes. Add the ground meat and cook, stirring, until browned, 12 to 15 minutes. Add the garlic, cloves, cinnamon, bay leaves, allspice, salt, and pepper and stir for a few minutes. Pour in the wine and then the tomatoes with their juices. Lower the heat, cover, and simmer for 45 to 50 minutes, adding a little more wine or water, if necessary, to keep the mixture moist but not liquid. About 5 minutes before turning off the heat, add the tomato paste. Simmer, uncovered, until all the liquid has been absorbed. Remove the skillet from the heat and cool slightly.

While the meat sauce is simmering, preheat the oven to 350°F. Line 2 rimmed baking sheets with parchment paper.

Brush the eggplant slices on both sides generously with olive oil and place on the lined baking sheets. Bake until soft, 10 to 12 minutes. Cool slightly before using.*

If opting for potatoes over bread crumbs, toss the potato slices in olive oil and bake on a rimmed baking sheet until soft but not browned.

When ready to assemble the moussaka, lightly oil an 11 x 15-inch baking pan or other large glass or ceramic baking dish.

Mix a ladleful of the béchamel into the meat sauce and stir to combine.

Spread the bread crumbs or slightly cooked potato slices on the bottom of the oiled baking pan. Place a third of the eggplant slices in an overlapping layer on top, patting down with a spatula or your palms. Spread a third of the meat mixture evenly over the eggplant. Place another overlapping layer of eggplant on top, and then another third of the meat sauce. Repeat with the last layer of eggplant and finish with a top layer of meat sauce. Pour the remaining béchamel over the meat sauce, spreading it with a spatula so that it is evenly dispersed over the surface. Sprinkle with the grated cheese and bake for 45 to 60 minutes, until the béchamel is set and golden brown on top. Remove, cool slightly, and serve.

*In the most traditional versions of moussaka, the eggplant slices are lightly fried to soften and then blotted dry on paper towels. I prefer to bake them (easier and lighter!), but if you want to go the traditional, old-fashioned route, pat the eggplant slices dry. In a large skillet, heat ¼ cup extra-virgin Greek olive oil for every 3 to 4 slices of eggplant. Working in batches, sauté the slices lightly, then drain on paper towels.

The Great Bourgeois Dishes of Athens

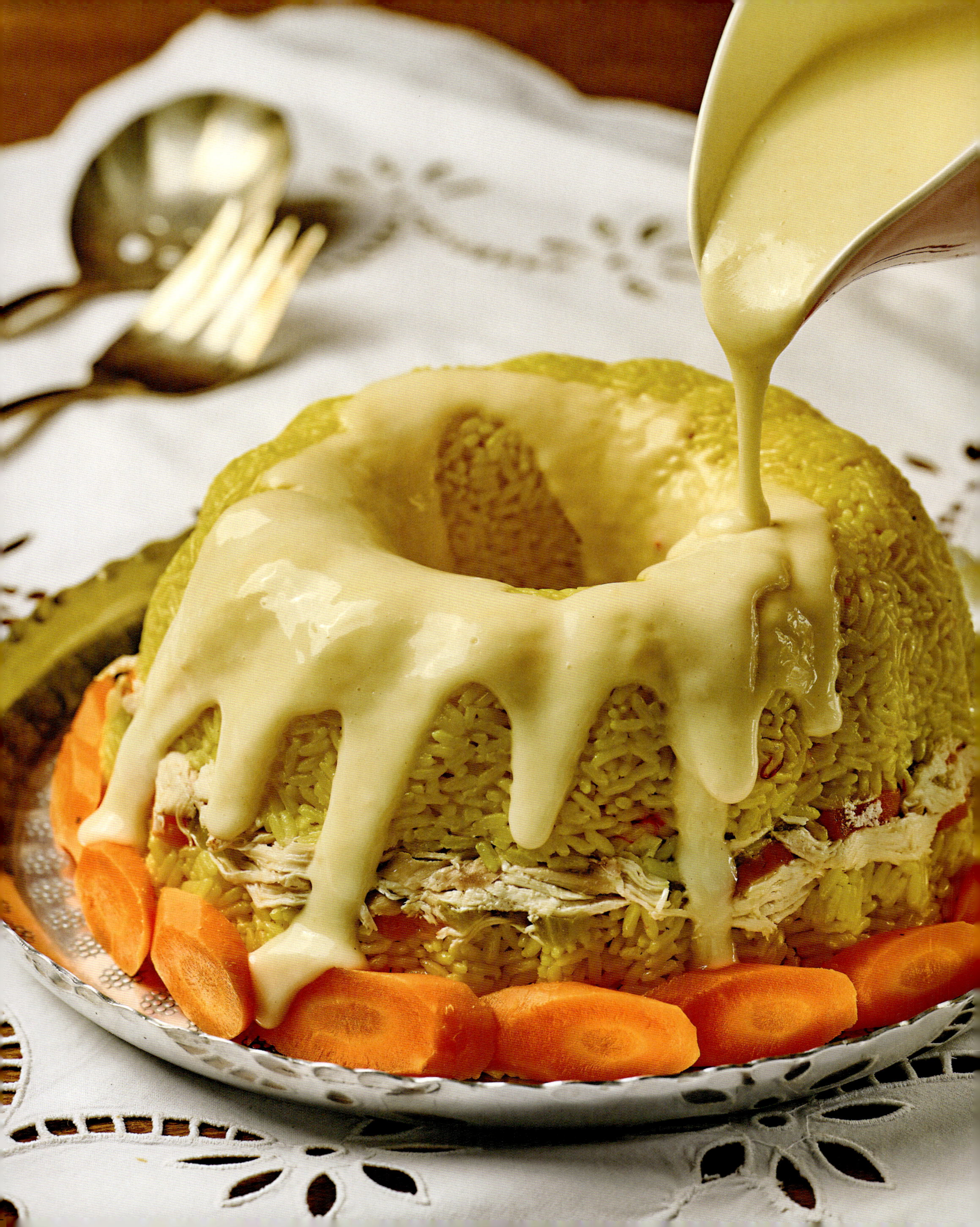

Kotopoulo (Chicken) Milanese

The world knows chicken Milanese as a breaded and fried thin piece of chicken breast, not unlike schnitzel. Somewhere between the Duomo and the Parthenon in the early twentieth century, the dish was transformed into a uniquely Greek affectation, combining chicken, rice, a Bundt pan, and a cascade of rich, Hellenized sauce suprême, one of the foundational sauces of French cuisine. It was the dish to cook if one's goal back in the day was to impress a guest and show off one's skill as the perfect homemaker and cook. Nikos Tselementes first published this recipe in his magazine Odigos Mageirikis (Cooking Guide) *way back in 1910, and for more than half a century it defined the oh-so-proper refinements of upwardly mobile Athenians. Purity or lack thereof notwithstanding, it's really delicious!*

MAKES 6 TO 8 SERVINGS

For the chicken

1 whole (4-pound) chicken

3 quarts water

Salt to taste

4 whole carrots

2 celery stalks

1 onion, halved

1 bay leaf

½ teaspoon whole black peppercorns

For the rice

Salt and freshly ground black pepper to taste

1 generous pinch Greek saffron (krokos Kozanis)

2 cups parboiled long-grain rice

1 tablespoon unsalted butter

Rinse the chicken inside and out. Remove and discard the skin and gizzards, and either leave the chicken whole or cut into large pieces. Place the chicken in a large pot, add the water, and bring to a boil. Skim the foam off the surface for the first 10 minutes. Season the water generously with salt and add the carrots, celery, onion, bay leaf, and peppercorns. Turn the heat down and cook at a gentle simmer for about 1 hour, or until the chicken meat falls off the bones. Using a slotted spoon, remove the chicken pieces and vegetables. Set aside to cool. When cool enough to handle, remove and discard the bones and shred the meat. Cut the cooked carrot into ½-inch rounds and set aside for garnish. Chop the cooked celery and onion and mix it into the chicken. Set aside until ready to use.

Measure out 1¼ quarts of the broth and transfer to a medium saucepan. Bring to a boil and season lightly with salt. While the broth is coming to a boil, measure out a shot glass more of it from the original pot—it should still be warm—and dilute the saffron in it.

Stir the rice into the simmering chicken broth and adjust the seasoning with a little salt if desired. Turn the heat down to a low simmer, cover, and cook for 20 to 25 minutes, or until the rice has absorbed all of the liquid and is tender. About 10 minutes before removing from the heat, add the butter and stir in the diluted saffron.

-recipe continues-

For the sauce suprême

4 tablespoons (½ stick) unsalted butter

¼ cup all-purpose flour

½ cup dry white wine

Strained juice of 1 lemon

1 cup heavy cream or crème fraîche

Salt and freshly ground black pepper to taste

Make the sauce: In a medium saucepan, heat the butter over medium heat until it bubbles and is completely melted but before it has the chance to brown. Whisk in the flour and continue whisking for 5 to 7 minutes so that the flour cooks. Whisk in ½ cup of the chicken stock, and as soon as that starts to thicken, add another ½ cup. Keep going until 2½ cups of stock are worked into the sauce, whisking all the while. Then, as it simmers and as you whisk, add the wine, then the lemon juice. Stir in the cream after 6 to 7 minutes, stirring the sauce to help it thicken. Season to taste with salt and pepper.

Lightly oil a 10-inch Bundt pan. Place half the rice on the bottom of the pan, pressing it flat with the back of a spoon. Add the chicken-vegetable mixture, pressing that in as well, then add the remaining rice, pressing it so that everything is as compact as possible inside the pan. Let the mixture stand in the pan for 10 to 15 minutes to firm up so that it retains its shape when unmolded.

To serve, place a platter, the circumference of which exceeds that of the Bundt pan by at least 3 inches, over the pan and carefully flip it. Gently remove the pan so that the rice sits decoratively on the plate, like a cake. Place the carrots around the base of the rice and gently spoon over the sauce, so that it looks almost like a glaze. Serve.

Delicious Liaisons...
Avgolemono

Greece's best-known sauce, a delicate, creamy liaison of eggs, lemons, and hot broth, has a complicated past. It most likely arrived on Greek shores with the Sephardic Jews, who, expelled from Spain in 1492 with the Inquisition, settled in large numbers in Ottoman Salonika, where they were free to practice their religion. Salonika, aka Thessaloniki, was essentially a Jewish city from the fifteenth century until World War II, when the community was decimated during the Holocaust. Avgolemono may be the evolution of a foundational Sephardic sauce called agristada, which was sour, typically made so with the addition of pomegranate juice or the juice of Seville (bitter) oranges. But lemons entered southern Europe around 1000 AD, and the Sephardic Jews may have brought them along on their exodus. Sometime in the last half millennium, avgolemono was born. But things come full circle, and nowadays, Athenian chefs experiment with this egg-citrus liaison by incorporating the juice of limes and, yes, bitter oranges, too, and add things like mastiha, white or sparkling wine, and saffron to the mixture.

The Great Bourgeois Dishes of Athens

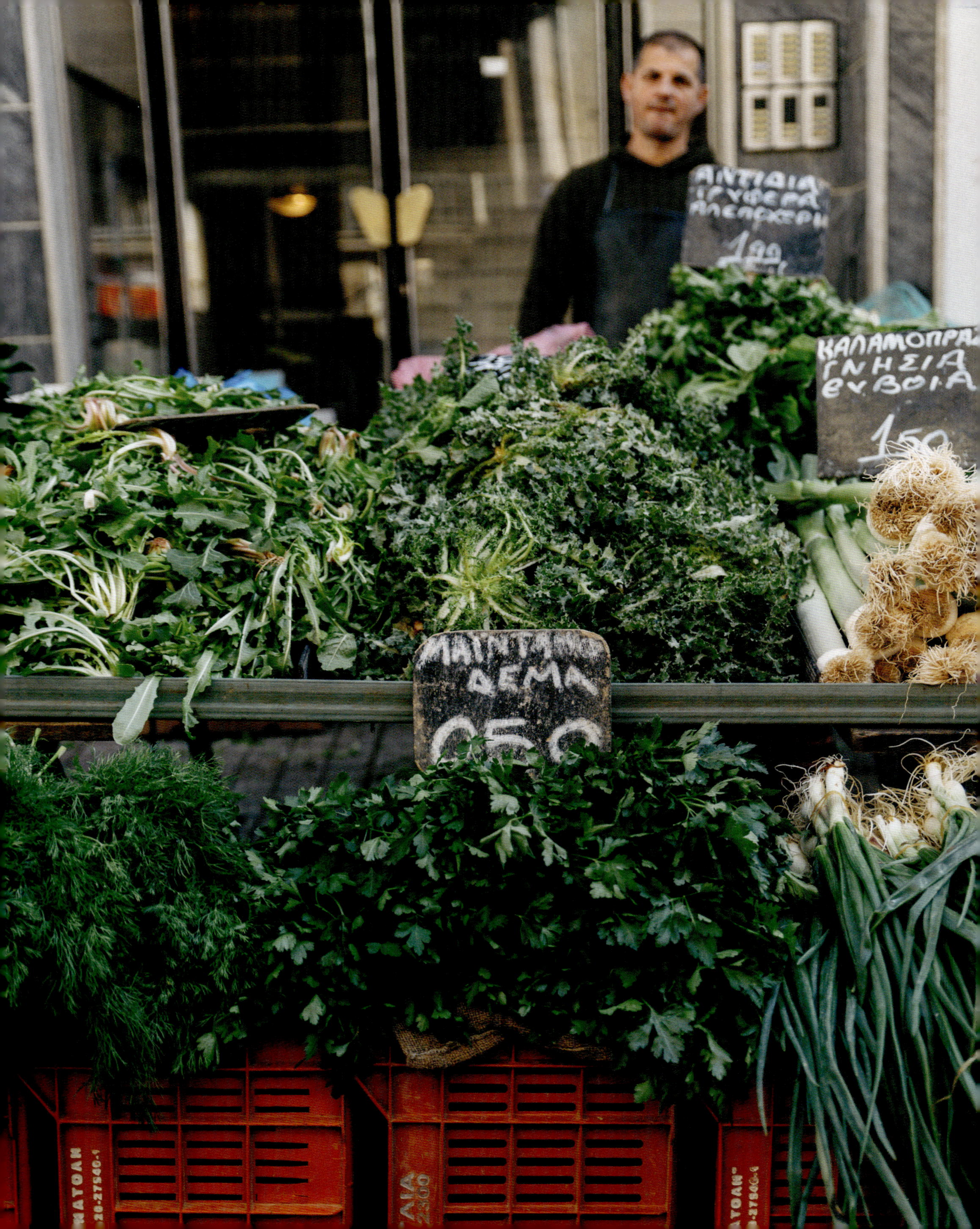
ΑΝΤΙΔΙΑ
ΚΑΛΑΜΟΠΡΑ
ΓΝΗΣΙΑ
ΕΥΒΟΙΑ
ΔΕΜΑ

A New Direction

Plant-Forward Athens

All one needs to do is walk past a neighborhood produce market, called *laiki agora*—"people's markets," to be exact—or even simply visit any supermarket or grocer to see firsthand the wealth, variety, and quality of produce grown in Greece and available in big urban centers like Athens. Indeed, much of the produce sold and consumed in Athens grows close by, in the Peloponnese and in Mesogeia, within just a few hours of the city.

The Mediterranean climate of temperate winters and plenty of sunshine is most conducive to growing delicious fruits and vegetables. It stands to reason that so much Greek food is traditionally and naturally plant-based. Greece boasts more plant-based recipes than any other cuisine in the Mediterranean. Almost unwittingly, Greeks are accidental vegetarians because of the incredible wealth of plant-forward and plant-based dishes people cook at home and restaurants offer on their menus.

There are some historical and cultural reasons for this wealth of plant-based dishes. For example, the Greek Orthodox fasting periods dictate going off animal products (with the exception of some seafood) for about half the year. Until the 1960s, meat was eaten sparingly anyway, reserved for Sundays and special occasions. But as the postwar generation got itself back on its feet and became more affluent, so did the Greek diet become more westernized. Steak houses, burger joints, and, of course, souvlaki places now abound in Athens, but so do vegan restaurants, as it's quite common these days to be a vegetarian or a vegan.

But it's also comforting to us Greeks to know that some of our favorite traditional plant-based recipes, the ladera (from *ladi*, for "oil"), typically one-pan dishes, are not only still a big part of so many taverna menus, but a new generation of chefs has embraced them and added their own globally inspired touches. There are traditional places all over the city renowned for their range of ladera, as well as new places featuring young chefs eager to leave a mark, creating the likes of zucchini stuffed with black rice and avgolemono (page 260) or classic stewed green beans yiahni in an onion-garlic-tomato sauce, enhanced with a daub of squid ink and a dusting of bottarga (page 259).

Being vegan is very cool in Athens these days. In the past five years the number of vegan restaurants in Athens has grown exponentially. And there is a Greek spin to trends: The supermarkets are stocked with nondairy yogurts, cheeses, and milks, and offer the likes of vegan tzatziki, vegan feta, and even vegan souvlaki.

Chefs are transforming classics like grape leaves yialantzi (a traditional rice-and-herb summer dish) by serving it with cashew-milk yogurt instead of traditional dairy-based yogurt. There are countless examples of this weaving of traditional recipes reworked anew with a whole world of plant-based ingredients with which to make or pair them. But my observation of the plant-based zeitgeist in Athens has shown me that the greater direction is the embrace of natural, unprocessed foods to create plant-based versions of familiar Greek dishes. Hence things like vegan moussaka with beans in the "meat" sauce, and veggie burgers that take traditional dishes like fava (puree of yellow split peas) and turn them into hearty, plant-based fare. This was something Greeks always did, anyway, long before it became a trend.

In this chapter, you will find plant-forward (neither vegan nor always purely vegetarian) Greek recipes, both traditional and contemporary, and you'll get a taste of some of the non-Greek influences that have insinuated themselves into Greek recipes.

Giant Beans
with a Grec-Mex Touch

I never thought I'd see the day when gigantes, Greek giant beans, got a Mexican makeover. But they have, and I've seen them in all sorts of recipes that combine the best-selling bean of Greece with decidedly foreign ingredients. They're great with cilantro, cumin, and chiles, as in the following recipe.

MAKES 6 SERVINGS

1 pound dried giant beans, soaked overnight and drained

2 bay leaves

2 tablespoons extra-virgin Greek olive oil

2 large red onions, finely chopped

6 garlic cloves, chopped

Sea salt and freshly ground black pepper to taste

1 (15-ounce) can diced tomatoes, about 2 cups

10 sun-dried tomatoes, soaked, drained, and chopped, liquid reserved

2 fresh chiles, whole or seeded and chopped, or 1 scant teaspoon red pepper flakes

⅓ cup Greek pine honey

2 to 3 tablespoons red wine vinegar

2 teaspoons ground cumin

1 small bunch cilantro, chopped

Chile-infused olive oil, for drizzling (optional)

Put the giant beans in a large pot and pour in enough cold water to cover by 3 inches. Add the bay leaves and bring to a boil over medium heat, then reduce the heat to a simmer and cook for 1 to 1½ hours, or until tender but al dente. You can skim the foam off the top as they simmer in the beginning.

While the beans are cooking, heat the olive oil in a large skillet over medium heat. Add the onions and garlic, give the mixture a swirl or two, and then reduce the heat to low. Season with a little salt. Cook, stirring occasionally, until the onions are golden brown and lightly caramelized, about 20 minutes. Add the diced tomatoes with their juices and cook for 5 to 8 minutes, until slightly thickened.

Preheat the oven to 375°F. Lightly oil a 9 x 13-inch baking dish.

Drain the giant beans, reserving the cooking liquid and discarding the bay leaves.

Place the beans, tomato sauce, sun-dried tomatoes, chiles, honey, vinegar, and cumin in the oiled pan and gently toss so that the sauce, honey, and spices are evenly distributed throughout the beans. Season lightly with salt and pepper. If the mixture seems like it needs more liquid, add the giant bean cooking liquid in increments of ½ cup. The mixture should be thick, but there should be enough liquid in the pan for the giant beans to expand some more and absorb the moisture. Cover with parchment paper then aluminum foil and bake for about 50 minutes, checking once or twice to see if you need to add more cooking liquid, or until the giant beans are thick and jammy. Taste and adjust the seasoning with salt and pepper. Stir in the chopped cilantro.

Remove and serve, either hot, warm, or at room temperature, drizzled, if desired, with a little chile-infused olive oil.

Giant Beans Baked
with Smoked Pork, Wine, and Graviera

We cook a lot of beans, and they're popular on Greek restaurant menus at every dining level, from simple tavernas to Michelin-starred establishments. Plant-forward means less meat and more plants, and this recipe with its specks of bacon is a good example of how old traditions, such as using—and stretching—a little protein in a pot of beans finds relevance today.

MAKES 6 SERVINGS

1 pound dried giant beans, soaked overnight and drained

8 tablespoons extra-virgin Greek olive oil, divided

2 large red onions, chopped

4 garlic cloves, chopped

Coarse sea salt and freshly ground black pepper to taste

⅓ pound Canadian bacon or other smoked pork of choice, cut into 1-inch pieces

1 heaping tablespoon tomato paste

3 good-quality red peppers in brine, drained and cut into 1-inch strips

1 (15-ounce) can diced canned tomatoes

½ cup dry red wine

6 fresh thyme sprigs

½ pound Greek graviera cheese, or any other mild yellow cheese, such as Gruyère, Compté, or Asiago, cut into ½-inch cubes

Put the giant beans in a large pot and pour in enough cold water to cover by 3 inches. Bring to a boil over medium heat, then reduce the heat to a simmer and cook for 1 to 1½ hours, or until tender but al dente. You can skim the foam off the top as they simmer in the beginning.

While the beans are cooking, heat 2 tablespoons of the olive oil in a large, deep skillet over medium heat. Add the onions and garlic, give the mixture a swirl or two, and then reduce the heat to low. Season with a little salt. Cook, stirring occasionally, until the onions are lightly golden, about 15 minutes. Add the bacon pieces and stir for a minute or two. Add the tomato paste and stir to combine well. Slide the red pepper strips into the pan, stir, then add the diced tomatoes with their juices. Bring to a simmer, then pour in the wine. Cook for 5 to 8 minutes, until slightly thickened.

Preheat the oven to 375°F. Lightly oil a 9 x 13-inch baking dish.

Drain the giant beans, reserving the cooking liquid. Place the beans and tomato sauce in the oiled baking dish. Mix in the remaining 6 tablespoons olive oil. Add some of the giant bean cooking liquid as needed, so the mixture is moist but not soupy. Season with salt and pepper and nestle the thyme sprigs in and around the giant beans. Bake for 45 to 50 minutes, checking once or twice to see if you need to add more cooking liquid, until the giant beans are very tender and most of the liquid in the pan has been absorbed. About 10 minutes before removing the beans from the oven, add the graviera cubes, nestling them into the beans evenly throughout the pan, and finish baking. Remove and serve immediately.

Black-Eyed Peas
with Preserved Lemon, Greens, and Capers

Subtle influences from North African cooking have worked their way into the regional Greek kitchen in places closest to the continent: Crete and the southern Dodecanese. But the use of preserved lemons, such a telltale ingredient in Moroccan cooking, exploded with flamboyance in Greek restaurants in the 1990s, a fun time to be a foodie in, as we thought of then, Anything-Goes Athens.

MAKES 6 SERVINGS

1 pound dried black-eyed peas

Sea salt and freshly ground black pepper to taste

½ cup extra-virgin Greek olive oil, divided

2 spring onions, trimmed and chopped

1 Spanish onion, finely chopped

1 leek, trimmed and chopped

1 fennel bulb, trimmed and chopped

1 tablespoon tomato paste

2 pounds Swiss chard or purslane, trimmed and coarsely chopped

½ preserved lemon, rinsed and finely chopped

1 bunch fresh dill, chopped

Place the black-eyed peas in a pot, pour in enough cold water to cover by 2 inches, and bring to a boil. Drain and rinse under cold water in a colander. Return the beans to the pot, cover with fresh water, and bring to a boil over high heat. Salt the beans lightly, reduce the heat to a simmer, and cook for about 20 minutes, or until al dente. Drain, reserving the cooking liquid.

In a Dutch oven, heat ¼ cup of the olive oil over medium heat. Add the spring onions, Spanish onion, leek, and fennel and sauté for about 8 minutes, until translucent and softened. Stir in the tomato paste. Stir in the black-eyed peas and chard. Add enough of the black-eyed pea cooking liquid to come about halfway up the contents of the pot. Season with salt and pepper, add the preserved lemon, cover, and simmer until the black-eyed peas are tender, about 15 more minutes. About 5 minutes before removing from the heat, stir in the dill. Adjust the seasoning with salt and pepper and serve, either hot, warm, or at room temperature.

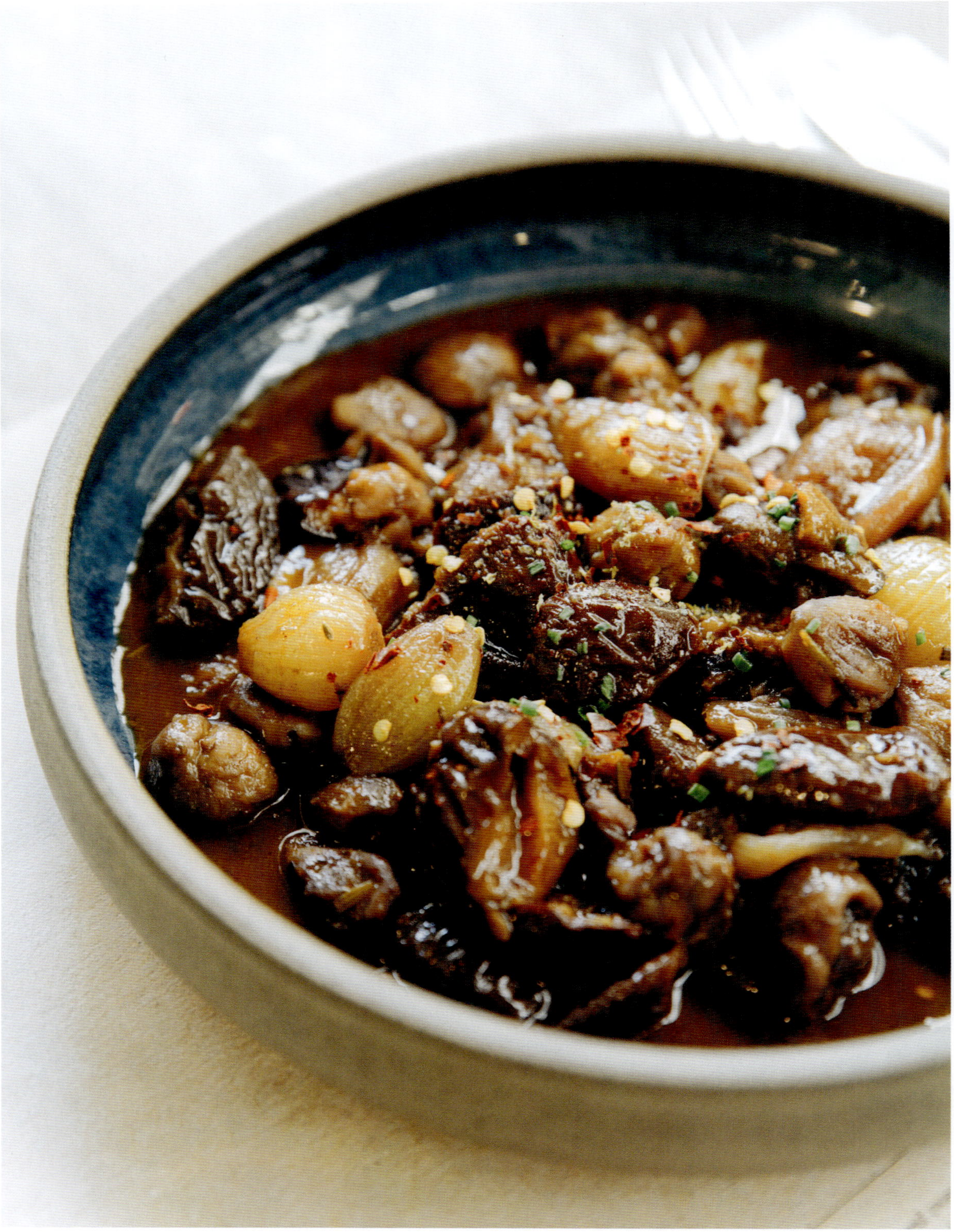

Nena's Chestnut Stifado
with Prunes

Chestnut stifado, a rich vegan stew whose origins are in the regional, traditional cooking of the Peloponnese and Crete, has become a modern classic in Athens, interpreted by chefs at some of the trendiest restaurants in town. Nena Ismyrnoglou prepares a favorite version, adding prunes to the mix, too.

MAKES 4 TO 8 SERVINGS

8 tablespoons extra-virgin Greek olive oil, divided

1 pound vacuum-packed or canned peeled chestnuts

1½ pounds peeled stewing onions or cipollini,* or 1¾ pounds medium onions, peeled and cut into ¾-inch pieces

3 medium carrots, peeled and cut into ½-inch pieces

1 cup dry red wine

Salt and freshly ground black pepper to taste

½-inch cinnamon stick

5 juniper or allspice berries, crushed

1 whole clove

1 bay leaf

1 teaspoon red pepper flakes

1½ teaspoons sweet paprika

¼ teaspoon hot paprika or cayenne

½ teaspoon black peppercorns

2 cups hot water

2 teaspoons finely chopped fresh rosemary or thyme, or 1 scant teaspoon dried rosemary or thyme

½ pound pitted prunes

2 tablespoons honey

2 tablespoons red wine vinegar

In a wide pot, heat 2 tablespoons of the olive oil over medium-high heat. Add the chestnuts and sauté for 2 to 3 minutes, then transfer with a slotted spoon to a bowl. Add the remaining 6 tablespoons olive oil to the pot. When slightly heated, add the onions and sauté for 8 minutes. Add the carrots and sauté for 3 minutes. Add the red wine, salt, cinnamon stick, juniper berries, clove, bay leaf, red pepper flakes, sweet and hot paprikas, and peppercorns and bring to a boil. Add the hot water, lower the heat to a simmer, cover the pot, and simmer for 1 hour.

Add the chestnuts and rosemary and continue cooking for 20 minutes. Add the prunes, honey, and vinegar and cook for 10 more minutes, or until the sauce thickens. Serve.

* To peel the onions: Boil them whole for 5 minutes from the moment the water starts boiling. Cool them slightly and let them become lukewarm. Cut off about ¼ inch of the root end—no more than that, or they'll fall apart during cooking. Squeeze from the opposite end of the cut, and they'll pop out clean!

Braised Chickpeas
with Olives, Pistachios, and Roasted Tomatoes

Chickpeas, one of the most ancient legumes in the eastern Mediterranean, have always been popular in Athenian kitchens, but while they were once the stuff of traditional soups, all thick and lemony, they're now the backdrop to countless salads and stews, with a mix of ingredients that run the gamut from Greek to global.

MAKES 4 SERVINGS

1 pound cherry tomatoes

8 tablespoons extra-virgin Greek olive oil, divided

2 tablespoons balsamic vinegar

1 tablespoon petimezi (grape molasses)

6 fresh thyme sprigs, stemmed and finely chopped

Generous pinch brown sugar

Coarse sea salt and freshly ground black pepper to taste

2 red onions, coarsely chopped

4 garlic cloves, finely chopped

2 (15-ounce) cans good-quality, low-sodium chickpeas

1 cup Greek throumbes olives or wrinkled black Moroccan olives

Finely grated zest of 1 lemon

⅔ cup salted roasted pistachios, coarsely chopped

Preheat the oven to 400°F. Lightly oil a small baking dish.

In a medium bowl, toss the cherry tomatoes with 2 tablespoons of the olive oil, the balsamic, petimezi, thyme, brown sugar, salt, and pepper. Transfer to the oiled baking dish and roast for 25 to 30 minutes, or until they start to dehydrate, blister, and char lightly. Turn them a few times over the course of the roasting time to be sure they don't burn or caramelize so much they stick to the pan. Remove and cool slightly.

Heat the remaining 6 tablespoons olive oil in a large, deep skillet or wide, shallow pot over medium heat. Add the onions and garlic and sauté for 12 to 15 minutes, until soft and lightly golden. Add the chickpeas and stir together for a few minutes to warm through. Stir in the olives and lemon zest. Add the roasted tomatoes and all their juices, then taste and adjust the seasoning as desired. Garnish with the pistachios and serve.

The People's Markets

At dawn on any given day of the week, winter, spring, summer, and fall, somewhere in Athens—somewhere, indeed, in all urban areas in Greece—vendors set up their tables and awnings, unload crate after crate of seasonal fruits and vegetables from the backs of their tented trucks, stack mounds of greens, pyramids of melons, apples, oranges, pomegranates, and other seasonal produce, trays of nuts, olives, and dried fruits, herbs, honey, flowers, fish and shellfish, bulk wine, and more, and open for business, sometime around 7:00 or 7:30 a.m.

Every neighborhood in Athens has its laiki agora, people's markets, once a week. Mine, in the Metaxourgeio neighborhood, is on Tuesdays, and going is a ritual. I walk the whole length of the market, eyeing what I want and what looks freshest, comparing prices, and chatting with neighbors and vendors whose weekly presence breeds familiarity and small talk. While most of these markets are straightforward, a few have become very hip and fun to just walk through. One of the largest, the market on Kallidromoiou, one of the city's most picturesque hilly streets in Exarcheia, is a magnet for street musicians. The cafés all around market day on Saturdays are abuzz with young and old sipping coffee and watching the world go by. The markets in Pangrati and Ambelokoipoi, both Athenian neighborhoods slightly further afield from the center, have large international populations, and the markets reflect their food needs, with offerings like galangal, bok choy, and daikon radishes. Wherever the laiki, the times are more or less the same: They open early and close down by 2:30 or 3:00 p.m., and the later one goes, the cheaper the produce—or whatever is left of it!

The laikes agores are a century-old tradition, started in 1929, between the wars and when the world economy was on the brink. Price gouging among the middlemen in Greece got so out of hand that it took a presidential decree to set up these markets, with much resistance from the farmers themselves, who feared retribution by their distributors. But cash won the day. The attraction for them was monetary, pure and simple: At the markets they'd be paid directly by the consumer without having to wait weeks or months, which was the case when working with middlemen. The first laiki agora opened in Athens at the end of January 1929 in Thisseion. Prime Minister Eleftherios Venizelos showed up and shopped, as did the Athens mayor and the finance minister, lending gravitas to this newfound concept. What began as a novel idea and way to fight price gouging became an overnight institution, with these markets spreading quickly all over the country. The middlemen snuck back in to some degree, as now these street markets aren't necessarily manned directly by the farmers, but nonetheless they're still the place to find the freshest and oftentimes least expensive produce. Today, in downtown Athens alone, there are forty-four people's markets.

Olympion's Chickpeas
with Eggplant, Lots of Onions, and Petimezi

Some of the best, most authentic fare in Athens can be found in the city's cafeneia, traditional multipurpose eateries that serve everything from coffee early in the morning to lunch and ouzo as the day wears on. They once populated every neighborhood and were, indeed, local hangouts, filled with regulars, old-timers, and, more and more of late, the twenty-to-forty-year-old set hungry for an Athens that's disappearing. There are just a few of these old stalwarts still around, and Olympion in Pangrati is not only one of them but arguably serves up some of the best food, traditional and with a twist or two, in the city. This is one of my favorite lunch bowls!

MAKES 6 TO 8 SERVINGS

1 pound dried chickpeas or 4 (15-ounce) cans good-quality, low-sodium chickpeas

½ cup extra-virgin Greek olive oil, divided

5 red onions, coarsely chopped

4 garlic cloves, chopped

3 medium eggplants, trimmed and cut into 1½-inch cubes

2 cups chopped fresh or canned plum tomatoes

1 heaping tablespoon tomato paste diluted in ¼ cup water

2 tablespoons grape molasses (petimezi)

1 cinnamon stick

6 fresh thyme sprigs

2 bay leaves

Salt and freshly ground black pepper to taste

If using dried chickpeas, soak them overnight, drain, and place in a large pot with enough fresh water to cover by 2 inches. Cook for 1 to 1½ hours or until tender, then drain. If using canned, rinse them under cold water in a colander, then drain.

Heat ¼ cup of the olive oil over medium heat in a Dutch oven. Add the onions and garlic and sauté until translucent, 8 to 10 minutes. Add the eggplant and stir gently to coat in the oil. Replenish the oil if needed, as the eggplant will absorb it quickly. Cook, stirring, until the eggplant begins to brown, 5 to 7 minutes. Add the chickpeas and toss everything gently together. Add the tomatoes, diluted tomato paste, petimezi, cinnamon stick, thyme, and bay leaves. Add enough water (or vegetable stock) to come about two-thirds of the way up the contents of the pot. Bring to a boil, reduce the heat to a simmer, cover, and cook for about 45 minutes, until most of the liquid has been absorbed and all the flavors have melded together. About 10 minutes before removing from the heat, season well with salt and pepper. Remove the bay leaves and serve either hot, warm, or at room temperature.

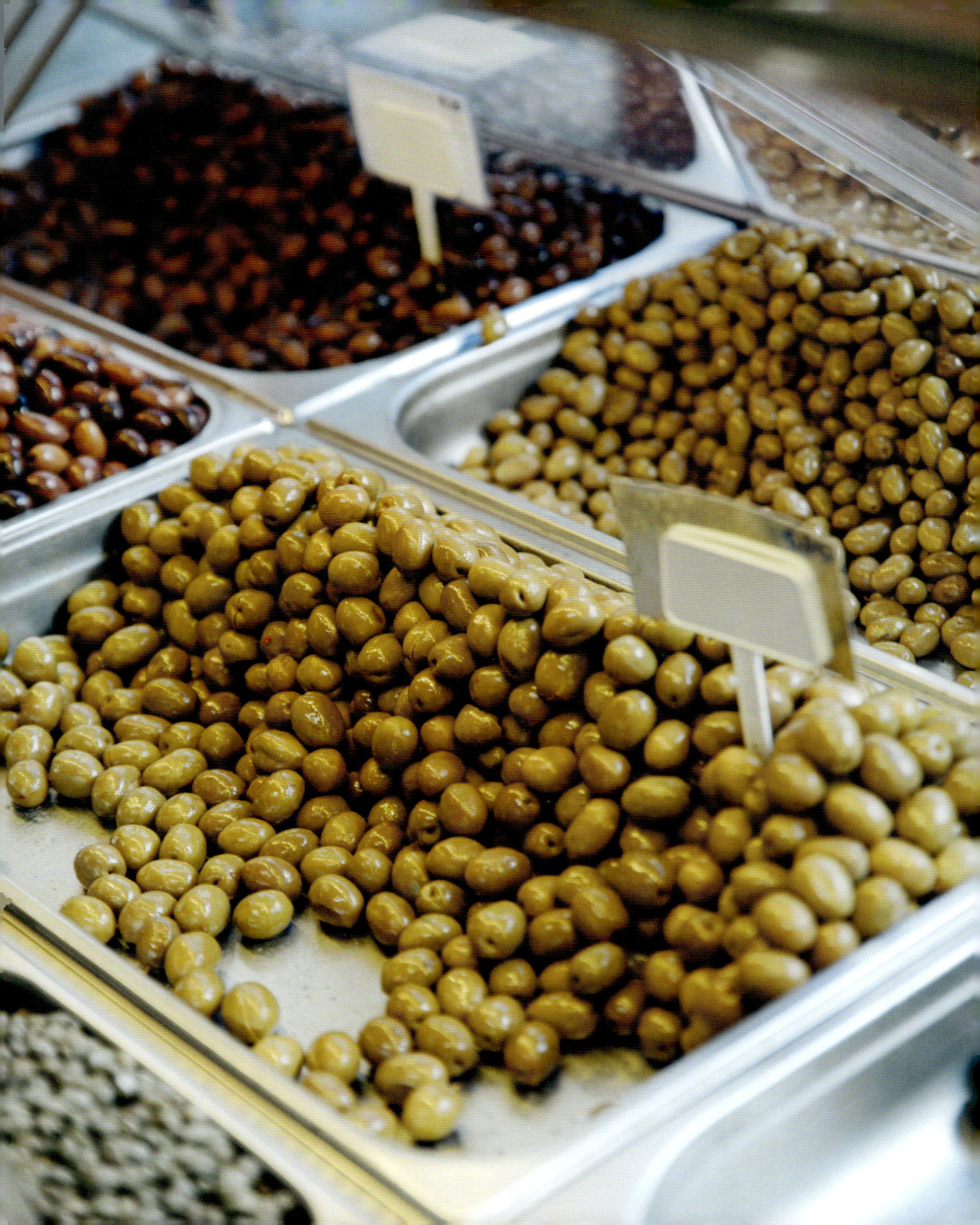

Lemony Chickpeas
with Turmeric and Fennel

Turmeric, kourkouma, known to the ancient Greeks, has found new life as a tasty panacea in modern Greek kitchens, and its use in bean dishes, like the one below, is more and more popular.

MAKES 6 SERVINGS

1 pound chickpeas, soaked overnight, or 4 (15-ounce) cans good-quality, low-sodium canned chickpeas, drained

⅔ cup extra-virgin Greek olive oil

1 large onion, finely chopped

1 large fennel bulb, trimmed and chopped

6 garlic cloves, minced

1 (1-inch knob) ginger, peeled and minced or grated

1 bay leaf

1 tablespoon ground turmeric

2 to 3 cups vegetable stock

Salt and freshly ground black pepper to taste

Strained juice of 1 lemon

If using dried chickpeas, soak them overnight, drain, and place in a large pot with enough fresh water to cover by 2 inches. Cook until tender but al dente, 1 to 1½ hours, then drain. If using canned, rinse them under cold water in a colander, then drain.

Heat 3 tablespoons of the olive oil in a wide pot over medium heat. Add the onion, fennel, garlic, and ginger and sauté, stirring occasionally, until soft, about 7 minutes. Add the chickpeas, bay leaf, and turmeric and stir well. Add enough vegetable stock to barely cover the chickpeas. Simmer for 30 to 45 minutes, or until thick and creamy. Season to taste with salt and pepper. Pour in the lemon juice and remaining olive oil and serve.

Chickpeas with Wild Mushrooms

INSPIRED BY AKRA

Akra means "edge," as in cutting-edge, perhaps, as chef-owners Yiannis Lucacos and Spyros Pediaditakis joined forces to create a sky's-the-limit reinterpretation of Greek cooking, taking traditions and catapulting them to modern sensibilities without, miraculously, forfeiting the soul of the cuisine. It takes knowledge and depth, a great palate, skill, and technique to do that. I find so many inspirations in the food at this hip place in Pangrati, with its handful of sidewalk tables and its wood-fired ovens and open grill in the back. There's a palpable excitement among the waitstaff, who seem genuinely thrilled to work here, serving up pretty amazing modern Greek fare. This simple chickpea and mushroom dish is inspired by something I ate there, a dish that requires good ingredients and basic cooking skills to prepare.

MAKES 6 SERVINGS

- ¼ cup extra-virgin Greek olive oil
- 1 medium red onion, chopped
- 4 garlic cloves, very thinly sliced
- 3 large portobello mushrooms, wiped clean with a damp cloth and cut into ½-inch slices
- ½ pound enoki mushrooms, trimmed
- ½ pound cremini mushrooms, wiped clean with a damp cloth and halved
- 2 tablespoons tomato paste
- 1½ tablespoons grape molasses (petimezi)
- 2 (15-ounce) cans good-quality, low-sodium chickpeas, drained and rinsed
- 3 cups mushroom or vegetable stock, plus more if needed
- ⅓ cup red wine vinegar or sherry vinegar
- 2 teaspoons soy sauce
- 1 bay leaf
- Coarse sea salt and freshly ground black pepper to taste

Preheat the oven to 350°F.

In a Dutch oven, heat the olive oil over medium heat. Add the onion and cook for 7 to 8 minutes, until softened. Stir in the garlic and cook for 2 minutes. Add the portobello mushrooms and cook for 4 minutes, until they begin to soften. Add the enoki and cremini mushrooms and cook for 2 to 3 minutes, until they soften and lose a little volume. Stir in the tomato paste, petimezi, and chickpeas, then add the stock, vinegar, soy sauce, and bay leaf. The liquid should come about three-quarters of the way up the contents of the pot; add more stock if needed. Season with salt and pepper.

Cover and bring to a simmer, then transfer to the oven. Braise for about 1 hour, or until there is almost no liquid left in the pot. Remove and discard the bay leaf, adjust the salt and pepper to taste, and serve.

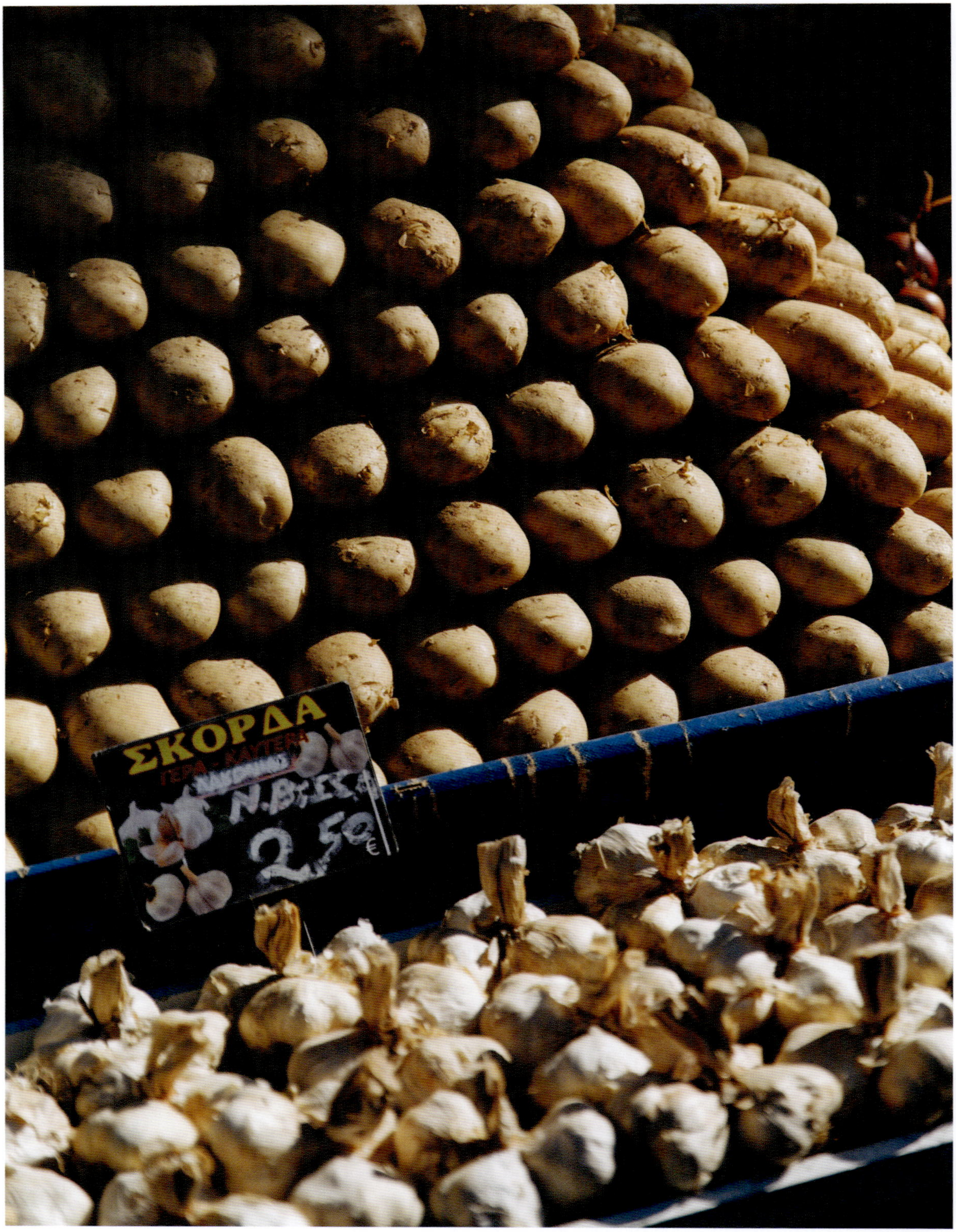
ΣΚΟΡΔΑ
2,50€

Vegan Root Vegetable Kapama

Kapama is one of the classic meat stews of Greece, made with regional variations all over the country. But here, root vegetables take the place of meat, making this dish a great representation of one of the keenest vegan trends in Athens: the reinterpretation of carnivorous pleasures not with laboratory meats but with other ingredients that are natural—real food.

MAKES 6 SERVINGS

½ cup extra-virgin Greek olive oil

3 large red onions, coarsely chopped

3 garlic cloves, chopped

3 large carrots, peeled, halved lengthwise, and cut crosswise into ½-inch slices

2 large turnips, peeled and cut into 1½-inch cubes

2 parsnips, peeled and cut into ½-inch rounds

1 cinnamon stick

6 whole cloves

6 allspice berries

2 bay leaves

3 fresh rosemary sprigs

Sea salt and freshly ground black pepper to taste

3 cups (1½-inch) butternut squash cubes

2 cups vacuum-packed or canned chestnuts

⅔ cup dry red wine

2 tablespoons balsamic vinegar

1 tablespoon Greek pine honey, or more to taste

½ cup dark seedless raisins

Heat the olive oil in a large, wide pot over medium heat. Add the onions, swirl for a few turns in the pan, turn the heat down to medium-low, and cook the onions until lightly browned, 12 to 15 minutes. Stir in the garlic. Add the carrots, turnips, parsnips, cinnamon stick, cloves, allspice, bay leaves, and rosemary, season lightly with salt and pepper, and cover the pot. Cook for about 5 minutes, checking occasionally and stirring if needed to avoid burning the vegetables.

Add the butternut squash and chestnuts, tossing gently to coat in the oil. Cook for 5 minutes, uncovered, then add the wine. As soon as it steams up, add enough hot water to come about halfway up the contents of the pot. Cover the pot, turn the heat up to medium-high, and bring to a simmer. Turn the heat back down to medium-low and cook until the vegetables are all tender and easy to pierce with a fork, 20 to 25 minutes. About 10 minutes before removing from the heat, stir in the balsamic vinegar, honey, and raisins. Remove and discard the bay leaves. Adjust the seasoning with salt and pepper and serve.

Lefteris Lazarou's Spanakopita Cream

During season 4 of My Greek Table, *I visited Lefteris Lazarou in his kitchen at Varoulko in Piraeus. It had been a while since we'd seen each other, and the chef, a close friend and the first chef I met in Greece when I was a young food reporter, is, in my mind, the father of modern Greek cooking. His penchant for turning ingredients and recipes once thought to be pedestrian—from monkfish, monkfish liver, and garfish to the Greek comfort food like cabbage or spinach rice—into delicate, refined, and brilliant dishes is what still sets him apart from the crowd. He has left a legacy that generations of young chefs strive to emulate. He turned a spanakopita, or spinach pie, into a luscious creamy delight for me, which I offer up here.*

MAKES 6 SERVINGS

3 frozen phyllo sheets, thawed and at room temperature

½ cup extra-virgin Greek olive oil

2 leeks, trimmed and chopped

2 pounds baby spinach

Salt and freshly ground black pepper to taste

6 ice cubes

1 bunch chopped fresh dill

Strained juice of 1 lemon

1½ cups crumbled Greek feta

1 tablespoon dried tarragon

Preheat the oven to 350°F.

Tear apart the phyllo sheets, place on a rimmed baking sheet, and bake until golden and crisp, 7 to 10 minutes. Remove and let cool.

Heat the olive oil in a large, wide pot over medium heat. Add the leeks and sauté for 5 to 7 minutes to soften. Add the spinach in batches, and as it loses volume keep adding the rest, stirring, until it's all used up. Season with salt and pepper. Cook for about 5 minutes, or until most of the pan juices have evaporated. Transfer the mixture to the bowl of a food processor or powerful blender. Add the ice cubes, which will help the spinach retain its bright green color, and puree the mixture until smooth.

Add the dill in handfuls, pureeing after each addition. Add the lemon juice in 3 doses, testing for acidity after the first addition before proceeding with the next one, and then again after the second addition, before adding the remainder. Add the feta and puree until smooth. Add the tarragon and puree again. Add 2 of the baked phyllo sheets and puree. Test the texture for density, and if it's too loose add the last sheet, if desired. Serve.

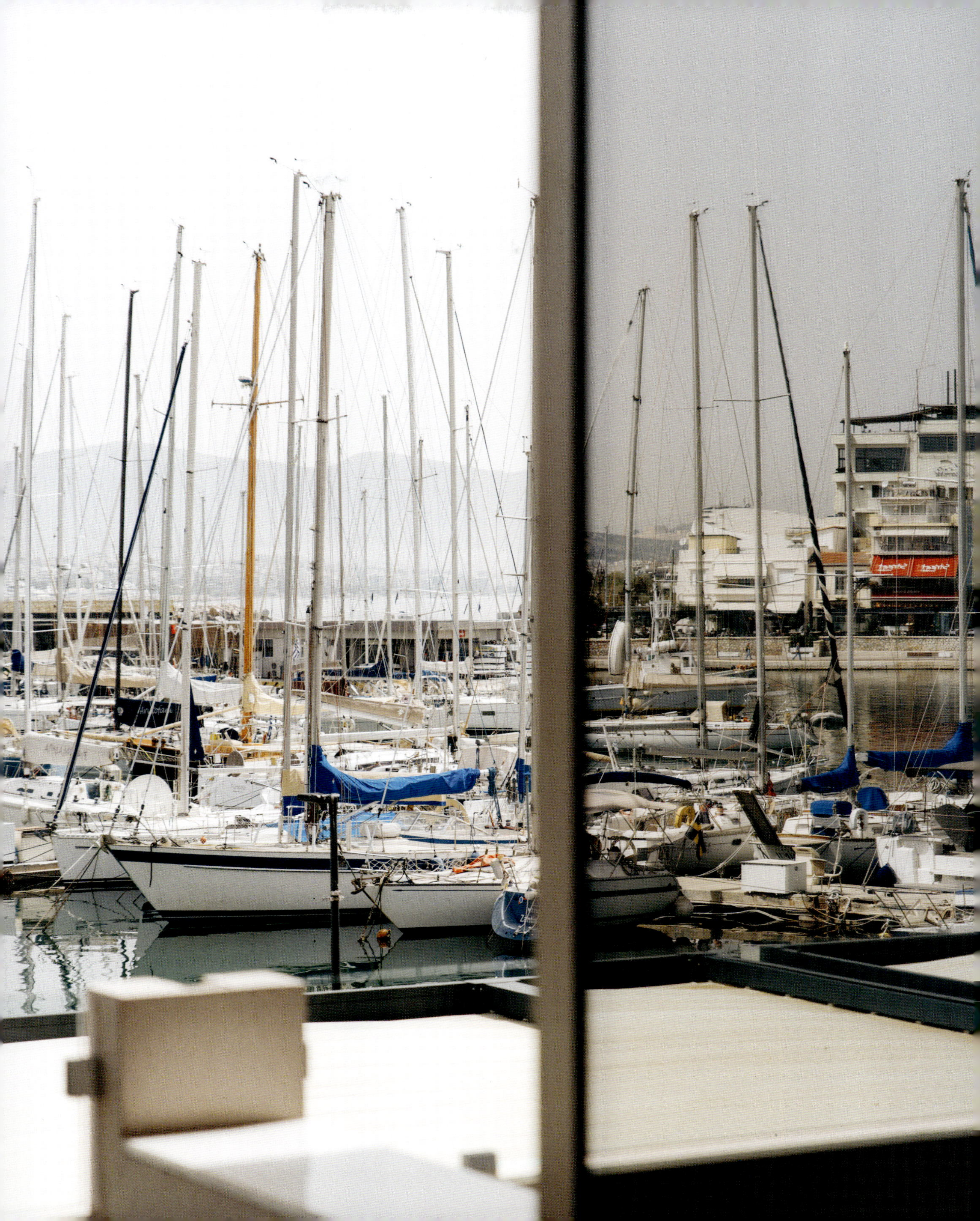

Lahanorizo Cream

"This is a poor person's recipe," Lefteris Lazarou told me the first time I tasted this reinvention of cabbage rice. He transformed this most pedestrian of Greek rice dishes, one that was often the bane of kids forced to eat it, into something luscious, sophisticated, and delectable, all the while keeping the flavor profile of this simple Greek recipe intact. Serve as is, or as an accompaniment to Filet Mignon with Mavrodaphne Sauce (page 328) or a grilled fish fillet.

MAKES 4 TO 6 SERVINGS

½ cup extra-virgin Greek olive oil

3 leeks, trimmed and chopped

½ head cabbage, coarsely shredded

⅔ cup white basmati rice

2 cups water

Salt to taste

Large pinch Greek saffron (krokos Kozanis)

⅔ cup chopped fresh mint

3 tablespoons strained fresh lemon juice

2 to 3 tablespoons apple cider vinegar

Heat the olive oil in a large, wide pot over medium heat. Add the leeks and sauté until soft, about 8 minutes. Add the cabbage in batches, so that it all fits in the pot. When the cabbage is wilted, after about 6 minutes, stir in the rice and then add the water. Season with salt to taste. Stir in the saffron. Cook until the liquid is almost completely absorbed, about 15 minutes, then stir in the mint and lemon juice. Cook for a few more minutes, until everything is tender.

Transfer the mixture to the bowl of a food processor or powerful blender. Process on high until the mixture is very smooth and creamy. Taste and adjust the acidity by adding a little of the apple cider vinegar as needed, and season with salt as needed. Serve.

Green Beans Yiahni
with Bottarga

What I love most about this dish is that it combines one of the most earthy and simple recipes for stewed green beans with one of the most esteemed, ancient, gourmet Greek ingredients, avgotaraho (bottarga), a marriage of opposites that works seamlessly.

MAKES 4 TO 6 SERVINGS

½ cup extra-virgin Greek olive oil, divided

2 large red onions, chopped

4 garlic cloves, minced

2 pounds fresh green beans, ends trimmed and stringy fibers removed

2 large potatoes, peeled and cut into 1½- to 2-inch cubes

2½ cups canned whole tomatoes

Sea salt and freshly ground black pepper to taste

2 teaspoons squid ink

½ cup chopped fresh flat-leaf parsley

8 to 12 paper-thin slices Greek avgotaraho (bottarga)

In a large pot, warm ¼ cup of the olive oil over medium heat. Add the onions and cook until translucent, 8 to 10 minutes. Stir in the garlic and green beans and toss to coat in the oil. Add the potatoes, tomatoes, salt, and pepper. Stir in the squid ink.

Add enough water to come about a third of the way up the contents of the pot. Cover and simmer for 35 minutes, or until the beans are tender. Right before removing from the heat, stir in the parsley and adjust the seasoning with additional salt and pepper as desired.

Serve topped with the shaved bottarga and drizzle with the remaining ¼ cup olive oil.

Zucchini Stuffed
with Black Rice, Fish, and Avgolemono

Black rice is a staple in China, the Philippines, Thailand, and other parts of East Asia. It was only a matter of time, what with the Filipino population in Athens at around forty thousand and the Chinese population, especially downtown, growing, that Athenians would start to venture into the ethnic food shops, curious about a whole new world of ingredients, black rice among them. And, of course, it is only natural that some of those ingredients would find themselves a new place in Greek restaurants, especially in the kitchens of young chefs less bound by tradition than generations past. And so it was that I first sampled this delectable if unrecognizable rendition of a beloved Greek classic, kolokythakia gemista me riz avgolemono (rice-stuffed zucchini) at Taverna ton Filon, a great place in the working-class neighborhood of Kolonos that raised the bar on Greek cooking ever since opening its doors to rave reviews in 2024. The dish inspired me to re-create my own version of it at home.

MAKES 6 TO 12 SERVINGS

6 zucchini (7 to 8 inches long), trimmed

5 tablespoons extra-virgin Greek olive oil, divided

2 red onions, minced

4 garlic cloves, finely chopped

⅔ cup black rice, rinsed in a colander

3 cups fish or vegetable stock, divided

½ cup dry white wine or ouzo

Sea salt and freshly ground black pepper to taste

1½ pounds white-fleshed fish fillets, such as swordfish, halibut, or cod

½ cup finely chopped fresh dill

½ cup finely chopped fresh flat-leaf parsley

2 large eggs, plus 2 large egg yolks

Strained juice of 1 large lemon

Cut the zucchini in half crosswise to get two cylinders. Using a teaspoon, carefully hollow out the zucchini pulp, leaving about a ¼-inch wall around the hollowed-out cylinders to hold the rice filling. Chop the pulp and set aside.

Heat 3 tablespoons of the olive oil in a large skillet over medium heat. Add the onions and garlic and sauté, stirring, for about 7 minutes, until softened. Add the rice and stir to coat in the oil. Add the zucchini pulp and stir all together. Add 1⅓ cups of the stock and the wine and bring to a simmer, then reduce the heat to low and simmer gently until the rice absorbs the liquid but is still moist, about 20 minutes. The rice should be about two-thirds of the way cooked. Season with salt and pepper.

In the meantime, heat the remaining 2 tablespoons olive oil in a nonstick skillet. Add the fish fillets and cook for about 4 minutes, turning once and seasoning with a little salt and pepper. Pour in ⅓ cup stock and cook until there is almost no liquid left, about another minute or so. Remove and cool, then shred the fish fillets and set aside.

Remove the rice from the heat and stir in the shredded fish, dill, and parsley.

Season the hollowed-out zucchini inside and out with a little salt and pepper. Fill each cavity with an equal portion of the rice mixture, mounding it over the top. Place upright, one cylinder snugly next to the other, in a wide pot. Pour the remaining 1⅓ cups stock into the pot and enough additional water to come about halfway up the height of the zucchini. Cover and bring to a simmer over medium heat. Simmer for about 35 minutes, or until the rice and zucchini are both tender.

Make the avgolemono: In a medium metal bowl, vigorously whisk the whole eggs and yolks until frothy, about 7 minutes. Slowly add the lemon juice, drop by drop and mixing all the while, until the mixture thickens, a few more minutes. Take a ladleful of the pot juices and very slowly, literally drop by drop, add it to the egg-lemon mixture, whisking all the while, then add a second and third ladleful in the same way, whisking constantly. Pour the avgolemono back into the pot, swirl it around to distribute it evenly, and serve.

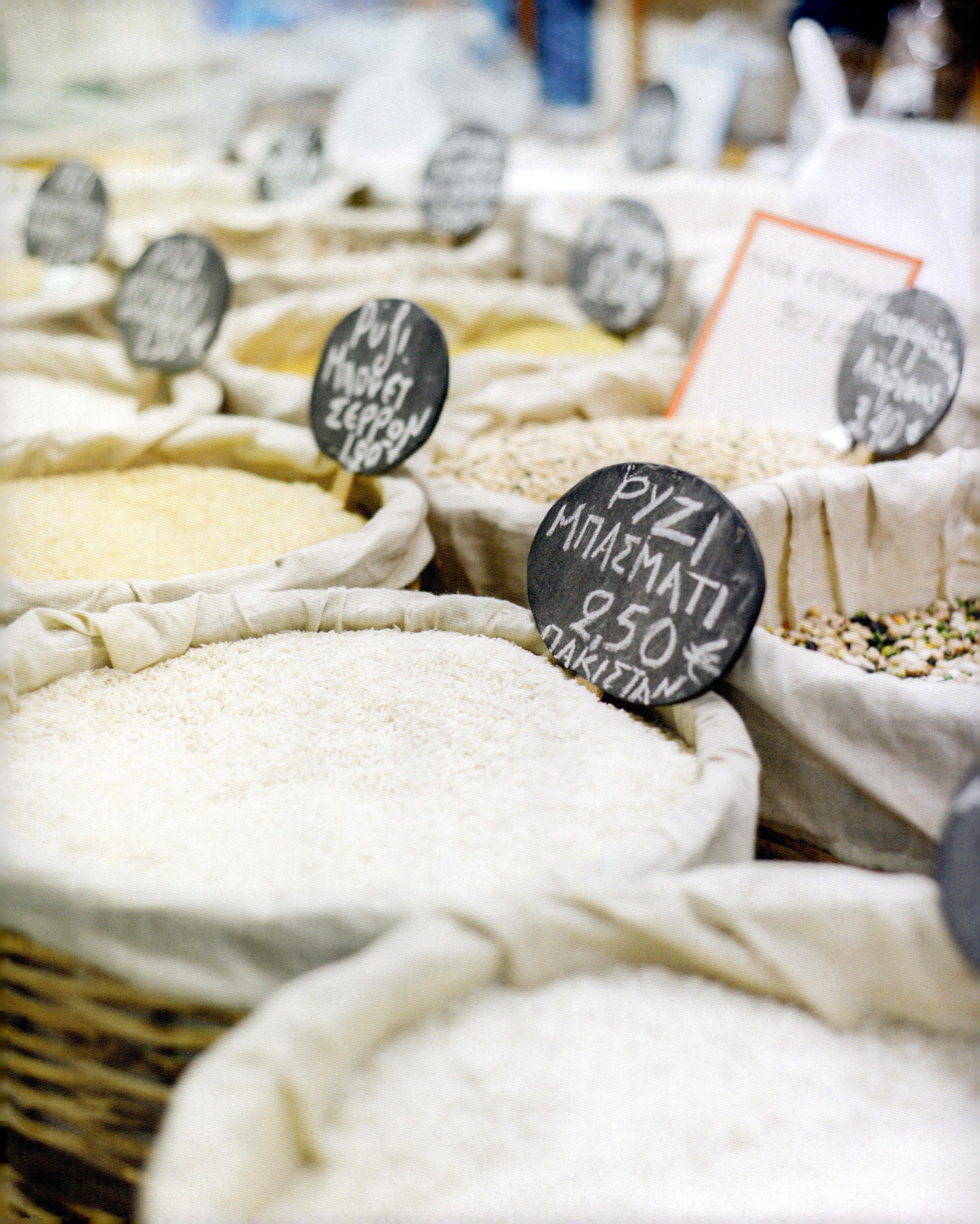
ΡΥΖΙ
ΜΠΑΣΜΑΤΙ
250€
ΠΑΚΙΣΤΑΝ

Carbs à la Athens

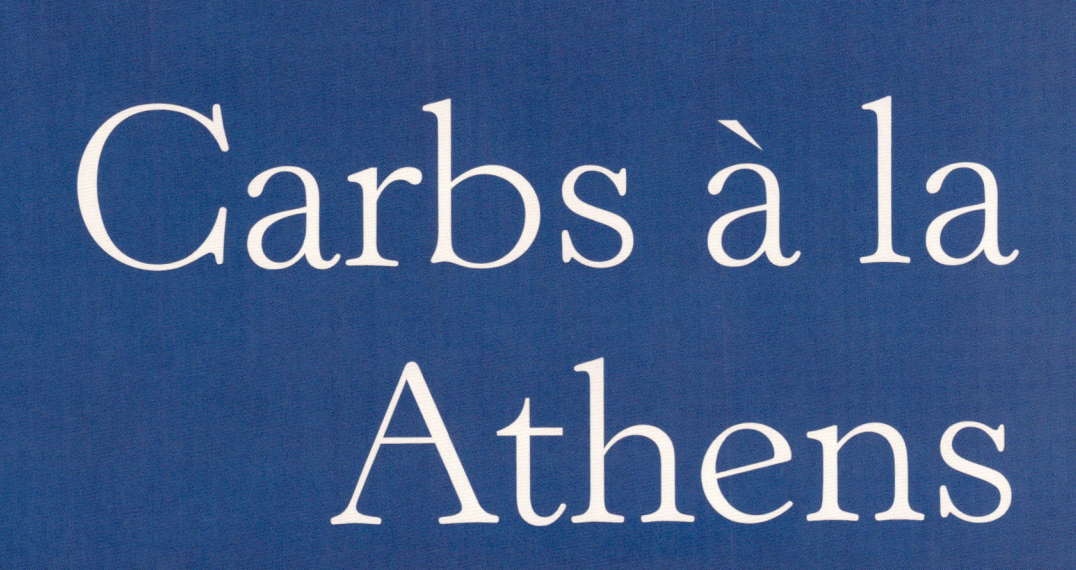

In my three decades as an adopted daughter of Athens, I've stood witness to many food trends, but perhaps none as radical as the way Greeks approach the cooking and consuming of carbs. When I first moved here, my point of reference was the family table, mostly that of my in-laws, and there were many a meal in which the main course was a plate of either macaronia or patates "mploum" (transliterated from the Greek spelling, and pronounced "bloom"). With less than perfect knowledge of Greek back then, I always thought this term referred to pasta or potatoes boiled to a sad and soggy end because everything was prepared this way (at least at the hands of my mother-in-law, who was not a great cook, and everything she put on the table was pretty much soft and tasteless). Mploum, however, is onomatopoeia for the sound, to Greek ears, of something hitting water—a splash! It generally refers to pasta and potatoes cooked in a lot of liquid, the better to soak up afterward with guilt-free chunks of bread, traditionally Greeks' favorite of all carbs. That's changed, too.

Now, soft pasta has been tossed out the window with the pasta water, to borrow from a familiar saying, and in its place al dente has stepped up. Older Greeks just can't embrace toothsome macaroni. It took the postwar generations, many of whom left to study elsewhere and returned with newly minted food experiences, to appreciate carbs with texture!

Other changes on the comforting carb front follow many of the global trends, including a slightly faddish aversion to carbs and the advent of all sorts of gluten-free options, most of which I am not crazy about and so have omitted by design.

Pasta bowls in Athens are a delicious mix these days, and it's easy to understand why. Pasta is by its very essence a carte blanche for so many sauces and toppings. The variety available in supermarkets and gourmet shops has expanded exponentially since I first moved here to include many Italian options, including fresh pasta; regional, artisanal Greek shapes; and, in the last decade or so, more and more Asian options.

A rather perfunctory, if delicious, swirl into the Athenian pasta bowl revealed to me a few other trends. Chefs are taking classic Greek and Italian dishes, for example, and tweaking them to the times by mixing place-specific pasta, such as egg noodles from Metsovo or Komotini or the Peloponnese, with hyperlocal Greek ingredients like singlino, a cured pork specific to the Mani, or one of countless great Greek regional cheeses. Regional pasta specialties have been deconstructed and reconstructed to meet the aesthetics of today's diners, eager to taste something creative but comforting, something new and yet familiar. A safe adventure. Even macaronia mploum has gotten a facelift. Scanning the pages of *Gastronomos*, the main Greek food magazine, I counted dozens of versions of these old dishes, all spiffed up with newfound purpose and, well, splash!

Alas, though, carbs are not limited to pasta. Rice is a biggie, too, and this city has embraced it in ways that would make the United Nations proud. Not long ago, all the great pilafs and vegetable-rice main courses were just about the limit when it came to the ways in which Greeks cooked rice. Sunday roasts were often accompanied by buttery rice pressed into a tube or Bundt pan and revealed with some Greek motherly drama at the table. But the ethnic makeup of Athens has broadened. Indian and Pakistani restaurants dot the center, serving up their delicious, traditional biriyanis, pilaus, and more. Risotto has become like a long-lost sibling returned home, embraced with abandon everywhere, and often rejiggered with Greek cheeses and Greek ingredients. Chinese, Japanese, Korean, and Thai restaurants exist in every neighborhood, bringing their rice specialties to the masses; for a time, Greek sushi (page 116) was the pinnacle of Athenian gastronomy.

In this chapter, I've focused mostly on pasta and rice, because other carbs are less prone to main-course status. I've tried to present a balanced bowl, focusing on a few local and traditional dishes that have all but disappeared, as well as on newer recipes that mirror the reinterpretation of Greek classics and the openness to once-obscure ingredients.

But, with my New York roots, I felt compelled to set aside some space for my personal favorite of all manifestations of comforting, beloved, if recently maligned carbs: pizza. Yes, there is an Athens story about that, too, and a recipe (page 286) or two to make!

Gkogklies

HANDMADE PASTA NUGGETS OF ATTICA

Think fresh gnocchi: That's what this old recipe for handmade pasta looks like. This combination of flour, salt, and water makes for the simplest of recipes, nuggets of dough boiled in salted water, drained, then drenched in melted, almost browned butter and a hard grated cheese called myzithra, *which was the de rigueur grating cheese for Greek pasta dishes long before Parmigiano ever entered the scene. This is a recipe from the Mesogeia, the inland area of the Attica peninsula, a specialty of the Arvanites (see page 267), who settled this area as well as parts of the Peloponnese and beyond in the fourteenth century.*

MAKES 6 TO 8 SERVINGS

4½ to 5 cups all-purpose flour

1 scant teaspoon salt, plus more for cooking

1 to 1½ cups water

1 cup (2 sticks) salted butter

Grated dried Greek myzithra or any other hard cheese, as desired

Combine 4½ cups of the flour with the salt in a large bowl. Slowly add the water, mixing by hand as you go, until a firm but pliant dough starts to take shape. The flour will absorb about a quarter of its volume in water, but this isn't an exacting art. It may take a little more, or the mixture may be too wet and need a little of the remaining flour. Knead and observe! The dough, when ready, should be dense, firm, and smooth, but pliant. Cover it in the bowl and let it rest for 30 minutes.

Shape the dough into a loaf and cut through the loaf at intervals of about 1 inch to create pieces that are all about the same size.

Lightly flour a work surface. Roll the first piece of dough into a rope about ¾ inch thick. Cut the rope at intervals of about 1 inch to create nuggets. Roll and press each nugget on the floured surface toward you, making a small indentation in each piece as you go. Set aside on a floured plate. Continue until all the dough is used up.

Bring a large pot of water to a rolling boil and add a generous amount of salt. Add the gkogklies in batches so as not to crowd the pot. Traditionally they boil for about 10 minutes (Greeks like soft pasta!). With a slotted spoon, skim them off the surface as they rise and place on a platter.

In the meantime, while the gkogklies are simmering, melt the butter in a small pot over medium heat to the point where it just starts to brown ever so lightly. As you skim off the gkogklies and transfer them to the platter, pour melted butter over them and sprinkle generously with grated cheese. Continue this way, layering the platter with gkogklies, melted butter, and cheese until done. Serve immediately.

Food Lore on Athens's Doorstep: Spata and Mesogeia

Spata, where the Athens International Airport is located, isn't a place most people think of when it comes to culinary traditions. The area is in Mesogeia, the interior part of the Attica peninsula. Its proximity to Athens and its decidedly contemporary suburban aura belies its long history. The area has been inhabited since Neolithic times but takes its name from a fourteenth-century Tosk Albanian despot named Gjin Bua Shpata (his surname means "sword"), who ruled western Greece. Albanian Christians like the Tosk tribe were invited into the country by the Byzantine and Frankish rulers of the time as a way to repopulate deserted areas and bolster their army. Now, generations later, the progeny of these early Albanian settlers are called Arvanites. They're totally Hellenized, and they have, like many regional Greeks, a cuisine all their own. Some of that survives today in Spata and its environs.

Agriculture and husbandry have been the main professions of the Arvanites in Mesogeia for centuries, and much of the traditional, hyperlocal food here, when you can find it, mirrors people's ties to the land. They excelled in viticulture, and the vine and all it offers are important parts of local culture even today. It is here that the famed Savatiano and Roditis grapes flourish, the stuff of Greece's well-known retsina. Grape growing is still a major source of income, so much so that to this day big events like weddings typically don't take place until after the harvest is complete, the crop sold, and the wine made, sometime after the middle of November, in other words. During the harvest, around the vineyards that blanket large swaths of land, despite the encroachments of highways and other accoutrements of twenty-first-century life, the sticky aroma of fermenting grapes is everywhere, as are the specialties made with must. The moustokouloura, ruddy grape-must cookies perfumed with cinnamon, are legendary in the Mesogeia, and one bakery in particular has been famous for them for the last three decades: Daremas, in Markopoulos.

The Arvanites farmers of Mesogeia grew legumes and grains, and for a time the barley that went into brewing Fix beer, an iconic Greek brand. Today, their cooking is still focused on the land, with many grain-based specialties prepared at home, such as a sweet trahana (made with whole milk); eggplants braised with trahana or snails; numerous pies, including fat spinach-cheese cigars rolled up with handmade phyllo; a local specialty called *mousounta*, which is spinach mixed with batter and baked; and a fried pie filled with feta called tiganopsomo, often served with a drizzling of petimezi (grape molasses), yet another gift of the vine.

There are others, too, like a luscious oniony baked cod dish studded with raisins and goat braised in tomato sauce, which typically followed a wedge of unique pastitsio (page 230) at wedding receptions, the better to warm one's bones with, since, as mentioned above, betrothals were generally postharvest winter affairs.

The Wedding Pastitsio of Spata

This rich dish and slight variation on the classic pastitsio theme, was served before the main course of tomato-braised goat at traditional weddings in Spata. This recipe is adapted from the book Traditional and Tasty Flavors of Spata *by Maria Kouloheri.*

MAKES 6 TO 8 SERVINGS

6 tablespoons extra-virgin Greek olive oil

1 large red onion, finely chopped

2 garlic cloves, finely chopped

2¼ pounds ground beef chuck

1 teaspoon ground nutmeg

1 teaspoon ground cinnamon, plus more for sprinkling

Salt and freshly ground black pepper to taste

1 heaping teaspoon tomato paste

1¼ pounds very ripe fresh tomatoes, grated

⅓ cup white Savatiano wine or another dry light wine such as pinot grigio

1 pound bucatini pasta

2 quarts whole milk, preferably sheep's milk

½ cup fine semolina flour

½ cup (1½ sticks) unsalted butter, 6 tablespoons chilled and 6 tablespoons at room temperature

8 cups Greek kefalotyri cheese, finely grated (about 2 pounds), divided

8 large eggs

Heat ¼ cup of the olive oil in a large, wide pot over medium heat. Add the onion and sauté until translucent and soft, about 8 minutes. Add the garlic and stir for a minute. Add the ground beef and cook, stirring to break up the meat, until all of it changes color, 8 to 10 minutes. Stir in the nutmeg and cinnamon and season with salt and pepper. Add the tomato paste and stir to thoroughly combine. Add the tomatoes and bring to a boil, then add the white wine. Bring back to a boil, then reduce the heat to a simmer. Cover and simmer for about 1½ hours, or until it is thick. Add a little hot water to the sauce if necessary during cooking to keep it from burning. The final texture should have a sheen from the slow cooking and release of so much fat and collagen in the meat.

While the sauce is simmering, bring a large pot of salted water to a boil, add the pasta, and cook until al dente. Drain, transfer to a large bowl, and mix in the remaining 2 tablespoons olive oil. Set aside.

Combine the milk and flour in a large saucepan and heat over medium heat, whisking vigorously so that the flour doesn't clump up, for about 5 minutes. Reduce to medium-low and continue whisking until it starts to thicken; this might take 20 to 30 minutes. It's done when large bubbles splatter on the surface of the sauce. Remove from the heat and whisk in the chilled butter and 2 cups of the grated cheese. Let the sauce cool down for 6 to 7 minutes. In a bowl, whisk 6 of the eggs until frothy. Slowly add the eggs to the sauce, whisking all the while.

Preheat the oven to 375°F. Take a little of the room-temperature butter and grease a large baking pan, either 10 x 15 inches or 12 x 18 inches.

Melt the remaining butter and add it to the pasta, mixing well. Whisk the last 2 eggs and mix them into the pasta as well, together with about a quarter of the ground meat sauce and 1 cup grated cheese.

Spread half the pasta inside the baking pan, sprinkle with half of the remaining grated cheese, and then spoon the remaining ground meat sauce on top, spreading it evenly over the surface. Add the remaining pasta mixture, and over that sprinkle the remaining cheese.

Using a ladle, spoon the béchamel evenly over the top. Sprinkle with cinnamon and bake for about 1 hour, or until the béchamel is set. Remove from oven and let the pastitsio stand for at least 30 minutes before serving.

Spaghetti with Avgotaraho

Bottarga—avgotaraho—the salted roe of grey mullet, typically preserved in beeswax, has been revered in Greece since at least the Byzantine era. But it wasn't until the 1990s that this once-rare treat exploded on the food scene, thanks in large part to the entrepreneurship of Zafeiris Trikalinos, who grew what was a small family business into a bristling gourmet success story, exporting his now-famous avgotaraho all over the world.

There are other producers, too, of course, but Trikalinos has expanded the concept by creating bottarga dust and an array of salts and other products from around the marshlands of Mesolonghi, on the western coast of Greece, whence the grey mullet goes to spawn and his familial roots are. He's also upped the ante on package design. The black and gold motifs speak of Greek luxury and pride, which Athenian chefs have embraced these past twenty years or so, folding the umami-intense, almost gelatinous paper-thin slivers of bottarga into pasta, dotting them over risotto or the fish roe dip taramosalata, slipping them between dried fig halves, or pairing them with apricots, among other things. Avgotaraho, indeed, is the crowning example of a very old Greek food that was reborn to fit the times, as Athens and Greece came into their own as culinary destinations.

MAKES 4 TO 6 SERVINGS

Salt

1 pound spaghetti

6 tablespoons extra-virgin Greek olive oil, or more, as desired

1 garlic clove, lightly smashed

4 to 5 ounces Greek avgotaraho (bottarga), cut into very thin slices

Grated zest of 1 lemon

Pinch fleur de sel

Coarsely ground black pepper to taste

Bring a large pot of water to a rolling boil and add a generous amount of salt. Add the pasta and cook according to the package directions until al dente.

While the pasta is cooking, warm the olive oil and garlic together in a shallow pan over low heat and swirl the garlic around to flavor the oil. Remove from the heat and remove and discard the garlic clove.

Drain the pasta, reserving ½ cup of its cooking liquid. Transfer the pasta to a large bowl and toss gently with the cooking liquid, garlic-infused olive oil, bottarga, lemon zest, fleur de sel, and black pepper and serve.

Seychelles' Signature Pappardelle
with Buffalo Meat

I am lucky to live a stone's throw from one of my favorite restaurants in Athens: Seychelles, a true pioneer of modern Greek comfort food. It took courage for original owners George Koutouzis and his partner, Anna Repousi, to open their doors, in 2015, in a simple, old, run-down house on the corner of Kerameikou and Akadimou Streets on Plateia Avdi in Metaxourgeio. This once-thriving historic working-class neighborhood a few minutes on foot from Omonoia was a mess, its open spaces and old buildings usurped by junkies and bordellos. But where urban blight spreads, artists (and a few pioneering restaurateurs and bar owners) move in, and the cycle of urban renewal begins, and so was it with Metaxourgeio, which today is one of the most fun and hip places to live and dine in the city.

Seychelles boasts many great dishes, but the one below is a beacon for pasta lovers all over the city. It calls for kavourma, a traditional charcuterie produced in northern Greece, from buffalo or pork or a combination of meats that are cut into chunks, slowly cooked, and preserved in their rendered fat and/or olive oil. It now can be found in Athenian and other Greek gourmet shops shaped into a log or loaf. You can substitute cured sausage meat, such as soppressata, or smoked ham, since kavourma will be hard to find outside of specific Greek markets.

MAKES 4 SERVINGS

¼ cup extra-virgin Greek olive oil

1 yellow onion, minced

½ pound Greek kavourma or cured sausage, such as soppressata, or smoked or cured ham, cut into 1-inch chunks

1 teaspoon brown sugar

5 tablespoons balsamic vinegar

Coarse sea salt and freshly ground black pepper

1 pound pappardelle

5 ounces Parmigiano, grated

3 tablespoons chopped fresh flat-leaf parsley

1½ cups fresh galomyzithra, or soft chèvre mixed with 1 to 2 tablespoons quark or full-fat Greek yogurt

Bring a large pot of water to a rolling boil.

While the water is heating, prepare the sauce: Heat the olive oil in a large, deep skillet over medium heat. Add the onion and sauté, stirring occasionally, until translucent and lightly browned, 10 to 12 minutes. Add the kavourma or other charcuterie, and turn to coat and mix with the onion. Sprinkle in the brown sugar. As soon as the sugar starts to caramelize, in about 1 minute, add the balsamic vinegar. Reduce the heat to very low and cook until the liquid in the pan is thick, almost syrupy, 3 to 4 minutes. Remove from the heat.

Season the boiling water generously with salt and cook the pappardelle for about 3 minutes less than is stated on the package directions. Drain, reserving 1 cup of the cooking liquid. Immediately add the pappardelle to the skillet, swish in about ½ cup of the pasta water together with the grated Parmigiano. Remove from the heat and stir in the parsley.

Serve in 4 individual bowls. Place a dollop of the Greek galomyzithra over the pasta and drizzle with a little olive oil. Serve immediately.

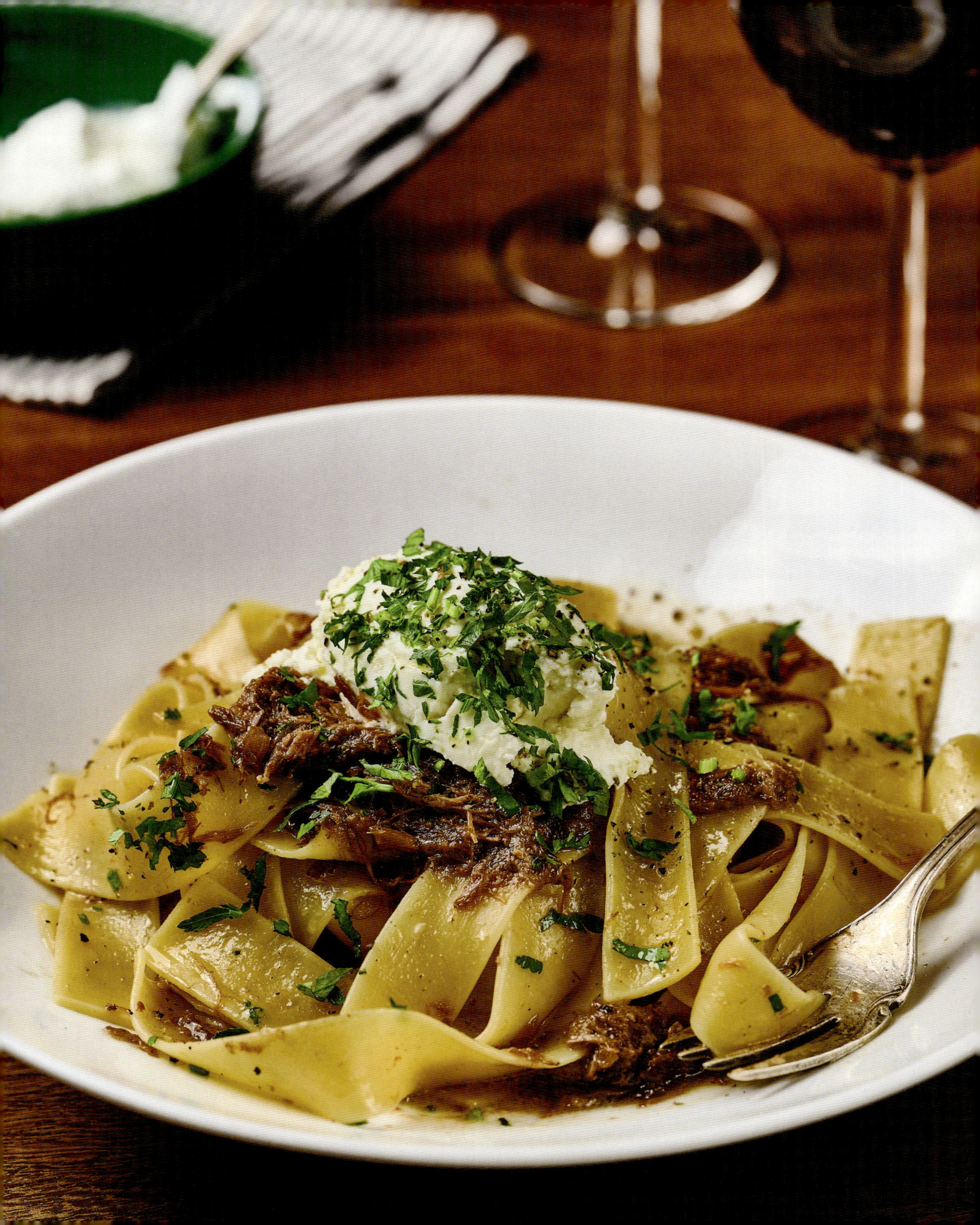

ΙΧΘΥΟΠΩΛΕΙΟ
ΤΣΙΠΟΥΡΕΣ
5.98
ΦΑΓΓΡΙΑ
6.98
ΙΧΘΥΟΠΩΛΕΙΟ
ΦΑΓΓΡΙΑ
6.99
ΤΣΙΠΟΥΡΕΣ
4.98
ΓΑΡΙΔΕΣ
8.99

Garidomakaronada

SPICY OUZO-SHRIMP PASTA

The sweet, succulent combo of shrimp, tomato sauce, and pasta is a destination dish in Athens (and beyond). Restaurants vie for a place on ten-best lists published every so often on food sites and in magazines. On Clean Monday, the start of Lent, mountains of this dish are served in tavernas up and down the coastline, as people head to the sea for all the traditional seafood dishes of Greek Lent. There are, literally, countless versions of shrimp pasta, but one thing is for sure: Somewhere in the not-too-distant past an enterprising cook embraced this Italian classic and christened it Greek, so much so that today it's a veritable tradition.

MAKES 4 TO 6 SERVINGS

3 tablespoons extra-virgin Greek olive oil

1 large red onion, finely chopped

Sea salt and freshly ground black pepper to taste

4 garlic cloves, minced

½ to 1 teaspoon red pepper flakes

4 cups canned diced tomatoes

1 cup water

½ cup ouzo, divided

1 (1-inch) strip orange zest

2 tablespoons unsalted butter

1 pound medium-large shrimp, peeled and deveined, heads and tails left on

1 pound spaghetti or linguine

2 teaspoons chopped fresh marjoram or oregano

In a deep skillet or saucepan, heat the olive oil over medium heat. Add the onion, season lightly with salt, and sauté for 7 to 8 minutes, until softened and translucent. Stir in the garlic, red pepper flakes, tomatoes, and water, turn the heat up to medium-high, and bring to a boil. Add ¼ cup of the ouzo and the orange zest, reduce the heat to a simmer, and season with additional salt and pepper. Cook the sauce for 20 to 25 minutes, until thickened.

While the sauce is simmering, in a large, deep skillet, melt the butter over medium heat. Add the shrimp and season with salt and pepper. When the shrimp start to turn pink on both sides, carefully pour in the remaining ¼ cup ouzo. Beware that it may flame up, which is normal. Cook for about 5 minutes all together, then remove from the heat.

Bring a large pot of water to a rolling boil and season generously with salt. Cook the pasta according to the package directions until al dente. Drain and reserve about 1 cup of the cooking liquid.

While the pasta is cooking, add the shrimp and all its pan juices to the tomato sauce. Heat for about 5 minutes. Stir in the marjoram and adjust the seasoning with salt and pepper.

Add the drained pasta to the sauce, loosening the mixture with some of the pasta water, and serve.

Surf 'n' Turf Pasta
with Pasturma, Shrimp, and Pistachios

Here's a personal interpretation of a no-holds-barred approach to modern Athenian pasta: a sauce that includes what would once have been considered an unthinkable duo, spiced pasturma and shrimp, dappled with the beloved pistachios from the nearby island of Aegina in the Saronic Gulf. But in Athens these days, anything goes, so long as it's tasty.

Pasturma (sometimes spelled bastirma *or* pastourma*) is a pungent, spiced, cured beef that is beloved in Greek, Turkish, and Armenian cooking. You can find it in specialty food shops that specialize in Greek or Middle Eastern products. The closest substitute would be pastrami.*

MAKES 4 TO 6 SERVINGS

Sea salt and freshly ground black pepper to taste

1 pound twisted pasta, such as Italian caserecce, trofie, strozzapreti, or Cretan schioufichta

6 tablespoons extra-virgin Greek olive oil, divided

1 leek, trimmed and chopped

3 shallots, finely chopped

3 garlic cloves, finely chopped

½ pound medium shrimp, heads and tails on, peeled and deveined

3 slices pasturma, minced

¼ cup dry white wine

1 cup hot vegetable or chicken stock

5 ounces Greek manouri or ricotta salata, crumbled or coarsely grated

¼ cup grated Greek kefalograviera, kefalotyri, or Parmigiano cheese

5 fresh thyme sprigs, stemmed and chopped

1¼ cups coarsely chopped salted pistachios, preferably from Aegina, toasted

1 scant teaspoon green peppercorns

Bring a large pot of water to a rolling boil and add a generous amount of salt. Cook the pasta according to the package directions until al dente.

While the pasta water is heating, in a large, deep skillet, warm 3 tablespoons olive oil over medium-high heat. Add the leek, shallots, and garlic and sauté for about 7 minutes, or until wilted and translucent. Add the shrimp and continue stirring over medium-high heat. Turn the shrimp to change color on both sides. Stir in the pasturma and deglaze the pan with the wine, stirring until the alcohol burns off, for about 3 minutes. Add the stock. Bring to a simmer and cook for about 2 minutes.

Drain the pasta, reserving 1 cup of its cooking liquid. Toss the pasta into the sauce and add the remaining 3 tablespoons olive oil and a little of the pasta water to the pan. Mix in the cheeses, thyme, and pistachios, give the peppermill a couple of turns over the mixture, crack the green peppercorns between your fingers into the mixture, toss, and serve.

Lobster Tail Yiouvetsi
with Roasted Red Peppers and Ouzo

Yiouvetsi comes in so many flavors in the Athenian kitchen, most traditionally with lamb or chicken, a favorite at many family-style tavernas and mageiria, and a classic of the bourgeois table, too. It's not hard to imagine why this total comfort dish, made with orzo, one of the world's most popular pasta shapes, has also won the hearts and minds of chefs and creative home cooks alike. From mushrooms to broccoli to seafood to Greek salad, there's a yiouvetsi recipe for everyone! This one, a Sunday special in my Athenian home, calls for lobster tails, notching up this traditionally homey recipe to a slightly higher level. In Greece I make it with Mediterranean lobster, or what the Greeks call astakos, *or with langoustines, which is in the lobster family and is prized for its delicate, sweet flesh. I've reworked this recipe, making it with Atlantic lobster tails instead.*

MAKES 8 SERVINGS

- 8 (4-ounce) lobster tails, thawed if frozen
- Sea salt and freshly ground black pepper to taste
- 3 tablespoons extra-virgin Greek olive oil
- 2 large yellow onions, finely chopped
- 3 garlic cloves, finely chopped
- 2 cups canned diced tomatoes
- 1 roasted red bell pepper, peeled, seeded, and pureed
- ½ cup ouzo
- Pinch cayenne or red pepper flakes
- 1 pound orzo
- 1 bunch flat-leaf parsley, stemmed and finely chopped
- 1 bunch basil, stemmed and cut into a chiffonade
- ¼ cup chopped fresh chives

You'll see a dark line running down the center of each lobster tail, which is the digestive tract. Using a sharp knife or kitchen shears, carefully cut along the length of the tail to expose the tract. Gently pull it out and discard it. Using kitchen shears, make a lengthwise cut down the center of the shell, stopping just before you reach the end of the tail. Carefully pull the lobster meat out of the shell, keeping it attached at the base to create a butterfly effect.

Bring a medium pot of water to a rolling boil, salt it generously, and carefully add the lobster tails. Poach the tails for about 4 minutes (or about 1 minute per ounce if using larger tails). Remove and set aside until ready to use. Reserve the water.

Heat the olive oil in a large, wide pot over medium heat. Add the onions and sauté until translucent and soft, about 8 minutes. Add the garlic and stir for about 1 minute. Add the tomatoes, red pepper puree, and 1 cup of the lobster cooking liquid. Stir in the ouzo and cayenne. Bring back to a simmer and cook for about 8 minutes, or until the alcohol evaporates and the sauce starts to thicken. Add the remaining lobster cooking water to the pot and bring to a boil. Taste and adjust salt. Add the orzo and simmer until the orzo is tender and the mixture juicy. Stir in the parsley and basil.

Carefully place the lobster tails in the pot and cook for 5 more minutes. Remove and serve, sprinkled with the chopped chives and a few grinds of black pepper.

Greek Salad Kritharoto

I don't know who first invented the Greek recipe called kritharoto, *which is orzo cooked in the manner of risotto, slowly and with the incremental addition of hot liquid. It was definitely part of the Athens foodscape as far back as the late 1990s, when I was a food writer for Ta Nea. I want to think it was one of those ideas in the air, so to speak, the kind of thing that springs up in various places at once. Favorite versions include additions like mushrooms and seafood.*

MAKES 4 TO 6 SERVINGS

1½ to 2 quarts vegetable stock

1 tablespoon unsalted butter

6 tablespoons extra-virgin Greek olive oil, divided

½ pound orzo

1 large red onion, chopped

1 large green bell pepper, seeded and coarsely chopped

Sea salt to taste

2 garlic cloves, finely chopped

6 cups chopped fresh, ripe tomatoes, with juices

1½ cups crumbled Greek feta or Cretan xynomyzithra cheese

½ cup sliced kalamata olives

2 tablespoons capers, rinsed and drained

3 tablespoons chopped fresh oregano

In a medium to large saucepan, bring the vegetable stock to a simmer.

In a wide, deep skillet, heat the butter and 1 tablespoon of the olive oil together over medium heat. Add the orzo and stir until it starts to brown a little. Add a ladleful of the hot stock, stirring until the liquid is absorbed. Repeat 6 to 8 more times, until the orzo is tender but al dente.

Meanwhile, in another large, deep skillet or wide, shallow pot, heat 3 tablespoons olive oil over medium heat. Add the onion and bell pepper, season with a pinch of salt, and sauté for about 8 minutes, or until soft and translucent. Add the garlic and stir for about 1 minute. Add the tomatoes and cook for about 10 minutes, until the tomatoes start to thicken.

Add the tomato mixture to the orzo, stir in the feta, olives, capers, and oregano, and keep stirring until the feta melts, about 3 minutes. If necessary, loosen the mixture a little before removing from the heat with ½ cup or so more of the hot stock. Drizzle in the remaining 2 tablespoons olive oil. Remove and serve.

Spinach-Chickpea Pasta
with Creamy Tahini

Pasta e fagioli is not "just" an Italian classic. Greeks also make similar dishes, especially in the southern Dodecanese (where there was, in fact, a decades-long Italian presence). Chickpeas and lentils are the two most prevalent legumes that one finds mixed into pasta, and bean soup variations elsewhere also sometimes call for short pasta to be mixed in, making all such dishes hearty, filling, and inexpensive. Athens is a melting pot of regional Greek traditions, and chefs experiment with them, rediscovering, reinventing, and ultimately creating something new. Sometimes traditions long forgotten reappear, intertwined and mixed up but still delicious. This dish is such an example. The use of tahini as pasta sauce is also distinctly from the southern Aegean, a very old combination that was served to nursing mothers to help them produce more milk!

MAKES 4 TO 6 SERVINGS

6 tablespoons extra-virgin Greek olive oil, divided

¼ cup tahini, preferably dark, from unhulled sesame seeds

Grated zest and strained juice of 1 lemon

4 garlic cloves, 2 smashed and 2 minced

2 scant teaspoons ground cumin, divided

Water as needed

Sea salt and freshly ground black pepper to taste

1 large red onion, minced

1 pound baby spinach

1 (15-ounce) can good-quality, low-sodium chickpeas, rinsed and drained

1 pound noodle-like or twisted pasta shape, such as tagliatelle, fettucine, strozzapreti, or caserecce

Smoked paprika or cayenne to taste (optional)

In the bowl of a food processor, pulse together 4 tablespoons of the olive oil, the tahini, lemon juice, the smashed garlic, and half of the cumin until very smooth and creamy. Add about ⅓ to ½ cup of water to the mixture to make a creamy, loose, but thick sauce, about the consistency of a medium batter. Season to taste with salt.

In a wide pot, heat 2 tablespoons olive oil over medium heat. Add the onion and minced garlic and sauté, stirring, until soft and translucent, about 7 minutes. Add the spinach to the pan in batches, if necessary. Season with salt and pepper and cook until the spinach wilts. Stir in the chickpeas and season with salt, pepper, and the remaining cumin. Add the lemon zest. Remove from the heat.

Bring a large pot of salted water to a boil. Cook the pasta according to the package directions until al dente. Drain, reserving 1 cup of the cooking liquid. Add the pasta to the spinach-chickpea mixture, stir in the tahini sauce, and add some of the pasta water if needed to loosen the consistency a little and create a creamy pasta dish. Serve sprinkled with a little smoked paprika or cayenne, if you like.

Athenian Carbonara

The very name of this dish might sound like an oxymoron at best, or a crime against tradition at worst! Carbonara slipped into Greek life via the pizzerias, the first of which opened in Athens in 1970. As the phenomenon spread (I mean, who doesn't like pizza?), these family eateries slowly expanded their offerings to include more "authentic" Italian fare, carbonara among them. It moved from there to the home kitchen, and Athenian mothers of my generation, myself included, would whip up carbonara for their kids, so by the early part of the 2000s it became an almost weekly Greek meal. There is now such a thing as Greek carbonara, even if it's open to interpretation. Sometimes the recipe appears with chopped sausages, other times with bacon or apaki (a vinegary Cretan preserved pork loin), and all manner of Greek regional cheeses and even different pasta shapes beyond the classic spaghetti. But the Greek version in almost every iteration almost invariably calls for cream. Here's my two cents when it comes to carbonara à la Greca!

MAKES 4 TO 6 SERVINGS

Salt and freshly ground black pepper to taste

1 pound whole wheat spaghetti

8 tablespoons (1 stick) unsalted butter

8 slices bacon, diced

¼ cup dry Greek white wine

1 cup grated Parmigiano

1 cup grated graviera or kefalograviera cheese

2 large egg yolks

½ cup heavy cream

Bring a large pot of water to a rolling boil and add a generous amount of salt. Add the pasta and cook according to the package directions until al dente.

While the pasta is cooking, melt the butter in a medium skillet over medium heat. Add the bacon and cook until lightly browned. Pour in the wine and let it cook off.

Place the grated cheeses in a large bowl and mix in the egg yolks. Add the bacon mixture slowly, stirring constantly so that you don't scramble the eggs.

Drain the pasta, reserving 1 cup of the cooking liquid. Toss the pasta in the bowl and drizzle in the heavy cream. Loosen the mixture as desired with a little of the pasta liquid and serve.

Mushroom-Spinach Fricasse Risotto
with Avgolemono

This dish is a modern Greek hybrid, so indicative of the mixing and matching of traditional techniques and recipes that now characterize modern Greek cooking. It's part risotto and part fricasse, the latter a category of recipes in the traditional Greek kitchen that combine protein and greens bound by the silky, creamy egg-lemon liaison, avgolemono.

MAKES 4 TO 6 SERVINGS

- ¼ cup extra-virgin Greek olive oil
- 1 bunch spring onions, trimmed and chopped
- 2 garlic cloves, thinly sliced
- ⅔ cup Arborio, Carnaroli, or Greek Carolina rice
- 1 pound oyster mushrooms, trimmed
- 4 portobello mushrooms, wiped clean with a damp towel and cut into ½-inch slices
- ½ pound fresh chanterelles, wiped clean
- ⅔ cup dry white wine
- 2 pounds fresh baby spinach or Swiss chard, trimmed and chopped
- Salt and freshly ground black pepper to taste
- 1 small bunch dill, trimmed and snipped
- 2 to 3 cups vegetable stock, mushroom stock, or water, divided
- 2 large egg yolks
- Strained juice of 1 lemon
- 1 teaspoon cornstarch

Heat the olive oil in a large, wide pot over medium heat. Add the onions and garlic and cook, stirring, until soft and translucent, about 8 minutes. Add the rice and stir to coat in the oil. Stir in the oyster mushrooms and portobellos, lower the heat to low, cover, and cook for 3 to 4 minutes. Stir in the chanterelles and cook for another 2 to 3 minutes. Deglaze the pan with the white wine, and as soon as the alcohol burns off, stir in the spinach, in increments, until the first batches cook down and lose volume and there is room for the remainder. Season to taste with salt and pepper. Add 2 cups of the stock or water and bring to a simmer. Cook, stirring, until everything is tender, about 15 minutes. Add some or all of the remaining stock or water if the mixture is too dense.

Meanwhile, in a medium metal bowl, vigorously whisk the egg yolks until creamy, then slowly drizzle in the lemon juice, drop by drop, until all of it is incorporated and the mixture is creamy. Very slowly, drop by drop, whisk in a ladleful of the hot pot juices. Repeat with a second ladleful, again very slowly. Pour the avgolemono into the pot, swirl or swivel from side to side, and serve.

Risotto
with Chestnuts, Winter Squash, Mavrodaphne, and Feta

This dish speaks to the Greek winter, and I make it when both winter squash and chestnuts come to the farmers' markets in Athens in the late fall. You can also use vacuum-packed or canned chestnuts, which are easier to work with and have pretty good flavor and texture.

MAKES 4 TO 6 SERVINGS

6 to 8 cups chicken or vegetable stock

1 pound winter squash, peeled, seeded, and coarsely grated

Salt to taste

3 tablespoons unsalted butter, divided

1 large red onion, finely chopped

1½ cups Arborio rice

⅓ cup Mavrodaphne or other sweet red wine, such as port

1½ cups vacuum-packed or canned peeled chestnuts, whole or halved lengthwise, as desired

4 fresh thyme sprigs, stemmed and finely chopped

2 fresh oregano sprigs, stemmed and finely chopped

1 teaspoon finely grated orange or tangerine zest

⅓ cup grated kefalotyri or Romano cheese

⅓ cup crumbled Greek feta

3 tablespoons chopped fresh flat-leaf parsley

In a medium saucepan, bring the stock to a simmer.

Set a fine-mesh colander in a bowl. Add the grated winter squash, sprinkle with a generous pinch of coarse sea salt, and knead to get as much of its liquid out as possible. Transfer the squash to a cheesecloth and wring it dry. Reserve the juices in the bowl.

Heat 2 tablespoons of the butter in a large, deep skillet or wide, shallow pot over medium heat. Add the onion, season with a pinch of salt, and sauté, stirring, until it is translucent and soft, about 8 minutes. Stir in the grated squash and cook for about 3 minutes. Stir in the rice and toss to coat in the butter.

Add a ladleful of the simmering stock, reduce the heat to medium-low, and stir until the liquid is absorbed. Repeat with a second and third ladleful, stirring after each addition until it is absorbed.

Pour in the wine. When that is absorbed, add about ½ cup of the winter squash liquid, tasting it first to be sure it isn't too salty. If it is, don't use it, and just continue with the stock. Add the chestnuts, thyme, oregano, and orange zest, and another ladleful of the simmering stock. Continue adding more stock until the risotto is cooked to al dente. Right at the end, stir in the cheeses and remaining 1 tablespoon butter and adjust seasoning with salt and a few turns on the peppermill. Serve, sprinkled with the chopped parsley.

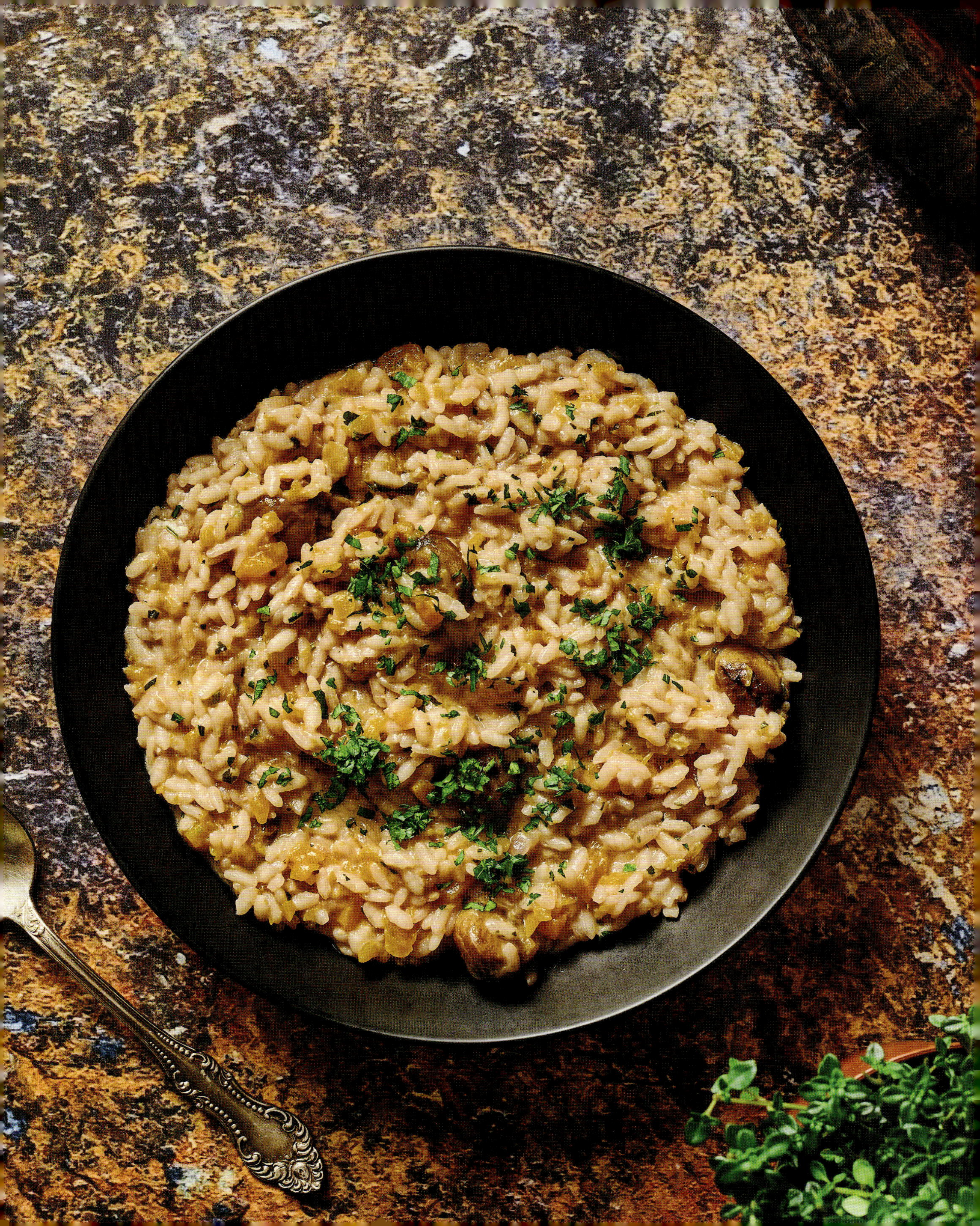

Pitsa, aka Pizza!

It was the summer of '72 and I had come to Greece with my older sister, Athena, and brother-in-law, Paul, who were more like parents to me than a sibling and her spouse. Athens was hot, dusty, and exciting to my twelve-year-old eyes, a city perhaps sensing the end of a stultifying dictatorship (it would end in two years), a time of tumultuous change palpably—and thankfully—ahead. We stayed in Agia Paraskevi, a big suburb just a few kilometers northeast of the city, guests in the home of Paul's aunt and uncle, Eleni and Maki. This was my brother-in-law's mother's sister and her husband, and they had been something akin to foster parents with a blood tie to another of Eleni's siblings' children, Thanassi, Yiani, and Nitsa, who were just a little older than I was. I kept company with them, trying to improve my almost nonexistent Greek, and they their nascent high school English.

Athens was in the throes of shaking off its postwar wariness, sensing a newfound era on the horizon, and building and building and building to meet the needs of an expanding urban population. Back then, there were chickens in the yards of people up in Agia Paraskevi. *The Mod Squad* and *Mission Impossible*, dubbed into English, were among the very meager offerings beyond the news on state television, the only kind. The programming stopped at midnight, replaced by the image of a ticking clock that marked the time until the morning, when the airwaves went live again. Fresh milk was impossible to find in food markets. Twentieth-century Greek urban children drank milk delivered to their doorsteps by the galata (milkman) or, more commonly, they were reared on condensed or—horror of cloying horrors—sweetened condensed milk. Nounou, the most famous brand, was established in 1929 and nourished the Greek army before delivering its iconic blue-and-white cans to the general public.

But, there was pitsa (mimicking the way the world's most popular food is still spelled in Grenglish). And when we first arrived in my relatives' home, it was a big thing, an emblem of something happy and modern, and a source of great pride, too, because the very first pizzeria in Greece opened within walking distance of their home, in the sprawling leafy plateia of Agia Paraskevi. It was called Portofino. More than half a century later, it's still there, albeit a little less illustrious, as so many waves of pizza styles have washed over Athens in the past few decades.

My newfound cousins and I walked to the square, together with the adults, of course, excited about pizza, each for our own reasons. For me, it was the comfort of having something familiar in a foreign country; for them, the advent of something new.

Greek pizza—actually sometimes called Canadian here—is a thing and it goes back to the origins of Portofino on that square, which was opened by two brothers who had emigrated to Canada in 1960, worked in pizzerias there, and returned a decade later to open their own. As for the name, it's simple: It came to them upon their return voyage, during which the boat they were on moored at Portofino!

I remember my very first sight and taste of it: Way smaller than a New York pie, my point of reference, at around 10 inches in diameter, and served in pans set down with gruff pomp by waiters in their black pants, white shirts, and black bowties, the serving garb of the day. When I picked up the first plump, overladen piece, attempting to fold it à la New York, my relatives stared at me and laughed. My New York pizza folding know-how obviously was useless. Greek pitsa was a different animal and it required a fork and knife to eat.

The crust was a little shiny, but crunchy and oily, too, with a discernable if subtle sweetness, and the topping was like a quilt of melted kasseri cheese, punctuated by the bright green of bell peppers and the insipid pink of fatty bacon strips, with no tomato sauce at all, a surprise to my twelve-year-old palate.

You had to order a pitsa with sauce, or order a margherita (no basil on the Greek version), if you wanted something remotely resembling what I, a Queens girl, identified as pizza. There were other offerings that were very popular, too: mushrooms (canned), which most Athenians and Greeks had actually never tasted before they popped up as a pizza topping; tessera tyria (four cheeses, one of them sometimes a harsh crumbled imitator of French Roquefort); as well as cheese (yellow, such as kasseri or regato) and zambon (ham) or pepperoni, another exciting newcomer to the Athenian palate.

Portofino, out there on the big sprawling square, became an overnight success, a place and a concept that appealed to everyone. Pizzerias became de facto family restaurants, the perfect place for multigenerational Greek family outings, where grandparents, adult children, and grandkids could all enjoy new and exciting pitsa together, with a happier future in sight. Before long, the pizzeria vied with souvlaki and gyro joints as popular foods-to-go establishments.

Granted, since 1970, much has changed, and the pizza front in Athens is a mosaic of those "traditional" Greek-style pies, but also veritable Neapolitan-style pizza, and even, nowadays, New York pizza (yeah, right!). There are also vegan and gluten-free offerings, which this Queens girl has not been able to embrace.

In its heyday, Portofino boasted many shops all over the city. Delivery was a given, as were the countless copycats who wanted, and succeeded at, getting a piece of the pie!

Athens-Style Classic Greek Pizza

You'll need two 10-inch pans that are about 1½ inches deep to make a traditional Athenian pizza. Kasseri cheese is the de rigueur melting option, in place of Naples's beloved mozzarella. The crust has a little sweetness, and the herb of choice is Greek oregano, far more widely used than basil in traditional Greek cooking.

MAKES 2 (10-INCH) PIES

For the dough

1 teaspoon active dry yeast

½ teaspoon sugar

⅔ cup tepid water

¼ cup extra-virgin Greek olive oil

½ teaspoon salt

2 to 2½ cups all-purpose flour

For the topping

4 firm ripe tomatoes (about 1 pound)

4 tablespoons extra-virgin Greek olive oil, divided

2 garlic cloves, crushed

Sea salt and freshly ground black pepper to taste

Pinch sugar

4 cups coarsely grated kasseri cheese

2 scant tablespoons dried Greek oregano

Prepare the dough: Combine the yeast and sugar in the bowl of a stand mixer outfitted with a dough hook (or in a separate bowl if you plan to knead the dough by hand). Add the warm water and olive oil and stir to combine. Cover with plastic wrap and let the yeast mixture stand in a warm place to proof for about 20 minutes.

When it's all bubbly, stir in the salt, then the flour in 1-cup increments, mixing at medium speed until a dough ball starts to take shape. Add more flour as needed to make a soft, pliant dough that doesn't stick, which will take about 8 minutes. Shape into 2 equal balls, place in a clean oiled bowl, cover with plastic wrap, and let stand in a warm, draft-free spot until the balls start to expand, about 20 minutes.

Knead each dough ball lightly again on a lightly floured surface and place back in the bowl, cover with plastic wrap, and let them stand in a warm, draft-free spot until double in bulk, 1 to 2 hours.

In the meantime, prepare the tomato sauce: Grate the tomatoes on the coarse side of a box grater. Heat 2 tablespoons of the olive oil in a medium pot over low heat. Add the garlic and cook, stirring, just to infuse the oil with its aroma. Remove the garlic and discard. Add the tomatoes, raise the heat to medium, season with salt, pepper, and sugar, and bring to a simmer. Turn the heat down to low and simmer until the sauce is thickened and textured, without any excess tomato water leaching out on the surface, about 25 minutes. (The time it takes to do this will vary depending on the tomatoes and how watery or firm they are.) Set the sauce aside to cool down to room temperature.

When the dough is doubled and the sauce cooked and cooled, preheat the oven to 400°F. Generously oil two 10-inch round baking pans.

Sprinkle flour lightly on a clean work surface and flatten one dough ball into a circle with the palm of your hand. Using a rolling pin, gently roll it out to a circle about 1 inch larger than the circumference of the pan. Lift it and place it in the pan. Brush the surface with 1 tablespoon olive oil, then spread half of the tomato sauce on top. Sprinkle half of the cheese over the surface and 1 scant tablespoon oregano. Repeat with the second dough ball and remaining ingredients.

Bake the pies for about 30 minutes, or until the dough is set, golden, and crisp and the cheese all bubbly and melted. Remove and serve hot.

Variations

To make a tessera tyria pitsa, use 4 cups of 4 different cheeses chosen from among the great cheeses of Greece: grated kasseri, kefalotyri, kefalograviera, and/or graviera; crumbled feta and/or rokfor (as blue cheese is called in Greece).

You can make a sort-of horitaki-inspired pizza by using crumbled feta, pitted kalamata olives, sliced fresh tomatoes, and dried Greek oregano.

If you want a vegetarian pizza, one popular Athenian variation uses mushrooms, green bell pepper rings, and kasseri cheese.

For meat lovers, the pizza can be very traditional, featuring sliced ham, crisp bacon, and pepperoni.

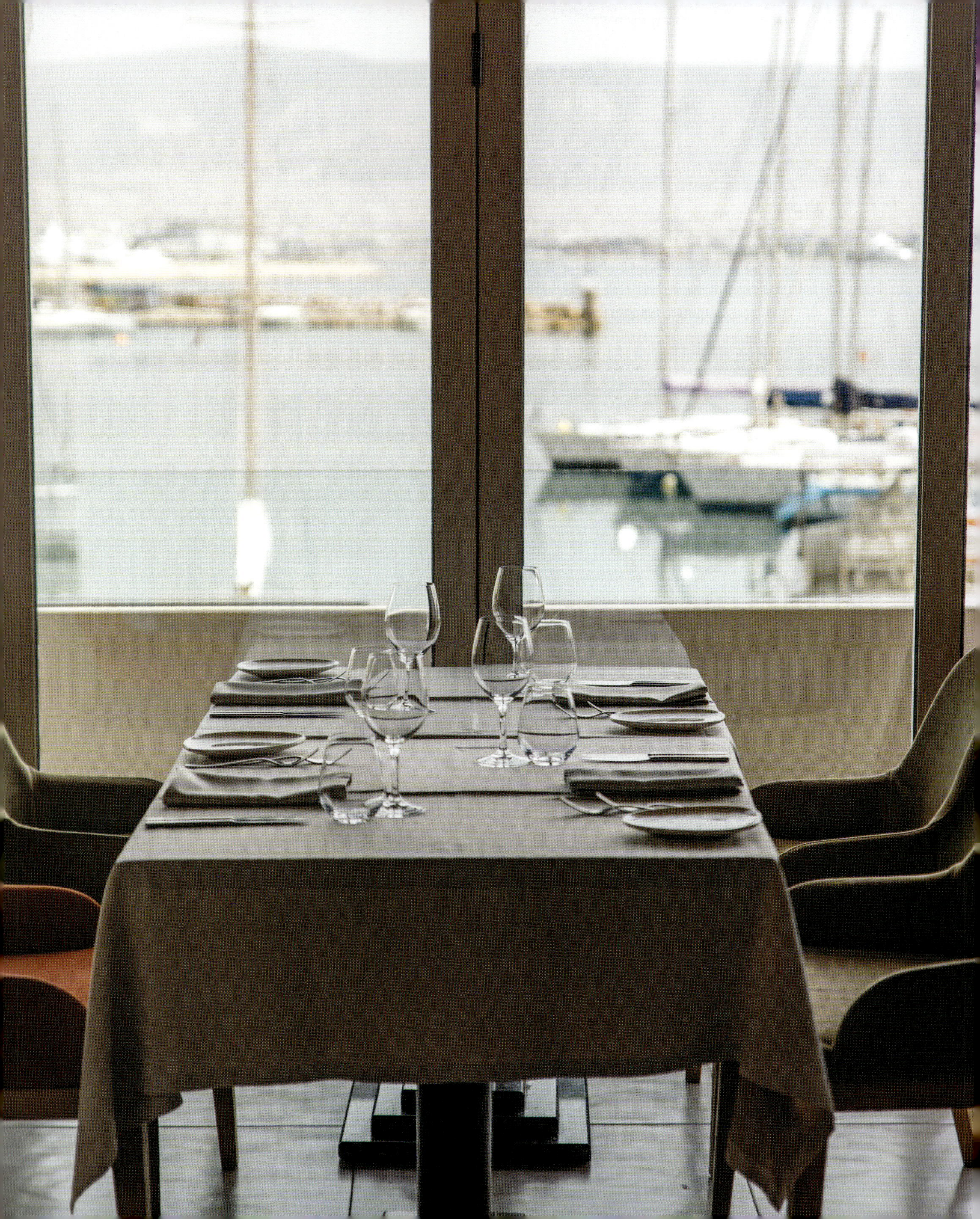

Athens & the Sea

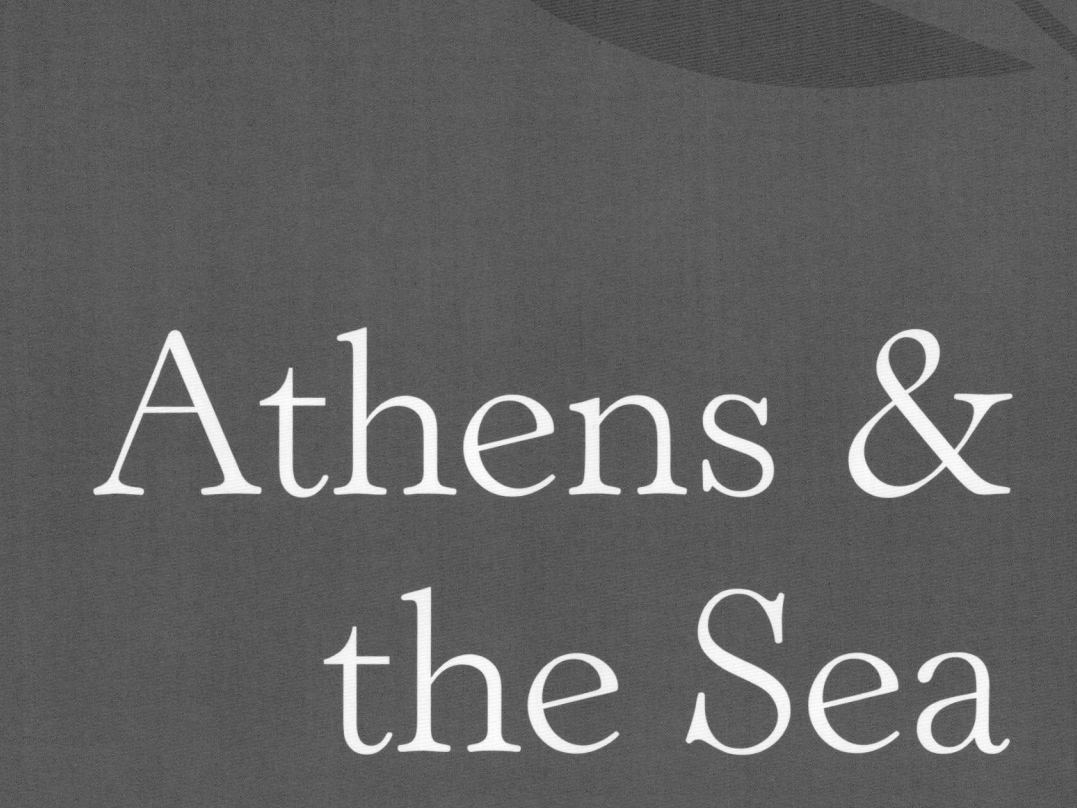

It doesn't take a great leap of imagination to understand just how important the sea is in the life of Athens. If you're a walker, the Bay of Faliron, the first coastal neighborhood, is about an hour away on foot or ten minutes by car, about six miles from Syntagma Square. Faliron marks the unofficial start of the Athenian Riviera, which stretches down Athens's southwestern coast, along the Saronic Gulf.

Living close to the sea is one of the things I love most about Athens. It's so easy to swim all year round; there are great restaurants and upscale suburbs along the coast, including the glitzy new development at Ellinikon, the old Athens airport site; and there's just something magical about being able to go for an afternoon walk with the Aegean at your side. That proximity has shaped the culture and identity of the Greek capital since ancient times.

Without the city's relationship to the Aegean, ancient Athens would never have evolved into a great trading and naval power. The port of antiquity, Piraeus, is still the port today. Indeed, it is the fifth busiest commercial port in Europe, after Rotterdam, Antwerp, Hamburg, and Valencia. In 2008, when the battered Greek economy was forced into "fire sale" mode, Piraeus was acquired by the Chinese state–owned entity COSCO. Most Chinese goods coming into Europe enter via Piraeus, which is also the largest passenger port in Europe, handling about fifteen million people a year. From the highest points of Athens, including the Acropolis, on a clear day Piraeus is easy to see.

But Athens's unique relationship to the sea goes beyond its ancient port. There are still points along the way where small fishing boats come in to anchor, selling their fresh catch along the docks. Even Glyfada, long one of the poshest suburbs on the coast, is the site of one such quaint market, and early in the morning local Greeks as well as a growing number of foreigners who now own property there are out buying their daily catch, with Chinese, Russian, and Arab denizens haggling with salty fishermen in broken Greek.

On the other side of the Attica peninsula is the Evian Gulf and the wider Aegean. On both sides there are literally dozens of beaches, more than fifty, where Athenians find respite.

The way in which the city's closeness to the water is manifested in the kitchen is not what one might expect. There aren't dozens of seafood specialties, for example, unique to Athens and its environs. The traditional seafood tavernas serve up pretty basic fare: fresh grilled whole fish on the bone, psarosoupa (fish soup; page 188), and a bevy of small fried fish (page 298), all crunchy and perfect for crisp white wine or light retsina, the traditional Attica wine (see page 371). Shrimp boats used to be a lot more plentiful along the Saronic, spilling their fresh catch in such abundance that half a century ago they spawned a whole restaurant phenomenon, ta garidadika—shrimp houses, along the Piraiki Coast (page 198). Shrimp and lobster pasta is something of a local specialty, but one finds that in the islands, too, and so are dishes like Athinaiki mayioneza (poached fish with homemade mayonnaise; page 217), and fish à la Spetsiota, in the style of Spetses, another island in the Saronic. In ancient times the Bay of Faliron teemed with fish and was mentioned by ancient writers; today to swim there is to understand firsthand the notion of an urban beach, relatively clean, and within a few minutes' walk from all the apartment blocks across Poseidonos Avenue, the main road along the coast.

Fish and shellfish in Athens are about abundance of product, something that a visit to the Varvakeios Fish Market will prove on any given day; it's also about the classics like grilled fresh fish cooked with respect to quality and garnished minimally (page 296), as well as novel ways with the fruits of the sea, spearheaded (pun intended) by masterful chefs like Varoulko's Lefteris Lazarou and his many acolytes and imitators over the years.

The range of seafood preparations has expanded tremendously since I first moved here three decades ago, when sushi had not yet arrived, raw fish was anathema to most Greeks, fish cookery equaled the grill or a few traditional, regional specialties, and sustainability wasn't a buzzword.

The recipes in this chapter represent a smattering of some of my favorite ways to enjoy fish, culled or created mostly from restaurant meals I've loved.

Fresh Cod or Halibut
with Braised Artichokes and Broad Beans

Braised artichokes and broad beans is a classic vegetable stew known as anginarokoukia; *fresh fish or shellfish of any sort is a new addition to the pot, a trend that started on restaurant menus as chefs looked to expand their offerings while delving into Greekness, in the years leading up to the 2004 Olympics. Perhaps they were taking a cue from some of the combinations of ladera (plant-based stews with olive oil) with fish that are traditional in Cretan cooking. Now the ocean's depths are the limit, so to speak, when it comes to combining seafood with old-school ladera retweaked for modern palates. This cod or halibut with anginarokoukia is but one.*

MAKES 4 SERVINGS

2 pounds fresh cod or halibut fillets

Salt and freshly ground black pepper to taste

1 pound fresh or thawed frozen broad beans

½ cup extra-virgin Greek olive oil, divided

2 large leeks, trimmed and chopped

2 scallions, trimmed and chopped

3 shallots, finely chopped

1 garlic clove, thinly sliced

8 to 10 new red potatoes, scrubbed and halved

2 to 4 cups fish stock or water

½ teaspoon saffron threads diluted in 2 tablespoons warm water

8 canned or thawed frozen artichoke hearts*

Grated zest and strained juice of 1 lemon

½ cup dry white wine

2 tablespoons chopped fresh dill

Season the fish lightly with salt and pepper and keep refrigerated until about 10 minutes before ready to cook.

If using fresh broad beans, open the pods and remove the beans (discard the pods). Bring a medium pot of lightly salted water to a boil and blanch the beans for 1 minute to loosen their skins. Have a bowl filled with ice water nearby, drain the beans, and transfer to the ice bath. Peel them.

Heat ¼ cup of the olive oil in a wide pot over medium heat. Add the leeks, scallions, and shallots and sauté, stirring, for about 8 minutes, until wilted and translucent. Add the garlic and cook, stirring, for about 1 minute. Add the potatoes and toss to coat in the oil. Add 2 cups of the stock and the saffron liquid. Bring to a gentle simmer and cook for 5 to 6 minutes, or until the potatoes begin to soften a bit.

Place the artichokes stem side up in the pan and scatter the broad beans evenly around them. There should be enough liquid in the pan to come about halfway up the contents. If the mixture needs more liquid, add a little more stock. Mix gently. Season with salt, pepper, and the lemon zest. Cook for about 10 minutes, until the artichokes are about halfway cooked.

Place the cod fillets in the pan, evenly distributed among the vegetables. Pour in the wine and let the alcohol cook off for about 5 minutes, then add the lemon juice. Cook for 12 to 15 minutes, or until the fish is fork-tender and flaky. Adjust the seasoning with salt and pepper. Gently stir in the dill, top with the remaining ¼ cup olive oil, and serve.

*You can also use fresh artichokes: First, remove their coarse outer leaves. Using a serrated knife, cut the tops off, leaving a base of about 1½ inches. Place each artichoke on its side and cut away any remaining leaves. Use a teaspoon to scrape out the purple fuzzy choke. Trim the stem, removing the tough outer part and a bit off the top to leave about 2 inches of the stem. Rub immediately with a cut lemon and place in a bowl of water.

One-Pot Fish Fillets
with Greek Salad and Greens

Greek salad takes shape in many different ways in the modern Athenian kitchen, its main ingredients finding their way into just about everything from soups like gazpacho to cooked dishes like this. The combination is delicious and could stand as a kind of exemplar of all that's perfect about the Greek and Mediterranean diet!

MAKES 4 SERVINGS.

¼ cup extra-virgin Greek olive oil, plus more for drizzling

1 large red onion, coarsely chopped

4 Yukon Gold potatoes, peeled and cut into ½-inch cubes

4 firm, ripe tomatoes, cored and cut into 6 wedges each

½ cup dry white wine

6 cups coarsely chopped fresh spinach or Swiss chard

Sea salt and freshly ground black pepper to taste

8 sun-dried tomatoes, soaked, drained, and chopped

16 kalamata olives, pitted

4 (8- to-10-ounce) white-fleshed fish fillets, such as Mediterranean sea bass, grouper, or red snapper

½ cup snipped fresh dill

½ cup chopped fresh flat-leaf parsley

Finely grated zest of 1 lemon

Heat the olive oil in a large, wide pot over medium heat. Add the onion and sauté until translucent and soft, about 7 minutes. Add the potatoes, cover the pot, and cook, shaking the pot back and forth every few minutes, for about 8 minutes, or until they start to soften. Add the tomatoes and wine, cover, and cook for about 5 minutes, until the alcohol steams off and the tomatoes start to soften a little. Gently stir in the spinach and season with salt and pepper. When the spinach loses about half its volume, stir in the sun-dried tomatoes and olives.

Season the fillets with salt and pepper. Gently stir the dill and parsley into the pot and place the fish fillets on top. Cover and cook for about 7 minutes, or until the fillets are white and fork-tender. Sprinkle the lemon zest on top. Remove and serve, drizzled with additional olive oil.

Slow-Cooked Peas and Shrimp

Aracas laderos, one of the classic old-style vegetable stews, shimmering with olive oil, is delicious with the "New Greek" addition of shrimp.

MAKES 4 TO 6 SERVINGS

6 tablespoons extra-virgin Greek olive oil, divided

1 large onion, halved and sliced

1 small fennel bulb, trimmed, halved, and sliced

2 garlic cloves, finely chopped

3 cups fresh or thawed frozen peas

2½ cup chopped fresh tomatoes or 1 (15-ounce) can diced tomatoes

Sea salt and freshly ground black pepper to taste

1 star anise

12 large shrimp, peeled and deveined, tails left on and heads optional

¼ cup ouzo

Grated zest of 1 lemon, divided

½ to ⅔ cup crumbled Greek feta (optional)

In a wide pot, heat 4 tablespoons of the olive oil over medium heat. Add the onion and fennel and cook until soft, 8 to 10 minutes, stirring occasionally. Stir in the garlic. Add the peas and toss to coat in the oil. Add the tomatoes with their juices. Season to taste with salt and pepper. Add enough water to come about a quarter of the way up the peas. Add the star anise. Cover partially and cook for 25 to 30 minutes, until everything is tender and the juices are almost cooked off.

About 10 minutes before the peas are ready, heat a large, deep skillet over medium-high heat. Add 2 tablespoons olive oil and in a few seconds add the shrimp. Cook for 1 minute on each side, pull the skillet off the flame, and slowly and carefully add the ouzo, away from the flame. It may flare up, so be cautious. Lower the heat a notch and cook the shrimp for another minute or two, until bright pink. Season lightly with salt and pepper and stir in the lemon zest.

Transfer the shrimp and all the pan juices to the pot with the peas and finish cooking them together. Serve, sprinkled with feta, if desired.

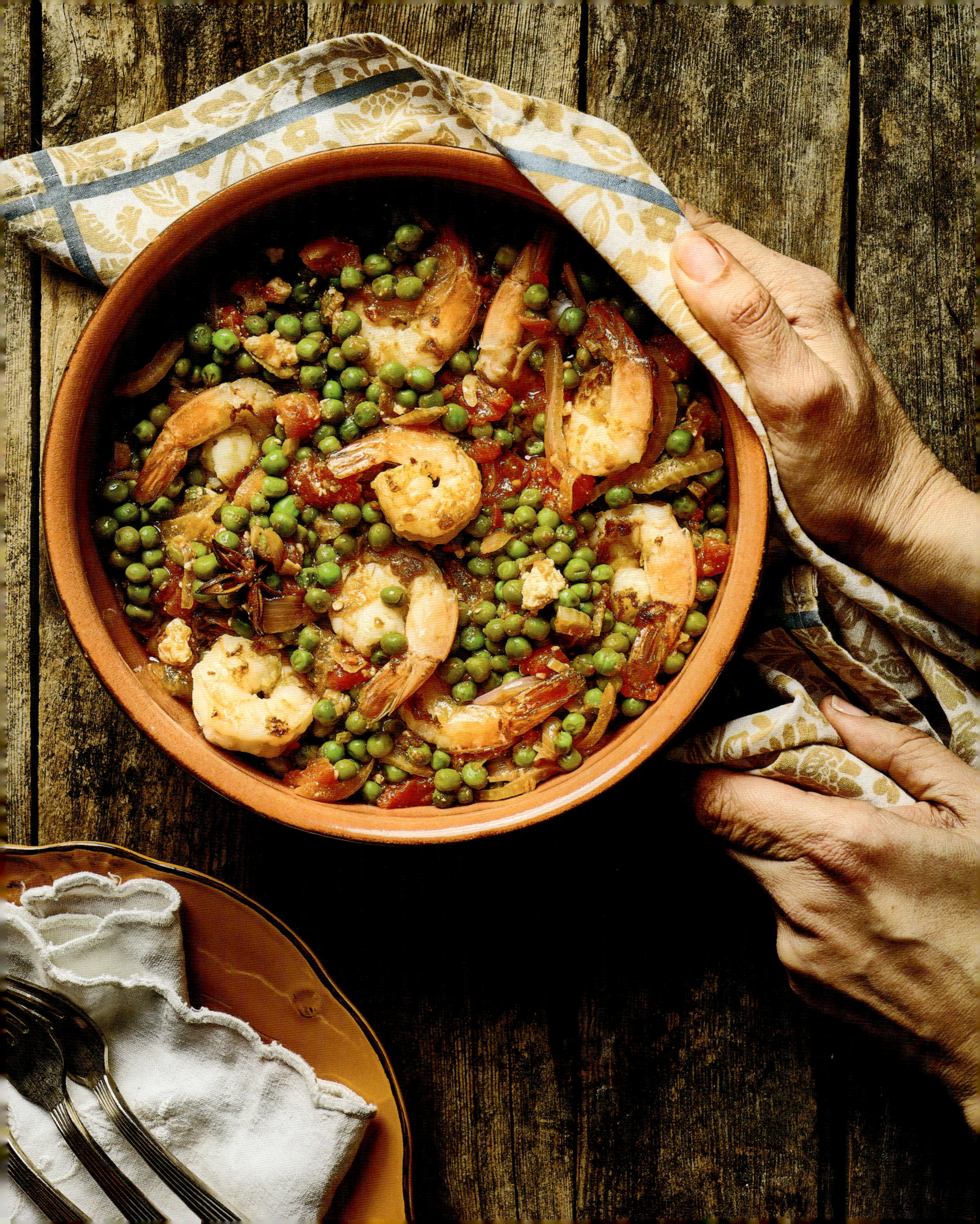

Ouzo Salmon Cooked over Greens

Salmon has been Hellenized! This ever-popular fish is in every fish store and supermarket fish counter, and on restaurant menus all over Athens. It's cooked up simply, on the grill with various sides, it's the recipient of thick Greek honey and other condiments, and it's cooked in new Greek dishes with things like greens and ouzo!

MAKES 4 SERVINGS

4 tablespoons extra-virgin Greek olive oil, divided, plus more for drizzling

1 large leek, trimmed and chopped

2 garlic cloves, finely chopped

¾ pound spinach, trimmed and coarsely chopped

¾ pound Swiss chard, trimmed and coarsely chopped

1 thin carrot, peeled and halved

½ cup snipped fresh dill

3 tablespoons chopped fresh mint

Sea salt and freshly ground black pepper to taste

4 (8-ounce) salmon fillets

¼ cup ouzo

¼ cup strained fresh lemon juice

In a large, wide pot, heat 2 tablespoons of the olive oil over medium heat. Add the leek and cook, stirring, until translucent and softened, about 7 minutes. Stir in the garlic. Add the spinach and chard to the pot, in increments if necessary, cooking it for a few minutes to lose some volume. Nestle the carrot halves among the greens. Stir in the dill and mint. Season the mixture lightly with salt and pepper.

Heat 2 tablespoons olive oil in a large nonstick skillet over medium-high heat. Place the salmon fillets in the pan, sear them on one side, then carefully turn to color on the other side. Pull away from the heat and pour in the ouzo. It may flare up, so be cautious. Place back on the heat, lower the heat to medium, and cook the salmon for another minute or two, until the alcohol burns off.

Carefully transfer the salmon fillets on top of the greens. Pour the pan juices into the pot, together with the lemon juice. Cover and cook for about 8 more minutes, or until the fillets are fork-tender. Remove and serve, drizzled with a little olive oil. Remove the carrots if desired. I like to get them in the pot for sweetness but don't like to eat them!

Married Sardines

Sardines are so popular in Greece—a healthy, oily fish that's sold everywhere and cooked up in dozens of different ways. When the term married *applies to them, they're usually coupled with the likes of herbs, scallions, and sometimes capers and tomatoes. The recipe below is a simple marriage of good things!*

MAKES 4 TO 6 SERVINGS

¼ cup extra-virgin Greek olive oil, plus more for drizzling

20 fresh sardines (1½ ounces each), scaled, gutted, filleted, and butterflied

Sea salt and freshly ground black pepper to taste

6 tablespoons finely chopped fresh flat-leaf parsley, divided

1 tablespoon finely chopped fresh oregano

2 scallions or spring onions, trimmed and minced

2 garlic cloves, minced

Finely grated zest and strained juice of 1 lemon

½ cup vegetable stock

¼ cup dry white wine

3 fresh rosemary sprigs

2 teaspoons cornstarch

⅔ cup water

Preheat the oven to 350°F. Lightly oil an ovenproof glass baking dish large enough to hold half the sardines in a single layer.

Place the sardines in the pan, skin side down, and butterflied open so that the flesh is exposed. Season with salt and pepper. Sprinkle 3 tablespoons of the parsley, the oregano, scallions, garlic, and lemon zest on top. Season the remaining sardines lightly with salt and pepper and place over the first layer, to make something akin to butterflied sardine "sandwiches."

Drizzle in the olive oil, stock, wine, and half of the lemon juice. Nestle the rosemary sprigs in a few different spots in the pan. Bake for about 12 minutes, or until the sardine flesh is fork-tender and white. Transfer to a serving platter and tent with aluminum foil to keep warm.

Strain the pan juices into a small pot and bring to a simmer over medium heat. Whisk the cornstarch with the water to dilute it completely. Add the cornstarch mixture to the pot and stir in the remaining lemon juice. Whisk for a few minutes to thicken. Pour the sauce over the fish, drizzle a little olive oil on top, and sprinkle with the remaining 3 tablespoons parsley. Serve.

Stacked Fried Sardines
with a Brush of Beets

Sardines hold a dear place on the table and in the hearts of both home cooks and professional chefs in Athens and throughout Greece. In the summer, when sardines are in peak season, the Varvakeios market is a virtual sardine fest, their silvery skin glistening in big Styrofoam bins, hawkers shouting out their virtues, and signs pointing both to their provenance (Kalloni in Lesvos, Evia, and elsewhere) and freshness, usually with a sign that just says "Morning," meaning caught that day. They're inexpensive and nutritious, but best of all sardines are also very versatile. The most common ways to eat them are grilled, baked with onions, garlic, and tomatoes, or fried, as below, a recipe inspired by something I sampled at one of the city's cult fish tavernas, Travolta, in the working-class neighborhood of Peristeri. Greek sardines are much smaller than their Spanish cousins.

MAKES 6 SERVINGS

- 2 large beets, scrubbed and trimmed
- 1 garlic clove, lightly smashed
- ½ teaspoon ground allspice
- 4 to 6 tablespoons extra-virgin Greek olive oil
- 2 large eggs
- 1 cup all-purpose flour
- Salt and freshly ground black pepper to taste
- 2 to 3 cups panko bread crumbs
- Finely grated zest of 1 lemon
- 1 tablespoon dried Greek oregano
- 24 medium sardines, scaled, gutted, filleted, and butterflied
- Vegetable oil, for frying
- ¼ cup finely chopped fresh flat-leaf parsley

Put the beets in a medium saucepan, cover with lightly salted water, and bring to a boil. Cover and simmer over medium heat until fork-tender, about 45 minutes. Set aside to cool, reserving their cooking liquid. Strain the cooking liquid through a sieve lined with a coffee filter.

Peel and coarsely chop. Place the chopped beets in the bowl of a food processor, add the garlic and allspice, and pulverize to a smooth paste. Add 3 to 4 tablespoons of the olive oil and pulse until very smooth and velvety but liquid enough to pour. Loosen the mixture if needed with a little of the beet cooking liquid. Using a small funnel, pour the beet cream into a squeeze bottle. Set aside until ready to use.

Lightly beat the eggs in a shallow bowl. Place the flour in another shallow bowl, and season it lightly with salt and pepper. In a third shallow bowl, mix together the panko, lemon zest, and oregano, and season with salt and pepper. Season the sardines with salt and pepper.

Heat about ½ inch of vegetable oil in a large, heavy skillet over medium-high heat. Press the first batch of sardines (as many sardines as will fit into the pan in one layer) into the flour, then egg, then panko mixture, coating on both sides. Slide the first batch into the pan using a spatula, fry on one side for about 1 minute, then turn to fry on the other for about another 1 to 1½ minutes. Remove with a slotted spatula and place on a paper towel–lined tray to blot them dry. Continue with breading and frying the remaining sardines.

Squeeze a 2-inch circle of the beet cream into the center of 6 serving plates. Using a fork or silicone brush, shape a larger circle inside the plate, leaving about 2 inches around the circumference. Stack 6 breaded fried sardines over the beet cream, sprinkle with parsley, and serve.

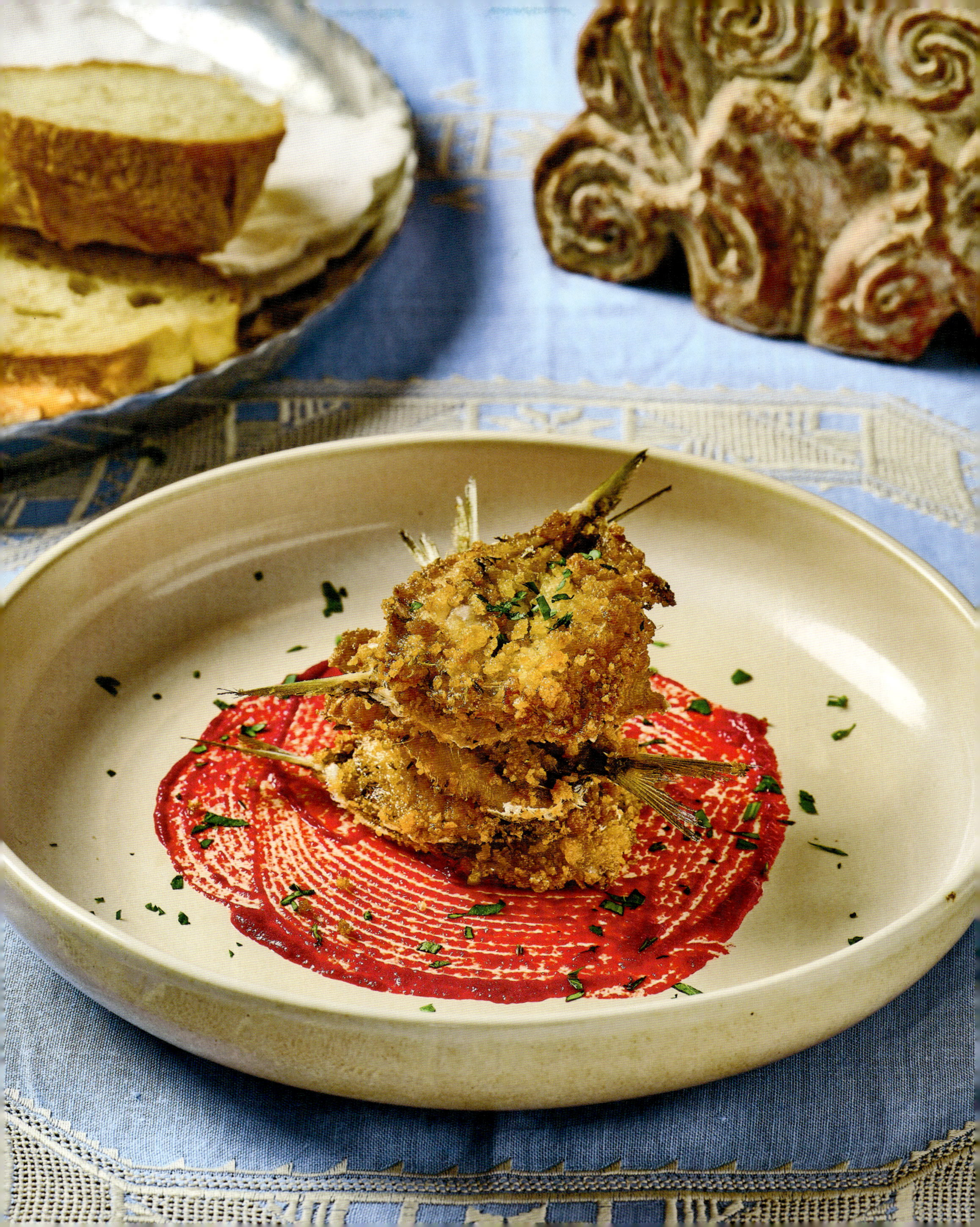

Lefteris Lazarou's Seared Fresh Squid
with Spanakopita Cream

Varoulko's Lefteris Lazarou, friend, lauded chef, and showman par excellence, prepared this recipe for us during an episode of My Greek Table, *season 4, which was devoted to him, "father of modern Greek cuisine," and his cooking.*

MAKES 2 OR 4 SERVINGS

8 fresh squid (about 6 inches long), cleaned

½ cup extra-virgin Greek olive oil

Sea salt to taste

2 teaspoons dried tarragon

2 to 4 tablespoons Spanakopita Cream (page 256)

½ cup microgreens and edible flowers

Score the cleaned squid tubes across the width, being careful not to cut all the way. You don't want separated squid rings, but the whole tube intact with the just top scored or slit. Place the cleaned, scored squid tubes and tentacles in a bowl and pour in the olive oil. Using a pastry brush, work the olive oil into the strands of the tentacles, too. Season with sea salt to taste.

Heat a large nonstick skillet over high heat. Add the tentacles, cook for about 1 minute, then turn to cook on the other side. Remove and set aside. Add the squid tubes and sear on one side. Season with salt and continue to brush with a little olive oil. Sprinkle with the dried tarragon. Turn the squid and remove when both sides are pink but still tender. This should take only about 4 minutes.

To serve, place the spanakopita cream on a platter and spread it across in a large swath. Place the grilled squid on top and sprinkle with the microgreens and edible flowers. Voilà!

Lefteris Lazarou, the Father of Modern Greek Cooking

We meet at the Renti Fish Market, south of Athens, en route to Piraeus, for a walk around and a lesson in Fish 101: what's fresh, what's not, what the gills teach us, how to know rigor. But mostly it's about how to love a monkfish, one of the sea's stranger creatures, and one Lefteris not only knows well but wrested from obscurity and catapulted to fame and high demand some thirty years ago. It's one of the many places we've convened over the years, usually to the accompaniment of some seafood meze and a clear glass of tsipouro, a favorite elixir of this most high-spirited chef.

I go back a long way with Lefteris Lazarou, chef-owner of Varoulko and arguably Greece's most renowned modern chef, and I love hanging with him. He's irreverent and avuncular at once, instantly recognizable anywhere in Greece, supremely gifted, and seemingly tireless at seventy-two, juggling restaurants, cooking classes, videos, and travel with the energy of a thirty-year-old. He was the first chef I ever met in Athens as a young writer for *Ta Nea*, and I still recall vividly the first meal I had at Varoulko, his restaurant: squid pesto with shoestring potatoes, a legacy dish in Athens back then, one of countless dishes that have written their own story on the stovetops and menus of this city. Others include his squid ink soups in all their iterations; artichokes à la polita with prawns, an early masterpiece; vegetable-rice dishes spun in a Thermomix to velvety elegance; and more, much more.

To my mind, he is the father of modern Greek cooking, and his path parallels the story of food over the last three decades in Athens, from humble roots to haute cuisine. Indeed, he is the first Greek chef to ever have been awarded a Michelin star, something that took fifteen years to achieve, from the opening of his first Varoulko location on a side street in Piraeus in 1987 to 2002, when he received the accolade.

Lefteris was at the helm of the transformation of Athens's food scene, and his creative energies helped push it from the simple cooking of a small provincial city to a world-class culinary destination. He was born in Piraeus with working-class roots and the sea in his blood. His father was a galley cook, and Lefteris himself started to cook on boats, in his father's kitchen, when he was fifteen. When he opened Varoulko at the age of thirty-five, it became an overnight sensation, with people swarming there from every corner of the Attica peninsula, so original and delicious was his food—and still is.

Humble to haute is a motif in his life and kitchen, the smooth-as-silk segue that takes some of the most common fish and transforms them into memorable, edible art, his particular genius. In his hands, forgotten fish like the garfish, a little-known species that is thin and has almost no flesh, and doesn't look like anything you've ever seen before, a thin strip that hovers in stillness in the sea and wiggles to move, are turned into artful dishes, several strips of its flesh braided beautifully and made succulent with a dark, sweet wine sauce. I remember the first bite of a grilled sardine "stuck" on toast with a spoonful of smoky eggplant salad, a new dish some fifteen years ago, ingenious in its technique and simplicity.

His genius is also in staying timely and keeping Varoulko afloat and flourishing for almost forty years. In that time, he's served statesmen, US presidents, and the Queen of England, cooked for Olympic teams, taught at the Culinary Institute of America, and year after year brings his brand to the Greek islands for summer visitors to enjoy, reinventing Greek cuisine in his own unique vision, always sharp, sensitive, sumptuous, and seaworthy.

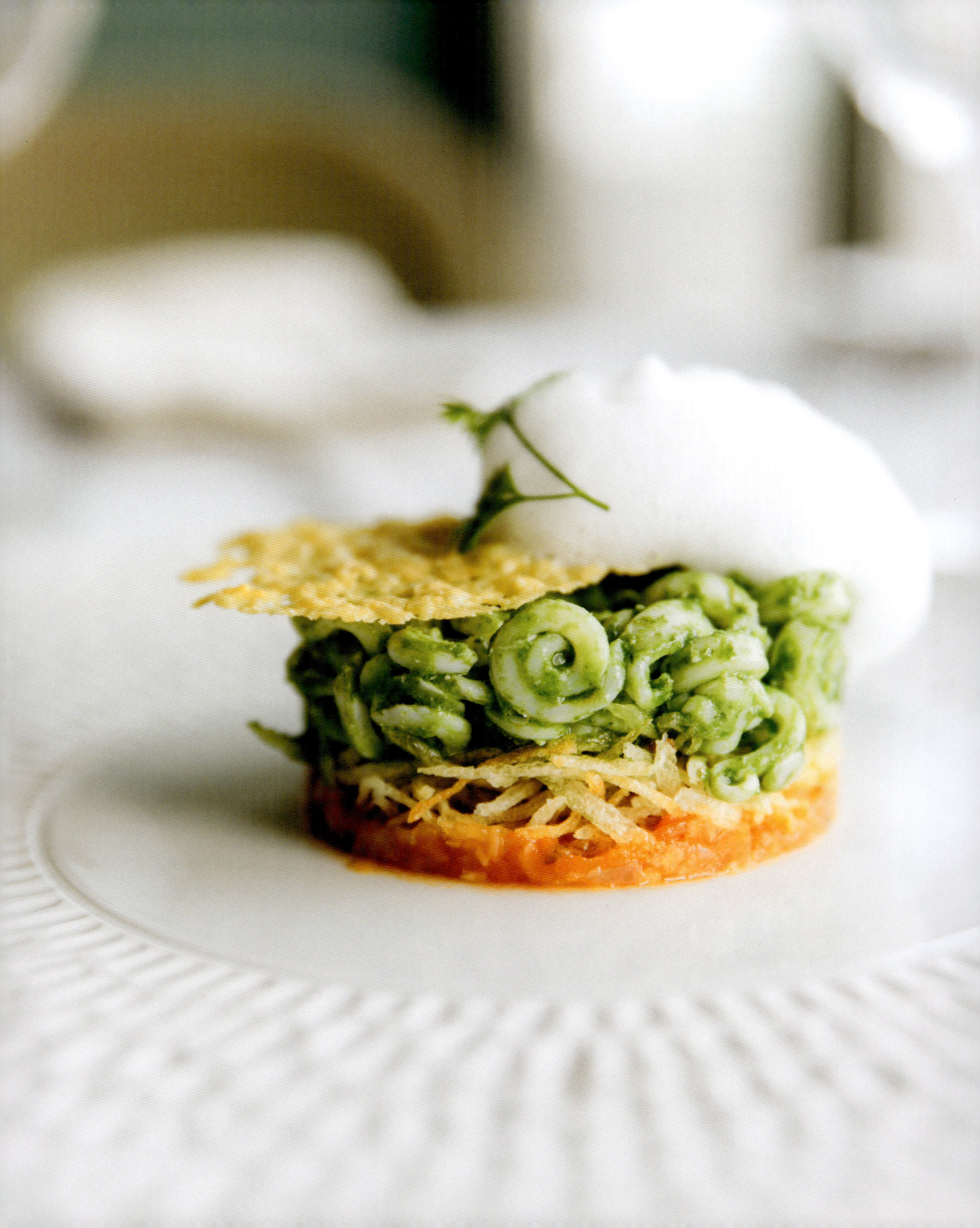

Lefteris Lazarou's Calamari Pesto

If there is one dish that I recall most fondly from all my years in Athens, it's probably this rendition of squid with pesto that is one of the long-standing signatures of Lefteris Lazarou. It's a dish he's been making and reimagining for decades, each new rendition more refined or more in tune with the times.

It hearkens back to his early experiences cooking in Italy, but it also weaves in his place as a Greek-focused chef, with the addition of both Aegina pistachios and ouzo, the latter of which he says he adds because it brings back memories of his father, who taught him that all cephalopods are easier to digest when you wash them down with Greece's favorite anise-scented distillation.

This recipe comes from the book I ghost-wrote with him in Greek many years ago.

MAKES 4 SERVINGS

For the pesto

3 bunches fresh basil leaves

1 scant cup grated Parmigiano

¾ cup shelled unsalted pistachios, preferably Aeginis

⅔ cup extra-virgin Greek olive oil

Freshly ground black pepper to taste

2 pounds fresh medium-size squid

¾ cup canola oil

¼ cup plus 1 tablespoon extra-virgin Greek olive oil, plus more for drizzling

2 large russet or Yukon Gold potatoes, peeled and cut into matchsticks

2 tablespoons ouzo

1 scant teaspoon cuttlefish ink powder (optional)

Make the pesto: In the bowl of a blender or food processor, pulse the basil, Parmigiano, and pistachios on high speed until the mixture is a dense paste. Gradually add the olive oil and a little pepper and pulse until the mixture is combined. The mixture may not absorb all the olive oil, so add it gradually. Measure out ¼ cup and reserve (save the rest for another use).

Remove the tentacles from the calamari, finely chop them, and wash them well. Using a small, sharp knife, slice each calamari lengthwise, and remove the viscera. Wash the calamari. Then, turn them inside out and, using a large, sharp knife, cut them into very thin, elongated strips, slightly thicker than spaghetti. Rinse the calamari again to remove their "saliva."

In a large nonstick skillet, heat the canola oil and ¼ cup of the olive oil over high heat. Blot the potato sticks dry and fry them in batches, turning gently, until golden and crisp, 4 to 5 minutes. Drain on paper towels.

While the potatoes are cooking, brush a nonstick pan with the remaining 1 tablespoon olive oil and heat it over high heat. Sauté the calamari bodies and tentacles for 1 minute, stirring, then deglaze with the ouzo. Add the reserved pesto and leave it for only 3 or 4 seconds (don't let it heat up more, as the pesto sauce will release its oil and make the dish heavy). Remove the pan from the heat.

Place a ring mold, 3 or 4 inches in diameter, in the center of each plate. Pat in a quarter of the fried potatoes and top with a quarter of the calamari mixture, pressing lightly to stabilize. Carefully lift the ring molds. Drizzle with a few drops of olive oil and garnish with a little cuttlefish ink powder, if desired.

"Honeyed" Octopus Braised in Sweet Wine and Vinegar

Honey and octopus are an unlikely but harmonious pairing that I first encountered at Papadakis Restaurant, prepared by the able hands of one of this city's few and most famous female chefs, Argiro Barbarigou. It continues to pop up around town on many menus, each version unique. There is something surprisingly simpatico about an almost caramelized octopus, and even though I cook less and less of this once signature Greek cephalopod, it's still popular.

MAKES 4 TO 8 SERVINGS

1 octopus (about 2½ pounds)

3 tablespoons extra-virgin Greek olive oil

1 large red onion, chopped

2 garlic cloves, finely chopped

2 tablespoons tomato paste

1½ cups semisweet red wine

¼ cup balsamic vinegar, or more to taste

1 tablespoon Greek pine honey

4 allspice berries

2 bay leaves

2 teaspoons dried Greek oregano

Salt and freshly ground black pepper to taste

To trim the octopus, remove the hood just below the eyes and squeeze or cut out the beak. Cut the octopus into 8 tentacles.

In a large, wide pot, heat the olive oil over medium-high heat. Add the onion and sauté until translucent and lightly golden, 10 to 12 minutes. Stir in the garlic. Stir in the tomato paste and cook for about 2 minutes. Add the octopus tentacles, reduce the heat to medium, and cover the pot. Cook the octopus for about 10 minutes, or until its color changes to a deep rose and it begins to exude its own juices.

Add the wine, vinegar, honey, allspice berries, and bay leaves. Keep the cover on the pot ajar and simmer the octopus for about 50 minutes, or until tender but not stringy. If the octopus is tender but with too much liquid in the pot, remove it with a slotted spoon and set it aside. Continue to cook the juices until they are reduced and almost the consistency of a thin syrup. Return the octopus to the pot and stir in the oregano and black pepper. Check for salt, but usually octopus doesn't need any. Serve.

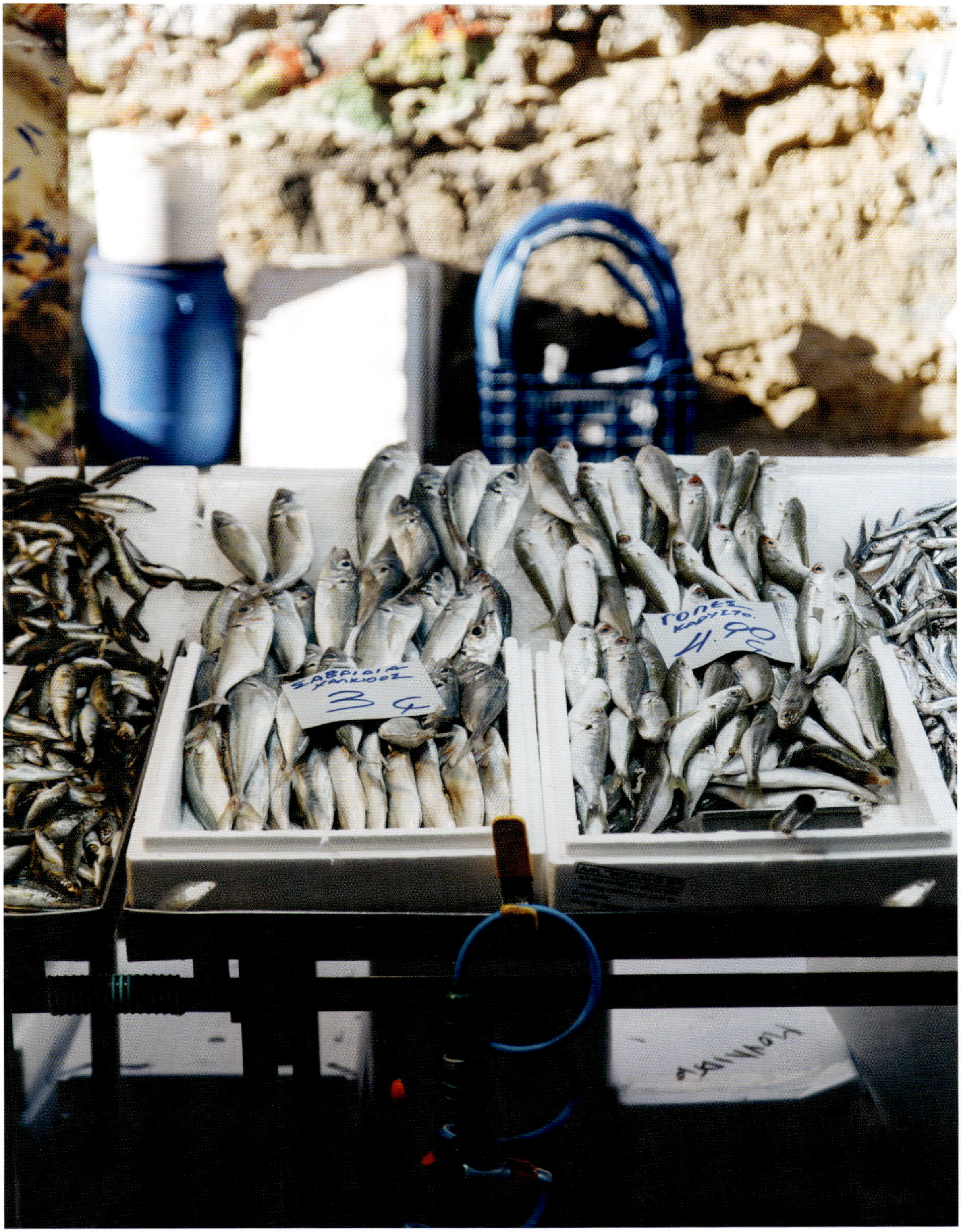
ΣΑΒΡΙΔΙΑ ΧΑΛΚΙΔΟΣ
3 €
ΓΟΠΕΣ ΚΑΡΥΣΤΟ.
4.90 €

Pan-Seared Monkfish Liver

It's hard to describe the rich, full flavor of monkfish liver, once the byproduct of a not-much-lauded fish and typically discarded. Then the awkward-looking monkfish was suddenly discovered (thanks to the visionary cooking of Lefteris Lazarou, whose name comes up a lot in this chapter) and its liver was suddenly a hot ticket item. The Japanese have long esteemed this treat as a rare delicacy, but for Greeks it was virtually unheard-of until the late 1990s. Granted, it's not that easy to find. You need to head to a high-end fishmonger or Japanese market, but it is well worth seeking out. Its flavor is an umami cross between butter and liver, something like foie gras of the sea. Each liver weighs between 2 and 4 ounces, depending on the size of the fish from which it is taken.

MAKES 4 SERVINGS

- ½ pound fresh or thawed frozen monkfish liver
- 6 tablespoons extra-virgin Greek olive oil
- 2 tablespoons apple cider vinegar
- 1 tablespoon strained fresh lemon juice
- Salt and freshly ground black pepper to taste
- 2 tablespoons finely chopped fresh flat-leaf parsley

Heat a large nonstick skillet over medium-high heat. Add the monkfish livers in a single layer. Sear on one side for about 3 minutes, then, using kitchen tongs, carefully turn to sear on the other side. Remove from the heat.

In a large bowl, whisk together the olive oil, vinegar, and lemon juice, seasoning with salt and pepper as you go. Marinate the seared monkfish livers in the sauce for about 5 minutes then serve, sprinkled with the parsley.

Fish Cakes with Tarama

Greeks love anything in a patty, from smash burgers (a new trend) to traditional vegetable patties and fritters, to all manner of fish and seafood cakes like these, flavored with dill, one of the most beloved herbs in the Greek kitchen, especially when it comes to seasoning anything from the sea.

MAKES 4 TO 5 SERVINGS

3 medium Yukon Gold potatoes, peeled

Salt

1 pound white-fleshed fish fillets, such as cod, halibut, or Mediterranean sea bass, shredded

1 tablespoon tarama

3 scallions, trimmed and finely chopped

1 garlic clove, minced

½ cup finely chopped fresh flat-leaf parsley

2 tablespoons snipped fresh dill

Grated zest and strained juice of 1 lemon

1 large egg, lightly beaten

¼ to ¾ cup plain bread crumbs

Sea salt and freshly ground black pepper to taste

Vegetable oil, for frying

All-purpose flour, for dredging

For serving

2 tablespoons chopped fresh flat-leaf parsley or 1½ cups frisée

Mayonnaise or tartar sauce (optional)

Place the potatoes in a medium pot and cover with ample cold water. Bring to a boil and season with salt. Cook over medium heat for 20 to 25 minutes, or until soft and flaky. Drain the potatoes and cool slightly. Place in a medium bowl and mash with a fork. They should be chunky, not smooth like mashed potatoes. Add the shredded fish, tarama, scallions, garlic, parsley, dill, and lemon zest. Taste and adjust seasoning with additional salt and pepper, as desired. Mix in the lemon juice and egg. Knead lightly and add enough of the bread crumbs so that when you form about 2 tablespoons of the mixture into a 3-inch patty, it holds its shape. Divide the mixture into 8 to 10 equal patties and place on a plate. Refrigerate for 15 minutes to firm them up.

Spread some flour in a shallow bowl and season lightly with salt and pepper. Dredge the patties.

Heat 1 inch of vegetable oil in a large, heavy skillet over medium heat. Slide a few of the patties into the skillet, being careful not to crowd it. Fry on one side until golden and then flip gently to fry on the other side. Remove and drain on paper towels. Repeat with the remaining patties.

Serve sprinkled with chopped parsley or garnished with frisée, with mayonnaise or tartar sauce, if desired.

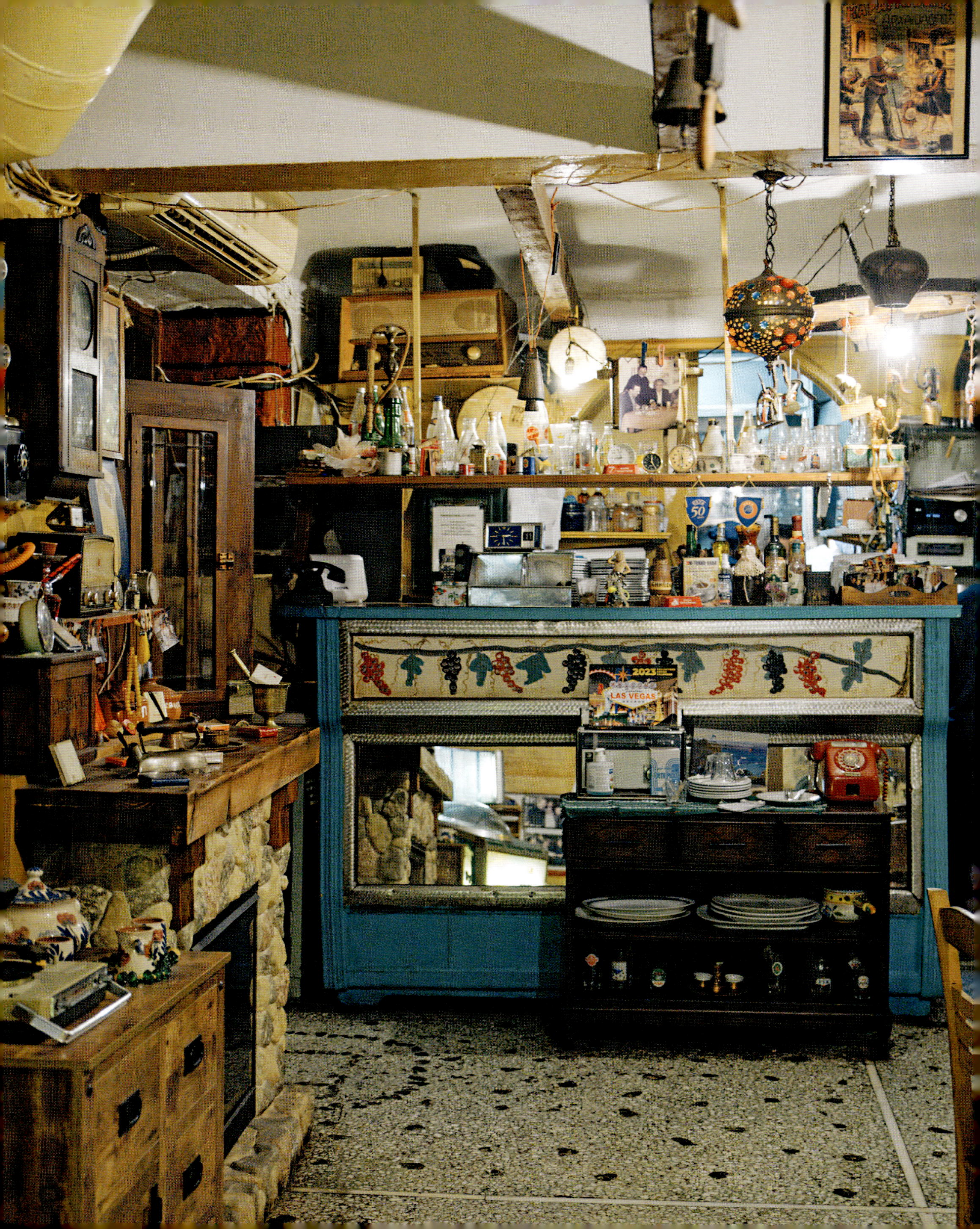
2023
LAS VEGAS

Meat Me... in Athens

Meat in Athens is such a huge subject. Even the most perfunctory look at the way this city and its denizens embrace carnivorous pleasures reveals that those pleasures are many and varied: succulent and smoked, stacked and wrapped, grilled and braised. Meat-loving Greeks wax poetic about their favorite souvlaki and gyro joints, some of which have cult status, like Elvis in Metaxourgeio, Hoocut on Agia Eirini Square, and the two Kostases (not related) at Syntagma and near Plateia Eirinis, respectively.

Athenians head to destination tavernas for everything from ribs and chops to meatballs, mutton or tripe soup, clay-baked shepherd's stews, and organ meats swaddled in intestines, then roasted or grilled to crunchy perfection. They salivate over fat burgers and smash burgers. And they spend fat money at steakhouses, for the likes of T-bones, Black Angus and Wagyu beef, and, more and more frequently, totally over-the-top tomahawks.

Whole areas outside the city are renowned for their grill houses, among them Pendelis, one of the mountains bordering the city; Ta Kalyvia, inland from the southern coast in Mesogeia; and Vari, along the southern coast, where you'll pass hawkers sometimes dressed up like tsoliades (skirt-clad Greek soldiers of yore) hawking menus and urging passersby to come in for dinner.

On the home front, although every supermarket has its meat section and in-house butcher, small neighborhood butcher shops are revered. The Central Market alone houses over a hundred butcher stalls, and every neighborhood has its own handful of butchers, avuncular and gruff all at once, and such a contrast to America, where the neighborhood butcher has all but disappeared. These mostly male professionals vie for attention by making life easy for the home cook, with their own special spice blends and marinades mixed into preshaped burgers, chicken breasts, and pork; they thread and sell fat chunks of pork, chicken, and beef onto skewers, often glistening with a marinade of their own creation, again making it easy to stop in, get home, and pop a few under the broiler for dinner. They know their customers by name, and home cooks feel secure in the knowledge that the butcher is their friend.

Greeks consume a bit more meat than their European neighbors, at about 7 pounds per person a month, compared to almost double the amount consumed in the United States. Pork, then chicken, are the two most popular meats in the Athenian and Greek kitchen, partly because they're less expensive than beef, which comes in third, and lamb and goat, traditional yet not nearly consumed in the same amounts, largely because they're associated with more seasonal eating, from Eastertime through the summer.

The recipes in this chapter are barely the tip of the iceberg when it comes to the many ways in which meat is cooked in the Athenian kitchen. Several renowned meat dishes, like Moscharaki Lemonato (page 222), Moscharaki Kokkinisto (page 223), and Yiouvetsi (page 226), are tucked into other chapters, carnivorous pleasures that to my mind belong under various other umbrellas, from meze treats to street food to bourgeois standard bearers. These next few pages represent a few of my favorite meat recipes, inspired by dishes I've enjoyed across the city all these years, in restaurants, tavernas, in my own home, and at friends' homes, too.

ΚΡΕΑΤΑ ΠΑΤΙΣ
ΝΤΟΠΙΟ ΦΡΕΣΚΟ ΜΟΝΟ ΕΔΟ
Γιδα ΝΤΟΠΙΑ ΧΕΡΑΚΙΑ 4.99
ΠΡΟΒΑΤΟ ΝΤΟΠΙΟ ΕΛΛΗΝΙΚΟ ΧΕΡΑΚΙΑ 4.99
ΖΥΓΟΥΡΙ ΜΑΛΑΚΟ ΧΕΡΑΚΙΑ 4.99
ΠΡΟΣΦΟΡΑ ΟΤΙ ΠΑΡΕΙΣ 4.99
ΚΡΕΑΤΑ ΝΤΟΠΙΑ ΦΡΕΣΚΑ ΤΡΙΠΟΛΗ

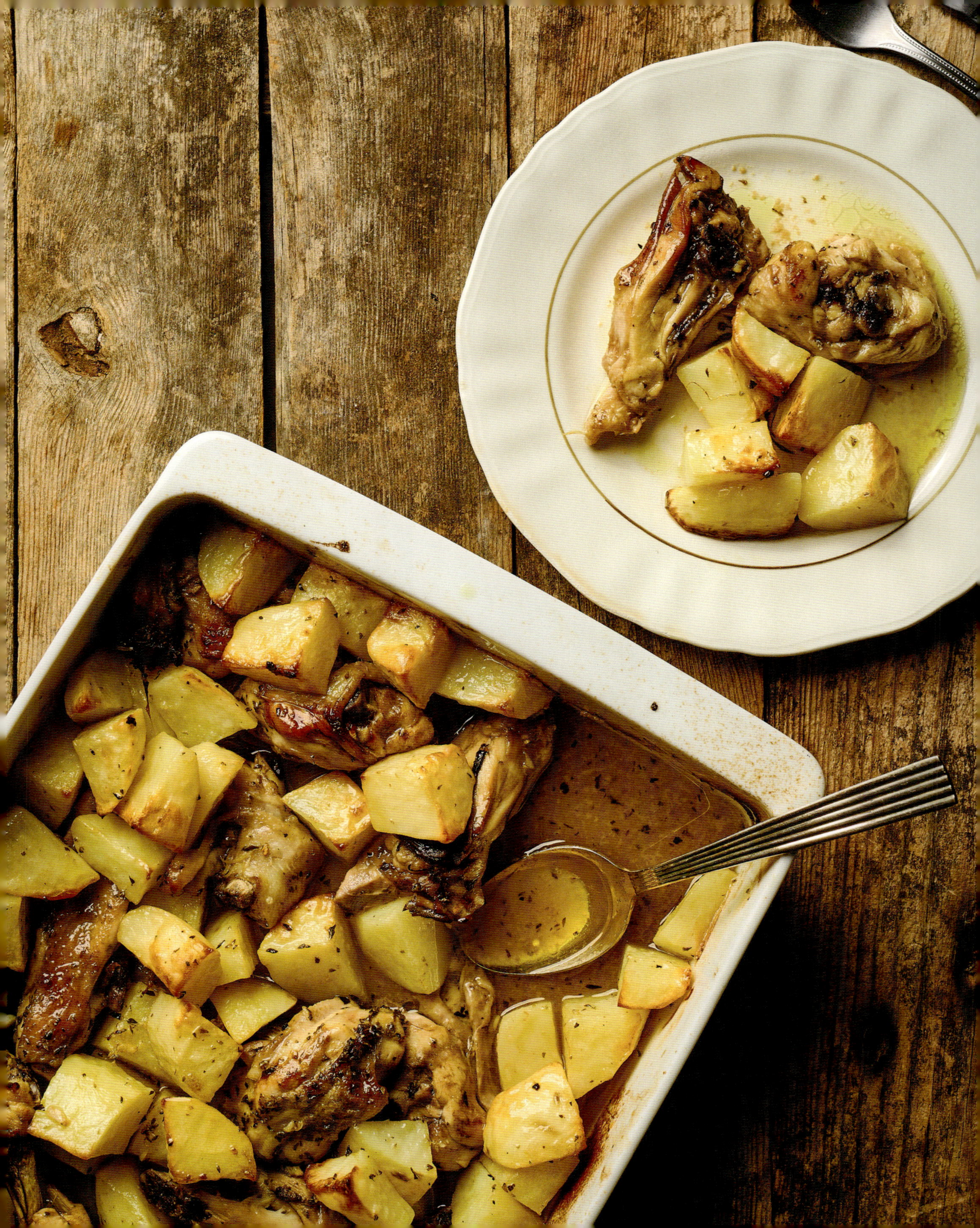

Lemony Chicken "Ribs"

Before I moved to Athens, I had never heard of chicken ribs, not the edible, finger-licking kind, anyway. But kotopoulo paidakia, essentially strips of chicken usually cut off the thigh, are a popular cut in Athens and all over Greece. They hold a special place in the childhood regimens of many an Athenian kid, one of those weeknight dinners that speaks to mommy food and storgi, the Greek word that refers specifically to a mother's love toward her child, wrapped with care and sealed with more than a little bit of indulging.

MAKES 4 TO 6 SERVINGS

6 tablespoons extra-virgin Greek olive oil

1 cup dry white wine

Strained juice of 1 lemon

⅓ cup strained fresh orange juice

2 tablespoons Dijon mustard

2 tablespoons grape molasses (petimezi) or Greek honey

4 garlic cloves, minced

1 heaping tablespoon dried Greek oregano

2 pounds boneless, skinless chicken thighs, cut into 2-inch-wide pieces

Coarse sea salt and freshly ground black pepper to taste

6 to 8 Yukon Gold or other roasting potatoes, quartered

In a large bowl, whisk together 3 tablespoons of the olive oil, the wine, lemon and orange juices, mustard, petimezi, garlic, and oregano. Add the chicken, cover, and marinate in the fridge for 30 minutes.

Preheat the oven to 350°F.

Remove the chicken from the fridge and let it stand at room temperature for 10 minutes, then transfer the chicken to a large baking dish, reserving the marinade. Season the chicken with salt and pepper. Toss the potatoes in a bowl with the remaining 3 tablespoons olive oil and a little salt and pepper and nestle between the chicken pieces. Drizzle the marinade over the chicken and potatoes. Cover with parchment paper, then aluminum foil, and bake for about 1 hour, or until the chicken is tender. About 15 minutes before removing from the oven, uncover the pan so that the chicken browns a little more. Remove and serve.

Grec-Mex Chicken Fajitas

In the "Foods that Unite Us" episode of My Greek Table, *season 4, Grec-Mex chicken fajitas is a favorite recipe mostly because it represents a new chapter in Athenian dining, the marriage of different ethnic cuisines with Greek. While there isn't a "Grec-Mex" restaurant per se, Greek flavors wend their way into the likes of fajitas, burritos, and more at new places like Amigos, Taqueria Maya, and Taco Loco, eateries that have spiced up the dining experience in the Greek capital. The two culinary traditions, despite being on opposite sides of the globe, complement each other beautifully.*

MAKES 4 TO 8 SERVINGS

4 tablespoons extra-virgin Greek olive oil, divided, plus more as needed

1 pound boneless, skinless chicken breasts or thighs, cut into thin strips

2 teaspoons dried Greek oregano, divided

1 teaspoon chili powder, or as desired, divided

1 teaspoon ground paprika, divided

1 teaspoon ground cumin, divided

1 teaspoon freshly ground black pepper, divided

¼ teaspoon cayenne pepper, divided

Sea salt to taste

1 large green bell pepper, seeded and cut into ⅛-inch-wide strips

1 large red bell pepper, seeded and cut into ⅛-inch-wide strips

1 large red onion, thinly sliced

3 garlic cloves, minced

8 (6-inch) flour tortillas

½ cup sliced kalamata olives

Crumbled Greek feta, for serving

Greek yogurt, for serving (optional)

Heat 2 tablespoons of the olive oil in a grill pan or a large skillet or wok over medium heat. Add the chicken and stir in half of all the spices. Cook, stirring, until about halfway done, 7 to 8 minutes. Add the bell peppers and onion and cook, stirring occasionally, until the onions are translucent, 7 to 8 minutes. Add the garlic and stir to soften. Cook until the vegetables are soft and the chicken is just about done, 3 to 5 minutes. Stir in the remaining spices, then adjust the seasoning with salt and pepper as needed. Cook, stirring, until everything is melded and the chicken is done, about 5 minutes more. Remove from the heat.

Place the tortillas on the grill or in a large skillet to warm them up.

To assemble the fajitas, fill the warmed tortillas with chicken, peppers, onions, olives, and feta. Serve with a dollop of Greek yogurt on the side, if desired.

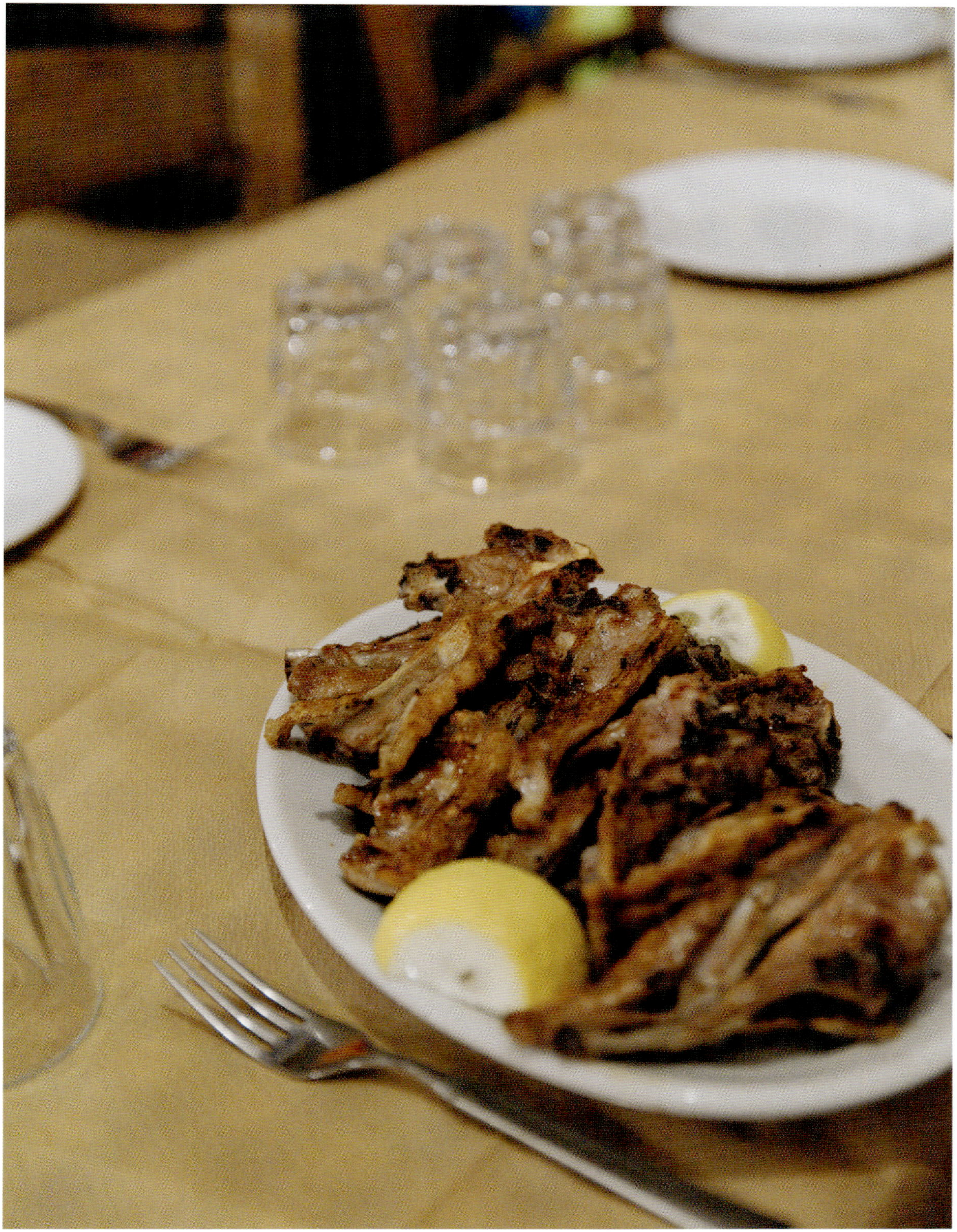

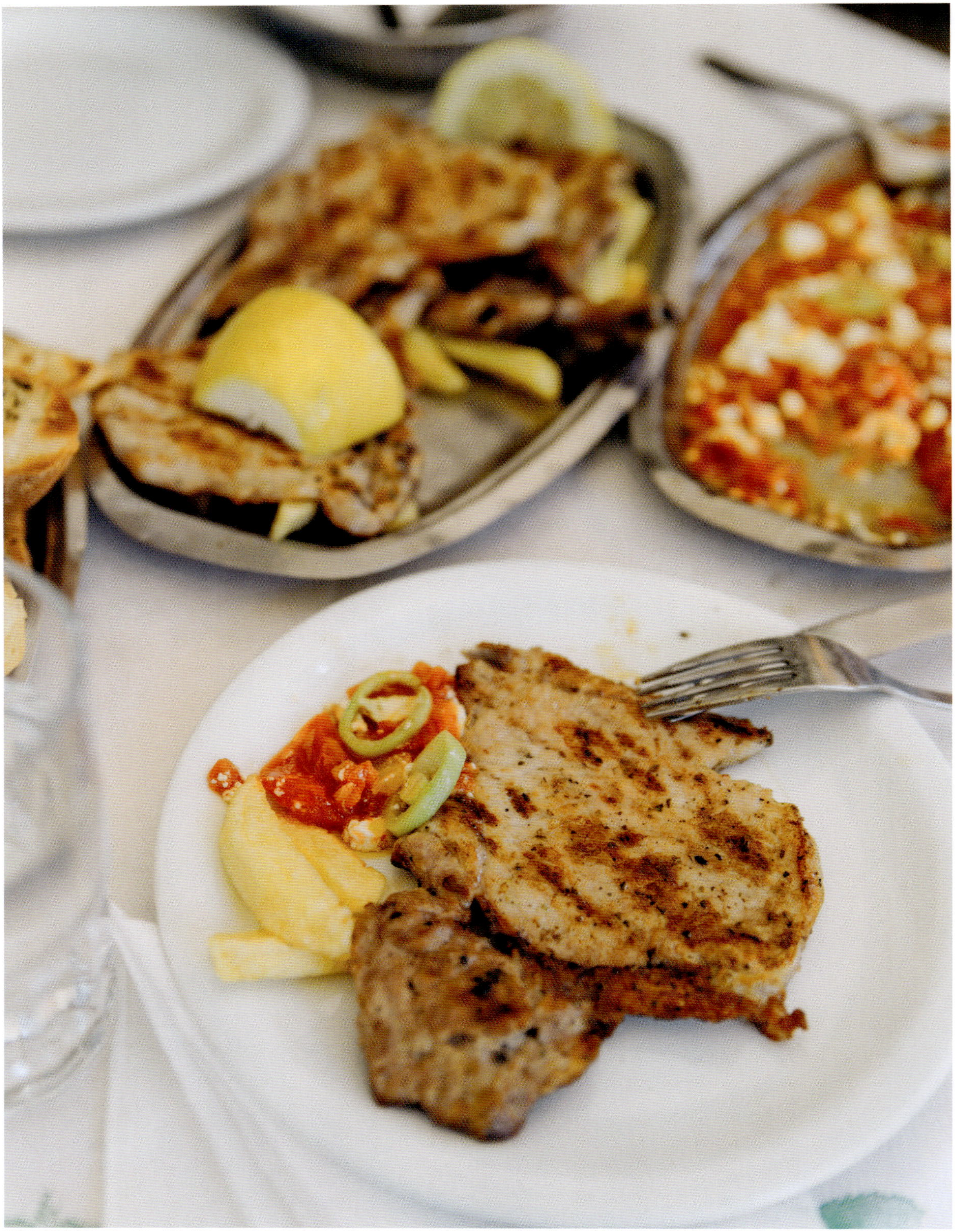

Schoolchildren's Greek Chicken Schnitzel

There's a lot going on in this title! As it happens, grandparents have a big place in the homes and hearts of their grandchildren in Athens and in Greece at large. We were the classic example of that, living in the family apartment house in a nice leafy suburb of Athens, two floors below my in-laws. My kids were up there all the time, and a treat for them, as for many of their friends in grade school at the time, was when yiayia or papou made schnitzel!

This classic Viennese dish is sold breaded and ready at every Greek supermarket, but some people still make their own, as my in-laws did, oftentimes letting the grandkids in on the dipping and breading fun, starting with a turn at the food processor or mortar and pestle to crumble the requisite frigania, mini store-bought toasts that have multipurpose use in the Greek kitchen. Needless to say, Greek oregano is incorporated into this easy recipe, and a twist of lemon, always a Greek favorite, helps lighten up the crunchy but dense mouthfeel of the crust. We usually serve this with homemade Greek fries and a salad.

MAKES 4 SERVINGS

1½ pounds boneless, skinless chicken breasts

1 cup all-purpose flour, or more as needed

Sea salt and freshly ground black pepper to taste

3 large eggs

1 heaping tablespoon Dijon mustard

1 heaping tablespoon dried Greek oregano

⅔ cup plain bread crumbs

½ cup extra-virgin Greek olive oil

Lemon wedges, for serving

Cut the breasts lengthwise into 2 pieces each. Using a kitchen mallet or the long side of a thick pestle, pound the breasts into cutlets about ½ inch thick.

Put the flour in a wide, shallow bowl and season with a little salt and pepper. In a second wide, shallow bowl, using a fork, beat together the eggs, mustard, oregano, salt, and pepper. Put the bread crumbs in a third wide, shallow bowl.

Heat the olive oil in a large, wide skillet over medium heat.

Dip and turn 2 chicken cutlets into the flour, coating both sides, then into the egg, turning to coat both sides, and finally into the bread crumbs. Place them in the skillet and pan-fry for about 4 minutes on each side, until golden and crisp. Transfer to a platter. Continue with the remaining cutlets until done and serve hot, with a few lemon wedges on the side.

Turkey-Stuffed Cabbage Rolls
with Avgolemono Cream Sauce

Many of the recipes that characterize Athens these days are a reflection of how much the supermarket and people's broadening tastes have changed in these past few decades. The advent of turkey as an everyday meat is one such change. This big awkward bird used to be a once-a-year treat, usually at New Year's. Its lean meat and mild flavor appeal to the calorie-counting set, and it is now widely available in many different cuts, including ground, and beloved as a substitution for red meat in many traditional Greek recipes such as these stuffed cabbage rolls.

But there is another new addition to this recipe, one of the many recent variations on the avgolemono theme (see page 220), this one a combination of Greece's most famous sauce with cream and butter. The turkey may be lean, but the sauce is rich!

MAKES 6 TO 8 SERVINGS

Salt and freshly ground black pepper to taste

1 large or 2 medium cabbages (about 5 pounds total)

2 tablespoons extra-virgin Greek olive oil, plus more as needed

1 tablespoon unsalted butter

2 large yellow onions, finely chopped

1½ pounds ground turkey or chicken

⅔ cup short-grain white rice

1⅓ cups chicken stock, or more as needed

½ cup chopped fresh flat-leaf parsley

½ cup chopped fresh dill

Bring a large pot of water to a rolling boil and season with salt. Cut the cabbage at its base to remove the stem. Gently plunge the cabbage head into the water and simmer it for 8 to 10 minutes, until the leaves are softened and translucent. Remove with a slotted spoon and set aside to cool.

While the cabbage is simmering, prepare the filling. Heat the oil and butter in a large skillet over medium heat until the butter melts. Add the onions and cook until translucent and soft, about 8 minutes. Add the ground meat and sauté, stirring, until it turns to a translucent white. Add the rice and stir to coat in the oil and to combine well with the meat. Add the stock, reduce the heat to low, and simmer until the rice has absorbed most of the liquid. Season with salt and pepper. Remove from the heat. Add the parsley and dill and set aside to cool slightly.

When the cabbage is cool enough to handle, gently pull apart the leaves. Halve the largest leaves if desired and trim the tough ribs so that the leaves roll more easily.

Oil the bottom of a large, wide pot. Strew the torn leaves or any that are too small to roll on the bottom of the pot. Place 2 to 3 teaspoons of the filling inside each cabbage leaf, depending on its size. Roll up the leaves to make cylinders, folding in the edges to keep the filling from spilling out. Place seam side down in the pot. Continue rolling and placing the rolls snugly next to each other. If there are more rolls than fit in one layer, start a second layer.

For the avgolemono cream sauce

2 large eggs yolks

Strained juice of 1 lemon

3 tablespoons unsalted butter

3 scant tablespoons all-purpose flour

½ cup heavy cream

Salt and freshly ground black pepper to taste

Add enough water or stock to cover the rolls by 1 inch and cover with an inverted plate. Bring to a simmer over medium heat, then reduce the heat and simmer gently for about 1½ hours, or until the cabbage is very tender and the rice cooked. There should be 1½ to 2 cups of liquid total left in the pot, which you'll need to make the avgolemono cream sauce.

To make the sauce, in a medium bowl, whisk the egg yolks until very frothy, then slowly whisk in the lemon juice until the mixture is frothy. Set aside for a few minutes. Take a ladleful of the hot pot juices and add them drop by drop to the egg-lemon mixture, whisking vigorously all the while, until you've incorporated the full ladle. Repeat with a second ladleful and with any pot juices that still might be left.

In a medium saucepan, melt the butter over medium heat. When it starts to bubble, whisk in the flour. Whisk vigorously for 3 to 4 minutes. Whisking all the while, add the cream, stirring to warm it through. Reduce the heat and add the egg-lemon mixture, whisking constantly. Season to taste with salt and pepper and immediately pour into the large pot with the cabbage rolls. Tilt it around to distribute evenly and serve immediately.

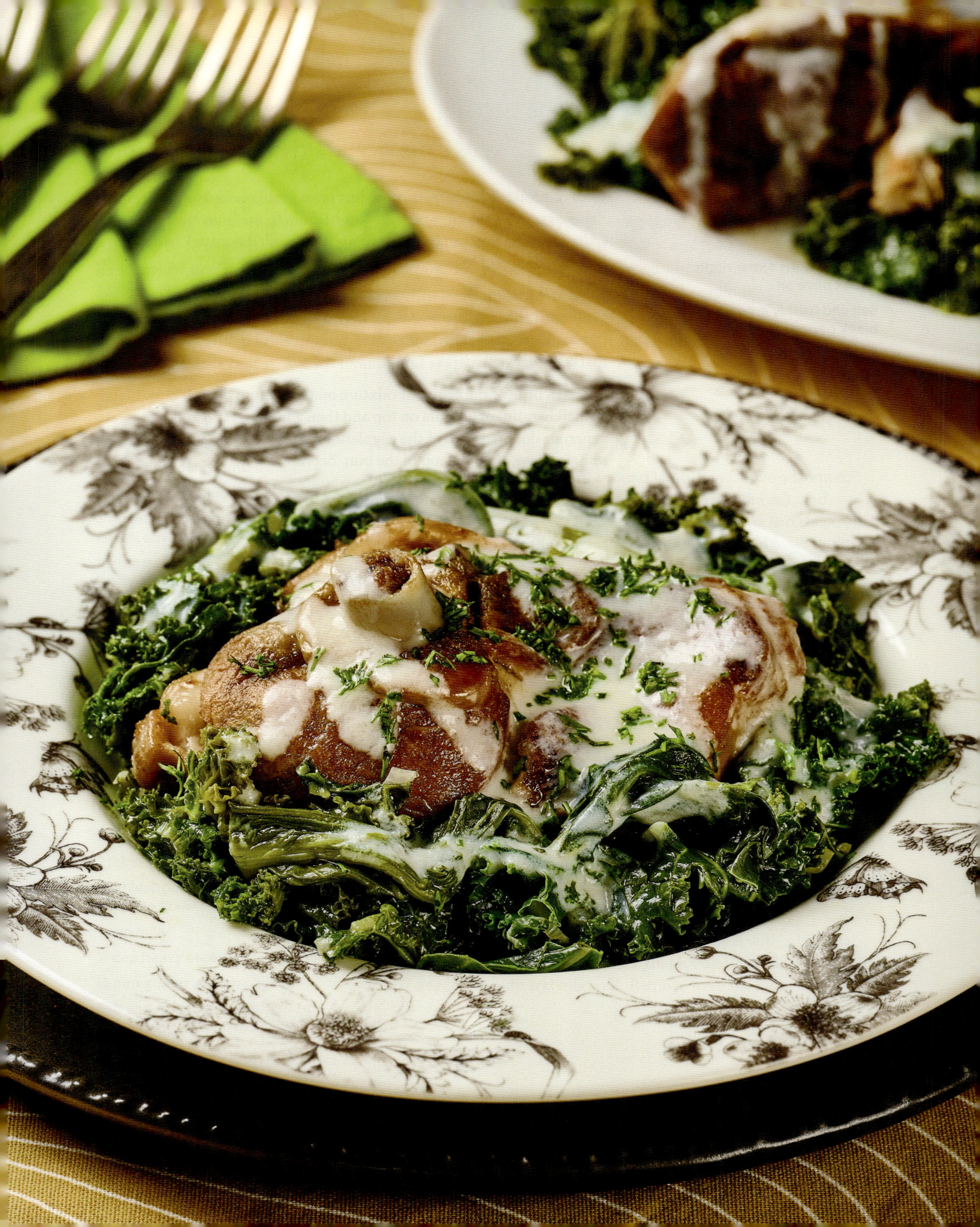

Lamb Fricasse
with Kale

Fricasse is one of the great dishes of Greek cuisine, a luscious concoction of lamb, pork, or fish cooked with greens and finished with avgolemono sauce. Romaine lettuce is the traditional choice for the greens, but in recent years kale, a newcomer in the brassica family, has won over home cooks and restaurant chefs alike.

MAKES 6 SERVINGS

½ cup extra-virgin Greek olive oil, or more as needed

3 pounds bone-in lamb shoulder, cut into roughly 2½-inch chunks

2 leeks, trimmed and chopped

3 scallions, trimmed and chopped

1 garlic clove, minced

1 scant teaspoon coriander seeds, crushed in a spice mill or with a mortar and pestle

Sea salt and freshly ground black pepper to taste

⅔ cup dry white wine

2 pounds kale, coarsely chopped

Grated zest and strained juice of 1 large lemon

2 large eggs

Heat the olive oil in a Dutch oven over medium-high heat. Using kitchen tongs, carefully place the lamb shoulder in the pot piece by piece, in one layer, and in batches if necessary so you don't crowd the pot. Sear on one side until well browned, about 10 minutes, then turn to sear on the other side and then all around. Transfer to a platter and repeat with the remaining lamb pieces, replenishing the olive oil if necessary.

Reduce the heat to medium, add the leeks and scallions, and cook, stirring occasionally, for 7 to 8 minutes, or until softened and translucent. Stir in the garlic.

Return the meat to the pot, season with the coriander, salt, and pepper, then pour in the wine. Stir the contents around, scraping up the bottom of the pot a little to get all the tasty bits that may have stuck there. Add enough water to come about halfway up the contents of the pot and bring to a simmer. Cover, reduce the heat to low, and cook for 1¼ hours. About halfway through cooking the meat, add the kale and lemon zest and stir to combine. Season with a little salt, cover, and continue cooking until the kale is wilted and tender and the lamb is cooked through.

Crack the eggs into a medium stainless steel bowl and whisk until very frothy, about 5 minutes. Very slowly add the lemon juice, drop by drop, whisking all the while. Take a ladleful of the pot juices and very slowly add them to the egg-lemon mixture, whisking vigorously. Repeat with a second ladleful. Pour the egg-lemon mixture into the pot, tilting it back and forth so that it is evenly distributed, and serve. Don't cover the pot because the eggs will set and you'll end up with an omelet!

Feminist Lamb and Potatoes

There are too many versions of this recipe to count, and I could have easily chosen any number of them, but instead opted to borrow one that goes back to 1887 and was published in the first feminist newspaper of Greece, Y Efimeris ton Kyrion *(The Ladies Journal), established in Athens that very same year by Kallirois Parren. Parren, born into a middle-class family in Rethymnon, Crete, educated in the best girls' schools of Athens and Piraeus at the time, and married to the Frenchman (Parren) who founded Agence France Press, was a brilliant, polyglot pioneer in the women's rights movement, especially in areas that fostered education and fought against child labor.*

Her legacy is a long one, in which patriotism, royalist leanings, and a visionary spirit are all woven together. The newspaper ran for three decades, finally shutting down in about 1916. She died in 1940. When I encountered this recipe for slow-cooked lamb in butter, which also calls for cooking the potatoes separately in butter until, to translate from the original, "they're nicely reddened like beautiful apricots, while their flesh will be soft like figs," I couldn't help but wonder if this decidedly French way of cooking meat and potatoes predates the man generally thought to have brought the marriage of French and Greek cuisines together, Nikos Tselementes (see page 228). The original recipe calls for baking the lamb in a hearth and covering the pot with ash, so I have adopted it here for modern kitchens.

MAKES 4 TO 6 SERVINGS

1 (4½- to 5-pound) bone-in lamb shoulder, cut into serving-size pieces

Sea salt and freshly ground black pepper to taste

3 generous tablespoons plus 8 tablespoons (1 stick) salted butter, divided

3 large, ripe tomatoes, cored and cut into chunks

2 pounds new potatoes, peeled

Preheat the oven to 325°F.

Season the lamb generously with salt and pepper and place it in a Dutch oven or, preferably, a copper pot with a lid. Place 3 generous tablespoons of the butter around the lamb, then add the tomatoes and a little pepper. Add enough water to come a little less than halfway up the lamb. Cover and bake for about 3 hours, or until the lamb is falling off the bones and all the pan juices are thick. Increase the oven temperature to 375°F, remove the lid, and continue roasting the lamb for about 20 more minutes, checking on it for moisture, until it browns a little.

When the lamb has about an hour left to go, start on the potatoes: Melt the remaining 8 tablespoons butter over low heat in a wide pot or deep skillet with a lid. Add the potatoes and season with salt and pepper. Cover and cook for 45 to 50 minutes, or until they're golden "like apricots" and soft "as figs"!

Serve the lamb and potatoes together.

Itinerant Shepherds, Attica Grill Houses, and a Misnomer

The sprawling grill houses along Attica's southern coast, on the edge of the Athenian Riviera, seem both kitschy and quaint at first glance, large places redolent of barbecue smoke and punctuated by the incongruous sight of full-grown men clad in white tights and pleated white foustaneles (the traditional skirts of nineteenth-century Greek soldiers) beckoning any potential customer to come in. Welcome to the Vlachika of Vari, one of three areas on the periphery of Athens where meat tavernas are a destination. Kalyvia, further inland from the coast, and Pendelis, the mountain bordering Athens to the north, are the other two destinations for the meat-loving crowd.

Vari is a bit different perhaps because it holds the most prominence as the place to go for traditional Greek grilling. The handful of places along this strip of the coast are called— incorrectly—Ta Vlachika. More on that in a second. It's hard to believe that this part of Attica, en route to Cape Sounion and now a Gold Coast, where real estate value has soared and foreign capital rules the roost, just a century ago was a no-man's-land of open fields, where local shepherds would descend in the cold months from the highlands of Pendeli and Parnitha to graze their flocks. These shepherds were Sarakatsanoi, or Sarakatsens, an ancient itinerant tribe that still exists, and once roamed all over Greece. Like all the once-itinerant shepherding tribes of Greece, at one point or another in the twentieth century, they settled into more permanent homes and regions. A few Sarakatsen families from Pendeli and Parnitha settled in Vari around 1917, still practicing the traditional profession of husbandry. But as it were, to those unschooled in such minutiae, they were referred to as Vlachs, the name of another tribe that roamed the Balkans and spoke a separate language. In 1962, one of those original Sarakatsen families opened the first taverna in what was until then one of several simple cafeneia, resting spots for shepherds on the move. By 1970, the road along this part of the coast was lined with similar restaurants, the resting spots were gone, and itinerant shepherding waned, but the aromas of meat on the grill wafted far enough afield and into the popular imagination, luring people from all over Attica.

Even the likes of Pelé and Brigitte Bardot have visited these meat meccas. They're still fun, and if you hanker after grilled protein and want to avoid the more touristy spots closer to Sounio, you'll enjoy this vintage aspect of local dining.

Grilled Lamb Chops Marinated
with Petimezi Barbecue Sauce

It's not typical for Greeks to grill at home. Most Athenians live in apartments and most do have balconies, but the preference is for cooking indoors and heading out to a specialty restaurant for a land-lover's meal of grilled meats. But these chops can be made in a grill pan on the stovetop, with a barbecue sauce that speaks modern Greek, in that it weaves ancient ingredients into a contemporary food aesthetic. Enjoy. And, yes, if you want to do these on the grill, you can!

MAKES 6 TO 8 SERVINGS

For the petimezi barbecue sauce

1 cup strained fresh orange juice

⅔ cup grape molasses (petimezi)

½ cup tomato juice

½ cup dry red wine

¼ cup extra-virgin Greek olive oil

¼ cup Dijon mustard

2 tablespoons balsamic vinegar

4 garlic cloves, minced

2 teaspoons finely chopped fresh rosemary

2 teaspoons finely chopped fresh oregano

1 teaspoon smoked paprika

½ teaspoon coarse sea salt

2 turns freshly ground black pepper

For the lamb chops

4 pounds single-cut lamb chops

Coarse sea salt and freshly ground black pepper to taste

2 tablespoons chopped fresh thyme

1 tablespoon dried Greek oregano

1 teaspoon extra-virgin Greek olive oil

Make the barbecue sauce: In a medium bowl, whisk together all of the ingredients until the mixture is smooth and emulsified. Set aside in a jar with a tight-fitting lid.

Place the chops in a large bowl and season well with the salt, pepper, thyme, and oregano. Let the chops sit in the refrigerator for 15 minutes. Pour in about a third of the barbecue sauce and toss the chops in it. Place back in the fridge for about 15 minutes.

Remove the chops from the fridge and have the remaining barbecue sauce nearby. Transfer about half of the remaining barbecue sauce to a bowl and set aside for serving. Have the rest near you for brushing the chops while grilling.

Brush a large ridged grill pan with the olive oil. Heat the grill pan over high heat and place as many chops as will fit in one layer. Sear them well, brushing with a little of the barbecue sauce, then turning when done and brushing the other side, too. The chops will take 3 to 4 minutes per side for medium-rare. Transfer to a platter and tent with aluminum foil to keep them warm. Continue until all the chops are done, brushing them lightly with some of the sauce as you grill them. Serve hot, with the reserved sauce on the side.

Beef Cheeks "Kokinisto"

Athenian chefs turned to beef cheeks when the Greek economy went south around 2009. Survival mode pervaded every aspect of life in the Greek capital, and keeping food costs down to create menus that people could afford was tantamount on chefs' minds. Pioneers like Christoforos Peskias, and Vasilis Kallidis, both reinterpreters of Greek cuisine for modern palates, started to use cheap but tender cuts of meat in classic Greek dishes like this kokinisto (tomato-braised) recipe. I actually tasted cheeks for the first time in Kallidis's restaurant Aneton in the northern suburb of Maroussi and was completely won over, for this often-discarded part of the animal just happens to be one of its tenderest.

MAKES 4 TO 6 SERVINGS

½ cup extra-virgin Greek olive oil

2 pounds beef cheeks, rinsed and patted dry

Salt and freshly ground black pepper to taste

2 large yellow onions, finely chopped

2 large carrots, peeled and chopped

2 celery stalks, trimmed and chopped

4 garlic cloves, finely chopped

2 tablespoons tomato paste

1 cup dry red wine

1½ cups chopped fresh or canned tomatoes

Pinch sugar

3 bay leaves

5 fresh thyme sprigs

4 allspice berries

3 cups chicken stock or bone broth, or more if needed

Heat the olive oil in a large, wide pan over medium-high heat. Using kitchen tongs, place the beef cheeks in the pan in a single layer. Sear them for 4 to 5 minutes on one side, then turn to brown on the other side. Season lightly with salt and pepper. Sear them in two batches, if necessary, for the cheeks to all fit in a single layer. Transfer to a plate.

Add the onions, carrots, and celery to the pan, season lightly with salt and pepper, and sauté, stirring occasionally, until translucent and softened, 8 to 10 minutes. Stir in the garlic and swirl it around in the pan to soften for about a minute. Add the tomato paste and stir it into the vegetables and cook for a couple of minutes. Return the beef cheeks to the pan and stir gently. Pour in the wine and bring it to a simmer. After about 2 to 3 minutes, when the alcohol has cooked off, add the tomatoes, sugar, bay leaves, thyme, allspice berries, and enough of the stock to come about three-quarters of the way up the contents of the pot. Season with additional salt and pepper to taste, cover, turn the heat down, and simmer gently for about 2 hours, until the cheeks are meltingly tender. Remove the bay leaves and serve.

Filet Mignon
with Mavrodaphne Sauce

This simple recipe for a luxury cut of meat, almost always saved for special occasions, marries one of the great dessert wines of Greece, Mavrodaphne, with one of the world's favorite cuts of steak.

MAKES 4 SERVINGS

For the mavrodaphne sauce

2 cups beef or chicken stock

1 cup Mavrodaphne or other sweet red wine, such as port

1 tablespoon balsamic vinegar

Sea salt and freshly ground black pepper to taste

3 tablespoons chilled unsalted butter

For the meat

1 tablespoon extra-virgin Greek olive oil

1 tablespoon unsalted butter

2 garlic cloves, crushed

Sea salt and freshly ground black pepper to taste

4 (½-pound) filets mignons

Place the stock, wine, vinegar, salt, and pepper in a small saucepan and bring to a boil. Turn the heat down to a simmer and cook the sauce for about 25 minutes, or until reduced by about half and thickened. Remove from the heat and whisk in the butter until the sauce is smooth and shiny. Cover and set aside.

Preheat the oven to 400°F.

Heat a cast-iron skillet over high heat. Add the oil, butter, and garlic. Reduce to medium heat and swirl the garlic around in the pan for about a minute or two. Remove and discard. Generously season the filets with salt and pepper on all sides. Place them in the skillet and sear for 2 to 3 minutes per side for medium-rare, or a little longer for medium. Transfer the skillet to the oven and bake for 4 to 10 minutes, depending on how rare or well-done you prefer your steaks. Remove and serve with the mavrodaphne sauce.

Ossobuco
with Greek Flavors

Ossobuco has taken over Athens. This cut of beef, so popular in Italian cooking, was not readily available in Greek butcher shops until recently. It's become very popular, and the shanks are usually cut from either veal calves or mature cows.

Every Athenian neighborhood has its butcher shops, which is the most likely place to find ossobuco, a gourmet cut. These shanks—the term ossobuco *literally means "bone with a hole"—weigh in at ¾ to 1 pound each, but the size and weight vary depending on the animal from which its cut, its age, and whether the piece is cut from the front or hind legs. Front-leg ossobuco is taller, shaped like a cone, and perfect for a dramatic presentation; the hind legs give you a flatter, wider piece, which is easier to manage and actually what most people, chefs included, prefer. In either case this cut needs long, slow braising, the better for all that delicious marrow and collagen to melt into the braising liquid, creating a dense, sumptuous sauce.*

The cut we choose depends on our desired result. The meat of a young animal is more tender and cooks faster, while the meat from an older one needs more time in the pot or oven, but has a richer, deeper flavor and aftertaste.

In this recipe for slow-braised ossobuco with Greek flavors, all the warm spices that usually go into meat stews are here, too, and so is a little surprise: a sweet white muscat wine.

MAKES 6 SERVINGS

- ¼ cup extra-virgin Greek olive oil, or more if needed
- 2½ to 3 pounds beef shank, cut into 6 cross-section pieces, about 2 inches thick
- Sea salt and freshly ground black pepper to taste
- 2 shallots, minced
- 1 garlic clove, finely chopped
- 1½ cups Samos Muscat or other sweet muscat
- 2 (15-ounce) cans diced tomatoes
- 1 cinnamon stick
- 2 star anise
- 2 whole cloves
- 6 to 8 allspice berries
- 2 bay leaves
- 6 fresh thyme sprigs
- 1½ cups beef or chicken stock or water

In a heavy, wide pot, heat the olive oil over high heat. Working in batches, add the shanks in a single layer and sear until browned, 7 to 10 minutes per side. Season each side with salt and pepper once it's seared. Transfer to a platter and repeat with the remaining pieces.

Replenish the oil if necessary and lower the heat to medium. Add the shallots and garlic and stir for about 2 minutes to soften. Lower the heat to medium-low, add the wine, and, using a wooden spoon, scrape up all the tasty bits that may be stuck to the bottom of the pan. Add the tomatoes with their juices, cinnamon, star anise, cloves, allspice, bay leaves, and thyme. Return the meat to the pot and pour in enough stock or water to barely cover it. Season with additional salt and pepper, cover, and reduce the heat to low. Simmer the meat for 1½ to 2 hours, or until it's very tender. Taste for salt and pepper and season as needed. Remove the bay leaves and serve.

Pork Roast Stuffed with Greek Cheeses and Dried Fruit

Rolo, as this stuffed, rolled, and bound piece of boneless pork is called, is one of the most popular meat preparations in Athens, something that's easy to find, with many variations, at almost every butcher shop and supermarket meat counter. This recipe calls for a rather large piece of pork loin, and it's usually reserved for holiday tables, especially Christmas and New Year's, but you can halve the recipe and make it with a smaller loin, too.

MAKES 6 TO 8 SERVINGS

For the pork

1 (5-pound) boneless pork loin, butterflied

Coarse sea salt and freshly ground black pepper to taste

2 tablespoons strained fresh orange juice

1 tablespoon extra-virgin Greek olive oil, plus more for greasing

1 tablespoon Dijon mustard

1 tablespoon grape molasses (petimezi) or Greek honey

6 ounces Greek graviera cheese or Gruyère, cut into ½-inch dice

10 pitted prunes, chopped

½ cup dark seedless raisins

4 fresh thyme sprigs, chopped

For the marinade

3 tablespoons extra-virgin Greek olive oil

2 tablespoons Greek honey

1 heaping tablespoon Dijon mustard

2 garlic cloves, minced

2 fresh rosemary sprigs, minced

1 (1½-inch) knob ginger, peeled and grated

Finely grated zest of 1 orange

Salt and pepper to taste

For the pan

2 cups dry red wine

Preheat the oven to 350°F.

Put the butterflied pork loin on a large cutting board and, using a kitchen mallet, pound the loin to flatten it a little, making it easier to roll. Season it inside and out with salt and pepper. Whisk together the orange juice, olive oil, mustard, and petimezi in a medium bowl. Brush about half of this mixture over the inside surface of the pork.

Add the graviera cubes, chopped prunes, raisins, and thyme to the same bowl and mix well with the remaining marinade. Spread the mixture evenly over the loin, leaving 1 inch or so around the edges. Cut a section of meat netting to fit the size of the loin roll.

Tuck in the short sides of the loin to keep the filling from falling out. Start the roll from one end, pushing any errant filling in while you go. When you get to the end and the roll is ready, carefully pull the netting over it to hold it in place.

Lightly oil a large baking dish. Place the pork in the baking dish. Whisk together all of the marinade ingredients in a medium bowl. Brush the exterior of the pork with it, saving some marinade to repeat during the roasting. Season the outside with more salt and pepper, as desired.

Pour the red wine in the pan, cover the pan with parchment paper and then aluminum foil, and roast for 1 hour 40 minutes to 2 hours (20 to 25 minutes per pound), or until the internal temperature of the pork is between 145°F and 160°F, depending on how well done you like it. Baste the pork with the wine a few times while roasting. About 30 minutes before it's done, remove the parchment and foil so that it gains some color as it continues to roast.

Remove, tent with foil, and let the meat rest for 20 minutes before removing the netting and slicing.

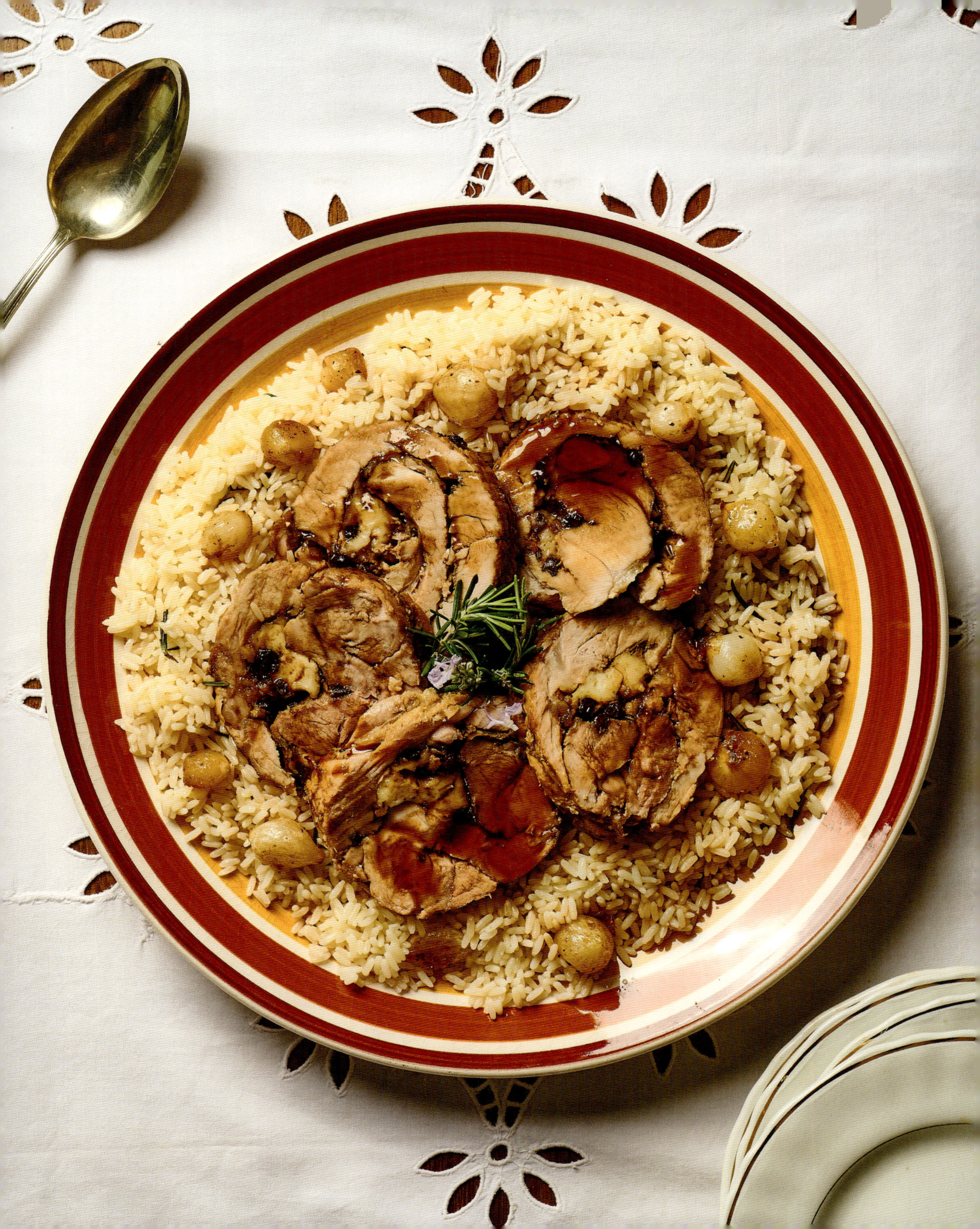

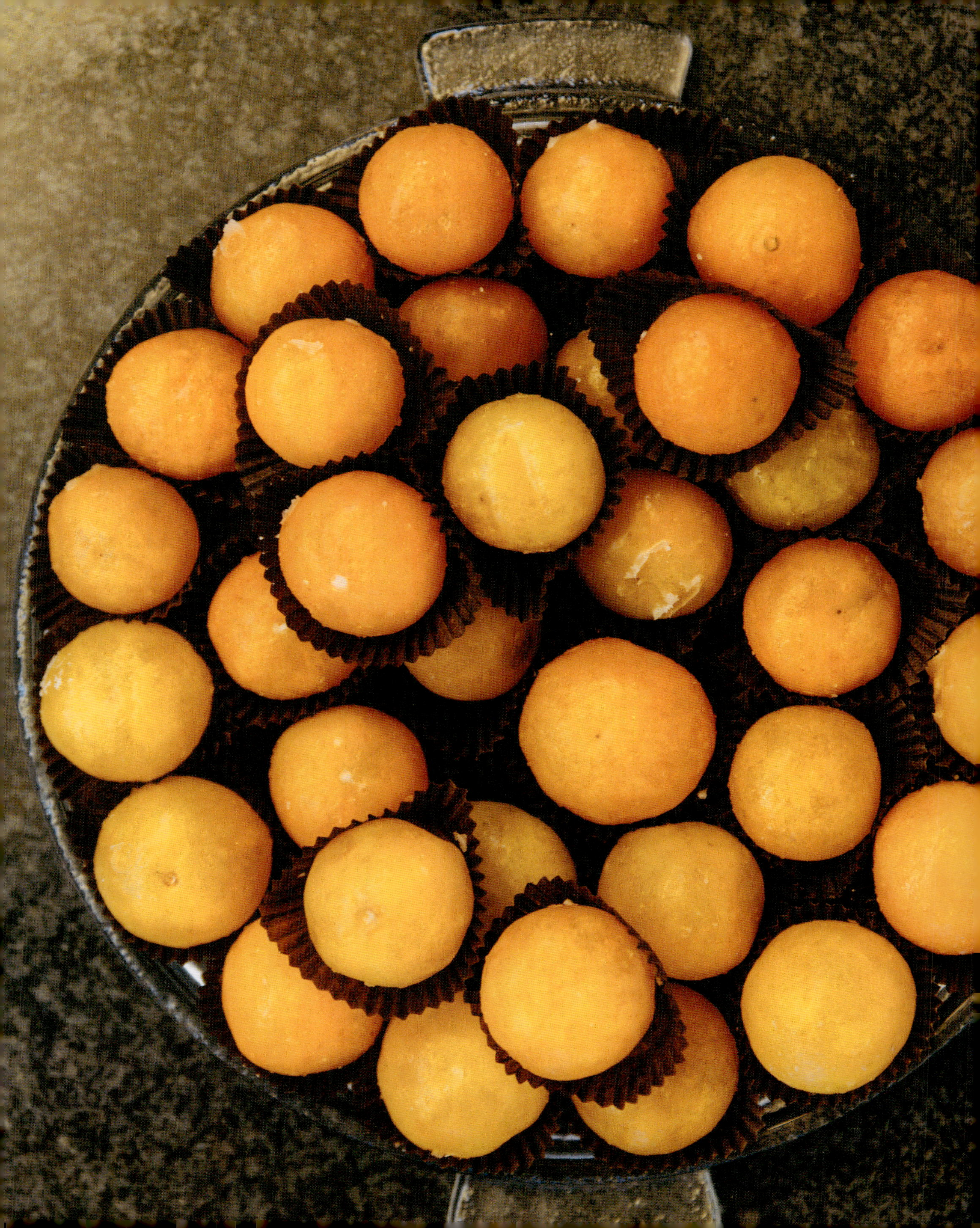

Desserts That Define Athens

How does one define a city by its sweets? New York: Cheesecake, Italian ice, and Mr. Softee? Palermo: Cannoli? New Orleans: Pralines? Honestly, I am not sure. What I do know is that for me, Athens and its sweets have been an ever-evolving story, weaving in major events of the nineteenth and twentieth centuries and trends of the young twenty-first.

As a transplant to this city, I had my own list of the honeyed or sugary treats that defined my experience of Athens, so much of that spun into the folds of my youth here, as a teenager visiting in the 1970s; later, in endless walks with a young beau (and, later, husband) in tow; with the sweet life I was lucky enough to have in my twenties, when I moved to the city on a lark, only to leave a few years later, newly married, then return to raise a family and write for a big-city newspaper in my thirties and forties. Athens, figuratively speaking, has been sweet to me over the many decades of my life here.

But I did also ask friends both native and new to this place, "When you think of Athens, what desserts come to mind?" In varying order of thought, their answers were reassuringly consistent: loukoumades, galaktoboureko, rice pudding, and a few French-style pastries like almond torte and sokolatina all topped the lists.

When I was a kid, the confection that beguiled me most was a plate full of crisp golden spheres dripping in dark, amber honey: loukoumades, which I knew from my own Greek home in New York but had experienced at a whole other level here, in shops that made them and only them, a treat that appealed to every generation, if my memory of old and young at packed round marble tables serves me well. Later, as a young woman in love, Athens was sweet with the likes of strawberry sorbet and parfait ice cream at Hara in Patissia, served on square metal plates, or with the long spoonsful of an ice cream sundae that was all the rage in the 1970s and into the mid-'80s, called Chicago (page 357). As a young food writer, I sought out things like the "mustard" ice cream of Toula in Pangrati, a famous old patisserie that created this ice cream flavor, something like salty caramel but named for its tawny color, the recipe for which I've never been able to either procure or find. It's delicious and they still make it. Other sweet, dreamy memories include billowy galaktoboureko, a classic cream-filled phyllo dessert that inspires passion in those who love it and intense opinions as to what pastry shop makes the best.

Athens is a city of old and new, living and dancing to its own tune, and that tango of past and present can be tasted in its sweets. I could easily have started a chapter on the desserts that define Athens by following the strands of honey and trail of nuts all the way back to its most ancient self, when those two most seminal ingredients informed the earliest confections. Koptoplakous, an assembly of nuts and honey layered between what was probably rough strips of griddled pastry, is considered among Greeks to be the ancestor to baklava; sesamous, a mixture of sesame seeds and honey sounds uncannily like pasteli, which we eat on the go today, an ancient energy bar created anew and available in food shops of every ilk all over the city. Ancient Athenian and Greek cheese pastries like plakountes (cheese pies sweetened with honey) are not that far a stretch from the honey-drizzled cheese cakes and Greek yogurt–honey mousses and panna cottas that are part of the contemporary Athenian sweet scene.

Fast-forward two millennia to the arrival of hundreds of thousands of Asia Minor Greek refugees to the city and the introduction of syrup-soaked phyllo pies and cakes called siropiasta—beloved galaktoboureko (page 352) among them. We wouldn't have the likes of these desserts if it weren't for the culinary heritage these Greeks carried in their hearts and committed to their memories and handwritten notebooks, and, luckily for the city, recreated in their new home.

Now, Athens is all of the above, a place of traditional sweets as well as of stevia-sweetened affectations (I am not a great fan) and vegan versions of the classics (see Vegan Galaktoboureko, page 355). It's also a city surrounded, until recent memory, by huge stretches of vineyards, grazing lands, and farmland, and the natural environment and history itself of Attica has informed a few well-known confections, too. Among these are the grape-must cookies moustokouloura (page 347), a specialty of the wine-making towns of Mesogeia, the most famous of which are made in a bakery in Markopoulos, and a local rendition of milk pie (page 363), the traditional sweet of Attica's ancient shepherds.

Whatever your sweet tooth might desire . . . from the old-world charm and unchanged recipes of generations past, still thriving in any number of its classic old pastry shops like Désiré in Kolonaki, Asimakopoulos (the oldest) on Harilaou Trikoupi in Exarcheia, and Bozas in Kypseli, to name but a few, to its hipper self of Greek-inspired gelati at Django in Koukaki and Kokkion in Psyrri, to the phantasmagorical creations of its most famous pastry chef, Stelios Parliaros, whose sweets have beguiled two generations on the list of who's who in this city . . . Athens has it.

In this chapter, I've presented some of my own favorites, a choice of just a few of its many sweets, but the ones that to my mind define Athens, past and present.

Desserts That Define Athens 335

Honeyed Fry-Pies, aka Loukoumades

"What sweet speaks of Athens to you?" I asked half a dozen friends, both native Athenians and Greek Americans who know the city well, and all of them, unequivocally, answered "Loukoumades" before naming anything else. I couldn't agree more, and instantly remembered the very first time I sampled these honeyed dough puffs, with my big sister Athena, back in 1972, on our first trip to Greece. We were wandering around the center, down Athens's grand avenue Panepistimiou and followed the scent, so to speak, to Aigaion, one of the original loukoumades shops in the city, housed in a nineteenth-century neoclassical building on the corner of Harilaou Trikoupi, near Omonoia and the University of Athens.

I was mystified at the making of these delectable sweets and remember watching a portly old guy, perhaps the son of the original owner, who had opened this historic shop in 1926, hovering over the gurgling hot oil as he plopped measured dough bits into it, scooping up the instantly puffed, crispy golden balls into a tray on the side. It was magic to my twelve-year-old eyes. Aigaion's round white marble tables, black French café chairs, and plain beige-tiled walls spoke to the simple elegance of another era, unchanged over time. But, alas, the shop closed its doors in 2017, yet another old Athenian victim of crisis debt and rising rents.

But loukoumades remain timeless, in every sense of the word, a sweet that likely is rooted in the most ancient Greek traditions, as honey, the world's oldest sweetener, was known and loved in the ancient Greek world. It is said that something similar, dubbed *honey tokens* by the ancient Greek poet Callimachus, was bestowed upon winners of the ancient Olympics; Aristotle mentions the gift pies awarded to victorious athletes. Archestratus, the first chronicler of all things gustatory, wrote of crispy dough balls flavored with honey and called *enkris*.

In its current etymological incarnation, the word comes from the Arabic *luqmat al Qadi*, which morphed into *lukma* or *lokma* in Turkish. It began to appear in Arabic cookbooks as early as the thirteenth century.

Fast-forward to Athens now. Two of the oldest shops for these honeyed fry-pies are still going strong: Krinos, opened in 1923, on Aiolou Street, and Ktistakis on Sokratous, famous for bringing a Cretan variation to the loukoumades theme by dipping the puffs in honey in such a way that it ends up on the inside of the puffs. Both are worth seeking out.

But loukoumades have also been catapulted into the global era of anything-goes toppings, and so we find myriad places around town, usually a small hole-in-the-wall serving up the puffs as sweet street food to go, slathered with the likes of chocolate syrup or white chocolate glaze or filled with mastiha cream filling, strawberry syrup, caramel-apple filling, and more. Chefs across town have sometimes usurped the name of this ageless treat and called even savory fried things loukoumades.

I am still beguiled by the traditional ones, and seek them out whenever I can.

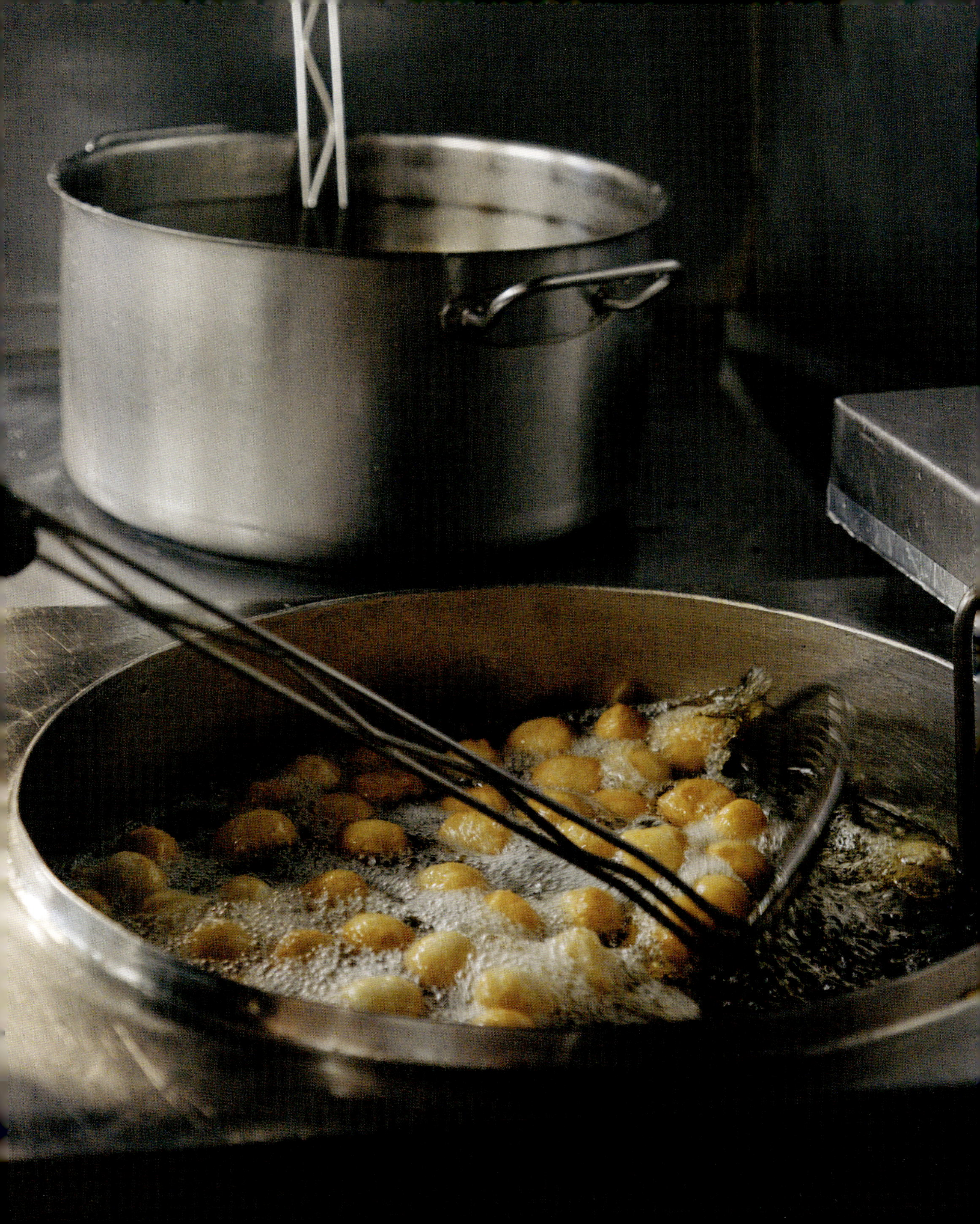

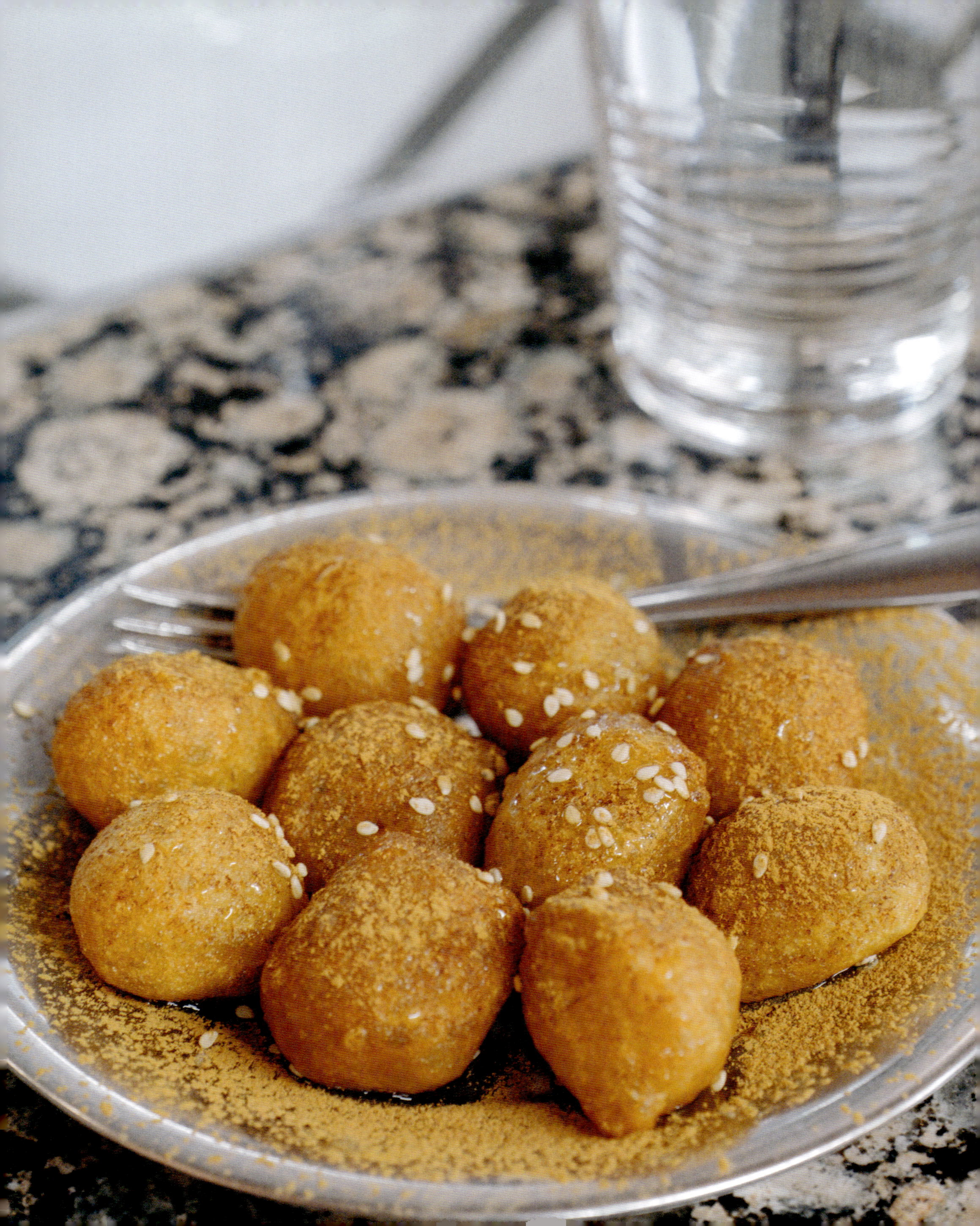

Loukoumades

These classic dough puffs with roots in ancient Greece are the sweetest street treat to go in Athens.

MAKES 6 TO 8 SERVINGS

2 cups warm water

1½ tablespoons active dry yeast

2 teaspoons sugar

4 to 5 cups all-purpose flour

½ teaspoon salt

2 tablespoons ouzo

Vegetable oil, for frying

Optional toppings

Greek pine honey and ground cinnamon

Greek pine honey, ground cinnamon, and sesame seeds

Chocolate-hazelnut cream, such as Nutella or Merenda

Chocolate syrup and walnuts

Combine the warm water, yeast, and sugar in a medium bowl, mix well, and let it proof for about 5 minutes, until bubbles start to form on the surface.

In a large bowl, combine 4 cups of the flour and the salt. Make a well in the center and add the yeast mixture and ouzo. Mix with a fork from the center of the well outward to combine. The mixture should be a smooth, dense, sticky batter-like mass, without knobs of undiluted flour anywhere. Cover the bowl with plastic wrap and let it rest in a warm, draft-free place for 35 to 40 minutes, or until doubled in bulk.

When ready to fry the loukoumades, heat 5 to 6 inches of vegetable oil in a heavy, wide pot over high heat. Take a tablespoon at a time of the loukoumades mixture and, using another tablespoon, push it into the hot oil. Repeat with a few more, being careful not to crowd the pot. Turn them carefully in the hot oil with a slotted spoon for about a minute or so, until golden and puffed. Remove and drain on paper towels. Continue until all the batter is fried.

Serve hot, drizzled with honey, chocolate-hazelnut cream, or chocolate syrup and sprinkled with cinnamon, sesame seeds, and/or walnuts, as desired.

Rice Pudding

If I don't make it myself, which is rarely, I head to one of two places for the best rice pudding, or rizogalo, in town: Varsos up north in Kifissia (see page 342), and Stani, a few minutes' walk from Omonoia Square. The recipe below is inspired by both, creamy and rich and comforting, the way only rice pudding can be. Imagine that this luscious dessert was once something fed only to the ill, since rice, an import until the 1950s, was expensive and so saved for special occasions or for the infirm.

MAKES 8 SERVINGS

⅔ cup Arborio, Greek Carolina, or glacé (glazed) rice

8 cups whole milk, divided

⅔ cup sugar

2 teaspoons vanilla extract

Grated zest of 1 lemon

3 tablespoons cornstarch

Ground cinnamon, for serving

Put the rice in a large saucepan and pour in enough water to cover the rice by ½ inch. Add ½ cup of the milk. Bring the mixture to a gentle simmer over medium-low heat, stirring on occasion, and cook for 20 to 25 minutes, or until the rice softens.

Add 7 cups of the remaining milk, the sugar, vanilla, and lemon and bring back to a simmer.

In a small bowl, dilute the cornstarch in the remaining ½ cup milk, whisking it until smooth, and add this slurry to the rice mixture, stirring it in well. Simmer until the mixture is thick and creamy, almost like a very dense porridge, 15 to 20 more minutes.

Remove from the heat and, using a ladle, pour into individual serving bowls. Let it cool in the bowls, then cover with plastic wrap and refrigerate for a few hours or overnight. Serve sprinkled with cinnamon.

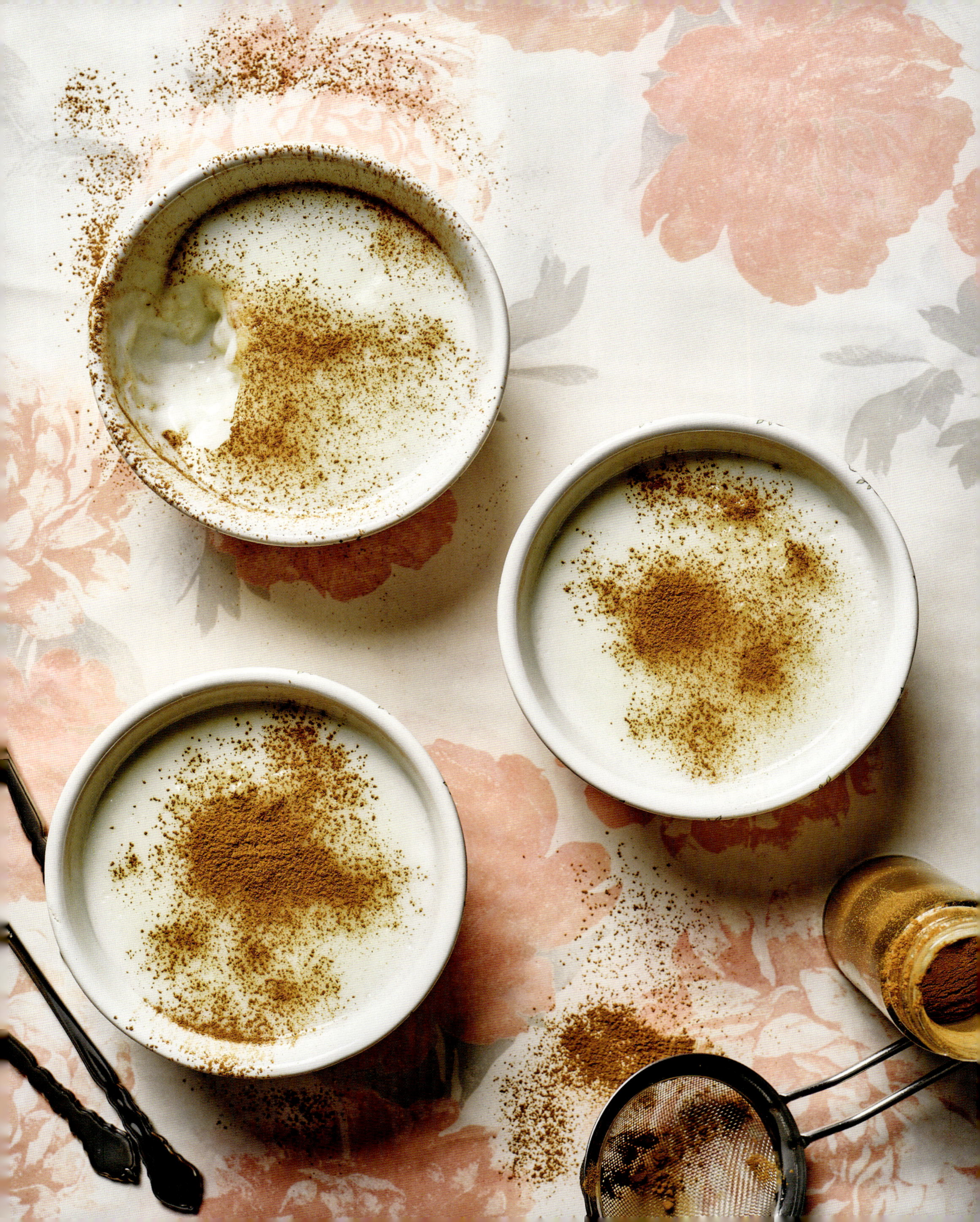

Varsos: Milk Men, the Philosopher's Suburb, and Desserts "Made for Kings"

I meet my friend Diana here for afternoon tea, and for a taste of old Athens in one of the few remaining places that still attracts an aristocracy of all persuasions: royal, political, artistic, literary. Varsos. A legend in Kifissia, with roots that stretch from the Greek countryside to Athens, across more than a century of existence.

Like so much of my experience in Athens, my first encounter with Varsos, indeed with Kifissia, was way back in the late 1980s, newly arrived as a young urban nomad, long before that was ever a thing. Vasili took me here for a walk and a date, and we meandered Kifissia's leafy streets and peered at its mansions through their gated grand entrances. He pointed out the belle epoque hotels, fashionable summer retreats for upper-crust Athenians from the late nineteenth century in newly freed Greece, through the interwar years, and then again in the 1960s and '70s. We sauntered past the sprawling resort cafés such as Blue Pine and Belle Helene on our long walk, then settled in downtown Kifissia at Varsos, cavernous, old, stately, and with so much tradition and history spilling off its shelves, it was hard to take it all in at once.

The scent of butter, cinnamon, and cooked sugar seemed to have seeped into its glossy beige walls and settled into the leather of its ornate café chairs. A sign above the sweet breads stacked over glass counters in the middle of the shop reads "Made for Kings." We sat by the windows in the back, an atrium of sorts, where whole choruses of parrots, themselves newcomers to the city, having escaped from a quarantine at the old airport and adapted brilliantly to the Attica climate, chirped nonstop. Waiters shuffled obsequiously from table to table and came to ours to take the order. We were there for two things: the rizogalo, or rice pudding, and Varsos's famously thick yogurt. Although the gamut of offerings in this historic old café is vast, from dozens of Greek cookies to famous meringues to tsourekia that the wives of Greek prime ministers were known to buy by the dozens, it's the milk and all that's prepared with it that has made Varsos such an institution.

It all started in 1892, when the pater familias, Vasilis Varsos, then just sixteen, and his brother, Yiorgos, fresh from the central Greek countryside, migrated to the new Greek capital with a few sheep in tow and settled into an area south of Omonoia. Before long, they opened a tiny milk shop called Parnassos on the corner of Santaroza and Panepistimiou Streets downtown. Word of the quality of their milk quickly spread among the denizens of the capital, and the small shop grew fast. They were industrious and visionary, and at one time had the largest ice box in Athens. But space was a problem and so, on the advice of the dairy farmers they worked with, they moved shop to Kifissia, next door to where Varsos sits today. By the early 1920s, Kifissia, once an ancient agrarian settlement, home to the ancient dramatist Menander and the rhetorician and philanthropist Herodes Atticus, for whom the ancient theater under the rock is named, and who built a villa and philosophers' retreat there during the reign of the Roman Emperor Adrian, had become a well-established retreat of another sort: The advent of the railroad in 1885, which still runs today, had catapulted Kifissia to its current status as a most desirable venue and summer respite for well-heeled Athenians, many of them in the aristocratic class, who migrated to Kifissia's cooler clime, occupying its grand belle epoque hotels, many of which still stand, and building the grand old mansions that my younger self discovered on those long walks with her beau.

By 1930, Vasilis's sons, Kostas and Yiorgos, had taken over the business. The war came, and with it the German occupation, and so the two brothers were arrested as Anglophiles, returning to their family business right after the war, a time of exponential growth for them, as for all of Greece. The whole family worked at Varsos. They had foresight to import dairy cows and a couple of bulls from Holland, and so, even in the annals of the Veterinary School of Athens, there's a mention of the pastry shop in Kifissia that first brought Holsteins to Greece.

Visions come and go, and life happens, too. On a trip to Paris in 1950, Kostas Varsos met a Greek Jew named Isaac Carasso, who invited him to move with his family to Paris so they could set up a yogurt business together.

Who knows what would have happened had Kostas accepted the invitation, for the company Karasos founded and named for his young son, Daniel, is what we know today as Danone, aka Dannon yogurt!

Two decades later, in 1970, Kostas lost a son to cancer, and with it, his interest in life. His brother Yiorgo picked up the reins and today the business, while no Danone, is still a thriving legend in Athens's poshest suburb, and the fourth generation of Varsos boys now run the show.

And so it is that, inside Varsos, site of first dates and dames both grand and plain sipping afternoon tea, that the urban history of Athens itself is folded into every spoonful of sweet things made here, "made for kings"—and a few discerning peons, too!

It's still great after all these years.

Tourta Amygdalou
ALMOND TORTE

This totally retro cake hearkens back to Athens circa 1960, when the city was in the midst of reinventing itself after the war. Things modern, from washing machines to electric ovens to the convenience foods of the day, were embraced in the collective consciousness, and among them was a most unlikely food item branded Μορφατ (pronounced, I kid you not, More Fat!). It is a shelf-stable nondairy cream, akin to American Cool Whip, but not frozen. Its blue-and-white can, replete with a Greek flag, was in the cupboard of every Greek homemaker, the stuff of Hellenized French pastries and homemade ice cream (one can each of Morfat, sweetened condensed milk, and evaporated milk whipped together and frozen, sometimes with a couple of tablespoons of instant Nescafé coffee mixed in if one wanted a mocha flavor). I first encountered it as a young bride in the 1980s, returning to Greece to visit my in-laws; invariably, my mother-in-law would whip up a tourta to welcome home her beloved son!

In the 1960s, French-style pastries started to become popular in the growing number of sweet shops in Athens; one in particular, Boza, in Kypseli, then one of the chicest neighborhoods in the city, was renowned for its tourta amygdalou, as well as other pastries of the era, like sokolatina, a layered chocolate cream cake soaked in syrup, most often garnished with chocolate sprinkles.

Tourta amygdalou was the birthday delight of the era, and there are a few different versions, including more recent ones with real whipped cream, but the original vintage cake calls for that 1960s-era blue can of Morfat, replaced here with Cool Whip!

MAKES 8 TO 10 SERVINGS

1¼ cups whole milk

2 large egg yolks

¾ cup plus 3 tablespoons sugar, divided

2 teaspoons cornstarch

1 teaspoon vanilla extract

¾ cup water

1¾ cups Cool Whip

1 recipe (2 rounds) Classic Yellow Sponge Cake (page 345) or from the bakery

1½ cups slivered almonds, lightly toasted

8 maraschino cherries

In a medium saucepan, combine the milk, egg yolks, 3 tablespoons of the sugar, and the cornstarch. Cook over medium-low heat, whisking continuously, for about 8 minutes, or until the mixture is thick and smooth and just before it comes to a boil. Remove and set aside. Whisk in the vanilla. Cover with plastic wrap and chill for 2 hours.

Meanwhile, in another medium saucepan, bring the water and remaining ¾ cup sugar to a simmer over medium heat and cook, stirring occasionally, for about 5 minutes, until the sugar is completely dissolved. Remove the syrup from the heat.

Remove the milk mixture from the fridge and whisk until smooth. Dollop by dollop, add the Cool Whip and whisk until smooth.

Cut the sponge cake bases to fit inside the circumference of a 12-inch springform pan. Place the first round inside the pan. Drizzle and brush with about a quarter of the syrup. Spread about half of the cream filling over the surface. Place the second sponge cake piece on top and drizzle and brush that with syrup, too. Spread about half of the remaining cream over the surface. Place the cake in the freezer for 2 hours. Cover and refrigerate the remaining cream.

Unhook the springform perimeter and remove it. Spread the remaining cream over the sides and top, using a pastry knife to form decorative waves and making sure to cover the cake completely. Reserve some of the cream to make decorative rosettes on the surface after the cake is garnished. Sprinkle the toasted almond slivers all over the cake. Transfer the reserved cream to a pastry bag and make 8 small rosettes on the surface of the cake. Top them with the maraschino cherries. Serve.

Classic Yellow Sponge Cake

MAKES 2 (10- OR 12-INCH) CAKES

1 cup (2 sticks) unsalted butter, softened

1 cup sugar

4 large eggs

1 teaspoon vanilla extract

1¾ cups all-purpose flour, sifted

2 teaspoons baking powder

½ teaspoon salt

¼ cup milk

Preheat the oven to 350°F. Grease and flour 2 (8-inch) round cake pans or line them with parchment paper.

In the bowl of a stand mixer outfitted with the paddle attachment, cream together the softened butter and sugar at medium-high speed until the mixture is light and fluffy, 3 to 5 minutes. Add the eggs, one at a time, mixing well after each addition. Add the vanilla.

In a separate bowl, whisk together the sifted flour, baking powder, and salt.

Gradually add the dry ingredients to the butter mixture, alternating with the milk, and mixing well after each addition.

Divide the batter evenly between the prepared cake pans. Smooth the tops with a spatula.

Bake for 25 to 30 minutes, or until a toothpick inserted into the center comes out clean. Allow the cakes to cool in the pans for about 10 minutes, then turn them out onto a wire rack to cool completely.

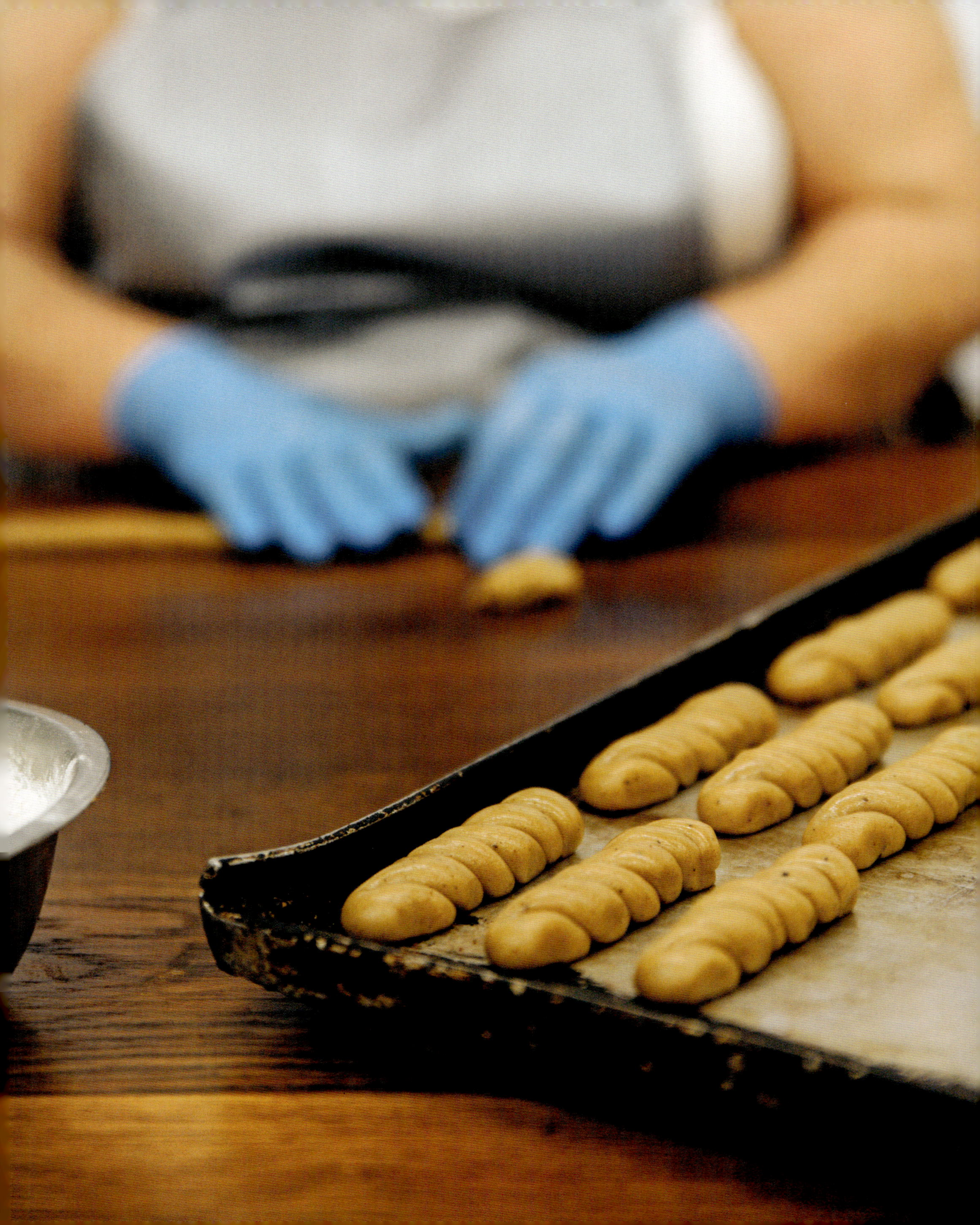

Moustokouloura

A cookie with a Michelin mention! Moustokouloura, or grape-must cookies, are a hallmark of the autumn in Athens, and the most famous ones hail from the Daremas family bakery in Markopoulo, in the heart of the Mesogeia region of Attica, famed since antiquity for its grapevines and wine. The region has changed dramatically—the Athens International Airport is here, and this once-agricultural back door to Athens, which for centuries provided wine and olive oil to the capital, is now, essentially, a suburb, connected by train and an easy commute from downtown. But farming still exists here, and Mesogeia is still the heart and soul of the Attica Wine Roads, and so it is that every autumn, when the grapes are harvested and pressed and the mousto—grape must—before it ferments into wine, Daremas is in full production. The whole square on which the bakery is located is permeated by the comforting aroma of grapey cookies baking, cinnamon wafting on the breeze.

The Daremas bakery is a must stop for any serious foodie in Athens. Now in its fourth generation, the business originally started as a small grocery and general store at the end of the nineteenth century, which lasted through 1948. The postwar years were a time of huge socioeconomic change, and women no longer baked bread at home. So the family transformed the store into a bakery. By now the second generation had taken over, and Sofia, wife to one of the two brothers now running the shop, started to bake a family recipe for these cookies. They became an instant success, and by the 1960s, as Athens evolved and seaside resorts like Porto Rafti attracted an ever-growing stream of urbanites who took to the sea there each summer, this small bakery became a de rigueur stop along the way. The rich and famous liked their moustokouloura with morning coffee; the cookies have been served to dignitaries and movie stars alike. These traditional amber-colored, coiled cookies, still twisted into shape by hand, baked on a lark two generations ago by a thoughtful wife wanting to lend a hand, have grown into a local legend. Even the Michelin Guide *mentions the cookies on the list of must-eats in greater Athens. This is not the Daremas secret family recipe, which would be impossible to extract, but a favorite of mine nonetheless. Vegans rejoice: These traditional cookies are always made with olive oil, not butter!*

MAKES ABOUT 4 DOZEN

2 cups extra-virgin Greek olive oil

1½ cups Saba or cooked grape must

½ cup brandy

1 cup sugar

1 teaspoon baking soda

2 teaspoons baking powder

1 scant teaspoon ground cinnamon

½ teaspoon ground cloves

6 cups all-purpose flour

2½ cups semolina flour

Sesame seeds, for garnish

-recipe continues-

In the bowl of a stand mixer outfitted with the whisk attachment, whisk together the olive oil, grape must, brandy, sugar, baking soda, and baking powder at medium-high speed until the sugar dissolves and the mixture lightens up in color.

Sift the cinnamon, cloves, and two flours together in a large bowl.

Remove the whisk attachment from the mixer and replace it with the dough hook. Slowly add the flours to the liquid, working the dough with the hook attachment on medium-low speed until enough of the flour is combined to create a soft dough that peels away from the sides of the bowl.

Preheat the oven to 350°F. Line 2 rimmed baking sheets with parchment paper.

Lightly flour a clean work surface. Break off one piece at a time of the dough mass, about 2 rounded tablespoons at a time, and shape into a rope about ½ inch thick and 6 inches long. Join both ends to form a circle, pinching the tops together to close. Place on the lined baking sheet and repeat with remaining dough. When all the cookies are shaped, sprinkle generously with the sesame seeds and bake for about 20 minutes, or until dark amber in color but still springy to the touch. Remove and cool. Store in a cool, dry place.

Greek Yogurt Panna Cotta

Greek yogurt is the basis of so many great Greek desserts these days, but panna cotta, all the rage in the Athens of the 1990s, those heady, delicious years leading up to the Olympics, is probably the most famous of all: elegant, familiar, and versatile.

MAKES 6 SERVINGS

1 teaspoon powdered gelatin

1 cup whole milk, divided

1 cup heavy cream

2 strips orange zest

¼ cup Greek honey

2 cups vanilla yogurt

For garnish

3 tablespoons chopped walnuts

2 tablespoons extra-virgin Greek olive oil

2 apples, cored and diced

2 tablespoons Corinthian currants

1 tablespoon brown sugar

Pinch sea salt

Pinch ground cinnamon

6 teaspoons thyme honey

Fresh mint sprigs

Soften the gelatin in 2 tablespoons of the milk for 10 minutes.

In a medium saucepan, gently heat the remaining milk. Add the cream and cook over low heat to warm through. Add the orange zest and the honey. Whisk for a minute or so, until everything is well combined. Remove from the heat and add the gelatin mixture, whisking to get out as much of the lumpiness as possible. Strain the mixture through a fine-mesh sieve into a large bowl. Slowly fold the yogurt into the bowl, gently stirring to combine well. The consistency should be really thick and creamy.

Fill 6 cups, ramekins, or glasses two-thirds of the way with the cream mixture. Refrigerate them for at least 1 hour or up to overnight to set.

Heat a dry skillet over low heat and add the walnuts to toast them lightly for a few minutes, stirring to keep them from burning. Add the olive oil and diced apples and stir it all around. Add the currants and brown sugar, season with the salt, and stir to coat. Sprinkle in the cinnamon. Keep stirring the mix so that the sugar doesn't totally caramelize the apples. The mixture is ready when the apples are soft.

Spoon 1 tablespoon of the apple mixture on each of the panna cotta cups and drizzle with 1 teaspoon thyme honey. Garnish with fresh mint and serve.

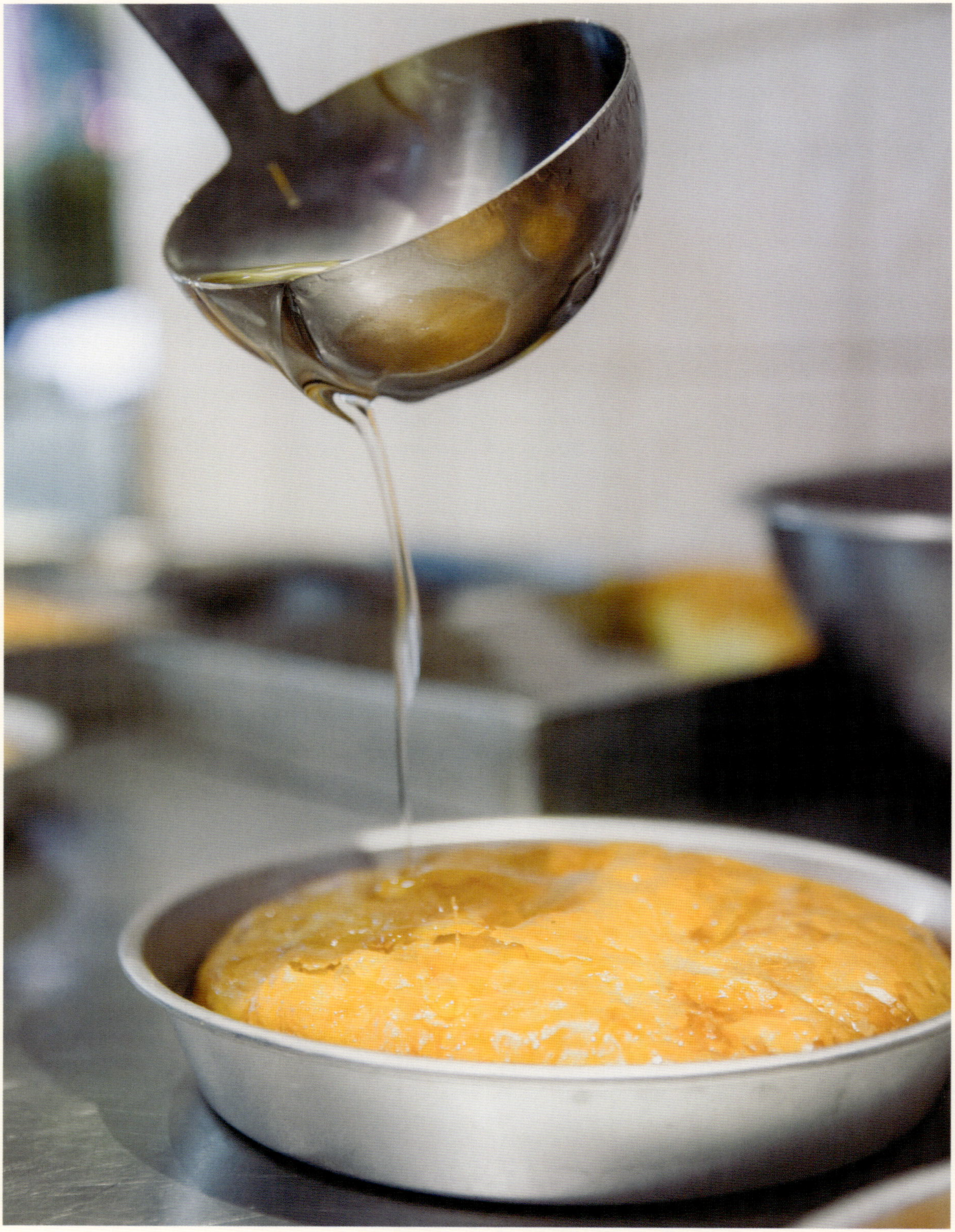

Galaktoboureko: The Stuff of Urban Legend

I asked a few of my closest Greek friends who know Athens well which desserts come to mind when they think of this city, and, invariably, galaktoboureko topped the list. This semolina custard–filled phyllo pastry moistened with a simple syrup is the stuff of urban legend, even though its origins are something of a dispute. To some it traces its roots to antiquity, but by most accounts it is clearly Anatolian, the hybrid child of urbane Greco-Turkish cuisine, something even its name evinces: *galakto* is from the Greek *gala*, "milk" (think galaxy, galactic, lactic, etc.), and *boureko* is from the Turkish *borek*, for "small phyllo pastry" or "pie."

It started to make its appearance in the Greek capital with the arrival of Asia Minor Greeks after the exchange of populations in 1922; it was a sweet known to the skilled and bourgeois home cooks of Smyrna (Izmir), who found fertile ground for re-creating it in Athens, where many settled. Greek desserts at the time were simple and agrarian. The syrup-soaked desserts of the Greeks of Anatolia were almost completely unknown before their arrival.

The raw ingredients of galaktoboureko are good milk and butter, two items that the new arrivals from Asia Minor found in abundance in the nearby region of Mesogeia, just outside Athens. Shepherds roamed with their flocks here in the lowlands in summer, then in Parnitha, the region's tallest mountain to the north of Athens, in the winter. They roamed, in other words, in close enough proximity to the city to make their dairy products accessible to the discerning home cooks who settled in and around Athens from the shores of Smyrna after their beloved city was burned to the ground.

It didn't take but a few years for Athenian dairy shops to begin producing creamy, crispy, syrupy galaktoboureko. The first one to start the trend was Lakafosis in Drosia, north of Athens, where many Asia Minor Greek refugees had settled, and which is close to Parnitha, hence to the shepherds and their milk-producing flocks. By the interwar years, galaktoboureko had become popular and demand for it was high, but the milk for making it was generally available for just a few months a year, around the end of winter, and then just after Easter, in tune with the nursing periods of the animals from which it was produced. For decades it was associated almost singularly with the Sunday before Lent, called Cheese or Dairy Sunday, and then again on or after Easter.

As milk became more readily available, so did the pans of galaktoboureko spread from patisserie to patisserie. One of the first pastry shops to produce it is also thought to be the oldest in Athens, the Asimakopoulos Brothers Pastry Shop in Exarcheia. Today, though, two names vie for the position of "best" galaktoboureko in the city: Kosmikon, which has been producing this creamy Greek-Anatolian dessert since 1961, and Galifianaki, which began producing its version of galaktoboureko with a kataifi (shredded wheat) crust in 1973.

The dessert has morphed again in more recent years, with chefs turning their creativity to its reinvention. Among the novel ways galaktoboureko is now represented in the city are open-faced galaktoboureko tarts and something unimaginable among those early home cooks of Smyrna, who sought out the best shepherds' milk and butter: a vegan version!

Classic Greek Galaktoboureko

Galaktoboureko needs almost no introduction. It is simply one of the best-loved, most-renowned phyllo desserts in Greece, filled with a creamy, lemony custard. It's a classic . . . no matter how you slice it!

MAKES 8 TO 12 SERVINGS

For the syrup
4 cups sugar
2 cups water
1 cinnamon stick
1 strip lemon peel zest

For the custard filling
4 large eggs
1 cup sugar, divided
1 cup heavy cream
3 cups whole milk
1 teaspoon vanilla extract
Pinch salt
1 cup fine semolina
7 tablespoons unsalted butter
2 teaspoons finely grated zest

For the phyllo
½ pound (2 sticks) unsalted butter, melted
½ pound (12 to 15 sheets) frozen #4 phyllo, thawed and at room temperature

Make the syrup: Combine the sugar, water, cinnamon stick, and lemon zest in a medium pot. Bring to a boil, stirring to dissolve the sugar. Simmer for 10 minutes. Remove from the heat and set aside to let cool.

Make the custard filling: In the bowl of a stand mixer outfitted with the whisk attachment, whisk the eggs and ½ cup of the sugar at medium-high speed for 3 to 4 minutes, until fluffy and thick. Set aside.

In a large pot, place the heavy cream, milk, vanilla, remaining ½ cup sugar, and salt and bring to a boil over medium heat. Slowly add the semolina in a steady, thin stream, whisking vigorously. Whisk for 3 to 4 minutes, until it thickens. When the mixture peels away from the sides of the pot, it's ready. Remove from the heat. Whisking constantly and vigorously, quickly pour in the egg-sugar mixture. Remove from the heat and whisk in the butter and lemon zests.

Preheat the oven to 350°F. Generously brush a large baking pan with some of the melted butter.

Place 1 sheet of phyllo in the pan and brush with melted butter. Repeat the same process with another 6 or 7 sheets of phyllo dough. Very gently press down on the phyllo with your hands. Brush the overhang with a little butter, too.

Spread the custard over the phyllo, spreading it evenly with a silicone spatula. Place the remaining phyllo sheets over the custard, drizzling and brushing each one with melted butter. Gather the overhanging phyllo from both the top and bottom layers and roll them along the rim of the pan to form a decorative edge. Brush that with butter, too.

Sprinkle the top layer of phyllo with a little cold water. Score the top of the pie into 10 or 12 pieces and then cut into them and pour any remaining butter on top. Bake for 45 to 60 minutes, or until golden brown. Remove from the oven and immediately pour the cold syrup over the pie. Let it sit for at least 30 minutes before serving.

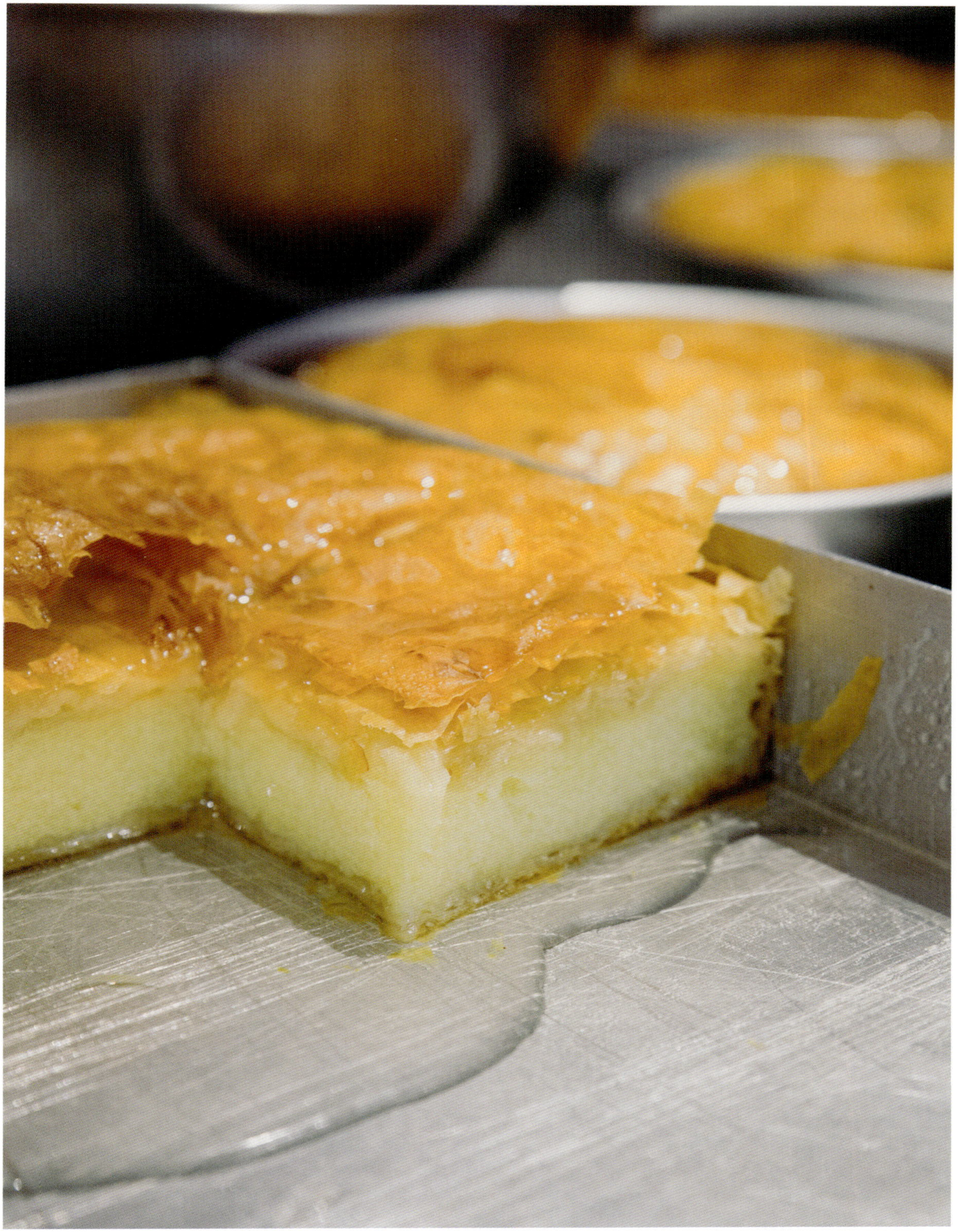

Galaktoboureko Tart

Here's a modern, elegant version of the Greek classic, and a rendition that's popped up around Athens in a few places.

MAKES 12 TARTS

For the syrup
4 cups sugar
2 cups water
1 cinnamon stick
1 strip lemon zest

For the custard filling
4 large eggs
1 cup sugar, divided
3 cups whole milk
1 cup heavy cream
1 teaspoon vanilla extract
Pinch salt
1 cup fine semolina
8 tablespoons (1 stick) unsalted butter, cut into 8 pieces
Grated zest of 1 orange
Grated zest of 1 lemon

For the phyllo
½ pound (2 sticks) unsalted butter, melted
1 pound frozen phyllo sheets, thawed and at room temperature
Ground cinnamon, for sprinkling

Make the syrup: Combine the sugar, water, cinnamon stick, and lemon zest in a medium pot. Bring to a boil, stirring to dissolve the sugar. Simmer for 10 minutes. Remove from the heat and set aside to let cool.

Make the custard filling: Whisk the eggs and ½ cup of the sugar in the bowl of a stand mixer outfitted with the whisk attachment for 3 to 4 minutes at medium-high speed, or until fluffy and thick. Set aside.

In a large pot, combine the milk, cream, remaining ½ cup sugar, vanilla, and salt and bring to a boil over medium heat. Slowly add the semolina in a steady, thin stream, whisking vigorously for 5 to 7 minutes, until it thickens. When the mixture peels away from the sides of the pot, it's ready. Turn off the heat. Whisking constantly and vigorously, quickly pour in the egg-sugar mixture. Remove from the heat and whisk in the butter and grated orange and lemon zests. Let the mixture cool for about 30 minutes.

Preheat the oven to 350°F. Generously brush 12 (4-inch) removable-bottom tart pans with melted butter.

Cut the phyllo stack across the center lengthwise and then across the center horizontally to quarter them. Depending on the brand of phyllo, you should have about 72 squares. Place 6 squares inside each tart pan, brushing each with butter and fanning them as you layer them, so that you get a fair amount of overhang evenly around each pan. Spoon equal amounts of the custard into each tart. Gently crinkle, pinch, or roll the overhang around the rim to form a decorative edge. Brush the rim with additional butter. Bake for about 25 minutes, or until the custard is set and the phyllo golden.

Remove and drizzle the cooled syrup into each of the tarts. Serve warm or at room temperature, sprinkled with cinnamon.

Vegan Galaktoboureko

Vegan galaktoboureko might set a few traditionalists on their heads, but this recipe is surprisingly satisfying. I learned how to make it as part of the vegan episode on season 4 of My Greek Table.

MAKES 8 TO 10 SERVINGS

For the syrup
2 cups water
2 cups brown sugar
Strained juice of ½ lime
½ teaspoon ground coriander
1 teaspoon ground ginger
10 cardamom pods, crushed

For the pastry
1 cup extra-virgin Greek olive oil, or as needed
½ ripe honeydew melon, peeled, seeded, and cubed
2 cups sweetened almond milk
1 cup fine semolina
1 pound frozen phyllo, thawed and at room temperature
2 tablespoons sesame seeds

Combine all of the ingredients for the syrup in a saucepan, bring to a boil, and cook until reduced by a third, about 8 minutes. Transfer to a bowl and refrigerate until needed.

Preheat the oven to 350°F. Oil a 9 x 13-inch glass baking dish.

Combine the melon and almond milk in a blender and puree until smooth. Transfer a quarter of the mixture to a large bowl. Add the semolina and mix until fully incorporated.

Transfer the remaining melon mixture to a large saucepan and bring it to a boil. Slowly add the semolina mixture in a steady flow, whisking constantly. Set aside to cool.

Fold 4 phyllo sheets lengthwise. Oil each sheet and place them so they come up the sides of the baking dish to cover the entire interior. Spread the melon cream evenly over the phyllo and top with 4 more sheets of phyllo, folding each one in half lengthwise and oiling each. Brush the top sheet with oil and fold the excess overhang around the inside edges of the pan to form a nice rim. Score into serving pieces with a sharp knife and sprinkle with the sesame seeds. Bake for 30 minutes. Remove from the oven and immediately pour the cold syrup over the entire surface of the pastry, then leave it to cool for about 1 hour. Serve.

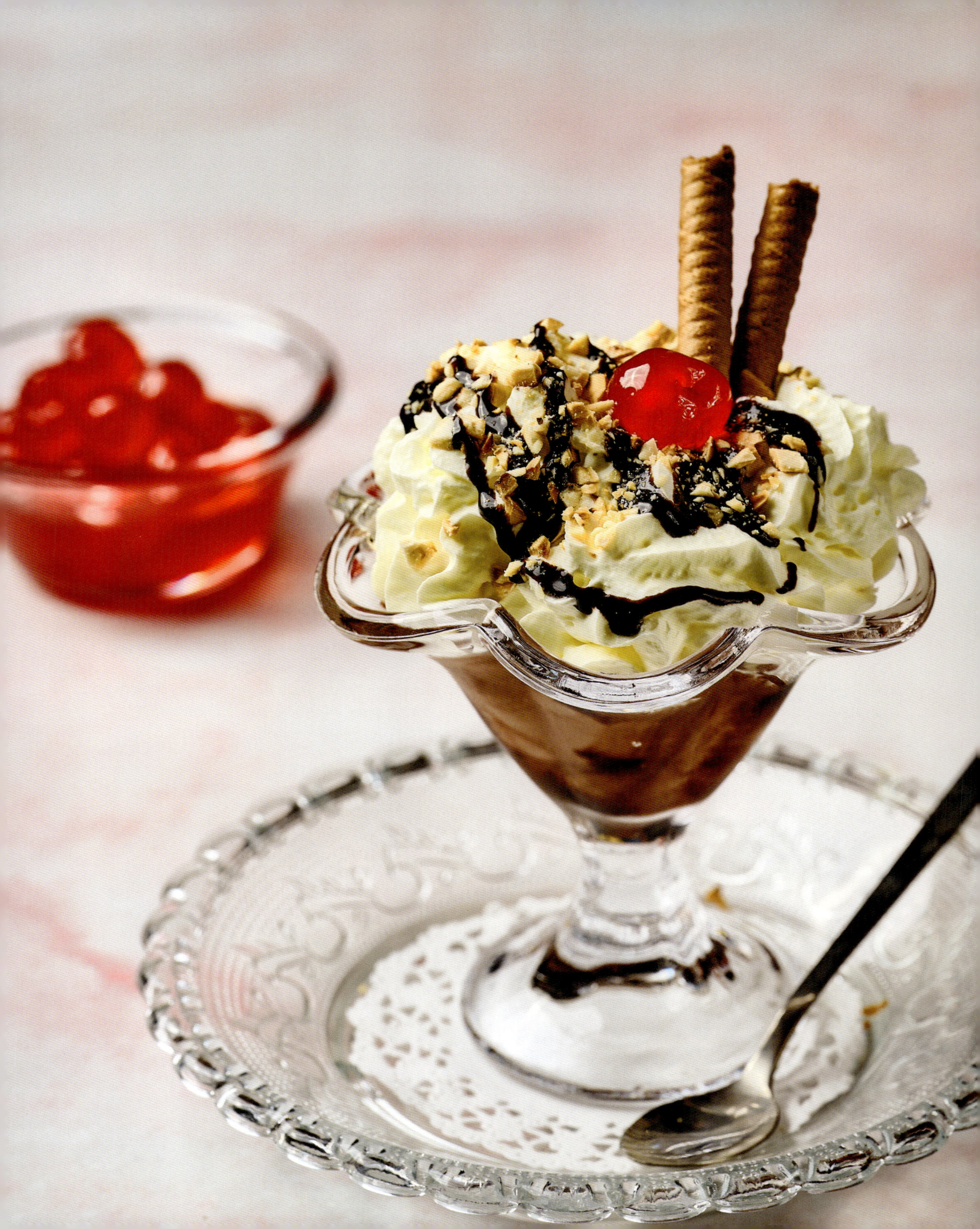

Chicago: An Athenian Ice Cream Sundae

I remember on my very first visits to Athens way back in the 1970s, my Greek relatives would take me for the city's most famous ice cream treat, the "sikagko," aka a Chicago-style ice cream sundae. Indeed, the sundae is said to have originated not too far from the Windy City, in Evanston, Illinois, as a way to get around a kind of blue law that forbade the sale of soda, and by extension the ice cream soda, on Sundays. A Greek chocolatier named Karolos Zonaras who lived in the United States embraced this ice cream delight, and when he returned to Athens in 1938 with a vision to open the best restaurant in the city, Zonar's, he put the sikagko on his menu. Zonar's went on to become the place to see and be seen in Athens, a reputation that lasted decades and was resuscitated in 2016 under different ownership. It's still the place where ladies go to lunch and others go to see and be seen.

MAKES 4 SERVINGS

For the ice cream

½ cup whole milk

1 cup heavy cream

½ cup sugar

3 large egg yolks

3 ounces dark chocolate

1 teaspoon vanilla extract

¾ cup blanched almonds, toasted and chopped

For the chocolate syrup

¾ cup water

¾ cup sugar

3 ounces unsweetened cocoa powder

½ cup heavy cream

For serving

1¼ cups heavy cream

½ cup blanched almonds, toasted and chopped

4 lady's finger cookies or wafer cigar cookies

To make the crème anglaise: In a medium saucepan, cook the milk, cream, and sugar over medium heat, stirring, until the mixture begins to simmer around the edges, about 8 minutes. Remove the pot from the heat.

Transfer about 3 tablespoons of the hot milk mixture to a bowl, add the egg yolks, and whisk well to combine. Pour the mixture back into the pot and stir with a silicone spatula over medium-low heat until the custard is thick enough to coat the spatula and reaches 160°F on an instant-read thermometer, 6 to 8 minutes. Stir in the chocolate and whisk until it is melted and blended. Stir in the vanilla. Don't let the mixture boil lest the yolks cook and curdle!

Transfer the mixture to a metal bowl set over a larger bowl filled with ice and let it cool for about 10 minutes. Mix in the chopped toasted almonds, then pour the mixture into a 9 x 13-inch stainless steel baking pan. Cover with plastic wrap and let the mixture freeze overnight in the freezer.

To make the sauce: In a medium saucepan, heat the water, sugar, and cocoa together over medium-high heat, stirring constantly, for about 3 minutes, or until it begins to simmer. Stir in the cream and cook for 1 minute, stirring. Let the chocolate sauce cool.

About 5 minutes before serving the Chicago, remove the ice cream from the freezer and let it sit at room temperature. Whip the cream with a hand mixer or in the bowl of a stand mixer with the whisk attachment. Scoop out 2 balls of ice cream and place inside each parfait glass. Top with chocolate syrup, whipped cream, and a little more syrup, then sprinkle with additional chopped toasted almonds on top. Garnish with a cookie and serve.

Ice Cream in Athens: The Scoop

It used to be that ice cream for most Greeks was a purely seasonal indulgence, one of those delights tempered by the belief that to eat something cold in the winter was unhealthy, in conflict with the needs of the season.

The truth is that ice cream got off to a rather tenuous start in the Greek capital as early as 1835, when an Italian hotel manager named Calvo, harboring ambitions to open a European-style pastry shop, served ice cream at a reception for the Bavarian ambassador. Unable to find natural colorings in the city at the time, he improvised, adding chemical dyes to his concoctions, causing his aristocratic audience to vomit everywhere. Ambitions, needless to say, dampened, he left town soon thereafter. By 1840, though, an industrious pâtissier named Yiorgos Karadamatis opened the first real sweet shop—until then, most sweets were simple and sold at bread bakeries—on the corner of Aiolou and Evripidou Streets in the heart of the market area. His treats became the talk of Athens and his success unrivaled for decades.

Like so much else in the annals of modern Greek food, so, too did the ice cream chronicles change with the arrival of Greek refugees from Asia Minor, whose cuisine was generally more sophisticated than that of their mainland brethren. With their arrival in 1922, ice cream carts started to pop up, and so did a popular flavor called dondourmas, a chewy, creamy ice cream that's been rechristened today as kaimaki.

Good ice cream requires good milk, something the Sourapa brothers, immigrants from Arcadia in the Peloponnese to Chicago and back, realized, and in 1934 upon their return to Greece, they established the Greek National Milk Company (EBGA), in the Botanikos area of Athens. Its name tells it all: This was Athens gardening, farming, and grazing ground (as in our word *botanical*), and proximity to cows meant access to great fresh milk. By 1936, they had introduced ice cream on a stick to the city, and by 1950, EBGA was a national phenomenon, opening nine hundred shops in Greek cities that year alone. Other ice cream and dairy behemoths soon followed, but ice cream still remained a mainly seasonal treat. In my early days in Greece, it was also the mark of a great home cook to make ice cream for the family, usually something called *parfait*, a creamy vanilla and chocolate. The recipe was a simple one: 1 can of sweetened condensed milk, 1 can of a nondairy cream called Morfat (see page 344), and 1 can of evaporated milk, all whipped up, placed in rectangular tin containers, frozen, and scraped a few times over the course of a day, before being served to family and friends. Pastry shops also made ice cream and sold it by weight. Among the most renowned are Hara in Patissia, still going strong since 1969, where I used to go with my beau for a scoop of its famous tutti-frutti, or a wedge of the "harem girl's" ice cream, vanilla wrapped in kataifi. Assimakopoulos on Harilao Trikoupi, said to be the oldest pastry shop in the city, is known for its ice creams and sorbets, too—the lemon and strawberry are favorites.

The scene started to change in the 1990s, with the first gelato shops popping up, and a whole new world of natural flavors with Italian finesse started to win over the city's ice cream lovers. Today, there are plenty of great places for a scoop, both old and new, and a decided trend toward the creative, incorporating Greek ingredients like honey, mastiha, local nuts, or composed flavors like quince with cinnamon or halva (both at my beloved purveyor of fine gelati, Django, on Veikou Street, not far from the Acropolis Museum). Frozen yogurt took the city by storm a few years back, too, but that's a story for another time.

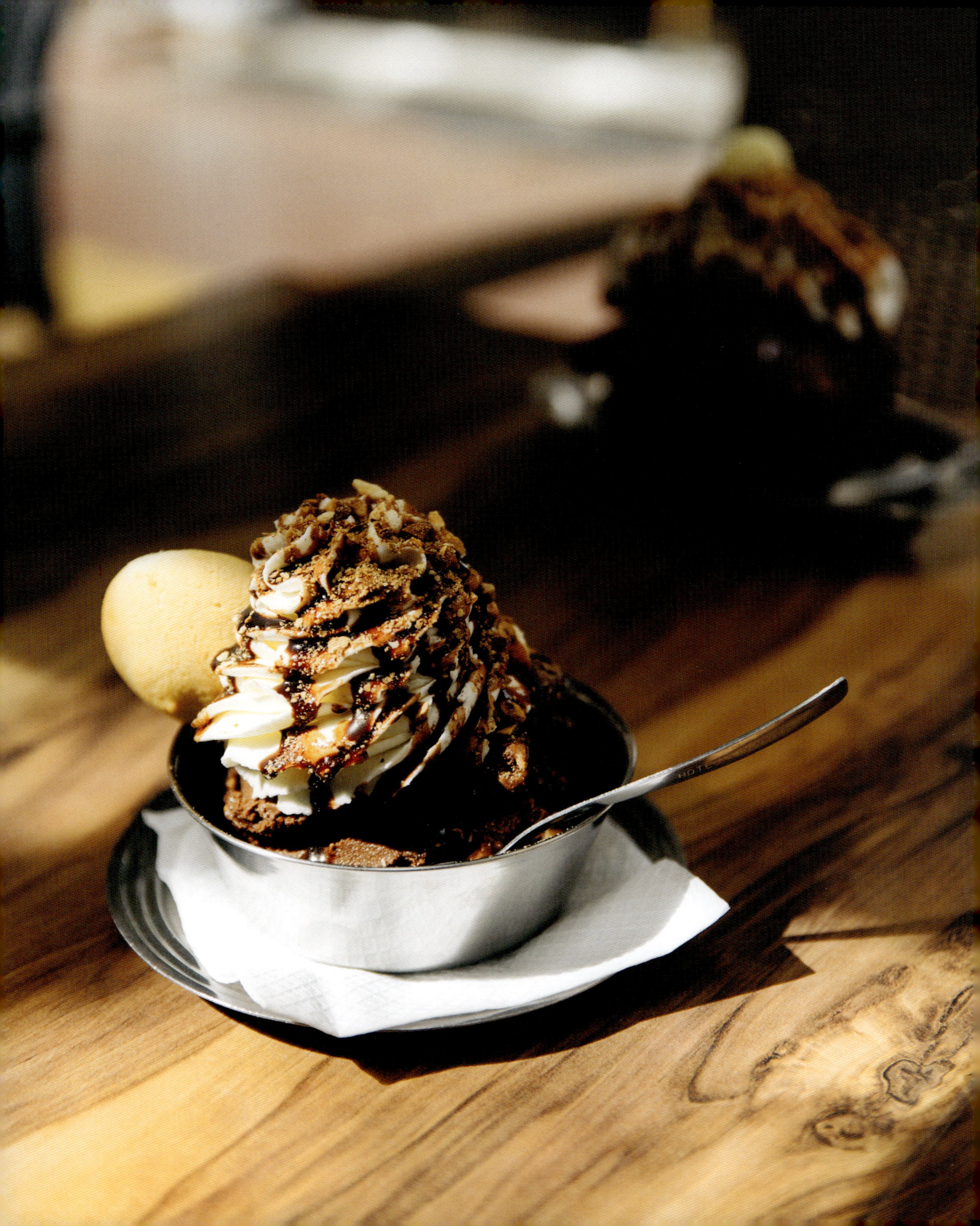

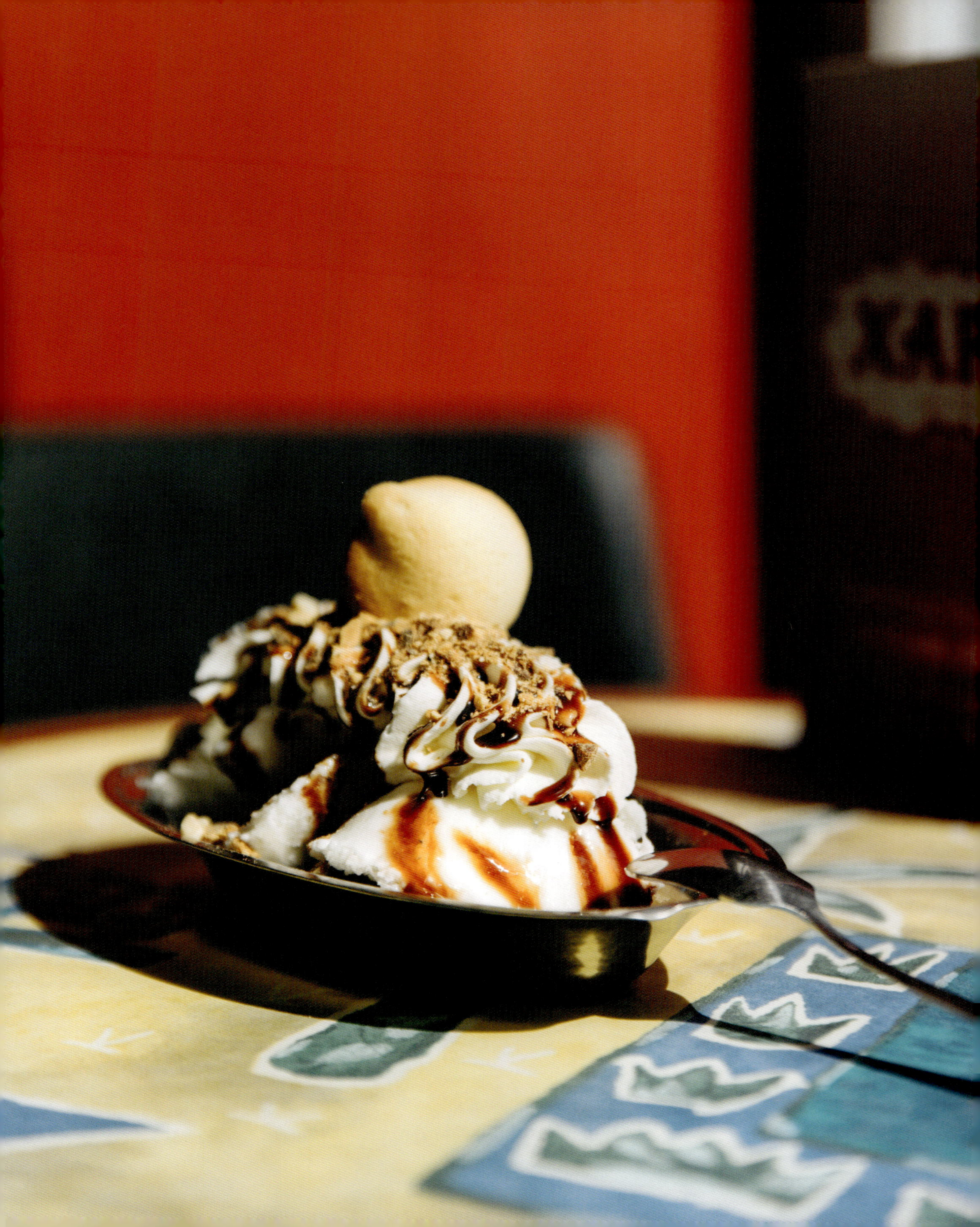

Melina's Sokolatina

I asked my friend, pastry chef Melina Milionis, about this chocolate pastry, so popular in sweet shops across town, and here's what she had to say: "When I think Athens desserts, the first one that comes to mind is a traditional sokolatina. A staple dessert in every bakery and cafe throughout Athens. Maybe it should be called sokol-Athina!" Sokolatina is an airy chocolate sponge cake with layers of chocolate custard and whipped cream, topped with chocolate ganache. A true chocolate lover's delight!

MAKES 8 TO 10 SERVINGS

For the chocolate custard

5 cups milk, divided

1½ cups granulated sugar, divided

8 large egg yolks

½ cup cornstarch

3 tablespoons unsweetened cocoa powder

1 tablespoon vanilla extract

Pinch salt

For the chocolate sponge cake

2½ cups cake flour

1½ cups unsweetened cocoa powder

2 teaspoons baking powder

1 teaspoon baking soda

Pinch salt

4 large eggs

2 cups granulated sugar

¾ cup extra-virgin Greek olive oil

½ cup lukewarm milk

1 tablespoon vanilla extract

½ cup brandy

Make the custard: In a small saucepan, whisk together 2½ cups of the milk and ¾ cup of the sugar over medium heat until steaming and starting to simmer. Remove from heat.

In a large bowl, beat the egg yolks, remaining ¾ cup sugar, and cornstarch with a hand mixer until light and fluffy. Add the cocoa powder and remaining 2½ cups milk and beat until everything is incorporated. Slowly whisk in the hot milk mixture.

Transfer the mixture to the same saucepan and heat over medium-low heat, whisking, until the mixture thickens to a custard consistency, 6 to 8 minutes. Pour the custard into a bowl, stir in the vanilla and salt, and cover with plastic wrap, pressing the plastic to the surface of the custard so that no film or skin forms. Set aside and allow to cool completely.

Make the chocolate cake: Preheat the oven to 350°F. Butter and flour a 9 x 14-inch baking pan.

In a medium bowl, whisk together the flour, cocoa powder, baking powder, baking soda, and salt.

In a large bowl, whisk the eggs, sugar, and olive oil until the sugar dissolves. Add the milk and vanilla.

Using a hand mixer, slowly add the dry ingredients to the wet, mixing until well incorporated. Pour the batter into the prepared pan, spreading it evenly, and bake for 30 to 40 minutes, or until set. While the cake is still hot, poke holes in the surface with a skewer, brush with the brandy, and let cool.

-recipe and ingredients continue-

For the chocolate whipped cream

4 cups heavy cream

¾ cup confectioners' sugar

6 tablespoons unsweetened cocoa powder

For the chocolate ganache

1½ cups heavy cream

1½ cups semisweet chocolate, chopped

½ teaspoon vanilla extract

Make the whipped cream: In a large bowl, beat the heavy cream, confectioners' sugar, and cocoa powder with a hand mixer just until thick peaks form—you don't want to make butter. (Keep in mind that you can keep some aside to dollop on the final dessert.)

Start to assemble the cake: Spread the custard over the cake and top with the chocolate whipped cream. Refrigerate for 2 to 3 hours, until the cream is set.

Make the ganache: Just before you are ready to take the cake out of the refrigerator, heat the heavy cream and chocolate in a small saucepan over medium heat, letting the chocolate melt for a few seconds before mixing to combine. Stir in the vanilla.

Finish assembling the cake: Take the cake out of the fridge and spread the ganache on top. Refrigerate for another 2 to 3 hours to set. If you want to be fancy before serving, take a pastry bag with a large piping tip and pipe the whipped cream on each slice, then add a maraschino cherry on top!

Poupeki

ATTICA-STYLE CRUSTLESS MILK PIE

The word poupeki *means "uncovered" in the local dialect of the Arvanites of Attica, descendants of Albanian settlers who migrated to the region between the thirteenth and sixteenth centuries and took up farming and husbandry. But this pie is also a specialty of the local Sarakatsani shepherds, who have herded their sheep in the region forever, moving to the lowlands in winter and to the highlands of Parnitha in summer. It is similar to galaktoboureko (page 354) in that the custard is a combination of milk, semolina, eggs, and sugar. Some versions call for lemon or orange zest, while others call for homemade phyllo on the bottom or no phyllo at all, as in this version, which is a kind of baked crustless custard pie sprinkled with a little sugar on top.*

MAKES 6 TO 8 SERVINGS

⅔ cup unsalted butter, at room temperature

4 cups milk, preferably sheep's or goat's milk

1 cup fine semolina

4 large eggs

1¼ cups sugar, divided

1 teaspoon vanilla extract

Grated zest of 1 lemon

Preheat the oven to 350°F. Butter a 9 x 13-inch baking pan.

In a small saucepan, bring the milk and semolina to a gentle simmer over low heat, whisking all the while so the mixture doesn't clump up. Remove from the heat.

In the bowl of a stand mixer outfitted with the whisk attachment, whisk the eggs and ¾ cup of the sugar together at medium-high speed until creamy and thick, 6 to 7 minutes.

Add half of the semolina mixture, in ¼-cup increments, to the egg mixture, whisking all the while, to temper the eggs. Pour the tempered egg mixture into the pot with the remaining milk-semolina mixture, scraping the bowl clean to get every last bit.

Add the butter, vanilla, and lemon zest and heat over low heat, whisking constantly, until the butter melts and the mixture is smooth, creamy, and thick.

Pour the mixture into the buttered baking pan. Bake for 40 to 45 minutes, or until set and lightly golden.

Slide the pan out of the oven and turn on the broiler. Sprinkle the poupeki with the remaining ½ cup sugar and broil for 3 to 5 minutes, or until the surface is caramelized. Remove, cool as desired, either slightly or completely, and serve either warm or at room temperature.

Athenian Lemon Pie
with Hints of Spetses

My friend Melina Milionis created this recipe for me after a trip to the beautiful island of Spetses in the Saronic Gulf, where lemon trees line the streets and gardens, their scent filling the air. It goes without saying that she brought some of the fruit back to the city with her, then created this version of lemon pie, using phyllo pastry, Greek yogurt, and olive oil. Versions of this pie, some crowned with meringue, others plain, are served in cafés all over the city.

MAKES 8 TO 10 SERVINGS

For the syrup

2 cups water

3 cups sugar

Strained juice of 4 lemons, plus the rinds

1 cinnamon stick

For the lemon pie

1 tablespoon butter, 1 tablespoon flour for the baking pan

1 pound frozen phyllo or kataifi, thawed and at room temperature

1 cup Greek yogurt

1 cup extra-virgin Greek olive oil

¾ cup sugar

1 tablespoon baking powder

2 teaspoons vanilla extract

5 large eggs

Grated zest of 2 lemons

Vanilla or coconut ice cream or gelato, for serving (optional)

Greek honey, for drizzling

Make the syrup: Add the water and sugar to a medium saucepan and heat over medium heat, stirring until the sugar is dissolved. Add the lemon juice, lemon rinds, and cinnamon stick, turn the heat down to low, and simmer for 8 minutes, or until slightly thickened. Remove from the heat and cool it completely.

Preheat the oven to 350°F. Line a rimmed baking sheet with parchment paper. Butter and flour a 9 x 13-inch baking pan.

If using phyllo sheets, cut into strips about the size of fettuccine noodles. If using kataifi, break it apart into individual strands. Place either on the lined baking sheet and bake for 10 to 30 minutes to dry them out a bit, keeping an eye on them so they don't burn. (The kataifi will take less time than the phyllo.) Remove and let sit at room temperature to cool.

In the bowl of a stand mixer outfitted with the whisk attachment, mix the yogurt, olive oil, sugar, baking powder, and vanilla at medium speed. Add the eggs, one at a time, and then the lemon zest, and whisk well to incorporate all the ingredients smoothly. Fold the phyllo strips or kataifi strands into the mixture with a spatula, making sure all are covered with batter.

Pour the batter into the prepared baking pan. Bake for about 40 minutes, until the top is light golden. Remove and immediately pour the cooled syrup on top. Let sit for 1 hour. Serve warm or at room temperature, with ice cream or gelato if desired, and drizzled with honey.

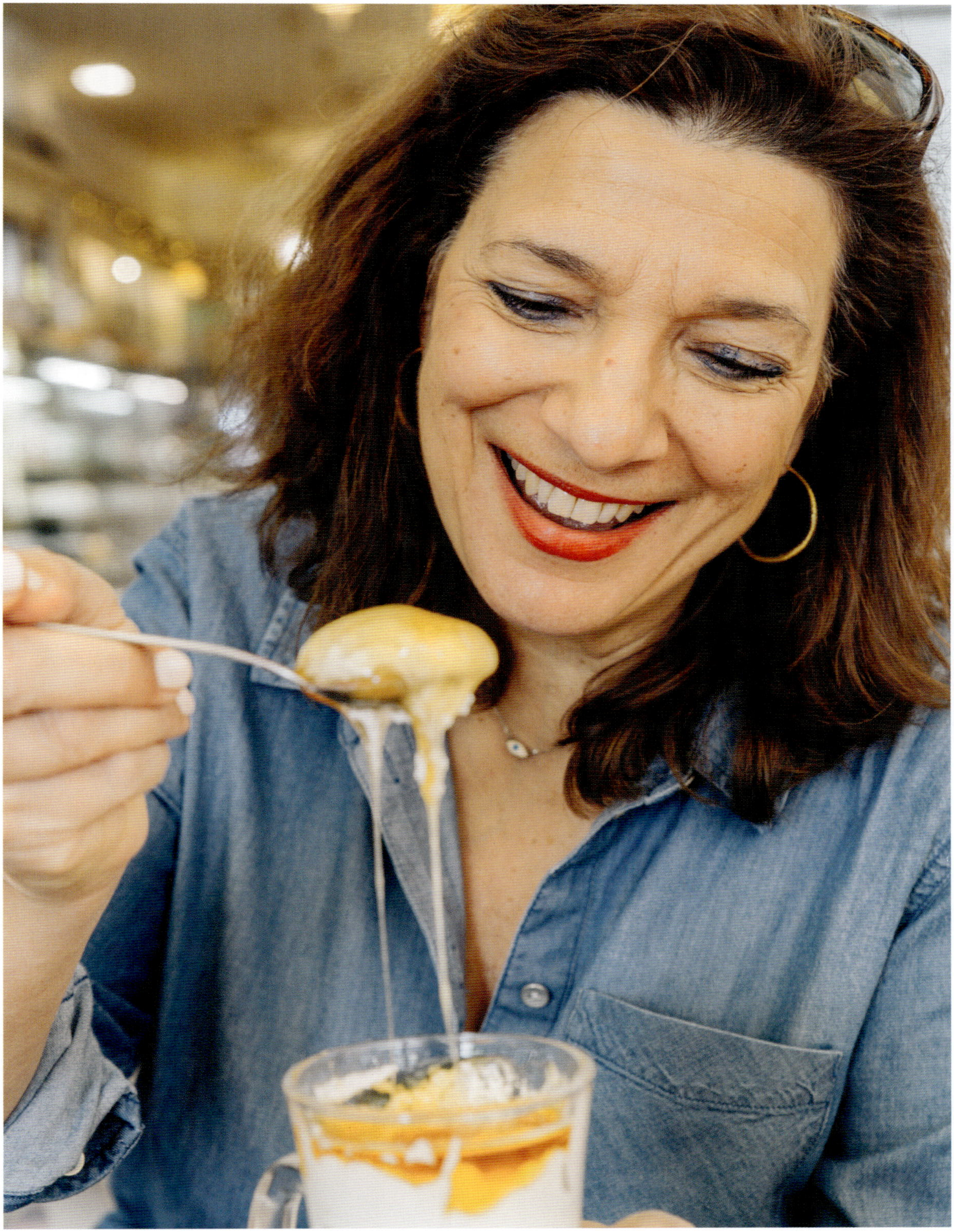

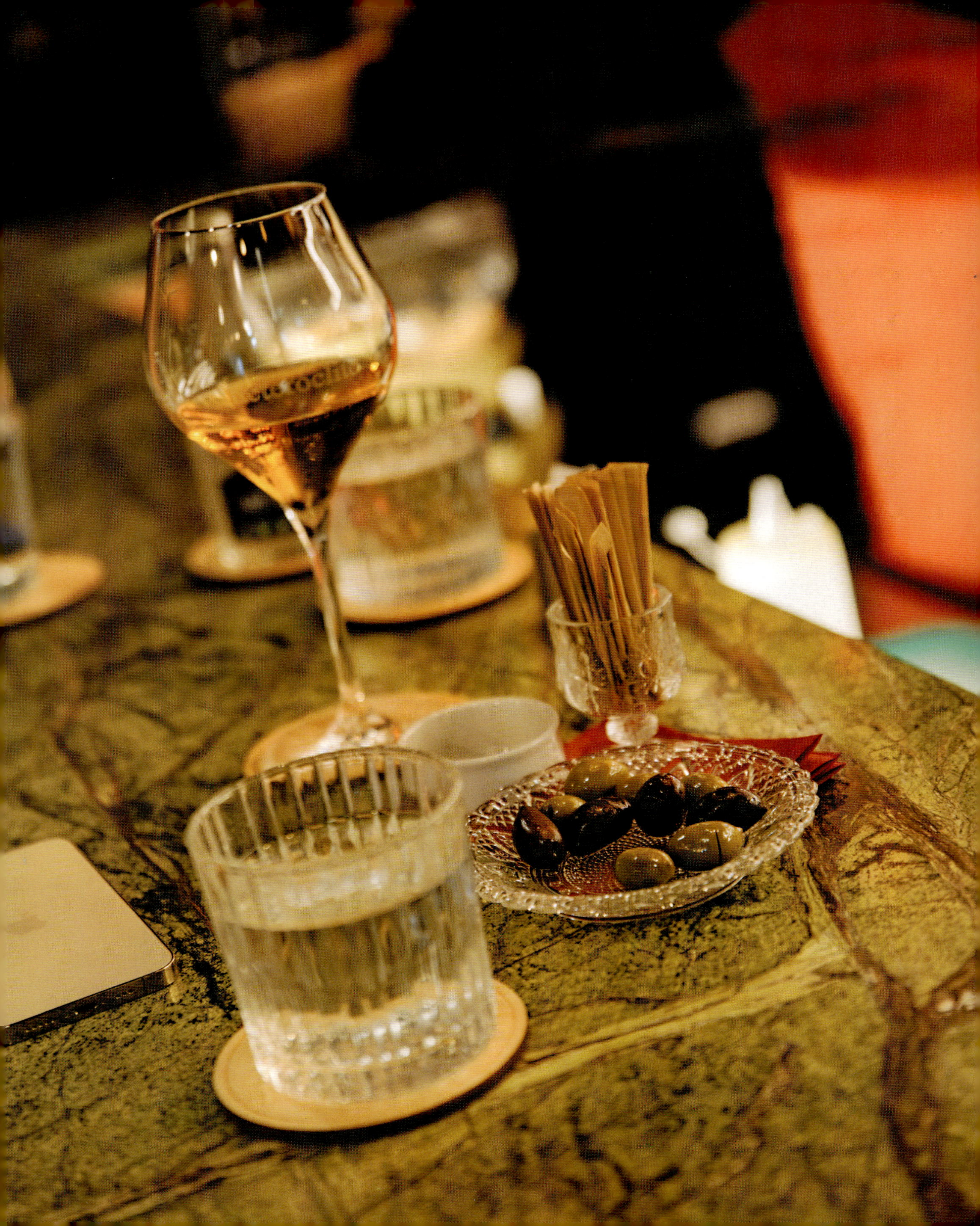

Cheers to Athens

Drinks

Athens has three, maybe four, life cycles each and every day, starting at dawn and ending at dawn. All you have to do is wend your way late in the evening, after ten o'clock, eleven o'clock, and well into the post-midnight hours, through the narrow streets of the center, along roads that once were lined with nothing but single-subject shops (doorknobs, paper, lighting supplies, fabrics, buttons, etc.), and you'll run into swarms of people outside its many bars, sharing a glass or two, meeting friends, and being the living proof of this city's special affinity for late nights out. I love it!

Social drinking is a deeply rooted Athenian tradition. One has to think only of the symposia of the ancient Greeks, essentially drinking parties for the cultivated citizens of the city (the word *symposium* means "to drink together"), to understand that the human connection forged over a glass or two of something alcoholic is part of the cultural DNA of the city. The concept of bars as a place for ordinary people to gather and drink might also be traced to the ancient kapeleia, social hubs where the working classes gathered, usually to drink wine. They eventually evolved into what we know today as tavernas.

Today, drinking together in Athens has many different forms, from American style bars (few and vintage at that) to some of the best cocktail bars in the world to the many wine bars that have multiplied these past few years, providing a venue where one can sample the hundreds and hundreds of world-class Greek wines.

The early "modern" history of the Athenian bar arguably began in 1909, when Mihalis Brettos opened his famous distillery in the heart of the Plaka, creating ouzo, liqueurs, and other distilled drinks with old recipes he had brought with him from Smyrna. Today, Brettos is no longer in the same family, but its colorful bottles, backlit on the walls, have become a landmark in the center, a spot photographed almost as frequently as the Acropolis!

In more contemporary times, the Athens bar story starts in 1958, with the opening of Au Revoir on Patission Avenue, which connected the then-posh neighborhood of Kypseli with the commercial center around Omonoia Square. This elegant watering hole, with its painted ceilings and rattan-covered walls, is newly discovered with each generation of young Athenians (including my own twenty-something children) as the place to come for a tipple. Its faded opulence speaks to the time when Kypseli, especially its main pedestrian street, Fokionos Negri, was the Park Avenue of Athens. I imagine that 1958 was a pivotal year, with people back on their feet and optimism finally permeating the city after the devastating years of World War II and then the Civil War. Perhaps Au Revoir was so named to say goodbye to the past, or perhaps it was christened in French as a nod to the well-heeled of the area, most of whom spoke the language of Balzac and embraced French culture and cuisine, to some extent, as a sign of civility and modernity. This glorious old place was designed by Aristomenis Provolegios, a famous Greek architect, and opened by two brothers, Lyssandros and Thodoris Papatheodorou. Almost seven decades later, it is still a beloved spot to have a classic cocktail. The dry martinis are legendary. It still attracts the Kypseli crowd, according to my daughter, Kyveli, a born-and-bred Athenian who lives nearby.

Au Revoir's spiritual cousin, and perhaps of greater heft when it comes to legendary bars, is the Galaxy on Stadiou Street (not to be confused with the now-defunct Hilton's

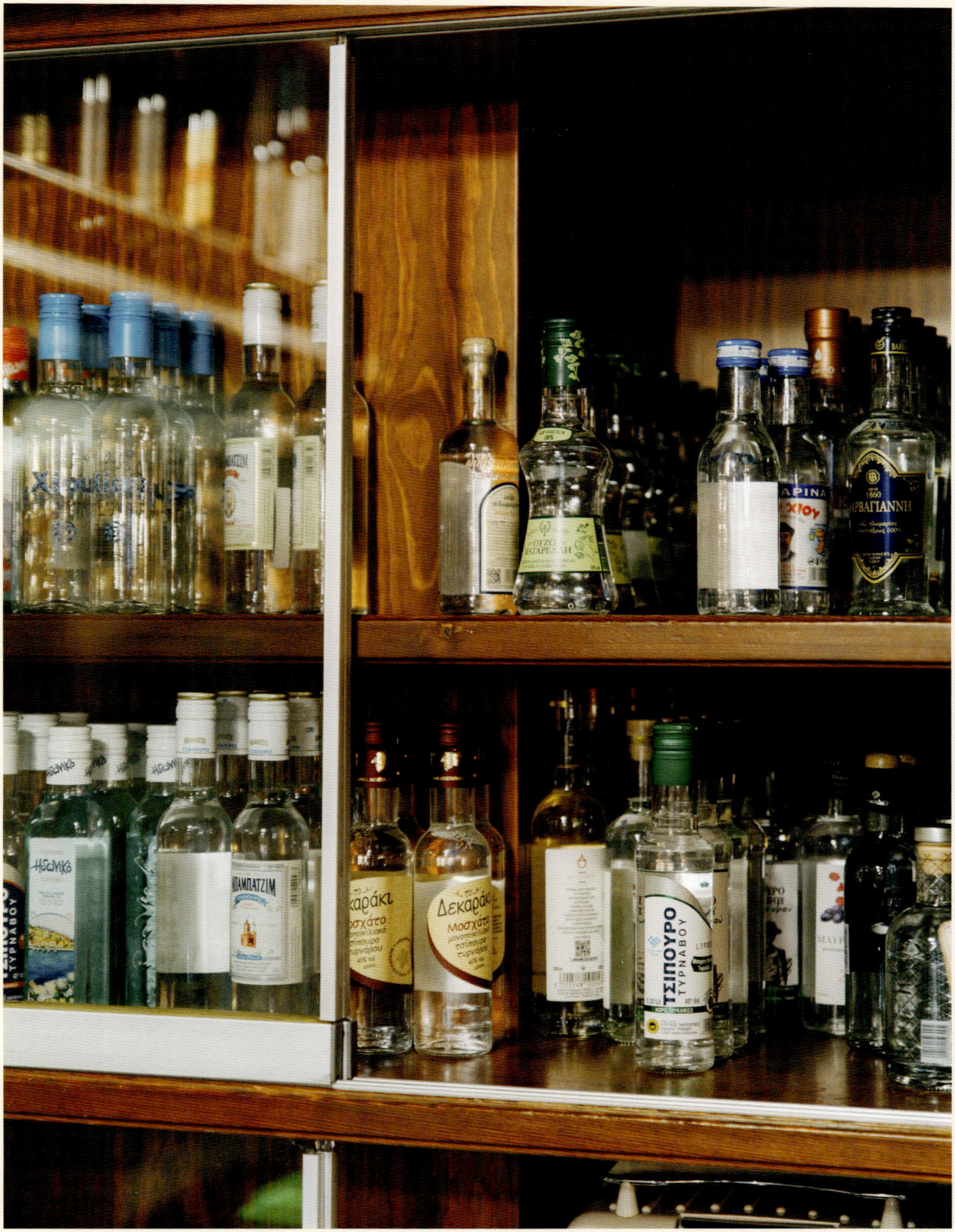

Δεκαράκι
Μοσχάτο
ΤΣΙΠΟΥΡΟ
ΤΥΡΝΑΒΟΥ
1860

rooftop Galaxy). It's a classy place and easy to find, across from the old Parliament building with the grand bronze statue of Greece's Revolutionary War hero, Theodoros Koloktronis, on his horse, pointing right at it from across the avenue.

The Galaxy, like Au Revoir, has remained unchanged for decades. Both are true landmarks in the city, discovered anew with each generation and embraced as Athens's own little secret spots. I used to go for a drink with my journalist buddies when I worked as a reporter for *Ta Nea*—the bar was conveniently located near the paper back then. I had to chuckle when my thirty-one-year-old daughter mentioned that it was one of her favorite places for meeting friends and asked if I had ever been.

By some accounts, the Galaxy is reminiscent of the American drinking houses that popped up in Athens after World War II, and locals refer to it as an "American" bar. It's so much more than that. Its deep wooden counter is dark and smooth with the patina of so many secrets spilled into it in these past fifty or so years. It's also cushioned around the edge, which makes it easy to relax into and sip a cocktail or two for hours, comfortably. The cocktails are classics, and Kostas, who is the conductor of all affairs at this beloved landmark, serves forth every round with a little meze—a salted cucumber, a wedge of bread and cheese on a stick, and more—hearkening back to the ancient concept of the symposia, in which it was considered barbaric to be drunk, and so food has always to be served with every tipple. The Galaxy's wall of fame is like a museum exhibition and testament to the twentieth-century intellectual and artistic life of the city, with photo after yellowed photo of the rich, famous, and infamous lined up and lit up by its trademark old globe lights dangling from the ceiling. Come here to sip a great Manhattan, Old-Fashioned, or Amaretto Sour.

Today, the Athens drinking scene is a frenzy of fun, creative places, some of which are counted among the best bars in the world, so lauded by publications that document such things. Newfound glory days define the drinking scene, which to some extent emerged with the financial crisis (in times of trouble, people drink) and grew into a vibrant part of the city's already lively nightlife, with some natural Greek entrepreneurship stirred in.

Cocktails started to conquer Athens in the mid-1990s, with a place called Bar Guru Bar, that opened on a decaying old street near the first City Hall, off Athinas. People flocked there, navigating between junkies (a huge problem in the Greek capital) and prostitutes, to sip mai tais and listen to jazz. But the real revolutionary was Baba au Rum, which opened on a side street in the fabric, button, and doorknob district of the historic city center, and with it a new era of cocktails, into which were mixed the likes of mastiha, tsipouro, and other Greek spirits, was born. Baba au Rum is still immensely popular, as is its closest rival, the Clumsies, on Praxitelous Street, where all the paper, lighting, and rubber stamp shops were located, again in the historic commercial center, which would see itself reborn with renovated building after building transformed into boutique hotels over the next decade or so.

Both Baba and the Clumsies are counted among the world's top fifty bars. Indeed, the Clumsies has bottled some of its most popular tipples, and you can find them in gourmet shops around town.

There are many other commendable watering holes with creative cocktails all around Athens, so much so that the annual bar show in Athens attracts an international audience, and several of its notable bartenders (aka mixologists) have been awarded international prizes for their creations.

Wine Bars of Athens

Wine drinking may go back six millennia in Athens, but the advent of wine bars is a twenty-first-century phenomenon, and like so much else, their arrival on this city's gustatory landscape is tied pretty closely to economics. The financial crisis decimated the city (and country) but didn't eviscerate Greeks' socializing spirit. At the start of the crisis in 2008 or so, wine bars started popping up in Athens. They offered a refuge for those of us wanting to go out without spending too much money, then evolved into more sophisticated places, beautifully appointed and often warm and cozy. But most important of all, they helped educate Greeks about their own world-class wines, as the Greek vineyard has evolved exponentially over the past two decades and more. Wine bars allowed us to sample unusual, often obscure, and regional varietals by the glass. They're a brilliant addition to the Athens drinkscape.

Now, the dozens of wine bars around town sometimes cater to specific interests, as in a few that serve only natural wines. And in this city and culture of nibbling imbibers, for whom alcohol is almost always accompanied with food, the wine bars are a natural place not only to sample Greece's stellar vintages (or international wines, if that's your interest) but also to nosh on some fine shared plates, too. The symposia have moved through space and time and settled anew in the twenty-first century, housed nowadays in the city's wine bars!

Wine Roads of Attica

One of the greatest things about Athens is its proximity to farmland, vineyards, the sea, and antiquities, all within about an hour's drive of the city and all doable in a day of varied, fascinating activities, with a stop or two for some delicious local food. The Wine Roads are one more reason why Athens is worth more than a perfunctory visit. There is so much to explore!

The Wine Roads of Attica wind their way through such a landscape—Attica, of course, being the prefecture in which Athens is located. There are twenty-six wineries along the route, but a few, like the Papagiannakos and Mylonas Wineries and the Costas Lazaridis Estate, stand out. There's a wine museum at Lazaridis, too, and that's worth a visit if wine is something that deeply interests you. There is also a great wine museum in Pallini, created by the Markou family, showcasing the history of wine in the region.

Attica is the oldest and largest wine-producing region in Greece, with the district of Mesogeia being the most prominent. (*Mesogeia* literally means "Middle Earth" or, if one doesn't want to sound so Hobbit-like, "Middle Land," so named since 508 BC, when the ten tribes of the region were divided into three territories by Cleisthenes, an Athenian statesman who is considered the father of Athenian democracy.) It is the interior portion of the Attica peninsula.

Attica's Mediterranean climate, with mild winters, plentiful sunshine, and cooling sea breezes, is what's made it such a perfect place for growing grapes. Most vineyards are located in the southeast, in Mesogeia, or to the north along the slopes of Mount Pendeli and Mount Parnitha, and to the west, in Megara and Mount Kitherona.

The white Savatiano grape rules here, covering about 90 percent of the area's 6,500 hectares (about 16,000 acres, or 25 square miles) of vineyards. That's an area about one and a half times the size of Manhattan. Other important grapes grown in Attica include Roditis, Malagouzia, and Assyrtico, among the whites, and Agiorgitiko, among reds. Some vintners and viticulturalists also grow international varieties like Cabernet Sauvignon, Chardonnay, and Sauvignon Blanc.

If there is one wine, though, that is most closely associated with Attica, it's the much-maligned resinated wine, retsina, made almost always with the Savatiano or Roditis grapes (or a combination thereof; see page 373). Retsina is vastly improved from what it was just a few decades ago, and it's very good, light, crisp, and elegant—the perfect wine for all the seafood you might enjoy at a stop along the coast as part of an outing to Middle Earth and beyond.

Attica's wine history is rich, and archeological finds have revealed countless drinking vessels, amphorae, and other relics all related to this gift of Dionysus, the god of wine, to humans.

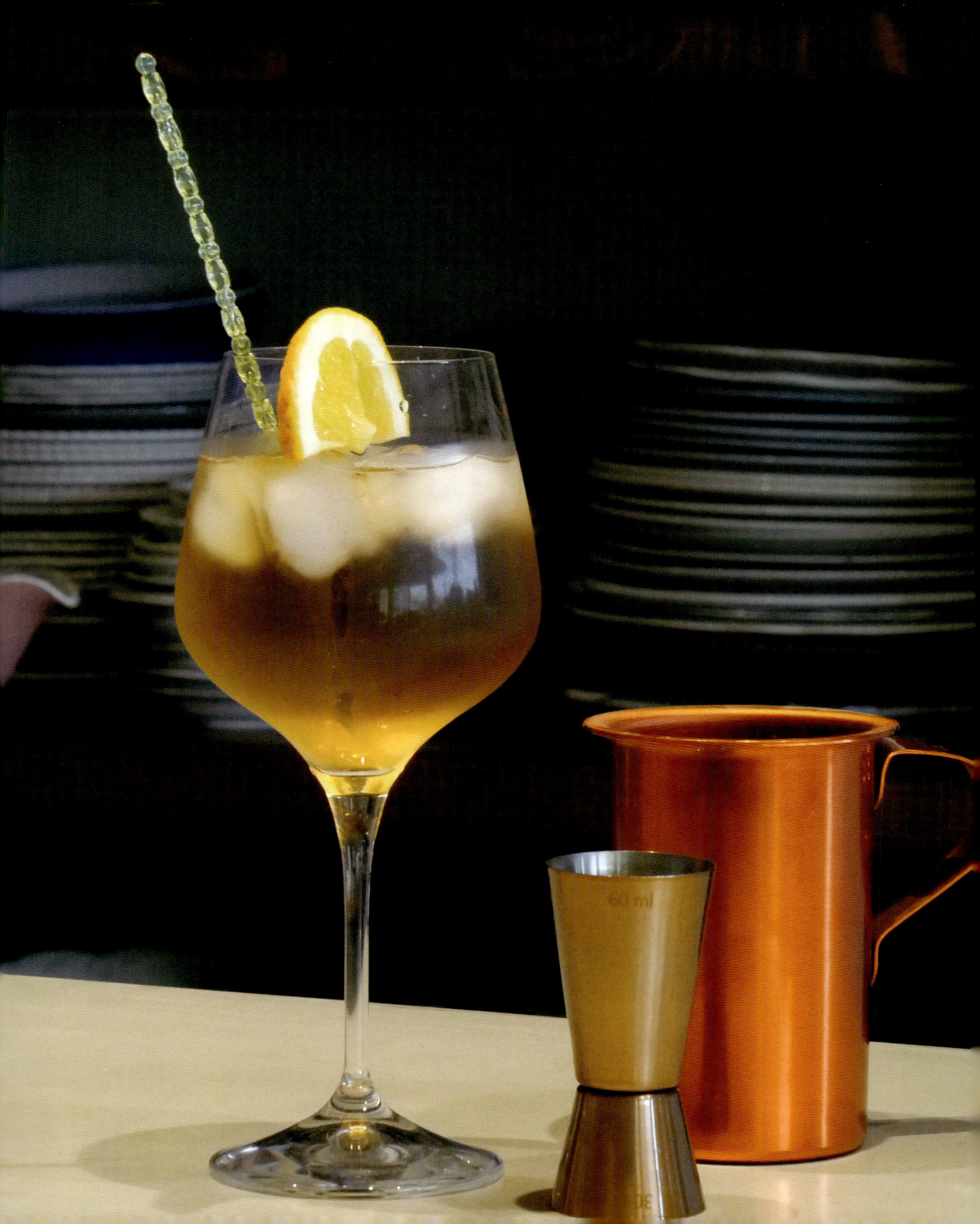
60 ml

Retsina

Retsina, the famed—and, to some, infamous—resinated wine for which Attica is most renowned, used to be one of those things that elicited a clear love-it or hate-it response. "Tastes like turpentine" was a common refrain among my wine-loving friends; "Gives us a bad rap" was another, especially among my wine-making friends. But things have changed, and retsina has seen something of a revival, thanks to a few brave and visionary winemakers who've lightened things up, rejiggered the formula, and created high-quality, lightly resinated wines that are easy to drink and delicious (see page 206 for more on today's resin tappers).

Retsina's story in Attica goes back possibly as far as 2,700 years ago, long before humans invented glass, which is, of course, impermeable, and long before the third century AD, when the Romans first started using barrels to store and transport wine. Resin tapped from Attica's sprawling Aleppo pine forests was used for centuries to seal the porous amphorae in which wine was stored and shipped in the ancient Greek world. It was a brilliant way to prevent wine from oxidizing and spoiling, and it added some flavor, too, which Greeks liked and so continued using the resin, even if the primary reason for doing so, as a sealant, was no longer needed. Retsina persisted, and as it continued to be produced, so did its volatile, love-it-or-leave-it perception grow.

The death-by-retsina of two Nordic monarchs during the Crusades probably didn't help its reputation. In 1103, en route to the Holy Lands, King Eric I of Denmark reportedly died after drinking an undiluted batch of retsina; some three decades later, another Nordic crusader king, Sigurd, reportedly died in Oslo, upon drinking some retsina he'd brought back with him from Greece, upon his return from Jerusalem. Between the eleventh and fifteenth centuries, many a traveler to Greece wrote about their unpleasant encounters with retsina, and the stain on this wine's reputation lasted for centuries, but ironically so did its appeal.

Today, retsina is not made by storing wine in resinated barrels; instead, it is produced using modern winemaking techniques, and small pieces of Aleppo pine are added during fermentation.

Why Aleppo pine, and why Attica? This resin of the Aleppo pine is known for being aromatic, with herby notes sometimes reminiscent of mastiha (another resin), thyme, rosemary, and even ginger. The forests, or what's left of them, are situated in close proximity to the sea, adding to their unique flavor. The trees are tapped in June, the best time to get the freshest, nonoxidized resin, which is what's used in today's fine retsinas. Aged resin is what may have given retsina such a bad reputation over the years, because it smells and tastes uncannily like turpentine.

Vintners who've braved the world of retsina and have lifted it out of its doldrums and into a respected place are making wines in which the resin is used lightly, its faint, refreshing qualities in perfect balance with the aromas of the Savatiano and Roditis grapes, both native to Attica, and the most traditional varieties used in producing retsina. This wine is still the best option for some of the headiest foods in Greece: the garlicky dips and fried fish found in the countless tavernas along the nearby coast.

Retsina Spritz

This recipe combines the bittersweet flavor of Campari with the unique pine resin notes of retsina.

MAKES 1 COCKTAIL

Ice cubes

2 ounces Campari

2 ounces retsina

2 ounces chilled sparkling water or club soda

Orange slice or lemon twist, for garnish

Fill a large wine glass or spritz glass halfway with ice cubes. Add the Campari and retsina. Add the chilled sparkling water. Stir gently to combine the ingredients.

Garnish with an orange slice or a lemon twist and serve.

Retsina Mojito

This Retsina Mojito is a Greek twist on the classic cocktail, replacing rum with retsina wine. The pine resin flavors of retsina complement the traditional mojito ingredients, creating a unique and refreshing drink. This cocktail is a great way to enjoy modern, high-quality retsina wines, which are smoother and more sophisticated than older versions. It's particularly good for those who may have had negative experiences with retsina in the past, as it presents the wine in a new, more approachable format.

MAKES 1 COCKTAIL

2 ounces retsina

1 ounce Finest Roots cinnamon liqueur (a Greek herbal liqueur)

1 ounce strained fresh lime juice

1 teaspoon Greek pine honey

Ice cubes

Dash ginger beer

Lime wedge and fresh rosemary or mint sprig, for garnish

In a cocktail shaker, combine the retsina, Roots, lime juice, honey, and ice. Shake well until the mixture is cold and the honey is dissolved.

Strain the mixture into a glass filled with ice. Top up with a dash of ginger beer.

Garnish with a lime wedge and a sprig of rosemary or mint and serve.

Variation

Use a honey-mint syrup instead of plain honey for a more pronounced mint flavor.

Ouzito

There are a few renditions of the classic Mojito on the Greek cocktail scene, mostly using Greek liqueurs like ouzo and mastiha. This one is particularly refreshing. Try adding a couple of ripe strawberries to the muddle, releasing their juices, and taking the fruity flavor of this great summer quaff up a few notches.

MAKES 1 COCKTAIL

1 tablespoon sugar or simple syrup

1 ounce strained fresh lime juice

7 fresh mint leaves, plus more for garnish

2 ounces ouzo

1 cup ice

2 ounces club soda

Fresh mint sprig and lime slices, for garnish

In a cocktail shaker, add the sugar, lime juice, and mint leaves. Gently muddle the ingredients together to release the mint's oils and dissolve the sugar. Pour in the ouzo and add ice to the shaker. Shake well to mix and chill the ingredients.

Pour the mixture (unstrained) into a highball glass or a tall glass filled with ice. Top off the drink with club soda and stir gently to combine. Garnish with a sprig of mint and lime slices and serve.

Mastiha Margarita

The unique flavor of mastiha, which is a little piney, adds a delicious twist on the classic margarita and complements the tequila and lime perfectly. You can adjust the sweetness by adding more or less simple syrup to taste. For a frozen version, blend all ingredients with crushed ice until smooth.

MAKES 1 COCKTAIL

Salt, for rimming (optional)

Ice

1½ ounces tequila

1 ounce mastiha liqueur

1 ounce strained fresh lime juice

½ ounce simple syrup

Lime slice, for garnish

If desired, rim a margarita glass with salt. Fill with fresh ice and set aside.

Fill a cocktail shaker with ice. Add the tequila, mastiha, lime juice, and simple syrup to the shaker. Shake vigorously for 10 to 15 seconds to chill and combine the ingredients. Strain the mixture into the prepared margarita glass. Garnish with a lime slice and serve.

Mastihatini

This Greek-inspired cocktail adds the piney notes of mastiha, a liqueur flavored and distilled from the resinous spice that is unique to the island of Chios, with the traditional martini structure. The lemon juice balances the sweet and herbal notes of the mastiha, while the simple syrup helps smooth out the flavors. You can adjust the sweetness by adding more or less simple syrup to taste.

MAKES 1 COCKTAIL

Ice
2 ounces vodka
1 ounce mastiha liqueur
½ ounce strained fresh lemon juice
½ teaspoon simple syrup
Lemon twist, for garnish

Fill a cocktail shaker with ice. Add the vodka, mastiha, lemon juice, and simple syrup and shake vigorously for 10 to 15 seconds to chill and combine the ingredients. Strain the mixture into a chilled martini glass. Garnish with a lemon twist and serve.

Aegean Negroni

This delicious cocktail was invented by Nikos Bakoulis, founder of the Clumsies, an Athenian landmark bar. I've tweaked it just a bit, to include a particularly herbaceous Greek gin called Stray Dog, which is available pretty widely in the United States.

MAKES 1 COCKTAIL

1 ounce Stray Dog gin
1 ounce white vermouth
1 ounce Italicus liqueur
Ice
1 lime leaf

In a cocktail shaker, shake together the gin, vermouth, Italicus, and ice. Strain into an ice-filled martini glass and garnish with the lime leaf.

Acknowledgments

I moved to Athens permanently with somewhat of a reluctant heart in the early 1990s. Inured back then to the frenetic pace of New York, my hometown, Athens, seemed so small and provincial. It was an adjustment, to be sure. My husband at the time, a native-born Athenian, never took to New York's particular brand of urban chaos. And so, I followed him to the Greek capital and set down roots. While I never gave up New York entirely (how can one?), I've never looked back either, forever grateful am I, indeed, for everything Athens has given me. It was destiny that called me here.

My kids were born and raised here, for one, and they are by all accounts true Athenians. I felt safe raising them here, free of so much of the fear we have learned to accept in daily life in the States. I saw my dream of being a newspaper reporter come to fruition in Athens, where I had a weekly food and restaurant column for twenty years at the city's largest daily newspaper. I saw another dream fulfilled, too, as the host of a cooking show called *What Are We Going to Eat Today, Mom?* It had ninety-eight episodes a season, which set the stage and gave me the courage and experience to create and host my PBS series, *My Greek Table*, years later. To Athens I owe all that and so much more.

This city is human-scale and the relationships between people reflect that. To my many dear friends here, lifelong friends at this point, with whom I've shared countless meals at home and at restaurants, life would be poor, lonely, and boring without you. Mary, Lizana, Romolo, Stratis, Ilya, Anna, Yianni, Andromachi, Peter and Mark, and others, thankfully too numerous to name (!), my Athens table is all the richer because of you and my sense of the city all the deeper.

I owe my big sister Athena, and brother-in-law Paul a huge thanks for bringing me here for the first time when I was just a kid, an experience that shaped me in ways I could never have imagined back then.

I must mention Peter Poulos, a truly amazing human being and good friend, whose love of Athens is infectious, who not only sees beauty everywhere, but points it out for others to see, too! Thanks, too, to Nikos Vatopoulos, an urban chronicler who taught me to look at my own neighborhood with new eyes and to discover the layers of Athenian architecture and history evident in every inch of this city.

I wish I could name each and every one of the shopkeepers, chefs, restaurateurs, fish and cheese mongers, food purveyors, butchers, spice, herb, and tea vendors, honey merchants and others who give Athens its life and vibrancy and make my own near-daily routine of going to the market so much fun and so human! Even now, in these rushed times, a little small talk precedes most interactions, and that's one of the things I love most about this city!

Much of my life in Athens culminates in the pages of this book, the idea for which was thrust rather enthusiastically upon me one day over lunch by my editor, Michael Flamini. It didn't take long to see that this was a book I had to do. It's not easy to capture a city in writing or in a picture of its food scene, especially one as complex as Athens and especially since everything is always in flux, ever evolving. I've done my best to present Athens as I know it, fully aware that there is also so much I don't know. And I have Michael to thank for that, for encouraging me to jump in and just do it.

Photos tell their own story, too. My talented friend Carolina Doriti, a great cook, teacher, and author, styled the recipes that Yiannis Sikianakis, food photographer par excellence, shot. Together, they created a gorgeous and varied selection of food images that I know capture the spirit and flavor of the city's culinary persona.

Athenian photographer Thomas Gravanis recreates the city in pictures so that armchair and would-be travelers alike will have a sense of the complex, fun, multifaceted, at times chaotic (a Greek word!) nature of the Greek capital.

I owe much to Janis Donnaud, my agent, for her smart approach to almost everything and for her support throughout the whole process of creating this book.

To the whole St. Martin's team, a huge thanks for putting up with me and putting together a beautiful book: assistant editor Claire Cheek; cover designer Olga Grlic, who captured the spirit of Athens brilliantly; designers Jan Derevjanik and Michelle McMillian; production editor Ginny Perrin; copyeditor Karen Wise and proofreader Melanie Gold; managing editor Chrisinda Lynch; publicist John Karle; and marketing manager Erica Martirano. Again, without a team as good as you, Athens wouldn't have happened.

I am grateful beyond words to my family in New York: Koko and Trif, Kat, Kristy, Tom, and George. If only you'd spend more time here, life in Athens would be even sweeter.

I can't in good conscience not mention the one person who, really more than anyone else, made Athens home for me, even if it's no longer a shared one, and helped me understand the city with a modicum of depth. Vasili, you're one of a kind, as unique and complex as the city in which you were born.

Finally, to Kyveli and Yiorgo, who are so much more Athenian than I will ever be, I love you to the end of the earth. You are without a doubt my greatest teachers. Thank you.

Bibliography

"A Guide to Laiki Agoras: Greece's Farmers' Markets." The Culture Trip. Accessed August 25, 2024. https://theculturetrip.com/europe/greece/articles/a-guide-to-laiki-agoras-greeces-farmers-markets/.

"Aiolou Street." Wikipedia. Last modified May 23, 2024. https://en.wikipedia.org/wiki/Aiolou_Street.

"Aiolou Street Has a Story of Its Own . . ." Archaeology Wiki. November 26, 2020. https://www.archaeology.wiki/blog/2020/11/26/aiolou-street-has-a-story-of-its-own/.

"Aiolou Street Has a Story to Tell." Greek News Agenda. April 14, 2021. https://www.greeknewsagenda.gr/aiolou/.

Asimov, Eric. "Retsina: Greece's Traditional Wine." *Quench*. December 6, 2018. https://grapecollective.com/articles/distinctly-greek-a-new-style-of-retsina-wines-is-revitalizing-one-of-the-worlds-longest-lived-wine.

Asimov, Eric. "Great Retsina: An Oxymoron No More." *New York Times*. January 17, 2019. https://www.nytimes.com/2019/01/17/dining/drinks/retsina-wine-greece.html.

Babiniotis, Giorgios. *Dictionary of Modern Greek* [in Greek]. Lexicology Centre in Greece, 1998.

Baker, Chris. *Athens: A Cultural and Historical Guide*. London: Thames & Hudson, 2010.

Ball, E. L. "Greek Food after Moussaka: Cookbooks, 'Local' Culture, and the Cretan Diet." *Journal of Modern Greek Studies* 21 (2003): 1–36.

Basbanelou, Alexandra. "The Sensational History of Retsina and 6 Recommendations for Drinking It" [in Greek]. *Athens Voice*. March 3, 2021. https://www.athensvoice.gr/life/geusi/wine-spirits/704418/i-syntaraktiki-istoria-tis-retsinas-kai-6-protaseis-na-tin-pieis/.

Benayon, M. "Avgolemono Soup: Traditional Greek Recipe." *196 Flavors*. January 22, 2016. https://www.196flavors.com/2016/01/22/greece-avgolemono-soup/.

Biris, Kostas. *Arvanites, the Dorians of Modern Hellenism: The History of the Arvanites*. Athens: Melisa, 1960.

Bouras, Dimitris. "Mikrolimano: A Historical Overview." *Journal of Hellenic Studies* 45, no. 2 (2020): 123–35.

Boutaris, Stelios. "Retsina: Greece's Traditional Wine." *Quench*. December 6, 2018.

Brekoulakis, Tasos, and Marina Petridou. *Souvlaki: A Gastronomic Journey from Homeric Times to Contemporary Street Food* [in Greek]. Pataki, 2019.

Cantina Team. "Frapé, The Story of Our National Coffee" [in Greek]. *Cantina*. October 15, 2017. https://cantina.protothema.gr/chrisima/themata-chrisima/frape-i-istoria-tou-ethnikou-mas-kafe/.

Chatzis, Andreas. "The Culinary Heritage of Piraeus: The Shrimp Houses of Mikrolimano." *Greek Gastronomy Review* 12, no. 1 (2021): 45–60.

Chrysopoulos, Philip. "The Ancient Roots of Greek Souvlaki: The World's First Fast Food." *Greek Reporter*. September 16, 2023. https://greekreporter.com/2023/09/16/ancient-roots-greek-souvlaki/.

Chrysopoulos, Philip. "'Time Out' Magazine Names Greek Cocktail Best in the World." *Greek Reporter*. August 7, 2019. https://greekreporter.com/2019/08/07/time-out-magazine-names-greek-cocktail-best-in-the-world/.

Clark, Bruce. *Athens: City of Wisdom*. New York: Pegasus Books, 2023.

Cloake, Felicity. "Everything You Need to Know about Moussaka, the Classic Greek Dish." *National Geographic*. August 23, 2023.

Clogg, Richard. *A Concise History of Greece*. 3rd ed. Cambridge: Cambridge University Press, 2013.

Dariotis, N. "Cooking to Suit the Occasion" [in Greek]. *To Vima*. April 25, 2012. www.tovima.gr/vimagourmet/kitchen/article/?aid=454749.

Daskalakis, A. *Culinary Traditions of the Arvanites: A Study of Ethnolinguistic Identity and Food Practices in Attica*. Athens: University of Athens Press, 2010.

Daskalakis, Nikos. "Piraeus: The Port of Athens." *Athens Historical Society* 38, no. 3 (2019): 78–89.

Davidson, Alan. *The Oxford Companion to Food*. Oxford University Press, 1999.

Dimaras, Dimitris. "Pezoulas in Tzitzifies: What and How We Ate in this Classic Taverna from 1951" [in Greek]. *Cantina*. April 6, 2022. https://cantina.protothema.gr/exodos/pezoulas-stis-tzitzifies-pos-kai-ti-fagame-stin-klasiki-psarotaverna-tou-1951/.

Dimitriou, Nena, Nicoleta Makrionitou, Georgia Papastamou, and Christina Tzialla. "The Best Galaktoboureka in Athens" [in Greek]. November 12, 2011. *Gastronomos*. https://www.gastronomos.gr/agora/ta-kalytera-galaktompoyreka-stin-athina/94370/.

Dimitriou, Nena, Nadia Liargova, Georgia Papastamou, and Marina Petridou. "Where Do We Eat the Best Cheese Pies?" [in Greek] *Gastronomos*. October 4, 2023. https://www.gastronomos.gr/agora/poy-trome-tis-kalyteres-tyropites-tis-athinas/167493/.

Dimitriou, Nena. "The All-Nighters' Oinomageirion" [in Greek]. *Gastronomos*. November 5, 2011. https://www.gastronomos.gr/magazi/to-oinomageireio-ton-xenychtidon/93078/.

Dioskouridis, Stavros. "The Athenian Taverna." *LIFO*. July 7, 2016. https://www.lifo.gr/culture/arxaiologia/i-athinaiki-taberna.

Doriti, Carolina. "Peinirli Ionias: Talking Dough." *Culinary Backstreets*. March 19, 2018. https://culinarybackstreets.com/cities-category/athens/2018/peinirli-ionias/.

Doriti, Carolina. "Retsina: The Fall and Rise of a Misunderstood Greek Classic." *Culinary Backstreets*. April 17, 2019. https://culinarybackstreets.com/cities-category/athens/2019/retsina/.

Doriti, Carolina. "Leloudas: Living Legend." *Culinary Backstreets*. January 20, 2023. https://culinarybackstreets.com/cities-category/athens/2023/leloudas-living-legend/.

Doukas, Babis. "The Story of the Athens Restaurant Scene" [in Greek]. *Esquire*. November 11, 2023. https://esquire.com.gr/geysi/estiatoria/26692/i-istoria-tis-athinaikis-estiatorikis-skinis.

Drenis, Lazaros. *The Greek Gastronomy: Quality Labels and Evaluation of Nutritional Units* [in Greek]. University of Thessaly, Diploma Thesis.

Epikouros. *The New Greek Cuisine* [in Greek]. Athens: Ikaros, 2012.

"Europe's Second Oldest Bar Is in Athens." XpatAthens. May 13, 2019. https://www.xpatathens.com/living-in-athens/taste-experience/pubs-bars-cafes/item/622-europe-s-second-oldest-bar-is-in-athens.

"Fish à la Spetsiota (Greek-Style Fish in Tomato Sauce)." *Larder Love*. August 2017. https://larderlove.com/fish-la-spetsae/.

Gagarin, Michael, ed. *The Oxford Encyclopedia of Ancient Greece and Rome*. New York: Oxford University Press, 2010.

Ghomenides, Christos. "Dining Out in Athens, Then and Now." Greece Is. January 5, 2023. https://www.greece-is.com/dining-out-then-and-now/.

Goldstein, Joyce. *Sephardic Flavors: Jewish Cooking of the Mediterranean*. Chronicle Books, 2000.

Greece and Grapes. "The Clumsies Aegean Negroni Cocktail." Greece and Grapes. Accessed May 15, 2024. https://www.greeceandgrapes.com/en/other-distillates-aegean-negroni-cocktail-clumsies.

Greek News Agenda. "Greek Cuisine: Its Evolution and Influences." Greek News Agenda. December 6, 2023. https://www.greeknewsagenda.gr/greek-cuisine-its-evolution-and-influences/.

Hatzopoulos, Miltiades B. *The City of Athens: A History*. Athens: University of Athens Press, 1998.

Higgins, Reynold. *The Modern History of Athens: From the 19th Century to Today*. Cambridge: Cambridge University Press, 2015.

Howitt-Marshall, Duncan. "Pastitsio: A Short History of a Greek Classic." *The Passionate Foodie*, December 15, 2020. https://passionatefoodie.blogspot.com/2020/12/pastitsio-short-history-of-greek-classic.html.

Howitt-Marshall, Duncan. "Firedogs and Skewers: Did the Ancient Greeks Eat Souvlaki?" Greece Is. February 16, 2023. https://www.greece-is.com/firedogs-skewers-ancient-greeks-eat-souvlaki/.

Kallidis, Vassilis. *The Athens Food Guide*. Patakis Publishers, 2018.

Karras, Christos. "13 Historic Bars in Athens" [in Greek]. *Athinorama*, January 2015.

Katsigeras, Mihalis. "Contribution to the History of Frapé" [in Greek]. *Kathimerini Newspaper*. September 6, 2017. https://www.kathimerini.gr/society/925538/symvoli-stin-istoria-toy-frape/.

Kavroulaki, Mariana. "Simit or Koulouri." *History of Greek Food*. June 9, 2008. https://1historyofgreekfood.wordpress.com/2008/06/09/simiti-or-koulouri/.

Kladis, Angelos. "The Belly of Athens: The Story of the Varvakeios Agora" [in Greek]. May 3, 2024. https://www.oneman.gr/onecity/urban/to-stomaxi-tis-athinas-i-istoria-piso-apo-ti-varvakeio-agora/.

Kochilas, Diane. "A Greek Cheese Pie Called Kourou." YouTube. October 27, 2022. https://www.youtube.com/watch?v=BSIp0DBzNSM.

Kochilas, Diane. "As Goes Greek Cuisine, So Goes the Greek Economy." *Washington Post*. June 12, 2010.

Kochilas, Diane. "Fish à la Spetsiota." Accessed August 28, 2024. https://www.dianekochilas.com/fish-a-la-spetsiota/.

Kochilas, Diane. "Seaside Saganaki." *Saveur*. June/July 2005.

Kokkinidis, Tassos. "Varvakeios: The Grand Food Market of Athens." *Greek Reporter*. September 29, 2023. https://greekreporter.com/2023/09/29/varvakios-food-market-athens/.

Koliopoulos, L., and T. Veremis. *Modern Greece: A History Since 1821*. Wiley-Blackwell, West Sussex, UK, 2010.

Konstantinidou, Vivi. "Here's Why There's So Much Buzz about Georgios Galyfianakis' Galaktoboureko!" [in Greek]. September 21, 2022. *Gastronomos*. https://www.gastronomos.gr/magazi/ma-giati-trechoyn-oloi-oi-athinaioi-sto-porto-rafti/155734/.

Konstantinidou, Vivi. "Daremas: The Best Moustokouloura in Attica Are Made at This Historic Bakery" [in Greek]. *Gastronomos*. September 28, 2023. https://www.gastronomos.gr/magazi/daremas-ston-istoriko-foyrno-toy-markopoyloy-psinontai-ta-kalytera-moystokoyloyra-tis-attikis/224855/.

Kopiaste. "Tyropita with Kourou Phyllo." *Kopiaste*. September 30, 2008. https://www.kopiaste.org/2008/09/tyropita-with-kourou-phyllo/.

Kossyfas, Dimitris. "Athens: A Homey Vibe from the Past at Leloudas." *Travel Food People*. November 22, 2023. https://travelfoodpeople.com/athens-a-homey-vibe-from-the-past-at-leloudas/.

Kotseli, Areti. "Greek and Turkish Debate over Origins of Koulouri/Simit." *Greek Reporter*. April 5, 2012. https://greekreporter.com/2012/04/05/greek-and-turkish-debate-over-origins-of-koulourisimit/.

Kouroupos, George. *Athens: The Making of a Modern City*. New York: Routledge, 2002.

Koutoupis, Maria. "The Transformation of Mikrolimano: From Ancient Port to Modern Destination." *Mediterranean Studies Journal* 10, no. 4 (2022): 211–25.

Koutsou, S. "The Role of Wild Greens in the Mediterranean Diet: A Case Study of the Arvanites." *Journal of Mediterranean Studies* 22, no. 3 (2015): 45–60.

Kremezi, Aglaia, and Anissa Helou. "What's in the Name of a Dish? The Words Mean What the People of the Mediterranean Want Them to Mean." In *Food and Language: Proceedings of the Oxford Symposium on Food and Cooking 2009*, edited by Richard Hosking, 2009.

Kremezi, Aglaia. "Horiatiki, the Peasant Roots of Greek Salad." June 25, 2022. https://www.aglaiakremezi.com/horiatiki-peasant-roots-greek-salad/.

Kremezi, Aglaia. "The Influence of Nikolas Tselementes on Modern Greek Cuisine." *Food and Travel*, 2023.

LaGrave, Katharine. "Nikolaos Tselementes Changed Greek Cuisine Forever—But for Better or Worse?" *Saveur*. October 30, 2019.

Laure, M. "Mikrolimano, the 'Little Port' of Piraeus." Live Athens. January 24, 2024. https://live-athens.com/mikrolimano-the-little-port-of-piraeus.html.

Lazarakis, Kontantinos. "The Vineyards of Attica and Their Centuries-Old History" [in Greek]. March 31, 2023. https://www.travel.gr/food_and_drink/wine-spirits/oi-ampelones-tis-attikis-kai-i-makraion/.

Leivadaros, Manos. "We Saw How Daremas' Must Cookies Are Made, Praised by the Michelin Guide: The Bakery in Mesogeia" [in Greek]. *Iefemerida*. July 10, 2022. https://www.iefimerida.gr/gastronomie/moystokoyloyra-darema-michelin-pos-ftiahnontai.

Matyszak, Philip. *24 Hours in Ancient Athens*. London: Michael O'Mara Books Limited, 2019.

Mavridis, George. "Garidadika: A Culinary Tradition in Mikrolimano." *Culinary History Review* 5, no. 2 (2023): 34–50.

Mavromatis, A. *Pies and Pastries of Greece: A Culinary Exploration of Regional Variations*. Thessaloniki: Hellenic Culinary Institute, 2018.

Melas, Spyros. "The Survival of Nikolaos Tselementes" [in Greek]. *Eleftheria*, March 5, 1958.

Meyer, Michael. *The Urban History of Athens: From Antiquity to the Present Day*. Chicago: University of Chicago Press, 2018.

Michalopoulos, George. "Pastitsio Recipe and History: Greek Baked Ziti." *Philosokitchen*. June 8, 2020. https://philosokitchen.com/pastitsio-recipe-greek-baked-ziti/.

Nasrallah, Nawal. "In the Beginning There Was No Musakka." *Food, Culture & Society* 13, no. 4 (2010): 595–606.

Neather, Andrew. "Nine Athens Wine Bars Championing Greece's Native Grapes." *Club Oenologique*. November 10, 2021. https://cluboenologique.com/story/best-athens-wine-bars/

Neos Kosmos. "Best Greek Cocktail: Time Out Votes the Clumsies Aegean Negroni as the Top Cocktail in the World." August 7, 2019. https://neoskosmos.com/en/2019/08/07/life/food-drink/best-greek-cocktail-time-out-votes-the-clumsies-aegean-negroni-as-the-top-cocktail-in-the-world/.

Nikolaidou, Eleni. *The Recipes of Hunger, Life in Athens during the Occupation* [in Greek]. Metaichmio Publishers, 2011.

"Our Grandparents Ate Here 100 Years Ago" [in Greek]. *Gastronomos*. November 5, 2021. https://www.gastronomos.gr/exodos/ta-aionovia-magazia-tis-athinas/93157/.

Panourgia, Neni. *Enfleshment of Memory*. Accessed October 19, 2024. https://www.documenta14.de/en/south/887.

Papacharalampous, Nafsika. *The Metamorphosis of Greek Cuisine 1st Edition: An Ethnography of Deli Foods, Restaurant Smells, and Foodways of Crisis*. Routledge Press, 2023.

Papadopoulos, Eleni. "The Role of Mikrolimano in the Maritime History of Greece." *Maritime History Review* 22, no. 1 (2020): 99–115.

Papadopoulos, G. *Herbs and Flavors of Greece: The Culinary Heritage of the Arvanites*. Athens: Greek Cultural Publications, 2017.

Papastamou, Georgia. "Karavitis: The Story of this Legendary Taverna" [in Greek]. *Gastronomos*. September 2, 2022. https://www.gastronomos.gr/magazi/karavitis-i-istoria-tis-thrylikis-tavernas-poy-katostarizei/152910/.

Papastamou, Georgia. "The History of the Greek Village Salad with Versions by Chefs" [in Greek]. *Gastronomos*. October 5, 2021. https://www.gastronomos.gr/topikes-kouzines/i-istoria-tis-choriatikis-salatas-kai-oi-ekdoches-ton-sef/87404/.

Papastrati, Sophia. "15 Tavernas from Old Athens, Straight Out of Greek Movies." *Gastronomos*. May 8, 2022. https://www.gastronomos.gr/exodos/15-tavernes-tis-palias-athinas-vgalmenes-apo-elliniki-tainia/130073/.

Paradeisi, Chrysa. *Illustrated Cooking and Pastry Making* [in Greek]. Vivlioekdotiki, Athens, 1959.

Paraskevoudi, Maro. "The Fried Cheese Pie of Dimitra Gounaridis Is Still Made with the Traditional Recipe" [in Greek]. May 11, 2023. https://www.oneman.gr/onecity/gefsi/i-tiganiti-tiropita-tis-dimitras-gounaridi-ftiaxnetai-akoma-me-tin-paradosiaki-sintagi/.

Paraskevoudi, Maro. "In Athens We've Been Eating Pan Pizza Since 1970." May 24, 2023. https://www.oneman.gr/onecity/gefsi/stin-athina-trome-pitsa-tapsiou-apo-to-1970/.

Parnell, Richard. "The Pasta Type You Need For Traditional Greek Pastitsio." *The Daily Meal*. January 6, 2024.

Parnell, Richard. "Wines of Attica Special and the Amazing 'Retsina Renaissance'." *The Buyer*. August 30, 2022. https://www.the-buyer.net/insight/wines-of-attica-special-and-the-amazing-retsina-renaissance.

Paster, Emily. "This Greek Chicken Soup Has a Surprising Sephardic History." *My Jewish Learning*. October 2, 2019. https://www.myjewishlearning.com/the-nosher/this-greek-chicken-soup-has-a-surprising-sephardic-history/.

Perry, Charles. "The Origins of Moussaka." *Culinary History Review*. 2017.

Petridou, Maria. "Pezoulas: The Best Fish Taverna in Athens, from 1951." *Gastronomos*. October 24, 2023. https://www.gastronomos.gr/magazi/pezoylas-i-kalyteri-psarosoypa-tis-athinas-apo-to-1951/229517/.

Petridou, Marina. "Katsogiannos: The Oldest Taverna in Drapetsona." *Gastronomos*. January 25, 2023. https://www.gastronomos.gr/magazi/katsogiannos-i-pio-palia-kai-istoriki-taverna-tis-drapetsonas/123056/.

Petridou, Marina. "A Shop in Agia Paraskevi Makes Sandwiches with . . . Beans." *Gastronomos*. May 25, 2022. https://www.gastronomos.gr/magazi/ena-magazi-stin-agia-paraskeyi-ftiachnei-santoyits-me-fasolada/134118/.

Pittas, Yiorgos. *The Coffee Houses of Athens* [in Greek]. Athens: Pub. Koilada Lefkon AE., 2013.

Pittas, Yiorgos. *The Athenian Taverna* [in Greek]. Athens: Indiktos., 2016.

Potamianos, Themis. *Cooking to Suit the Times* [in Greek]. Reprint 2012. Athens: Estia.

Psihouli, Eleni. "Diporto: The Whole History of Athens in a Basement." *Cantina.* January 20, 2017. https://cantina.protothema.gr/estiatoria-bars/diporto-oli-i-istoria-tis-athinas-se-ena/.

Rentoulas, Angelos. "Stani in Omonoia: The Most Tender Shop in Omonoia" [in Greek]. *Gastronomos.* September 28, 2021. https://www.gastronomos.gr/magazi/i-stani-stin-omonoia/86452/.

Roden, Claudia. *The Book of Jewish Food: An Odyssey from Samarkand to New York.* New York: Knopf, 1996.

Sarant. "Kuruou" [in Greek]. https://sarantakos.wordpress.com/2018/03/06/kuru/.

Sitaras, Thomas. *Old Athens Lives, Feasts and Eats, 1834–1938* [in Greek]. Athens: Okeanidou, 2011.

Slice of Gourmet. "Tiropita Kourou." March 7, 2023, https://sliceofgourmet.com/side-dish/breads/tiropita-kourou/.

Sofianopoulos, Christos. "The Shrimp Houses of Mikrolimano: A Taste of Tradition." *Greek Food and Culture* 7, no. 3 (2021): 56–70.

Souvlaki for the Soul. "Tiropitakia Kourou: Shortbread Cheese Pies." November 17, 2009. https://souvlakiforthesoul.com/shortbread-cheese-pies/.

Stoili, Melissa. "The Authentic Pastitsio" [in Greek]. *To Vima.* September 25, 2012.

Sutton, David. "Let Them Eat Stuffed Peppers: An Argument of Images on the Role of Food in Understanding Neoliberal Austerity in Greece." Edited transcript of a talk given by David Sutton on March 16, 2016, at the School of Oriental and African Studies, University of London. *Gastronomica: The Journal of Critical Food Studies* 16: 8–17.

Thanasoulas, Dionysis. "Christos Lentzos: The King of Frapé Drank Espresso!" [in Greek]. *Protothema.* https://www.protothema.gr/greece/article/1448364/hristos-ledzos-o-vasilias-tou-frape-epine-espreso/.

Trivolis, Despina. "Peinirli: It Came From the Black Sea." *Culinary Backstreets.* August 4, 2012. https://culinarybackstreets.com/cities-category/athens/2012/peinirli/.

Trivolis, Despina. "Stani: Home of the 'Real' Greek Yogurt." *Culinary Backstreets.* October 30, 2012. https://culinarybackstreets.com/cities-category/athens/2012/stani/.

Tsangas, Eleni. "Yiorgos Varsos: The Bitter Moments of a Sweet Story." [in Greek]. September 24, 2021. https://www.bigpost.gr/lifestyle/article/64137/giorgos-varsos-oi-pikres-stigmes-mias-glykias-istorias/.

Tsibiridou, F., and V. Yiakoumaki. *Report for the Research Programme Greek Traditional Foods and the Industrialization of their Production titled European Food Policy and the Definition of Tradition.* 2007.

Tsoukalas, Dimitris. "Historical and Cultural Significance of Mikrolimano." *Piraeus Cultural Journal* 15, no. 2 (2022): 88–102.

Tsoukalas, Costas. *Modern Greece: A History of Athens and its Role in the Balkans.* Athens: Hellenic Ministry of Culture, 2006.

Tsoukalas, K. "Food and Identity: The Arvanite Community in Modern Greece." *Journal of Ethnic Foods* 8, no. 1 (2021): 12–25.

Vasilakis, T. *Traditional Sweets of Greece: A Journey Through Time and Culture.* Crete: Cretan Culinary Press, 2019.

Vatopoulos, Nikos. *Perpatontas stin Athina (Walking in Athens)* [in Greek]. Metaichmio, 2018.

Velidakis, Loukas. "Christos Lentzos: The Master of Frapé in the Sphere of Myth" [in Greek]. *Kathimerini.* December 20, 2023.

Vlaikos, Dimitris. "Peinirli in Drosia Has 3 Generations of History" [in Greek]. *Gastronomos.* Updated August 2, 2022. https://www.gastronomos.gr/magazi/gia-peinirli-sti-drosias/63392/.

Wikipedia. "Avgolemono." Last modified July 15, 2024. https://en.wikipedia.org/wiki/Avgolemono.

Wikipedia. "Arvanitika." Last modified October 10, 2024. https://en.wikipedia.org/wiki/Arvanitika.

Wikipedia. "Laiki Agora." Last modified September 8, 2024. https://en.wikipedia.org/wiki/Laiki_agora.

Yiakoumaki, V. 2006. "Local, Ethnic and Rural Food: On the Emergence of Cultural Diversity in Greece since Its Integration in the European Union." *Journal of Modern Greek Studies* 24: 415–45.

Yonan, Joe. "Greek Salad Is Perfect, If You Make It Right. Here's How." *Washington Post.* July 28, 2024. https://www.washingtonpost.com/food/2024/07/28/greek-salad-classic-diane-kochilas/.

Zerva, Ioanna. "Stani A 90 Year Old Dairy Shop in Omonoia That All Tourists Visit." October 8, 2021. *Cantina.* https://cantina.protothema.gr/estiatoria-bars/reportaz-estiatoria-bars/stani-ena-galaktopoleio-90-eton-stin-om/.

Zgourides, C. "Inviting Writing: The Secret of Lemon Soup." *Smithsonian.* March 2011. https://www.smithsonianmag.com/arts-culture/inviting-writing-the-secret-of-lemon-soup-30492851/.

Zouraris, Christos. *Deipnosofist* [in Greek]. Athens: Ikaros, 2008.

Zouraris, Christos. *The Second Deipnosofist* [in Greek]. Athen: Ikaros, 2001.

Index

Aegean Negroni, 376
Agia Eirini Square, 13, 56, 310
Agia Paraskevi, 40, 284
Agios Panteleimonas, 13, 26
Aiolou Street, 12–13, 336, 358
Akra, 70, 253
Aleppo pine, 206, 373
All-Nighter's Patsas (Tripe Soup), 178
almonds
    Almond Torte, 344
    in Athenian Ice Cream Sundae, 357
    in Homemade Granola with Greek Flavors, 62
Al Zaim, 26
Anchovies Sofrito from Laki's Ouzerie, 128
anthotyro
    in Greek Gelatin Salad, 150
    in Moussaka with Metsovone Béchamel, 234
    in Pastitsio, 230
    in Spanakopita Grilled Focaccia, 35
apples
    in Bibb Lettuce Salad with Winter Fruit and Walnuts, 155
    in Greek Yogurt Panna Cotta, 349
apricots, dried
    in Homemade Granola with Greek Flavors, 62
    in Trahana Breakfast Bowl, 63
aracas laderos, 294
Arancini, Grape Leaf, 141
Argoura, 86, 115, 116, 118
Artichokes and Broad Beans, Fresh Cod or Halibut with Braised, 292
arugula
    Baby Arugula and Chickpea Salad with Raw Red Onion, Hard-Boiled Eggs, and Tahini Ladolemono, 159
    Beet and Arugula Salad with Sultanas and Chèvre, 158
    Focaccia Sandwich with Fava, Arugula, and Grilled Eggplants, 39
    in Vegan Peinirli with Hummus, 49
Arvanites, 266, 267, 363
Asimakopoulos Brothers Pastry Shop, 351
asparagus, in Cuttlefish Ink and Crab Soup, 187
Athenian Carbonara, 278
Athenian Housewife's False Soufflé, 227
Athenian Ice Cream Sundae, 357
Athenian Lemon Pie with Hints of Spetses, 364

Athenian Mayonnaise, 217
Athenian Pot Roast, 224
Athens Central Market Beef Soup, 172
Athens Olympics (2004), 4, 112, 148, 167, 185, 229, 292
Athens-Style Avocado Toast with Mashed Feta, Tomatoes, and Jammy Eggs, 76
Athens-Style Classic Greek Pizza, 286
Athinaiki Mayioneza, 217
Athinaiki Salata, 144, 162
Athinaikon, 102, 124
Attica, 266
    fish tavernas, 195
    grill houses, 325
    resin tappers of, 206, 373
    Wine Roads of, 290, 371
Attica-Style Crustless Milk Pie, 363
Au Revoir, 368
Avgolemono
    about, 239
    Lahanodolmades, 220
    Mushroom-Spinach Fricasse Risotto with, 279
    Turkey-Stuffed Cabbage Rolls with Avgolemono Cream Sauce, 318
    Zucchini Stuffed with Black Rice, Fish, and, 260
avgotaraho. *See* bottarga
avocados
    Athens-Style Avocado Toast with Mashed Feta, Tomatoes, and Jammy Eggs, 76
    Watermelon Salad with Jalapeños, Avocado, and Feta, 154

Baba au Rum, 370
Baby Arugula and Chickpea Salad with Raw Red Onion, Hard-Boiled Eggs, and Tahini Ladolemono, 159
bacon
    in Athenian Carbonara, 278
    in Giant Beans Baked with Smoked Pork, Wine, and Graviera, 244
Bairaktaris, 50–51
Bakoulis, Nikos, 376
Barbarigou, Argiro, 304
Bar 17, 234
Bean Soup Sandwich, 40
beef
    about, 310
    in All-Nighter's Patsas (Tripe Soup), 178
    in Athenian Pot Roast, 224

Athens Central Market Beef Soup, 172
    in Bean Soup Sandwich, 40
Beef Baked with Orzo, 226
Beef Cheek and Mushroom Soup, 171
Beef Cheeks "Kokinisto," 327
Beef Stew, 223
    in Cabbage Rolls with Egg-Lemon Sauce, 220
    in Cheese-Stuffed Taverna Burgers, 200
Filet Mignon with Mavrodaphne Sauce, 328
    in Karamanlidika's Giant Beans Bouryioundi with Feta and Spicy Sausage, 133
    in Keftedes with Ouzo and Diced Tomatoes, 203
    in Kimadopita, 31
Leloudas's Poor Man's Plate of Greek Fries with Ground Meat Sauce and Grated Myzithra, 136
Lemony Braised Beef, 222
    in Moussaka Pita Wrap, 57
    in Moussaka with Metsovone Béchamel, 234
Ossobuco with Greek Flavors, 329
    in Pastitsio, 230
    in Sweet Potato Skordalia, 91
beets
    Beet and Arugula Salad with Sultanas and Chèvre, 158
    Beet Risotto with Beet Greens and Feta, 281
    in Bibb Lettuce Salad with Winter Fruit and Walnuts, 155
    Nena Ismyrnoglou's Beet Taramosalata with Lime and Mint, 88
    Stacked Fried Sardines with a Brush of Beets, 298
Beis, Vangelis, 138
bell peppers, red
    in Fiery Feta Cream, 98
    Katsogiannis's Grilled Eggplant Dip with Roasted Red Peppers, 89
Berry Sauce, Crunchy Feta in Phyllo with Tahini and, 111
Bibb Lettuce Salad with Winter Fruit and Walnuts, 155
Biftekia, 200
Black-Eyed Peas with Preserved Lemon, Greens, and Capers, 245
Black Salami, 35
Botsaris, 122

Index   383

bottarga
    about, 269
    Creamed Trahana with Dried Figs and Bottarga, 185
    Green Beans Yiahni with Bottarga, 259
    in Spaghetti with Avgotaraho, 269
    Sweet Potato Taramosalata with Bottarga, 86
Boureki, Harry's Strapatsada, 23
"bourgeois" cuisine, about, 212–14
Boza, 335, 344
Braised Beef, Lemony, 222
Braised Chickpeas with Olives, Pistachios, and Roasted Tomatoes, 248
breakfast, about, 60–61
Bream in Citrus Juice with Tomato, Olives, and Red Onion, Gilt-Head, 114
Brekoulakis, Tasos, 50
Broad Beans, Fresh Cod or Halibut with Braised Artichokes and, 292
Buffalo Meat, Seychelles' Signature Pappardelle with, 270
Bulgur Salad with Fresh Fruit and Figs, 164
burgers
    Cheese-Stuffed Taverna Burgers, 200
    Lamb Burgers with Smoked Eggplant Cream, 320
Burrata, Olive Oil, and Herbs, Carob Rusk Tomato Salad with, 153
butternut squash
    Roasted Butternut Squash Soup with Greek Figs, 174
    in Vegan Root Vegetable Kapama, 255

cabbage
    Greek Taverna Cabbage-Carrot Salad with a Tomato Rose, 156
    in Lahanorizo Cream, 258
    in Mixed Greens Salad with Tangerine-Olive Oil Dressing, 167
cabbage rolls
    Cabbage Rolls with Egg-Lemon Sauce, 220
    Turkey-Stuffed Cabbage Rolls with Avgolemono Cream Sauce, 318
Café Neon, 66
cafés, about, 66
Calamari
    Pesto, 303
    Souvlaki, 56
Camp, John, 8, 50
cannellini beans
    Bean Soup Sandwich, 40
    in Greek Vegetable Soup with Jammy Eggs, 191
Carbonara, Athenian, 278
carbs, about, 264–65
Carpaccio over Grape Leaves, Sea Bass, 118

carrots
    Greek Taverna Cabbage-Carrot Salad with a Tomato Rose, 156
    in Vegan Root Vegetable Kapama, 255
Central Market, 94, 127, 172, 175, 177, 181, 310
cheese pies. See also kourous; tyropites
    about, 18
    Graviera Cheese and Ham Pie, 28
    Mouzilo's Fabulous Tyropita, 20
Cheese-Stuffed Taverna Burgers, 200
chestnuts
    Nena's Chestnut Stifado with Prunes, 247
    Risotto with Chestnuts, Winter Squash, Mavrodaphne, and Feta, 282
    in Vegan Root Vegetable Kapama, 255
chèvre
    Beet and Arugula Salad with Sultanas and Chèvre, 158
    in Mouzilo's Fabulous Tyropita, 20
Chicago, 105, 334, 357
chicken
    Chicken Milanese, 237
    Epirus's Lemony Pulled Chicken Soup, 177
    Grec-Mex Chicken Fajitas, 314
    Homemade Chicken Gyro, 54
    Lemony Chicken "Ribs," 313
    Schoolchildren's Greek Chicken Schnitzel, 317
chickpeas
    Baby Arugula and Chickpea Salad with Raw Red Onion, Hard-Boiled Eggs, and Tahini Ladolemono, 159
    Braised Chickpeas with Olives, Pistachios, and Roasted Tomatoes, 248
    Chickpea Soup That Emulates Diporto's Legendary Revithada, 182
    Chickpea Soup with Pasturma, 184
    Chickpeas with Wild Mushrooms, 253
    Lemony Chickpeas with Turmeric and Fennel, 252
    Mushroom Chickpea Tigania with Soy Sauce and Honey, 130
    Olympion's Chickpeas with Eggplant, Lots of Onions, and Petimezi, 250
    Spinach-Chickpea Pasta with Creamy Tahini, 277
Christoforidi, Virginia, 138
Classic Greek Pizza, Athens-Style, 286
Classic Tavernisio Tzatziki, 98
Classic Yellow Sponge Cake, 345
Clay-Baked Whole Eggplants with Feta and Tomatoes, 197
Clumsies, the, 32, 370, 376
coffee, about, 61, 66–67
Cookoovaya, 56
crabmeat
    Cuttlefish Ink and Crab Soup, 187
    in Shrimp Croquettes with "Sos Pikant," 124

Creamed Trahana with Dried Figs and Bottarga, 185
crepes
    about, 72
    Greek Salad, 75
    Spanakopita, 73
Crispy Fried Feta Triangles from Nea Ionia, 25
Croissant, Spinach Pie Meets, 32
Croquettes, Shrimp, with "Sos Pikant," 124
crudo, Athenian Style, 115
Crunchy Feta in Phyllo with Tahini and Berry Sauce, 111
cucumbers
    in Classic Tavernisio Tzatziki, 98
    in Greek Gelatin Salad, 150
    Greek Salad with Cucumber Granita, 149
    in The Not-So-Classic Greek Horiatiki Salata, 145
Cuttlefish Ink and Crab Soup, 187
Cycladic Eggs on Toast, 78
Cycladic Museum, 78

Da Capo, 60
Daremas, 267, 347
desserts. See also Galaktoboureko
    about, 334–35
    Almond Torte, 344
    Athenian Ice Cream Sundae, 357
    Athenian Lemon Pie with Hints of Spetses, 364
    Greek Yogurt Panna Cotta, 349
    Loukoumades, 339
    Melina's Sokolatina, 361
    Moustokouloura, 347
    Poupeki, 363
    Rice Pudding, 340
Diporto, 127, 181, 182
dips
    about, 84
    Fiery Feta Cream, 98
    A Fish Taverna's Taramosalata, 85
    Garlicky Fava with Red Wine and Herbs, 95
    To Kafeneion's Delicious Eggplant Dip with Olives and Honey, 92
    Katsogiannis's Grilled Eggplant Dip with Roasted Red Peppers, 89
    Melitzanosalata with Miso, Tahini, and Petimezi, 90
    Mung Bean Fava with Tahini and Za'atar, 94
    Nena Ismyrnoglou's Beet Taramosalata with Lime and Mint, 88
    Sweet Potato Skordalia, 91
    Sweet Potato Taramosalata with Bottarga, 86
    Taramosalata with Tomato Paste, 87
    Yellow Split-Pea Fava with Smoked Eel, Caramelized Tomatoes, and Onions, 97

Dodoni, 14, 17
Dolmades, Greek Sushi, 116
doughnuts. *See* loukoumades
Drapetsona, 89, 203
drinks
    about, 368–71
    Aegean Negroni, 376
    Mastiha Margarita, 375
    Mastihatini, 376
    Ouzito, 375
    Retsina Mojito, 374
    Retsina Spritz, 374

Edible Athens, 24
Eel, Yellow Split-Pea Fava with Caramelized Tomatoes, Onions, and Smoked, 97
eggplants
    Clay-Baked Whole Eggplants with Feta and Tomatoes, 197
    Focaccia Sandwich with Fava, Arugula, and Grilled Eggplants, 39
    To Kafeneion's Delicious Eggplant Dip with Olives and Honey, 92
    Katsogiannis's Grilled Eggplant Dip with Roasted Red Peppers, 89
    Lamb Burgers with Smoked Eggplant Cream, 320
    in Melitzanosalata with Miso, Tahini, and Petimezi, 90
    in Moussaka Pita Wrap, 57
    in Moussaka with Metsovone Béchamel, 234
    Nena's Grilled Squid with Smoked Eggplant Salad, 113
    Olympion's Chickpeas with Eggplant, Lots of Onions, and Petimezi, 250
eggs
    Athens-Style Avocado Toast with Mashed Feta, Tomatoes, and Jammy Eggs, 76
    Baby Arugula and Chickpea Salad with Raw Red Onion, Hard-Boiled Eggs, and Tahini Ladolemono, 159
    Cycladic Eggs on Toast, 78
    Greek Vegetable Soup with Jammy Eggs, 191
    Hangover Eggs, 81
    in Harry's Strapatsada Boureki, 23
    in Kayianas on Toast 2 Ways, 77
    Saganaki with Pasturma and Eggs, 105
    in Traditional Peinirli, 48
Elliott, Sloane and Drossoula, 3
Elytis, Odysseas, 66
Epirus, 31, 172, 175, 177, 178
Epirus's Lemony Pulled Chicken Soup, 177
Exarcheia, 2, 35, 72, 102, 124, 194, 249, 335, 351

Fajitas, Grec-Mex Chicken, 314
False Soufflé, Athenian Housewife's, 227

fava
    Focaccia Sandwich with Fava, Arugula, and Grilled Eggplants, 39
    Garlicky Fava with Red Wine and Herbs, 95
    Mung Bean Fava with Tahini and Za'atar, 94
    Yellow Split-Pea Fava with Smoked Eel, Caramelized Tomatoes, and Onions, 97
Feminist Lamb and Potatoes, 324
fennel
    Lemony Chickpeas with Turmeric and Fennel, 252
    in Lightest Shrimp Meze with Capers, Ouzo, and Orange, 121
    Mixed Greens Salad with Tangerine-Olive Oil Dressing, 167
    in Sea Bass Carpaccio over Grape Leaves, 118
    Sweet Potato Taramosalata with Bottarga, 86
feta
    Athens-Style Avocado Toast with Mashed Feta, Tomatoes, and Jammy Eggs, 76
    in Bean Soup Sandwich, 40
    Beet Risotto with Beet Greens and Feta, 281
    Clay-Baked Whole Eggplants with Feta and Tomatoes, 197
    Crispy Fried Feta Triangles from Nea Ionia, 25
    Crunchy Feta in Phyllo with Tahini and Berry Sauce, 111
    in Cycladic Eggs on Toast, 78
    in Grape Leaf Arancini, 141
    in Graviera Cheese and Ham Pie, 28
    Greco-Russian Piroski Stuffed with Feta Mashed Potatoes, 26
    in Greek Gelatin Salad, 150
    in Greek Salad Crepes, 75
    in Greek Salad Kritharoto, 276
    in Greek Salad with Cucumber Granita, 149
    in Hangover Eggs, 81
    Karamanlidika's Giant Beans Bouryioundi with Feta and Spicy Sausage, 133
    in Katsogiannis's Grilled Eggplant Dip with Roasted Red Peppers, 98
    in Kayianas on Toast 2 Ways, 77
    in Mouzilo's Fabulous Tyropita, 20
    in The Not-So-Classic Greek Horiatiki Salata, 145
    in Octopus Saganaki, 108
    Pancakes Stacked with Ham and Feta Cream, 70
    in Panko-Crusted Saganaki, 106
    Risotto with Chestnuts, Winter Squash, Mavrodaphne, and Feta, 282
    Saganaki Risotto with Feta and Oregano, 280
    in Spanakopita Cream, 256
    in Spanakopita Crepes, 73
    in Spinach Pie Meets Croissant, 32
    in Tyropitakia Kourou, 14
    Watermelon Salad with Jalapeños, Avocado, and Feta, 154
Fiery Feta Cream, 98
figs
    Bulgur Salad with Fresh Fruit and Figs, 164
    Creamed Trahana with Dried Figs and Bottarga, 185
    in Homemade Granola with Greek Flavors, 62
    Roasted Butternut Squash Soup with Greek Figs, 174
    in Trahana Breakfast Bowl, 63
Filet Mignon with Mavrodaphne Sauce, 328
fish and seafood. *See also* calamari; lobster; mussels; shrimp; tuna
    about, 290–91
    Anchovies Sofrito from Laki's Ouzerie, 128
    Athinaiki Mayioneza, 217
    Athinaiki Salata, 162
    crudo, Athenian Style, 115
    Fish à La Spetsiota, 215
    Fish Cakes with Tarama, 307
    A Fish Taverna's Taramosalata, 85
    Fresh Cod or Halibut with Braised Artichokes and Broad Beans, 292
    Gilt-Head Bream in Citrus Juice with Tomato, Olives, and Red Onion, 114
    "Honeyed" Octopus Braised in Sweet Wine and Vinegar, 304
    Lefteris Lazarou's Cuttlefish Ink and Crab Soup, 187
    Married Sardines, 297
    Nena's Grilled Squid with Smoked Eggplant Salad, 113
    Octopus Saganaki, 108
    One-Pot Fish Fillets with Greek Salad and Greens, 293
    Ouzo Salmon Cooked over Greens, 296
    Pan-Seared Monkfish Liver, 306
    Potatoes Yiahni with Smoked Herring, 129
    Sea Bass Carpaccio over Grape Leaves, 118
    Seared Fresh Squid with Spanakopita Cream, 300
    Stacked Fried Sardines with a Brush of Beets, 298
    Taverna Fish Soup, 188
    Warm Giant Beans with Smoked Mackerel and Red Onions, 135
    Zucchini Stuffed with Black Rice, Fish, and Avgolemono, 260

Index   385

focaccia sandwiches
  about, 35
  Focaccia Sandwich with Fava, Arugula, and Grilled Eggplants, 39
  Grilled Focaccia Sandwich with Greek Olives, Manouri Cheese, Tomato Vinaigrette, and Fresh Basil, 36
  Grilled Spanakopita Focaccia, 35
Fokionos Negri, 47, 138, 368
frappes, about, 66–67
Fresh Cod or Halibut with Braised Artichokes and Broad Beans, 292
Fresh Tomato-Onion Salad with an Extra Grated, Juicy Tomato, 151
fricasses
  Lamb Fricasse with Kale, 323
  Mushroom-Spinach Fricasse Risotto with Avgolemono, 279
  Pork Fricasse with Celery and Leeks, 233
Fried Feta Triangles from Nea Ionia, Crispy, 25
Fried Mussels, 199
Fried Sardines with a Brush of Beets, Stacked, 298
Fried Whole Shrimp, The Simplest, 198
Fries, Leloudas's Poor Man's Plate of Greek, with Ground Meat Sauce and Grated Myzithra, 136

Galaktoboureko
  about, 351
  Classic Greek, 352
  Tart, 354
  Vegan, 355
Galaxy, The, 368, 370
garidadika, 122, 198, 290
Garidomakaronada, 273
Garlicky Fava with Red Wine and Herbs, 95
Gastronomos, 88, 121, 264
giant beans (gigantes)
  Giant Beans Baked with Smoked Pork, Wine, and Graviera, 244
  Giant Beans with a Grec-Mex Touch, 243
  Karamanlidika's Giant Beans Bouryioundi with Feta and Spicy Sausage, 133
  Warm Giant Beans with Smoked Mackerel and Red Onions, 135
Gilt-Head Bream in Citrus Juice with Tomato, Olives, and Red Onion, 114
Gjin Bua Shpata, 267
Gkogklies, 266
Glyfada, 20, 290
granita
  Greek salad, 148
  Greek Salad with Cucumber Granita, 149

Granola with Greek Flavors, Homemade, 62
grape leaves
  Grape Leaf Arancini, 141
  in Greek Sushi Dolmades, 116
  Sea Bass Carpaccio over Grape Leaves, 118
  yialantzi, 242
grape molasses. *See* petimezi
graviera
  in Athenian Carbonara, 278
  in Athenian Housewife's False Soufflé, 227
  in Cheese-Stuffed Taverna Burgers, 200
  Giant Beans Baked with Smoked Pork, Wine, and Graviera, 244
  Graviera Cheese and Ham Pie, 28
  in Kaseropita Kourou, 17
  in Pork Roast Stuffed with Greek Cheeses and Dried Fruit, 330
Grec-Mex Chicken Fajitas, 314
Greek Civil War, 122, 212, 213, 368
Greek Gelatin Salad, 150
Greek meatballs. *See* keftedes
Greek salad. *See* Horiatiki Salata
Greek Salad and Greens, One-Pot Fish Fillets with, 293
Greek Salad Crepes, 75
Greek Salad Kritharoto, 276
Greek Salad with Cucumber Granita, 149
Greek Sushi Dolmades, 116
Greek Taverna Cabbage-Carrot Salad with a Tomato Rose, 156
Greek Vegetable Soup with Jammy Eggs, 191
Greek War of Independence, 122, 212
Greek yogurt
  about, 60, 64, 342
  in Athenian Lemon Pie with Hints of Spetses, 364
  in Classic Tavernisio Tzatziki, 98
  Pancakes with Baklava-Flavored Greek Yogurt, 68
  Panna Cotta, 349
Green Beans Yiahni with Bottarga, 259
Grilled Eggplant Dip with Roasted Red Peppers, Katsogiannis's, 89
Grilled Focaccia Sandwich with Greek Olives, Manouri Cheese, Tomato Vinaigrette, and Fresh Basil, 36
Grilled Lamb Chops Marinated with Petimezi Barbecue Sauce, 326
Grilled Sausage "Plaki," 138
Grilled Spanakopita Focaccia, 35
Grilled Squid with Smoked Eggplant Salad, Nena's, 113
Ground Beef and Vegetable Pie (Kimadopita), 31
Guru Bar, 370
gyros
  about, 50–52
  Homemade Chicken Gyro, 54

halloumi
  in Pan-Fried Cheese with Mastiha and Lemon, 112
  in Panko-Crusted Saganaki, 106
ham
  in Athenian Housewife's False Soufflé, 227
  Graviera Cheese and Ham Pie, 28
  Pancakes Stacked with Ham and Feta Cream, 70
Handmade Pasta Nuggets of Attica, 266
Hangover Eggs, 81
Hara, 334, 358
Harry's Strapatsada Boureki, 23
Hiliadaki, Georgianna, 148
Homemade Chicken Gyro, 54
Homemade Granola with Greek Flavors, 62
Homey, Comforting Beef Baked with Orzo, 226
Honeyed Fry-Pies. *See* loukoumades
"Honeyed" Octopus Braised in Sweet Wine and Vinegar, 304
Hoocut, 56, 310
Horiatiki Salata
  about, 146
  Greek Gelatin Salad, 150
  Greek Salad with Cucumber Granita, 149
  Not-So-Classic Greek, 145
  variations on, 148
Hummus, Vegan Peinirli with, 49

ice cream
  about, 334, 358
  Athenian Ice Cream Sundae, 357
  Melina's Sokolatina, 361
Ismyrnoglou, Nena, 9, 88, 113, 121, 247

Jalapeños, Avocado, and Feta, Watermelon Salad with, 154

kafekopteia, 66
kalamata olives. *See* olives
Kale, Lamb Fricasse with, 323
Kallidis, Vasilis, 327
Kallisti, 88, 113
Kapama, Vegan Root Vegetable, 255
Kapetan Mihalis, 102
Karadamatis, Yiorgos, 358
Karagiorgos, Thanasis, 64
Karamanlidika's Giant Beans Bouryioundi with Feta and Spicy Sausage, 133
Karamanlis, Konstantinos, 50
Karavitis Taverna, 201
Kaseropita Kourou, 17
kasseri
  in Athenian Housewife's False Soufflé, 227
  in Athens-Style Classic Greek Pizza, 286
  in Graviera Cheese and Ham Pie, 28

386   Index

kasseri (*continued*)
   in Ground Beef and Vegetable Pie, 31
   Kaseropita Kourou, 17
   in Kimadopita, 31
   in Pastitsio, 230
   in Pasturmadopita from Karamanlidika, 134
   in Traditional Peinirli, 48
katiki, in Cycladic Eggs on Toast, 78
Katsogiannis's Grilled Eggplant Dip with Roasted Red Peppers, 89
Katsogiannis Taverna, 89, 203
Kayianas on Toast 2 Ways, 77
kefalograviera
   in Athenian Carbonara, 278
   in Beet Risotto with Beet Greens and Feta, 281
   in Grape Leaf Arancini, 141
   in Grilled Spanakopita Focaccia, 35
   in Moussaka with Metsovone Béchamel, 234
   in Panko-Crusted Saganaki, 106
   in Shrimp Saganaki Risotto with Feta and Oregano, 280
   in Surf 'n' Turf Pasta with Pasturma, Shrimp, and Pistachios, 274
kefalotyri
   in Athenian Housewife's False Soufflé, 227
   in Moussaka with Metsovone Béchamel, 234
   in Pastitsio, 230
   in Tyropitakia Kourou, 14
   in Wedding Pastitsio of Spata, 268
keftedes
   about, 201
   with Ouzo and Diced Tomatoes, 203
Kifissia, 340, 342–43
Kimadopita, 31
Kitsoulas Taverna, 201
Kolonaki Square, 60–61, 66
Kontizas, Sotiris, 9, 148, 170
Kostas, 12–13, 51, 310
Kotopoulo (Chicken) Milanese, 237
Koukaki, 3, 87
koulouri
   about, 9, 12, 43, 148
   recipe, 44
Koumoundouros, Alexandros, 122
kourous
   about, 18
   Kaseropita, 17
   Tyropitakia, 14
Koutouzis, George, 270
Krikzonis, Fotis, 234
Kritharoto, Greek Salad, 276

Lahanodolmades Avgolemono, 220
Lahanorizo Cream, 258
laiki agora, about, 242, 249
Laki's Ouzerie, 128
lamb
   Feminist Lamb and Potatoes, 324
   Grilled Lamb Chops Marinated with Petimezi Barbecue Sauce, 326
   Lamb Burgers with Smoked Eggplant Cream, 320
   Lamb Fricasse with Kale, 323
   The Simplest Pan-Seared Lamb Chops, 208
Lazarou, Lefteris, 9, 115, 291, 301, 306
   recipes, 187, 256, 258, 300, 303
Leeks, Pork Fricasse with Celery and, 233
Lefteris Lazarou's Calamari Pesto, 303
Lefteris Lazarou's Cuttlefish Ink and Crab Soup, 187
Lefteris Lazarou's Seared Fresh Squid with Spanakopita Cream, 300
Lefteris Lazarou's Spanakopita Cream, 256
Leloudas's Poor Man's Plate of Greek Fries with Ground Meat Sauce and Grated Myzithra, 136
Leloudas Taverna, 136
Lemon Pie with Hints of Spetses, Athenian, 364
Lemony Braised Beef, 222
Lemony Chicken "Ribs," 313
Lemony Chickpeas with Turmeric and Fennel, 252
Lemony Pulled Chicken Soup, Epirus's, 177
Lentzos, 66–67
Lesvos, 102, 115
Lightest Shrimp Meze with Capers, Ouzo, and Orange, 121
lobster
   about, 290
   Lobster Tail Yiouvetsi with Roasted Red Peppers and Ouzo, 275
Lombotesis, Anastasios, 18
loukoumades
   about, 13, 334, 336
   recipe, 339
Lucacos, Yiannis, 253

mageiritsa, 175
Manouri Cheese, Grilled Focaccia Sandwich with Greek Olives, Tomato Vinaigrette, Fresh Basil, and, 36
Margarita, Mastiha, 375
Married Sardines, 297
mastiha
   Margarita, 375
   Mastihatini, 376
   Pan-Fried Cheese with Mastiha and Lemon, 112
Mastihatini, 376
mavrodaphne
   Filet Mignon with Mavrodaphne Sauce, 328
   Risotto with Chestnuts, Winter Squash, Mavrodaphne, and Feta, 282

meat. *See also* beef; chicken; lamb; pork
   about, 310
Melina's Sokolatina, 361
melitzanosalata, 9, 84, 113
   with Miso, Tahini, and Petimezi, 90
Meraklidis, Isaac, 50–51
Mesogeia, 181, 195, 208, 266, 267, 335, 347, 351, 371
Metaxourgeio, 13, 141, 148, 194, 249, 270
meze
   about, 102–3
   Anchovies Sofrito from Laki's Ouzerie, 128
   Crunchy Feta in Phyllo with Tahini and Berry Sauce, 111
   Gilt-Head Bream in Citrus Juice with Tomato, Olives, and Red Onion, 114
   Grape Leaf Arancini, 141
   Greek Sushi Dolmades, 116
   Grilled Sausage "Plaki," 138
   Karamanlidika's Giant Beans Bouryioundi with Feta and Spicy Sausage, 133
   Leloudas's Poor Man's Plate of Greek Fries with Ground Meat Sauce and Grated Myzithra, 136
   Lightest Shrimp Meze with Capers, Ouzo, and Orange, 121
   Mushroom Chickpea Tigania with Soy Sauce and Honey, 130
   Mussels with Turmeric, 127
   Nena's Grilled Squid with Smoked Eggplant Salad, 113
   Octopus Saganaki, 108
   Pan-Fried Cheese with Mastiha and Lemon, 112
   Panko-Crusted Saganaki, 106
   Pasturmadopita from Karamanlidika, 134
   Potatoes Yiahni with Smoked Herring, 129
   Saganaki with Pasturma and Eggs, 105
   Sea Bass Carpaccio over Grape Leaves, 118
   Shrimp Croquettes with "Sos Pikant," 124
   Shrimp Mikrolimano, 122
   Sweet Potato Saganaki, 107
   Warm Giant Beans with Smoked Mackerel and Red Onions, 135
Mihail, Nikos, 86, 115, 116, 118
Mikrolimano, Shrimp, 122
Milionis, Melina, 72, 361, 364
Milk Pie, Attica-Style Crustless, 363
Miso, Tahini, and Petimezi, Melitzanosalata with, 90
Mitropoleos Street, 50–51, 124
Mitsos, Barba, 181
Mixed Greens Salad with Tangerine-Olive Oil Dressing, 167
Mojito, Retsina, 374

Index 387

Monastiraki Square, 50–51
Monkfish Liver, Pan-Seared, 306
Moscharaki Kokinisto, 223
Moscharaki Lemonato, 222
Moussaka
    with Metsovone Béchamel, 234
    Pita Wrap, 57
Moustokouloura, 347
Mouzilo's Fabulous Tyropita, 20
Mung Bean Fava with Tahini and Za'atar, 94
mushrooms
    Beef Cheek and Mushroom Soup, 171
    Chickpeas with Wild Mushrooms, 253
    Mushroom Chickpea Tigania with Soy Sauce and Honey, 130
    Mushroom-Spinach Fricasse Risotto with Avgolemono, 279
mussels
    Fried Mussels, 199
    Mussels with Turmeric, 127
My Greek Table, 50, 148, 256, 300, 314, 355
myzithra
    in Crispy Fried Feta Triangles from Nea Ionia, 25
    in Handmade Pasta Nuggets of Attica, 266
    Leloudas's Poor Man's Plate of Greek Fries with Ground Meat Sauce and Grated Myzithra, 136

Nea Ionia, 18, 25
Negroni, Aegean, 376
Nena's Beet Taramosalata with Lime and Mint, 88
Nena's Chestnut Stifado with Prunes, 247
Nena's Grilled Squid with Smoked Eggplant Salad, 113
Noua, 224
Ntylan, 138

octopus
    "Honeyed" Octopus Braised in Sweet Wine and Vinegar, 304
    Octopus Saganaki, 108
Odigos Mageirikis, 228, 237
olives
    Braised Chickpeas with Olives, Pistachios, and Roasted Tomatoes, 248
    Delicious Eggplant Dip with Olives and Honey, 92
    Gilt-Head Bream in Citrus Juice with Tomato, Olives, and Red Onion, 114
    in Greek Gelatin Salad, 150
    in Greek Salad Crepes, 75
    in Greek Salad Kritharoto, 276
    Grilled Focaccia Sandwich with Greek Olives, Manouri Cheese, Tomato Vinaigrette, and Fresh Basil, 36

    in The Not-So-Classic Greek Horiatiki Salata, 145
    in One-Pot Fish Fillets with Greek Salad and Greens, 293
    in Vegan Peinirli with Hummus, 49
Olympion's Chickpeas with Eggplant, Lots of Onions, and Petimezi, 250
One-Pot Fish Fillets with Greek Salad and Greens, 293
orzo
    Beef Baked with Orzo, 226
    in Greek Salad Kritharoto, 276
    in Lobster Tail Yiouvetsi with Roasted Red Peppers and Ouzo, 275
Ossobuco with Greek Flavors, 329
Otto of Bavaria, 7, 195, 212
Oursa, 40
Ouzerie Tou Laki, 102, 128
Ouzito, 375
ouzo
    Keftedes with Ouzo and Diced Tomatoes, 203
    Lightest Shrimp Meze with Capers, Ouzo, and Orange, 121
    Lobster Tail Yiouvetsi with Roasted Red Peppers and Ouzo, 275
    Ouzito, 375
    Ouzo Salmon Cooked over Greens, 296
    Spicy Ouzo-Shrimp Pasta, 273
Overoll, 32

paidakia, 208, 313
pancakes
    about, 60
    Athens Style, 65
    with Baklava-Flavored Greek Yogurt, 68
    Cornmeal Pancakes with Grape Molasses, 71
    Stacked with Ham and Feta Cream, 70
Pan-Fried Cheese with Mastiha and Lemon, 112
Pangrati, 66, 70, 98, 195, 201, 249, 250, 253
Panko-Crusted Saganaki, 106
Panna Cotta, Greek Yogurt, 349
Pan-Seared Lamb Chops, The Simplest, 208
Pan-Seared Monkfish Liver, 306
Papadakis Restaurant, 304
Papandreou, Andreas, 3
Papatheodorou, Lyssandros and Thodoris, 368
Pappardelle with Buffalo Meat, Seychelles' Signature, 270
Parliaros, Stelios, 335
Parren, Kallirois, 324
parsnips, in Vegan Root Vegetable Kapama, 255
pasta. *See also* Pastitsio
    about, 264–65
    Athenian Carbonara, 278

    Handmade Pasta Nuggets of Attica, 266
    Lobster Tail Yiouvetsi with Roasted Red Peppers and Ouzo, 275
    Seychelles' Signature Pappardelle with Buffalo Meat, 270
    Spaghetti with Avgotaraho, 269
    Spicy Ouzo-Shrimp Pasta, 273
    Spinach-Chickpea Pasta with Creamy Tahini, 277
    Surf 'n' Turf Pasta with Pasturma, Shrimp, and Pistachios, 274
Pastitsio, 230
    about, 232
    Wedding Pastitsio of Spata, 268
pasturma
    about, 274
    Chickpea Soup with Pasturma, 184
    Pasturmadopita from Karamanlidika, 134
    Saganaki with Pasturma and Eggs, 105
    Surf 'n' Turf Pasta with Pasturma, Shrimp, and Pistachios, 274
    in Traditional Peinirli, 48
Patissia, 2, 24, 195, 334, 358
Patsas (Tripe Soup), 178
pears
    in Bibb Lettuce Salad with Winter Fruit and Walnuts, 155
    in Bulgur Salad with Fresh Fruit and Figs, 164
Peas and Shrimp, Slow-Cooked, 294
Pediaditakis, Spyros, 253
peinirli
    about, 47
    Traditional Peinirli, 48
    Vegan Peinirli with Hummus, 49
Pendelis, 12, 310, 325
people's markets, about, 242, 249
Peskias, Christoforos, 9, 90, 148, 185, 327
Pesto, Calamari, 303
petimezi (grape molasses)
    Cornmeal Pancakes with Grape Molasses, 71
    Grilled Lamb Chops Marinated with Petimezi Barbecue Sauce, 326
    Melitzanosalata with Miso, Tahini, and Petimezi, 90
    Olympion's Chickpeas with Eggplant, Lots of Onions, and Petimezi, 250
Petridou, Marina, 50
Pezoulas, 85, 97
piroski (pierogi), 13
    Greco-Russian Piroski Stuffed with Feta Mashed Potatoes, 26
pistachios
    in Bulgur Salad with Fresh Fruit and Figs, 164
    in Homemade Granola with Greek Flavors, 62
    Surf 'n' Turf Pasta with Pasturma, Shrimp, and Pistachios, 274

Pita Wrap, Moussaka, 57
pitsa (pizza)
    about, 284–85
    Athens-Style Classic Greek Pizza, 286
Plaka, 4, 8, 146, 194
plant-based dishes, about, 242
Plateia Avdi, 24, 60, 270
Plateia Proskopon, 70
Pontos, 31
pork
    in Bean Soup Sandwich, 40
    in Cabbage Rolls with Egg-Lemon Sauce, 220
    in Cheese-Stuffed Taverna Burgers, 200
    Giant Beans Baked with Smoked Pork, Wine, and Graviera, 244
    in Grilled Sausage "Plaki," 138
    Keftedes with Ouzo and Diced Tomatoes, 203
    Moussaka Pita Wrap, 57
    Pork and Leeks with Red Pepper Flakes and Herbs, 205
    Pork Fricasse with Celery and Leeks, 233
    Pork Roast Stuffed with Greek Cheeses and Dried Fruit, 330
    in Seychelles' Signature Pappardelle with Buffalo Meat, 270
    in Sweet Potato Saganaki, 107
    in Sweet Potato Skordalia, 91
potatoes
    in Athens Central Market Beef Soup, 172
    in Athinaiki Mayioneza, 217
    in Athinaiki Salata, 162
    in Beef Cheek and Mushroom Soup, 171
    Feminist Lamb and Potatoes, 324
    in Fish Cakes with Tarama, 307
    in Fresh Cod or Halibut with Braised Artichokes and Broad Beans, 292
    Greco-Russian Piroski Stuffed with Feta Mashed Potatoes, 26
    in Greek Vegetable Soup with Jammy Eggs, 191
    in Green Beans Yiahni with Bottarga, 259
    in Grilled Sausage "Plaki," 138
    Leloudas's Poor Man's Plate of Greek Fries with Ground Meat Sauce and Grated Myzithra, 136
    in Lemony Chicken "Ribs," 313
    in Moussaka Pita Wrap, 57
    in Moussaka with Metsovone Béchamel, 234
    in One-Pot Fish Fillets with Greek Salad and Greens, 293
    Potatoes Yiahni with Smoked Herring, 129
    in Taramosalata with Tomato Paste, 87
Pot Roast, Athenian, 224

Poulos, Peter, 178
Poupeki, 363
Praxitelous Street, 32, 370
Provolegios, Aristomenis, 368
prunes
    Nena's Chestnut Stifado with Prunes, 247
    in Pork Roast Stuffed with Greek Cheeses and Dried Fruit, 330
psistaries, 208
purslane
    in Black-Eyed Peas with Preserved Lemon, Greens, and Capers, 245
    in Greek Salad with Cucumber Granita, 149

radicchio, in Mixed Greens Salad with Tangerine-Olive Oil Dressing, 167
Renti Fish Market, 301
Repousi, Anna, 270
resin tappers of Attica, 206
Retro Rice and Tuna Salad, 163
retsina
    about, 206, 373
    Mojito, 374
    Spritz, 374
rice. See also risotto
    about, 264–65
    in Cabbage Rolls with Egg-Lemon Sauce, 220
    Chicken Milanese, 237
    in Grape Leaf Arancini, 141
    in Greek Sushi Dolmades, 116
    Retro Rice and Tuna Salad, 163
    Rice Pudding, 340
    in Sea Bass Carpaccio over Grape Leaves, 118
    in Turkey-Stuffed Cabbage Rolls with Avgolemono Cream Sauce, 318
    Zucchini Stuffed with Black Rice, Fish, and Avgolemono, 260
risotto
    Beet Risotto with Beet Greens and Feta, 281
    with Chestnuts, Winter Squash, Mavrodaphne, and Feta, 282
    Mushroom-Spinach Fricasse Risotto with Avgolemono, 279
    Shrimp Saganaki Risotto with Feta and Oregano, 280
Ritsos, Yannis, 66
Roasted Butternut Squash Soup with Greek Figs, 174
Root Vegetable Kapama, Vegan, 255
Rusk Tomato Salad with Burrata, Olive Oil, and Herbs, Carob, 153

saganaki
    about, 105
    Octopus, 108
    Panko-Crusted, 106
    with Pasturma and Eggs, 105

Shrimp, Risotto with Feta and Oregano, 280
Sweet Potato, 107
salads. See also Horiatiki Salata
    about, 144
    Athinaiki Salata, 144, 162
    Baby Arugula and Chickpea Salad with Raw Red Onion, Hard-Boiled Eggs, and Tahini Ladolemono, 159
    Beet and Arugula Salad with Sultanas and Chèvre, 158
    Bibb Lettuce Salad with Winter Fruit and Walnuts, 155
    Bulgur Salad with Fresh Fruit and Figs, 164
    Carob Rusk Tomato Salad with Burrata, Olive Oil, and Herbs, 153
    Fresh Tomato-Onion Salad with an Extra Grated, Juicy Tomato, 151
    Greek Gelatin Salad, 150
    Greek Salad with Cucumber Granita, 149
    Greek Taverna Cabbage-Carrot Salad with a Tomato Rose, 156
    Mixed Greens Salad with Tangerine-Olive Oil Dressing, 167
    One-Pot Fish Fillets with Greek Salad and Greens, 293
    Retro Rice and Tuna Salad, 163
    Spanakopita Salad, 161
    Watermelon Salad with Jalapeños, Avocado, and Feta, 154
Salmon Cooked over Greens, Ouzo, 296
sandwiches. See also focaccia sandwiches
    about, 30
    Bean Soup Sandwich, 40
    Koulouri, 44
sardines
    Married Sardines, 297
    Stacked Fried Sardines with a Brush of Beets, 298
Schoolchildren's Greek Chicken Schnitzel, 317
sea bass
    in Gilt-Head Bream in Citrus Juice with Tomato, Olives, and Red Onion, 114
    Sea Bass Carpaccio over Grape Leaves, 118
seafood. See fish and seafood
Seared Fresh Squid with Spanakopita Cream, 300
Seychelles' Signature Pappardelle with Buffalo Meat, 270
shrimp
    about, 290
    in Athinaiki Salata, 162
    Lightest Shrimp Meze with Capers, Ouzo, and Orange, 121
    Shrimp Croquettes with "Sos Pikant," 124
    Shrimp Mikrolimano, 122

Index   389

Shrimp Saganaki Risotto with Feta and Oregano, 280
The Simplest Fried Whole Shrimp, 198
Slow-Cooked Peas and Shrimp, 294
Spicy Ouzo-Shrimp Pasta, 273
Surf 'n' Turf Pasta with Pasturma, Shrimp, and Pistachios, 274
"sikagko," 357
Simplest Fried Whole Shrimp, 198
Simplest Pan-Seared Lamb Chops, The, 208
Skordalia, Sweet Potato, 91
Slow-Cooked Peas and Shrimp, 294
Smoked Eggplant Cream, Lamb Burgers with, 320
Smoked Eggplant Salad, Nena's Grilled Squid with, 113
Smoked Herring, Potatoes Yiahni with, 129
Smoked Mackerel, Warm Giant Beans with Red Onions and, 135
Smoked Pork, Wine, and Graviera, Giant Beans Baked with, 244
Sokolatina, 361
soups
  about, 170
  All-Nighter's Patsas (Tripe Soup), 178
  Athens Central Market Beef Soup, 172
  Beef Cheek and Mushroom Soup, 171
  Chickpea Soup That Emulates Diporto's Legendary Revithada, 182
  Chickpea Soup with Pasturma, 184
  Creamed Trahana with Dried Figs and Bottarga, 185
  Cuttlefish Ink and Crab Soup, 187
  Epirus's Lemony Pulled Chicken Soup, 177
  Greek Vegetable Soup with Jammy Eggs, 191
  Roasted Butternut Squash Soup with Greek Figs, 174
  Taverna Fish Soup, 188
soutzouk
  in Pasturmadopita from Karamanlidika, 134
  in Traditional Peinirli, 48
souvlaki
  about, 12–13, 50–52
  Calamari, 56
Spaghetti with Avgotaraho, 269
Spanakopita
  Cream, 256
  Crepes, 73
  Grilled Focaccia, 35
  Salad, 161
  Seared Fresh Squid with Spanakopita Cream, 300
Spata, 267, 268
Spetses, 215, 290, 364
Spicy Ouzo-Shrimp Pasta, 273
spinach. *See also* Spanakopita

Mushroom-Spinach Fricasse Risotto with Avgolemono, 279
in One-Pot Fish Fillets with Greek Salad and Greens, 293
in Ouzo Salmon Cooked over Greens, 296
Spinach-Chickpea Pasta with Creamy Tahini, 277
Spinach Pie Meets Croissant, 32
Spritz, Retsina, 374
squid
  in Calamari Souvlaki, 56
  Nena's Grilled Squid with Smoked Eggplant Salad, 113
  Seared Fresh Squid with Spanakopita Cream, 300
Stacked Fried Sardines with a Brush of Beets, 298
Stani, 64, 340
stews
  Athenian Pot Roast, 224
  Beef Baked with Orzo, 226
  Beef Stew, 223
  Fresh Cod or Halibut with Braised Artichokes and Broad Beans, 292
  Green Beans Yiahni with Bottarga, 259
  Lemony Braised Beef, 222
  Nena's Chestnut Stifado with Prunes, 247
  Ossobuco with Greek Flavors, 329
  Pork Fricasse with Celery and Leeks, 233
  Slow-Cooked Peas and Shrimp, 294
  Vegan Root Vegetable Kapama, 255
Strapatsada Boureki, Harry's, 23
Stratis, Dimitris, 40
street food. *See also* souvlaki
  about, 12–13
  Bean Soup Sandwich, 40
  Crispy Fried Feta Triangles from Nea Ionia, 25
  Focaccia Sandwich with Fava, Arugula, and Grilled Eggplants, 39
  Graviera Cheese and Ham Pie, 28
  Greco-Russian Piroski Stuffed with Feta Mashed Potatoes, 26
  Grilled Spanakopita Focaccia, 35
  Harry's Strapatsada Boureki, 23
  Kaseropita Kourou, 17
  Kimadopita, 31
  Koulouri, 44
  Lamb Burgers with Smoked Eggplant Cream, 320
  Moussaka Pita Wrap, 57
  Mouzilo's Fabulous Tyropita, 20
  Spinach Pie Meets Croissant, 32
  Traditional Peinirli, 48
  Tyropitakia Kourou, 14
  Vegan Peinirli with Hummus, 49
Surf 'n' Turf Pasta with Pasturma, Shrimp, and Pistachios, 274

Sushi Dolmades, Greek, 116
Sushi Mou, 115
sweet potatoes
  Sweet Potato Saganaki, 107
  Sweet Potato Skordalia, 91
  Sweet Potato Taramosalata with Bottarga, 86
Swiss chard
  in Black-Eyed Peas with Preserved Lemon, Greens, and Capers, 245
  in Greek Vegetable Soup with Jammy Eggs, 191
  in Ouzo Salmon Cooked over Greens, 296
Syntagma Square, 212

tahini
  Baby Arugula and Chickpea Salad with Raw Red Onion, Hard-Boiled Eggs, and Tahini Ladolemono, 159
  Crunchy Feta in Phyllo with Tahini and Berry Sauce, 111
  Melitzanosalata with Miso, Tahini, and Petimezi, 90
  Mung Bean Fava with Tahini and Za'atar, 94
  Spinach-Chickpea Pasta with Creamy Tahini, 277
Ta Karamanlidika, 133, 134, 184
Ta Nea, 3–4, 167, 175, 181, 276, 301, 370
tangerines
  in Lightest Shrimp Meze with Capers, Ouzo, and Orange, 121
  Mixed Greens Salad with Tangerine-Olive Oil Dressing, 167
tarama. *See also* Taramosalata
  Fish Cakes with Tarama, 307
Taramosalata
  about, 85
  Beet Taramosalata with Lime and Mint, 88
  A Fish Taverna's, 85
  Sweet Potato Taramosalata with Bottarga, 86
  with Tomato Paste, 87
Tart, Galaktoboureko, 354
taverna, about, 194–95
Taverna ton Filon, 260
Testis, Panayiotis, 24
Theatrou Street, 127, 181
tigania
  Mushroom Chickpea Tigania with Soy Sauce and Honey, 130
  Pork and Leeks with Red Pepper Flakes and Herbs, 205
To Kafeneion's Delicious Eggplant Dip with Olives and Honey, 92
tomatoes
  about, 146
  in Athens Central Market Beef Soup, 172

tomatoes (*continued*)
  Athens-Style Avocado Toast with Mashed Feta, Tomatoes, and Jammy Eggs, 76
  in Athens-Style Classic Greek Pizza, 286
  in Beef Cheeks "Kokinisto," 327
  in Beef Stew, 223
  Braised Chickpeas with Olives, Pistachios, and Roasted Tomatoes, 248
  Carob Rusk Tomato Salad with Burrata, Olive Oil, and Herbs, 153
  Clay-Baked Whole Eggplants with Feta and Tomatoes, 197
  in Fish à La Spetsiota, 215
  Fresh Tomato-Onion Salad with an Extra Grated, Juicy Tomato, 151
  in Giant Beans with a Grec-Mex Touch, 243
  Gilt-Head Bream in Citrus Juice with Tomato, Olives, and Red Onion, 114
  in Greek Gelatin Salad, 150
  in Greek Salad Crepes, 75
  in Greek Salad with Cucumber Granita, 149
  Greek Taverna Cabbage-Carrot Salad with a Tomato Rose, 156
  in Greek Vegetable Soup with Jammy Eggs, 191
  Grilled Focaccia Sandwich with Greek Olives, Manouri Cheese, Tomato Vinaigrette, and Fresh Basil, 36
  in Harry's Strapatsada Boureki, 23
  in Kayianas on Toast 2 Ways, 77
  Keftedes with Ouzo and Diced Tomatoes, 203
  in The Not-So-Classic Greek Horiatiki Salata, 145
  in One-Pot Fish Fillets with Greek Salad and Greens, 293
  in Pastitsio, 230
  in Shrimp Mikrolimano, 122
  in Slow-Cooked Peas and Shrimp, 294
  in Spicy Ouzo-Shrimp Pasta, 273
  in Vegan Peinirli with Hummus, 49
  Yellow Split-Pea Fava with Smoked Eel, Caramelized Tomatoes, and Onions, 97
To Oinomageireio Epirus, 175
To Steki tou Theatrou, 127
Tourta Amygdalou, 344
trahana
  about, 60, 63
  Breakfast Bowl, 63
  Creamed Trahana with Dried Figs and Bottarga, 185
Trikalinos, Zafeiris, 269
Tripe Soup, 178
tsalafouti cheese, in Mouzilo's Fabulous Tyropita, 20
tsaletia, 71
Tsarouchis, Yannis, 66
Tselementes, Nikos, 213, 215, 228–29, 230, 232, 237, 324
tuna
  in Greek Sushi Dolmades, 116
  Retro Rice and Tuna Salad, 163
Turkey-Stuffed Cabbage Rolls with Avgolemono Cream Sauce, 318
turmeric
  Lemony Chickpeas with Turmeric and Fennel, 252
  Mussels with Turmeric, 127
turnips, in Vegan Root Vegetable Kapama, 255
tyrokafteri, Fiery Feta Cream, 98
Tyropitakia Kourou, 14
tyropites
  about, 3, 18
  Mouzilo's Fabulous, 20
  Tyropitakia Kourou, 14
tzatziki
  about, 52, 84
  Classic Tavernisio, 98

Vakondios, Dimitris, 66
Vari, 325
Varoulko, 9, 115, 256, 291, 300, 301
Varsos, 340, 342–43
Varvakeios Fish Market, 102, 291, 298
Vasilopoulos, Stefanos, 20
vegan, about, 242
Vegan Galaktoboureko, 355
Vegan Peinirli with Hummus, 49
Vegan Root Vegetable Kapama, 255
vegan sandwiches. *See* focaccia sandwiches
Vegetable Soup with Jammy Eggs, Greek, 191
Venizelos, Eleftherios, 249

walnuts
  Bibb Lettuce Salad with Winter Fruit and Walnuts, 155
  in Homemade Granola with Greek Flavors, 62
  in Pancakes with Baklava-Flavored Greek Yogurt, 68
  Warm Giant Beans with Smoked Mackerel and Red Onions, 135
  Watermelon Salad with Jalapeños, Avocado, and Feta, 154
wine. *See also* retsina
  about, 370–71
  Garlicky Fava with Red Wine and Herbs, 95
  Giant Beans Baked with Smoked Pork, Wine, and Graviera, 244
Wine Roads of Attica, 290, 371
winter squash
  Risotto with Chestnuts, Winter Squash, Mavrodaphne, and Feta, 282
  Roasted Butternut Squash Soup with Greek Figs, 174

Yellow Split-Pea Fava with Smoked Eel, Caramelized Tomatoes, and Onions, 97
yellow split peas. *See* fava
yiahni
  Green Beans Yiahni with Bottarga, 259
  Potatoes Yiahni with Smoked Herring, 129
Yiotis, Alexandros, 146
Yiouvetsi
  Beef Baked with Orzo, 226
  Lobster Tail Yiouvetsi with Roasted Red Peppers and Ouzo, 275
yogurt. *See* Greek yogurt

Zaharatos, 66, 212
Zonaras, Karolos, 357
zucchini
  in Athens Central Market Beef Soup, 172
  in Moussaka Pita Wrap, 57
  Zucchini Stuffed with Black Rice, Fish, and Avgolemono, 260

About the Author

Yulia Koval

Diane Kochilas is a *New York Times* bestselling author and the host of *My Greek Table* on Public Television. She runs the Glorious Greek Kitchen cooking school on her native island Ikaria, as well as food and culture tours throughout Greece. She is the author of thirteen books on Greek and Mediterranean cuisine. She divides her time between Athens, Ikaria, and New York.

www.dianekochilas.com

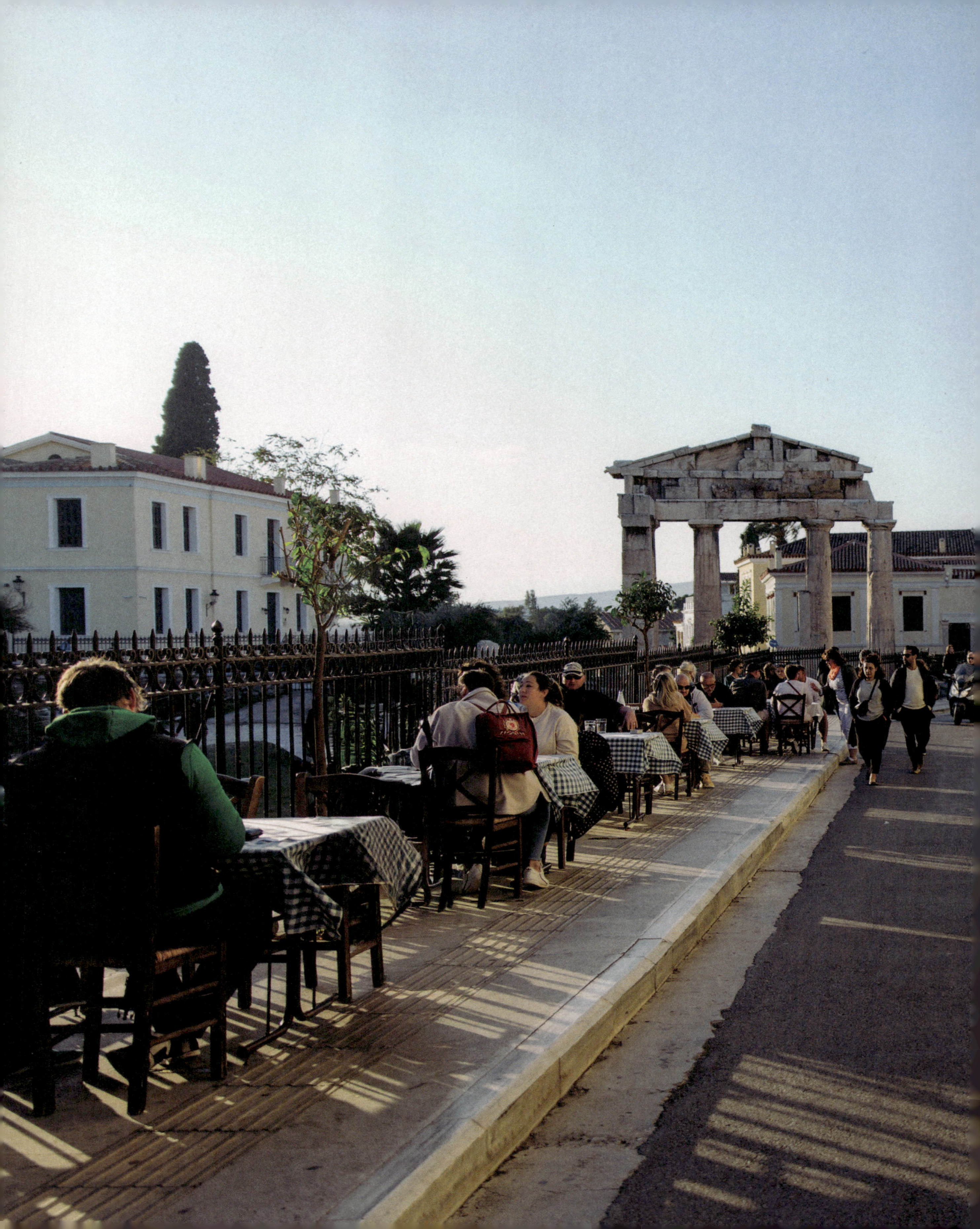